# GET THE FULL PICTURE WITH *LONE STAR POLITICS!*

**Delve deeply into Texas's rich political traditions as *Lone Star Politics* explores how myth clashes with the reality of modern governance.**

Explaining who gets what, and how, this Nacogdoches author team uses the comparative method to set Texas in context with other states' constitutional foundations, institutions, electoral practices, and policymaking. Its examination of winners and losers provides critical food for thought as students consider the political process.

This new **Fourth Edition** includes expanded coverage of the impact of the state's growing diversity on political participation and behavior; Rick Perry's legacy as governor; and important policy discussion around fracking, education reforms, and immigration. **New full-page infographics** visually capture a chapter's key concepts, making the abstract understandable and comparisons easy.

## KEY FEATURES

**Chapter opening vignettes** hook students in with current, relatable stories relevant to Texas government.

# KEY FEATURES

**Chapter objectives** and **Core Assessment questions** align with the Texas Higher Education Coordinating Board's (THECB) curriculum standards, reinforcing chapter content and ensuring that learning outcomes are achieved.

the preservation of the right of local self-government, unimpaired to all the States." In this chapter we will explore the constitutional arrangement of federalism and the development of the Texas Constitution more generally. We will first outline the federalist structure of the national government and how Texas fits into that structure. We then survey how the Texas Constitution has evolved over time, reflecting our rich history and culture. Finally, we discuss the problems of the current constitution and examine the prospects for constitutional reform.

### Chapter Objectives

★ Explain the purpose of a constitution and how the Texas Constitution developed.

★ Describe how federalism affects the choices made by state government.

★ Discuss the evolution of Texas's previous constitutions and the historical events that influenced them.

★ Explain how Texas's current constitution organizes its government.

★ Identify problems with the current Texas Constitution.

★ Assess who wins and who loses in Texas given its environment of distrust of the government.

## TEXAS AND THE FED ON *Marijuana*

Texans favor a justice system that's tough on crime, and social conservatives have long warned against the potential dangers of marijuana use. Yet one of the current significant trends across the country is a move away from the criminalization of marijuana. Sixteen states have decriminalized marijuana, meaning possession is now treated as a minor offense involving a small fine. Another two states, Colorado and Washington, have legalized marijuana. When these states first chose to legalize marijuana, it created an interesting paradox since possession of the substance was still against federal law. Since then, however, the federal government has said it will only prosecute possession in those two states if it is tied to other criminal activity or involves minors in possession. More recently, President Obama referred to marijuana policy as a state's rights issue.

The choice to incarcerate people for possession and use of marijuana entails significant costs to Texas. It cost Texans an estimated $378,820 a day to incarcerate people for simple drug possession.[1] While Texas law no longer deems it a felony to possess even a small amount of marijuana, state law can still seem draconian. Jacob Lavoro made national headlines in 2014 when he was arrested for making a batch of pot brownies. Although Lavoro used 2.5 grams of THC in his brownies, the Texas teen was originally charged for the entire weight of the brownies—one and a half pounds—which carried with it a maximum punishment of life in prison.

The most significant change in Texas law to date came in 2006 when the state's legislature passed a law allowing local police to issue a citation and court date for possession without mandatory arrest. While cities such as Austin have decreased initial arrests, Dallas has continued to employ mandatory arrest for possession. In the 83rd legislative session, the state's legislature considered, but did not pass, changing marijuana possession to a class C misdemeanor. This change would have meant that Texans found guilty of possession would face a fine but not imprisonment. Although more Texans are embracing the notion of decriminalization, social conservatives still vehemently oppose any move toward legalization. Former governor Perry had suggested he would support decriminalization, but Governor Abbott has clearly stated that he favors existing drug laws and prefers focusing on compliance. Both Perry and Abbott, however, agree that marijuana laws are issues for states to decide.

★ To what extent should local governments have authority over marijuana laws?

★ Given the costs of incarceration, is the state of Texas fiscally irresponsible in continuing to criminalize marijuana use? Explain your answer.

★ How likely do you think it is that marijuana will be decriminalized or legalized in Texas in the next decade?

★ How does the federal government's authority over security clash with state governments' power over marijuana laws?

1. "High Time for Texas to Decriminalize Marijuana" *Daily Texan*, January 30, 2014, www.dailytexanonline.com/opinion/2014/01/30/high-time-for-texas-to-decriminalize-marijuana (accessed August 20, 2014).

*New* **Texas and the Fed** boxes examine contemporary policies on topics of national concern, like immigration, abortion, and marijuana, and consider how they affect Texas and how Texas seeks to influence them.

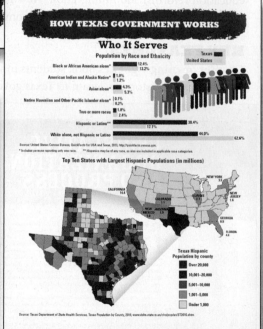

*New* **How Texas Government Works** infographics are eye-catching visual comparisons, broadening students' understanding of such topics as the state's demographic diversity and its energy use and production.

**Sam Houston**

By the time he became a Texan and led Texas to independence, Sam Houston had gone through two wives and lots of alcohol and was, in the words of Texas historian James L. Haley, "considered in respectable circles as unsavory as he was colorful."[i] However, no one better reflects the reality that the greatness of Texas's legends can be found in less-than-perfect people, as Houston guided Texas through some of its most dramatic transitions.

In his youth, Houston generally preferred sneaking away to live among the Indians to working in the family business. Houston distinguished himself during the War of 1812, serving bravely and winning the admiration of General Andrew Jackson. Houston followed Jackson, his new mentor, into politics and was sometimes mentioned as a successor to President Jackson. However, Houston's first marriage abruptly ended in

1827 in the middle of his term as governor of Tennessee and just two months after his wedding. His marriage over and his political career in ruins, Houston went to live again among the Cherokees. During this time, he took a Cherokee wife without entering into a formal Christian marriage. Over time, Houston's state of mind deteriorated and his Indian hosts eventually stripped him of his original Indian name ("The Raven") and began to call him Oo-tse-tee Ar-deetah-skee ("The Big Drunk").[ii] After abandoning his second wife and returning to public life in America, Houston narrowly avoided jail after assaulting a member of Congress who had insulted his integrity. Brought before Congress to face charges, Houston delivered an impassioned defense on his own behalf, allegedly because his lawyer, Francis Scott Key, was too hungover to speak.

During the Texas Revolution, gossips frequently attributed Houston's disappearances to drinking binges rather than military missions. Some questioned his bravery and military leadership during the war. Many Texans wanted Houston to turn and fight the Mexican Army sooner, despite Houston's protest that his troops were undertrained and outnumbered. While most Texans sided with Houston after his victory at San Jacinto, criticisms of his conduct of the war reappeared in political campaigns for the rest of his career.

After leading Texas through the revolution, Houston continued to play a major role in the changes in the state while serving as Texas's first president during its years as an independent nation. Houston struggled in the years after the Texas Revolution to protect the Tejanos who had served alongside him during the war. Similarly, his years among the Cherokees and his continued fondness for them left him at odds with many Anglos who preferred to see Native Americans driven off or killed.

After playing a central role in winning Texas's entry into the United States, Houston's final political act was the struggle to keep Texas from seceding and joining the Confederacy. Houston disliked slavery and defied state law by freeing his own slaves. He had been one of few southern senators to speak out against slavery, a sentiment that led the Texas Legislature to vote against his return to the Senate. His final departure from politics came when he refused to support the secession of Texas in the American Civil War and, as a result, was forced by the legislature to resign his governorship. If Texans had followed Houston's leadership, the lives of many Texas soldiers would have been saved and the state spared postwar Reconstruction.

Houston finally settled down after marrying his third wife and finding redemption, but he never denied his faults. When asked if his sins had been washed away at his river baptism, Houston joked, "I hope so. But if they were all washed away, the Lord help the fish down below."[iii]

However numerous his sins, Houston's principles make him a much more heroic historical figure than many of his more sober peers. From the moment Houston arrived in Texas, he became a central figure in the transformation of the state, and for thirty years he guided Texas through its most turbulent times. While Houston might not be able to be elected today, he did more to shape modern Texas than any other person.

i. James L. Haley, *Passionate Nation: The Epic History of Texas* (New York: Free Press, 2006), 107.

ii. James E. Crisp, *Sleuthing the Alamo: Davy Crockett's Last Stand and other Mysteries of the Texas Revolution* (New York: Oxford University Press, 2004), 29.

iii. Haley, *Passionate Nation*, 277.

**Texas Legends** boxes showcase figures and events that have shaped—and continue to influence—Texas politics. Examples include revolutionary Sam Houston; the state's first African American legislator, Barbara C. Jordan; the League of United Latin American Citizens; and Texas Supreme Court Justice Raul Gonzalez.

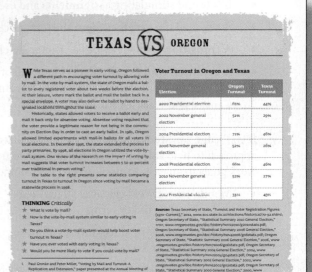

## TEXAS (VS) OREGON

While Texas serves as a pioneer in early voting, Oregon followed a different path in encouraging voter turnout by allowing vote by mail. In the vote-by-mail system, the state of Oregon mails a ballot to every registered voter about two weeks before the election. At their leisure, voters mark the ballot and mail the ballot back in a special envelope. A voter may also deliver the ballot by hand to designated locations throughout the state.

Historically, states allowed voters to receive a ballot early and mail it back only for absentee voting. Absentee voting required that the voter provide a legitimate reason for not being in the community on Election Day in order to cast an early ballot. In 1981, Oregon allowed limited experiments with mail-in ballots for all voters in local elections. In December 1995, the state extended the process to party primaries. By 1998, all elections in Oregon utilized the vote-by-mail system. One review of the research on the impact of voting by mail suggests that voter turnout increases between 5 to 10 percent over traditional in-person voting.[i]

The table to the right presents some statistics comparing turnout in Texas to turnout in Oregon since voting by mail became a statewide process in 1998.

**THINKING** *Critically*

★ What is vote by mail?

★ How is the vote-by-mail system similar to early voting in Texas?

★ Do you think a vote-by-mail system would help boost voter turnout in Texas?

★ Have you ever voted with early voting in Texas?

★ Would you be more likely to vote if you could vote by mail?

i. Paul Gronke and Peter Miller, "Voting by Mail and Turnout: A Replication and Extension," paper presented at the Annual Meeting of the American Political Science Association, Chicago, Illinois, August 20, 2007.

**Voter Turnout in Oregon and Texas**

| Election | Oregon Turnout | Texas Turnout |
|---|---|---|
| 2000 Presidential election | 66% | 44% |
| 2002 November general election | 51% | 29% |
| 2004 Presidential election | 71% | 46% |
| 2006 November general election | 52% | 26% |
| 2008 Presidential election | 66% | 46% |
| 2010 November general election | 52% | 27% |
| 2012 Presidential election | 33% | 43% |

**Sources:** Texas Secretary of State, "Turnout and Voter Registration Figures (1970–Current)," 2012, www.sos.state.tx.us/elections/historical/70-92.shtml; Oregon Secretary of State, "Statistical Summary 2010 General Election," 2010, www.oregonvotes.gov/doc/history/nov2010/g3osstats.pdf; Oregon Secretary of State, "Statistical Summary 2008 General Election," 2008, www.oregonvotes.gov/doc/history/nov2008/go8stats.pdf; Oregon Secretary of State, "Statistic Summary 2006 General Election," 2006, www.oregonvotes.gov/doc/history/nov2006/go6stats.pdf; Oregon Secretary of State, "Statistical Summary 2004 General Election," 2004, www.oregonvotes.gov/doc/history/nov2004/go4stats.pdf; Oregon Secretary of State, "Statistical Summary 2002 General Election," 2002, www.oregonvotes.gov/doc/history/nov2002/go2stats.pdf; Oregon Secretary of State, "Statistical Summary 2000 General Election," 2000, www.oregonvotes.gov/doc/history/nov2000/genstats.pdf [all Web sites accessed on September 8, 2014]; some calculations made by authors.

**Texas vs. _____** boxes are an extension of the book's comparative method, encouraging students to think about how Texas differs vis-à-vis other states when it comes to such topics as election processes, tax rates, and the death penalty.

★ Is the potential taxpayer burden of refusing federal funds for national health care reforms worth the state insisting on its independence?

★ Have controversies over issues such as abortion and privatization hurt health care services for Texas residents?

★ How does the state reconcile its provision of health care and social welfare programs with the Texas culture of independence?

**Critical thinking questions** at the end of the "Winners and Losers" sections encourage critical evaluation, presenting a balanced and realistic approach to the state's politics.

**SAGE edge for Instructors** supports teaching by making it easy to integrate quality content and create a rich learning environment for students.

- **Test bank** provides 975 updated questions linked to Bloom's Taxonomy and tied to learning objectives and page references; also with Respondus™ test generation capabilities

- Editable, chapter-specific **PowerPoint® slides** offer complete flexibility for creating multimedia presentations

- Carefully selected **video** and **multimedia content** enhance classroom-based exploration of key topics

- **Instructor manual** summarizes key concepts and links content to the Texas Higher Education Coordination Board curriculum standards

- Chapter-specific **discussion questions** help launch classroom interaction

- Lively and stimulating **assignments** and **exercises** that can be used in-class or for online teaching

- A set of all the **graphics from the text** for class presentations

- A **transition guide** provides a chapter-by-chapter outline of key changes to the fourth edition

- A **common course cartridge** includes all of the instructor resources and assessment material from the student study site, for easy upload in learning management systems such as Blackboard™, Angel®, Moodle™, Canvas, and Desire2Learn™

**SAGE edge for Students** provides a personalized approach to help students accomplish their coursework goals in an easy-to-use learning environment.

- Mobile-friendly **eFlashcards** strengthen understanding of key terms

- Mobile-friendly practice **quizzes** allow for independent assessment

- An **action plan** includes tips and feedback on progress through the course materials, allowing students to individualize their learning experience

- **Chapter summaries** with **learning objectives** reinforce important material

- Carefully selected **video links** and **multimedia content** enhance exploration of key topics

# LONE STAR POLITICS

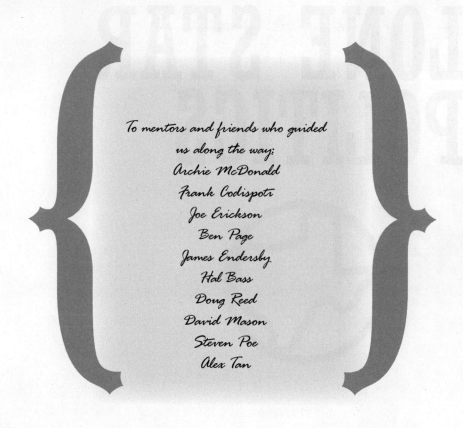

To mentors and friends who guided
us along the way:
Archie McDonald
Frank Codispoti
Joe Erickson
Ben Page
James Endersby
Hal Bass
Doug Reed
David Mason
Steven Poe
Alex Tan

# LONE STAR POLITICS

## TRADITION AND TRANSFORMATION IN TEXAS | FOURTH EDITION

Ken Collier | Steven Galatas | Julie Harrelson-Stephens

STEPHEN F. AUSTIN STATE UNIVERSITY

Los Angeles | London | New Delhi
Singapore | Washington DC | Boston

Los Angeles | London | New Delhi
Singapore | Washington DC | Boston

FOR INFORMATION:

CQ Press

An Imprint of SAGE Publications, Inc.

2455 Teller Road

Thousand Oaks, California 91320

E-mail: order@sagepub.com

SAGE Publications Ltd.

1 Oliver's Yard

55 City Road

London EC1Y 1SP

United Kingdom

SAGE Publications India Pvt. Ltd.

B 1/I 1 Mohan Cooperative Industrial Area

Mathura Road, New Delhi 110 044

India

SAGE Publications Asia-Pacific Pte. Ltd.

3 Church Street

#10-04 Samsung Hub

Singapore 049483

Acquisitions Editor:   Sarah Calabi
Senior Development Editor:   Nancy Matuszak
Digital Content Editor:   Allison Hughes
Editorial Assistant:   Raquel Christie
Production Editor:   Laura Barrett
Copy Editor:   Shannon Kelly
Typesetter:   C&M Digitals (P) Ltd.
Proofreader:   Theresa Kay
Indexer:   Judy Hunt
Cover Designer:   Michael Dubowe
Marketing Manager:   Amy Whitaker

Printed in Canada

*Cataloging-in-publication data is availble for this title from the Library of Congress.*

ISBN 978-1-4833-5277-0

This book is printed on acid-free paper.

15 16 17 18 19 10 9 8 7 6 5 4 3 2 1

# BRIEF CONTENTS

Contents / x
Preface / xix
About the Authors / xxviii

**CHAPTER 1**
**INTRODUCTION** / 2

**CHAPTER 2**
**TEXAS CONSTITUTION** / 38

**CHAPTER 3**
**TEXAS LEGISLATURE** / 76

**CHAPTER 4**
**LEGISLATIVE ORGANIZATION AND PROCESS** / 112

**CHAPTER 5**
**TEXAS GOVERNORS** / 154

**CHAPTER 6**
**THE PLURAL EXECUTIVE AND BUREAUCRACY IN TEXAS** / 182

**CHAPTER 7**
**TEXAS JUDICIAL SYSTEM** / 216

**CHAPTER 8**
**TEXAS-SIZED JUSTICE** / 244

**CHAPTER 9**
**CAMPAIGNS AND ELECTIONS, TEXAS STYLE** / 268

**CHAPTER 10**
**POLITICAL PARTIES** / 314

**CHAPTER 11**
**ORGANIZED INTERESTS** / 344

**CHAPTER 12**
**LOCAL GOVERNMENT IN TEXAS** / 370

**CHAPTER 13**
**FISCAL POLICY** / 410

**CHAPTER 14**
**EDUCATION AND SOCIAL POLICY** / 440

**CHAPTER 15**
**TRANSFORMING TEXAS: ENERGY, ENVIRONMENT, TRANSPORTATION, AND IMMIGRATION POLICIES** / 474

Appendix
  Declaration of Independence of the
  Republic of Texas / 504
Notes / 507
Glossary / 524
Index / 534

# CONTENTS

Preface                                                                          xix
About the Authors                                                                xxviii

## CHAPTER 1                                                                      2
### INTRODUCTION
**Texas Geography**                                                              4
**History: The Birth of Texas Traditions**                                       6
   *Mexican Independence*                                          9
   *The Texas Revolution*                                          10
   *The Republic of Texas*                                         12
**Texas Statehood**                                                              13
*Texas Legends*: **Sam Houston**                                                 14
   *Texas in the Confederacy*                                      15
   *Reconstruction in Texas*                                       16
   *The End of Reconstruction and Rise of the "Redeemers"*         17
   *Era of Reform*                                                 18
   *The Great Depression and the New Deal in Texas*                21
*Texas Legends*: **Bob Bullock**                                                 22
**Transitions to the Twenty-first Century**                                      23
   *Texas Today*                                                   23
**A Tradition of Change**                                                         27
**Winners and Losers**                                                           33
***Texas versus Vermont***                                                       34
**Conclusion**                                                                   36
**Key Terms**                                                                    37
**Core Assessment**                                                              37

## CHAPTER 2                                                                      38
### TEXAS CONSTITUTION
**Constitutional Government**                                                    40
**The Federal System of the United States**                                      41
   *Vertical Federalism*                                           42
   *Horizontal Federalism*                                         44
   *The Evolving Idea of Federalism*                               46
***Texas and the Fed on Abortion***                                              47
**Texas Constitutions**                                                          52
   *Immigration Rights*                                            53
   *The Republic of Texas: The Constitution of 1836*               54
   *Statehood: The Constitution of 1845*                           56

*Secession and the Confederacy: The Constitution of 1861*    57

*Texas Legends:* **James Collinsworth**    **58**

*The First Reconstruction: The Constitution of 1866*    58

*The Second Reconstruction: The Constitution of 1869*    59

*Texas Legends:* **E. J. Davis**    **60**

**The Current System: The Constitution of 1876**    **61**

*Individual Freedom*    62

*The Legislative Branch*    63

*The Executive Branch*    63

***Texas versus Connecticut***    **64**

*The Texas Judiciary*    65

*Civil Rights in Texas*    65

*Distrust of Government*    66

**Criticisms of the Texas Constitution**    **66**

*Amending the Constitution*    67

*Constitutional Revision*    68

***Texas versus Massachusetts***    **69**

**Winners and Losers**    **73**

**Conclusion**    **74**

**Key Terms**    **75**

**Core Assessment**    **75**

## CHAPTER 3    76

### TEXAS LEGISLATURE

**The Texas Legislature in Context**    **78**

**Typologies of State Legislatures**    **86**

**Qualifications for Office and Length of Terms**    **88**

**Theories of Representation**    **92**

*Texas Legends:* **Barbara C. Jordan**    **98**

**Winners and Losers**    **99**

**Electing the State Legislature**    **99**

*Single-Member District versus Multi-Member District*    100

*Redistricting Games*    101

***Texas versus North Dakota***    **105**

***Texas versus Arizona***    **108**

**Winners and Losers**    **109**

**Conclusion**    **110**

**Key Terms**    **111**

**Core Assessment**    **111**

## CHAPTER 4    112

### LEGISLATIVE ORGANIZATION AND PROCESS

**Legislative Organization**    **114**

*Presiding Officers*    115

*Political Parties in Texas Legislative Organization*    117

*Special Legislative Caucuses*    122

**Texas versus Nebraska** 124

*Committees* 126

**Texas versus New South Wales** 132

**Winners and Losers** 135

**Legislative Process** 136

*Introducing Bills in the Legislature* 137

*Introducing Resolutions in the Legislature* 137

*Legislation in Committee* 138

*Debate in the Legislature* 142

*Voting on Passage* 144

*Texas Legends:* **The Killer Bees** 145

*Trends in Legislative Activity* 146

**Winners and Losers** 150

**Conclusion** 152

**Key Terms** 152

**Core Assessment** 153

# CHAPTER 5 154

## TEXAS GOVERNORS

**The Office of the Governor** 156

*Qualifications* 157

*Texas Legends:* **Ann Richards** 162

*Terms* 163

*Succession* 164

*Compensation* 164

*Impeachment* 165

**Powers of the Governor** 166

*Executive Roles* 166

*Legislative Roles* 170

*Judicial Roles* 173

*Other Roles* 174

*Military Roles* 174

*Texas Governor: Weak?* 176

**Informal Powers** 176

**Winners and Losers** 178

**Texas versus Louisiana** 179

**Conclusion** 179

**Key Terms** 180

**Core Assessment** 180

# CHAPTER 6 182

## THE PLURAL EXECUTIVE AND BUREAUCRACY IN TEXAS

**The Plural Executive** 185

*Lieutenant Governor* 186

*Attorney General* 187

AP Photo/David J. Phillip

AP Photo/Todd Yates/
Corpus Christi Caller-Times

Comptroller of Public Accounts 190
Agriculture Commissioner 192
Land Commissioner 194
Secretary of State 195
**Boards and Commissions** 197
Texas Department of Transportation 197
Department of State Health Services 200
**Texas versus Georgia** 201
Railroad Commission of Texas 201
*Texas Legends:* **Railroad Commission of Texas** 202
Texas Department of Criminal Justice 203
State Board of Education 204
Public Utility Commission of Texas 205
**Texas versus Bavaria** 206
Staffing the State Government 208
**Bureaucratic Accountability** 210
**Winners and Losers** 212
**Conclusion** 213
**Key Terms** 214
**Core Assessment** 214

## CHAPTER 7 216

### TEXAS JUDICIAL SYSTEM

**Judicial Federalism and Texas Courts** 218
**Texas versus Kansas** 220
**Local Trial Courts** 221
Municipal Courts 221
Justice of the Peace Courts 222
**County-Level Trial Courts** 222
*Texas Legends:* **Judge Roy Bean** 223
Constitutional County Courts 223
County Courts at Law and Statutory Probate Courts 226
**District Courts (State-Level Trial Courts)** 226
**Appellate Courts** 227
**Courts of Appeals (Intermediate Appellate Courts)** 228
**Texas's Highest Appellate Courts: The**
**Court of Criminal Appeals and the Supreme Court of Texas** 228
**Judicial Selection** 229
*Texas Legends:* **Raul A. Gonzalez Jr.** 230
Judicial Appointment 232
Judicial Removal 233
**Texas Judges** 234
**Problems with the Texas Judiciary** 236
**Alternative Systems of Judicial Selection: Appointment and Merit** 237
**Criminal Justice in Texas** 238

Texas Court of Criminal Appeals

Texas versus Missouri                                    239
Winners and Losers                                       241
Conclusion                                               242
Key Terms                                                243
Core Assessment                                          243

## CHAPTER 8                                             244
### TEXAS-SIZED JUSTICE
Justice in Texas                                         246
Incarceration in Texas                                   247
*Texas Legends:* The Texas Rangers                       248
*Shift to Rehabilitation*                                249
*Texas and the Fed on Marijuana*                         250
*Prison Conditions*                                      250
*Privatization of Prisons*                               252
*Texas Legends:* Chicken Ranch                           253
Rights of the Accused                                    254
Law and Punishment                                       255
*Tort Reform*                                            255
*Castle Doctrine*                                        257
*Capital Punishment*                                     258
*Texas versus California*                                262
Winners and Losers                                       265
Conclusion                                               265
Key Terms                                                266
Core Assessment                                          266

## CHAPTER 9                                             268
### CAMPAIGNS AND ELECTIONS, TEXAS STYLE
Democracy, Representation, and Elections in Texas        271
*Voter Qualifications and Registration*                  271
Voting Rights in Texas                                   273
*Legal Barriers to Voting in Post-Reconstruction Texas*  273
*Eliminating Barriers to Voting for African Americans*   275
*Hispanics and Voting Rights*                            278
*Voting Rights for Women, Members of the
Armed Forces, and Younger Voters*                        280
Winners and Losers                                       282
Types of Elections in Texas                              282
*Texas Legends:* Landslide Lyndon                        283
*Primary Elections versus General Elections*             284
*Texas versus Oregon*                                    286
*Direct Democracy Elections*                             288
*Texas versus Louisiana*                                 290
*Too Much Democracy?*                                    291
Voting, Voter Registration, and Turnout                  292

AP Photo/Mayra Beltran, Houston Chronicle

AP Photo/Eric Gay, File

*Electronic Voting in Texas* — 293
*Contemporary Voter Registration and Turnout* — 295
*Who Votes?* — 298
**Electoral Competition in Texas Elections** — 300
*Campaigns in Texas History* — 303
*Campaigns in Texas Today* — 303
**Campaign Finance in Texas** — 306
*Regulating Campaign Finance* — 306
*Contribution Disclosure* — 308
*Judicial Campaign Contributions* — 309
*Campaign Spending* — 309
**Winners and Losers** — 311
**Conclusion** — 312
**Key Terms** — 313
**Core Assessment** — 313

## CHAPTER 10     314

### POLITICAL PARTIES

**The Development of Political Parties in Texas** — 316
*Texas versus New York* — 318
*Parties, Competition, and Voter Participation* — 320
**Political Parties in Texas** — 323
*Party Loyalty and Identification* — 325
*Functions of Parties* — 326
*The Consequences of Weak Parties* — 328
*Texas Legends:* **Pappy O'Daniel** — 330
**Party Organizations** — 331
*Local Parties* — 333
*State Parties* — 335
*Nominating Presidential Candidates* — 337
*The State Parties and the National Parties* — 339
*Texas versus Iowa* — 340
**Winners and Losers** — 341
**Conclusion** — 342
**Key Terms** — 343
**Core Assessment** — 343

© LM Otero/AP/Corbis

## CHAPTER 11     344

### ORGANIZED INTERESTS

**Organized Interests in Texas Politics** — 346
*Interest Group Formation* — 347
*Texas Legends:* **James Leininger** — 348
*Types of Interests in Texas* — 350
*What Organized Interests Contribute to the Political Process* — 352
**Influencing Policy in Texas through Organized Interests** — 353
*Organized Interests' Spending on Elections* — 353

AP Photo/Will Weissert

# CONTENTS

*Texas Legends*: **The League of United Latin American Citizens**    **354**

*From Activism and Litigation to Lobbying*    **357**

*Lobby Regulation*    **361**

*Lobbyists' Relationship with Texas Legislators*    **362**

*Texas versus Washington*    **364**

**The Relationship between Organized Interests and Parties**    **365**

**Winners and Losers**    **366**

**Conclusion**    **367**

**Key Terms**    **368**

**Core Assessment**    **368**

## CHAPTER 12    370
### LOCAL GOVERNMENT IN TEXAS

**Local Government: The Basics**    **372**

**County Government, Texas-Style**    **376**

*History and Function of Counties in Texas*    **376**

*Governing Texas Counties*    **379**

*County Finances and Operations*    **382**

**Cities**    **385**

*Texas Legends*: **Tommy Joe Vandergriff**    **387**

*Forms of City Government*    **388**

*Texas versus Ohio*    **391**

*City Elections*    **392**

*Issues in City Government*    **395**

*Texas Legends*: **The Galveston Hurricane**    **397**

*Homeowners Associations: Not Quite a Government, but Close*    **399**

*Texas and the Fed on Same-Sex Benefits*    **400**

**Other Forms of Local Government**    **401**

*Public Education as Local Government*    **401**

*Special Districts*    **403**

*Texas versus Tennessee*    **404**

**Winners and Losers**    **406**

**Conclusion**    **407**

**Key Terms**    **408**

**Core Assessment**    **408**

## CHAPTER 13    410
### FISCAL POLICY

**The Policymaking Process**    **412**

**Sources of State Revenue: Taxes**    **413**

*Texas and the Fed on Fiscal Federalism*    **414**

*Taxes in Texas History*    **414**

*State Taxes Today*    **415**

*Texas versus New Jersey*    **416**

*Property Taxes*    **419**

**Winners and Losers**    **423**

AP Photo/Tony Gutierrez

© San Antonio Express-News/ZUMA

Sources of State Revenue: Other Resources ....... 424
   *Federal Grants* ....... 425
   *Interest, Licensing, and Lottery Funds* ....... 426
Spending and Budgeting ....... 427
   *State Budgeting* ....... 427
   *State Spending* ....... 429
   *The Rainy Day Fund* ....... 430
   *The Legislative Budget Board* ....... 432
Fiscal Policy Tools ....... 434
   *Tax Expenditures* ....... 434
   *Subsidies* ....... 435
Winners and Losers ....... 436
Conclusion ....... 438
Key Terms ....... 438
Core Assessment ....... 439

## CHAPTER 14      440
### EDUCATION AND SOCIAL POLICY

Education Policy ....... 442
   *Public Education in Grades K–12* ....... 443
*Texas Legends:* **Neither Separate Nor Equal:**
**Hispanics in the Education System** ....... 445
   *Funding for K–12* ....... 446
*Texas Legends:* **Mansfield High** ....... 447
   *Accountability and Reform in K–12* ....... 449
Winners and Losers ....... 452
*Texas and the Fed on Education Policy* ....... 453
   *Higher Education* ....... 454
*Texas Legends:* **Governor James Ferguson and the University of Texas** ....... 458
   *Access to Higher Education* ....... 459
   *Costs of Higher Education* ....... 461
   *Accountability in Higher Education* ....... 464
   *Universities' Other Contributions* ....... 466
Winners and Losers ....... 466
Health and Human Services ....... 467
   *Social Welfare Programs* ....... 467
   *Health Care* ....... 469
Winners and Losers ....... 471
Conclusion ....... 473
Key Terms ....... 473
Core Assessment ....... 473

## CHAPTER 15      474
### TRANSFORMING TEXAS: ENERGY, ENVIRONMENT, TRANSPORTATION, AND IMMIGRATION POLICIES

Oil and Gas in Texas ....... 476

| | |
|---|---|
| *Oil's Influence on Texas* | 476 |
| *Texas Legends:* **Hot Oil** | **478** |
| *The Natural Gas Boom and Fracking* | 479 |
| **Environmental Policy** | 481 |
| **Texas Air Quality** | 482 |
| *Texas versus California* | 483 |
| **Water and Scarcity** | 484 |
| *Texas Legends:* **Private Property and Takings** | **485** |
| **Alternative Energy** | 485 |
| **Hazardous Waste** | 486 |
| **Winners and Losers** | 488 |
| **Transportation Policy** | 488 |
| *Railroads* | 489 |
| *Roads* | 490 |
| *Mass Transit* | 495 |
| **Winners and Losers** | 496 |
| **Immigration Policy** | 496 |
| *Costs and Benefits of Undocumented Workers* | 498 |
| *Texas and the Fed on Immigration* | 499 |
| **Winners and Losers** | 501 |
| **Conclusion** | 502 |
| **Key Terms** | 503 |
| **Core Assessment** | 503 |
| | |
| Appendix | |
| Declaration of Independence of the Republic of Texas | 504 |
| Notes | 507 |
| Glossary | 524 |
| Index | 534 |

# PREFACE

*As has often been said, there is no State in the Union whose history presents such varied and romantic scenes as does that of Texas. This alone would recommend it to the general reader and the earnest student. But there is in addition to its interest a weighty reason why every school in the State should give Texas History a place in its course of study. No one who learns well the lessons taught can fail to become a better and wiser citizen.*[1]

Anna J. Hardwicke Pennybacker,
*A New History of Texas for Schools* (1888)

**M**rs. Pennybacker's "new" history of Texas presents a traditional view of the state's history. The copy we used when writing this book originally belonged to Earl B. Persons, the great-uncle of one of the authors. In the century since young Earl Persons first read this quotation in his schoolbook, Texans have written some new history and revised some old. Mr. Persons served in World War I before taking part in the rise of the oil business in East Texas—a period during which he saw his pastures become more valuable for the oil under them than the cattle that grazed on them. The next generation of Texans saw America through World War II, the Cold War, and the space race directed from NASA in Houston. That generation grew up on *Texas History Movies,* a comic version of Texas history sponsored by an oil company. Another generation saw the high-tech boom take root in the state. Texans born today may never own a printed book on the state's politics and history, and thus they will be unlikely to leave their names scrawled in a textbook to remind descendants of the Texas their ancestors knew. (However, today's students can still preserve the Texas they know by buying copies of this text and setting them aside so that their children and grandchildren can share the fun of Texas circa 2015—please contact CQ Press for inquiries regarding bulk sales.)

The economic, demographic, and political changes in the state continually introduce new ways of life to its citizens. Over the past century, as Texans moved from the ranches and farms of the countryside into more urban areas, these cities, suburbs, and exurbs became the natural habitat of Texans. As small towns gave way to cities, Texans found themselves living closer and closer together, meaning that they had to cooperate more with neighbors and fellow citizens. The farmer's lonely but simple commute from farmhouse to field has been replaced by long treks to work on crowded superhighways. For Texans of an earlier time, commerce meant the weekly trip into town to sell goods, buy supplies, and check the mail at the post office. Social networking meant gathering at the local coffee shop to swap stories over breakfast. Today, many Texans remain in constant contact with other Texans, other Americans, and other people from around the world. Many Texans have trouble working when their Internet connection goes down even briefly.

Clearly, we Texans aren't what we used to be. However, our image of ourselves has not changed quite as much as the circumstances of our lives. During the century since Mrs. Pennybacker wrote those words reproduced above, most Texans have looked again at our history and found a much more nuanced view of our conflicts with the Mexican government during the revolution and with the U.S. government during and after the U.S. Civil War. Although scholars have reviewed and revised the stories of Texas, Texans have often clung to the more romantic version of our history. At the same time, Texans seamlessly blend together many of the traditions and cultural traits that find their way into the state. One can't help to think about the blending of cultures when revising chapters over a breakfast of jalapeño cheddar biscuits, which combine the state's southern and Mexican heritages, in the familiar confines of Whataburger, a modern chain restaurant with roots in Corpus Christi that has become a Texas tradition of its own. In Texas, we often take the blending of cultures for granted. Such a meal is neither Mexican nor southern—it's Texan.

Our state's government is in the unenviable position of having to keep pace with all the changes in the state while still remaining true to our traditions and legends. Texas government needs to be both lean and modern, capable of managing the affairs of almost 27 million Texans while still retaining a small-town feel and the frontier spirit. Texas leaders must be both engaged and rooted, nimble enough to respond to global competition and regional hurricane devastation but still able to ride a horse and swap stories with fellow Texans, whether over the counter of the local diner or over the Internet on Reddit, Facebook, or Twitter.

One of the most remarkable things about teaching Texas politics is that, although many Texas students only take the course because it's required, and so many instructors have trepidations about teaching it, the subject is actually pretty enjoyable. As Molly Ivins said, "I believe politics is the finest form of entertainment in the state of Texas: better than the zoo, better than the circus, rougher than football, and more aesthetically satisfying than baseball."[2] Generations of textbooks have stepped into the breach between these reluctant participants, often with mixed results. Textbooks about Texas politics tend to be rather dry, but the topic can be spicy, as our state's history is full of legends, criminals, preachers, hucksters, and even comedians. Somehow, when all is said and done, the life is too often taken out of Texas politics, and we think that's a true Texas tragedy.

We've tried to breathe a little of that life back into the study of Texas politics. We can't engage in storytelling for storytelling's sake. However, any effort to put together a dry, story-free (i.e., "serious") textbook on Texas politics would lead us to forget the role that the state's legends and myths play in shaping how Texans think and how our politicians behave. You can't tell the story of Texas without revisiting a few tall tales, debunking some persistent myths in the state, and captivating the readers with the true stories that are often more interesting than the legends.

## READING BETWEEN THE LINES OF LONE STAR POLITICS

The plan for the book is relatively simple. We open with an introduction to the state and its history in Chapter 1. While much of this story will be familiar to many readers, we feel it bears repeating to bring focus to the political history of the state and to refresh the memories of Texas students who haven't read much about their state's history since middle school. Building on the state's history, Chapter 2 examines the birth and rebirth of the state through its constitutions. That chapter emphasizes that while the Texas Constitution continues to evolve, it has not been able to keep pace with a rapidly changing state. Chapter 3 looks at how the Texas Legislature is elected and how it functions, and Chapter 4 looks at the legislative process. The legislature, which is at the heart of Texas democracy, is a fine example of how changes have been slow to come. Next, Chapter 5 visits the Texas governor's mansion to see if the governor's office is ready to keep up with the dynamic state. Chapter 6 examines many of the organizations that make up the Texas bureaucracy. Chapter 7 considers the court system of Texas, and Chapter 8 looks at the process of dispensing justice in Texas. Chapter 9 examines how Texans elect their officials, including discussion of how candidates campaign for those offices. Chapter 10 looks at how Texans work together (sometimes) through parties, and Chapter 11 explores the impact of organized interests in the state. Chapter 12 considers local government in Texas (including those pesky homeowners associations). Chapter 13 begins our discussion of what government produces: policy. That chapter focuses on our fiscal policy—how and why we tax citizens and how that money is spent. Chapter 14 focuses on the public education system (K–12), higher education, and the state's role in health care. Finally, Chapter 15 investigates what Texas is doing in the areas of transportation, natural resources, the environment, and immigration. It also concludes the book and revisits a few themes.

## FEATURING OUR FEATURES

This text is designed to draw readers into the key issues of politics in Texas. Several features of the text are designed to bring the reader's attention to an issue, often helping the reader to see it in a new light.

### Texas Legends

John Steinbeck observed after his first visit to Texas, "Like most passionate nations Texas has its own history based on, but not limited by, facts."[3] We have made a discussion of Texas legends a recurring feature of this text. When we look at the characters and stories that fill Texas politics, we often find that Texas's legends differ from reality. These legends play a role in shaping Texans' self-image whether or not they can be proven true. One historian, who suggested that the real Davy Crockett surrendered rather than died fighting—unlike Fess Parker's heroic portrayal of Crockett in Disney's movie version of the battle of the Alamo—was told by an angry reader that the "Fess Parker image has done more for children than your book can."[4] Discussing what has been termed the "Texas creation myth," one writer concluded, "The mythic Alamo of the American collective imagination has become far more important than the Alamo

of tedious historical fact."[5] It is odd that Texans have allowed Davy Crockett, Jim Bowie, and other legends of the Alamo to be recast (especially by Walt Disney). Many of the men who defended the Alamo were brave, but their lives were not necessarily family fare. For example, Bowie partnered in a slave-smuggling ring with pirate Jean Lafitte before arriving in Texas,[6] and William Travis abandoned a young son and a pregnant wife before he came to the state.

That these men and women lived hard lives and made serious errors is not the point of retelling their stories. Texas is a place where people come to start over and find a new identity. The celebrated Baron de Bastrop was really a Dutchman named Philip Hendrik Nering Bögel who invented the title when he arrived in San Antonio with very little money. When Moses Austin came to Texas in 1820 to win the right to form colonies in Texas, only to be sent packing by a Spanish governor who distrusted foreigners, it was the baron who persuaded the governor to forward Austin's proposal to the Spanish government. As one author put it, "He was among the first, but certainly not the last, loser to come to Texas to reinvent himself and emerge in prominence."[7]

The flaws in Texas's leaders remain evident today. George W. Bush was honest—if not always specific—about the mistakes in his past. Despite those flaws, Texans twice chose him as their governor before recommending him to a nation that then twice elected him as president.

Even as the legends of our history reinvented themselves, we Texans have reinvented our own history. Our recollection of history is less fixed than we care to admit. After the Texans won the Battle of San Jacinto with the battle cry, "Remember the Alamo," the Alamo itself would lie in neglect for half a century, a forgotten monument that was used to store onions and potatoes before being restored and elevated as the "Shrine of Texas Liberty."

Our explorations of Texas legends are not an attempt to resolve the debate between views of "Disneyland Davy" and other versions of Texas history. Texans need not be sidetracked by the debate about whether or not their state's heroes were perfect. They were not. Neither were the founders of the United States. What we need to understand is how important these images are to the people of Texas. Describing the "passionate nation" that is Texas, John Steinbeck noted that "rich, poor, Panhandle, Gulf, city, county, Texas is the obsession, the proper study and the passionate possession of all Texans."[8]

The aspirations embedded in our myths play a role in how the state approaches change. Because our legends are about who we once were, retelling these stories now reminds us who we are today and keeps us from drifting too far from our values. At the same time, these legends can tell us a great deal about who we want to be and where our hopes come from. As Steinbeck wrote, "I have said that Texas is a state of mind, but I think it is more than that. It is a mystique closely approximating a religion."[9]

### Winners and Losers

Politics involves the distribution of goods and by its nature produces winners and losers. While Texas's history, culture, and predilections may seem vague and distant to students today, the politics that spring from them have ramifications that are very real for the citizens of the state. This text is intended to encourage students to think critically about Texas politics, identify problems, and look ahead to solutions. We will frequently pause and look at who gets what from government by looking at winners and losers in Texas politics and featuring questions that encourage critical thinking. This is especially valuable in studying Texas political history because the victories won by a group in one era most often lay the groundwork for the next battles. Texas is in a constant state of change, and citizens need to consider what issues need to be addressed to deal with these changes and how their fellow Texans might be affected by them.

## Texas versus . . .

We will occasionally pause to compare Texas to other states, often focusing on those states that provide the most dramatic or interesting contrasts to Texas. We want to illustrate how Texas is different and why that difference is significant. Because most citizens of a state seldom consider their options, we felt it was important to illustrate the possibilities of state government and to illustrate the consequences of choices that people face. Comparisons were selected to provide examples from potentially familiar settings, such as Louisiana or California, as well as settings that Texans may have little exposure to, such as Vermont or North Dakota. It is our hope that students will come to appreciate why Texas is just a little bit different. Our comparison of Texas to other states is a good place to highlight critical thinking. We pose a set of questions after each comparison to encourage students to look at options and ponder what would best serve the state.

## Texas and the Fed

Chapter 2 introduces the topic of federalism, but it's nearly impossible to leave behind the relationship between the state and federal governments. Federalism permeates a diverse set of issues covered throughout the book, and now students can get to know that relationship more intimately. This new box feature explores how Texas and the federal government relate on topics including abortion, marijuana, voting rights, same-sex benefits, education policy, and immigration. These are important contemporary issues that deserve greater scrutiny. Questions at the end of each box encourage students to think actively about what they've just read and engage in debate or draw their own conclusions.

## How Texas Government Works

With every edition, we try to ensure a good representation of visual material because we know that some people simply process information better that way. We also understand that sometimes a picture really is worth a thousand words. We haven't taken those words out of the book, because not everyone gets what the picture is saying, but we have added full-page infographics to this edition—one for each chapter. They focus on processes and structures that convey how Texas government works, and they provide big-picture perspective in showing how Texas compares to the rest of the United States or even internationally. Students will come away with a better understanding of not only how Texas government functions but how it fits into this wider world we live in.

## NEW TO THE FOURTH EDITION

You can't talk about Texas government without talking about the relationship between the state government and the federal government. We've added a federalism box feature called **Texas and the Fed** to explore a lot of contemporary issues relevant to and of interest to students today that can't get the attention they deserve shoehorned into a discussion about how the courts are structured. This new feature appears in half of the book's chapters and has been carefully developed to compare the state and federal approaches on a topic. These discussions also encourage students to think critically about the state and federal relationship and probe beyond what they may hear with half an ear on the news or read in a tweet on Twitter.

**How Texas Government Works** infographics appear in every chapter, offering engaging visual illustrations of key chapter concepts and processes, such as how a Texas bill becomes a law and how organized interests approach lobbying. These new, full-page graphic displays are also a great way to make comparisons, such as how today's state demographics compare to the rest of the country, how the state measures up on voter turnout, and where Texas sits globally when it comes to death penalty executions.

In addition to these brand new features, we've added some new **Texas Legends**, spotlighting individuals such as the first Supreme Court of Texas justice Raul A. Gonzalez Jr., organizations such as the League for Latin American Citizens, and the social movement behind Hispanics' fight for equal education in the state. We've heard your calls for more positive representations of Hispanics and for more diversity coverage in the book overall. Concerns such as these, along with a conscious attempt to widen our discussion to acknowledge the current and growing diversity of Texas's population and interests, have been a main drive behind this edition.

We're also very aware of the impact of the Texas Higher Education Coordinating Board's (THECB's) new curriculum standards and kept them in mind throughout the revision process. We honed our narrative, our chapter objectives, and our probing questions to provide content that students can learn from without being distracted by blatant check marks down a list of requirements. *Lone Star*'s comparative approach provides a wealth of opportunity to get students thinking from a variety of angles, and we've added more questions—crafted particularly with THECB standards in mind—to ensure students develop these skills. The end of each chapter now includes **Core Assessment** questions that address these new standards and serve as a jumping-off point to more targeted study that can be found on the book's companion website. We realize, though, that instructors may want something more, and we've arranged for that in the expanded offerings in our instructor resources, available from SAGE edge for CQ Press.

## SAGE EDGE FOR CQ PRESS

http://edge.sagepub.com/collier4e

**S**AGE edge offers a robust online environment featuring an impressive array of tools and resources for review, study, and further exploration, keeping both instructors and students on the cutting edge of teaching and learning. SAGE edge content is open access and available on demand. This edition comes with a full range of high-quality instructor and student ancillaries prepared by Alexander B. Hogan, Lone Star College-CyFair. Learning and teaching has never been easier!

**SAGE edge for Students** provides a personalized approach to help students accomplish their coursework goals in an easy-to-use learning environment.

- Mobile-friendly **eFlashcards** strengthen understanding of key terms and concepts.
- Mobile-friendly practice **quizzes** allow for independent assessment by students of their mastery of course material.
- A customized online **action plan** includes tips and feedback on progress throughout the course and materials, which allows students to individualize their learning experience.
- **Chapter summaries** with **learning objectives** and **review questions** reinforce the most important material.
- Carefully selected chapter-by-chapter **video links** and **multimedia content** enhance classroom-based explorations of key topics.

**SAGE edge for Instructors** supports teaching by making it easy to integrate quality content and create a rich learning environment for students.

- A **Test bank** provides a diverse range of pre-written options as well as the opportunity to edit any question and/or insert personalized questions to effectively assess students' progress and understanding.
- Editable, chapter-specific **PowerPoint® slides** offer complete flexibility for creating a multimedia presentation for the course.
- **Multimedia content** includes videos that appeal to students with different learning styles.
- An **instructor manual** summarizes key concepts and identifies content to THECB curriculum standards by chapter to ease preparation for lectures and class discussions.
- Chapter-specific **discussion questions** help launch classroom interaction by prompting students to engage with the material and by reinforcing important content.
- Lively and stimulating **assignments** and **exercises** can be used in class or in online teaching to reinforce active learning and key features from the text. The activities apply to individual or group projects.
- A set of all the **graphics from the text**, including all of the maps, tables, and figures, is available in PowerPoint, pdf, and JPEG formats for class presentations.
- A **transition guide** provides a chapter-by-chapter outline of key changes to the fourth edition.
- A **common course cartridge** includes all of the instructor resources and assessment material from the student study site, making it easy for instructors to upload and use these materials in learning management systems such as Blackboard™, Angel®, Moodle™, Canvas, and Desire2Learn™.

PREFACE

## ACKNOWLEDGMENTS

**O**bviously, we didn't do this by ourselves. We did make all the mistakes. Against all odds, a small band of dedicated people tried their best to detect these mistakes and set us right.

We also benefited from many small favors from other colleagues and new friends. Clint Walker and our other Facebook friends from "The History of Six Flags" page helped us figure out the names of some of the rides from the early days of Six Flags Over Texas.

While the book's heart came from Texas, we got some help from friends in Washington, D.C. As parts of this book were being written at a small-town Whataburger, the good people at CQ Press, located far from Texas, labored to keep us on schedule and under control. Despite the fact that they still haven't found the pictures we wanted of the "Los Conquistadors Coronado Burro Ride" at the Six Flags Over Texas amusement park (or hid them from us if they did), we would like to thank senior development editor Nancy Matuszak, editorial assistant Raquel Christie, copy editor Shannon Kelly, and production editor Laura Barrett for their benevolence, patience, and diligence. We'd also like to thank the reviewers who offered up a valuable balance of criticism and encouragement:

Alicia Andreatta, Cisco College

Gabriel Bach, North Lake College (Irving, TX)

Leda Barnett, Our Lady of the Lake University

Annie Benifield, Lone Star College–Tomball

Brian Cravens, Blinn College

Richard Daly, St. Edward's University

Kevin Davis, North Central Texas College

Cecil Dorsey, San Jacinto College–South

Henry Esparza, University of Texas at San Antonio

Richard Hoefer, University of Texas at Arlington

Floyd W. Holder IV, Texas A&M University–Kingsville

Jeff Justice, Tarleton State University

Heidi M. Lange, Houston Community College SWC

Mary Linder, Grayson County College

Hamed Madani, Tarrant County College–Southeast

Maurice Mangum, Texas Southern University

Thomas Miles, Texas Women's University

Eric Miller, Blinn College

Brian Naples, Panola College

Sharon A. Navarro, University of Texas at San Antonio

**xxvi** LONE STAR POLITICS

William Parent, San Jacinto College

Lisa Perez-Nichols, Austin Community College

Paul J. Pope, University of Texas at Brownsville

Jo Marie Rios, Texas A&M University–Corpus Christi

Robert Rodriguez, Texas A&M University–Commerce

Debra St. John, Collin County Community College

Raymond Sandoval, Richland College

Gino Tozzi, Jr., University of Houston–Victoria

Christopher L. Turner, Laredo Community College

Joel Turner, Western Kentucky University

Glenn Utter, Lamar University

M. Theron Waddell, Galveston College

## NOTES

1. Mrs. Anna J. Hardwicke Pennybacker, *A New History of Texas for Schools* (Tyler, Tex., 1888), v.

2. Molly Ivins, *Nothin' But Good Times Ahead* (New York: Random House, 1993), 55–56.

3. John Steinbeck, *Travels With Charley: In Search of America* (New York: Bantam Books, 1961), 226.

4. James E. Crisp, *Sleuthing the Alamo: Davy Crockett's Last Stand and Other Mysteries of the Texas Revolution* (New York: Oxford University Press, 2004), 142.

5. Ibid., 144.

6. Ibid., 17.

7. James L. Haley, *Passionate Nation: The Epic History of Texas* (New York: Free Press, 2006), 70.

8. Steinbeck, *Travels With Charley*, 226.

9. Ibid., 227.

# ABOUT THE AUTHORS

**Ken Collier** is an associate professor at Stephen F. Austin State University, with a PhD from the University of Texas at Austin. He is the author of *Between the Branches: The White House Office of Legislative Affairs* and is currently writing on presidential speechwriting and leadership. He has published articles in such journals as *Journal of Politics, White House Studies, Presidential Studies Quarterly, Public Choice, and Social Science Quarterly.*

**Steven Galatas** is an associate professor at Stephen F. Austin State University, with a PhD from the University of Missouri. He has published articles in *Journal of Politics, Public Choice, Party Politics, Politics and Policy,* and *PS: Political Science and Politics.* His research and teaching concern comparative elections, voting behavior, and campaign finance.

**Julie Harrelson-Stephens** is an associate professor at Stephen F. Austin State University, with a PhD from the University of North Texas. She has co-edited, with Rhonda L. Callaway, *Exploring International Human Rights: Essential Readings* and has been published in *Conflict and Terrorism, PS: Political Science and Politics, Human Rights Review,* and *International Interactions.* Her primary research interests include human rights, regime theory, and terrorism.

**SAGE** was founded in 1965 by Sara Miller McCune to support the dissemination of usable knowledge by publishing innovative and high-quality research and teaching content. Today, we publish more than 750 journals, including those of more than 300 learned societies, more than 800 new books per year, and a growing range of library products including archives, data, case studies, reports, conference highlights, and video. SAGE remains majority-owned by our founder, and after Sara's lifetime will become owned by a charitable trust that secures our continued independence.

Los Angeles | London | Washington DC | New Delhi | Singapore | Boston

# 1 INTRODUCTION

After watching immigrants stream across the border into Texas year after year, government officials on the Texas side began to worry that their state was being transformed into a part-Mexican, part-Anglo society that would prove unmanageable and ungovernable as the growing number of immigrants asserted their political power. Some immigrants entered lawfully, patiently working through the government's cumbersome process; others came without regard for the laws, exploiting a border that was too long and too remote to be effectively monitored. Most of the new immigrants proved both hard-working and enterprising additions to Texas's society and economy. Many brought their families for a chance at a better life or planned to bring family along as soon as they earned enough money to do so. A few crossed the border to escape legal and financial problems back home and contributed to criminal enterprises or squandered their wages on alcohol and vice, eventually abandoning their families. Established residents worried that they would become foreigners in their own country or doubted that their new neighbors would ever prove anything but a challenge since many newcomers refused to assimilate or adopt the politics and culture of their new home. Many of the new arrivals stubbornly clung to their native tongue; some even began to demand that official business be conducted in it.

The government felt that much of the problem lay on the other side of the border. Some of these immigrants seemed to be entering the state to foment change, and many had strong ties to political leaders back home. Sam Houston, the former governor of Tennessee, was a close political and personal friend of U.S. president Andrew Jackson. Davy Crockett, also a product of Jackson's Democratic Party in Tennessee, had served in the U.S. Congress and was one of the more dynamic political figures of the day. It seemed likely that his political ambitions followed him to Texas.

Many of the early Texans who fought for independence from Mexico came to Texas against the expressed wishes of the Mexican government. Whereas early American colonists along the Eastern Seaboard settled among, and then pushed aside, the more loosely organized Native American populations, some early Texans violated a border officially recognized by the American government as they brushed aside Mexican law. The immigration issue—today as then—represents the challenge of governing a rapidly changing state. While immigrants today generate a great deal of revenue for the

state through sales and income taxes, they also cost the counties and local governments a great deal in services. Immigrants contribute greatly to the economic success of the state by meeting the demand for inexpensive labor, but they sometimes do so at the expense of native-born labor.

The 55-foot Big Tex, which presides over the Texas State Fair, is an icon to all Texans, no matter their origin. The 2010 Census found that about 61 percent of Texans were born in Texas, 23 percent were born elsewhere in the United States, and 16 percent were foreign born.

Immigration, then and now, shows us that Texas's placement at the crossroads between new and old has been one of the few constants in the politics of the state. Texas has relished its growth but often been uncomfortable with the new arrivals who have fueled it. Texans have enjoyed the prosperity that growth brings but only reluctantly accepted the new Texans and the changes they have triggered.

While change may be inevitable, a society is rooted by the stories citizens share and hand down from generation to generation. We Texans are especially attached to our state's history and its legends of larger-than-life people and events. Stories from Texas history are more than dramatic scenes we retell and re-create for entertainment; these stories define who we are and remind us of our values. Texas's unique relationship with its history is reflected in a favorite theme park, Six Flags Over Texas, an amusement park originally constructed around Texas history themes and which at one time featured rides such as "La Salle's River Boat Adventure" in the French section and "Los Conquistadores Mule Pack Coronado Trek" in the Spanish section.[1] Like the state it represents, the theme park has undergone constant change since its inception. Today, the legends portrayed at Six Flags Over Texas are decidedly modern, and tourists are more likely to pose for pictures with Batman and Bugs Bunny in front of gleaming metal roller coasters than with the costumed deputies who duel horse thieves in front of the replica county courthouse.

Legends are stories passed down for generations—but stories that are often presented as history. While not always entirely true, legends play an important role in politics. Legends reveal a desire to be culturally connected to our fellow citizens and to a larger entity, and they also tell us a great deal about who we want to be.

So where, between legend and reality, is the true Texas? Even as it takes care to project a rustic frontier image, Texas today is home to many of the most innovative businesses in the global marketplace. Greg Abbott launched his campaign in La Villita near the Alamo in San Antonio, but he did so in front of a large video screen that flashed his message digitally to the crowd. Thus, even as they remember the Alamo and the rest of Texas's past, the leaders of Texas today embrace new technology as well as the state's oldest traditions.

In this chapter, we will chart the contours of this gap. We will start by looking at Texas history and geography, casting an eye toward the traditions and transformations that have shaped the state's politics. We will examine some of the legends behind Texas politics and highlight the differences between Texas and another one-time independent U.S. state. We will conclude the chapter by focusing on the state of Texas today—its people, economy, and culture.

## Chapter Objectives

★ Describe how the state's geography and demographics shape its politics.

★ Discuss the role of tradition and legend in Texas politics.

★ Evaluate the role that political parties played in the origin and development of Texas.

★ Describe the political culture of Texas and its impact on Texas government.

★ Explain the context of Texas's increasingly diverse population.

★ Assess who wins and who loses in a changing Texas.

## TEXAS GEOGRAPHY

The landmass of Texas defines the state's image as much as it has determined the course of its history. With a land area totaling 263,513 square miles, it is the second largest of the U.S. states, behind Alaska's 663,276 square miles. From east to west the state spans 773 miles and from north to south 801 miles. The 785-mile drive from Marshall to El Paso takes a traveler from the Piney Woods of East Texas to the sparse landscape of the West Texas desert. Driving the 900 miles north from Brownsville to Texline takes the traveler from the border of Mexico and the Gulf of Mexico to the borders of Oklahoma and New Mexico. The Texas Gulf Coast consists of shoreline and marshy areas, while the Trans-Pecos region includes the arid desert of Big Bend and Guadalupe Peak, the highest point in Texas at 8,749 feet.

Texas runs the full gamut from urban to rural. The state's most populous county, Harris County, which contains Houston, had 4,336,853 residents in 2013, making it more populous than half of the states in the United States. Texas also has some of the nation's least populated counties, with Loving County's 677 square miles in the Panhandle occupied by only ninety-five residents. The state has eight counties with populations under 1,000, and about one-third (eighty-nine) of Texas's 254 counties have populations under 10,000.

Texas's size encourages more than bragging rights. V. O. Key, a native Texan and one of the founders of modern political science, pointed out that the geographic size of the state has limited the face-to-face interactions needed to develop closely knit political organizations. While this helped inoculate Texas from the large party machines that corrupted politics in many other places during the nineteenth century, it has also inhibited the formation of beneficial groups that would bring together more benevolent forces from across the state.

The state's size makes campaigning expensive for candidates trying to win votes statewide and has left the state's politicians more dependent on those capable of financing a statewide campaign. The sheer size of the state has also rewarded a dramatic style. As Key observed after surveying the electoral history of his home state, "Attention-getting antics substituted for organized politics."[2] In the absence of closely knit state political networks, and given Texans' fondness for independence, the path to power for the political outsider may be a little bit easier. The ability to quickly grab the imagination of voters has given Texas politics a colorful cast of characters rivaled by few other places. Texas's political candidates are often larger than life, and while change has been a constant in Texas politics, subtlety is often lacking. These colorful characters often make for good storytelling, but they do not always make for good government. As former lieutenant governor Ben Barnes once mused as he looked out at the Texas Senate, "There were more eccentric, unpredictable, and flat crazy characters than you'd find in any novel."[3]

Size has contributed to the state's mentality in other ways. With its seemingly endless frontier, Texas represents limitless potential to many. At the same time, its spaciousness offers an escape that reinforces Texans' sense of independence and freedom. With Texans dispersed across such an extensive landscape, history and legends become even more important as a shared culture. The vast geographic distances and the differences in human geography leave many wondering exactly what it is that binds so tightly all these people from all these places and makes them into such fiercely loyal Texans. The answer, of course, is Texas's unique history. As John Steinbeck wrote, "There is no physical or geographical unity in Texas. Its unity lies in the mind."[4]

While Texas's history unites its citizens, it also represents a long string of transitions that brought with them conflict between old and new. As we will see, the Texas political system has often resisted the needs and wishes of new arrivals because those that preceded them were reluctant to give up the power they had earned or fought for. While this pattern is not unique to Texas, Texas's history offers a vivid tableau of upheaval along the hard road of change.

# HISTORY: THE BIRTH OF TEXAS TRADITIONS

The first wave of change began about 12,000 years ago when humans who had drifted across the Bering Strait land bridge into North America some 20,000 years ago eventually found their way into Texas. These earliest Texans hunted mammoths before those large animals became extinct. Later, bison served as a primary food source on the grassy plains that covered present-day West Texas. As changes in the climate began to warm the plains, the land could no longer support the large mammals that the hunting tribes depended on, and, as a result, hunter-gatherer tribes became more prevalent.

As with native people from other parts of the continent, the Native American tribes of Texas were diverse. About 1,500 years ago, the Caddo people developed agricultural tools and practices that gave them a more stable food supply, which meant less need to roam and more time to form a society with social classes and to establish trading relations with other tribes. By 1500, an estimated 200,000 Caddos inhabited a society that was extensive enough to lead some historians to call the Caddos the "Romans of Texas."[5] Along the Gulf Coast, the Karankawa tribe relied on fish and shellfish for much of their diet. Dubbed cannibals by some, the Karankawas ate only their enemies and were in fact so shocked to learn that the Spanish survivors of the Narváez Expedition had cannibalized each other that some Karankawas expressed regret at not having killed the Spanish explorers when they first came ashore.[6] Coahuiltecan tribes roamed the area southwest of the Karankawas, surviving on a diverse diet of whatever they could gather or catch. Because subsistence needs forced them to move about the prairies, these small hunter-gatherer bands lacked the cohesive society that developed among tribes such as the Caddos. The Apaches, who inhabited areas of what would become the Texas Panhandle, lived in large, extended families in a peaceful and well-ordered society.

Christopher Columbus's first voyage brought great change to the Texas region as the Spanish Empire in America began to take root in the Caribbean, Central America, and the Southwest. As would many others after them, the conquistadores Álvar Núñez Cabeza de Vaca and later Hernando Cortéz visited the region seeking wealth. One of the most significant instruments of change the Spanish brought with them was the horse. Even though the Spanish forces were never a large enough presence to transform the region, the horses they brought changed Indian society by giving some tribes the means to move their camps more quickly and become more effective hunters and warriors.

The French, led by René-Robert Cavelier and Sieur de La Salle, managed only a brief presence in Texas. La Salle, who, in the view of one historian, had the sort of personality and exhibited the kind of behavior that "led many to question his mental stability,"[7] had an ambitious plan to build a series of posts down the Mississippi River to the Gulf of Mexico, claim all of the land drained by the Mississippi, and name it Louisiana in honor of the French king Louis XIV. La Salle's venture into Texas failed, and La Salle himself was killed in an ambush. However, La Salle's incursions spurred the Spanish to increase their settlement of East Texas to counter any future French arrivals.

Although relative newcomers themselves, the Spanish, like the Indian tribes before them, were suspicious of the motives of new arrivals and sought to bar outsiders; they attempted to strengthen their hold on the area by encouraging their own people to

**MAP 1.1**    **Independent Texas**

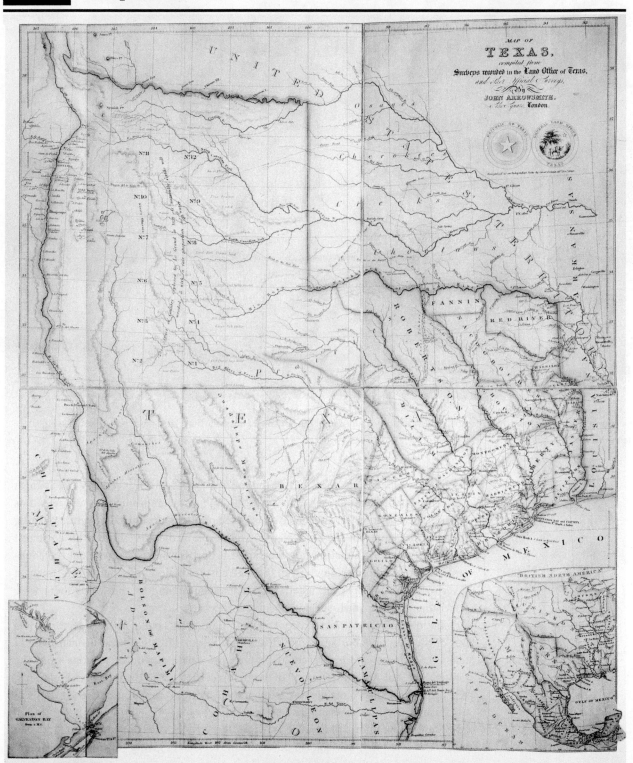

The Alamo, the most famous historic site in Texas, was originally part of the network of missions that the Spanish hoped would establish their presence in Texas.

establish or expand settlements. Over the course of the eighteenth century, the Spanish gradually established themselves in Texas through a system of missions and presidios (forts). The missions were designed to bring the Indians closer to God while pushing the French away from the area. Native Americans in the area showed little interest in converting to Catholicism, however, and the Spanish had to supplement their religious outposts with presidios. Given the high costs of maintaining these forts, Spanish investments in the area ultimately proved inadequate, and by the 1790s there were fewer than 3,200 Spanish-speaking people in Texas.

Building a border wall to keep American immigrants out of Spanish territory was out of the question, but Spanish officials declared in 1795 that local officials should take "the utmost care to prevent the passage to this kingdom of persons from the United States of America."[8] In one of the first recorded verbal assaults on immigrants, one Spanish official colorfully warned that the American immigrants "are not and will not be anything but crows to pick out our eyes."[9]

Despite the efforts of Spanish officials, the tides of change proved too strong to resist, and eventually the Spanish government resorted to giving citizens of the United

States land grants to settle in Louisiana (before the territory was acquired by France in 1800). While recruiting Anglo settlers from the United States to serve as a buffer against intrusion by the U.S. government seems self-defeating, the Spanish government had little choice. Many in Spain realized that closing off Texas was futile. Spanish officials hoped that by abandoning Florida and negotiating the Adams-Onís Treaty of 1819, which established clear boundaries between Spanish and U.S. claims, American interest would be diverted away from Texas long enough for Spain to build a stronger presence there.

The Spanish legacy in Texas can be seen on any Texas map, as every major river except the Red River bears a Spanish name. Spanish rule also left a different, but particularly Texan, kind of mark: a 1778 Spanish proclamation stated that all unbranded cattle were property of the king, which led to the practice of cattle branding to identify ownership.[10]

The roots of the organized Anglo settlement of Texas in the early nineteenth century can be traced to the last years of Spanish rule in Texas. A Missouri resident, Moses Austin, visited Texas in 1820 in hopes of winning the legal right to form colonies in the area. Unfortunately, the return trip took its toll on Austin after his horses were stolen, and he died soon after returning to Missouri, though not before expressing the hope that his son Stephen would carry on the endeavor. In fact, Stephen F. Austin had little interest in serving as an **empresario** (an entrepreneur who made money colonizing areas), and Texas was initially a somewhat unwanted inheritance. However, Austin, a canny businessman, came to see the potential of the land and ultimately warmed to his task.

**Empresario**
an entrepreneur who made money colonizing areas of the Mexican territories.

## Mexican Independence

The next round of change began on September 16 (still celebrated by many Tejanos—Texans of Mexican origin—as Diez y Seis de Septiembre) when Father Miguel Hidalgo y Costilla launched the Mexican War of Independence against Spain through his revolutionary "Call of Hidalgo" (also known as the "Grito de Dolores"), which demanded that those born in the New World be endowed with the same rights as those born in Europe. Mexican independence ended Spanish control of Texas, but it did not end the desire of local authorities to stop the growing trickle of immigrants from the United States. The fledgling Mexican government eventually approved Austin's colonization plan in the hope that legal settlers brought by authorized empresarios like Austin would become loyal to the Mexican government rather than their U.S. roots.

By 1824, Austin had assembled the 300 families allowed under his initial contract and began to settle in Texas. While these colonists suffered more than their share of hardships, Austin's colonies prospered so much that he received four additional contracts to bring settlers to the area over the next seven years. In what would become a familiar problem in Texas, the same opportunities that drew legal settlers and other empresarios to the colonies of Austin also drew illegal immigrants unwilling to deal with the encumbrance of law. Soon Austin and other empresarios found themselves laboring to protect their legal colonies from a flood of illegal squatters.

By the 1830s, there were about 10,000 Anglo settlers in Texas. Some came to Texas hoping to make money quickly in land speculation, but most were subsistence farmers looking for a chance to own their own land and control their own destiny. Some were fleeing financial ruin brought on by the Panic of 1819; others came to Texas to escape legal problems in American states. Tensions between the Anglos and the Mexican government developed as a result of differences in political culture and the Mexican government's insistence on Spanish as the official language. In addition, many Anglo settlers were Protestants who resented the Mexican government's requirement that they become Catholics. Finally, some wanted to use their land to produce cotton, a cash crop that depended heavily on the labor of the approximately 1,000 slaves they brought with them. This too created conflict as the Mexican government was opposed to slavery. In fact, the risk of losing their slaves kept many wealthy southern plantation owners from moving into Texas.

## The Texas Revolution

The tension between the Mexican government and the Anglo settlers eventually turned into that most dramatic political transformation—revolution. Initially, Anglo settlers were divided on the issues of revolution and independence. Stephen F. Austin and many of the established settlers advocated a moderate course, asking for separate statehood within the Mexican nation. Mexico's constitution required that Texas have a population of 80,000 before becoming a state, a number far greater than the 30,000 inhabiting the area at the time. During the early 1830s, the Mexican government granted some of the Anglos' other requests: the right to trial by jury and the official use of the English language. Despite these concessions, many Anglos remained unhappy and began to openly defy the Mexican government. When Texans in Gonzales fired on Mexican troops who came to take away the cannon the town used for its defense, the Texas Revolution began.

Tejanos were in a difficult position. In the 1820s, about 4,000 Tejanos inhabited the region, including many former soldiers who had been stationed in the area and remained after leaving military service. Many had become community leaders and owned large ranches. While Anglo settlers were unhappy about life under the Mexican government, Tejanos were uneasy about the possibility of living under the rule of Anglo settlers, many of whom considered Mexicans and their culture inferior. At the same time, Tejanos shared the concerns of Anglo settlers who did not want a central government in Mexico City controlling their fate and hampering their economic development.

The politics of the independence movement was often chaotic. When Mexican president Antonio López de Santa Anna became less tolerant toward the Texans' aspirations and sent troops to enforce his laws, the Texans began to mobilize politically, calling for a meeting to organize their response. They termed the meeting the "Consultation" of the people of Texas to avoid drawing the ire of Mexican officials with the label "convention," which implied the authority to rewrite the constitution. The Consultation assembled on November 1, 1835, and on November 13 passed the

Organic Law. This law created a government with a governor, lieutenant governor, and the General Council, which was comprised of representatives from each geographic district. Henry Smith, the leader of the more radical group favoring immediate independence, was elected governor by a 30–22 vote, beating out Stephen F. Austin, who clung to a more moderate course. Perhaps Texans should have worried more about their choice. Smith had been married to—and quickly widowed by—two sisters in succession, only to marry a third sister, the twin of his second wife. Smith's political relationships died even more quickly than his romantic relationships. Smith resisted compromise and suspended the General Council. Meanwhile, the council impeached him after less than four months in office. The effect of all this was a government paralyzed.

The revolution was further hamstrung when the council created a regular army under the command of Sam Houston without formally bringing the volunteers already in the field under Houston's command. The volunteers were notorious for their autonomy and lack of discipline, as Austin would find out on November 23 when he ordered them to attack Mexican troops in Béxar, only to have his order refused.

Voters on February 1, 1836, elected representatives to serve as delegates to a new convention that began deliberations on March 1. Shunning most of the more cautious men who had served in the earlier Consultation and in the General Council, Texans chose younger men, many of whom were newcomers—nearly half of the fifty-nine delegates had lived in Texas less than two years. They met in the town of Washington (on the Brazos River) in part because local business owners provided a building without charge. There the delegates adopted, without debate, a declaration of independence drafted by George C. Childress, who had been in Texas for less than eight months. The convention continued meeting until it completed the Constitution of the Republic of Texas on March 17. The constitution protected slavery and permitted a freed slave to live in Texas only with the permission of the Texas Legislature. A government ad interim, composed of the members of the constitutional convention, was empowered to run the affairs of the state. One of the first orders of business was the election of David G. Burnet as Texas's first president. For vice president the convention selected Lorenzo de Zavala, who had served as Mexican minister to Paris under Santa Anna but left his post when Santa Anna claimed dictatorial powers in 1835.

While united by their struggle against the Mexican government, the revolutionary leaders of Texas often fought among themselves even after independence was won. After Houston's ankle was shattered in the Battle of San Jacinto on April 21, 1836,

# TEXAS FOREVER!!

The usurper of the South has failed in his efforts to enslave the freemen of Texas.

The wives and daughters of Texas will be saved from the brutality of Mexican soldiers.

Now is the time to emigrate to the Garden of America.

A free passage, and all found, is offered at New Orleans to all applicants. Every settler receives a location of

## EIGHT HUNDRED ACRES OF LAND.

On the 23d of February, a force of 1000 Mexicans came in sight of San Antonio, and on the 25th Gen. St. Anna arrived at that place with 2500 more men, and demanded a surrender of the fort held by 150 Texians, and on the refusal, he attempted to storm the fort, twice, with his whole force, but was repelled with the loss of 500 men, and the Americans lost none. Many of his troops, the liberals of Zacatecas, are brought on to Texas in irons and are urged forward with the promise of the women and plunder of Texas.

The Texian forces were marching to relieve St. Antonio, March the 2d. The Government of Texas is supplied with plenty of arms, ammunition, provisions, &c. &c.

An 1836 flyer offers free transportation and land to new settlers in hopes of reinforcing the Anglo presence in Texas.

President Burnet denied the victorious general permission to leave for New Orleans to seek medical treatment. Burnet eventually relented when the captain of the boat Houston was set to embark on refused to take anyone at all if he was not allowed to take Houston.

## The Republic of Texas

On September 5, 1836, Sam Houston was elected president of the Republic of Texas by a landslide, receiving 5,119 votes compared to 743 for Henry Smith and only 586 for Stephen F. Austin. The Republic of Texas Constitution also won approval from voters, as did a referendum on pursuing annexation to the United States. With over 3,000 citizens voting to seek annexation and fewer than 100 objecting, Texas's interest in joining the United States was clear from its first day of independence.

The government was temporarily located in Columbia but soon moved to a new town located on Buffalo Bayou that backers, much to the new president's delight, suggested be named Houston. The new capital city, like much of the republic, was improvised; the legislature met in an unfinished capitol building with tree branches forming the roof.

While the period of Texas independence was relatively brief, it was neither simple nor quiet. The population of Texas doubled. Just after the revolution in 1836, Texas had about 30,000 Anglos, 5,000 black slaves, 3,470 Tejanos, and 14,500 Indians. By 1847 its "white" population (including 12,000–14,000 persons of Mexican descent) had soared to 102,961, and its black population had climbed to 39,048 (38,753 slaves and 295 freed blacks).

Change was not limited to population. While the republic's second president, Mirabeau B. Lamar, helped develop the Texas education system, his administration proved disastrous for the Indian tribes living in Texas. Houston had worked to build friendships with Texas's tribes, but Lamar sought to eradicate them. During the three years of the Lamar administration, the Republic of Texas's debt skyrocketed from $2 to $7 million, and the value of its currency plummeted. Lamar opposed annexation by the United States at a time when the United States was expressing doubts of its own. Sam Houston returned to the presidency only after a bruising political battle. Once back in office, Houston helped make peace with the Indians and brought fiscal discipline back to government, spending one-tenth of what Lamar had spent.

The path to statehood would not be as simple as Houston hoped. In the United States, northern interests in the U.S. Congress, led by John Quincy Adams, balked at bringing another slave state into the nation. Houston managed to stir U.S. interest by making overtures to European powers—a course of action designed to pique the United States' jealousy and make it wary of foreign intervention along its borders. As threats from Mexico continued into the 1840s, Texas turned to England and France for help in obtaining the release of Texas soldiers imprisoned in Mexican jails. Houston also positioned Texas for future bargaining by claiming for the republic disputed land reaching west and north as far as Wyoming, including portions of the Santa Fe Trail used for trade between the United States and Mexico. The Texas Congress went even further and passed (over Houston's veto) a bill that claimed all the land south of the forty-second parallel and west of Texas to the Pacific, as well as portions of Mexico—a claim that would have made Texas larger than the United States at the time.

## TEXAS STATEHOOD

The issue of the annexation of Texas eventually became central to the 1844 U.S. presidential election when James K. Polk, the candidate backed by Andrew Jackson, campaigned for the acquisition of Texas. Texas's expansive claim to territory was resolved when Henry Clay crafted a compromise whereby Texas accepted its present borders in return for a payment of $10 million. While the joint resolution inviting Texas to join the United States passed the U.S. House easily, it barely squeaked through the Senate, 27 to 25. John Quincy Adams and Texas's opponents made one final, last-ditch effort to stop Texas statehood by asserting that the admission of Texas through a joint resolution was unconstitutional because that method of admission was not spelled out in the U.S. Constitution.

Texas called a convention for July 4, 1845, to approve annexation and draft a constitution to accommodate Texas's new role as a U.S. state. The only vote in the Texas Legislature against entering the United States came from Richard Bache, who allegedly voted against annexation because he had come to Texas to escape his ex-wife and did not care to live in the same country with her again.[11] Texas was able to retain ownership of its public lands, a term of annexation that other new states did not enjoy. The U.S. Congress accepted the state's new constitution in December, and President James K. Polk signed the bill on December 29, 1845. Texas formally entered statehood on February 19, 1846.

A telling part of the residual folklore of Texas's admission is the notion that Texas retains the right to secede—and if it so chooses, to reenter the United States as five separate states. The origins of this idea come from a compromise designed to overcome objections in the U.S. Congress to the original admission of Texas. The joint resolution that admitted Texas to the Union provided that Texas could be divided into as many as five states. New states north or west of the Missouri Compromise lines would be free; in states south of the compromise lines, a popular vote would determine the legality of slavery. However, the power to create new states ultimately rests with the U.S. Congress, and the right to divide was not reserved to Texas.

J. Pinckney Henderson earned the honor of serving as Texas's first governor after winning election by a large margin. Texas sent Sam Houston and Thomas Jefferson Rusk to serve as the state's first two U.S. senators. Texas's only Jewish member of Congress for 130 years was among its first: David Kaufman of Nacogdoches, a Philadelphia-born Jew who had worked as a lawyer in Mississippi before arriving in Texas, distinguishing himself as an Indian fighter, and then serving two terms as the Speaker of the Republic of Texas's legislature. Kaufman was only the second Jewish member of the U.S. House, taking office the year after Lewis C. Levin became the nation's first Jewish representative in 1845. Passed over in the selection of Texas's first congressional delegation was Anson Jones, who had been sworn in as president of Texas on December 9, 1844. Jones was embittered by this perceived slight and set about putting together his own volume

## Sam Houston

By the time he became a Texan and led Texas to independence, Sam Houston had gone through two wives and lots of alcohol and was, in the words of Texas historian James L. Haley, "considered in respectable circles as unsavory as he was colorful."[i] However, no one better reflects the reality that the greatness of Texas's legends can be found in less-than-perfect people, as Houston guided Texas through some of its most dramatic transitions.

In his youth, Houston generally preferred sneaking away to live among the Indians to working in the family business. Houston distinguished himself during the War of 1812, serving bravely and winning the admiration of General Andrew Jackson. Houston followed Jackson, his new mentor, into politics and was sometimes mentioned as a successor to President Jackson. However, Houston's first marriage abruptly ended in

1827 in the middle of his term as governor of Tennessee and just two months after his wedding. His marriage over and his political career in ruins, Houston went to live again among the Cherokees. During this time, he took a Cherokee wife without entering into a formal Christian marriage. Over time, Houston's state of mind deteriorated and his Indian hosts eventually stripped him of his original Indian name ("The Raven") and began to call him Oo-tse-tee Ar-deetah-skee ("The Big Drunk").[ii] After abandoning his second wife and returning to public life in America, Houston narrowly avoided jail after assaulting a member of Congress who had insulted his integrity. Brought before Congress to face charges, Houston delivered an impassioned defense on his own behalf, allegedly because his lawyer, Francis Scott Key, was too hungover to speak.

During the Texas Revolution, gossips frequently attributed Houston's disappearances to drinking binges rather than military missions. Some questioned his bravery and military leadership during the war. Many Texans wanted Houston to turn and fight the Mexican Army sooner, despite Houston's protest that his troops were undertrained and outnumbered. While most Texans sided with Houston after his victory at San Jacinto, criticisms of his conduct of the war reappeared in political campaigns for the rest of his career.

After leading Texas through the revolution, Houston continued to play a major role in the changes in the state while serving as Texas's first president during its years as an independent nation. Houston struggled in the years after the Texas Revolution to protect the Tejanos who had served alongside him during the war. Similarly, his years among the Cherokees and his continued fondness for them left him at odds with many Anglos who preferred to see Native Americans driven off or killed.

After playing a central role in winning Texas's entry into the United States, Houston's final political act was the struggle to keep Texas from seceding and joining the Confederacy. Houston disliked slavery and defied state law by freeing his own slaves. He had been one of few southern senators to speak out against slavery, a sentiment that led the Texas Legislature to vote against his return to the Senate. His final departure from politics came when he refused to support the secession of Texas in the American Civil War and, as a result, was forced by the legislature to resign his governorship. If Texans had followed Houston's leadership, the lives of many Texas soldiers would have been saved and the state spared postwar Reconstruction.

Houston finally settled down after marrying his third wife and finding redemption, but he never denied his faults. When asked if his sins had been washed away at his river baptism, Houston joked, "I hope so. But if they were all washed away, the Lord help the fish down below."[iii]

However numerous his sins, Houston's principles make him a much more heroic historical figure than many of his more sober peers. From the moment Houston arrived in Texas, he became a central figure in the transformation of the state, and for thirty years he guided Texas through its most turbulent times. While Houston might not be able to be elected today, he did more to shape modern Texas than any other person.

i. James L. Haley, *Passionate Nation: The Epic History of Texas* (New York: Free Press, 2006), 107.

ii. James E. Crisp, *Sleuthing the Alamo: Davy Crockett's Last Stand and Other Mysteries of the Texas Revolution* (New York: Oxford University Press, 2004), 29.

iii. Haley, *Passionate Nation*, 277.

of the history of the republic, published posthumously a year after Jones shot himself on the steps of the old capitol in Houston.

Americans who had resisted the admission of Texas for fear of provoking war with Mexico soon saw those fears realized when fighting broke out in 1846. Many historians believe that U.S. President Polk orchestrated the Mexican-American War by ordering Gen. Zachary Taylor into territory near the mouth of the Rio Grande that Mexican officials had claimed was part of Mexico. Mexico responded by declaring a defensive war on April 23, with the United States responding with its own declaration of war on May 13. The Mexican-American War ended after troops under the command of U.S. general Winfield Scott moved into Mexico City. The **Treaty of Guadalupe Hidalgo** was signed on February 2, 1848, recognizing the Rio Grande as the official boundary between Texas and Mexico. While the treaty offered assurances that the rights of erstwhile Mexican citizens who suddenly found themselves citizens of the United States would be protected, this promise proved fragile.

The rapid population growth following Texas's annexation further transformed the state. However, not every group grew at an equal rate. Despite the general population surge, the Tejano population declined, and by the 1847 census, the 8,000 Germans in Texas were the largest ethnic minority in a state with a total population of around 142,000, including 40,000 slaves and only 295 free people of color. Even though the Tejanos had fought for independence, many were forced to move to Mexico as the clash of Mexican and Anglo cultures intensified, marking one of just a few times in its history that Texas saw people moving away.

## Texas in the Confederacy

The rise of cotton farming in Texas increased the importance of slavery to the Texas economy as production of cotton grew from 40,000 bales in 1848 to 420,000 bales in 1860.[12] By 1860, Texans held 182,566 slaves, compared to a total population of 604,215.[13] While much of Texas was becoming dependent on slave labor, Sam Houston battled slavery and in 1855 became one of the few southern members of Congress to publicly oppose it. Once again, Houston's personal popularity was undone by an unpopular stand on the burning issue of the day. In 1857, two years before his term expired, the Texas Legislature voted to not return Houston to the Senate for another term, leaving Houston to serve the remainder of his term as a lame duck. Houston responded to the insult by running for governor in 1857. Over the course of this campaign, he traveled over 1,500 miles, visited forty-two cities, and gave endless speeches, many lasting as long as four hours. Despite his efforts, Houston lost the election to Hardin R. Runnels by a vote of 32,552 to 28,678. Houston's loss came in part from his association with the anti-immigrant Know Nothing Party, which proved unpopular among voters of Mexican and German ancestry who might otherwise have sympathized with Houston's anti-slavery stance.

After serving out the remainder of his term, Houston left the U.S. Senate in 1859 to run once again for governor, hoping that when the South seceded from the Union he could lead Texas back to independence. This time, Houston was successful, defeating

**Treaty of Guadalupe Hidalgo** signed on February 2, 1848, this agreement between the United States and Mexico ended the Mexican-American War and recognized the Rio Grande as the boundary between Texas, now part of the United States, and Mexico.

Runnels 33,375 to 27,500. Nonetheless, over the objections of Governor Houston, the Secessionist Convention was subsequently convened, and, on February 1, 1861, it voted overwhelmingly in favor of secession. A few weeks later, voters statewide approved a secession ordinance by a three-to-one margin. The Secession Convention approved a requirement that all state officers swear an oath of loyalty to the Confederacy. After Houston refused to take the oath, the governor's office was declared vacant.

The Confederate regime in Texas was a disaster for many. Not only were free blacks victimized, but Germans were targeted for harassment because of their opposition to slavery. Tejanos saw their land seized, and many Tejanos chose to align themselves with the Union. Some enlisted, becoming the heart of the Union's Second Cavalry, while others fought as pro-Union guerrillas. Many pro-Union Anglos were forced to flee the state. William Marsh Rice, whose wealth would one day endow Rice University, had to leave Houston and move his businesses to Matamoros in Mexico.

## Reconstruction in Texas

Northern rule arrived with the end of the Civil War on June 19, 1865, when Union forces under Gen. Gordon Granger arrived in Galveston, bringing with them a proclamation ending slavery in Texas. That date, known as "Juneteenth" in Texas, was the day on which the slaves in Texas were actually freed, despite President Abraham Lincoln's having signed the Emancipation Proclamation in January 1863. While many transformations in Texas history involved the arrival of new citizens from outside the state, the end of slavery meant that former slaves were now new citizens in their old state. Joining with a small number of Anglo Republicans, African Americans helped elect Republicans to statewide offices and constitutional conventions.

Freedom proved a mixed blessing for the "freedmen." While legally they were free, in practical terms freedmen endured horrendous intimidation and exploitation. State law would not recognize any marriage involving African American Texans until 1869. Although the Freedmen's Bureau was created to help former slaves, the bureau's efforts were sometimes limited by administrators who, while supporting the end of slavery, doubted the goal of racial equality. Texas, like other southern states, passed so-called Black Codes that were designed to limit the rights of the former slaves. In Texas, any person with one-eighth or more of Negro blood could not serve on a jury or vote. With local law enforcement often in the hands of Confederate sympathizers, African Americans relied on Union troops for protection. As elsewhere in the former Confederate states, the Ku Klux Klan became a vehicle for terrorizing former slaves and those sympathetic to their cause, as well as "carpetbaggers" (people from the North who came south to assist or cash in on Reconstruction) and "scalawags" (Republicans of local origin).

In January 1866, Texans elected delegates to a convention to draft a new state constitution aimed at winning the state readmission into the United States. However, the Texas Legislature seemed to have missed the news that the South lost the war: the legislature refused to ratify the Thirteenth Amendment (ending slavery) and Fourteenth Amendment (guaranteeing equal rights) and instead drafted a framework of laws limiting the rights of freed slaves. The Constitution of 1866 failed to meet the demands of the Radical Republicans, who had won control of the U.S. Congress in the

1866 election. While much has been made of the influx of carpetbaggers during this time, in fact the political transition to Republican control of Texas government during Reconstruction resulted less from an influx of outsiders from the northeast and more on the right of freed slaves to vote at the same time that supporters of the Confederacy lost their right to vote or hold office after Congress passed the Second Reconstruction Act. With most white Democrats purged both from office and from voting lists, the next constitutional convention was dominated by Republicans, who accounted for seventy-eight of the ninety delegates. The resulting Constitution of 1869 won for Texas readmission to the United States by including many provisions granting rights to freed slaves: the rights to vote, run for office, serve on juries, testify in court against whites, and attend public schools.

## The End of Reconstruction and Rise of the "Redeemers"

Texas politics was transformed again when Reconstruction ended and more Confederate sympathizers were allowed to vote. The Democrats (the party of the white Confederate sympathizers) won control of the legislature in the election of 1872. Like the emancipation of the slaves, this transformation of Texas politics did not arise from an influx of new Texans, but rather resulted from the renewal of citizenship of old citizens. Republican E. J. Davis was widely despised by Democrats, who considered him at best a symbol of northern oppression and at worst incredibly corrupt. Once in control of Texas government, the Democrats proclaimed themselves "Redeemers" and removed the last remnants of Republican rule. On August 2, 1875, the Texas Legislature authorized a new constitutional convention and elected three delegates each from the state's thirty senatorial districts. None of the ninety members of the 1875 convention had been members of the convention that drafted the 1869 constitution, and the partisan composition was dramatically different. Seventy-five members were Democrats while only fifteen were Republicans. At least forty were members of the Patrons of Husbandry, also called the Grange, an economic and political organization of farmers. Voters ratified the constitution on February 15, 1876, by a vote of 136,606 to 56,652.

The rise of the Redeemers and the impact of the Grange are especially important transitions in Texas politics because the constitution of this era remained in force long after the politics and politicians responsible for it had vanished. Texas has continued to change and grow, but the Texas Constitution has not been replaced since, only amended—piecemeal changes resulting in minor alterations to the basic design of 1876. The twenty-five years that followed the Civil War spawned the cowboy imagery that Texans still relish. It was during this brief period that the frontier truly existed, when Texas was in fact home to the quintessential rugged cowboy who tended large ranches and oversaw herds of cattle—a stereotype that has remained rooted in the Texan persona ever since. And even then, the image of Texas as the "Old West" was based on the lives of only a small number of Texans. Although Texans hold the legend of the cowboy in high esteem, the cowboy's life was anything but glamorous. Most were young. About one-third were Hispanic or African American. The ranch owners generally regarded them as common laborers on horseback, and the men who rode the range and drove the cattle were paid less than the trail cooks.[14] By the 1890s, the fabled trail drives had come to an end, finished by drought, quarantines, barbed-wire fencing across the open range, and competition from the railroads.

The state government encouraged immigration in the last half of the nineteenth century to help settle and populate the western part of the state and drive off Indian tribes. Some state officials saw the immigration of white settlers and farmers as a means of counteracting the increase in former slaves, many of whom had become sharecroppers. Germans flooded into Texas, their numbers surging from 41,000 in 1870 to 125,262 in 1890; at this time, Texans of Mexican ancestry numbered only 105,193. While Texas west of Austin may have resembled the Wild West, most Texans resided in the eastern portion of the state, which resembled the "New South" that was emerging elsewhere out of the former Confederacy and was characterized by railroad networks and urbanized cities, such as Dallas.

## Era of Reform

As Texas transitioned from the farming and ranching of the nineteenth century to the industrial and oil economy of the twentieth century, the state began to struggle with the limits of the Constitution of 1876. In 1890, Attorney General James Stephen Hogg decided that his office lacked the resources to adequately enforce regulations on the state's railroads. Hogg's call for the creation of a railroad commission became a centerpiece of his campaign for governor. The railroads labeled Hogg "communistic," but his economic and political reforms proved popular, and his election represented the first stirrings of the reform movement in Texas. While the creation of the Texas Railroad Commission was heralded as a means to achieve fair competition, in practice it was often used to restrict out-of-state railroads and protect Texas-based businesses from international competitors.

Although glamorized in movies and television shows, cowboys, or *vaqueros*, led a hard life and were often shunned by civilized society.

Frustrated by the lack of responsiveness from the Democrats to their needs, farmers organized the People's Party, more commonly known as the Populist Party. While the populists were short-lived, their call for radical reforms, including public ownership of the railroads, and their willingness to reach out to black voters rattled the political order. After the populists were absorbed into the Democratic Party, the progressives took up the role of reform party. In contrast to the populists' narrow base in agricultural communities, the progressives emerged in the 1890s as a broader reform movement attacking both the railroads that bedeviled the farmers and the big industries that challenged urban labor.

While progressive candidates for governor won elections, their legislative victories were limited. Thomas Campbell won the governorship in the election of 1906 only to see much of his progressive agenda hijacked or sidetracked by the legislature. Most crucially, Campbell was unable to win approval of statewide referenda and recall. Legislation requiring that insurance companies invest 75 percent of their premiums in Texas did change the way insurance companies operated, but this mainly benefited Texas businesses and drove foreign insurers from the state.

The progressive movement in Texas became consumed by the alcohol prohibition issue, in part because Texas politics lacked the large corporations and big city political machines that energized the efforts of progressives in the North. Much of the prohibitionists' efforts took place at the local level; they were especially successful at winning local option elections that outlawed drinking. In 1891, the Texas Legislature put a prohibitionist constitutional amendment before the state's voters. The campaign was intense, and voters turned out at more than twice the rate they had in the previous gubernatorial election to narrowly reject the amendment by a 237,393 to 231,096 vote.

While the emergence of a new Texas economy early in the twentieth century and the reforms of the progressive movement captured the attention of many voters, others remained fixated on the old issues of race and the Civil War. In a struggle that foreshadows today's battle over the history that is taught in Texas's classrooms, Governor Oscar Branch Colquitt struggled in his 1912 reelection bid because he had criticized the state textbook board for rejecting a history book because it contained a photograph of Abraham Lincoln. Meanwhile, voters flocked to see Colquitt's opponent, William Ramsay, who played upon southern sentiments in his speeches and had bands play "Dixie" during campaign events. Prohibition was a hotly contested issue on its own and reflected old racial hatreds as alcohol was portrayed as a vice of the Germans and Mexicans.

No one better personifies the failures of Texas progressives to produce reform in the state than James E. "Pa" Ferguson. While the rest of the Texas political system obsessed over prohibition, "Farmer Jim" shunned the issue and instead won office with promises of capping how much rent tenant farmers could be charged by their landlords. Ferguson's tenant farmer law was ultimately ruled unconstitutional, but he remained a hero to the state's small farmers. Ferguson could be charming, but his politics were often petty. For example, he used appointments to the board of Prairie View Normal and Industrial College to remove Principal Edward Blackshear, who had had the temerity to support a political rival. Ferguson also took his personal political fight to the University of Texas, demanding the removal of William J. Battle, the president of the university. When asked his reason for wanting Battle's removal, Ferguson proclaimed, "I don't have to give any reason. I am Governor of the State of Texas."[15] Later, Ferguson vetoed appropriations for the university. After Ferguson was elected to a second term in 1916, his battle with the university and its allies ultimately brought him down. On July 23, 1917, the Speaker of the Texas House called for a special session to consider impeachment, and in August the Texas House voted on twenty-one articles of impeachment, including charges dealing with Ferguson's personal finances, especially bank loans. The Senate found him guilty on ten charges, primarily those dealing with his finances. While impeachment removed Ferguson from the governor's office and disqualified him from holding other public office, Texas was not so easily rid of his influence.

Ferguson's departure made passage of statewide prohibition easier. The presence of military training camps in Texas led prohibitionists to argue that patriotism required that the state protect young recruits from liquor. Initially, the Texas Legislature simply made it illegal to sell alcohol within ten miles of a military base. The next year, in May 1919, Texas voters approved an amendment to the Texas Constitution that brought prohibition to Texas a year before it went into effect nationwide.

As with other states, prohibition in Texas proved unworkable as many Texans refused to give up alcohol. The legislature contributed to the failure of the initiative by providing very little funding for the enforcement necessary to make prohibition a success. Organized crime thrived on the revenue that illegal alcohol distribution and sales brought and allegedly worked with prohibitionists to keep alcohol illegal. During prohibition over 20 percent of all arrests in the state were related to prohibition.[16] Galveston became a major center for liquor smuggling as foreign ships anchored along "Rum Row," a line just beyond U.S. territorial waters where boats dropped anchor to distribute alcohol just out of the reach of American law.

While voters were approving prohibition, they also rejected an amendment that would have embraced another item on the progressives' list of reforms: the right of women to vote in all elections. Some of the resistance was based solely on gender discrimination, but some southern voters believed that granting equal rights to women would open the door to "Negro rule" and socialism.

The economic changes that came with the new century resulted from a flood of oil, not of new citizens. While oil's presence in Texas had been noted since Spanish explorers used natural tar seeps to patch their boats, its impact on the state was not realized until the early twentieth century. A few wells were drilled in Texas in the 1890s, but the state lacked the refinery capacity to make use of the oil. After the first refinery was built in Texas, interest in oil exploration increased, but the state remained a minor producer. That changed in 1901 when the Spindletop oil rig near Beaumont hit oil and gas, eventually producing 100,000 barrels of oil a day. Investors began streaming into the state in search of oil; by 1928, Texas was leading the nation in oil production, providing 20 percent of the world's supply. By 1929, oil had replaced "King Cotton" as the largest part of the Texas economy.

Just as oil investors transformed much of the Texas countryside and economy, oil revenues had a huge impact on Texas government, contributing almost $6 million to state accounts by 1929 and reducing the need for other state taxes. Texas's other major business was lumber, which grew dramatically early in the twentieth century, eventually topping 2.25 billion board feet in 1907 before overcutting slowed production. Highway construction boomed in Texas, and by the end of the 1920s Texas had almost 19,000 miles of highway. Fruit trees were introduced into southern Texas, providing a new segment of the economy and planting the seeds for future immigration as seasonal, migratory labor was needed to harvest these fruits. By the 1920s, Texas seemed well on its way to establishing a strong and diverse economy—a trend that would be undone by the Great Depression.

## The Great Depression and the New Deal in Texas

By the late 1920s, Texans were beginning to show a little independence from the Democratic Party. The state went for a Republican presidential candidate for the first time in 1928 when Texans shunned Democrat Al Smith, a Catholic New Yorker who drank. However, many Texans regretted their vote for Republican Herbert Hoover as Texas was hit hard by the depression that many blamed on him. As many as one-third of farmers in some areas were driven from their farms by the depression, and the Texas oil boom did little to spare the state. Overproduction of oil caused prices to fall to as low as three cents a barrel. When the Railroad Commission refused to act to reduce overproduction, Governor Ross S. Sterling declared martial law and used National Guardsmen to shut down the East Texas oil fields. The desperation of the times brought about the repeal of national prohibition, with "wets" arguing that repeal would aid recovery.

Burdened with a depressed economy and the overproduction of oil and cotton, Governor Sterling ran for reelection against "Pa" Ferguson's legacy, his wife, Miriam "Ma" Ferguson, who trounced Sterling at the ballot box. While the Fergusons finally departed the governor's office for good in 1935, it wasn't long before another character, Wilbert Lee "Pappy" O'Daniel, ushered in a new brand of populist politics. O'Daniel, a former sales manager for a flour mill, became known statewide as the host of a radio show that featured the music of the Light Crust Doughboys, mixed with inspirational stories. Purportedly encouraged by listeners' letters urging him to run—although some suggested that wealthy business interests and a public relations expert had done the urging—O'Daniel declared his candidacy, proclaiming the Ten Commandments as his platform and the Golden Rule as his motto. He won the Democratic nomination without a runoff and, facing no real opposition, won the general election with 97 percent of the vote.

Although a colorful personality on the campaign trail, O'Daniel accomplished little of importance once in office as he lacked the skill to work with legislators and tended to appoint less-than-qualified people to office. After winning reelection to the governorship in 1940, O'Daniel shifted his sights to Washington, D.C., when the death of Sen. Morris Sheppard created a vacancy in 1941. O'Daniel won the special election to replace Sheppard, narrowly edging out a young ex-congressman named Lyndon Johnson in a disputed election.

## Bob Bullock

When Texas governor George W. Bush delivered the eulogy for Bob Bullock in June 1999, he honored him as "the largest Texan of our time." Although the state's historical museum in Austin now bears his name, Bullock's path to legendary status was neither steady nor straight. Bullock began his political career aligned with segregationists, transformed himself into a liberal Democrat, and then metamorphosed into one of Republican George W. Bush's most important political allies. Bullock was very much like Sam Houston, a Texan who transcended personal failing to rise to greatness and become a state icon. As Bullock quipped when Hill Junior College put his name on a building, "I'm so happy that they named a gym after me instead of a prison."[i]

Bullock grew up in Hillsboro, Texas, where it seemed to many that he was more likely to end up inside the walls of one of the state's penal institutions than atop its political institutions. Some in Hillsboro attribute to a young Bob Bullock a prank right out of

*American Graffiti*. One night someone wrapped a chain around the rear axel of a police cruiser, tied it to a telephone pole, and then called the police to tell the officer on duty that evening about a big fight at a local cafe. When the officer leapt into his car, the car lurched as far as the end of the chain before its rear end was yanked clear off.

Bullock battled his way through Texas government as legislator, lobbyist, staffer for Governor Preston Smith, and secretary of state. Even as he worked his way up in Texas politics, he chain smoked and drank a fifth of whiskey daily. In 1974, Bullock won statewide election to the position of comptroller of public accounts, and he modernized the office's accounting practice by replacing paper and pencil account ledgers and mechanical adding machines with computers. Bullock won an expanded budget for his office by promising legislators that, with a few more million dollars provided for auditors and enforcers, he would find a few hundred million more in revenue that the legislature could appropriate. Bullock used these resources to stage dramatic, highly visible seizure raids at some businesses. The raids encouraged other delinquent businesses to settle their accounts. Bullock never shied from a battle, once forcing the Texas Council of Campfire Girls to pay $13,284 for sales taxes on their fund-raising candy sales. He also used the comptroller's ability to generate tax revenue estimates that effectively served as a cap on legislative spending as a tool for influencing state policy.

As much as Bullock mastered political office, he was unable to master his appetites. Bullock occasionally showed up at work drunk and traveled around the state on business accompanied by a companion selected from the secretarial pool. Once,

after being caught using a state airplane for personal use, Bullock proclaimed, "Yeah, I'm a crook, but I'm the best comptroller the state ever had."[ii] While he could be blunt in his politics, he wasn't interested in having too much truth reported. When pressed too insistently by reporters at a press conference, Bullock warned, "I keep files on reporters, too. I could name your girlfriends and where they live and what flowers you buy them . . . if I wanted to tell that to your wives."[iii] When the paper began reporting on his use of public funds for a new truck, Bullock mailed boxes of cow manure to the *Dallas Morning News*, a move his spokesman later defended by saying, "He did it on his own time, on his own money."[iv]

By the time he was elected lieutenant governor in 1990, Bullock had put most of his troubled past behind him, telling one person, "There is nothing left for me to do but what's good for Texas." When George W. Bush became governor, he immediately realized that Bullock's years of experience, fund-raising skills, and legislative connections made him an indispensable partner, especially for a governor new to state government. Working closely with Bullock, Bush built the record of bipartisan legislative success that helped propel him to the White House. The endorsement of Bullock, a long-time Democrat, gave Bush an important boost. Known for closing his remarks with "God bless Texas," Bullock found a way to move beyond the personal controversy that often swirled around him and help Texas forge ahead.

i. Dave McNeely and Jim Henderson, *Bob Bullock: God Bless Texas* (Austin: University of Texas Press, 2008), 16.

ii. Ibid., 7

iii. Ibid., 114.

iv. Ibid., 141.

# TRANSITIONS TO THE TWENTY-FIRST CENTURY

Texas spent the rest of the twentieth century in transition, shedding some old habits. Even with the landmark *Brown v. Board of Education* Supreme Court decision in 1954, Texas managed to resist desegregation, despite the Court's mandate of instituting it with "all deliberate speed." Many Texas schools remained segregated well into the early 1970s when federal courts ordered them to desegregate. In 1954, Texas women belatedly won the right to serve on juries, but further progress toward equality was slow. In the 1960s, only six women served in the Texas Legislature, and the state failed to ratify the national Equal Rights Amendment (ERA). However, in 1972, voters approved an equal rights amendment to the state constitution, and the legislature voted to ratify the ERA (although it would fail to get the required three-quarters of states nationally). In 1975, Liz Cockrell was elected mayor of San Antonio, making her the first woman mayor of a major Texas city.

By the 1960s, the partisan legacy of the Civil War was finally beginning to wear off. In 1961, John Tower was elected to the U.S. Senate, becoming the first Republican to win statewide office since Reconstruction. With the Republican Party showing signs of viability, many conservative Democrats shifted their allegiance to the Republican Party in state elections. This followed years of dividing their loyalty by voting for Republicans in national elections while supporting Democrats for state and local offices, a practice labeled **presidential republicanism.** The career of Texas governor John Connally is a case in point. Connally, although friendly with Lyndon Johnson and elected governor as a Democrat, served in the cabinet of Republican president Richard Nixon before eventually seeking the presidency himself as a Republican candidate. Texas did not seat its first Republican governor until 1978 when William P. Clements won an upset victory. While Clements' narrow victory was the only statewide race the Republicans won that year, it proved a significant first step as Texas Republicans thereafter began to score more and more successes. Once conservatives saw that they could win elections under the Republican banner, they began to shift their party affiliation. By the 2000 elections, Republicans dominated, winning every statewide office on the ballot.

## Texas Today

Texas can be viewed through a variety of lenses. In a political science course it is natural to look at the boundaries that define Texas politically. Such boundaries may be the most visible delineations of the state, but this is not the only way of looking at Texas and its citizens. If Texas is, as John Steinbeck suggested, as much a state of mind as a geographic state, then we may need to look at who we are and where we come from.

For generations, waves of people have come to Texas to make new lives for themselves; in the process they have brought with them new ideas and new customs. Texas has always been a meeting ground for different ambitions and cultures. These cultures have clashed, blended, and evolved into a complicated modern state that can be a challenge to govern.

In a classic study of political life in America, Daniel Elazar focused on political culture. **Political culture** is the shared values and beliefs about the nature of the political world that give us a common language that we can use to discuss and debate ideas.[17]

**Presidential republicanism**
the practice in the South of voting for Republicans in presidential elections but voting for conservative Democrats in other races; this practice continued until animosity over Reconstruction faded and the Republicans demonstrated their electability in the South.

**Political culture**
the shared values and beliefs of citizens about the nature of the political world that give the public a common language as a foundation to discuss and debate ideas.

# HOW TEXAS GOVERNMENT WORKS

## Who It Serves

### Population by Race and Ethnicity

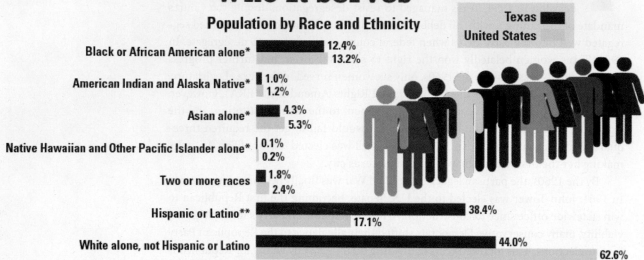

Legend: Texas (dark) / United States (light)

| | Texas | United States |
|---|---|---|
| Black or African American alone* | 12.4% | 13.2% |
| American Indian and Alaska Native* | 1.0% | 1.2% |
| Asian alone* | 4.3% | 5.3% |
| Native Hawaiian and Other Pacific Islander alone* | 0.1% | 0.2% |
| Two or more races | 1.8% | 2.4% |
| Hispanic or Latino** | 38.4% | 17.1% |
| White alone, not Hispanic or Latino | 44.0% | 62.6% |

Source: United States Census Bureau, QuickFacts for USA and Texas, 2013, http://quickfacts.census.gov.

\* Includes persons reporting only one race.    \*\* Hispanics may be of any race, so also are included in applicable race categories.

## Top Ten States with Largest Hispanic Populations (in millions)

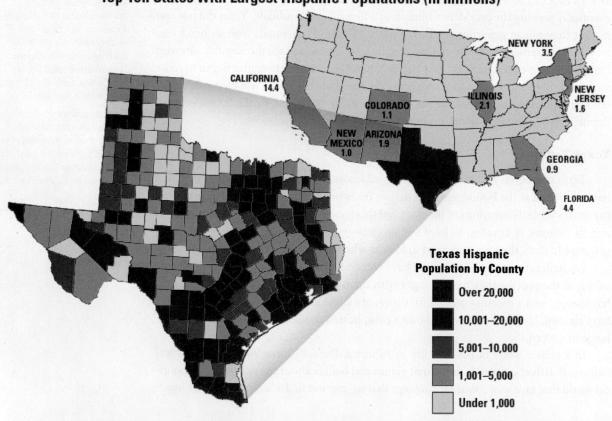

NEW YORK 3.5

CALIFORNIA 14.4

COLORADO 1.1

ILLINOIS 2.1

NEW JERSEY 1.6

NEW MEXICO 1.0

ARIZONA 1.9

GEORGIA 0.9

FLORIDA 4.4

**Texas Hispanic Population by County**

- Over 20,000
- 10,001–20,000
- 5,001–10,000
- 1,001–5,000
- Under 1,000

Source: Texas Department of State Health Services, Texas Population by County, 2010, www.dshs.state.tx.us/chs/popdat/ST2010.shtm.

The **individualistic political culture** that many observers attribute to Texans holds that individuals are best left largely free of the intervention of community forces such as government, which should attempt only those things demanded by the people it is created to serve.[18] The individualistic subculture is most dominant in western parts of the state where frontier living fostered independence and a general distrust of government. Texans, initially attracted to the state by the promise of land, were often forced to develop and protect that land without help from the government. Instead, they had to depend on themselves for basic services, often including law enforcement and justice. From these roots, a preference for as little government as possible and a general distrust of government persists today across much of the state.

In contrast, the **traditionalistic political culture** sees government as having a limited role concerned with the preservation of the existing social order. The traditionalistic culture can be seen in areas such as East Texas that were more heavily influenced by the traditions of the Old South. Finally, the **moralistic political culture** sees the exercise of community forces as sometimes necessary to advance the public good. In this view, government can be a positive force and citizens have a duty to participate. While this view can be found in many places in New England and other parts of the United States, it is rare in Texas.

While the discussion of distinct cultures or nations within Texas or the United States might seem foreign at first, it reflects an ongoing discussion in political science about distinguishing *nations* from *states*. This language may be more familiar to viewers of the *Colbert Report*, as Stephen Colbert frequently refers to his audience as the "Colbert nation." In the worlds of Colbert and of political science, a nation is "groups of people who share—or believe they share—a common culture, ethnic origin, language, historical experience, artifacts and symbols."[19] On the other hand, a state represents a sovereign political entity with defined political boundaries.

Colin Woodard has argued that the United States includes eleven such nations, four of which can be found in Texas: the Deep South, Greater Appalachia, the Midlands, and El Norte. (See Map 1.2.) El Norte is actually part of the oldest area of civilization on the continent. It took root when Columbus arrived in the New World and witnessed the Spanish expeditions that had viewed the Smoky Mountains of Tennessee and the Grand Canyon by the time the English arrived in Jamestown. This nation, which includes parts of northern Mexico as well as southern Texas, shares a language, cuisine, and societal norms that are distinct from both other parts of Texas and from the interior of Mexico. While the political divisions created by the Texas revolution may have tried to divide El Norte, like the *noretños* of northern Mexico, Tejanos value a reputation for being more independent, self-sufficient, adaptable, and work-centered than residents of the interior of Mexico.

Parts of Texas are also included in the Deep South nation, a tradition where the remnants of aristocratic privilege and classical Republicanism can still be seen in the notion that democracy is a privilege of the few. The Deep South is internally polarized on racial grounds and deeply at odds with other nations over the direction of the state and the country. Greater Appalachia runs through much of the northern part of the state and shares some of the Deep South's resistance to the intrusion of northern nations via the Civil War, Reconstruction, and subsequent social and economic

**Individualistic political culture** the idea that individuals are best left largely free of the intervention of community forces such as government and that government should attempt only those things demanded by the people it is created to serve.

**Traditionalistic political culture** the idea, most prevalent in the parts of Texas most like the Old South, that government has a limited role concerned with the preservation of the existing social order.

**Moralistic political culture** rare in Texas, the view that the exercise of community pressure is sometimes necessary to advance the public good; it also holds that government can be a positive force and citizens have a duty to participate.

MAP 1.2 Texas within Colin Woodward's American Nations

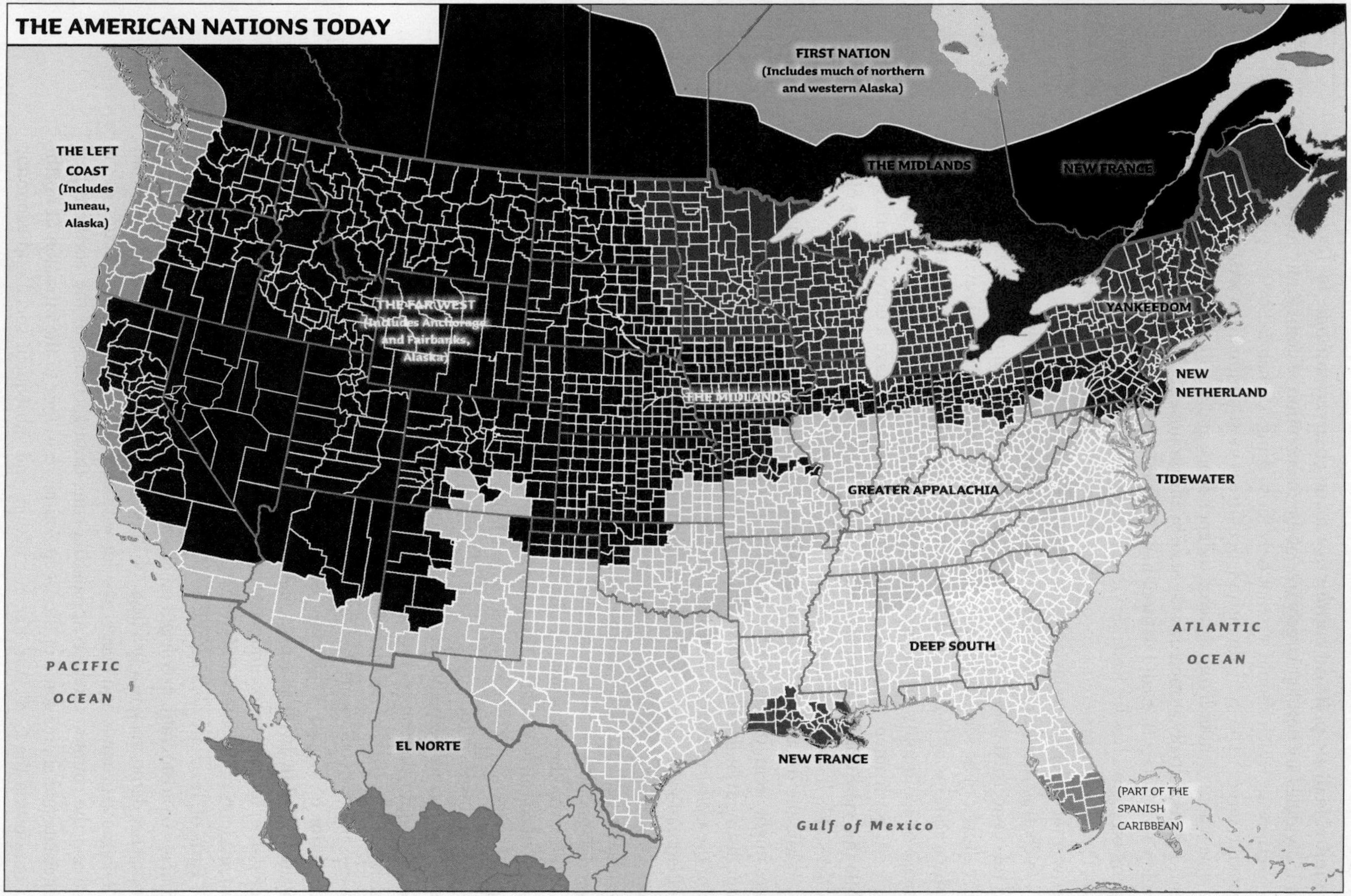

## THE AMERICAN NATIONS TODAY

**THE LEFT COAST** (Includes Juneau, Alaska)

**FIRST NATION** (Includes much of northern and western Alaska)

**NEW FRANCE**

**THE MIDLANDS**

**THE FAR WEST** (Includes Anchorage and Fairbanks, Alaska)

THE MIDLANDS

NEW NETHERLAND

YANKEEDOM

TIDEWATER

GREATER APPALACHIA

DEEP SOUTH

EL NORTE

NEW FRANCE

**ATLANTIC OCEAN**

**PACIFIC OCEAN**

(PART OF THE SPANISH CARIBBEAN)

Gulf of Mexico

reforms. Greater Appalachia holds a deep commitment to individual liberty and personal sovereignty but is as adverse to the aristocrats of the Deep South as it is to social reformers from the northeast. The Midlands, which is comprised of only the northernmost counties of the state, is skeptical of government but subscribes to the idea that it should benefit ordinary people. Residents of the Midlands are moderate and at times even apathetic about politics and care little about either ethnic or ideological purity.

While some skeptics would argue that these political cultures or nations within the state would be erased by the infusion of citizens from other countries or states, it may be the case that other forces are at play. Many observers decry the rise of polarization in national politics and lay the blame partially at the feet of partisan redistricting. Other scholars have argued that what is really happening is that migration patterns are creating communities that are more politically and socially homogeneous. In his book *The Big Sort*, Bill Bishop argues that Americans now have enough financial freedom and mobility to have unprecedented choice over where they live.[20] Freed from restraints of economics and family, Americans are choosing communities that share their political and social values.

The mixing of cultures in Texas has produced entirely new cultures unique to the state. In no place is this unique mixture more evident than in Laredo's annual George Washington's Birthday celebration, a month-long festival created in 1896 that takes an American-style celebration and unites it with the city's diverse roots. Today, Mexican food and colonial gowns both star in this celebration of the city's bicultural roots, and Laredoans and their guests move easily from jalapeño-eating contests to formal colonial pageants. In this sense, Laredo perfectly embraces the tradition of change that defines Texas. Much was made of Texans' independent streak after Governor Perry tossed around language about secession. However, a 2009 Rasmussen Poll taken after Perry's comments revealed that 75 percent of Texans wanted to remain part of the United States and only 18 percent would support secession.[21] Clearly, Texans love being Americans just as much as they love being Texans.

The diverse range of legends underlying modern Texas has given Texans a choice of legends from which to draw on. According to historian Randolph B. Campbell, Texans have opted to draw upon the rugged individualism of the cowboys of the cattle drive rather than the slavery, secession, and defeat of the Old South.[22] Even then, the lonely cowboy driving cattle across the open plains is an uncertain guide for Texans trying to find their place in the state today. Texans' identity and expectations of their government are grounded in images of the past that may not be entirely true. Thus, we have to wonder how our understandings of our past are shaping the state's future.

## A TRADITION OF CHANGE

Texas continues its tradition of change. For hundreds of years, people left their old lives to build new ones in Texas, leaving behind them signs declaring "Gone to Texas." While these generations of new Texans brought different languages and cultures, all consistently brought one thing—change. Such change has defined Texas since the 1500s when newly arrived Spanish explorers turned the Caddo word for friend (*techas*) into *Tejas,* a term describing the Caddo tribe.[23] In the centuries since, waves of people have come to Texas seeking opportunity and bringing change.

The changes have not always been welcomed by established Texans. When explorer Francisco Vasquez de Coronado's expedition arrived and proudly proclaimed to the Zuñi Indians who lived in Texas that the tribe now enjoyed protection as subjects of the Spanish king, the Zuñis answered with a volley of arrows.[24] The arrows bounced off the Spanish armor, and today immigrants arriving from across the nation and around the world generally receive a better reception. Still, new arrivals have often been seen by many Texans as competitors rather than partners in the state's future.

New arrivals remain a constant in Texas. The state's population has increased about a hundredfold since joining the United States, growing at an average of just over 40 percent each decade (see Figure 1.1). The Census Bureau estimated that there were 26,448,193 Texans in 2013 and that there will be over 27 million people living in the state by 2025. Seven counties in Texas grew more than 50 percent in the ten years between the 2000 and 2010 censuses: Rockwall (81 percent), Williamson (69 percent), Fort Bend (65 percent), Hays (61 percent), Collin (59 percent), Montgomery (55 percent), and Denton (53 percent).

According to Office of the State Demographer, Texas will do a lot more growing in the next four decades. Changes in immigration and birth rates make predictions difficult, but the state could have as many as 32 million citizens in 2050, even if there is zero migration into the state. If migration into the state continues at the pace seen

| FIGURE 1.1 | **Population and Percentage of Growth in Texas since 1850** |

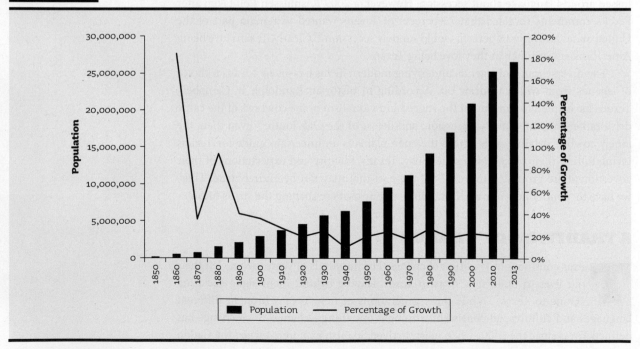

*Source:* Data from U.S. Census Bureau, "State and County QuickFacts: Texas," http://quickfacts.census.gov/qfd/states/48000.html

from 2000 to 2010, 2050 could see just over 55 million Texans.[25] How today's Texans make room for the 8 million new residents expected over the next two decades will be an important part of the state's politics.

Change is especially difficult for a political system that must meet the needs of a large, diverse, and ever-shifting population. Political systems tend to represent the status quo, and established groups are inherently threatened by changes to the government's base of power. Because politics is, in the words of a classic definition, about who gets what, newcomers compete against established residents, leaving the government to resolve the conflict and determine who wins and who loses. Politics becomes a battle between the old and the new, and this battle is often repeated in Texas. The Texas Revolution, which came about when Mexican officials refused to meet the needs of Anglo settlers, is probably the most dramatic—and ultimately literal—example of politics as a battle.

A current snapshot of Texas reveals increasing population diversity as the state grows. In 2005, Texas became a "majority-minority" state, joining Hawaii, New Mexico, and California as states in which the nation's majority (Anglos) make up less than half of a state's population. In Texas today Anglos account for 45 percent of the state's population. While about 70 percent of Texas residents describe themselves as "white," this category includes both Anglos and Hispanics (see Figure 1.2). About 16 percent of Texans (compared to 12.7 percent of Americans) are foreign born, and just over one in three Texans speaks a language other than English at home (compared to one in five Americans).[26]

The state's future will be even more diverse. The state demographer estimates that from 2010 to 2050, Texas's Hispanic population will grow from just under 10 million to just over 30 million. During that same time, the Anglo population is expected to stay relatively unchanged at 11 to 12 million.[27] While some of the rise of Hispanics in Texas may result from immigration, the number will rise even if immigration ends because the state's Hispanic population is much younger than its Anglo population. In 2010 the number of Hispanics in Texas under age thirty-seven outnumbered Anglos in the same age group. Thus, the Texans most likely to make baby Texans in the immediate future are Hispanic.

Another measure of the "new normal" of Texas is that today married Texans make up only about half of the population. In 2012, 48 percent of women and 50.9 percent of men in Texas were married.[28]

While much has been made of the emergence of a Latino majority in Texas, we have to remember how broad these racial categories are and how many differences exist within such groups. The term *Hispanic* includes many recent immigrants who may share a language but have origins that go beyond those of the Mexican-Americans usually considered Hispanics in Texas. In fact, Texas has seen immigration from both Central and South America. While Hispanics that come from countries in these regions may share a language, the nations are very different. At the same time, some Hispanics in Texas trace their lineage to before the United States, Texas, or even Mexico existed. These Texan families represent some of the state's oldest and including them in the same category with the state's newest arrivals illustrates the problems of relying on such broad categories.

**FIGURE 1.2**   **Race and Ethnicity in Texas, 2010**

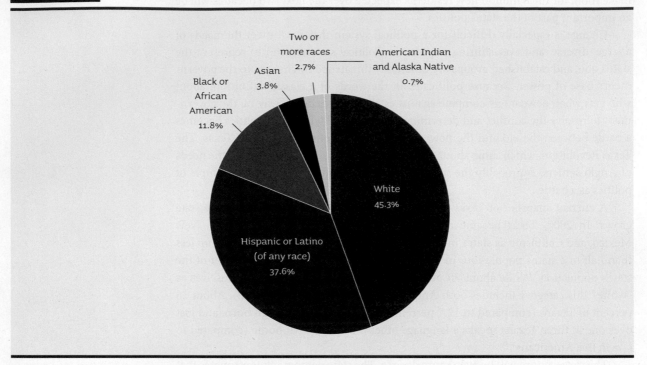

Two or
more races
2.7%

American Indian
and Alaska Native
0.7%

Asian
3.8%

Black or
African
American
11.8%

White
45.3%

Hispanic or Latino
(of any race)
37.6%

*Source:* Data from U.S. Census Bureau, "State and County QuickFacts: Texas," http://quickfacts.census.gov/qfd/states/48000.html

It was less than a century ago that German Americans were considered distinct and foreign enough to generate fear among some that they would align themselves with Germany during World War I. Many of 2050's Hispanics will be the product of several generations of living in America and all of the socialization inherent in the public school system, media, and other culture.

Many observers believe that the rising number of Hispanics will lead inevitably to a Democratic electoral majority in Texas. Gallup has found evidence that Hispanics in Texas have slightly different tendencies than those presented in the national picture. While nationally Hispanics favor Democrats over Republicans 51 percent to 21 percent, in Texas the Democrats' margin is slimmer at 46 percent to 27 percent.[29] Of course, the popularity of the two parties among Hispanics will turn on a variety of policy issues. Hispanics, like German Americans and other groups, will continue to evolve and eventually become a natural part of political life in Texas.

The state's rural nature has been transformed, and today about 80 percent of Texans live in 1,210 cities or suburbs. In fact, Texas has four of the country's fifteen largest cities: Houston (#4), San Antonio (#7), Dallas (#9), and Austin (#13). Texans aren't simply moving to big cities. Census figures reveal that eight of the fifteen fastest-growing cites of 100,000 people or more are in Texas, and many of those are largely suburban areas such as Round Rock, Plano, McKinney, Frisco, and Carrolton.[30] While the Texas population is growing, this growth is not occurring in every part of the state.

In fact, the 40 percent of the state located along and east of Interstate 35 contains 86 percent of the state's population and saw 92 percent of the state's population growth in 2011 and 2012. Indeed, about the only significant population growth west of the I-35 corridor came in and around El Paso, Midland, and Odessa. In fact, Midland (#1) and Odessa (#5) joined Austin (#7) in the ten fastest-growing metro areas in percentage growth in the nation from July 1, 2011, to July 1, 2012.[31]

Texans often quip they are "the buckle in the Bible Belt," reflecting a strong Christian presence in the state. While most Texans might generally fall under the label "Christian," the more specific practices that fall under that broad category are quite diverse. For example, one recent poll found that the percentage of Catholics (20 percent) and Baptists (19 percent) was roughly equal in Texas.[32] (See Figure 1.3.)

The state's economy is as diverse as its people. While the state still has more farms (247,000 farms encompassing about 130,400,000 acres) and ranches than any other state,[33] more Texans work in the information industry than agriculture. While Texas as a ranching and farming behemoth remains the preferred image, in fact, residents today are engaged in providing virtually every kind of product and service (see Table 1.1). Educational services and health care are the biggest industries, while agriculture, despite the image, is the smallest.

**FIGURE 1.3**   **Religious Traditions in Texas, 2014**

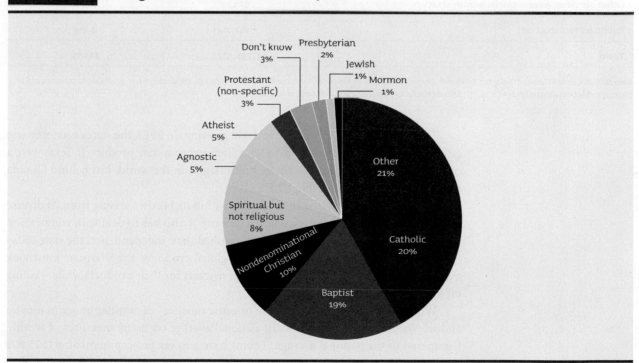

**Source:** Data from UT-Austin/*Texas Tribune*, Texas Statewide Survey, June 2014, http://s3.amazonaws.com/static.texastribune.org/media/documents/uttt-jun2014-summary-all.pdf (accessed August 25, 2014), 21.

## TABLE 1.1 Texas Civilian-Employed Population, Sixteen Years and Older, 2012

| Employment | Number Employed | Percentage of Employed |
|---|---|---|
| Agriculture, forestry, fishing and hunting, and mining | 396,204 | 3.4% |
| Construction | 925,163 | 7.9% |
| Manufacturing | 1,085,234 | 9.3% |
| Wholesale trade | 331,573 | 2.8% |
| Retail trade | 1,369,963 | 11.7% |
| Transportation and warehousing; utilities | 645,214 | 5.5% |
| Information | 204,380 | 1.7% |
| Finance and insurance; real estate and rental and leasing | 776,037 | 6.6% |
| Professional, scientific, and management services; administrative and waste management services | 1,277,165 | 10.9% |
| Educational services; health care and social assistance | 2,539,598 | 21.6% |
| Arts, entertainment, and recreation; accommodation and food services | 1,039,161 | 8.9% |
| Other services, except public administration | 624,711 | 5.3% |
| Public administration | 517,014 | 4.4% |
| **Total** | **11,731,417** | **100%** |

**Source**: U.S. Census Bureau, "Selected Economic Characteristics: 2012 American Community Survey," http://factfinder2.census.gov/faces/tableservices/jsf/pages/productview.xhtml?pid=ACS_12_1YR_DP03&prodType=table (accessed September 3, 2014).

The Texas economy is massive and still growing. In 2013, the state's economy was estimated to have produced almost $1.5 trillion in gross state product. If Texas were a country, its economy would be the eleventh largest in the world, just behind Canada and ahead of Russia. (See Table 1.2.)

Even as Texas grapples with challenges within its borders arising from its diverse and growing population and expansive economy, it also has to deal with competition from overseas. While Texans have always relished their independence, the state today must work to ensure its place in a growing global economy. Even farmers must look overseas as they attempt to cultivate foreign markets for their products while warding off foreign competitors.

While the wealthy Texas oil baron or cattle rancher is a familiar image in movies and television, Texans fall below the national average on many measures of wealth. Compared to the national average, Texans have a lower per capita income ($25,809 versus $25,051 in 2012), a higher poverty rate (17.4 percent versus 14.9 percent of all Americans), and a lower rate of home ownership (63.9 percent versus 65.5 percent).

While Texas may be a land of great wealth, it is also a land of great need. One study found that Texas ranked first or second in income inequality, depending on whether you measured inequality between the highest income group and the bottom income group or between the highest and middle income groups.[34]

Texas's years of transformation are not over, as the state continues to change rapidly. In the 1990s, the Texas population grew by 22.8 percent, and between 2000 and 2010 it grew another 20.6 percent. Texas is now second in U.S. state population, with an estimated 26,448,193 residents in 2013, though it is still well behind California's 38,332,521 residents.

Thus, the state with a constitution that was authored in the nineteenth century by isolated farmers who formed the Grange in order to connect with other farmers has become a booming high-tech center with citizens connected to each other and to the wider world through Facebook, Twitter, Instagram, and Pinterest. Visitors arriving in the Texas capital will not find lonely cowboys astride horses on the open plains; instead, they will encounter computer engineers and game programmers checking social networks on their smartphones while stuck in traffic.

## WINNERS AND LOSERS

Certainly one of the most significant forces of change that has shaped Texas's past, present, and future is immigration. Texas is a state defined by its ever-changing and constant immigrant population. In understanding Texas's past and trying to prepare Texas for the future, no immigrant population is more integral to the state than the Hispanic population. As the historical overview in this chapter makes clear, Tejanos in early Texas were central to its development. As Anglos came to dominate the state, historical revisionists overlooked early cooperation between Anglos and Tejanos, emphasizing and often exaggerating the tensions between the two groups. Just as many Tejanos were driven out of Texas after the revolution against Mexico, their contributions to the war on both sides of the conflict were driven from the pages of Texas history. At some point the Mexican flag failed to appear in the Alamo's "Hall of Honor" that commemorates the country of birth of the Alamo's defenders, allowing Texans to forget that nine of the eleven defenders of the Alamo born in the Mexican territory of Texas had Hispanic origins. Juan Nepomuceno Seguín, who neither wrote nor spoke English, was a close friend of Stephen F. Austin and helped drive Mexican forces from San Antonio before slipping out of the Alamo to seek reinforcements. Later, Seguín joined Sam Houston's army at the decisive battle of San Jacinto. As one historian put it, "'Remember the Alamo' became a formula for forgetfulness."[35] A rapidly anglicizing Texas replaced the legend

| TABLE 1.2 | Gross Domestic Product, 2013 | |
|---|---|---|
| **Rank** | **Nation** | **Millions of Dollars** |
| 1 | United States* | 16,720,000 |
| 2 | China | 8,939,000 |
| 3 | Japan | 5,007,000 |
| 4 | Germany | 3,593,000 |
| 5 | France | 2,739,000 |
| 6 | United Kingdom | 2,490,000 |
| 7 | Brazil | 2,190,000 |
| 8 | Russia | 2,113,000 |
| 9 | Italy | 2,068,000 |
| 10 | India | 1,825,000 |
| 11 | Canada | 1,758,000 |
| 12 | Australia | 1,488,000 |
| 13 | **Texas**** | **1,482,000** |
| 14 | Spain | 1,356,000 |
| 15 | Mexico | 1,327,000 |

**Source:** Texas Comptrollers of Public Accounts, March 2014.

* United States, including Texas.

** If an independent country.

# TEXAS (VS) VERMONT

A comparison of Texas and Vermont illustrates the diversity of states within the United States. Vermont, a northeastern state, got its start when Ethan Allen and the Green Mountain Boys rebelled against attempts by New York and New Hampshire to exert control over the region after the American Revolution. On January 15, 1777, the independent Republic of New Connecticut was declared; later, the name was changed to the Republic of Vermont. Vermont sent ambassadors to France, the Netherlands, and the United States. In 1791 Vermont entered the United States as the fourteenth state to balance the admission of slave-holding Kentucky as the fifteenth state.

While both Texas and Vermont share a history of independence before joining the United States, the similarity ends there. Geographically, Vermont is quite small, at 9,250 square miles. Vermont's size is smaller than the combined area of the largest two Texas counties (10,957 square miles is the combined area of Brewster and Pecos counties in West Texas). Vermont's landscape is dominated by the Green Mountains, abundant forests, and plentiful rivers and streams. As the second-largest state by area, Texas covers a vast territory that varies tremendously in land formations, water resources, and natural resources.

The demographics of the two states are also strikingly different. Settled by the English and some French colonists from nearby Quebec, Vermont remains among the most homogeneous states in the United States. In 2012 Vermont held the distinction of being one of the "whitest" states in the United States, with 94 percent of its residents describing themselves as white and not of Hispanic origin; Texas, in contrast, was among the most racially and ethnically diverse states.

Vermont also consistently ranks as one of the smallest states in population. In 1850, the first census in which Texas participated, Vermont had a slightly larger population than Texas. Immigration over the following decade saw Texas surpass Vermont in population by the 1860 census, at which point Texas already had over 600,000 residents. It would take Vermont 140 years to reach that level of population. By the time it did, in 2000, Texas recorded over 22 million residents.

Large cities are found throughout Texas; three of the nation's ten largest cities are located in Texas. Vermont's largest city,

## Texas versus Vermont: Ethnic Makeup

| Population Group | Texas | Vermont |
|---|---|---|
| White alone, not of Hispanic origin | 44.5% | 94.0% |
| Hispanic/Latino | 38.2% | 1.6% |
| African American | 12.3% | 1.1% |
| Asian American | 4.2% | 1.4% |

*Sources:* Population Division, U.S. Census Bureau, "Quick Facts: Texas" and "Quick Facts: Vermont," 2013, http://quickfacts.census.gov/qfd/index.html (accessed August 27, 2014).

Burlington (42,282 in 2012), is so small that it would rank seventy-fifth in city size in Texas. Even the images of the two states generate contrasts. Texas is the land of open plains, oil wells, cattle, gun-slinging cowboys, and big-time football. Vermont is the land of maple syrup, ice cream, fall foliage, and quaint towns.

Obviously, to govern a diverse population spread over a vast geographic area with extensive mineral wealth, Texas requires a fundamentally different approach than Vermont. In many instances, Texas politics is vastly different in practice than Vermont's political system. However, these differences may not be exactly what we expect.

## THINKING Critically

In several places, this textbook presents discussions, tables, and figures to offer comparisons between Texas and other states. At this point, think about the heritage and demographics of your community or hometown.

★ Is your community more like a typical Texas or Vermont community?

★ What have your experiences in politics been like?

★ How would they compare to those in a state like Vermont?

of heroic Tejanos with a legend that emphasized dictatorial Mexican rulers seeking the expulsion of the Anglos.

The Tejano population of Texas declined from the time of the revolution until a repressive regime in Mexico, coupled with decades of revolution within that country, created a new wave of immigrants. This tripled the Mexican population in Texas from 1900 to 1920. While these immigrants played an important role in cotton production, they were often not welcomed and took their place somewhere between Anglos and African Americans, unaccepted in either community. Techniques such as "white primaries," which were used to exclude African Americans from voting, were eventually also employed against Tejanos. As the state continued to change, and immigrants continued to move into Texas, Hispanics were marginalized in the political process as well as in the history books.

One of the enduring legends of early Texas history is how Anglo order and hard work saved the state from Mexican chaos. According to this view, it was immigrants from the United States who, in the words of one public school textbook from the 1880s, "changed Texas from a wilderness into a civilized state: Mexico had nothing but fear and hatred."[36] Like other legacies, this historical "truth" ignores some aspects of history and exaggerates others. So far, Hispanics have been the losers in the formation of historical legend.

By 1930, the Tejano population of Texas had begun to rise with the rest of the population, reaching almost 684,000. Reflecting the return of Tejanos to Texas politics, the League of United Latin American Citizens (LULAC) was formed in Corpus Christi in 1929. LULAC quickly became a major factor in Texas politics. In 1956 Henry B. González became the first Tejano in over half a century to hold a seat in the Texas Senate. During the 1957 legislative session, González set the record for a filibuster in the Texas Senate as he fought laws backing segregation in Texas public schools. In 1961 González broke ground again by winning a seat in the U.S. House of Representatives. By that time half a dozen Tejanos were serving in the Texas Legislature and a Tejano was serving as mayor of El Paso. Tejanos won their first statewide office when Dan Morales was elected attorney general in 1992. Hispanics are both the largest and fastest-growing group in the state and today hold a variety of offices. In 2009 Eva Guzman became the first Hispanic woman to serve on the Texas Supreme Court when Governor Rick Perry appointed her to fill a vacancy on the court. Tejanos are increasingly successful in organizing and exerting political pressure in Texas. As the Hispanic population continues to increase and organize its interests within the state, Hispanics are in a position to be the winners in a future Texas.

Today, Texas is again dealing with immigrants whose numbers are increasing so rapidly that they form a majority in some parts of the state. The struggle to deal with this change is part of what defines Texas as a state. As we will see throughout this text, legends tend to be static and are often at odds with the changing nature of the state. The myth that Texas's story is a primarily Anglo one ignores others' contributions. What's more, the myth of Anglo primacy remains the dominant legend in Texas's history books. Throughout the rest of this book, we will continue to explore this tension between legend and change.

★ How accurate should our Texas legends be? Can Texas afford to keep it real?

★ Why is there tension between the rapidly changing nature of Texas and our legends?

★ How does Texas's size affect its politics?

★ How will changes to the population and economy shape Texas state government in the future?

## CONCLUSION

Texas faces fresh challenges as it continues to change. The rising political clout of Republicans, Hispanics, and women at the close of the twentieth century has been only partially reflected in changes to the Texas political system. At the same time, Texas now faces many political issues that have been long deferred by the state's leaders. The funding of public schools, in dispute for over a decade, was only partially resolved by a special session of the legislature in 2006. Texas continues to grapple with air quality, an issue that it did not even begin to address until 1965. Toll roads and mass transit have become major issues as the state tries to keep its rapidly growing population and economy moving.

In 2004 Republicans redistricted the state of Texas to correct what they saw as the underrepresentation of their party in the Texas delegation to the U.S. House. Hispanic leaders continue to struggle to elect officials in proportion to their share of the population. Despite a few highly visible women representing the state in the U.S. Senate or as Texas comptroller, women remain dramatically underrepresented in state offices, composing only 21 percent of the Texas Legislature in 2013. The struggle of Republicans, women, and Tejanos exemplifies the reality that changes in the state's politics often lag well behind other changes—demographic, social, and economic.

Texans' struggle to define themselves was revived in March 2010 as they witnessed another round of fighting for control of the Alamo. This struggle, played out in Austin rather than San Antonio, was over who among the defenders of the Alamo 174 years earlier would be featured in the Texas public school curriculum. The Texas State Board of Education, the fifteen-member elected board that approves curriculum for the state's public schools, was revising what students must learn about history. The board had previously approved a draft standard for fourth-grade classes that included discussion of the Tejanos who died defending the Alamo, but that wording was removed in the March meeting. While the majority on the board approved language that they felt was very inclusive and avoided "number counting and quotas" by focusing on "leaders" at the Alamo, Mary Helen Berlanga asked, "What did James Bowie and Davy Crockett do that the Tejanos did not do?"[37]

Finding a place in the Alamo is an important part of finding a place in Texas politics. The sacrifice of the Alamo's defenders defines the state as much as any single event. While Texans share a fondness for the state's history, what they choose to see in that history can be very different.

Like all democracies, Texas government takes its flavor from the people it represents. As this chapter demonstrates, the meaning of the word *Texan* has changed over the state's history, and today the meaning conjures a different image in each corner of the state. And yet, despite the changes in those who call themselves Texans, and the changes in the places where they live and how they work, the basic structure of Texas government has remained largely unchanged.

While Texans relish their colorful history, the state today must work to ensure its place in a competitive, global, high-tech economy. A constitution written in 1876 by isolated Texas farmers who had little interest in government, growth, diversity, big business, or the modern world leaves a government that must struggle to meet the needs of a state that is rapidly growing and increasingly diverse and that features an economy driven by large multinational corporations on the cutting edge of the information age.

Change does not make the state's history less important. The rapid transformations occurring in the state today make understanding Texas's history of change even more important as Texans grapple with difficult issues such as immigration. Following the legacy of a declaration of independence written by men who had lived in Texas only a few years, Texans must both acknowledge the potential contributions of new arrivals and protect what previous generations have created. In the following chapters, we will look at how Texas politics and government have adapted to the waves of change over the course of the state's history and consider how well Texas is prepared for the changes ahead.

for CQ Press

Sharpen your skills with **SAGE edge** at **edge.sagepub.com/collier4e**. **SAGE edge for students** provides a personalized approach to help you accomplish your coursework goals in an easy-to-use learning environment.

## KEY TERMS

empresario (p. 9)

individualistic political culture (p. 25)

moralistic political culture (p. 25)

political culture (p. 23)

presidential republicanism (p. 23)

traditionalistic political culture (p. 25)

Treaty of Guadalupe Hidalgo (p. 15)

## CORE ASSESSMENT

1. How much do Texans need to know about the history of their state? What role should that history play in shaping how Texans think about the state's future?

2. Does the shared identity as Texans reinforce individualism or create obligations to each other and the community?

3. When should a state that has seen such a rapidly expanding population stop encouraging growth? What obligations do current Texans have to create opportunities for new Texans coming from other states and other countries?

# TEXAS CONSTITUTION

When Texas joined the Union in 1845, its residents wanted a federal government that could help them control their remote frontier, but they did not particularly want much else. A few years later, the election of President Abraham Lincoln, who Texans feared would threaten the institution of slavery, pushed the state toward secession. Texans were concerned that the federal government would come and take their slaves, and most Texans at the time preferred to leave the Union rather than remain on what they viewed as such unjust grounds. The rhetoric in Texas leading up to the Civil War was filled with speeches about states' rights and federal intrusion. The Ordinance for Secession drafted by Texans at the 1861 Secession Convention indicated the general mood in the state:

> The recent developments in Federal affairs, make it evident that the power of the Federal Government is sought to be made a weapon with which to strike down the interests and prosperity of the people of Texas and her Sister slaveholding States, instead of permitting it to be, as was intended, our shield against outrage and aggression.

Frontier Texans lived a hard life, but one in which they largely made their own destiny and provided for their own defense. Today's Texans continue to want the federal government to control their border but otherwise stay out of their lives. In the past few years, Texas politicians have once again focused on federal policies that they view as too intrusive and as a loss of sovereignty at the state level. Texans don't want the federal government to tell them how to conduct their business, whether the business in question is elections, guns, clean air, or social services and health care. Texans have long been individualistic, espousing a "pull yourself up by your bootstraps" approach to life and holding individuals responsible for their own welfare. In fact, the only thing that Texans appear to want from the federal government, then as now, is a secure frontier.

Politicians across the state continue to reflect the sentiment that the federal government and its policies are hostile to state interests. As governor, Rick Perry became the poster boy for the fight against big government in Texas. Senator Ted Cruz advocated obstructionism at the federal level, and former attorney general Greg Abbott

Tea Party protests against the growth and intrusiveness of the federal government illustrate an increasing anti-Washington mood in Texas. This protest, which took place in front of the Alamo, protested the federal bailouts.

based his political identity on challenging federal policy in almost every policy area. As attorney general, Abbott sued the federal government more than thirty times over everything from federal air quality regulations to the state's voter identification law. Abbott also joined several other states in a suit challenging the constitutionality of the Affordable Care Act (ACA). During his time as attorney general, Abbott was famous for saying he woke up, went to work, sued the federal government, and went home. In true Texas style, Abbott's response to disputed land along the Texas-Oklahoma border was to tell the Federal Bureau of Land Management that they could come and take it, a reference to the flag raised over Gonzales during the Texas Revolution threatening the Mexican government.

Today's Texans continue to oppose national policies in almost all issue areas, although the religious right is much more likely to approve government involvement in social issues (such as marriage and abortion) than other Tea Party and Tenther groups that often oppose national government.

The sharing of power between the national government and state governments remains a highly contentious issue. These concerns have to do with a fundamental constitutional arrangement: How much power should the national government have compared to the states? Many Texans believe that the national government has become overlarge and too involved and that state governments should more actively protect their power vis-à-vis the national government. Citizens worry about national tyranny and have often preferred more local policy control. In fact, Article 1, Section 1 of the current Texas Constitution embodies this very idea, stating that "Texas is a free and independent State, subject only to the Constitution of the United States, and the maintenance of our free institutions and the perpetuity of the Union depend upon the preservation of the right of local self-government, unimpaired to all the States." In this chapter we will explore the constitutional arrangement of federalism and the development of the Texas Constitution more generally. We will first outline the federalist structure of the national government and how Texas fits into that structure. We will then survey how the Texas Constitution has evolved over time, reflecting our rich history and culture. Finally, we discuss the problems of the current constitution and examine the prospects for constitutional reform.

## Chapter Objectives

★ Explain the purpose of a constitution and how the Texas Constitution developed.

★ Describe how federalism affects the choices made by state government.

★ Discuss the evolution of Texas's previous constitutions and the historical events that influenced them.

★ Explain how Texas's current constitution organizes its government.

★ Identify problems with the current Texas Constitution.

★ Assess who wins and who loses in Texas given its environment of distrust of the government.

## CONSTITUTIONAL GOVERNMENT

**Constitution**
a written document that outlines the powers of government and the limitations on those powers.

The founding fathers created a government based on a written **constitution** that outlines the powers of government and limitations on those powers to protect the rights of citizens. Ideally, a constitution should be a brief, flexible document that broadly defines what the government can and cannot do. The government, in turn, works within the boundaries of the constitution as it goes about day-to-day operations. The legislature, for example, passes laws that do not violate the basic principles outlined in the constitution. The more fundamental the constitution's provisions, the less likely it will need to be updated over time. The U.S. Constitution, for instance, has lasted over 200 years, with Congress passing and repealing more specific laws to reflect the changing times. Ideally a constitution should protect citizens' rights while being flexible enough to remain relevant as society changes.

Our country's founders believed that a constitutional government was necessary to prevent tyranny. James Madison wrote in *Federalist* No. 51 that

if men were angels, no government would be necessary. If angels were to govern men, neither external nor internal controls on government would be necessary. In framing a government which is to be administered by men over men, the great difficulty lies in this: you must first enable the government to control the governed; and in the next place oblige it to control itself.

The founders, concerned with tyranny often displayed by the monarchs at the expense of the people, set out to create a new form of government. The U.S. Constitution checked potential tyranny in several ways: by creating different levels of government (federalism), by separating power among different branches of government (separation of powers), and by empowering the people to check the government (popular sovereignty). While the U.S. Constitution was revolutionary in the eighteenth century, today written constitutions are the norm. Since independence, Texas has followed the U.S. model and created government based on a written constitution.

The idea of **popular sovereignty**, or creating a government in which the power to govern is derived from the will of the people, is a critical aspect in limiting tyranny. This idea stands in sharp contrast to the prevailing norm 200 years ago when the U.S. Constitution was written. Monarchs ruled with little concept of popular representation in government, instead claiming a divine right to rule derived from the will of God. With the memories of a rebellion against monarchy fresh in their minds, the founders included popular sovereignty in the preamble to the U.S. Constitution with the words "We the people." Similarly, the Texas Revolution invoked memories of the American Revolution; Texas wanted independence from Mexican rule, and Santa Anna was cast as the tyrant. The Texas Constitution reflects the idea of popular sovereignty with its preamble, which states that the people of Texas establish the constitution. Popular sovereignty is also manifest in Texas in the election of almost all state officials, including members of the legislative, executive, and judicial branches. Texas voters must also approve amendments to the state's constitution, further extending popular rule to the state's fundamental law.

The United States invented modern constitutional government, and the U.S. Constitution is a model of brevity and flexible language. It remains relatively short, has been amended only twenty-seven times, and outlines the fundamental functions and limits of government while leaving the legislature to pass more specific legislation.

Of course, such an ideal constitution is rarely achieved. The Texas Constitution by contrast is extremely long and specific, creates a relatively weak executive, and undergoes constant amendment as the government tries to keep up with a rapidly growing and changing state. The current Texas Constitution, Texas's sixth since its independence from Mexico, reflects Texas's historical experiences under Mexico and Spain, its reaction to the Civil War and Reconstruction, and the still-prevailing preference for limited government. The current constitution also represents the federal nature of the U.S. government.

**Popular sovereignty**
a government in which the power to govern is derived from the will of the people.

## THE FEDERAL SYSTEM OF THE UNITED STATES

Federalism—the sharing of powers between two levels of government—is a uniquely American creation. The North American colonies had relatively little influence in decisions made by the central government back in London. The founders were frustrated over lack of representation in the British government, and they believed that governmental tyranny could be checked by separating the powers of government. In an attempt to limit the potential for tyranny, the framers divided powers among the branches of government as well as between the levels of government. The federalist concept specifies a division of powers between the central or national government and the lower levels or state governments.

In creating a federal system, the framers compromised between two alternative ideal systems: unitary and confederal. A **confederal system** is a governmental arrangement where the lower units of government retain decision-making authority. The United States experienced a confederacy twice: first under the Articles of Confederation and later in the short-lived Confederacy created by southern states during the Civil War. In both cases, the states retained decision-making authority, leaving a relatively weaker national government. A modern-day example of a confederacy is the United Nations, where member countries can participate in various treaties, choose to opt out of treaties, or withdraw from the organization at any time.

A **unitary system**, by contrast, vests power in a central government; lower units of government only have power that is granted to them by the central government. For instance, the North American colonies had only the powers granted to them by the British government. Today, about 75 percent of governments are unitary, making this the most prevalent type of government in the world. An example of a unitary government close to home is the relationship between Texas and its local governments. Cities and counties in Texas are granted only limited lawmaking authority by the state constitution and the state legislature.

The founders, having experienced both a unitary and confederal government, created an alternative form of government known as federalism. **Federalism** is a system of government where power is shared between the national and state governments, and it represents a compromise between a unitary and confederal system. The U.S. Constitution created a federal system by vesting certain powers in the national government while reserving other powers for the states. Theoretically, dividing power among levels of government prevents the national government from imposing "one-size-fits-all" standards that may not make sense for a particular state or region. On the one hand, federalism allows states to experiment with new policies and permits flexibility as states pass laws that represent their distinct political culture. Ideally, a federal system allows each state to pass laws representing its particular political preferences. On the other hand, federalism imposes significant costs on the United States since different levels of government create policy for the same issue areas, often at the taxpayer's expense. The founders believed that the prevention of tyranny was more important than the inefficiency that different levels of government create. Moreover, federal intervention is often necessary to prevent majority rule from overwhelming minority rights. As Madison explained in *Federalist* No. 10, larger governments are more likely to respect minority rights, a fact we learned during the fight against slavery and the subsequent civil rights movement.

## Vertical Federalism

Although the founders generally believed that dividing powers among levels of government would be beneficial, the exact division of power within our federal system is unclear. **Vertical federalism**, or the distribution of power between the national government and the state governments, has been highly contested for much of our

**Confederal system**
a type of government in which the lower units of government retain decision-making authority.

**Unitary system**
a type of government in which power is vested in a central governmental authority.

**Federalism**
a form of government based on the sharing of powers between the levels of government; in the United States, between the national and state governments.

**Vertical federalism**
the distribution of power between the national government and state governments.

# HOW TEXAS GOVERNMENT WORKS

## The Federal System

| Legislature | Executive | Judiciary |
| --- | --- | --- |

### National Government

| U.S. Senate<br>U.S. House of Representatives | President | U.S. Supreme Court<br>Federal Circuit Courts<br>Federal District Courts |
| --- | --- | --- |

### State Government

| Texas Senate<br>Texas House of Representatives | Governor<br>Lieutenant Governor<br>Agriculture Commissioner<br>Attorney General<br>Comptroller<br>Land Commissioner<br>Secretary of State | Supreme Court of Texas \| Texas Court of Criminal Appeals<br>Texas Appellate Courts<br>Texas District Courts |
| --- | --- | --- |

### County Government

| County Commissioner's Court | | Constitutional County Courts<br>Statutory County Courts<br>Statutory Probate Courts<br>Justice of the Peace Courts |
| --- | --- | --- |

### City or Municipality Government

| City Council | Mayor<br>City Manager | Municipal Courts |
| --- | --- | --- |

history. The difficulty in describing the federal nature of the U.S. government is best exemplified by juxtaposing the supremacy clause and the reserved powers clause of the U.S. Constitution. The **supremacy clause** guarantees that the national government is the supreme law of the land. Thus, the U.S. Constitution and laws created by the national Congress supersede state laws and state constitutions. States can make laws within their territory so long as those laws do not conflict with national laws or the U.S. Constitution. The Tenth Amendment, or reserved powers clause, however, declares that "the powers not delegated to the United States by the Constitution, nor prohibited by it to the States, are reserved to the States respectively, or to the people." This provision creates a class of powers called **reserved powers**, although the Supreme Court has interpreted these powers narrowly in recent times. These two constitutional clauses have generated opposing views of the division of powers between the national government and the state governments. The reserved powers clause seems to indicate a federal system in which states have most of the power, whereas the supremacy clause points to a government where most of the power rests with the national government.

The U.S. Constitution gives the national government exclusive authority over coining money, establishing a navy, declaring war, and regulating interstate commerce, among other things. These **enumerated powers** expressly granted to the national government are listed in Article I, Section 8 of the U.S. Constitution. In 1819, the Supreme Court ruled in *McCulloch v. Maryland* that the "necessary and proper clause" of the U.S. Constitution created **implied powers**. Thus, in addition to those powers specified in the Constitution, the national government was given broad discretionary powers to enact any law necessary and proper to carry out its enumerated powers. The idea of implied powers creates a category of powers that are unspecified and thus constantly expand our understanding of the powers of the national government. The U.S. Constitution also outlines explicit roles for the states with regard to the conduct of elections, the selection of electors to the Electoral College, the establishment of voter qualifications, and the approval of constitutional amendments. Moreover, Article I, Section 10 of the U.S. Constitution explicitly prohibits states from entering into treaties, coining money, or granting letters of marque or titles of nobility, among other things. Other powers, such as the power to tax and spend, to establish courts, or to charter banks, are **concurrent powers** shared by the national and state governments (see Figure 2.1).

## Horizontal Federalism

**Horizontal federalism** refers to the relationship between states. Certain provisions within the U.S. Constitution regulate the relations among states. The founders specified certain state obligations to other states, in part to create a sense of national unity among them. For instance, states are required to grant the same **privileges and immunities** to citizens of other states as they grant to their own citizens. This provision means that states may not fundamentally treat citizens of other states differently than their own citizens. The privileges and immunities clause makes travel between states easier and prevents discrimination against citizens of other states. However, exceptions to the privileges and immunities clause have been recognized in two cases.[1] First, states may deny the right to vote to nonresidents. Thus, the laws of

## FIGURE 2.1 Distribution of Powers between the National Government and the States in the U.S. Constitution

| DELEGATED POWERS (to the national government) | Admit new states to the Union |
| | Coin money |
| | Conduct foreign affairs |
| | Declare war |
| | Establish courts inferior to the Supreme Court |
| | Make laws that are necessary for carrying out the powers vested by the U.S. Constitution |
| | Raise and maintain armies and navies |
| | Regulate interstate and foreign commerce |

| | CONCURRENT POWERS (shared by the national government and the states) |
| Borrow and spend money for the general welfare | |
| Charter and regulate banks; charter corporations | |
| Collect taxes | |
| Establish courts | |
| Establish highways | |
| Pass and enforce laws | |
| Take private property for public purposes, with just compensation | |

| RESERVED POWERS (to the states) | Conduct elections and determine voter qualifications |
| | Establish local governments |
| | Maintain militia (National Guard) |
| | Provide for public health, safety, and morals |
| | Ratify amendments to the federal constitution |
| | Regulate intrastate commerce |

| | DENIED POWERS (to the states) |
| Abridge the privileges or immunities of citizens or deny due process and equal protection of the laws (Fourteenth Amendment) | |
| Coin money | |
| Enter into treaties | |
| Keep troops or navies | |
| Levy import or export taxes on goods | |
| Make war | |

*Source:* Adapted from Christine Barbour and Gerald C. Wright, *Keeping the Republic*, 4th brief ed. (Washington, D.C.: CQ Press, 2011), 84.

one state cannot be unduly influenced by citizens from neighboring states. In addition, states may distinguish between residents and nonresidents in the distribution of certain state-subsidized benefits that may differ from state to state, such as in-state tuition rates or welfare payments. This exception has been deemed reasonable since "individuals could benefit from subsidies without being subject to the taxes that pay the subsidies."[2] The **full faith and credit clause** creates an additional obligation between states. States are required to give full faith and credit to the acts, records, and judicial decisions of other states. This means that court judgments or legal contracts from one state will be honored by all other states. Thus, debt or child support

**Full faith and credit clause**
the constitutional requirement that court judgments or legal contracts entered into in one state will be honored by all other states.

**Extradition**
the constitutional requirement that a state deliver someone suspected or convicted of a crime in another state back to the state where the crime allegedly occurred so the accused can face trial or sentencing.

**Dual federalism**
the theory of federalism that suggests state governments and the national government have separate spheres of policy influence and restrict their involvement to policies in their areas.

**Cooperative federalism**
the theory of federalism that suggests that both levels of government cooperate across various policy areas rather than maintaining distinct policy arenas.

**Devolution**
returning power to state governments.

payments cannot be avoided by moving to another state. Finally, the U.S. Constitution requires that states deliver someone suspected or convicted of a crime in another state back to the state where the crime is alleged to have occurred so the accused can face trial and sentencing. This process, known as **extradition**, was designed to keep criminals from escaping justice by moving from state to state.

### The Evolving Idea of Federalism

Creating a new type of government generated a significant amount of uncertainty. It is clear that America's founders sought to produce a system of government in which powers are shared between two levels of government. It is considerably less clear exactly what that distribution of power was supposed to look like. From its inception, the idea of federalism has generated a good deal of controversy, culminating, in part, in a civil war less than a century after the republic was founded. Very few policy areas have escaped this tension.

The idea of sharing power between the national government and the states was an ambiguous one from the beginning. The tension of trying to reconcile the supremacy clause and the Tenth Amendment continues to create different outlooks on how big the national government should be and exactly what it should do. Not surprisingly, those who focus on the supremacy clause view the national government as more powerful, whereas those who focus on the Tenth Amendment view the national government's power as exceedingly limited. In the past, this tension led to a theory of **dual federalism**, in which state powers and federal powers were separate and distinct. However, since the New Deal, those natural policy distinctions began to erode as the federal government developed policies in areas traditionally left to state governments, such as civil rights. As the strict separation between levels of government gave way to both levels of government being involved in the same policy areas, dual federalism gradually transformed into what political scientists refer to as **cooperative federalism**. This moniker suggests that the national government and the states cooperate in various policy areas. In reality, the national government is often leading the policy change and state governments often engage in active resistance to federal policy.

Today, the United States continues to grapple with exactly which powers belong to the national government and which should be reserved for the states. Sentimental attachment to the idea of federalism is often usurped by a preference for efficiency and uniformity. The result is that, over time, the power of the states has eroded significantly. Most notably, states have historically enjoyed policy control over issues such as police power, marriage, education, and election laws. Yet in the last half century, the national government has begun to encroach on policy areas traditionally reserved for the states. Proponents of a system of government that vests more power in the national government than the states point to issues such as slavery and civil rights that were unlikely to improve without national intervention. On the other hand, Texans often long for a return to a system of government where the states hold most if not all of the power. Proponents of state power support **devolution**, or the idea that power should be returned to the states. Negotiating these competing views continues to be a source of conflict within the United States.

# TEXAS AND THE FED ON *Abortion*

In 1973, the U.S. Supreme Court ruled in *Roe v. Wade* that state laws prohibiting abortion violated a woman's right to privacy. Since then, pro-life advocates have searched for ways to undo *Roe*. At the heart of the issue for pro-life supporters is the argument that all life is sacred. A secondary issue is whether the national government or the state governments have the power to decide whether or not to allow abortions. Pro-choice advocates argue that basic rights, from voting rights to privacy rights, must be protected at the national level to protect interests that may face discrimination locally. Indeed, James Madison argued in *Federalist* No. 10 that minority rights are more likely to be protected when a government covers an expanded sphere. Yet critics argue that abortion is a states' rights issue. From this point of view, issues such as abortion that are not directly addressed in the U.S. Constitution are left to state governments, which should adopt policies that reflect their state's cultural preferences.

Supporters of states' rights realized a significant victory when the U.S. Supreme Court ruled in *Webster v. Reproductive Health Services* (1989) that states could place restrictions on abortion. Since then, numerous states have attempted to limit or deny abortions by passing onerous legal requirements on facilities that provide abortions. In 2013, the Texas Legislature passed House Bill 2, which, among other things, required that doctors who provide abortions have admitting privileges at nearby hospitals and that clinics that provide abortions meet the same standards as ambulatory surgical centers. The effect of the law was immediate—nearly half of the thirty-four abortion providers in the state closed or stopped providing abortions once the requirement that doctors have nearby hospital privileges went into effect. Since most of the remaining facilities would have to undergo multimillion-dollar renovations to meet the standards required of an ambulatory surgical center, only a few clinics are expected to remain open once that

requirement also goes into effect. In 2014, the Supreme Court ordered Texas to stop enforcing the law until the appeals process was exhausted. The closure of these clinics disproportionately affects rural and poor Texans. Texans who live in the South and the West have been hit particularly hard, as it can now take them more than five hours to drive to a clinic. The affected clinics are also key providers of contraception, sexually transmitted disease (STD) testing, and cancer screening.

Initial estimates suggest that the number of abortions in Texas has fallen by 13 percent since the law went into effect.[i] Yet there is also preliminary evidence of a rise in sales of misoprostol, a drug sold over the counter in Mexico that is sometimes used to self-induce an abortion.[ii]

★ To what extent is abortion a federalist issue?

★ How should government weigh the predominant political culture against minority rights?

★ In drafting its restrictions against abortion, does the Texas Legislature have a responsibility to consider the impact of the legislation on women's access to other services offered at these facilities?

★ Who wins and who loses when the effects of legislation are felt beyond the specific activity or group a bill was meant to address?

---

i. Brian M. Rosenthal, "Texas Abortions Down 13% Due to New Law, Study Says," *Houston Chronicle*, July 23, 2014.

ii. Erica Hellerstein, "The Rise of the DIY Abortion in Texas. A Pill That Revolutionized Reproductive Rights in Latin America Is Now Gaining Ground on the Black Market in South Texas," *The Atlantic*, June 27, 2014, www.theatlantic.com/health/archive/2014/06/the-rise-of-the-diy-abortion-in-texas/373240/ (accessed August 23, 2014).

---

Perhaps the most effective tool the national government uses to gain control of state policy areas is money. With the creation of a national income tax in 1913, the national government enjoyed a significant increase in revenues. Since that time, Congress has used its financial advantage to control issues that were traditionally considered state policy areas. Use of financial incentives to encourage policies at the state or local level is referred to as **fiscal federalism**. The national government has awarded two types of grants to state and local governments. The **categorical grant** is money given to states and local governments that must be spent for specific activities. When the national

**Fiscal federalism**
use of financial incentives by the national government to encourage policies at the state or local level.

**Categorical grant**
national money given to states and local governments that must be spent for specific activities.

government specifies how the money is to be spent, it can then set national policy goals in traditionally state-controlled policy areas. In response to this, Republican administrations have favored the **block grant** in an attempt to return policy control back to the states. A block grant is given to state and local governments for a broader purpose and imposes fewer restrictions on the states regarding how the grant money is to be spent. In the 1970s, President Richard Nixon reorganized existing categorical grants into block grants to continue the flow of money from the national government to the states while allowing the states to exert more discretion on how the money was spent.

A current example of a categorical grant is Medicaid. Medicaid was established to provide health care to the children of low-income families, the elderly, and individuals with disabilities, among others. As long as states meet the guidelines set by the national government, they receive national funds that supplement state funds to cover the cost of the program. Currently, Texas receives $60 in federal matching funds for every $40 it spends on Medicaid in the state.[3] Governor Perry suggested that the national government convert Medicaid into a block grant. This would continue the flow of money from the national government to the state without the current federal requirements. Proponents of changing Medicaid to a block grant argue that it would give states more flexibility as to how to spend the money and that the state and the national government would save money. Opponents worry that removing the requirements attached to Medicaid dollars would allow states to discontinue covering certain groups or medical services. While block grants are a popular means of reviving state power, they have been politically difficult to achieve. Members of Congress prefer to allocate money attached to specific policies, making it easier for them to take credit for the resulting goods provided to their home states.

One example of the national government's use of grants to intrude on state policy issues occurred in the 1980s when Congress wanted to establish a national drinking age. Congress, faced with increasing pressure from the organization Mothers Against Drunk Driving, and absent clear constitutional authority to establish a national drinking age, passed legislation that would take away 10 percent of a state's federal highway funds if the state did not raise its drinking age to twenty-one within two years. South Dakota sued the national government, arguing that the policy amounted to coercion and was a blatant intrusion on states' rights. In *South Dakota v. Dole*, the U.S. Supreme Court ruled that the national government could reasonably attach conditions to national grants. In a dissenting opinion, Justice Sandra Day O'Connor concurred with South Dakota that the law violated the spirit of federalism, arguing that "the immense size and power of the Government of the United States ought not obscure its fundamental character."[4] Nonetheless, Texas, along with most states in the Union, raised its drinking age to twenty-one as a result of the law. This case illustrates how the national government has used its substantial tax base to considerably increase its policy authority beyond its delegated powers.

Another controversial way that the national government infringes on state policy areas is its reliance on unfunded mandates. An **unfunded mandate** occurs when the national government passes legislation that imposes requirements on state and local governments that then bear the cost of meeting those requirements. Some examples include requirements that all states, including Texas, ensure equal access to public facilities for disabled persons, guarantee civil rights, provide public assistance for single

Texans in Corpus Christi protest the Affordable Care Act, claiming it is a federal intrusion into states' rights. The Supreme Court upheld the law in 2012, but a new challenge will be heard by the Court in 2015.

parents, and enforce clean air standards.[5] In each of these cases, the states and local governments must pay for a significant portion of these regulations that are imposed on them by the national government.

The debate over the appropriate division of power between the national government and state governments has accelerated in recent years. The expansion of the national government, first with the wars in Afghanistan and Iraq and later with the bailouts of American financial and automobile industries, renewed America's interest in the proper role and size of the national government. The subsequent stimulus package, followed by the divisive passage of the Affordable Care Act, once again put the issue of federalism at the forefront of the political debate in America. Other issues, such as gay marriage, education policy, and responses to natural disasters such as Hurricane Katrina, serve to highlight the differing views of Americans concerning the responsibilities of government.

One of the most contentious debates over federalism currently involves the states' customary authority over marriage. Traditionally, states have enjoyed almost complete control over rules governing marriage, including defining licensing requirements, establishing an age of consent, providing for common law marriages, and determining general guidelines for divorce. Recently, this control has been challenged by the issue of same-sex marriage. In 2000, Vermont became the first state in the country to approve civil unions. Three years later, Massachusetts became the first state to allow same-sex marriage. Currently, thirty-two states and the District of Columbia allow same-sex marriage, and appeals are pending in federal court to overturn gay marriage bans in every other state. Under the full faith and credit clause of the U.S. Constitution, states have honored marriages performed in other states so long as they did not violate the state's own marriage guidelines. The Massachusetts law caused a national uproar as opponents of same-sex marriage feared that the full faith and credit clause would result in the legalization of gay marriages across the United States. The national government responded by passing the 1996 Defense of Marriage Act, which allows states to adopt legislation excluding same-sex marriages in their territories. With this act, the national government is explicitly attempting to relieve the states of their obligation to grant full faith and credit to public acts in other states. At the state level, many states began to pass laws explicitly denying the validity of same-sex marriages within their state. Thirty-one states amended their state constitutions to only allow marriage between a man and a woman. Texas did so in 2005 when voters overwhelmingly approved a constitutional amendment defining marriage as a union between a man and a woman. Since then, gay couples have filed legal challenges to these bans in every state. Early in 2014, a federal judge overturned Texas's ban on gay marriage, ruling that "without a rational relation to a legitimate governmental purpose, state-imposed inequality can find no refuge in our U.S. Constitution."[6] However, Texas is not issuing same-sex marriage licenses yet since the judge issued a stay on the decision until it is through the appeals process.

While the battle over same-sex marriage has been contentious, the battle over the passage of a national health care policy has taken the conflict over federalism to a whole new level. A national health care system has been a goal of the Democratic Party since President Harry Truman proposed a national health insurance plan in 1945. Indeed, health care reform was the hallmark of Massachusetts senator Ted Kennedy's nearly five decades in Congress. Hillary Clinton made national health care central to her presidential campaign after championing a similar proposal as First Lady. When Barack Obama was elected president in 2008, he promised to make health care reform a priority. While national health care has been popular among Democrats for some time, it has been equally unpopular among Republicans. Even as President Obama signed the Affordable Care Act into law on March 23, 2010, the Republican opposition to the bill was still growing. Though many of the provisions of the ACA are quite popular, undoubtedly the most controversial provision requires all citizens to either purchase insurance or pay a penalty. Ironically, this provision originated among conservatives as a way to prevent free riders in health care. Nonetheless, Texans, who tend to distrust government in general, by and large don't want anything approaching universal health care. A University of Texas/*Texas Tribune* poll conducted when the bill was passed showed that 60 percent of Texans opposed the new bill and only 28 percent supported it. Only a few hours after the bill passed, Governor Rick Perry released a statement suggesting that "Texas leaders will continue to do everything in our power to fight this federal excess and find ways to protect our families, taxpayers and medical providers from this gross federal overreach."[7] From the beginning of the battle over the ACA, Perry described the bill as an encroachment on state's rights and "the largest unfunded mandate in American

# MAP 2.1 The United States, 1837

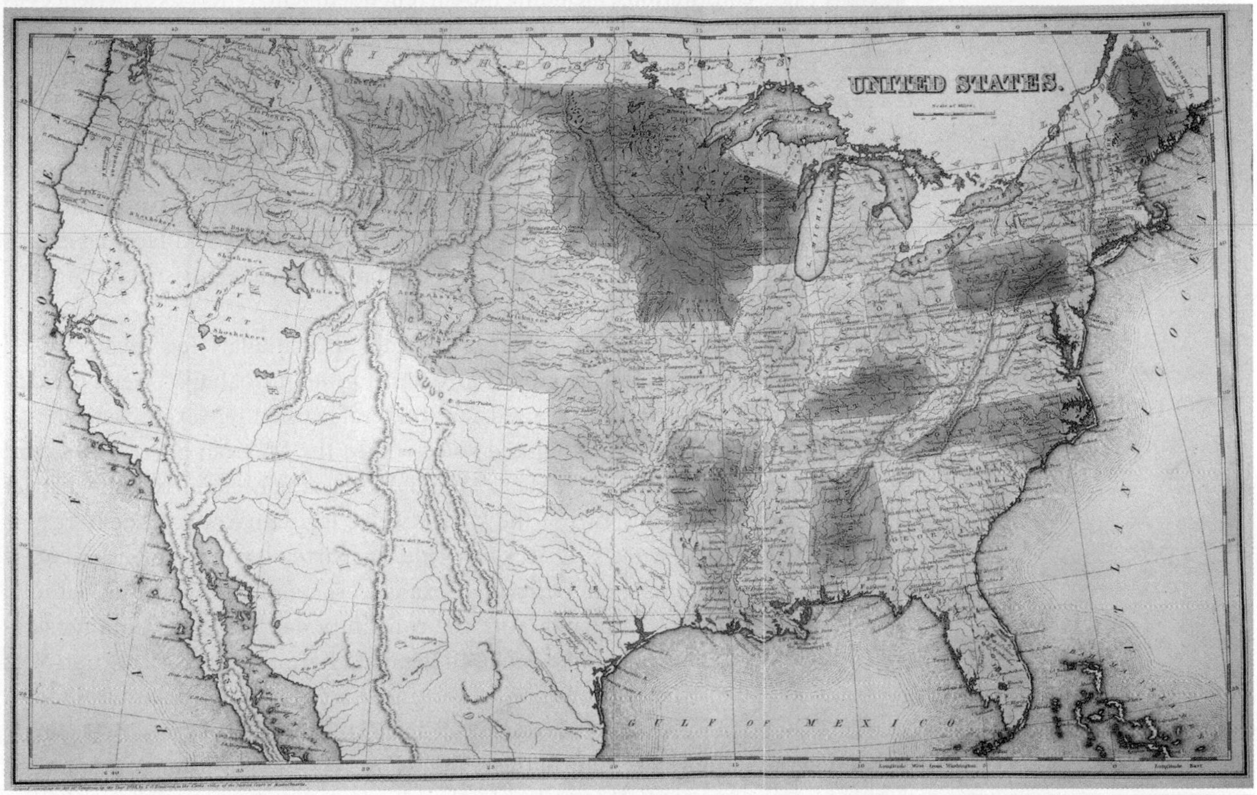

The northern part of Mexico in 1837 extended across most of what is today the American Southwest and most of California.

history."[8] In that spirit, Perry championed a bill reaffirming Texas's commitment to the Tenth Amendment. The so-called Tenthers contend that policies such as national health care reform, Social Security, and Medicare are an unconstitutional violation of the Tenth Amendment. According to a statement posted on his Web site when he was attorney general, Greg Abbott joined other states in suing the federal government "to protect all Texans' constitutional rights, preserve the constitutional framework intended by our nation's founders, and defend our state from further infringement by the federal government."[9] When the Supreme Court upheld the ACA in 2012 as a constitutional tax, Governor Perry responded that "freedom was frontally attacked by passage of this monstrosity—and the Court utterly failed in its duty to uphold the Constitutional limits placed on Washington."[10] As we can see, after 200 years, federalism in the United States continues to evolve. How much power the national government should have and how much power should be retained by the states remains an issue as contentious today as it was at our nation's founding. States have also continued to become more involved in the day-to-day lives of their citizens. Nevertheless, state constitutions vary greatly in their length and specificity, the amount of power they confer to each branch of government, and the structure of their state judiciary, among other things.

## TEXAS CONSTITUTIONS

Texas's constitutions, including the current document, reflect its experiences as a province of Spain and later Mexico. For almost three centuries, Texas was part of the Spanish Empire, its population was relatively sparse, and no written constitution existed. This period of Spanish rule left an indelible mark on Texas law. In contrast to English common law, property rights for women were well defined under Spanish law and included the right to hold property, the right to half of all property accumulated during a marriage, and the right to manage their own financial affairs.[11] In addition, Spanish law traditionally protected a debtor's home and farming equipment from seizure for repayment of debt, and this protection has persisted throughout Texas's constitutions under the homestead provisions.

Under Mexican rule, Texas, as part of the state of Coahuila y Tejas, experienced its first federal constitution when the 1827 Constitution of Coahuila y Tejas divided the state into three districts and created a unicameral legislature. Texans were always somewhat frustrated with their limited voice within the Mexican government, and most felt underrepresented in the state. Although they largely comprised the district of Bexar, Texans held only two of the state's twelve legislative seats. Anglo-Texans also resented certain aspects of Mexican rule, in particular the establishment of Catholicism as a state religion. Officially, Texans were required to join the Catholic Church. Texans also were unhappy with the constitutional provisions limiting slavery, although they largely ignored them. In general, Texans favored local control of government and distrusted centralized government, a preference that endures today. As more Anglos moved to Texas for access to cheap land, Mexico became increasingly worried about its ability to control the region. The Mexican government responded to this concern by attempting to bar further immigration from the United States. While the central Mexican government saw further Anglo immigration as a threat to its control over the region, Anglo-Texans saw attempts to stop such immigration as a threat to their continued existence. Texans, both Anglos and Tejanos, began to favor the creation of a separate Texas state. The central government, which had long looked the other way as Texans brought slaves into the region, also moved to outlaw all forms of slavery.[12] However, it was a change in tactics by Mexican president Antonio López de Santa Anna that undoubtedly made independence from Mexico inevitable. President Santa Anna, originally favored in Texas because of his commitment to federalism, abolished the Mexican Constitution and moved to centralize power.[13] When the Mexican Army arrived in the town of Gonzales in the fall of 1835 to collect a cannon they had loaned the town, Texans attached a flag with the words "Come and Take It" to the cannon. The clash in Gonzales marked the point of no return.[14] Texans, Anglos, and Tejanos alike moved to fight for independence from Mexico. After several months of fighting, including the ill-fated battle of the Alamo, Texans finally turned the tides of the revolution at San Jacinto. On April 21, 1836, Texans defeated Santa Anna at the Battle of San Jacinto, and both sides signed the Treaty of Velasco, which granted Texas its independence.

## Immigration Rights

When Texans declared independence from Mexico, they brought up a lengthy list of complaints, including unfairness in the judiciary, a lack of adequate political representation, and the imposition of a state religion. White Texans were frustrated with Mexican laws that seemed to ignore their needs. Texas was given only two seats in the legislature, and the Mexican judicial system often seemed to disregard the concerns of the new settlers. But much of the Texans' frustration with Mexico was that Mexico simply didn't represent the cultural preferences of its white settlers. Immigration issues were high among the grievances that fueled Texans' impetus to separate from Mexico.

The Mexican Texans' concern with immigration might seem strange to modern-day Texans. Ironically, much the way the modern economy of Texas depends on its immigrant population, Mexican Texas depended on immigration for the security of the sparsely populated state and initially encouraged immigration from both America and Europe. Under Spain and during the early years of the Mexican Republic, immigration laws were quite liberal. However, Mexican authorities became increasingly concerned with the growing influence of Anglos in Texas. Eventually, Mexico sought to halt American immigration with the Law of April 6, 1830, although a significant number of Americans continued to enter Texas illegally.[15]

Anglo immigrants to Texas under Mexico faced a variety of difficulties arising from their inability to speak or write Spanish. Indeed, one of the complaints of the Anglos about the judicial system was their inability to understand the laws or Spanish law books. Stephen F. Austin, in an attempt to avoid revolution, wrote to the Mexican government that "with only two measures Texas would be satisfied, judges who understand English . . . and trial by jury."[16] The basic difficulties of English-speaking immigrants living under a Spanish-speaking government were a primary concern of Anglos in Texas. One of the demands Texans made at the Consultation of 1832 was that the Mexican government create bilingual primary schools with instruction in both English and Spanish. In 1834, Santa Anna, responding to the unrest in Texas, passed several reforms, including making English the official language of the state of Coahuila y Tejas.[17] Nevertheless, Santa Anna soon abolished the constitution and concentrated power in the central government in Mexico. Once independent, Texans would not forget their experiences under Mexico, and they resolved to have their new constitution and subsequent laws passed translated into Spanish.

Anglo-Texans' experiences as an immigrant minority were manifest in the Constitution of 1836, which established extraordinarily liberal immigration policies. It declared that "all persons, (Africans, the descendants of Africans, and Indians excepted,) who were residing in Texas on the day of the Declaration of Independence, shall be considered citizens of the Republic."[18] Furthermore, the constitution made the following provision for future immigrants: "After a residence of six months, [if the immigrant] make oath before some competent authority that he intends to reside permanently in the same, and shall swear to support this Constitution, and that he will bear true allegiance to the Republic of Texas, [the immigrant] shall be entitled to all the privileges of citizenship."[19]

Before Texas declared its independence from Mexico, Anglo-Texans complained that they were inadequately represented in Mexico. Thus, the framers of the new Texas constitution sought to grant immigrants the right to vote, regardless of citizenship. That right has persisted to the current constitution of Texas, which authorized "male persons of foreign birth" to vote in the state so long as they had "resided in this State one year next preceding an election, and the last six months within the district or county in which he offers to vote" and had declared their "intention to become a citizen of the United States."[20] Originally, Texas constitutions were designed to ensure that future immigrants could easily and reasonably attain both citizenship and the right to participate in the government. This provision remained in force until 1921, when Texans, by a slim majority (52 percent in favor; 48 percent opposed), approved a constitutional amendment allowing only citizens to vote.

Hispanics in Texas today fight for many of the same rights that Anglos demanded under Mexican rule more than a century ago. Immigrants in modern-day Texas make similar demands for easing citizenship requirements and for language rights. Anglo-Texans today, sufficiently distanced from their own experience as an immigrant population, have, in many cases, forgotten the difficulties they faced as the immigrant minority. Nevertheless, the immigration issue was as critical in the independence movement of Texas as it is in Texas politics today.

## The Republic of Texas: The Constitution of 1836

No episode has contributed to the mythical history of Texas more than its brief period as an independent country. Delegates from across the state met at Washington-on-the-Brazos to write a constitution for the future Republic of Texas. Of the fifty-nine delegates, almost half had been in Texas less than two years, and most of them had emigrated from southern states. The constitutional convention occurred in the midst of the revolution, and delegates hurriedly wrote the new constitution, well aware that the conflict was in danger of arriving at their doorstep at any moment.[21] The resulting document was largely influenced by the U.S. Constitution in that it was relatively brief and flexible, provided for three branches of government, and established a system of checks and balances. The president was elected to a three-year term, prohibited from serving consecutive terms, and appointed commander in chief of the Texas military. A bicameral legislature was established, with one-year terms in the House and three-year terms in the Senate. The short legislative terms and the nonconsecutive presidential term reflected Texans' distrust of government in general, an attitude that continues to dominate state politics today. At the end of the constitution was a declaration of rights, which enumerated individual rights similar to those found in the national Bill of Rights, such as freedom of speech, press, and religion. While white and Hispanic males were given a broad range of freedoms, free persons of African descent were prohibited from residing in the state without the consent of the Texas Legislature.

There were, however, some notable differences between the U.S. Constitution and the Republic of Texas Constitution. For instance, Texas's constitution was distinctly unitary rather than federal in nature since the Republic of Texas did not create lower units of government with any independent power. In a reaction to the establishment of Catholicism as the state religion under Mexico, the republic's constitution prohibited priests from holding office. Perhaps the most important feature of the new constitution was its legalization of slavery, a provision that had irreversible consequences for both Texas and the United States. Immigrants moving to Texas were permitted to bring their slaves with them, and Texas slave owners were prohibited from freeing their slaves without the consent of the legislature. However, the constitution stopped short of allowing the slave trade in Texas. When Texas was a part of Mexico, its slave population was relatively small. Once Texas left Mexico, and with annexation into the United States seen as inevitable by many, the slave population exploded in Texas, rising from an estimated 5,000 slaves (12 percent of the population) in 1836 to 58,161 (27 percent of the population) by the 1850 census and 182,566 (30 percent) of the population by 1860.[22]

A flag from the Republic of Texas, representing Texas's time as an independent country.

Texas voters overwhelmingly supported the new constitution as well as annexation by the United States. However, annexation was not immediate. There were two significant obstacles to Texas joining the United States. First, Texas's claim of independence was precarious. Upon his return to Mexico, Santa Anna renounced the Treaty of Velasco and reiterated Mexico's claims to Texas. Any attempt by the United States to annex Texas could potentially provoke a war with Mexico. Second, Texas's constitutional protection of slavery made annexation controversial within the United States. Abolitionists objected to the addition of another slave state; at the same time, existing slave states saw the admission of Texas into the United States as a guarantee of the future of slavery. Initially at least, the annexation of Texas was unpopular in the United States, particularly outside of the South. Thus, a first annexation treaty failed to receive Senate ratification. Eventually, though, the idea of **Manifest Destiny**, or the inevitability of the expansion of the United States across the continent, won out. James K. Polk campaigned for the presidency based on expanding the United States through immediate annexation of Texas and expansion into Oregon. In 1845, Texas was finally admitted into the United States. According to the annexation agreement, Texas retained responsibility for its debt as well as the rights to its public land. In addition, Texas could divide itself into as many as five states as the population continued to expand and then be admitted to the United States under the provisions of the national constitution.

Some of the greatest legends in Texas are built on this brief period of independence. Today Texans speak fondly of a time when they were masters of their own domain. According to popular imagery, Texas's time as an independent country makes it exceptional among the states. In truth, the Republic of Texas, though unique, was also relatively short-lived, poor, and unproductive. Much of Sam Houston's presidency was spent trying to convince the United States to annex Texas while simultaneously attempting to secure international recognition of Texas's independence by the United States, Great Britain, and France, as well as trying to procure financial aid from

**Manifest Destiny**
the belief that U.S. expansion across the North American continent was inevitable.

these governments.[23] As noted above, Texans overwhelmingly preferred joining the United States. It was the United States that hesitated in bringing Texas into the Union. Offshoots of this legend continue to prevail throughout the state. For instance, many Texans believe that Texas is the only state permitted to fly its flag at the same height as the U.S. flag as an indication of its unique status. In truth, U.S. flag code permits all states to fly their flags at a height equal to that of the U.S. flag.

## Statehood: The Constitution of 1845

Once Texas was admitted into the United States, a new constitution was necessary. The statehood constitution continued to specify separation of powers and a system of checks and balances while recognizing the federal nature of the United States. The terms for legislators were lengthened to two years for the Texas House and four years for the Texas Senate, although the legislature would now meet biennially, or every other year. The governor's term was shortened to two years, and the governor was prohibited from serving more than four years in any six. The governor's appointment power was expanded to include the attorney general, the Supreme Court of Texas judges, and district court judges, in addition to the secretary of state. Texans' experiences under both Spain and Mexico were evident in the guarantees of property rights for women and homestead provisions in the new constitution.

The new constitution reflected the experience of Texans in other ways as well. Most Texans were in debt and highly distrustful of creditors, and, indeed, many individuals, including Stephen F. Austin, came to Texas to try to get out of debt. Thus, the statehood constitution established guarantees against imprisonment for debt. The bill of rights was moved to the beginning of the constitution, an indication of the importance Texans placed on individual freedom and limited government. Most of the republic's constitutional guarantees, such as freedom of speech and press and protections for the accused, were continued. At the same time, the provisions protecting slavery remained and the Texas Legislature was prohibited from emancipating slaves without compensation. Voting rights for African Americans and women were not considered in the deliberations, although there was a vigorous debate over enfranchising all free "white" men. Historically, the category of "white" had included both Native Americans and native Mexicans, though some of the delegates expressed concern that the term might now be used to exclude those populations.[24] In the end, the right to vote was conferred on "every free male person who shall have attained the age of twenty-one years . . . (Indians not taxed, Africans and descendants of Africans excepted)."[25] In addition, the constitution mandated that one-tenth of the state's annual revenue be set aside to create a permanent school fund. Overall, the statehood constitution was relatively brief and flexible. Daniel Webster, a U.S. senator at the time, referred to the framers of this constitution as the "ablest political body assembled in Texas," producing the best constitution of the day.[26]

With the election of Abraham Lincoln as U.S. president, however, secessionist movements erupted in many southern states, including Texas. When Texas voted to secede, Angelina County in East Texas was opposed, but in the rest of East Texas, where slavery dominated the economy, there was almost universal support for secession (see Map 2.2). Although the movement to secede was strong in Texas, Governor Sam Houston led a substantial opposition. Several counties in Central Texas and North

**MAP 2.2** **Texas Secession Vote, 1861**

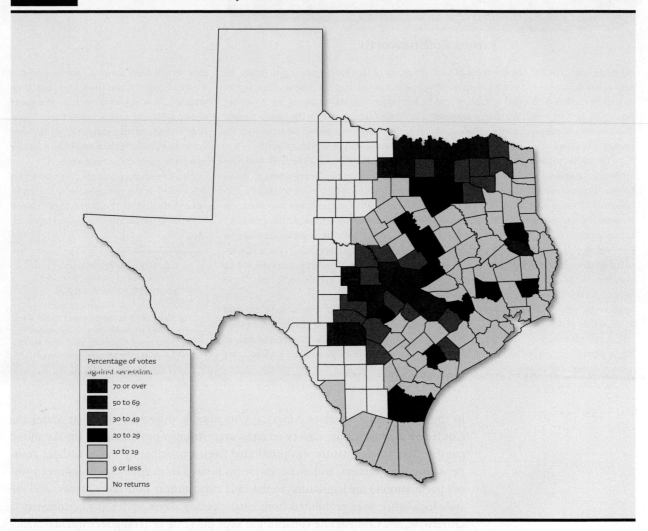

Percentage of votes
against secession.

- 70 or over
- 50 to 69
- 30 to 49
- 20 to 29
- 10 to 19
- 9 or less
- No returns

**Source:** Annals of the Association of American Geographers, "Vote on Secession, 1861," www.lib.utexas.edu/maps/atlas_texas/texas _vote_secession_1861.jpg (accessed September 25, 2012).

Texas voted against secession. The Central Texas frontier relied on protection from the U.S. Army, and the ethnic German population there opposed slavery, making secession less popular. Secession was also unpopular in North Texas, where slavery was virtually absent.[27] Nonetheless, on February 23, 1861, Texas voted to secede and joined the Confederate States of America.

### Secession and the Confederacy: The Constitution of 1861

Joining the Confederacy meant that a new constitution was needed. However, the 1861 Confederate constitution was primarily a revised version of the 1845 statehood constitution, replacing references to the United States with references

## James Collinsworth

On December 16, 1836, the Congress of the Republic of Texas chose James T. Collinsworth as the republic's first chief justice of the Supreme Court of Texas. The thirty-year-old Collinsworth's rise to prominence in Texas had been remarkable.

In some regards, Collinsworth was eminently qualified. In the earliest days of the Texas Revolution, he organized a company of men that captured La Bahia Presidio in the revolution's first military action against a Mexican military installation. He signed both the Texas Declaration of Independence and the republic's new constitution. After that, Collinsworth took the field and helped to ensure his new nation's freedom by serving alongside Sam Houston at the Battle of San Jacinto.

Collinsworth was well read, boasting a library of 175 books, many on the subject of law. Before coming to Texas, he spent five years as U.S. district attorney for Tennessee's Western District. In November 1836, he was elected to the Texas Senate, only to resign two weeks later to take his place on the state's Supreme Court.

In June 1838, Collinsworth allowed himself to be nominated for president of Texas. In doing so, he stepped into the highly divisive contest to succeed Sam Houston. On one hand, Collinsworth faced the animosity of Houston's political enemies because he was seen as Houston's chosen successor. On the other hand, Houston's supporters were divided between Collinsworth and Peter Grayson.

On July 11, 1838, Collinsworth drowned in Galveston Bay. While opinions are mixed on whether he fell off his boat accidentally or jumped in a fit of despair, all sources agree that he had been drinking heavily, with one friend noting, "I was here and had been with him...and he was under the influence of Ardent Spirits for a week before hand."[i] Peter Grayson had committed suicide two days earlier in Tennessee, leaving Mirabeau B. Lamar to win the presidency unopposed.

Collingsworth County (the name was misspelled in the law passed by the legislature establishing the county) was named in James Collinsworth's honor on August 21, 1876.[ii]

---

i. James L. Haley, *The Texas Supreme Court: A Narrative History, 1836–1986* (Austin: University of Texas Press, 2013), 19.

ii. Joe E. Ericson, "Collinsworth, James," Handbook of Texas Online, June 12, 2010, www.tshaonline.org/handbook/online/articles/fc097 (accessed August 23, 2014). Published by the Texas State Historical Association.

---

to the Confederate States of America. One notable difference was that under the Confederate constitution, slavery received even stronger protection. In the statehood constitution, the legislature was prohibited from emancipating slaves without compensating their owners, and owners were prohibited from emancipating slaves without permission of the legislature. In the 1861 constitution, both slave owners and the state legislature were prohibited from emancipating slaves under any circumstance. Otherwise, the Confederate constitution kept the same general governmental structures as the 1845 statehood constitution.

### The First Reconstruction: The Constitution of 1866

With the end of the Civil War, Texas needed a new constitution that recognized the new political reality of the defeated Confederacy and reconstituted Union. Lincoln assigned a provisional governor, A. J. Hamilton, who immediately called for a constitutional convention. Adult white males who swore an oath of allegiance to the United States of America could participate in electing delegates to the convention. Once again, the approach of the drafters at the 1866 constitutional convention was to amend the 1845 statehood constitution rather than write an entirely new constitution. The 1866 constitution specifically renounced secession, repudiated the debts associated with fighting the Civil War on the side of the Confederacy, and acknowledged that slavery was "terminated by this State, by the Government of the United States, by force of arms."[28]

Although slavery was ended, African Americans were not granted voting rights in the 1866 constitution, and other provisions expressly prohibited them from holding office. In addition, the scope of the governorship was altered. Positions that had been previously appointed by the governor, such as the attorney general and state level judges, were now to be elected. The governor's term was extended to four years, with the stipulation that the governor serve no more than eight years in any twelve-year time period. In addition, the governor was granted a line-item veto for appropriations bills. Perhaps the most significant contribution of the 1866 constitution was a clause that made it legal for individuals to acquire the mineral rights of their property, a provision that persists today.[29] In the end, though, this constitution was short-lived as Radical Republicans, frustrated with the lack of any substantive change in the South, gained control of the national Congress and passed the Reconstruction acts designed to punish southern states.

### The Second Reconstruction: The Constitution of 1869

The Reconstruction acts passed by Congress divided the South into military districts and assigned military leaders. Texans were required by Congress to write a new constitution in which African Americans realized full political rights, and they were required to ratify the Thirteenth and Fourteenth Amendments in order to end military rule in the state. Moreover, the Radical Republicans who gained control of Congress prevented ex-Confederates, including anyone who had held a political office during the Confederacy, from either participating as delegates at this convention or voting on the resulting constitution. The result was that only six of the ninety delegates that participated in the 1866 constitutional convention attended the 1869 convention.[30] The delegates then, most of whom were unionist Republicans, were viewed with suspicion and resentment by the majority of Texans who had supported the Confederacy. Thus, the 1869 constitution is perhaps best viewed as an anomaly in Texas's constitutional development, as many of its provisions were more radical than the average Texan preferred. For instance, the office of the governor was again given broad appointment powers, including the power to appoint Texas's Supreme Court justices, district court justices, the attorney general, and the secretary of state. The governor's salary was increased and the line-item veto was retained. The 1869 constitution also created a plural executive that consisted of eight offices, including the governor. Perhaps a more radical development for Texans was the 1869 constitution's institution of a broader range of social services and corresponding taxes than Texans had previously experienced. For example, the constitution created a road tax that funded bridge building and road improvements in Texas. In addition, this constitution made elementary education compulsory and funded it with one-fourth of the state's annual tax revenues, along with a poll tax and monies from the state's public lands. Adult males were guaranteed the right to vote, regardless of race, color, or previous condition, and both slavery and systems of peonage were outlawed. The delegates also proposed the creation of a new state of West Texas, although this was ultimately defeated.[31]

To protest the exclusion of ex-Confederates while including African Americans in the creation of the 1869 constitution, many Democrats boycotted the election to ratify the constitution. Nonetheless, in November 1869, the participating voters approved

## E. J. Davis

Texas State Library and Archives Commission

According to Texas legend, Texas needed the "Redeemer" constitution of 1876 to cleanse the state of the despotism endured under Republican governor E. J. Davis. Davis represented the more extreme branch of

the Republican Party and narrowly won the gubernatorial election in 1869 with the backing of black voters. This connection to both ex-slaves and the Republican Party no doubt helped to alienate former slave owners. In the eyes of many, Davis ballooned the debt, declared martial law in much of the state with his control of the state militia and state police, and sold out the state's farmers to big business, including railroads, at the expense of the mainly agrarian population. And, to add insult to injury, when it became clear that Republicans would likely lose the next election, Davis postponed the legislative election and initially refused to leave office after losing the governor's race. This version of events allowed Texans, still stinging from their loss of the recent "War of Northern Aggression," to blame the North for the economic decline of the state and erase from memory the Confederates' military defeat. It also gave birth to the legend of Democrats as redeemers who saved the state from a corrupt "foreign" invader.

However, if we examine some of the particulars of this story, we get a much more complicated history. Davis sought to create a compulsory education system for all children throughout the state. Any such system and its accompanying taxes would have been seen as exorbitant by Texans who preferred government to stay out of their daily lives. It was also the first time that tax dollars would pay for the education of African Americans in the state, and it was the education of African Americans that led to the claims of waste. Although Democrats saw the policy as wasteful, Texas became one of the first states to adopt a compulsory public education system.

It is true that Davis increased the debt of the state, but this is only part of the story. The state of Texas had been financially devastated by the Civil War and would have faced a lack of revenue regardless of who occupied the governor's office. Davis advocated an expansion of social services favored by the Republican Party, which necessarily translated into higher state taxes.

the new constitution and Republican E. J. Davis was elected governor of Texas. The climate in which the 1869 constitution was written had lasting effects. After all, the national Congress had mandated many of the provisions of the new constitution, and many Texans had not participated in the election of the convention members, the vote to ratify the constitution, or the subsequent election of Governor Davis. Davis would remain the only Republican elected as governor in the state until the 1970s. Because the events surrounding the 1869 constitution occurred during a period of military administration of the state, most Texans doubted the legitimacy of both the new constitution and the new governor from the outset.

E. J. Davis would prove to be one of the most controversial governors in the state's history. The taint of illegitimacy was impossible for Davis—and, for the next century, the Republican Party—to overcome. After Reconstruction ended and former Confederates were again eligible to vote, Democrats won back control of the state legislature and the governorship, ousting Davis and replacing him with Democrat Richard Coke in the 1873 gubernatorial election. With a Democrat safely in office, Texans immediately set out to write a new constitution. Some sought to prevent a "tyrant" such as Davis from

The Republican policies were no doubt more progressive than Texas Democrats preferred. That does not necessarily translate into wastefulness or dishonesty, though. Moreover, both taxes and state debt were actually higher under the succeeding Democratic administrations.[i]

Davis also used the state police and the state militia to deal aggressively with lawless areas in Texas. Texas still had large expanses of frontier to protect. There was also a good deal of resistance remaining from the Civil War. For instance, Davis declared martial law in Hill County in January 1871, following the arrest of a state policeman. The policeman had offended locals when he attempted to arrest the son of the county's largest landowner for killing a freedman and his wife.[ii] Similarly, racially motivated attacks and murders in Limestone County, along with a mob threatening the state police, led Davis to declare martial law there in 1871. So, while it is true that Davis used expanded police powers to maintain order in the state, often the disorder was the result of whites attempting to repress the newly freed African American minority and reject the authority of the Republican-dominated state government and police.

Given that many Democrats were disenfranchised during punitive Reconstruction, Davis knew that Republican control of both the governorship and the legislature would be short-lived. Although Davis postponed the legislative and congressional elections, when they finally did take place, the Democrats won decisively. The new Democratic-controlled legislature passed a law calling for the election of state and local offices, including the governor, to be held on December 2, 1873. In that election, Davis was overwhelmingly defeated by Democrat Richard Coke. However, the validity of the election was challenged by Republicans in the *Ex parte Rodriguez* case in the Supreme Court of Texas. The 1869 constitution stated that "all elections for State, district and county officers shall be held at the county seats of the several counties, until otherwise provided by law; and the polls shall be opened for four days, from 8 o'clock, a.m., until 4 o'clock, p.m., of each day."[iii] Democrats argued that the constitution allowed the legislature to change either the allotted time or the place of the election. Republicans argued that the semicolon after the phrase "provided by law" created two independent clauses, and though the legislature could change the

location of the polls, it could not change the time allotted for the elections. The Supreme Court of Texas sided with the Republicans, thus earning the nickname "the Semicolon Court." Although the Supreme Court of Texas ruled that Coke's election was invalid, Democrats ignored the ruling and inaugurated Coke. Davis, unwilling to resort to force to protect his position, vacated the office.

In many ways, vilifying the Davis administration extended the tensions of the Civil War, as Democrats blamed Republican unionists for all of the state's problems. That we still see many textbooks repeat the one-sided view of the Davis administration even today is a testament to the pervasiveness of the anti-Republican and anti-northern myth.

---

i. Janice C. May, *The Texas State Constitution: A Reference Guide* (Westport, Conn.: Greenwood Press, 1996); see also Randolph B. Campbell, *Gone to Texas* (New York: Oxford University Press, 2004).

ii. For more details of this incident, see Handbook of Texas Online, "Hill County Rebellion," www.tshaonline.org/handbook/online/articles/jchka (accessed September 3, 2014).

iii. Texas Constitution (1869), art. 3, sec. 6.

ever again gaining so much power in Texas. Others leapt at the opportunity to replace the constitution that the national government and the Republican Party had imposed on them. Either way, Texans were once again writing a constitution.

# THE CURRENT SYSTEM: THE CONSTITUTION OF 1876

The current constitution of Texas emerged from the tangled mess left by the demise of Radical Republican rule and the return to power of the Democrats. The 1876 constitution created three branches of government, with separation of power between the branches and a system of checks and balances. Texas's constitution is based on the idea of popular sovereignty, evidenced in the preamble: "Humbly invoking the blessings of Almighty God, the people of the State of Texas do ordain and establish this Constitution." The constitution also embodies the principle of federalism in recognizing that Texas is free, "subject only to the Constitution of the United States."[32]

Several clashes created the context for the current Texas Constitution. First, the Civil War and the subsequent Reconstruction fostered considerable resentment toward northern Republican interests throughout the South. The Reconstruction era in Texas saw a Radical Republican–dominated government exclude the majority of Texans from participating in the creation of the constitution and in the state's political processes in general. Thus, the Republican Party spent the next 100 years almost completely shut out of the state's political arena. Second, a preference for independence and individual freedom, along with a deep-seated distrust of government, has always characterized the state's political culture. With the exception of the 1869 constitution, Texas has consistently sought to restrict the powers of government. While the current constitution represents the most extreme attempt at restricting Texas government, all of the constitutions, with the exception of the 1869 one, sought to create a government that would generally stay out of the lives of average Texans. The constitution drawn up in 1876, in reaction to its comparatively progressive predecessor, went further than any previous constitution in specifying exactly what the government could and could not do. Delegates to the convention that created the current constitution were overwhelmingly Democrats who distrusted government, favored local control, preferred fiscal restraint, and wanted to fix the perceived injustices of the Republican-created 1869 constitution. Third, the delegates who wrote the current constitution were primarily concerned with protecting agrarian interests, as most Texans in 1876 engaged in farming. Indeed, close to half of the delegates were members of the Grange, an organization created to protect the interest of farmers. These farmers sought to limit the power of the railroads, which they relied on to deliver their crops and livestock to market. The Davis administration's policies aided the expansion of the railroads in Texas, which led to increased rail rates that frustrated the farmers in the state. The resulting constitution is one of specific limitations on governmental power rather than a fundamental set of laws.

### Individual Freedom

Texans have always placed a high value on individual freedoms. Since 1845 a bill of rights has been the first article in each Texas constitution, demonstrating the importance Texans place on individual freedom (see Table 2.1). The Texas Constitution carries over rights from the previous constitution, such as freedom of speech, press, and assembly, along with the right to bear arms. It also includes protections against unreasonable search and seizure and cruel and unusual punishment and guarantees a trial by jury.

Texans' experiences during the Civil War also influenced the writers of the current constitution. Because President Lincoln had suspended habeas corpus during the war so that people who were suspected of disloyalty could be arrested and held indefinitely without being charged, the framers of the current Texas constitution specified that the right to habeas corpus shall never be suspended. The authors kept the provisions for freedom of religion while adding a requirement that state officeholders "acknowledge the existence of a Supreme Being." Moreover, the current constitution prohibits public money from being used for the benefit of "any sect, or religious society, theological or religious seminary." Long-standing prohibitions against imprisonment for debt and provisions for community property and homesteads were retained in the new constitution.

## The Legislative Branch

Consistent with Texans' preference for small government and their distrust of politicians, the current constitution was designed to create a part-time citizen legislature. The constitution restricts the legislature to biennial sessions for only 140 days. The idea was that, rather than having professional politicians, any citizen could participate in a legislature that met so infrequently. To discourage professional politicians further, the constitution originally spelled out a modest salary for state legislators, a salary that required a constitutional amendment to change. This restriction persisted until 1991 when the constitution was amended to create the Texas Ethics Commission to set legislative salaries, subject to voter approval. The legislative branch is composed of a Texas House of Representatives with 150 members and a Texas Senate with thirty-one members. Members of the House continue to be elected every two years, while the terms of the senators were shortened to four years. While the legislature is limited to a relatively short session, thirty-day special sessions can be called by the governor, who sets the agenda for those sessions.

Much of the Texas Constitution is a list of things that the legislature is specifically prohibited from doing. For instance, the constitution spells out the types of taxes the legislature can and cannot levy. It explicitly prohibits the state from passing a property tax and sets ceilings on the amount of property taxes that local governments can collect. The constitution further forbids the government from imposing a state income tax without approval by a majority of voters. The legislature is additionally prohibited from passing a bill that contains more than one subject and is required to place the subject of the bill in the title. A reading of the current constitution makes clear that the main goal of the framers was to expressly limit the government rather than create a broad governing mandate.

## The Executive Branch

Under Reconstruction, supporters of the Confederacy were banned from voting and participating in the creation of the constitution. In the resulting government, the Republican governor centralized power often to deal with Texans who resisted extending rights to newly freed slaves. Governor E. J. Davis declared martial law in parts of the state where the Ku Klux Klan and other local groups controlled the local government. As soon as all Texans were once again permitted to participate in elections and write a constitution, the reaction was swift. They wasted no time writing a new constitution that severely stripped the powers of the governor. In doing so, it created an institutionally weak governor, distributing traditional executive powers into several offices. According to Article 4, the executive branch is divided between a governor, lieutenant governor, secretary of state, comptroller, agriculture commissioner land commissioner, and attorney general.[33] Thus, in contrast to the U.S. executive, the Texas Constitution creates a plural executive, an institutional arrangement where traditional functions of the executive branch are divided among several officeholders rather

| TABLE 2.1 | Articles of the Current Texas Constitution |
|---|---|
| Preamble | |
| Article 1 | Bill of Rights |
| Article 2 | The Power of Government |
| Article 3 | Legislative Department |
| Article 4 | Executive Department |
| Article 5 | Judicial Department |
| Article 6 | Suffrage |
| Article 7 | Education |
| Article 8 | Taxation and Revenue |
| Article 9 | Counties |
| Article 10 | Railroads |
| Article 11 | Municipal Corporations |
| Article 12 | Private Corporations |
| Article 13 | Spanish and Mexican Land (repealed August 5, 1969) |
| Article 14 | Public Lands and Land Office |
| Article 15 | Impeachment |
| Article 16 | General Provisions |
| Article 17 | Mode of Amending the Constitutions of this State |

# TEXAS (VS) CONNECTICUT

The constitutions of Texas and Connecticut date from very different eras in the country's history. The Texas Constitution, the state's sixth, was written in 1876 and reflects the agrarian, rural nature of the state at the time. Connecticut's constitution is one of the country's newer state constitutions, having been written and adopted in 1965. It is the state's third, following the Fundamental Orders of Connecticut (1638) and the Connecticut Constitution (1818).

Connecticut's constitution reflects in many ways the world of the 1960s. Its language is less formal and archaic than that of either the Texas Constitution or the U.S. Constitution. An extensive list of civil rights and liberties takes center stage in Connecticut's constitution. We might expect issues surrounding the free exercise of religion and separation of church and state to be reflective of the time and to therefore be more pronounced in the Connecticut Constitution than in the Texas Constitution. After all, Connecticut wrote and adopted its constitution after the U.S. Supreme Court eliminated mandatory prayer and mandatory religious instruction in public schools.

In fact, the Texas and Connecticut constitutions share a number of characteristics regarding religious liberty. For example, both guarantee freedom of worship, prohibit compulsory attendance at religious services, and prohibit any requirement that individuals give money to build places of worship. The constitutions of both states also contain a number of prohibitions on their respective state governments. Yet the two documents differ in a number of respects, too. The Connecticut Constitution features specific language that guarantees the right of ministers and religious teachers to pursue their professions. Texas lacks such language in its constitution. In Texas, public lands cannot be given to religious organizations; a similar provision does not appear in the Connecticut Constitution.

The table in this box lists key provisions of the Texas and Connecticut constitutions in the area of religious liberty.

## THINKING Critically

★ Which state provides the most guarantees of religious liberty?

★ Which state places the strongest limitations on government in the area of religious liberty?

★ Which state imposes a greater degree of separation between church and state?

★ Are your answers surprising or unexpected? Why or why not?

## Religious Liberty: Texas Constitution (1876) and Connecticut Constitution (1965)

| Issue/Topic | Texas Constitution | Connecticut Constitution |
|---|---|---|
| Freedom of worship guaranteed | ✓ | ✓ |
| Attendance at services cannot be compelled | ✓ | ✓ |
| Contributions to build places of worship cannot be required | ✓ | ✓ |
| Preference to any religious society cannot be conferred | ✓ | ✓ |
| Equality of denominations guaranteed | ✓ | ✓ |
| Equal protection of the law cannot be denied based on religion | ✗ | ✓ |
| Alternative voting permissible where religion forbids action on Election Day | ✗ | ✓ |
| Right of ministers and religious teachers to pursue their profession guaranteed | ✗ | ✓ |
| Religious tests as a prerequisite to holding office are not permitted | ✓ | ✗ |
| Disqualification as a witness in court based on religion is not permitted | ✓ | ✓* |
| State funds cannot be given to religious organizations | ✓ | ✗ |
| Public lands cannot be given to religious organizations | ✓ | ✗ |

* In equal protection clause.

than a single person. Moreover, offices that had previously been appointed by the governor would now be elected in order to further limit the power of the governor. In fact, the only significant state-level appointment left to the governor is the secretary of state. The delegates of the constitutional convention also shortened the term of office for the governor, decreased the governor's salary, and limited the number of terms that a governor could hold office. Later amendments increased the governor's term to four years and removed the term limits. Clearly, though, one of the main goals of the delegates creating the current constitution was to limit the power of the governor.

## The Texas Judiciary

Article 5 of the Texas Constitution created a judicial branch with county courts, commissioners courts, justice of the peace courts, district courts, and appellate courts, as well as "such other courts as may be provided by law." It also specified the creation of two high courts, the Supreme Court of Texas to hear final civil appeals, and the Court of Criminal Appeals to hear final criminal appeals.[34] Moreover, the constitution specified the election of all state judges, although judicial vacancies are filled by gubernatorial appointment. The result is a judiciary whose members are constantly raising campaign funds in order to get reelected. This is in sharp contrast to the federal judiciary, which is appointed for the purpose of creating an independent judiciary.

## Civil Rights in Texas

Two of the most controversial subjects at the 1876 constitutional convention dealt with suffrage and education. One Reconstruction reform that could not be undone was the extension of suffrage to African Americans in Texas, which was now mandated by the U.S. Constitution. There were those at the convention, however, who favored a poll tax in order to vote, ostensibly in an attempt to disenfranchise African Americans in Texas. However, the Grange and other poor

A crowd prevents seventeen-year-old Steve Poster from entering Texarkana Junior College in 1956. During this period southern states resisted federal mandates to desegregate schools.

AP Photo

farmers objected to the poll tax, which would also disenfranchise poor whites in Texas. In the end, the convention delegates defeated the poll tax. They also refused to grant women's suffrage. Interestingly, the current constitution protects voters from arrest on their way to and from the polls on Election Day.

Perhaps an even more controversial topic than voting rights was the educational system, which was mandated in the 1869 constitution. During the Reconstruction period, education was compulsory, regardless of race, and was paid for with tax revenue. At a time when the Texas economy had been devastated by the Civil War, a majority of Texans saw a universal educational system as excessive. Opposition to this system was widespread, as white landowners objected to paying for the education of African American children, and farmers in general favored local control of education, which could be tailored to the needs of particular communities while corresponding to crop cycles.[35] Thus, the 1876 constitution ended compulsory education and required segregated schools. Texas would not reinstate compulsory education until 1915. The Texas Constitution does provide a provision to prevent discrimination based on sex; in 1972, it was amended to guarantee equality under the law regardless of "sex, race, color, creed or national origin"—the so-called Texas equal rights amendment. A similar amendment failed at the national level. Undoubtedly, the most important constitutional change to civil rights in recent years has been the constitutional amendment designed to prevent same-sex marriages in the state. In 2005, Texas voters overwhelmingly voted to define marriage as "the union of one man and one woman," although in 2014 a federal judge called the constitutionality of this amendment into question.

### Distrust of Government

The most prominent feature of the current Texas Constitution is the general distrust of government. Article 1 underscores the attitudes of most Texans that "all political power is inherent in the people, and all free governments are founded on their authority . . . they have at all times the inalienable right to alter, reform or abolish their government in such manner as they may think expedient." We see evidence of Texans' distaste for government throughout the document. For example, the circumstances under which the government can tax and incur debt are spelled out in the Texas Constitution. In order to keep the government small, the powers, terms, and salaries of the executive and legislature are strictly limited. Instead, the framers of the Texas Constitution created a system in which political power is retained by the people. The result of attempting to keep all political power with the people in Texas is the **long ballot**, a system in which almost all positions in the state are elected rather than appointed. This distrust of government continues to pervade Texans' attitudes today and is one of the main reasons why a complete constitutional revision has failed to get support in the state.

**Long ballot**
a system in which almost all of the positions in a state are elected rather than appointed.

## CRITICISMS OF THE TEXAS CONSTITUTION

The state's current constitution was written in the era of cowboys and cattle drives. Today's Texas is one of computers and commuters. The population in the 1880s was slightly over 1.5 million people, whereas in 2013 the U.S. Census

Bureau estimated Texas's population at 26.4 million. Hispanic and African American populations comprised the two largest minorities in Texas in the 1880s. The Hispanic population has increased significantly since then, but the African American population has declined, and other minorities, such as Asian immigrants, have a greater presence in the state today. Economically, Texas in 1876 was agrarian, with small farms and ranches dominating the state. Today, the state's economy is one of the most diverse in the United States and continues to diversify. Texas has a substantial aerospace and defense industry, a significant telecommunications and computer sector, and is an important center of finance, shipping, energy, and other big business. It is not surprising, then, that the current constitution is considered outdated and inadequate for such a large and diverse state.

The desire of the framers to eliminate the last vestiges of Reconstruction, rather than the goal of writing a long-lasting constitution, shaped the current Texas Constitution. One of the most frequently cited criticisms is the amount of specific detail in the document. The Texas Constitution is a long list of specific rules rather than a set of fundamental legal principles for state law. For instance, in 2003, Texans approved twenty-two constitutional amendments, including one permitting cities to donate their surplus fire-fighting equipment to volunteer fire departments. Similarly, of the sixteen constitutional amendments voters passed in November 2007, one was a proposal to create and fund a cancer research institute. While both of these amendments may be commendable, they are the sort of specific policymaking ideally originating in the state legislature rather than being embedded in a constitution.

Including such specific detail in the state's constitution leaves Texas with the second-longest constitution in the United States, one that is both disorganized and unwieldy. The problem is compounded because the more detailed the constitution is, the more likely that enactment of new statutes will require constitutional amendment rather than passage in the legislature. The result is a constitution that continues to grow; it is now approximately 87,000 words.

In addition, the constitution severely limits the government. The formal power of the executive is limited, leaving Texas's governor one of the institutionally weakest executives in the United States. Moreover, the legislature's session is limited to 140 days every other year. While that may have been desirable in 1876 agrarian Texas, today's Texas is the second-largest state in the United States and has an increasingly diverse population and economy. Extremely low legislative pay means that average Texans cannot afford to take the job. Instead of being a citizen legislature, the Texas Legislature is dominated by wealthy individuals and big business. Finally, judges in Texas constantly have to raise money for reelection, which creates a climate of mistrust in the Texas judiciary. The result is a judiciary that most Texans believe is overly influenced by money.

## Amending the Constitution

The current Texas Constitution outlines the process by which it can be amended. Both houses of the Texas Legislature must approve any proposed amendments by a two-thirds vote. Once approved, the amendment must be published twice in major newspapers and posted in each county courthouse thirty days prior to Election Day. Finally, the amendment must be approved by a simple majority of voters. The Texas

Constitution has been amended 483 times, making it one of the most frequently amended constitutions among the states.[36] Alabama's state constitution has been amended the most, passing 880 amendments, while Rhode Island's constitution has been amended the least, with a mere ten amendments. (See Table 2.2 for comparison of other facts about the constitutions of the fifty states.)

As Figure 2.2 illustrates, the overwhelming majority of proposed constitutional amendments in Texas are approved by electors; 87 percent of all proposed amendments have been adopted since 1985. Almost all constitutional amendments are put on the ballot in odd years or in special elections. Unfortunately, the voter turnout during special elections is significantly lower than during general elections (see Figure 2.3). Since 1985, the average turnout in elections with constitutional amendments has been 8.3 percent of the entire voting-age population.[37] Voter turnout remains alarmingly low even when the proposed amendment is relatively popular or controversial. For example, in 2007, when 88 percent of voters approved school tax relief for the elderly and disabled in Texas, less than 7 percent of potential voters actually participated in that election. In 2003, voters approved twenty-two constitutional amendments, including a controversial limit on medical malpractice lawsuits, with a mere 9.3 percent turnout rate. In 2005, 76 percent of voters approved a constitutional amendment defining marriage as a union between a man and a woman. An amendment this controversial was based on a 14 percent voter turnout. Amending the fundamental state law with such low turnout rates raises serious questions about the nature of popular sovereignty in Texas.

## Constitutional Revision

Distrust of government has generally translated to suspicion of change in Texas. The current constitution has been criticized since its inception. Demands for constitutional revision have been almost continuous in Texas, with early calls for constitutional conventions occurring in 1913, 1917, 1949, 1957, and 1967.[38] As early as 1922 Governor Pat Neff urged the legislature to write a new state constitution, arguing that the 1876 constitution had become a "patch-work"—this after only thirty-nine amendments.[39] However, it wasn't until the early 1970s, in reaction to the Sharpstown Scandal, a banking and stock fraud scandal involving officials at the highest levels of government, that Texas came close to substantial constitutional revision. The legislature created a constitutional revision commission that proposed sweeping changes to the current Texas Constitution. The proposal included providing annual sessions for the legislature, increasing the power of the governor, creating a single high court, and changing the selection process of the judiciary. The proposed document would have contained only 14,000 words and would have reduced the number of articles from seventeen to eleven. The final proposal was considered a well-drafted constitution and contained many of the changes constitutional experts continue to propose today. In the end, though, a joint meeting of both houses of the legislature failed by three votes to get the two-thirds vote necessary to pass. In its next regular session, the legislature revived most of those proposals in the form of eight amendments to the constitution, but Texas voters overwhelmingly rejected each of the amendments.

# TEXAS VS MASSACHUSETTS

The Massachusetts Constitution of 1780, which predates the U.S. Constitution by nearly ten years, is the oldest written constitution still in use not only in the United States but also anywhere in the world. The framers of the Massachusetts Constitution included three heroes of the American Revolution: John Adams, Samuel Adams, and James Bowdoin. These larger-than-life heroes established a pattern that many states now follow for state constitutions: a preamble, a declaration of the rights of citizens, a framework for government, and amendments to the constitution. The virtues of the relatively broad language of the Massachusetts Constitution have served the state well, as opposed to the highly specific and technical language of the Texas Constitution. Fewer constitutional amendments (120 total) have been passed in Massachusetts than in almost half of the states—certainly fewer than Texas's 483 amendments. Also unlike Texas, Massachusetts still uses its original document, while Texas is on its fifth constitution since statehood (and its sixth if you add the short-lived Constitution of the Republic of Texas).

## THINKING *Critically*

★ Why do you think the Massachusetts Constitution is a model for other states?

★ What aspects of the Massachusetts Constitution seem unusual to you?

★ What aspects seem familiar?

★ Do some features in the Texas Constitution seem preferable to you?

## A Constitutional Comparison of Massachusetts and Texas

| Feature | Massachusetts | Texas |
|---|---|---|
| Year adopted | 1780 | 1876 |
| Word length | 45,000 | 87,000 |
| Amendments | 120 | 483 |
| Major sections | 4 | 17 |
| Executive offices elected | | |
|   Governor | ✓ | ✓ |
|   Lieutenant governor | ✓ | ✓ |
|   Secretary of state | ✓ | ✗ |
|   Attorney general | ✓ | ✓ |
|   Treasurer/Comptroller | ✓ | ✓ |
|   Other | ✓ (1) | ✓ (2) |
| Legislature | General Court | Texas Legislature |
|   Senate | | |
|     Size | 40 | 31 |
|     Length of term | 2 years | 4 years |
|   House | | |
|     Size | 160 | 150 |
|     Length of term | 2 years | 2 years |
| Judiciary | Appointed | Elected |
| Statewide referendum to amend constitution | ✓ | ✓ |
| Statewide referendum to make general laws | ✓ | ✗ |
| Initiative petition to amend constitution | ✓ | ✗ |
| Initiative petition to make general laws | ✓ | ✗ |

Another serious attempt at significant constitutional revision came in 1998, spearheaded by Sen. Bill Ratliff and Rep. Rob Junell. The Ratliff-Junell proposal also reduced the document to about 18,000 words, granted expanded appointment power to the governor, increased the length of legislators' terms while imposing term limits, created

## TABLE 2.2 Comparison of State Constitutions

| State | Number of Constitutions | Date of Current Constitution | Approximate Word Length |
|---|---|---|---|
| Alabama | 6 | 1901 | 376,006 |
| Alaska | 1 | 1959 | 13,479 |
| Arizona | 1 | 1912 | 47,306 |
| Arkansas | 5 | 1874 | 59,120 |
| California | 2 | 1879 | 67,048 |
| Colorado | 1 | 1876 | 66,140 |
| Connecticut | 2 | 1965 | 16,401 |
| Delaware | 4 | 1897 | 25,445 |
| Florida | 6 | 1969 | 56,705 |
| Georgia | 10 | 1983 | 41,684 |
| Hawaii | 1 | 1959 | 21,498 |
| Idaho | 1 | 1890 | 24,626 |
| Illinois | 4 | 1971 | 16,401 |
| Indiana | 2 | 1851 | 11,476 |
| Iowa | 2 | 1857 | 11,089 |
| Kansas | 1 | 1861 | 14,097 |
| Kentucky | 4 | 1891 | 27,234 |
| Louisiana | 11 | 1975 | 69,876 |
| Maine | 1 | 1820 | 16,313 |
| Maryland | 4 | 1867 | 43,198 |
| Massachusetts | 1 | 1780 | 45,283 |
| Michigan | 4 | 1964 | 31,164 |
| Minnesota | 1 | 1858 | 11,734 |
| Mississippi | 4 | 1890 | 26,229 |
| Missouri | 4 | 1945 | 69,394 |
| Montana | 2 | 1973 | 12,790 |
| Nebraska | 2 | 1875 | 34,934 |
| Nevada | 1 | 1864 | 37,418 |
| New Hampshire | 2 | 1784 | 13,060 |
| New Jersey | 3 | 1948 | 26,360 |
| New Mexico | 1 | 1912 | 33,198 |
| New York | 4 | 1895 | 44,397 |
| North Carolina | 3 | 1971 | 17,177 |
| North Dakota | 1 | 1889 | 18,746 |
| Ohio | 2 | 1851 | 53,239 |

| State | Number of Constitutions | Date of Current Constitution | Approximate Word Length |
|---|---|---|---|
| Oklahoma | 1 | 1907 | 81,666 |
| Oregon | 1 | 1859 | 49,016 |
| Pennsylvania | 5 | 1968 | 26,078 |
| Rhode Island | 2 | 1986 | 11,407 |
| South Carolina | 7 | 1896 | 27,421 |
| South Dakota | 1 | 1889 | 27,774 |
| Tennessee | 3 | 1870 | 13,960 |
| **Texas** | **5** | **1876** | **87,000** |
| Utah | 1 | 1896 | 17,849 |
| Vermont | 3 | 1793 | 8,565 |
| Virginia | 6 | 1971 | 21,899 |
| Washington | 1 | 1889 | 32,578 |
| West Virginia | 2 | 1872 | 33,324 |
| Wisconsin | 1 | 1848 | 15,102 |
| Wyoming | 1 | 1890 | 26,349 |

**Source:** Data from *The Book of the States*, vol. 46 (Lexington, Ky.: Council of State Governments, 2014), table 1.1.

a salary commission appointed by the governor to set compensation for legislators (without voter approval), and reorganized the judiciary with a single high court and gubernatorial appointment of judges followed by a retention election. Ratliff and Junell argued that the current constitution is clearly broken and imposes an intolerable cost on the state. Ratliff suggests that "[voters know] that any document you have to try to amend 20 times every other year is broke. It's sort of a Texas tragedy, actually, that we can't seem to come to grips with the fact that we need a new, basic document going into the next century and the next millennium."[40] Moreover, the cost of the frequent elections necessary to amend the constitution is considerable, manifesting itself in the forms of "voter fatigue and the temptation for special-interest groups to push amendments that aren't in the public interest."[41] Unfortunately, the Ratliff-Junell proposal unceremoniously died from neglect in the legislature. As with previous attempts at constitutional revision, Texans resisted change and chose to continue to patch up the old constitution. The constitution thus remains mired in legislative detail, and Texas politicians remain unwilling or unable to create a constitution designed for the diversity and complexities of our state.

Absent a constitutional convention, constitutional revision can occur in a variety of other ways. In Texas, constitutional revision has been accomplished primarily through amending the constitution. This incremental change in Texas, while not ideal, has been necessary since many Texans resist more sweeping changes, such as wholesale revision through constitutional conventions. Theoretically, change could also be accomplished with the voter-led initiative and referendum. An **initiative** occurs when voters gather signatures on a petition in order to place either statutes or constitutional amendments

**Initiative**
a mechanism that allows voters to gather signatures on a petition in order to place statutes or constitutional amendments on a ballot.

FIGURE 2.2 Texas Constitution of 1876: Amendments Proposed and Adopted, 1879–2013

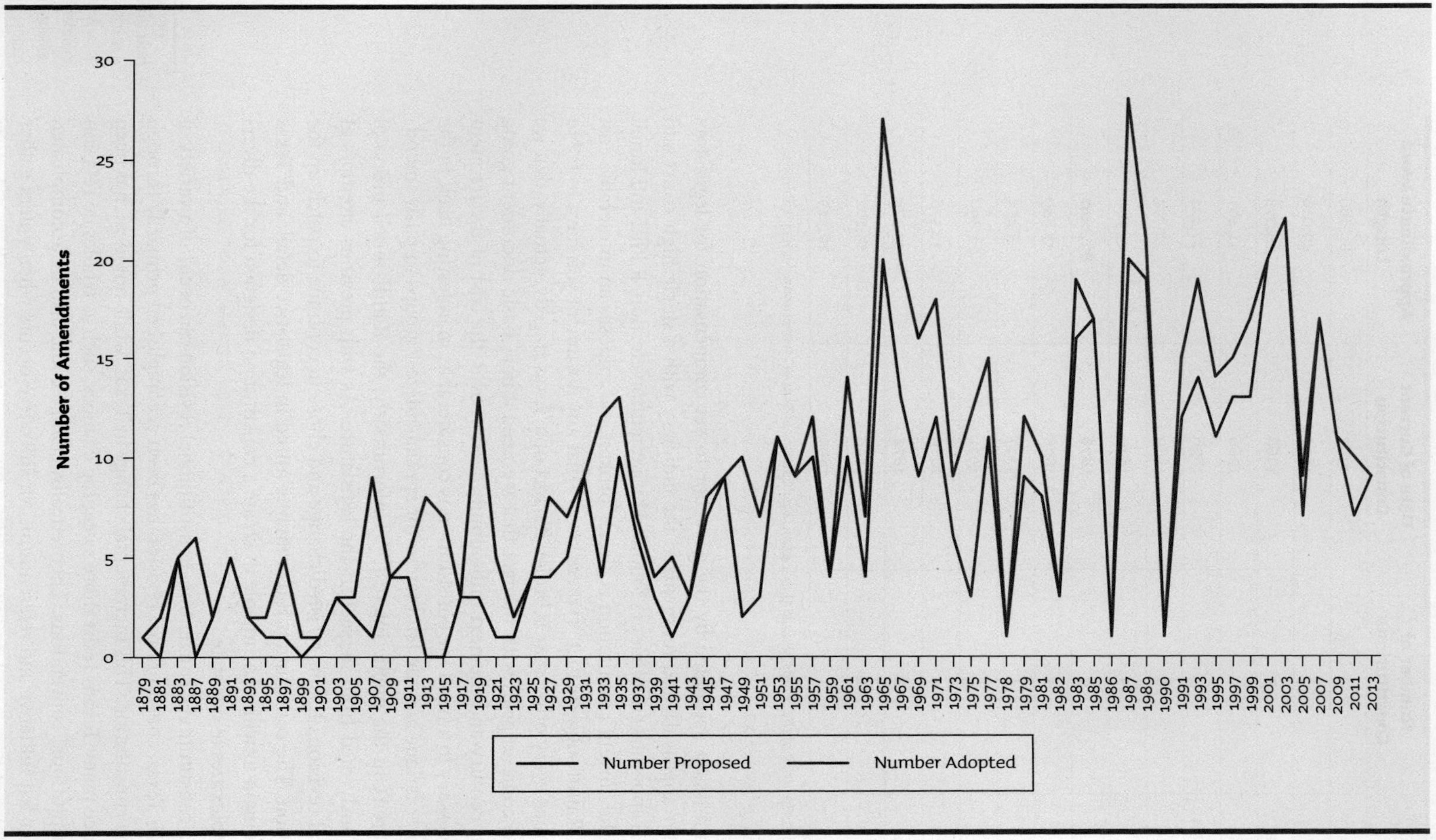

Number Proposed — Number Adopted

Number of Amendments

*Source:* Texas Legislative Council, www.tlc.state.tx.us (accessed September 16, 2014).

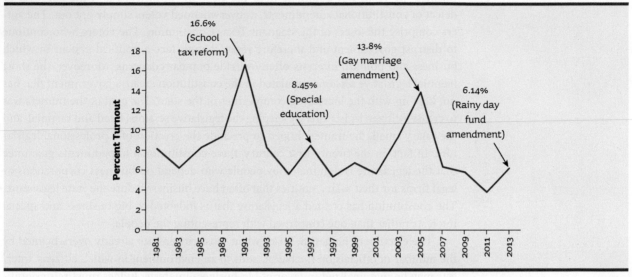

**Source:** Texas Secretary of State, www.sos.state.tx.us/elections/historical/70-92.shtml (accessed August 8, 2014).

on a ballot. A **referendum** allows voters to cast a popular vote on statutes passed by the legislature. These two voter-led mechanisms are consistent with Texans' legendary preference for limited government and popular control. So it is particularly surprising that the Texas Constitution does not have provisions for either procedure. While Texans' preference for limited government may be notorious, in this case it is apparently trumped by their equally entrenched resistance to change. In the end, prospects for constitutional change seem limited. Most Texans, even as they acknowledge the problems with the current constitution, still distrust more the potential problems of a new one.

> **Referendum**
> a mechanism that allows voters to cast a popular vote on statutes passed by the state legislature; the legislature can place measures on the ballot for voter consideration.

## WINNERS AND LOSERS

In Texas, the general distrust of government and resulting resistance to change has created an environment in which the fundamental law is unyielding—a difficult situation for one of the nation's most rapidly changing states. The authors of the current Texas Constitution distrusted the Reconstruction government, which they viewed as the government of an occupying army. Their reaction was to create a constitution intended to limit the power of government, curb the potential for abuse by business, and preserve the power of citizens in the state. Ironically, the constitution entails such a high democratic cost to Texas citizens that the goals of the framers were guaranteed to fail. In an effort to safeguard the power of individuals, voters in Texas routinely face a long ballot and are literally overwhelmed by the number of offices and constitutional amendments put before them at each election. Instead of ensuring popular control of government, such a burden on citizens ensures voter fatigue and apathy. When citizens don't play their role to keep government in check, professional politicians and narrow special interests fill the gap.

The winners of the current constitutional rules tend to be big-business interests. Business in Texas can dominate both the elections of officials and the approval or defeat of constitutional amendments, as overwhelmed voters simply opt out. The voters comprise the losers of the stagnant Texas Constitution. The voters, who continue to distrust government and therefore resist change, face a political system in which business and political interests often override popular concerns. Moreover, the short biennial legislative sessions stipulated in the constitution create a government that has not kept up with the increasing complexities of the state. The goal of the framers was to create a citizen legislature. By keeping the legislative sessions fixed and biennial, and the salary small, the framers hoped to preclude the creation of a professional legislature. In fact, in the twenty-first century, these constitutional impediments guarantee that the legislature is dominated by people who depend on business corporations or legal firms for their salary, entities that often have business before the state legislature. The constitution has created a legislature that is indebted to big business and special interests rather than one concerned with representing the people.

The election of judges in Texas, when most citizens are already overwhelmed by the number of officials on the ballot, adds to an environment in which citizens' interests may be marginalized in favor of big-business interests. Judges must raise significant amounts of money to be elected in the state, even as most citizens are simply not paying attention to judicial elections. Big business and other special interests are willing to fill that gap. In general, the Texas Constitution as it currently stands does not effectively empower the people in the state, and the general distrust of government means the people do not favor changing the constitution.

★ How does Texas's mistrust of government and resistance to change manifest itself in the current constitution? How does this conflict with the political preference for limited government?

★ To what extent does the Texas Constitution create a citizen legislature?

★ What are the pro and con arguments for making changes to the Texas Constitution?

## CONCLUSION

Texans continue to cling to a constitution written well over 100 years ago at a time when the state was largely dominated by agriculture. Texas has undergone constant and dramatic change since the constitution was written, and there is no sign that this change is slowing down. Gone are the days of the rugged frontier. In today's Texas you are more likely to see a computer chip than a longhorn. Yet even as the state continues to change, Texans cling to the myth that the constitution continues to serve them. Mistrust of government overrides concerns over an unresponsive governmental structure. Texas continues to face increasingly complex issues, but Texans' tradition of mistrust undermines the ability of the government to respond to the state's transformations. Reliance on its outdated constitution will not serve Texas in the future.

for CQ Press

Sharpen your skills with **SAGE edge** at **edge.sagepub.com/collier4e**. **SAGE edge for students** provides a personalized approach to help you accomplish your coursework goals in an easy-to-use learning environment.

## KEY TERMS

block grant (p. 48)

categorical grant (p. 47)

concurrent powers (p. 44)

confederal system (p. 42)

constitution (p. 40)

cooperative federalism (p. 46)

devolution (p. 46)

dual federalism (p. 46)

enumerated powers (p. 44)

extradition (p. 46)

federalism (p. 42)

fiscal federalism (p. 47)

full faith and credit clause (p. 45)

horizontal federalism (p. 44)

implied powers (p. 44)

initiative (p. 71)

long ballot (p. 66)

Manifest Destiny (p. 55)

popular sovereignty (p. 41)

privileges and immunities (p. 44)

referendum (p. 73)

reserved powers (p. 44)

supremacy clause (p. 44)

unfunded mandate (p. 48)

unitary system (p. 42)

vertical federalism (p. 42)

## CORE ASSESSMENT

1. With the current constitutional structure, to what extent do you have a responsibility to participate in elections that include amendments to the Texas Constitution?

2. How can we safeguard majority rule while protecting minority rights?

3. What changes should we make to the current Texas Constitution?

# TEXAS LEGISLATURE

Can you imagine speaking for eleven hours without stopping for a break? Wendy Davis (D–Fort Worth) captured national media attention at the end of the first special session of the 83rd Texas Legislature in June of 2013 when she engaged in such a speech. This type of speech, called a filibuster, is a legislative tool used in the Texas Senate to prevent a vote on a bill by engaging in unlimited debate and refusing to yield the floor to another member. Davis's filibuster ended when the 140-day regular session of the Texas Legislature came to a close. The subject of Davis's impassioned speech was a bill before the legislature that attempted to place a number of restrictions on abortions in Texas. As a pro-choice Democrat, Davis wanted to prevent the pro-life, Republican majority from passing the abortion bill, which would have been one of the most restrictive abortion laws in the country. Filling the visitors' gallery was a significant number of women, and some men, who supported Davis's pro-abortion position. These crowds cheered Davis throughout her eleven-hour ordeal. While Davis's speech thrust her into the national spotlight and led to calls for her eventual decision to run for governor in 2014, it also spotlighted the issue of women's representation in the Texas Legislature.[1]

One opinion piece painted a scathing picture of the Texas Legislature as an Old Boys' network dominated by sexist politicians that enacted anti-women's legislation, such as restrictive abortion laws, and provided little funding for women's health initiatives, including policies to aid low income, poorly educated women.[2] This opinion piece was referenced on editorial pages in Texas newspapers such as the *Dallas Morning News* and the *Lubbock Avalanche-Journal,* as well as by national media outlets such as the *Huffington Post.*[3] Some progressive and liberal opinion leaders have focused at times on the low number of women in the Texas Legislature as one of the causes of the general lack of emphasis by members on women's issues. The assumption is that if more women were elected to the Texas Legislature, policies in Texas would change on issue such as abortion and public health funding. This belief rests on some prior assumptions, of course, such as all women are pro-abortion and favor expansion of public health funding.

Whether these assumptions are correct, Davis's filibuster and the related media coverage and opinion pieces did highlight a few key issues for political science and students of government. The first is the relative lack of women in the Texas Legislature.

**Senator Wendy Davis (D-Fort Worth) celebrates as time runs out on the Texas Legislature's consideration of an abortion bill in 2013. Davis filibustered the bill for eleven hours to prevent a vote on it.**

Edith Williams became the first woman elected to the Texas Legislature in 1922, but she served only a single term. In the decades that followed, only a handful of women were elected to the legislature. Until the 1960s, fewer than a dozen women served during any given session of the legislature. In 2013, Wendy Davis was one of six women serving in the Texas Senate, and only thirty-one women served in the Texas House of Representatives that year.

Second, women are elected to the legislature when they actually appear on the ballot. Yet in 2012, only fifty-four women ran either as a Democrat or Republican for the 150 seats in the Texas House of Representatives and thirty-one seats in the Texas Senate that year.[4] Thus, if women's issues are being ignored or underfunded and if electing more women to the legislature is the answer, then the political parties need to recruit more women to run for office. In fact, in the primary elections to nominate candidates for the general election for the 84th Legislature in November 2014, no challenger to a male incumbent in the Texas Senate faced a female opponent, and no female candidates contested the open seats available. In addition, Wendy Davis's exit from the Texas Senate to run for governor and Leticia Van de Putte's decision to run for lieutenant governor may leave the Texas Senate with two fewer women in 2015.[5] In an unusual race for the 83rd Legislature in the 2012 elections, the 134th District for the Texas House of Representatives, which includes the Houston areas of River Oaks and Bellaire, featured Republican incumbent Sarah Davis versus Democratic challenger Ann Johnson.[6] A state legislative race featuring a woman nominated by each major political party is a rarity in Texas politics.

Finally, the issue of the number of women serving in the Texas Legislature, or in any elected capacity, raises a number of important theoretical issues for students of government and political science. Key among these issues is the exact meaning or purpose of "representation." Is representation about geography, or is representation about demographics such as sex/gender, income, race/ethnicity, religion, and educational background? How we answer this affects whether we think a legislature is "representative" and whether we believe the government is responsive to its citizens. We return to this issue later in the chapter.

## Chapter Objectives

★ Describe the form and function of the Texas Legislature.

★ Identify the different types of state legislatures.

★ Relate the qualifications for legislative office and the implications of term limits.

★ Explain the differences between microcosm theory of representation and principal-agent theory of representation.

★ Assess who wins and who loses in how Texas's legislature functions.

★ Discuss how the Texas Legislature is elected.

★ Assess who wins and who loses under Texas's single-member district system.

## THE TEXAS LEGISLATURE IN CONTEXT

The U.S. Congress, as the legislative branch of the U.S. government, serves as a model for most legislative branches of state governments. The Texas Legislature is no exception. (See Table 3.1 for a comparison of some of the characteristics of the U.S. Congress and the Texas Legislature.) The legislative branch in Texas is usually referred to as the Texas Legislature, or simply *the* legislature. The Texas Legislature is **bicameral**, consisting of two separate chambers or houses. The lower house is called the House of Representatives, and the upper house is called the Senate. This approach parallels the number and naming of chambers in the U.S. Congress. References to "upper" and "lower" houses developed from the British Parliament, in which the House of Lords represented the nobility of the "upper" class and the House of Commons represented the ordinary citizens of the "lower" class. These terms

**Bicameral**
a legislature that consists of two separate chambers or houses.

## TABLE 3.1  U.S. Congress and the Texas Legislature: A Comparison

| Characteristic | U.S. Congress | | Texas Legislature | |
| --- | --- | --- | --- | --- |
| | U.S. Senate | U.S. House | Texas Senate | Texas House |
| Size of chamber | 100 | 435 | 31 | 150 |
| Term in office | 6 years | 2 years | 4 years | 2 years |
| Staggered terms | Yes | No | Yes | No |
| Minimum age for election | 30 | 25 | 26 | 21 |
| Resident of state | Yes | Yes | 5 years | 2 years |
| Resident of district | N/A | No | 1 year | 1 year |

carried over into the American, and Texan, experience. States vary slightly in the names of the two chambers. For example, in Virginia the lower house is called the House of Delegates. Most states, however, employ the naming convention that Texas also uses. Forty-nine states possess a bicameral legislature in the state government. Nebraska is the only state with a single-chamber, or unicameral, state legislature.

The decision to have a dual-chambered state legislature reflects more than just a simple desire to mirror the U.S. Congress. James Madison suggested in the *Federalist Papers* that the protection of liberty from passionate majorities rests in part with dividing the power of the legislature.[7] Requiring any new law to pass in two chambers makes it more difficult for a majority to abuse its power. This "divide and subdue" technique of allocating the power of the legislature across two chambers is enhanced because each chamber is chosen by a different means. For example, members of the U.S. House of Representatives are chosen by popular vote based on small geographic districts, while U.S. senators are chosen by statewide popular vote. Another reason, historically, to employ a bicameral legislature is to ensure the adequate representation of different groups. Originally, state governments were directly represented in the U.S. Congress because state legislatures, as opposed to the states' voters, chose the members of the U.S. Senate. In 1913, the Seventeenth Amendment to the U.S. Constitution made the U.S. Senate directly elected by the citizens of the state the senator represents. The shift reflected the desire among Progressives at the time to make senators accountable to voters, not state legislatures.

One interesting fact is that other federal systems beyond the United States lack consistency between the national legislature and regional/state legislatures in terms of the number of chambers. While all federal systems in the world have bicameral national legislatures, many have unicameral regional/state legislatures. For example, all of the ten provincial legislative assemblies in Canada are unicameral, while the national parliament remains bicameral. Similar arrangements occur in Mexico, where each state in Mexico has a unicameral state legislature even though the national Congress in Mexico is bicameral. Outside of North America, unicameral state legislatures are found in Austria, Brazil, Germany, and Malaysia. The case of Germany is interesting because state governments are directly represented in the upper house of the national parliament. More specifically, the upper house of the German national parliament, the Bundesrat, consists of members of each state's executive branch. Members of the Bundesrat sit in the chamber by state, not by political party, and votes are cast by state, not by individual members. As a result, this structure cannot be replicated in the German states. The Australian state of Queensland also has a unicameral legislature, while the rest of Australia's states are bicameral.

In the past, some U.S. states mirrored the relationship between the two houses in the U.S. Congress by making counties the basis of representation in the upper house of the state legislature. However, with 254 counties, Texas never really did this. Today, the use of counties as a basis for representation in state legislatures is no longer employed in any state. The U.S. Supreme Court rejected counties and other local governments as a basis for representation in state legislatures in *Baker v. Carr* (1962), ruling that the equal protection clause of the Fourteenth Amendment asserts the principle of "one person, one vote."[8] The *Baker* decision meant that the population of state legislative districts must be roughly equal and may not differ in population by more than, give or take, 5 percent. Using counties as the basis of representation for state legislatures clearly violated this concept since counties can and do vary tremendously in population size. For example, if counties were used to determine the makeup of the Texas Senate, Harris County, which includes the city of Houston, would have one state senator for approximately 4 million people, while Loving County in West Texas would have one senator for its eighty-two residents. Obviously, people in Loving County would be dramatically overrepresented compared to those living in Harris County. In *Reynolds v. Sims* (1964), the U.S. Supreme Court extended this logic by requiring that both houses of state legislatures represent the population of a state on a one-person, one-vote basis.[9]

Each of the forty-nine states in the United States with a bicameral state legislature has an upper house that is smaller than the lower house. The smaller size of the upper house again mirrors the U.S. Congress; the U.S. Senate, with 100 members, is considerably smaller than the 435-member U.S. House of Representatives.

The size of the membership of a state's legislature, however, is not proportional to the population of the state. Large-population states such as Texas, Florida, and California do not always have the largest state legislatures. New Hampshire, one of the smallest states, has the largest lower house among the forty-nine bicameral state legislatures, with 400 members.

What may matter more is the relationship between the number of citizens and the size of the legislature. Where there are more legislators relative to the population, each legislator represents fewer people; in some sense the legislator is closer to the people. As shown in Table 3.2, the relationship between the size of the state legislature and the number of representatives is more complex than might be expected. In Texas, with the eleventh-largest legislature and the second-largest population, each member represents around 139,000 people. When comparing the ratios of representation to population, Texas ranks forty-ninth in the United States. Thus, Texans are less represented in their own state legislature than citizens of almost every other state. Only California has fewer state representatives per person than Texas. Of course, the relative sizes of both houses of legislature change the dynamic a bit. The Texas Senate's thirty-one members each represent about 815,000 people, but in the Texas House of Representatives the ratio is about 193,000 per member.

States vary in the size of their legislature and ratio of legislators to people because each individual state determines the size of its own legislature. Often this number is set in state constitutions and therefore is difficult to change as the state population grows. The Texas Constitution says that the Texas Senate has exactly thirty-one members. In contrast, the Texas Constitution gives a minimum number for the Texas House of Representatives: ninety-three. The

The Texas state capitol in Austin is the source of a Texas legend. The building was designed to be slightly taller than the U.S. Capitol building in Washington, D.C. The Texas capitol is allegedly taller when measured from the tip of the statue at the top of the dome to the lowest level at the back of the building, which is a partially exposed basement level. However, from the front, as shown here, the Texas capitol is shorter than the national capitol.

Texas Legislature has the power to add additional seats if so desired. As the population of Texas has grown, the legislature has increased the size of the Texas House of Representatives over time to the current size of 150. In 1999, Texas voters amended the state constitution to limit the size of the Texas House of Representatives at 150. Finally, a practical limitation on the ratio of legislators to population is the fact that extremely large legislatures are difficult to organize. If Texas used the same ratio as New Hampshire, where each member of the state legislature represents just over 3,000 people, the Texas Legislature would have to seat over 80,000 members. In general, there is a trade-off between representation and efficiency, as larger legislatures tend to be less efficient.

The Texas Legislature is one of a handful of state legislatures that does not meet yearly for a regular session, instead convening every two years. State legislatures in Montana, Nevada, and North Dakota also meet biennially.[10] In these states, and in Texas, the length of the legislative session is set so that the legislature meets only in a single year. In 2008, voters in the state of Arkansas amended that state's constitution to shift the Arkansas Legislature from biennial to annual meetings. While the state constitutions of a few states, such as North Carolina and Tennessee, stipulate that the legislatures are supposed to meet every other year, these legislatures are permitted to divide the regular session across two years, allowing them in practice to meet annually for regular business.[11] A few other states, such as Maine, Minnesota, and Wisconsin, allow their legislatures to carry over sessions across the two-year period while technically considering their legislatures to be biennial. When in **regular session**, the Texas Legislature meets for 140 days, making the length of its session the fourteenth-longest in the country. Thirteen states, including large-population states such as California, Michigan, New York, North Carolina, Ohio, and Pennsylvania, do not limit the length of state legislative sessions.[12]

**TABLE 3.2** **Size of State Legislatures**

| State | Total Members of the State Legislature | | | | Population Per Legislator | | Population | |
|---|---|---|---|---|---|---|---|---|
| | Upper House | Lower House | Total Members | Rank | Ratio | Rank | In Millions | Rank |
| New Hampshire | 24 | 400 | 424 | 1 | 3,116 | 50 | 1.321 | 42 |
| Pennsylvania | 50 | 203 | 253 | 2 | 50,336 | 13 | 12.735 | 6 |
| Georgia | 56 | 180 | 236 | 3 | 41,219 | 20 | 9.728 | 9 |
| New York | 62 | 150 | 212 | 4 | 91,609 | 4 | 19.421 | 3 |
| Minnesota | 67 | 134 | 201 | 5 | 26,442 | 30 | 5.315 | 21 |
| Massachusetts | 40 | 160 | 200 | 6 | 32,798 | 23 | 6.560 | 14 |
| Missouri | 34 | 163 | 197 | 7 | 30,515 | 27 | 6.011 | 18 |
| Maryland | 47 | 141 | 188 | 8 | 30,797 | 26 | 5.790 | 19 |
| Connecticut | 36 | 151 | 187 | 9 | 19,153 | 34 | 3.582 | 29 |
| Maine | 35 | 151 | 186 | 10 | 7,167 | 45 | 1.333 | 41 |
| **Texas** | **31** | **150** | **181** | **11** | **139,602** | **2** | **25.268** | **2** |
| Vermont | 30 | 150 | 180 | 12 | 3,502 | 49 | 0.630 | 49 |
| Illinois | 59 | 118 | 177 | 13 | 72,680 | 7 | 12.864 | 5 |
| Mississippi | 52 | 122 | 174 | 14 | 17,116 | 38 | 2.978 | 31 |
| North Carolina | 50 | 120 | 170 | 15 | 56,269 | 11 | 9.566 | 10 |
| South Carolina | 46 | 124 | 170 | 15 | 27,329 | 28 | 4.696 | 24 |
| Kansas | 40 | 125 | 165 | 17 | 17,356 | 37 | 2.864 | 33 |
| Florida | 40 | 120 | 160 | 18 | 118,130 | 3 | 18.901 | 4 |
| Indiana | 50 | 100 | 150 | 19 | 43,344 | 16 | 6.502 | 15 |
| Iowa | 50 | 100 | 150 | 19 | 20,359 | 33 | 3.054 | 30 |
| Montana | 50 | 100 | 150 | 19 | 6,629 | 46 | 0.994 | 44 |
| Oklahoma | 48 | 101 | 149 | 22 | 25,268 | 31 | 3.765 | 28 |

| State | Total Members of the State Legislature | | | | Population Per Legislator | | Population | |
|---|---|---|---|---|---|---|---|---|
| | Upper House | Lower House | Total Members | Rank | Ratio | Rank | In Millions | Rank |
| Michigan | 38 | 110 | 148 | 23 | 66,970 | 9 | 9.912 | 8 |
| Washington | 49 | 98 | 147 | 24 | 45,941 | 15 | 6.753 | 13 |
| Louisiana | 39 | 105 | 144 | 25 | 31,625 | 24 | 4.554 | 25 |
| North Dakota | 47 | 94 | 141 | 26 | 4,794 | 48 | 0.676 | 48 |
| Alabama | 35 | 105 | 140 | 27 | 34,307 | 22 | 4.803 | 23 |
| Virginia | 40 | 100 | 140 | 27 | 57,412 | 10 | 8.038 | 12 |
| Kentucky | 38 | 100 | 138 | 29 | 31,526 | 25 | 4.351 | 26 |
| Arkansas | 35 | 100 | 135 | 30 | 21,676 | 32 | 2.926 | 32 |
| West Virginia | 34 | 100 | 134 | 31 | 13,879 | 41 | 1.860 | 37 |
| Ohio | 33 | 99 | 132 | 32 | 87,640 | 5 | 11.568 | 7 |
| Tennessee | 33 | 99 | 132 | 32 | 48,299 | 14 | 6.375 | 17 |
| Wisconsin | 33 | 99 | 132 | 32 | 43,168 | 17 | 5.698 | 20 |
| California | 40 | 80 | 120 | 35 | 311,183 | 1 | 37.342 | 1 |
| New Jersey | 40 | 80 | 120 | 35 | 73,396 | 6 | 8.808 | 11 |
| Rhode Island | 38 | 75 | 113 | 37 | 9,338 | 43 | 1.055 | 43 |
| New Mexico | 42 | 70 | 112 | 38 | 18,458 | 35 | 2.067 | 36 |
| Idaho | 35 | 70 | 105 | 39 | 14,986 | 39 | 1.573 | 39 |
| South Dakota | 35 | 70 | 105 | 39 | 7,807 | 44 | 0.820 | 46 |
| Utah | 29 | 75 | 104 | 41 | 26,642 | 29 | 2.771 | 34 |
| Colorado | 35 | 65 | 100 | 42 | 50,449 | 12 | 5.045 | 22 |
| Arizona | 30 | 60 | 90 | 43 | 71,252 | 8 | 6.413 | 16 |
| Oregon | 30 | 60 | 90 | 43 | 42,762 | 19 | 3.849 | 27 |
| Wyoming | 30 | 60 | 90 | 43 | 6,314 | 47 | 0.568 | 50 |
| Hawaii | 25 | 51 | 76 | 46 | 17,985 | 36 | 1.367 | 40 |
| Nevada | 21 | 42 | 63 | 47 | 43,007 | 18 | 2.709 | 35 |
| Delaware | 21 | 41 | 62 | 48 | 14,530 | 40 | 0.901 | 45 |
| Alaska | 20 | 40 | 60 | 49 | 12,025 | 42 | 0.722 | 47 |
| Nebraska | 49 | 0 | 49 | 50 | 37,384 | 21 | 1.832 | 38 |

**Sources:** Audrey S. Wall, ed., *Book of the States*, vol. 44 (Lexington, Ky.: Council of State Governments, 2012), 83, table 3.3; Kristin D. Burnett, "2010 Census Briefs: Congressional Reapportionment" (Washington, D.C.: United States Census Bureau, 2011), 2, table 1; some calculations by author.

The length and frequency of legislative sessions directly influences the ability of a legislature to work. Legislatures that meet annually may be more likely to manage the state budget because they are able to review the budget each year and make adjustments. In contrast, the Texas Legislature has to pass a budget that covers two years of revenue and spending. The legislators have to predict how much the state will receive in taxes and other sources of revenue and also how much the state needs to spend for the those two years. In addition, annual legislatures handle new issues each year, while in Texas the legislature cannot handle new issues as often. The infrequency of legislative sessions in Texas reflects in part the general distrust of government consistent with Texas's political culture and values. A legislature that meets infrequently cannot do as much work—or, theoretically, pass as many laws—perhaps keeping the state government smaller.

State legislatures are typically not limited to meeting during their regular sessions. Often, state governments find it necessary to have the legislature meet beyond the required sessions. These **special sessions** of the legislature may occur after an unexpected event, such as a financial crisis or a natural disaster. In some cases, a special session may be called to have the legislature pass legislation that did not pass during the regular session. States vary in how the legislature is called back for a special session. In some states, such as Alaska and Florida, a **supermajority** of legislators (for example, two-thirds of the members of each chamber) must agree to hold the special session by filing a petition. Some states, such as Idaho, allow the presiding officers of each chamber to call the legislature into special session. Finally, in some states, the legislature may not call itself into session, but the governor may call the legislature back. Almost every state allows the legislature to determine the subject of the special session, including the topics that may be debated and on which the legislature may pass new laws. Moreover, a majority of states do not limit the number of days that the legislature meets in special session.[13]

Like other state legislatures, the Texas Legislature is not limited to meeting during its regular session every two years. The legislature may be called into special sessions. However, the special sessions are limited to thirty days. In addition, the power to call special sessions in Texas does not rest with the legislature. That power rests with the governor. The governor also determines the topics that the legislature may discuss during special sessions and may add topics to the agenda during the special sessions. To bring the legislature into special session, the governor issues an official document referred to as "the call." This document states when the legislature will begin meeting for the special session and the topics it will consider. If the governor is not satisfied with the work of the Texas Legislature during a special session, the governor may call the legislature back into session as often as he or she wishes. When the legislature is in regular session or special session, its members possess certain rights and privileges that they do not possess otherwise. For example, the Texas Constitution states that "Senators and Representatives shall, except in cases of treason, felony, or breach of the peace, be privileged from arrest during the session of the legislature, and in going to and returning from the same." Another right is designed to allow members an expansive freedom of speech while engaged in legislative debate: "No member shall be questioned in any other place for words spoken in debate in either House." Essentially, what

**Special session**
meetings of a legislature that occur at times other than those required by a constitution or law; in Texas, special sessions are called by the governor and last for up to thirty days.

**Supermajority**
a majority that is larger than a simple majority of 50 percent plus one; supermajorities include requirements of 60 percent, two-thirds, three-fourths, or 80 percent to make a decision.

is said in the legislature supposedly stays in the legislature. Of course, what is said in the legislature may still come back to haunt a member during the next election.

When the legislature meets for its biennial session, a tremendous amount of work needs to be accomplished. Certain issues come up every legislative session, such as the state budget. During most sessions, the legislature must approve interim appointments made by the governor to fill vacancies that occurred while the legislature was not in session. Other issues vary markedly from session to session. In the mid-2000s, the legislature spent a great deal of time unsuccessfully addressing the funding formula for public elementary and secondary schools. The 81st Legislature, which met in 2009, faced several controversial issues. One was the impact of the meltdown in the U.S. banking and financial services sector following the collapse of the U.S. housing market in 2008. The resulting economic recession across the United States affected the Texas economy. As in 2009, the 2011 session required the legislature to address major shortfalls in the state budget, and it slashed spending by $15.2 billion, the largest budget cuts in state history.[14] Such cuts were necessary absent a willingness by a majority of legislators to raise taxes or to dip into the Rainy Day Fund. The impact of the cuts included significant reductions in state funding for school districts across the state and in support for the state's public universities.

The most significant issue addressed by the legislature in 2011 was arguably redistricting. Every ten years after U.S. Census data is released, the state legislature redraws the lines for election districts for the Texas Senate and Texas House of Representatives. New maps are also drawn to elect members of the Texas State Board of Education. This process is not without controversy, because population growth is not equal across the state. Some areas in Texas grow faster than others, so districts have to be shifted from one part of the state to another. We will return to this issue later in the chapter. In the end, the legislature passed a law that drew new district boundaries for both houses of the legislature and for the State Board of Education. However, the legislature was unable to come to an agreement on new election districts for Texas's seats in the U.S. House of Representatives. These districts were ultimately drawn by federal courts.[15]

More recently, in 2013, legislators grappled once again with the state budget, which passed after considerable debate over projected revenue from taxes and fees and projected expenses. Texas, like most U.S. states but not the national government, must maintain a balanced budget based on provisions of its state constitution. Budget debates focused on whether to restore funding for transportation, public education, and other state services to levels of spending prior to the recession of 2008–2012.[16] Additionally, a legislative overhaul of the high-stakes STAAR tests required of all students in Texas public schools reduced the number of high school courses required to be tested in the STAAR system from every course to just five courses, with school districts able to elect whether to test in two other subjects, English III and Algebra II.[17] While bills allowing concealed weapons to be carried on college and university campuses failed to pass in 2013, the legislature did approve those with concealed handgun licenses to store guns and ammunition in locked cars on campus.[18]

In reaction to U.S. Supreme Court decisions upholding the Patient Protection and Affordable Care Act, also known as Obamacare, Texas lawmakers passed a number of bills in 2013, some of which limited the growth of Medicare and Medicaid expected to occur under the act. Other bills attempted to reduce fraud in the health care system. In another high-profile issue, the Texas Legislature's attempts to address the issue of immigration failed. Bills to allow undocumented aliens to drive, to encourage the U.S. Congress to reform the national immigration system, and to ask the U.S. Congress to create a path to "legal status" so some undocumented immigrants could eventually receive citizenship did not receive the votes needed to become laws.

Because the regular session ended without completing work on three key issues that Governor Perry wished to see the legislature act, he called legislators back to Austin for a special session from May 27 to June 25, 2013. He asked for laws to place restrictions on when and where abortions may be performed, to prioritize and fund transportation projects, and to pass a final redistricting plan for the state legislature and Texas's seats in the U.S. House of Representatives. When the filibuster by Texas senator Wendy Davis discussed at the beginning of this chapter blocked legislative action at the end of the first special session on the abortion issue, Perry called the legislature back into session again in July, and this time it passed abortion legislation. A third special session in August was called by the governor to focus exclusively on transportation funding.

## TYPOLOGIES OF STATE LEGISLATURES

**B**ased upon factors such as length of legislative session, compensation for legislators, and professional resources, state legislatures may be classified as one of three types: citizen, professional, or hybrid. A **citizen legislature** seeks to limit the role of a state legislator to a part-time function so that many or most citizens can perform it. Typically, citizen legislatures meet every other year or for only a few weeks each year. Compensation is minimal for citizen legislators, and in some cases amounts to no more than reimbursement for travel expenses and some meals. The amount of time that a member of a citizen legislature spends in session, committee work, election campaigns, and constituency service is about half of the time they spend on a regular, full-time job. Staffing and other professional resources are minimal. North Dakota and Rhode Island are examples of states that have citizen legislatures.

In contrast, a **professional legislature** meets annually, often for as much as nine months of the year. In these states, being a member of the state legislature is a full-time occupation. As a reward for devoting so much time to state government, members of the legislature are well compensated, averaging $68,599 among the eleven state legislatures classified as professional.[19] Generous allowances are also provided so that members of the legislature can hire and maintain extensive staffs that typically include secretarial support and researchers. These legislatures average 8.9 staff members per legislator. California and New York are examples of states that have professional legislatures. Given the size and scope of state government, especially in high-population states, the development of professional state legislatures is not surprising.

In between these two extremes are hybrid legislatures. In states such as Louisiana and Missouri, the legislature typically meets annually for a couple of months. Members of the legislature receive some compensation. Average compensation for states with

**Citizen legislature**
a legislature that attempts to keep the role of a state legislator to a part-time function so that many or most citizens can perform it; normally, a citizen legislator is provided minimal compensation, offered few staffing resources, and has short or infrequent legislative sessions.

**Professional legislature**
a legislature that meets annually, often for nine months of the year or more; a professional legislator is provided a professional-level salary and generous allowances to hire and keep support and research staffs.

this type of legislature is $35,326.[20] In addition, members of the legislature receive some funds to hire a small personal staff—on average three staff members per legislator.

The base pay for members of the Texas Legislature is only $7,200. Members also receive $150 per day for personal expenses while the legislature is in session, meaning that they earn a total of $28,200 in years with a regular session.[21] The commission reviews the rates of compensation prior to every session of the legislature and changes them as needed. In addition, members of the legislature also receive compensation at a rate of $.56 per mile for travel from their home district to Austin for the session. If the legislator takes a personal airplane, the legislator receives $1.33 per air mile. The daily rates for personal expenses are set by the Texas Ethics Commission, while rates for reimbursement for travel are set by the comptroller for public accounts. The pay and compensation for the Texas Legislature is much less than that of California or Michigan, where legislator base pay is over $95,000 per year and $70,000 per year, respectively. At the low end, Kansas pays its legislators a base of $88.66 per day the legislature is in session, plus $.50 per mile for travel and a per diem of $123 for housing and meals.[22]

The salary for members of the Texas Legislature is especially tough on representatives from outside Austin because they must pay for a place to live in the capital during the session. To help compensate for the relatively low pay, members of the Texas Legislature enjoy one of the most generous retirement plans among the fifty state legislatures. To qualify, a legislator must serve eight years in the legislature. At age sixty, he or she can start receiving the retirement benefit upon leaving the legislature. Legislators may start receiving retirement benefits at age fifty if they have served at least twelve years in the legislature. The pension formula—that is, the amount contributed from the state government and budget—is based on 2.3 percent of the base compensation to state district judges times the length of service in the legislature.[23] In 2005, the salary of the district judge was $125,000. This would make the minimum benefit $23,000 per year after eight years of service in the legislature. In addition, members of the legislature may contribute up to 8 percent of their salary per year while they serve in the legislature toward their pension. Note that participation in the retirement plan is optional, but many legislators choose to join it. Members of the Texas Legislature receive coverage in the state health insurance plan that is offered to all state employees.

In terms of staffing resources, members of the Texas Senate receive an allowance of $25,000 per month to pay for the costs of maintaining offices in Austin and in their district. These funds are used to purchase office equipment and supplies, pay for office space, and provide salaries and other compensation for office workers. On average, members of the Texas Senate keep six staffers employed year round. Members of the Texas House of Representatives receive $8,500 per month for staff support, enough to provide each representative an average staff size of three persons. To supplement their regular paid staff, members of the legislature rely on student interns and volunteers to carry out their day-to-day activities.

Although the framers of the Texas Constitution sought to establish a citizen legislature, the Texas Legislature today is classified as a hybrid legislature. This labeling takes into account the pension and staffing resources, not just base salary and infrequency of meetings. Peverill Squire, a researcher who developed an index of state legislatures

In a show of civic interest, the rotunda of the Texas Legislature is filled with members of the public who turned out to observe proceedings on an abortion bill prior to a vote by the legislature in 2013.

based on the criteria of salary and compensation, staffing and similar resources, and time devoted to legislative activities, found that since 1979 the Texas Legislature has consistently ranked in the middle of state legislatures.[24] Texas was ranked neither in the top third of the list in terms of high salaries and extensive amounts of time spent doing legislative business nor in the bottom third where compensation is low and members of the legislature devote little time to doing legislative business. Absent the generous retirement benefits, the Texas Legislature is structurally similar to a citizen legislature. The low level of pay means that most legislators must maintain other forms of income during their legislative careers or before vesting in their retirement. The attempt to have a largely citizen nature to the Texas Legislature is consistent with the mythology of Texas, which demands that government be staffed by average citizens in order to keep legislators honest and serve the people better. In reality, legislators in Texas hold jobs outside the legislature that allow them to take time off when the legislature is in session, often in professions or industries that have a vested interest in state policy. Most Texans simply cannot leave their job for 140 days every other year to serve in the legislature. Thus, many ordinary Texas citizens simply cannot afford to be a legislator.

## QUALIFICATIONS FOR OFFICE AND LENGTH OF TERMS

Individuals elected to the state legislature must meet both formal and informal requirements. Formal requirements are the legal criteria established in the state constitution. To be elected to the Texas House of Representatives, a candidate must be at least twenty-one years of age and have been a resident of Texas for two years and a resident of the district for at least one year. Election to the Texas Senate requires that a candidate be at least twenty-six years of age and have been a resident of Texas for five years and a resident of the district for at least one year. Both senators and representatives must be U.S. citizens and qualified to vote in the state of Texas.[25]

However, some informal elements appear to exist as well. For example, members of the state legislature are typically elected with a **party affiliation**. Members identify themselves to voters as a Democratic candidate, a Republican candidate, or a member

**Party affiliation**
a candidate's identifiable membership in a political party, often listed on an election ballot.

of some other political party. Of course, a party label typically means that the candidate competed in a primary election to win the right to campaign as the party's candidate in the general election. Often another extra-constitutional requirement, then, is a successful run in a **party primary**. This requirement is essential for candidates seeking to run with a Democratic Party label or a Republican Party label. Candidates from other parties, such as the Libertarian Party, need only win the nomination at a party convention. To compete in a party primary requires candidates to be well financed. Once a candidate wins his or her party's nomination in the primary, he or she can then campaign in the general election. While independent candidates do occasionally win election to the legislature without a party label or a primary election, this situation is quite rare.

Like other legislatures, the Texas House of Representatives and the Texas Senate possess the legal right to refuse to seat a winning candidate. Such refusals are extremely rare, however. Several decades ago, a representative from Gillespie County was elected as a write-in candidate. The losing candidate appealed to the Texas House, requesting that it not seat the winner because he had not competed in the primary, had never announced his candidacy, and had never paid a filing fee. The House refused to consider the appeal.[26] The power to decide whether or not an election is valid resides with the legislature. As stated in the Texas Constitution, "Each House shall be the judge of the qualifications and election of its own members; but contested elections shall be determined in such manner as prescribed by law."[27]

The term of office for members of the Texas House of Representatives is two years. Texas senators are elected every four years, but the elections are staggered so that one-half of the Texas Senate is chosen every two years. An exception to this rule involves **redistricting**. After the U.S. Census data is released and the redistricting process to adjust election districts for the legislature is completed, the entire Texas Senate is elected at the next election. Thus, the entire Texas Senate was elected in 2012. Then, by lottery, one-half of the Texas Senate comes up for reelection after just two years—2014 in this case. These individuals then serve a four-year term ending in 2018. The other half of the Texas Senate began a four-year term in 2012. These members are up for reelection in 2016. This process is highly unusual among state legislatures in the United States. Only the legislatures of Illinois and New Jersey have similar arrangements.[28] Typically, terms in office are fixed and are not affected by the redistricting process every decade. Most states have legislatures in which the lower house serves a two-year term and the upper house serves a four-year term.

The timing of elections to the state legislature also varies significantly by state. Some states hold elections simultaneously with elections for the U.S. president and U.S. Congress. Other states hold elections to coincide with midterm elections to the U.S. Congress, for example, in 2006 and 2010. A few states, including Louisiana, conduct elections to the state legislature in the year before elections for U.S. president, such as in 1999, 2003, and 2007. In Texas, elections for the state legislature occur simultaneously with U.S. presidential elections and with midterm elections to the U.S. Congress.

In the 1980s, some states began imposing term limits on their elected representatives. A **term limit** is a legal limitation whereby legislators are limited to a specific number of terms after which they are no longer eligible to serve in the state legislature.

**Party primary**
an electoral contest to win a political party's nomination for the right to appear as its candidate on the ballot in the general election.

**Redistricting**
the periodic adjustment of the lines of electoral district boundaries.

**Term limit**
a legal limitation on the number of terms an elected official may serve in office.

Term limits are typically the result of a **citizen initiative**, or petition drive, rather than self-imposed limits that the legislature itself has enacted. Six states enacted term limits by simply passing a new law, while fifteen states passed term limits by amending their constitutions. Currently, fifteen states have term limits. Some states limit the amount of time an individual may serve in a specific chamber of the legislature. Arkansas and Michigan are typically considered to have the most restrictive limits on the amount of time someone may serve in the state legislature: six consecutive years for the lower house of the state legislature and eight consecutive years for the upper house. Thus, an individual may serve a total of fourteen years in these legislatures, six in one chamber, plus eight in the other. Other states place a limit on the total number of years a person may serve in either chamber of a state legislature. California, since 2012, and Oklahoma, since 1999, allow an individual to serve only twelve years. This limit is cumulative across both houses of their respective legislatures. This time in office may be in a single chamber or across both chambers. Thus, an individual might serve four years in the lower house, plus eight years in the upper house.

Some states simply impose limits on the number of consecutive terms that an individual may serve rather than limit the total number of years. For example, Florida limits members of both houses of its state legislature to a total of eight years. On the surface, this limit seems to be more restrictive than the examples above. However, members of the Florida State Senate hold office for four years. A legislator may serve two consecutive terms, so that she or he served eight years. The legislator may then sit out a term and then be reelected to the Florida State Senate for two more terms. Texas, along with thirty-four other states, does not have term limits.[29]

Proponents of term limits argue that these limits encourage **turnover** in office by requiring incumbents (those currently in office) to step down after a specified number of terms or years in office. Turnover is viewed as important to prevent careerism among politicians who make serving in an elected office their primary occupation and who thereby allegedly lose touch with the needs and concerns of the average voter.

Opponents of term limits often point to their antidemocratic nature. If voters choose to reelect the same person over and over again, that should be their decision to make; voters should not be denied a chosen representative by an arbitrary limit on the number of terms a person may serve. In addition, the experience incumbents acquire through their years of service in the state legislature is often invaluable.

Interestingly, six states abandoned term limits after their adoption. Of these six states, five of them had adopted term limits simply by passing a new law. In three of these states—Massachusetts, Washington, and Wyoming—their respective state supreme courts overturned the term limits as a violation of the state constitution. Idaho and Utah eliminated term limits by action of the state legislature repealing the term limits law. In Oregon, the Oregon Supreme Court found that the amendment to the state constitution that imposed term limits violated another part of the state constitution. Interestingly, the legislators' actions in these states did not lead to a massive outcry by voters. It also did not lead to an anti-incumbency trend to vote out the members of the legislatures who repealed the limits on their own terms in office.

Do term limits actually increase the rate of turnover in office? Evidence from the 2006 elections suggests that they do. Among the fifteen states with the highest rates of turnover in their legislatures, twelve have term limits. California and Nebraska had the highest rates of turnover, at 40.8 percent. Both states have term limits. By comparison, Texas ranked twenty-eighth in the United States in turnover. Sixteen percent of seats in the Texas Legislature changed hands in the 2006 election. Of the fifteen states with the lowest rates of turnover, only Louisiana imposed term limits on its state legislators.[30] Proponents of term limits point to these higher rates of turnover as evidence that term limits are effective in ending political careerism and returning state legislatures to citizen control.

In 2012, turnover in state legislatures averaged 26.6 percent. While this rate was somewhat higher than in prior elections, it reflects the fact that this election was the first for state legislatures since the redistricting process associated with the 2010 census. On average, the fifteen states with term limits had higher rates of turnover, at 35.5 percent, compared to states without term limits. However, New Hampshire, which does not have term limits, led the nation in turnover, and two other states without term limits, Kansas and Idaho, were also in the top ten states in terms of state legislative turnover.[31]

While turnover is often useful to measure the extent of change in membership from one session of the legislature to another, turnover is calculated using election results from legislative election districts in which a sitting official, or incumbent, lost the election and from legislative election districts in which the seat was open. An open seat may occur when the incumbent chooses to retire or dies in office prior to the election. In contrast to turnover, rates of incumbency measure the number of legislators who previously served and were reelected. In general, the rates of incumbency in the Texas Legislature are quite high, never dropping below 70 percent for either chamber since 1997. However, the 2012 election saw the lowest rate of incumbency in the recent history of the Texas House of Representatives. This rate of incumbency reflected the 2011 redistricting of the legislature, which shifted seats from rural areas in western Texas and Deep East Texas to higher-growth areas, such as the Dallas-Fort Worth Metroplex, Houston, and the I-35 corridor from San Antonio through Austin. Usually Texas senators are equally or more likely to be reelected than their counterparts in the Texas House. This trend held despite redistricting for the 2012 election. These rates of incumbency are quite different from the U.S. Congress, where the U.S. Senate has a lower rate of incumbency than the U.S. House. Another low rate of incumbency since 1997 occurred in the 78th Texas Legislature, which met in 2003. In the elections for that legislature in November 2002, Republicans won enough seats to win control over both houses. Each chamber went Republican for the first time in more than 100 years.

The 2008 elections returned 85.3 percent of incumbents to the Texas House of Representatives and 93.5 percent of senators to the 81st Texas Legislature; these rates are the highest rates for the legislature since 1997.[32]

One interesting effect of term limits is an apparent reduction in the number of women serving in state legislatures. In Missouri, Ohio, Arizona, and Florida, each of which observes term limits, the number of women serving in the legislature has gone down. Ironically, the expectation was that term limits would increase the number of women representatives because more open seats would be available. It appears, however, that when female legislators are term-limited out, the candidates recruited

**TABLE 3.3** **Rates of Turnover for the Texas Legislature, 1997–2013**

| Legislature | Year Legislature Met | Year of Election | Rate of Incumbency | |
| --- | --- | --- | --- | --- |
| | | | TX House of Representatives | TX Senate |
| 83 | 2013 | 2012 | 70.7% | 80.6% |
| 82 | 2011 | 2010 | 75.3% | 93.5% |
| 81 | 2009 | 2008 | 85.3% | 93.5% |
| 80 | 2007 | 2006 | 83.3% | 83.9% |
| 79 | 2005 | 2004 | 88.0% | 100.0% |
| 78 | 2003 | 2002 | 75.3% | 77.4% |
| 77 | 2001 | 2000 | 92.7% | 96.7% |
| 76 | 1999 | 1998 | 92.7% | 93.5% |
| 75 | 1997 | 1996 | 82.7% | 80.6% |

*Source:* Adapted from Legislative Reference Library of Texas, "Membership Statistics for the 83rd Legislature," 2013, www.lrl.state.tx.us/legeLeaders/members/memberStatistics.cfm (accessed June 7, 2014).

to run for the open seats are often men. In contrast, states without term limits, such as Maryland and Virginia, have seen an increase in the number of women serving in the legislature.[33]

# THEORIES OF REPRESENTATION

One of the key functions of a legislature is **representation**, or the relationship between the people and their representatives. **Principle-agent theory of representation** suggests that the citizens, or principles, choose someone to speak or act on their behalf. The person speaking or acting on behalf of the principles is called an agent. An analogy is found in our court systems, where a lawyer is hired as an agent to speak to the courts for his or her client, who is the principle. Likewise, actors or sports figures, as principles, hire agents to negotiate contracts and represent them. In principle-agent theory of representation, the agent or representative simply has many, many principles, or citizens who elect the agent. Within principle-agent theory, there are three views on what constitutes an appropriate relationship between a representative and the electorate. According to the **delegate** approach, the people elect a representative to present the views of the district.[34] The legislator as delegate is expected to carry out specific tasks and hold specific positions, regardless of personal beliefs, on issues such as public school funding, crime, and abortion. Essentially, the representative becomes the agent of the majority who elected him or her to office, though majorities can shift as the issues change. In contrast, the **trustee** approach begins by assuming that elected officials have access to information that voters do not.

**Representation**
the relationship between an elected official and the electorate.

**Principle-agent theory of representation**
theory that citizens, or principles, choose someone to speak or act on their behalf in the government.

**Delegate**
an elected official who acts as an agent of the majority that elected her or him to office and carries out, to the extent possible, the wishes of that majority.

**Trustee**
an elected official who is entrusted to act in the best interests of the electorate based on his or her knowledge; he or she is understood to be generally better informed than the broader electorate.

As a result, the representative understands issues from the broader perspective of the best interests of the entire district, state, or country. In this case, the people trust their representative to make the best choices for them when voting in the state legislature. Therefore, the representative, who is better educated about the issue, may go against the wishes of the majority. Finally, the **politico** approach asserts that a representative follows the wishes of the voting majority on the most important issues while on other issues he or she has more leeway.[35] In the latter case, the representative's personal beliefs may conflict with those of the majority, and the representative then must choose between conscience and constituency.

In the United States, representation is connected to the single-member district plurality (SMDP) election system that is used to elect both houses of the U.S. Congress and most state legislatures. This election system implies a certain type of representation: geographic. Texans, and indeed most Americans, assume that a representative serves a specific geographic area. The Texas Senate consists of thirty-one members elected from thirty-one geographic areas of the state (see Map 3.1). So, state senator Charles Schwertner was expected to reflect the views of the people in the ten central Texas counties from which he is elected, while Wendy Davis, whose story opens this chapter, was expected to reflect the views of the people from the portions of Tarrant County who elected her. For the 150 members of the Texas House of Representatives, the size of the district that each member represents is smaller (see Map 3.2). For example, El Paso County contains five districts, while Dallas County contains twelve districts. Thus, Rep. Naomi Gonzalez represented the citizens of a portion of El Paso in the 83rd Legislature, while Joe Moody represented citizens in a different part of the city. However, even in the larger House, a member such as Ken King must still sometimes represent multiple counties because the population is quite low in rural western Texas.

The advantage of geographic representation is the direct connection it provides between the representative and the voters. The voters living in a specific geographic area, or election district, know exactly who their representative is. Voters are assumed to share political values and beliefs based upon where they live, with geography as the primary focus or point of representation. An elected official's gender, race or ethnicity, social economic status, and so forth are not assumed to matter significantly because the representative is from the same community as her or his constituents. On the other hand, this theory assumes that a representative can reflect the view of every person, or at least a majority of the people that elected him or her. Of course, this is not always possible in view of the large number of issues confronting today's legislators. The passage of a **bill**, or a new law or change to an existing law, typically involves numerous and complex considerations. Further complicating matters is the fact that voters often are economically and socially diverse; race, ethnicity, religious background, and other factors shape their understanding of politics, often in opposing ways. Pragmatically, a single representative is unlikely to be able to adequately reflect all of these views.

An alternative approach to representation is the microcosm theory. John Adams, the second president of the United States and an early proponent of the theory, believed that a legislature should look like the larger society.[36] The aim is to have the legislature be as close to a perfect representative sample as possible.[37] The microcosm theory proceeds from the view that, while each individual member cannot truly represent the

**Politico**
an elected official who is expected to follow the wishes of the electorate on some issues but on others is permitted more decision-making leeway; a hybrid of the trustee and delegate.

**Bill**
a proposed new law or change to existing law brought before a legislative chamber by a legislative member.

**MAP 3.1** State Senate Districts in Texas for the November 2014 Elections

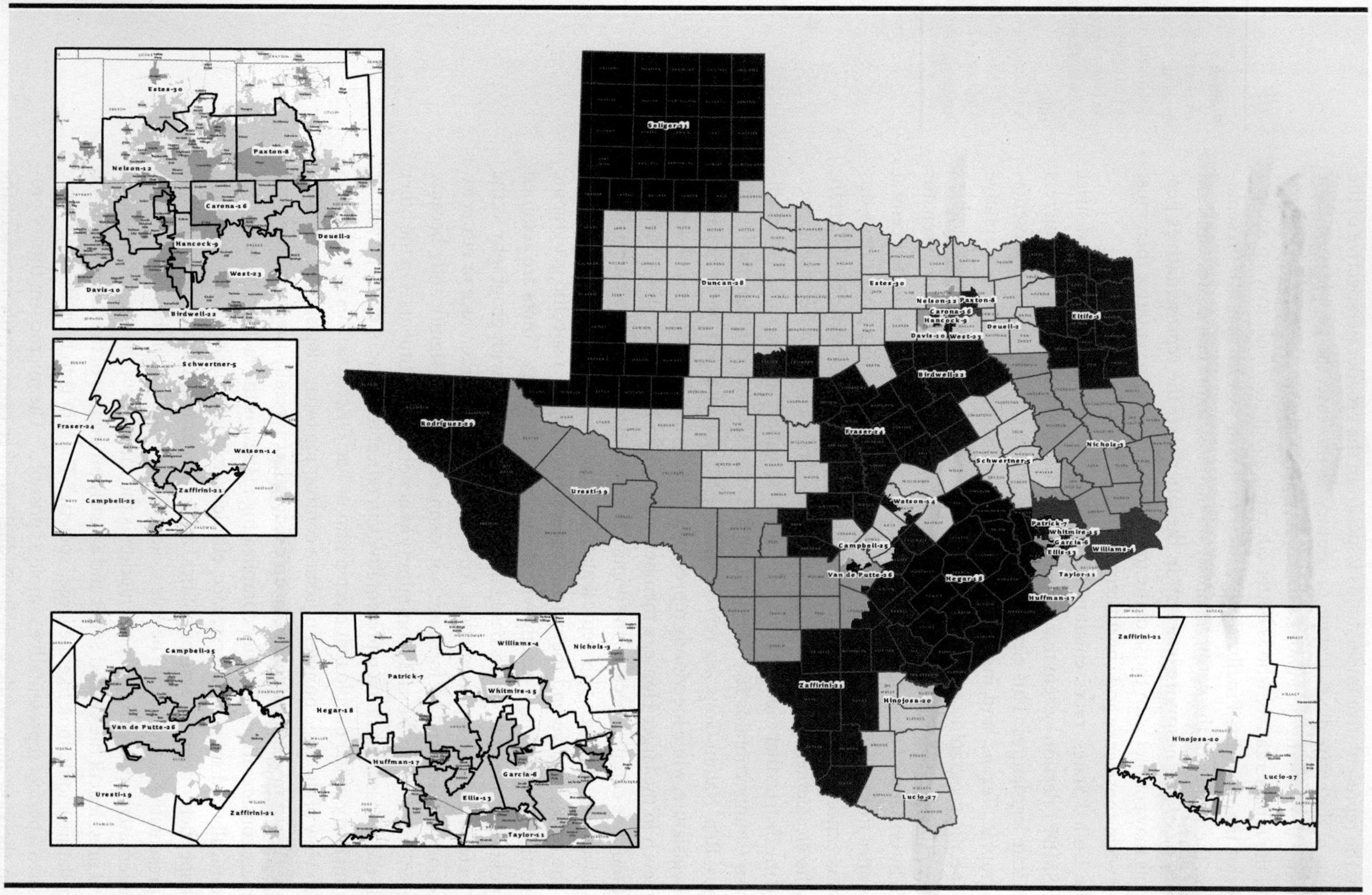

**Source:** Texas Legislative Council, "State Senate Districts, 83rd Legislature, 2013–2014," http://www.tlc.state.tx.us/redist/pdf/senate/map.pdf (accessed August 27, 2014).

**MAP 3.2** State House Districts in Texas for the November 2014 Elections

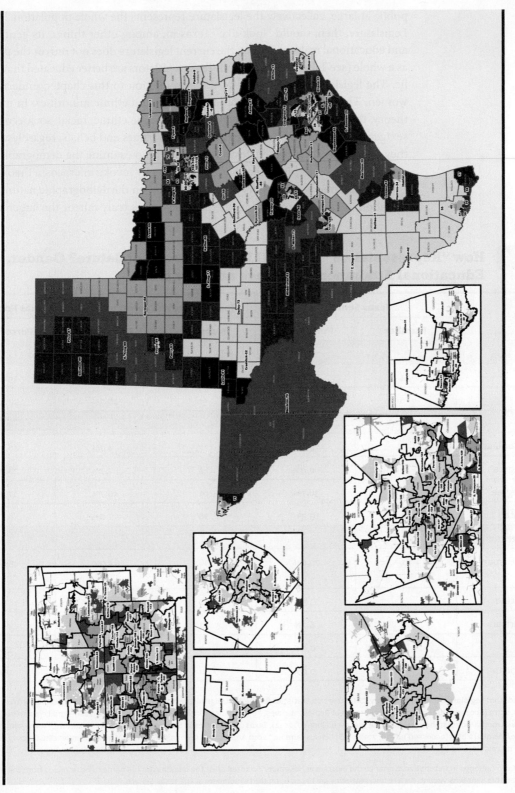

**Source:** Texas Legislative Council, "State House Districts, 83rd Legislature, 2013–2014," http://www.tlc.state.tx.us/redist/pdf/house/map.pdf (accessed August 27, 2014).

public at large, collectively the legislature represents the whole population. The Texas Legislature, then, should "look like" Texas in, among other things, its gender, racial, and educational makeup. In fact, the current legislature does not mirror the population as a whole (see Table 3.4). In general, Texas legislators are better educated than the public. The legislature, as discussed in the introduction to this chapter, underrepresents women. This same observation holds for racial and ethnic minorities. In microcosm theory, the assumption is that people with the same ethnic, racial, socioeconomic, or sex/gender background hold the same political values and beliefs, regardless of where they live. Thus, critics of the Texas Legislature who examine the demographic imbalance of the membership of the legislature indirectly invoke microcosm theory.

Because microcosm theory focuses attention on the demographic nature of representation, it raises awareness of whether legislatures truly mirror the larger society. If

**TABLE 3.4** **How "Representative" Is the 2013–2014 Texas Legislature? Gender, Educational Attainment, and Race and Ethnicity**

| | Texas Senate* | | Texas House of Representatives | | Texas Population |
|---|---|---|---|---|---|
| | Number | Percentage | Number | Percentage | Percentage |
| **Sex** | | | | | |
| Male | 24 | 80.0% | 119 | 79.3% | 49.6% |
| Female | 6 | 20.0% | 31 | 20.7% | 50.4% |
| **Education** | | | | | |
| High school or less | 0 | 0.0% | 7 | 4.7% | 46.0% |
| Two-year degree | 0 | 0.0% | 4 | 2.7% | 28.3% |
| Four-year degree | 11 | 36.7% | 61 | 40.7% | 17.3% |
| Post-graduate | 19 | 63.3% | 78 | 52.0% | 8.5% |
| **Race and Ethnicity** | | | | | |
| White, Non-Hispanic Caucasian | 21 | 70.0% | 96 | 64.0% | 45% |
| Hispanic/Latino | 7 | 23.3% | 30 | 20.0% | 38% |
| African American | 2 | 6.7% | 21 | 14.0% | 12% |
| Asian | 0 | 0.0% | 3 | 2.0% | 4% |
| Native American | 0 | 0.0% | 0 | 0.0% | 1% |

**Sources:** Adapted from Legislative Reference Library, "Membership Statistics for the 83rd Legislature," 2013, www.lrl.state.tx.us/legeLeaders/members/memberStatistics.cfm (accessed June 7, 2014); Texas House of Representatives, "Biographical Data: House of Representatives—83rd Legislature," 2013, www.house.state.tx.us/_media/pdf/members/biodata.pdf (accessed June 10, 2014); Texas Senate, "Texas Senators of the 82nd Legislature," www.senate.state.tx.us/75r/Senate/Members.htm (accessed July 16, 2012); U.S. Census Bureau, "2010 American Community Survey," http://factfinder.census.gov (accessed June 3, 2010); some calculations by author.

* The death of Mario Gallegos in October 2012 prior to the election in November occurred after the deadline for his name to be removed from the ballot. Thus, he was elected, but his seat was vacant. As a result, statistics are based upon thirty members of the Texas Senate.

we assume that a legislator's income, education, race, religion, and gender all shape the decisions that he or she makes, then microcosm theory offers a starting point to address whether the legislature is truly representative of the population. If the legislature looks like the larger society, citizens may accept its legitimacy and decisions more readily. If the legislature does not seem to mirror the larger society, then legitimacy and decisions may be questioned.

Certainly, the Texas Legislature in 2013–2014 did not resemble the larger society of Texas. The legislature collectively was better educated than the average Texan, as shown in Table 3.4. An overwhelming majority of the members of both houses of the Texas Legislature had completed at least a four-year college degree. This stands in sharp contrast to the 17 percent of Texans who had a degree from a four-year institution of higher learning. In addition, most legislators were male, despite the fact that a majority of Texas's population is female.

Similarly, the racial and ethnic makeup of the Texas Legislature is not reflective of the wider population. The legislature is significantly more white/Caucasian compared to the general population. Asian Americans and African Americans in particular were underrepresented in the 2013–2014 legislature. Moreover, despite gains in the overall population, Hispanic representation in the Texas Legislature continues to lag behind that in the wider society.

In addition, the Texas Legislature does not mirror the wider population of Texas in religious identification, as evidenced by the 82nd Legislature (2011–2012). While Roman Catholics in the legislature appear to mirror their concentration in the general population, the number of self-identified Protestant Christians at first glance seems to be underrepresented. However, a significant number of members of the legislature at the time—30 percent—refused to disclose their religious preference or left their preference unspecified. It is quite possible that some in that 30 percent were Protestant Christians but failed to report their preference. In addition, the term *Protestant Christian* is an overarching one that covers a wide range of different members and organizations of Christianity, including Assemblies of God, Baptists, Churches of Christ, the Church of God, Episcopalians, Lutherans, Methodists, Pentecostals, Presbyterians, and nondenominational Christians, among others. These groups differ significantly in their understanding of the role of religion in public life and their orientations toward social issues such as abortion and gay rights. Even within a particular grouping of denominations, differences exist. For example, the Evangelical Lutheran Church in America, the nation's largest Lutheran denomination, is open and accepting of gays and lesbians, as illustrated by its support for gay clergy. However, the nation's second-largest Lutheran denomination, the Lutheran Church-Missouri Synod, is against gay rights. In Texas, these two groups are roughly equal in membership. Whether the legislature reflects these nuances is difficult to tell.

| TABLE 3.5 Religious Affiliation of the 82nd Texas Legislature (2011–2012) | | |
|---|---|---|
| **Religious Affiliation** | **Texas Legislature** | **Texas Population** |
| Protestant Christian | 41% | 57% |
| Catholic Christian | 22% | 24% |
| Other Christian (Orthodox, Jehovah's Witness, etc.) | 5% | 2% |
| Jewish | 2% | 1% |
| Mormon | 0% | 1% |
| Muslim | 0% | 1% |
| Other | 0% | 2% |
| Unspecified/Refused | 30% | 12% |

**Sources:** National Conference of State Legislatures, "Legislator Demographics: State-by-State: Texas," 2012, www.ncsl.org/legislatures-elections/legisdata/legislator-demographic-map.aspx (accessed July 15, 2012); Pew Forum on Religion in Public Life, "Religious Composition of Texas," 2012, religions.pewforum.org/maps (accessed July 15, 2012); U.S. Census Bureau, "2010 American Community Survey," http://factfinder.census.gov (accessed June 3, 2010).

## Barbara C. Jordan

© Everett Collection Inc / Alamy

Barbara Jordan's career in Texas politics represents both personal and institutional victories. Jordan graduated from Boston University Law School. Her first two efforts at winning a seat in the Texas House of Representatives were foiled by a system that chose the twelve members of the House from Harris County at large through a countywide vote that diluted the political strength of minorities. Under this system, even though about 20 percent of Houstonians were African American, none of Harris County's representatives were black. However, the *Baker v. Carr* (1962) and *Reynolds v. Sims* (1964) U.S. Supreme Court decisions required that members of the state legislature had to be elected from districts that were roughly equal in population, thus putting an end to the at-large system. Helped by the newly drawn single-member districts mandated by the Court's decisions and by the removal of the poll tax as a barrier to voting, Jordan was elected to the Texas Senate in 1966 and became the first woman to serve in the Texas Senate and the first African American to serve since 1881.

Initially, Jordan faced insults from some legislators, who called her "Mammy" or "the washerwoman" behind her back.[i] However, Jordan's intelligence and political skills won over many of her fellow legislators, and the Texas Senate unanimously elected her as president pro tempore in 1972. Later that same year, Jordan became the first black woman from the South to win election to the U.S. House of Representatives.

While in the U.S. Congress, Jordan became an important player in the impeachment of President Richard Nixon, delivering a speech in which she declared, "My faith in the Constitution is whole; it is complete; it is total. And I am not going to sit here and be an idle spectator to the diminution, the subversion, the destruction, of the Constitution." In 1976, she became the first African American woman to deliver the keynote address at the Democratic National Convention, delivering what many observers consider one of the best speeches given at a party convention.

While much of what Barbara Jordan accomplished resulted from her character and intelligence, her political career would not have been possible without the Supreme Court opening the door to more representative legislative bodies through its redistricting decisions that protected the representation of minorities.

---

i.  James L. Haley, *Passionate Nation: The Epic History of Texas* (New York: Free Press, 2006), 545.

Proponents of microcosm theory, including at least one U.S. founder, would point toward distrust of the state government as a result of the gap between the makeup of the legislature and the population of Texas. Public policy that results from a nonrepresentative legislature cannot be an accurate reflection of what Texans want from their state government. Yet critics of microcosm theory point out that representation is not just about social and demographic characteristics of voters and legislators. Representation is about geography, values, and beliefs. Just because a representative differs from the wider population in his or her educational background, ethnicity, etc. does not mean that that representative does not share the same values and beliefs of those who elected him or her. After all, enough people supported the representative to get her or him elected.

## WINNERS AND LOSERS

In creating the Texas Legislature, the framers of the Texas Constitution were thinking about who wins and who loses in politics. In theory, citizen legislatures ensure that citizens do not lose in the contest of politics; their purpose is to protect citizen interests over those of the special interests that so frequently dominate legislatures. Unfortunately, in Texas there are several institutional constraints that preclude the establishment of a true citizen legislature. The low level of financial compensation forces most legislators to maintain outside sources of income. Those individuals with higher levels of education, higher incomes, and more flexible work schedules may be in a more favorable position to serve in the Texas Legislature. Given the relatively high cost of campaigns, legislators also need to be able to spend time fund-raising to seek reelection. The average citizen simply can't afford to take the job. Thus, the effort to maintain a "citizen" legislature may result in a legislature that does not in fact "look like" Texas.

If Texas lacks a true citizen legislature, it is reasonable to ask just how representative the state's legislature is. Evaluating the legislature based on microcosm theory suggests that it is unrepresentative, particularly in terms of gender. Hispanics and African Americans in the state are underrepresented as well, though representation of minorities has improved recently and may continue to do so.

★ How do the assumptions of principle-agent theory and microcosm theory differ?

★ How do delegate and trustee theories of representation differ?

★ How would additional increases in the number of women and minorities change the Texas Legislature?

## ELECTING THE STATE LEGISLATURE

Elections to most state legislatures are similar to elections to the U.S. House of Representatives. Typically, states employ some type of **single-member district (SMD)** system—usually the state (or the entire nation in the case of the U.S. House of Representatives) is divided into a number of election districts equal to the membership of the chamber. Thus, for elections to the Texas Senate, the state of Texas is divided into thirty-one districts. Each district elects one and only one person to the chamber. For the Texas House of Representatives, the state is divided into 150 districts. Voters cast a single vote for their most preferred candidate on the ballot. In general

**Single-member district (SMD)** an election system in which the state is divided into many election districts, and each district elects just one person to the state legislature.

**Plurality election**
a type of election in which the candidate with the most votes wins the election.

**Majority election**
a type of election in which a candidate must receive 50 percent of the vote plus one additional vote to be declared the winner; simply winning the most votes is not sufficient.

**Runoff election**
a type of election in SMDM that is held when an election fails to yield a clear majority winner in the initial balloting; the runoff is limited to the top two vote-getters from the initial election, ensuring a majority win.

**Instant runoff**
a type of election in which second-place votes are considered in instances where no candidate has received a majority of the vote; a winner is determined by adding together the first- and second-place votes.

**Multi-member district (MMD)**
an election system in which the state is divided into many election districts, but each district elects more than one person to the state legislature.

elections in Texas, as in most other states, the candidate with the most votes wins the election and the seat in the legislature. This approach is called a **plurality election** and is often called the single-member district plurality (SMDP) system. Other states use a single-member district majority (SMDM) system, which requires the winning candidate to receive a majority of the vote, or 50 percent of the vote plus one additional vote. In a **majority election**, if no candidate receives a majority on the initial vote, a **runoff election** is held, usually two weeks to one month later. Because only the top two candidates from the initial election are included in the runoff election, a majority outcome is guaranteed. This system is used in a handful of states, such as Georgia and Louisiana. A variation of this approach is called the **instant runoff**. In this type of election, voters indicate, in addition to their first choice, who they prefer as a second choice. If no candidate receives a majority at the initial election, the second-place votes are considered and a winner is determined by adding the first- and second-place votes. This system is used to elect the lower house of the Australian national parliament.

The main advantage to SMDM elections is that the winner is selected by the majority of the voters who show up. Texas uses both systems: it uses the SMDP system for general elections to the state legislature, U.S. House of Representatives, and U.S. Senate and the SMDM system for primary elections to state and local offices and to the U.S. Senate and U.S. House of Representatives.

### Single-Member District versus Multi-Member District

Some states use the **multi-member district (MMD)** system to elect their state legislature. In an MMD system, the state is divided into many election districts, but each district elects more than one person to the state legislature. Voters normally cast a single vote for their most preferred candidate on the ballot. After the votes are counted, the candidates with the highest vote totals equal to the number of seats in the district are elected. The advantage of the MMD system is that candidates from more than one political party (or faction of a political party) are able to win a seat from the district. Theoretically, this logic applies to racial and ethnic minorities as well. In practice, at least in the American South (including Texas), multi-member districts have diluted minority representation and allowed whites to overwhelm the state legislature with their candidates. This issue will be explored in more detail below.

For the Texas Senate, the requirement to use the SMDP system was part of the original wording of the Constitution of 1876.[38] However, election districts for the Texas House of Representatives were originally a combination of SMDP and MMD; the MMD system was used sometimes when a county contained enough people to qualify for more than one member of the Texas House of Representatives. Instead of creating separate districts within the county, two or more representatives would represent the entire county. The issue of the impact of these multi-member districts became an important one during the civil rights era of the 1960s. When the U.S. Congress passed the Voting Rights Act of 1965, one of the provisions—discussed later in this chapter—forced a shift in Texas and other states away from the MMD system and to the SMDP or SMDM systems.[39] While the U.S. Supreme Court initially held that the U.S. Constitution's Fourteenth Amendment, specifically the equal protection clause, did not require the use of single-member district election systems in *Fortson v. Dorsey* (1965),[40] the courts found that the MMD system used for the Texas Legislature appeared to depress representation among African Americans and Hispanics.[41] This finding was reinforced a generation later in *Thornburg v. Gingles* (1986).[42] In contrast, the SMDP or SMDM systems can be used to concentrate minority voters into election districts with smaller populations by creating majority-minority districts. In such districts a majority of the population comes from a historically underrepresented racial or ethnic minority. As a result of this concentration of minority voters, more minorities are elected to the legislature, and candidates are more responsive to minority voters. Texas has used the SMDP system since the 1970s for both houses of its legislature.

The use of MMD or SMD to elect the state legislature has additional consequences for demographic representation. Evidence exists that the use of MMD systems may increase the number of women elected to state legislatures. For example, in 2013, five of the ten states with the highest levels of women in the state legislature used MMD for one or both houses. More systematic studies over the past few decades have found that MMD systems tend to be associated with higher rates of women being elected to state legislatures, while states that switched from MMD to SMD experienced declines in the number of women elected.[43]

## Redistricting Games

One of the challenges of the single-member district (SMD) system is the regular need to redraw district lines. This need occurs because population changes over time. Population change occurs at uneven rates within a state. If election district lines for the state legislature remain fixed, then over time some areas will have many more people per representative than other areas. Consider the fact that Nacogdoches County in eastern Texas, home of the oldest city in the state, had a population of 9,614 residents in 1870, just prior to the creation of the current state constitution. That same census found that Dallas County had 13,314 residents.[44] By 2000, Nacogdoches County, with a population of 59,203,[45] had nowhere near the population of Dallas County, at 2,218,899.[46] In 1876, Dallas County and Nacogdoches County were equally represented in the Texas House of Representatives, with one member each. Obviously, if redistricting never occurred, Nacogdoches County would be drastically overrepresented in the state legislature today, and Dallas County would be drastically underrepresented. This situation violates the principle of **one person, one vote**, which requires that the vote of any one person carry the equivalent weight of the vote of any other person. Without any redistricting, a resident of Nacogdoches in an election would carry greater weight than a resident of Dallas. Redistricting in Texas normally occurs every ten years, after the results of the U.S. Census are provided to the states.

Historically, state legislatures in many states were redistricted by simply adding new seats as the state's population grew and shifted. Growing counties were rewarded with more seats; those with declining populations or no population growth did not lose representation. Texas followed this pattern in the late 1800s and early 1900s. Between 1921 and 1951, the Texas Legislature neither redistricted nor added new seats, despite periods of rapid population growth in some parts of the state and population decline

**One person, one vote**
shorthand term for the requirement of the U.S. Supreme Court that election districts should be roughly equal in population.

# Redistricting Process in Texas

## Texas Legislature

| | |
|---|---|
| **Redistricting Texas's seats in the U.S. House of Representatives** | **Redistricting itself and other agencies like the Texas State Board of Education** |

↓

**U.S. Court approves the plan or rejects it and sends it back to the legislature to fix**

**State or federal court invalidates the Texas Legislature's plan and sends it back to the legislature to fix**

**OR**

**Texas Legislature cannot agree to a redistricting plan**

↓

**Legislative Redistricting Board (LRB), comprised of the lieutenant governor, Speaker of the Texas House, attorney general, comptroller of accounts, and commissioner of the General Land Office, takes on redistricting**

↓

**LRB draws up a redistricting plan**

↓

**LRB submits its plan to the Texas Legislature for approval**

↓

**The final plan by the legislature is enacted or used in the next election after approval by state or federal court**

in others. The Texas Constitution specified that the Texas Senate contain thirty-one members, and the Texas House of Representatives originally held ninety-three members. Since a 1999 amendment was added to the Texas Constitution, the membership of the Texas House of Representatives has been set at 150.[47]

Because the Texas Legislature can no longer simply add seats to either chamber, one of the challenges is to ensure one person, one vote by drawing districts of roughly equal size based upon population. The Texas Legislature is responsible for drawing the lines for its own election districts as well as those for the state's board of education and the state's seats in the U.S. House of Representatives. Counties, cities, and other local governments also redistrict every ten years, but these governments are responsible for their own redistricting. The state legislature must abide by a number of federal rules and guidelines when drawing election districts. First, the landmark Voting Rights Act of 1965 (VRA) and similar laws seek to ensure the fair representation of minorities who have historically faced discrimination. While the VRA initially applied to African Americans, the law has since expanded to include Asian Americans, Native Americans, and Hispanics. A key provision of the VRA was that the federal government must approve any change to election laws in states with a history of discrimination. However, in the summer of 2013, the U.S. Supreme Court eliminated the requirement that states receive prior approval from the U.S. Department of Justice before passing a redistricting plan.[48] The U.S. Department of Justice can still bring court cases against states for redistricting if the redistricting engages in discrimination, but the action by the national government must occur after the fact. In addition, the burden of proof shifts from states with a history of discrimination proving that they are not engaged in discrimination to the national government proving that a state continues to engage in discrimination.

In a second guideline intended to boost the number of minorities that win election to the state legislature, the federal government encourages the creation of majority-minority districts. A **majority-minority district** is an election district in which the majority of the population comes from a racial or ethnic minority. In Texas, majority-minority districts have been established to benefit African American or Hispanic populations. In *Hunt v. Cromartie* (1999),[49] the U.S. Supreme Court ruled that while race can be one factor in drawing Texas's district lines, it cannot be the only factor. The Supreme Court in this case reaffirmed earlier decisions, such as *Shaw v. Reno* (1993)[50] and *Miller v. Johnson* (1995).[51] Yet the Court continued to rule that the drawing of district lines for partisan advantage remains acceptable as long as the principle of one person, one vote established by the U.S. Supreme Court in *Baker v. Carr* is followed. Interestingly, just because a district is drawn to be majority-minority does not necessarily mean that a racial or ethnic minority will win the seat. In 1991, Gene Green, an Anglo Democrat, won a newly drawn Hispanic majority seat for the U.S. House of Representatives from the Houston area. Likewise, El Paso voters in the largely Hispanic 16th Congressional District threw out incumbent Silvestre Reyes in the Democratic primary for Robert O'Rourke.[52]

The Texas Constitution imposes its own restrictions on redistricting in the Texas Legislature. First, districts must be contiguous, meaning that a person should be able to travel from one part of the district to another without leaving the district. In other words, a district must be a single, unbroken entity and cannot be divided into two or more parts separated

**Majority-minority district**
an election district in which the majority of the population comes from a racial or ethnic minority.

AP Photo/Eric Gay

Lydia Camarillo, co-chair of the Texas Latino Redistricting Task Force, addresses the media following a hearing in federal court on Wednesday, February 15, 2012, in San Antonio. The task force was one of several civil rights groups that raised concerns about the redistricting process used by the Texas Legislature during the 2011 regular session.

entirely by other districts. Second, districts must respect county boundaries as much as possible. Third, districts should be drawn to be as compact as possible, meaning that the district should not be dispersed across wide geographic areas unless unavoidable. Finally, the state must now use the SMDP system. The MMD system is not permitted.

Redistricting at the state level occurs through one of three methods. The most simple is that the legislature itself conducts the redistricting. Many states allow the legislature to draw and redraw district lines. Obviously, the ability of members of the state legislature to define their own election districts encourages incumbents to draw district lines to their political advantage, a process referred to as **gerrymandering**. In some states, a commission separate from the legislature develops a redistricting plan that the legislature must later approve on a final vote with little or no amendment to the plan. These states attempt to remove politics from the process as much as possible and, more importantly, to prohibit the members of the state legislature from drawing their own district lines. In doing so, the expectation is to limit gerrymandering and incumbency. Several types of commissions exist. Some states, such as Alaska, Colorado, and Vermont, establish a commission from nominations made by the governor, state supreme court justices, and/or members of the legislature. In states such as Arkansas and Ohio, members of the state executive branch, such as the governor and attorney general, make up the commission that develops the redistricting plan. Some states, including Idaho, New Jersey, and Pennsylvania, have commissions appointed by the legislature itself. Finally, a few states rely on a **nonpartisan or bipartisan independent commission**. These states, which include California and Arizona, remove direct political control from the process even more extensively by having unelected government officials appoint the redistricting commission. In all of these cases and types, the commission must develop the redistricting plan for the legislature to approve.

In Texas, the state legislature is responsible for redistricting, with one important modification. If the legislature is unable to pass a redistricting plan, the process is handed over to the **Legislative Redistricting Board (LRB)**. This system, and similar ones in states such as Connecticut, Mississippi, and Oklahoma, is called a hybrid system because the redistricting occurs through a combination of the legislature and some other body that includes membership from outside the legislature. The redistricting commission or board in this system only serves in an advisory capacity and only when the legislature

# TEXAS (VS) NORTH DAKOTA

Texas and North Dakota could not be more different. Texas is the second-largest state in the country in terms of population. North Dakota, with 675,905 people, ranks forty-eighth; only Vermont and Wyoming have fewer people. Population growth rates in Texas make the Lone Star State one of the fastest-growing states in the nation. North Dakota ranks near the bottom in growth. Texas is a highly urbanized state. North Dakota remains essentially rural.

Another difference between the two is found in their election processes. In North Dakota and a few other states, the lower house of the state legislature is chosen through a multi-member district (MMD) system. Each election district chooses two members of the lower house of the North Dakota Legislature. Each voter in North Dakota casts two votes in his or her election district. The top two vote-getters win seats in the North Dakota House of Representatives. The ninety-four members of the North Dakota House are selected every four years from forty-seven election districts. Elections are staggered so that odd-numbered districts elect their representatives in a given election year, followed two years later by even-numbered districts choosing their representatives. Other states using this system include Idaho, New Jersey, South Dakota, Washington, and West Virginia.

Because each district elects more than one representative, the possibility exists that candidates from both political parties will be elected to office. In some elections, as many as one in three election districts elects one Republican and one Democrat to serve in the North Dakota House. In such cases, voters from both political parties have a representative from their district.

The MMD system may encourage greater party competition than the single-member district system used in Texas. Parties have a greater incentive to run candidates. Getting elected in North Dakota means securing either first or second place, not just first place. Of course, parties also have an incentive to run more than one candidate in each district. In contrast to Texas, as discussed in Chapter 10, North Dakota has relatively few districts in which the two major parties do not compete. In 2008, for example, every district saw both Republican and Democratic candidates competing for office. In 2006, only three districts lacked a candidate from both major parties.

## Split Results in Recent Elections to the North Dakota House of Representatives

| Result | 2012 | 2010 | 2008 | 2006 | 2004 | 2002 |
|---|---|---|---|---|---|---|
| Two Republicans elected | 75% | 71% | 57% | 42% | 61% | 62% |
| One Republican, one Democrat elected | 13% | 13% | 17% | 33% | 22% | 17% |
| Two Democrats elected | 13% | 17% | 26% | 26% | 17% | 21% |

*Sources:* North Dakota Secretary of State, "General Election—November 5, 2002," https://apps.nd.gov/sec/emspublic/gp/electionresultssearch.htm?searchType=STATE&electionDate=11052002&cmd=Search&showMap=N (accessed August 28, 2014); North Dakota Secretary of State, "General Election—November 2, 2004," https://apps.nd.gov/sec/emspublic/gp/electionresultssearch.htm?searchType=STATE&electionDate=11022004&cmd=Search&showMap=N (accessed May August 28, 2014); North Dakota Secretary of State, "General Election—November 7, 2006," https://apps.nd.gov/sec/emspublic/gp/electionresultssearch.htm?searchType=STATE&electionDate=11072006&cmd=Search&showMap=N (accessed August 28, 2014); North Dakota Secretary of State, "General Election—November 4, 2008," https://apps.nd.gov/sec/emspublic/gp/electionresultssearch.htm?searchType=STATE&electionDate=11042008&cmd=Search&showMap=N (accessed August 28, 2014); North Dakota Secretary of State, "General Election—November 2, 2010," http://results.sos.nd.gov/ (accessed August 28, 2014); North Dakota Secretary of State, "General Election—November 6, 2012," http://results.sos.nd.gov/resultsSW.aspx?eid=35&text=Race&type=LG&map=DIST (accessed June 7, 2014).

## THINKING *Critically*

★ Do you think the MMD system in North Dakota encourages greater party competition?

★ What do you think are advantages of the MMD system?

★ What do you think are advantages of the SMD system?

★ Are there any drawbacks to either system?

★ Which system would you prefer?

★ Do you think Texas should maintain its SMD system of elections for the Texas House of Representatives? Why or why not?

itself fails to pass a redistricting plan on its own. The LRB in Texas, which was created by a 1948 amendment to the state constitution, is composed of the lieutenant governor, the Speaker of the Texas House of Representatives, the attorney general, the comptroller of accounts, and the commissioner of the General Land Office. The LRB develops a plan for redistricting that is submitted to the state legislature for approval. The board also becomes involved in redistricting the state legislature when a state or federal court invalidates a plan approved by the state legislature. However, the LRB redistricts only the state legislature. The task of drawing election districts for the members of the U.S. House of Representatives from Texas remains the exclusive domain of the state legislature.

Recent efforts at redistricting in the past decade illustrate the politics behind the redistricting process. In 2000, Texas faced the unusual situation of divided control over the state legislature, with Republicans controlling the Texas Senate and Democrats controlling the Texas House of Representatives. This transition occurred with the rise of the Republican Party and the end of the era of Democratic Party dominance. An impasse developed. The two chambers could not reconcile their differences to pass a final redistricting plan. When the legislature was unable to pass a redistricting plan, the LRB developed a proposal that became the basis of redistricting the Texas Legislature. This plan was authored by Attorney General John Cornyn, a Republican, and passed on a 3 to 2 vote in the LRB with support from Comptroller Carole Keeton Rylander and Land Commissioner David Dewhurst. The plan ensured that Republicans increased their majority in the Texas House of Representatives.[53]

However, redistricting for U.S. House of Representatives seats also became a contentious issue. With the Texas Legislature unable to arrive at a consensus, the federal courts stepped in and drew the lines to favor both Democratic and Republican incumbents. Following the 2002 elections, Republicans gained control of the Texas House of Representatives and retained control over the Texas Senate. With Republicans now in charge of both houses of the state legislature and the governorship, U.S. House of Representatives Majority Leader Tom DeLay (R–Sugarland) proposed to Republican leaders in the state legislature a plan to redistrict Texas. DeLay sought to increase the number of Texas seats controlled by Republicans. After intense debate in the state legislature during the regular session, Governor Rick Perry called the Texas Legislature into special session three times in order to complete redistricting. In the middle of this political drama, Democratic members of the Texas House fled to Oklahoma and later to New Mexico in attempts to prevent the quorum necessary to conduct business. However, the state legislature did eventually pass a mid-decade redistricting plan. In the 2004 elections, the new district lines yielded Texas Republicans a net gain of six seats in the U.S. House of Representatives.

Almost immediately, this mid-decade redistricting plan was challenged in federal courts by civil rights groups in Texas. Remember that due to the state's past history of discrimination redistricting maps must be approved by the federal government before Texas can use the new districts in an election. Attorneys for the civil rights groups identified three issues for the U.S. Supreme Court to examine. First, did the mid-decade redistricting violate the U.S. Constitution? Second, did the new districts disenfranchise minority voters by diluting their votes and downplaying their growing strength in violation of the Voting Rights Act of 1965? Third, were the district lines drawn in such a partisan manner as to violate earlier U.S. Supreme Court rulings? In 2006, the U.S. Supreme Court issued a decision in *LULAC v. Perry* (2006).[54] The Court stated that the mid-decade redistricting was permissible and held that the Texas districts were not drawn in an excessively partisan manner so as to completely dilute Democratic voters. Finally, the Court did find that some of the district lines violated the Voting Rights Act of 1965, primarily by reducing the strength of Hispanic voters in at least one district. These unacceptable district lines were redrawn to solve the problem identified by the U.S. Supreme Court. Thus, the transition to Republican Party control of the Texas Legislature ushered in a new era of partisan politics. Redistricting battles shifted from the tradition of defending the reelection chances of incumbents of both parties to securing partisan control over the U.S. House of Representatives and the Texas Legislature for the majority party.

Remember that the Texas Legislature is tasked with passing redistricting plans for itself, the Texas seats in the U.S. House of Representatives, and other agencies, such as the Texas State Board of Education. When the 82nd Legislature tackled the issue of redistricting after the 2010 census during the 2011 regular session, the process was quite different from that in 2003. With Republicans firmly in control of both houses of the Texas Legislature, the redistricting debates were less rancorous. As mentioned above, the Texas Legislature had to shift seats in the Texas House of Representatives away from rural areas in the state to faster-growing regions. For example, East Texas grew at rates far slower than the Dallas-Fort Worth Metroplex, the I-35 corridor in Central Texas, and the Greater Houston area. As a result, East Texas lost representation in the Texas House of Representatives so that seats might be shifted toward higher-population areas of the state. Such decisions are not without consequences, and they sometimes create intraparty rivalries. For example, redistricting directly affected several members of the state legislature in early 2012 when the first primary elections using the new districts for the Texas Legislature occurred. Wayne Christian, a long-serving member of the Texas House of Representatives, lost his primary election bid to the former mayor of Marshall, Chris Paddie. Christian lost a significant part of his old district and picked up several counties along the Texas-Louisiana border—areas in which he was less known and in which he had to campaign for the first time.[55] A similar battle occurred in West Texas, a Republican-dominated area of the state with many long-serving Republicans. There were no opportunities to keep all of the Republican incumbents by reducing the number of seats dominated by Democrats.[56] In an interesting development, some long-serving Republicans found themselves in drastically redrawn districts even in urban areas of the state. Representative Barbara Nash (R–Arlington) was given a significantly altered district by her own party in which only about 20 percent of the redrawn district was in her original district. Many voters in her newly drawn district lived in surrounding communities in the eastern portions of Travis County, including Mansfield and Grand Prairie, where her opponents in the Republican primary election, Pat Carlson and Matt Krause, were better known.[57] Ultimately, Nash lost the primary to Krause.

While the legislature passed bills into law during the 2011 session that redrew the districts for both houses of the Texas Legislature, the attempt to redistrict Texas's seats in the U.S. House of Representatives failed. The issue reemerged during the 2011 special session in June, but again the legislature struggled to pass a redistricting plan that both houses could agree upon. Ironically, the task of redistricting the seats in the U.S. House of Representatives should have arguably been the easiest task. As a result of population growth that outpaced all other states in the United States, Texas gained four new seats in the U.S. House, boosting the Texas delegation to thirty-six. No sitting member of

# TEXAS (VS) ARIZONA

Redistricting in Texas leaves the process in the hands of the Texas Legislature and the Legislative Redistricting Board (LRB), all elected officials with a vested interest in engineering district lines. For members of the legislature, protecting incumbents of both parties or securing gains for their party in the legislature can be important. For members of the LRB, assisting their party in gaining or retaining control of the legislature also matters. However, the implications for wider issues, such as partisan control over state delegations to the U.S. House of Representatives, are apparent from the recent battles in Texas.

Arizona voters in 2000 approved Proposition 106, which amended the Arizona Constitution to create an independent commission to oversee redistricting for the state legislature and U.S. House of Representatives. The Arizona Independent Redistricting Commission consists of five persons.[i] By law, two members are Democrats, two members are Republicans, and one member is independent. All five must have maintained the same party affiliation, or no affiliation in the case of the independent, for at least the previous three years. In addition, all five members cannot have served as public officials, lobbyists, campaign workers, or political party officials in the three years prior to their appointment. Nominees are compiled by another independent commission charged with making nominations to Arizona appellate courts and are presented to the leadership of the Arizona Legislature for final appointment.

Proposition 106 contains explicit language to specify how the commission carries out the redistricting process.[ii] For example, the initial mapping of electoral districts cannot consider party affiliations of voters or the history of voting in existing districts. The commission must follow the guidelines of the Voting Rights Act of 1965, other legislation passed by Congress, and relevant rulings by the courts. District lines are to be compact and to respect the boundaries of existing communities, counties, and cities. Also, districts are expected to be competitive between Democratic and Republican candidates. This provision is tested only after the initial plan is developed. Thus, highly gerrymandered districts that clearly favor one party or another are not possible in Arizona.

## THINKING *Critically*

★ How does the system of the Arizona Independent Redistricting Commission attempt to depoliticize the redistricting process?

★ Does Arizona's system accomplish this goal? Why or why not?

★ Has redistricting affected your hometown? Would you like to see your state adopt such a plan?

---

i. Arizona Independent Redistricting Commission, "Frequently Asked Questions," www.azredistricting.org/?page=faq (accessed August 28, 2014).

ii. Arizona Independent Redistricting Commission, "Proposition 106," http://azredistricting.org/2001/Prop-106.asp (accessed August 28, 2014).

---

the U.S. House of Representative faced elimination of his or her district as occurred in slow-growth states, such as Michigan. In the political wrangling that occurred in the special session, the Texas Senate narrowly passed Senate Bill 22, which created an independent redistricting commission of citizens similar to the system used in Arizona (see Texas versus Arizona Box for details). If the bill had passed the Texas House of Representatives, future decisions would have been made by the commission, with the legislature merely approving the plan. However, the bill died in the Texas House. The political drama continued into the fall of 2011 and spring of 2012. Federal courts, including the U.S. Supreme Court, were pulled into the fray as the courts began drawing districts as a result of legal challenges to the proposed districts. The Mexican American Legislative Caucus (MALC), consisting of Mexican Americans in the Texas Legislature, also filed challenges to the maps that the legislature approved for itself. The challenge from the MALC and other Hispanic civil rights groups was that the districts were designed to dilute Hispanic votes and decrease Hispanic representation. The MALC charged that the districts violated the Voting Rights Act of 1965 and the Fourteenth

Amendment's equal protection clause. These accusations seemed more credible given the large increases in the Hispanic population relative to the Anglo population and the relative discrepancy that already existed between the makeup of Texas's population and the makeup of the Texas Legislature. African American civil rights organizations, such as the NAACP, also raised concerns about the effects of redistricting. The federal district court in San Antonio convened a three-judge panel that threw out the work of the Texas Legislature and drew new lines for the Texas Senate, Texas House of Representatives, and Texas's seats in the U.S. House of Representatives that complied with federal laws and U.S. Supreme Court rulings—or so it thought. However, the U.S. Supreme Court blocked the use of the districts drawn by the court in San Antonio in order to hear arguments from the state of Texas, represented by Texas attorney general Greg Abbott, on the intent of the legislature during the redistricting process.[58] In the end, the MALC reached agreement with Abbott, who was tasked with representing the state government and legislature before the courts, but the NAACP did not.[59] While negotiations took place between the attorney general and the various civil rights groups, the spring 2012 primary elections for the political parties to nominate their candidates for the Texas Legislature and U.S. Congress were placed in jeopardy, as were the presidential primaries. Agreement was reached on new maps in late February. The primaries were pushed back from March into April, and finally to May 29 to meet the timetables for nominating candidates, voter registration, and ballot preparation.

The Texas Legislature addressed the redistricting issue again during its 2013 session, seeking to replace the court-imposed plan used for the 2012 elections with a legislative-approved plan for elections beginning in November of 2014. As mentioned at the start of the chapter, the failure to pass a redistricting plan during the regular session of the legislature resulted in the issue being added to the call by Governor Perry for the first special session. In that session, the Texas Legislature passed final redistricting plans for both houses of the legislature and the thirty-six Texas seats in the U.S. House of Representatives. These plans were similar to plans introduced in the 2011 session of the 82nd Legislature. After the U.S. Supreme Court overturned parts of the 1965 Voting Rights Act in *Shelby v. Holder*, the Texas Legislature passed its redistricting plans, and Governor Perry asked the federal courts to dismiss the pending cases challenging redistricting in Texas because the Court had invalidated the need for preclearance, a key reason for the pending cases.[60] A San Antonio panel of federal judges permitted the new plans adopted during the special session to be used for the 2014 elections and beyond.[61]

## WINNERS AND LOSERS

The type of electoral system used can have substantial impacts on the degree of representation in a state. In Texas, the use of SMD has the advantage of increasing representation of ethnic and racial minorities, in part through the creation of majority-minority districts. By contrast, multi-member districts are theoretically more likely to give more women a voice in the political system. Thus, the use of the SMD system, while favoring Hispanics and African Americans in Texas, may sacrifice more equal representation for women. The legitimacy of a democracy is based, in part, on equal representation in government. That means that when we have a government in which racial and ethnic minorities and women are well represented, all Texans are winners. Decisions about election systems are not always about win-win solutions. By using SMD, Texas may be unintentionally trading greater representation for Hispanics and African Americans for less representation for women. A possible solution would be to encourage more women of all racial and ethnic groups to run for office.

Historically, the redistricting process for both houses of the Texas Legislature and the Texas districts in the U.S. House of Representatives resulted from bipartisan cooperation to protect incumbents. This approach resulted in a political powerhouse in the U.S. House that was able to deliver goods for Texans regardless of party. Since 2000, redistricting battles have both highlighted and exacerbated the increased divisiveness in the Texas Legislature. The 2000 battle to redistrict the Texas Legislature was followed by the 2002 fight to redraw the map for the Texas delegation to the U.S. House. Dominance of the Texas Legislature in 2011 and 2013 by Republicans allowed them to control the process in ways to favor their party through gerrymandering. Historically, bipartisan cooperation in the Texas Legislature created norms of cooperation that carried over to the U.S. congressional delegation, allowing Texas's congresspeople to secure a greater share of U.S. government spending and greater influence over national legislation. The rise of partisanship within the Texas Legislature is likely to make all Texans losers if such norms are reinforced in an increasingly partisan U.S. Congress.

★ How important is minority representation in government?
★ Does Texas need more minority representation?
★ What are the likely costs of increased partisanship in the Texas Legislature?

## CONCLUSION

The Texas Legislature is a mixture of tradition and transformation. It remains an outlier in terms of its biennial sessions and relatively low pay, and it is significantly more homogeneous than the wider population it represents. The legislature is more male, better educated, and more Anglo than Texas as a whole. Finally, the legislature continues to experience relatively high rates of incumbency and low rates of turnover, a characteristic it shares with many other state legislatures. Continuity with the past is still present, but transformation is occurring, if slowly. Over the past few decades, the percentage of women in the legislature has increased, even though this number still lags behind that of other state legislatures. Changes in the makeup of Texas's population, including a rise in the number of Hispanics, challenge the demographic makeup of the legislature, especially in light of the microcosm theory. Yet the single-member district system focuses attention on geographic representation and on principle-agent theories of representation. The battles over redistricting in the 2011 and 2013 sessions reflect the changing nature of Texas, which is challenged by the need to accommodate the increasingly diverse state population in terms of representation and to reflect the population shift from rural East Texas and West Texas to more urbanized, metropolitan areas.

for CQ Press

Sharpen your skills with **SAGE edge** at **edge.sagepub.com/collier4e**. **SAGE edge for students** provides a personalized approach to help you accomplish your coursework goals in an easy-to-use learning environment.

## KEY TERMS

bicameral (p. 78)

bill (p. 93)

citizen initiative (p. 90)

citizen legislature (p. 86)

delegate (p. 92)

gerrymandering (p. 104)

instant runoff (p. 100)

Legislative Redistricting Board (LRB) (p. 104)

majority election (p. 100)

majority-minority district (p. 103)

multi-member district (MMD) (p. 100)

nonpartisan or bipartisan independent commission (p. 104)

one person, one vote (p. 101)

party affiliation (p. 88)

party primary (p. 89)

plurality election (p. 100)

politico (p. 93)

principle-agent theory of representation (p. 92)

professional legislature (p. 86)

redistricting (p. 89)

regular session (p. 82)

representation (p. 92)

runoff election (p. 100)

single-member district (SMD) (p. 99)

special session (p. 84)

supermajority (p. 84)

term limit (p. 89)

trustee (p. 92)

turnover (p. 90)

## CORE ASSESSMENT

1. Does Texas need to develop a more professional legislature like that of California and New York?

2. What disadvantages are there to Texas developing a more professional legislature?

3. Which demographic characteristics of the Texas Legislature are most similar to the state's population? Which ones are the least similar?

4. How does the lack of diversity in the Texas Legislature potentially impact the types of laws considered and passed?

5. Suppose you are a member of the Texas Legislature. How would you balance your personal political beliefs with the need to represent all of your constituents?

# 4 LEGISLATIVE ORGANIZATION AND PROCESS

Following the selection of the Speaker of the Texas House of Representatives in January 2013 at the opening of the 83rd Texas Legislature, the House appeared to return to normalcy after a decade of wandering around a metaphorical "Oz" in which competition for the Speaker position was abundant. The incumbent Speaker, Joe Straus (R–San Antonio), was reelected on a unanimous voice vote of acclamation. Not a single member of the Texas House abstained or voted against Straus.[1] Challenges to his leadership by Bryan Hughes (R–Mineola) and David Simpson (R–Longview) had materialized between the November 2012 election and the opening day of the 83rd Legislature in January 2013. However, by mid-December 2012, Straus was claiming that more than 100 of the 150 members of the Texas House backed his reelection, more than enough to thwart attempts by Hughes and Simpson to unseat him.[2]

Behind-the-scenes politicking by Straus ensured his reelection to the Speakership for a third term, and Hughes and Simpson withdrew from the contest. In his nomination speech in support of Straus, which was delivered on the floor of the Texas House at its first meeting in January 2013, John Zerwas (R–Fort Bend) highlighted Straus's conservative credentials of fiscal management, local control over educational institutions, and leadership style. Another nomination speech from René Oliveira (D–Cameron County) highlighted Straus's ability to build consensus, a theme echoed by Senfronia Thompson (D–Humble).[3]

The reelection of Straus reflected a return to the traditionally unanimous, perfunctory election of the Speaker of the Texas House. For example, the last Democratic Speaker, Pete Laney, received unanimous support from the 150 members of the chamber for his election in January 2001. Laney and his supporters had used a series of behind-the-scenes discussions since the November 2000 election to build bipartisan support for his reelection when the legislature met for its regular session in January. Not only did every Democratic member of the Texas House vote for Laney, every Republican member did as well, despite the fact that he was a candidate from the opposition party. Unanimous or near-unanimous election was the norm in the Texas House of Representatives prior to 2002.

Pete Laney's tenure ended not because of dissatisfaction within his own party over his leadership but because of the loss of the Democratic majority; the advent

of Republican control over the chamber in 2003 resulted in the first Republican Speaker in the modern era, Tom Craddick (R–Midland). However, Craddick's autocratic style of leadership garnered him many critics. Craddick was accused of using procedural tricks to deny opponents in his own party the right to speak during procedural motions,[4] and he also claimed he had the absolute power to recognize members during regular debates or procedural motions.[5] Craddick alienated his fellow Republicans, resulting in 20 percent of the Texas House voting against him for Speaker in January 2007,[6] an unusually high level of opposition in the modern era. This, coupled with the loss of seats to the Democrats during the November 2008 election for the legislature, changed the dynamics of support for the Speaker. Attitudes within the Texas House and in the general public seemed to shift in favor of a more bipartisan approach to the workings in the House. Two years later, as the 81st Texas Legislature opened its session in January 2009, the members of the Texas House replaced Craddick with relative newcomer Joe Straus III (R–San Antonio) on a unanimous vote.[7]

Joe Straus was reelected Speaker of the Texas House by a unanimous vote in 2013. The Speaker is one of the most powerful positions in Texas government.

Straus's embrace of "normal" operations—that is, a more bipartisan approach in which the majority party works with the minority party to produce a broader consensus approach to legislation—reflects the style used by Speakers such as Pete Laney and his predecessors in the Democratic-controlled House throughout most of the twentieth century. This bipartisanship was the subject of Republican dissatisfaction during the 2009 House session, and some planned to replace Straus with an even more conservative leader prior to the start of the 82nd Legislature in January 2011.[8] Although Straus was in fact reelected,[9] fifteen members of the Texas House—almost all Republican— voted against him, and Straus's Speakership continued to cause controversy within the Republican Party in the spring of 2012.

During the Republican primaries in May 2012, three of Straus's key supporters lost their elections to more conservative Republicans who opposed Straus.[10] By the Texas Republican Convention in June 2012, grassroots opposition to Straus included complaints about his perceived bipartisanship, softness on immigration, advocacy of airport pat-downs, and lack of commitment to pro-life positions.[11] In the end, Straus was able to quell opposition and be reelected as Speaker the normal way—by a voice vote of unanimous support—by the time of the regular session that started in the spring of 2013. But as a glance at the last few years will show, it was a long battle.

The Speaker of the Texas House is one of the most powerful positions in Texas government. He or she exercises tremendous power and influence over which bills become law, which members of the Texas House receive which committee assignments, and ultimately what the legislature accomplishes during its relatively brief biennial session. If politics is a game about who gets what and how, the Speaker is a key player.

In this chapter, we will examine the organizational structure of the Texas Legislature. An overview of the various types of committees is given, and the roles and structures of these committees are discussed. Then we examine the role of chamber leadership and the role and organization of political parties in the Texas Legislature. We also examine the impact that special legislative caucuses, such as the Mexican American Legislative Caucus and the Rural Caucus, have on legislation. Finally, we examine the legislative process, comparing the similarities between the Texas Senate and Texas House of Representatives. We also note key differences in the two chambers, such as calendars, blocking bills, and filibusters used in shaping legislation.

## Chapter Objectives

★ Describe the leadership roles in Texas's legislative organization.

★ Evaluate who wins and who loses in how the Texas Legislature is organized.

★ Explain the process for a bill becoming law in the Texas Legislature.

★ Assess who wins and who loses when growing partisanship influences the Texas Legislature.

## LEGISLATIVE ORGANIZATION

State legislatures rely on a system of processes, called legislative organization, that helps them carry out their functions. These functions include developing new bills, revising existing laws, and overseeing the activities of the executive branch. Legislatures are typically organized around the chamber leadership (presiding officers), party organization, committee structure, and special legislative caucuses. These institutional features shape and mold legislation in profound ways by offering opportunities for a legislator to alter a bill to his or her liking. While this ability to mold legislation is most evident in the committee system, chamber leadership positions offer another opportunity for a handful of members to exercise strong influence over bills. More importantly, in the last decade or so, party organization has emerged as a new form of legislative organization that is becoming increasingly relevant to which bills become law. Party organization and special legislative caucuses have resulted in legislative transformation that offers students of Texas government a new perspective on legislative organization and process absent in Texas's past. In the end, institutional "rules" or "organizations" determine what becomes law and who wins and who loses in the legislature itself. Because laws affect citizens throughout the state, legislative organization also influences the daily lives of Texas as well.

## Presiding Officers

Leadership of each chamber of the Texas Legislature is especially important. These leaders include the Speaker of the Texas House of Representatives and the president of the Texas Senate. Individuals holding these positions possess important powers to shape and to mold the agendas of the chambers. This ability to control the agenda influences the likelihood that a bill becomes a law.

### Lieutenant Governor

The president of the Texas Senate is the **lieutenant governor**. This is the most common arrangement in U.S. state legislatures, used in twenty-six of the fifty states. In these states, the lieutenant governor is elected by voters across the state, thus the upper house lacks any control over who serves as its presiding officer. Texas is no different. Most states with this arrangement limit the power of the lieutenant governor to control the upper house. Exceptions to these limits are found in the South, including in Texas, where the lieutenant governor is unusually powerful. Twenty-four states typically allow the membership of the state's upper house to select one of its members as the presiding officer.

As mentioned above, in Texas the lieutenant governor is directly elected by the voters of the state, denying senators the choice of their presiding officer. If the lieutenant governor's position is vacant, as when Lt. Gov. Rick Perry became the governor after George W. Bush was elected president of the United States, then the Texas Senate can elect a senator to perform the duties of lieutenant governor until the next general election. When the lieutenant governor is unable to attend sessions, the **president pro tempore** takes over as the presiding officer. The president pro tempore is elected by the membership of the Texas Senate.

The lieutenant governor is an important actor in the Texas executive branch, and his or her election by the voters of Texas in a statewide election gives the position tremendous political clout. Unlike the members of the Texas Legislature, the lieutenant governor may claim a statewide mandate in favor of his or her political agenda, including legislation that he or she wants the legislature to pass. Theoretically, the lieutenant governor can frame the issues before the legislature. Those pieces of legislation, and positions on bills, that the lieutenant governor favors must reflect the will of the people of Texas because all Texas elected him or her. Thus, the lieutenant governor can claim that those opposed to him or her in the Texas Legislature are defending the

**Lieutenant governor**
the presiding officer of the Texas Senate, elected directly by the voters. Also serves as a member of the Texas executive branch and assumes the duties of the governor when the governor is out of state, dies in office, resigns from office, or is impeached.

**President pro tempore**
a presiding officer elected by the members of the Texas Senate; takes over when the lieutenant governor is unavailable.

narrow interests of only the district that each member of the legislature represents, not the broad general interest of all Texans. In this respect, the lieutenant governor is similar to the governor.

The lieutenant governor also exercises power in the Senate. The lieutenant governor assigns each bill introduced in the Texas Senate to one of the standing committees. As the presiding officer, he or she recognizes speakers during debates on the floor of the Texas Senate and also interprets the rules of debate in the Texas Senate. The lieutenant governor appoints, without limitation, members of the standing committees of the Texas Senate and selects the chairs of those committees. However, the lieutenant governor votes in the Texas Senate on bills, resolutions, and procedural motions only to break a tie.

The lieutenant governor also serves on the Legislative Redistricting Board (LRB). As discussed in Chapter 3, when the Texas Legislature is unable to pass a plan to redistrict the state legislature every ten years, the LRB develops the plan for the legislature. The lieutenant governor also sits on the **Legislative Budget Board (LBB)**. We discuss the role and function of the LBB later in this chapter.

Arguably, like the governor in Texas, the lieutenant governor is constitutionally weak. Much of the power of the lieutenant governor derives from the norms and traditions of the Texas Senate, which typically places significant authority in the hands of the lieutenant governor to appoint committees and committee chairs, negotiate compromises on bills, and interpret the rules of debate. Some of these norms and traditions are embedded in the rules of the Texas Senate. At the beginning of each session, the Senate agrees on a set of procedures and ways to conduct business that is called the rules. A successful lieutenant governor is adept at using the rules—and often networking, personal charm, and powers of persuasion—to get things done in the Senate. Yet lieutenant governors are often limited by their approach to leadership. Alienating or isolating key members of the Texas Senate may cause a backlash against the lieutenant governor.

### Speaker of the House

The **Speaker of the House** presides over sessions of the Texas House of Representatives. This title is the most common for the presiding officer of the lower house of state legislatures. In Texas, the Speaker is elected by the membership of the House as the first order of business at the beginning of the legislative session in January, following the elections for the entire state legislature in November, as discussed at the beginning of this chapter. Although the election is often by secret ballot, candidates for the position of Speaker campaign for weeks before the vote is taken. Historically, this process involves a system in which members of the Texas House sign cards pledging their support to a candidate before the legislature meets. Thus, a candidate for the Speaker position largely knows which members are going to vote for her or him before the balloting occurs.[12]

Unlike in the U.S. House of Representatives, the vote for the Texas Speaker is usually bipartisan and lopsided. As mentioned at the opening of this chapter, current Texas Speaker Joe Straus was elected by a unanimous vote. In 1999, James "Pete" Laney was unanimously elected to the position as well. Even controversial figures such as Tom Craddick have received significant bipartisan support.

From the end of Reconstruction in the 1870s through the 1980s, near-unanimous bipartisan votes reflected the reality of Texas politics: the Democratic Party controlled the chamber. As a result, the Republicans in the Texas House often found that supporting the eventual Democratic winner created opportunities for them to have bills and amendments that they favored considered by the majority party. A more pragmatic reason exists for members of both parties to support the Speaker. The powers of the Speaker are extensive, and maintaining a favorable relationship with the Speaker is important. As a consequence, the tradition of near-unanimous bipartisan votes continues. For now, the transition to Republican control over the Texas House has not produced a shift away from bipartisan support for the election of the Speaker, because the powers of the Speaker, regardless of party affiliation, remain extensive.

Powers of the Speaker include presiding over debates and controlling them by deciding whether to recognize a member to speak or introduce a motion. The Speaker's power also extends over interpretation of the standing rules by which the legislature operates—a power that may be used to help some legislators and hurt others. The Speaker serves on the Legislative Redistricting Board and appoints part of the membership of the LBB. In addition, the Speaker appoints some standing committee members, the chairs of standing committees, and members of conference committees from the Texas House. The Speaker may also create select committees and interim committees. Thus, the Speaker has the ability to influence the size and shape of election districts and the items included in the state budget.

The Speaker also assigns bills to the committees. To be in favor with the Speaker helps ensure a member of the Texas House positive consideration of pet bills and favorable committee assignments. However, unlike the lieutenant governor in the Texas Senate, the power to appoint committee members by the Texas Speaker is limited, since one-half of the makeup of some standing committees is determined by seniority. The Speaker appoints a **Speaker pro tempore** to preside when the Speaker is unable to be at the capitol.

One recent study of presiding officers across the state legislatures in the United States offers a comparison of the Texas Speaker to his or her colleagues in other states. The Texas Speaker's overall appointment powers place him or her among the most powerful presiding officers in the country, and certainly the most powerful in the South. This concentration of power is partially a result of the infrequent meetings of the Texas Legislature. The ability to appoint interim committees while the legislature is not in session strengthens the power of the Speaker. However, the seniority system of appointments to the standing committees in the Texas House places some limitations on the power of the Speaker. Thus, the Texas Speaker is quite a bit less powerful with regards to control over standing committees, even in comparison to other states in the South.[13]

## Political Parties in Texas Legislative Organization

Political parties can provide a basis for organizing the legislature as a means by which to rally support. Because political parties bring together people with similar political beliefs, the parties assist in **structuring the vote**—that is, aligning support for or opposition to bills. They also sometimes play an important role in the selection of

**Speaker pro tempore**
officer that presides over the House of Representatives when the Speaker is unavailable; akin to the president pro tempore in the Texas Senate.

**Structuring the vote**
the way in which political parties align support for or opposition to bills.

committees and the organization of the work of committees, and they can form a base of support for the election of the Speaker of the Texas House. Outside the legislature, the political party provides a mechanism for raising needed campaign funds and functions as a tool for mobilizing voters on Election Day.

The **party legislative caucus** plays an important role in many state legislatures. At its most basic level, the political party in each house of the Texas Legislature *is* the party legislative caucus. A party legislative caucus is simply the members of a specific chamber of the legislature who belong to a specific political party. Normally, the term is shortened to *party caucus*. Throughout this chapter, we use the term *party caucus* to refer to a party legislative caucus. Members of the caucus must pay dues to join. These dues allow the caucus to pay for its operation, expenses, and staff.

**Party legislative caucus**
the organization of the members of a specific legislative chamber who belong to the same political party; normally shortened to party caucus.

### Democratic Party Organization in the Texas House

The historic pattern in Texas has been an absence of party caucuses in the legislature. Several reasons account for this lack of party organization. First, the dominance of the Democratic Party in Texas meant that party caucuses were unnecessary. Texas, like the rest of the single-party states in the American South prior to the 1970s, had patterns of behavior among legislators that reflected divisions within the Democratic Party itself. Another factor that contributed to the absence of party caucuses was the strength of the leadership positions. The powerful Speaker of the Texas House and the lieutenant governor in the Texas Senate historically commanded their respective chambers, rewarding supporters and circumventing the need for party organization. In the Texas House, the creation of the Democratic Party caucus in 1981 signaled a shift in the party system within the legislature. The growing number of Republicans spurred Democratic members to increase awareness within their party of policy issues and impelled them to discuss bills and discipline party members.[14] From 1981 until 1993, many Democratic members did not join the party caucus, and conservative Democrats often worked on bills in a bipartisan manner with Republicans. By 1993, most Democratic members found that working on a common position on bills within their own party helped to get legislation passed and served as a counterbalance to the growing influence and importance of the Republican Party in the chamber. Additionally, differences between the two political parties were becoming more evident, reflecting the growing trend of partisan politics at the national level. The transition to a more competitive two-party legislature led the Texas Democratic Party, at that time still in the majority, to institutionalize, or formalize, its party organization in the legislature in order to meet a growing Republican challenge. The Democratic Party hoped that by increasing the level of party organization in the legislature, it could deliver policies and bills more effectively and prevent the loss of additional seats to the Republican Party.

### Republican Party Organization in the Texas House

Although sometimes more cohesive in voting than the Democrats, Republicans did not formally create a party caucus in the Texas House until 1989. Republicans resisted forming party caucuses in the legislature in part because they feared focusing on party differences would lead to a loss of influence over legislation. While

Democratic control over both chambers of the Texas Legislature existed for many decades, Republicans nevertheless received influential positions on committees, were appointed chairs of committees, and acquired positions of leadership in the chamber. Intensified partisanship associated with the Democratic Party's response to the increased number of Republicans elected to the Texas Legislature in the late 1980s and early 1990s was assumed to put Republican access to these positions in jeopardy. After all, why would Democrats allow an increasingly large and electorally successful Republican Party to have influence over legislation? However, both houses of the Texas Legislature continued to operate in a bipartisan manner, consistent with long-standing tradition. This situation also reflected the Democratic Party's reluctance to embrace the changes that were occurring in the legislature and in the electorate. Democrats appeared to be ignoring their declining numbers in the legislature and the erosion of voter support at the ballot box.

The continued bipartisanship that remained also reflected the power of the Speaker of the Texas House and the lieutenant governor. Both of these presiding officers continued to wield tremendous power and remained able to reward Republicans who were loyal to their presiding officer, even when that officer was a Democrat. Thus, Republicans had an incentive to maintain a degree of bipartisan support for the presiding officers in each chamber of the legislature. Democrats also hoped that continued bipartisanship while they remained in the majority would be rewarded with similar treatment if and when the Republicans became the majority party.

While battles over taxation and spending in the late 1980s led to the formation of the Republican caucus in 1989, Republican fears of loss of influence were unfounded during the waning years of Democratic control over the legislature. Beginning in 2003, Republican control over the legislature, especially the Texas House, launched a series of debates and fights within the Republican Party over just how much influence should be granted to the now-minority Democratic members and to what extent Republicans should shut out the Democratic Party. Among some Republicans, a "to the victor go the spoils" approach began to take root. Republicans were now in charge, so why was bipartisanship necessary? Also important among Republicans was the desire to fundamentally change the nature of state government by significantly reducing its size and balancing the state budget without raising taxes. Bipartisanship meant compromise with the Democrats on these key issues and meant that key goals of the party, and many Republican voters, went unfulfilled. Those factions within the Republican Party caucus in the Texas House of Representatives have continued to fight since 2003 over the extent to which Republicans ought to work with the Democratic minority in the chamber.

### Party Organization in the Texas Senate

Formation of party caucuses in the Texas Senate occurred much later than in the Texas House of Representatives, in part because the Texas Senate is so much smaller. Each party typically has less than twenty members, so getting to know other members of a political party in the Texas Senate is much easier. In addition, the Texas Senate has historically been more informal, less structured, and more consensus oriented than the Texas House. Following the previous creation of party legislative caucuses in the Texas House, the Republicans in 1999 created the first party caucus in the Texas Senate, with Democrats following suit in 2001.[15] With this background, the Texas Senate defies the findings of at least one major study of party caucuses in state legislatures. Political scientist Wayne Francis found that party caucuses were more important in small chambers with nearly evenly matched parties.[16] However, another study that focused just on the southern states, where the Democratic Party held power for decades, found that as the Republican Party became more competitive electorally, the party caucuses became more institutionalized and more formal.[17] While both of these studies occurred before the party caucuses were fully developed in the Texas Legislature, Texas certainly appears to offer support for the latter study and remains consistent with the pattern of other southern states.

### Party Caucus Organization and Functions

Today, both parties maintain party caucuses in both houses of the Texas Legislature to provide communication among members of the caucus, to discuss bills and amendments, and to raise money for campaigns.[18] Each party caucus also elects a **party caucus chair**. The party caucus chair is elected by the caucus to oversee the day-to-day operation of the party. The party caucuses in the Texas House of Representatives also have a **floor leader** elected by the caucus membership. Deputy floor leaders assist the floor leader. These deputy positions are normally appointed by the caucus chair and often go to first-term legislators and those with less tenure to help them get to know other legislators and to gain experience in the legislative process. The job of the floor leaders and deputy floor leaders is to remind members of the party caucus of the party's position on a bill or amendment and to encourage members to vote with the rest of the party caucus. The Texas House Republican Caucus in the 2011 session had fifteen floor leaders, while the Democratic House Caucus had five. Similar levels of organizational structure existed in the 2013 session.

The party caucuses are increasingly using new media to carry out their activities. For example, the Texas House Democratic Caucus uses text messaging to remind members about upcoming votes. It is attempting to find ways to use Twitter as a tool for greater communication as well[19] and has also created a Facebook page to promote its legislative agenda and to raise public awareness of issues that it supported during the legislative session. Thus, not only does the party caucus support members, it aims to generate support outside the legislature and promote candidates with the public. The Texas Republican House Caucus maintains a Web site and Twitter feed to alert the public of important matters, and its Facebook page serves a similar purpose to that of its Democratic counterparts.

The party caucuses in the Texas House of Representatives work to find speakers on major state bills or individuals to ask specific questions during floor debates. Party caucuses also review bills and propose amendments to them. Often the caucuses review analyses of the impact of each bill and the costs associated with them. Both party caucuses in the Texas House also maintain a small staff to assist the caucus chair and membership with meeting logistics, such as finding a place to meet or having photocopies

**Party caucus chair**
a party leader whose main job is to organize party members to vote for legislation on the floor.

**Floor leader**
a party member who reminds legislators of the party's position on a bill and encourages members to vote with the rest of the party caucus; the floor leader is assisted by one or more deputy floor leaders.

of bills and amendments made. The staff also prepares bills and amendments, develops press releases, and performs other tasks to inform the wider public of bills. To fund their activities, the party caucuses may charge dues on their members.[20]

In addition, the Texas House Republican Caucus contains a policy chair appointed by the chair of the state Republican Party. This individual helps to steer members on crucial issues. Because the Republican Party is the majority party in Texas, pressure is placed to vote with the party to ensure bills become law.[21] Yet even in the Republican Party, the independence of members is respected when a vote places the individual member of the legislature in conflict between the party caucus's position and the wishes of the member's constituents back home. In this case, satisfying the constituents back home trumps party.[22]

For the Texas House Democratic Caucus, certain social issues, such as abortion, are more contentious within the party caucus, and members were pressured less to vote the party line on such issues in the 2011 session.[23] The media attention to this issue due to Wendy Davis's (D–Fort Worth) filibuster in the Texas Senate during the 2013 first special session placed greater pressure on Democrats in both chambers to toe the line on the abortion issue in 2013. Greater unity and cohesion occurred on economic issues and voter ID laws. Another interesting development regarding the Texas House Democratic Caucus was the creation of a political action committee (PAC) to help reelect its members during the 2012 elections. The caucus was active in recruiting individuals to run for the Texas Legislature, training candidates, and producing advertising materials to help the election of those running for office for the first time. These efforts were independent of the Democratic Party's state organization.[24] By the 2013 session, the Texas House Democratic Caucus was affected by its shrinking size, which weakened its impact. The willingness of Speaker Joe Straus to work with Democrats on some issues allowed the party some influence greater than its caucus size.[25]

Because the Texas House of Representatives is larger than the Texas Senate, party organization there is more developed and more relevant. The Texas Senate Democratic Caucus lacks floor leaders and whips and appears to be less of an organizing tool than its Democratic counterpart in the House and its Republican counterpart in either chamber. The caucus does not work as much to line up speakers during debates or to help reach common positions. Less pressure is placed on individual members to vote a particular way on most bills. The caucus is more active on the more controversial and specific issues, such as voter ID laws and women's health issues.[26]

This approach by the Texas Senate Democratic Caucus may reflect the smaller size of the Texas Senate and the status of the Democratic Party as the minority party. As one staffer stated, "The Senate is more of an individual sport, while the House of Representatives is more of a team sport."[27] Moreover, just like the Texas House Democratic Caucus, the Texas Senate Democratic Caucus seems to serve as more of an informational tool and is focused on putting out press releases, holding press conferences, and sending out daily tweets on Twitter to inform the public of issues, debates, and bills in the legislature.[28] The less formal nature of the Texas Senate Democratic Caucus may be a deficit to the Democratic Party and its agenda in the legislature because the collapse of the party at the state level, including the lack of any statewide elected officials, has created a vacuum and leaves the party at a distinct disadvantage.

In contrast, the Texas Senate Republican Caucus appears more organized and more cohesive. This is critical because the Republicans are in the majority and therefore need stronger cohesion to ensure important legislation is passed. As the majority party, there is more pressure to deliver legislation to keep party supporters and constituents happy.

Before the emergence of a Republican majority in the Texas Legislature, one study of party caucuses in state legislatures suggested that, compared to other states, party cohesion was relatively weak in Texas.[29] Given the internal divisions within the Republican Party over how to work with the Democratic minority, the need for bipartisan cooperation, and whether to pursue consensus politics, party cohesion remains a challenge. Another limitation on the development of well-organized, highly structured political parties is the effectiveness of the caucus leadership and its leadership style.[30] Under Democratic Party dominance, party cohesion mattered less and legislators could afford to be more independent minded, and, indeed, the individualistic nature of Texas political culture calls upon legislators to exert a degree of independence from their party. Historically, the powers and influences of the Speaker and lieutenant governor in their respective chambers have produced their own centralized system of legislative organization. The emergence of the party legislative caucuses has challenged this centralized system, especially in the Texas House of Representatives where a more party-centered model may be developing. Disagreement within the Republican Party caucus in the Texas House over the continuation of bipartisanship has pitted Speaker Joe Straus and his allies against more conservative, less compromise-oriented members of the Republican caucus.

### Additional Compensation for Legislative Leadership

Texas, unlike some other states, provides its legislative leaders no additional compensation beyond their base salary. This lack of additional pay applies to both the Speaker of the Texas House and the state's lieutenant governor. Party leadership positions, including party caucus chairs, floor leaders, and deputy floor leaders in the Texas Legislature, are also uncompensated. However, leadership positions do receive additional pay in other states. For example, Oklahoma provides $12,364 per year to the majority party and minority party leaders (what Texas refers to as the party caucus chairs) in both houses of the Oklahoma Legislature. Utah gives $2,000 per year to its party whips (also referred to as floor leaders and deputy floor leaders in Texas). North Dakota gives between $10 and $307 per day the legislature is in session, depending on the position. North Carolina provides over twenty different leadership positions with additional compensation ranging between $13,000 and $34,000 per year, depending on the position. Texas is one of only seventeen states that do not provide additional compensation to those who assume leadership positions.[31]

### Special Legislative Caucuses

**Special legislative caucus**
an organization of members of the state legislature who share a common interest or have constituencies with a common interest.

While party legislative caucuses are organized on party lines, a **special legislative caucus** is comprised of legislative members who share a common interest. Special legislative caucuses may include members of both chambers of the Texas Legislature and may have both Democratic and Republican members. These groups meet regularly to discuss important topics of mutual interest to them and their constituents. Three types of special legislative caucuses exist in the Texas Legislature, the oldest of which are **minority and women's caucuses**. These caucuses exist to represent the unique concerns and beliefs of women and ethnic groups across a broad spectrum of policy areas and political issues. They include the Texas Legislative Black Caucus (TLBC), the Texas Women's Political Caucus, and the Mexican American Legislative Caucus (MALC). These caucuses bring together members of the Texas Legislature that share a bipartisan desire to discuss issues affecting women, African Americans, and Hispanics. Often the groups assist in developing new bills or building support for bills that the caucus members believe to be important. For example, in the 2011 regular session, the TLBC and the MALC were very active on bills associated with redistricting the Texas Legislature and Texas's congressional districts. Both of these groups sought redistricting plans that maximized minority representation. When the legislature failed to approve such plans, the MALC especially was active in appearing before federal courts to argue in favor of redistricting plans that created more majority-minority districts, as discussed in Chapter 3. Interestingly, the Texas Women's Political Caucus became inactive in recent sessions of the legislature because the more conservative members and the more liberal members were heavily divided over the issues of abortion and public funding for birth control. As a result, several liberal Democratic members of the legislature formed the Women's Health Caucus to promote their positions on these issues and others.[32]

A second type of special legislative caucus is an **ideological caucus**, which is designed to promote a broad ideological agenda. In 1985, when the Democratic Party held the majority, conservative members of the Texas Legislature created the Texas Conservative Coalition. Likewise, after Republicans gained the majority, the Legislative Study Group was created in 1993 to promote liberal policies. The Texas Progressive Caucus met during the 2011 session to promote issues important to liberals, and the Tea Party Caucus organized to advance more conservative issues in line with the wider, national Tea Party movement. This group supported massive reductions in the size of government, significant cuts in spending, and lower taxes.

The final type of special legislative caucus is the **issue caucus**. An issue caucus exists to promote bipartisan and cross-chamber support for policies and bills that advocate positions in a relatively narrow range of policy areas or political issues that are important to key constituents. One example is the Rural Caucus, which advocates for health care, transportation, and education policies favorable to rural Texas. The Sportsmen's Caucus promotes and protects hunting and fishing rights, and the House Environmental Caucus and Texas Carbon Management Caucus support policies for environmental protection and conservation of natural resources. Some caucuses, such as the Texas High Speed Rail Caucus, focus on a very narrow issue. (See Table 4.1 for a list of the special legislative caucuses in the Texas Legislature.)

### Structuring the Vote

Some members of the Texas House find the special legislative caucuses especially important in efforts to make other members of the legislature more aware of issues under consideration.[33] As part of this effort at raising awareness, members of special

**Minority and women's caucuses**
special legislative caucuses in the state legislature that represent the unique concerns and beliefs of women and ethnic groups across a broad range of policy issues.

**Ideological caucus**
a special legislative caucus in the state legislature that promotes an ideological agenda.

**Issue caucus**
a special legislative caucus in the state legislature that promotes bipartisan and cross-chamber support for policies and bills advocating positions inside a relatively narrow range of policy areas or political issues.

# TEXAS VS NEBRASKA

As mentioned in Chapter 3, Nebraska possesses the only unicameral state legislature in the United States. All other state legislatures, including Texas, are bicameral. The history of Nebraska's unicameral legislature dates back to the time of the 1930s and the Great Depression. U.S. senator George William Norris (R–Nebraska) suggested that Nebraska change its state legislature from a bicameral to a unicameral one. According to Norris, bicameralism was a result of the British system, in which the House of Commons and House of Lords represented different citizens' social classes (aristocracy and commoner), but Nebraska lacked such classes, so there was no reason to have a bicameral state legislature.[i] Norris campaigned all over the state advocating a single-chambered legislature. Voters apparently agreed, and they amended the state's constitution in 1934 to abolish the lower house, retaining only the upper house. Almost 60 percent of voters approved of the change.[ii] As a result, the costs of operating the legislature fell in half when the newly unicameral legislature met for the first time in 1937.[iii]

In addition, the Nebraska Legislature sits as a nonpartisan legislature. Unlike in Texas, where legislative candidates run with clear party affiliations, candidates in Nebraska do not do so, and during their campaigns prior to Election Day, candidates do not refer to political party affiliation. The top two candidates in the primary election compete in the general election, with the candidate with the most votes winning the election to the state legislature.[iv] Once elected to the Nebraska Legislature, the legislators sit according to geographic location in the state, not by party affiliation as they do in the Texas Legislature and in all other state legislatures. It is important to note that the Republican Party at various levels of government in Nebraska does list candidates running for the Nebraska Legislature who have Republican support.[v] Democratic Party organizations within the state do the same thing.[vi]

The nonpartisan nature of the Nebraska Legislature is also a result of the efforts of Norris, the "Father of Unicameralism." He believed the lack of partisanship allowed the legislators to focus on their own beliefs, not the wishes of party leaders. Norris also believed the nonpartisan approach resulted in legislators paying attention to the needs of their districts, which would better serve the people of Nebraska.[vii] This nonpartisan approach was consistent with the Progressive Era belief that political parties were controlled by party leaders, who in turn were assumed to be dominated by big business, labor unions, and organized interests, not the broader body of citizens.

Since the Nebraska Legislature is unicameral and nonpartisan, its legislative process differs as well. For example, a nonpartisan legislature does not need to worry about the balance between Democratic and Republican members on standing committees, as the Texas Legislature does. In addition, the issue of which party controls the chair of each standing committee does not exist. Finally, there is no need to reconcile bills using a conference committee, as in all other states, including Texas. This approach also reflects Norris's approach to politics. Norris noted that in Nebraska during the days of bicameralism, conference committees consisted of six members who met in secret without any public record of their decisions and produced a bill that legislators could not amend. This suggested to Norris that the political parties were able to hide their agendas and not be accountable to voters. As a result, he believed that conference committees increased the power of interest groups.[viii]

## THINKING Critically

★ How do Norris's claims about the origins of bicameralism differ from the reasons typically associated with the framers of the U.S. Constitution? (See especially pages 78–79 in Chapter 3.)

★ What potential advantages exist to the Nebraska nonpartisan arrangement?

★ What advantages and disadvantages exist in a unicameral state legislature?

★ Should Texas consider adopting a unicameral, nonpartisan state legislature? Why or why not?

i. Nebraska Legislature, "History of the Nebraska Unicameral," http://nebraskalegislature.gov/about/history_unicameral.php (accessed September 18, 2014).

ii. Ibid.

iii. Nebraska Legislature, "On Unicameralism," http://nebraskalegislature.gov/about/ou_experience.php (accessed September 18, 2014).

iv. Nebraska Legislature, "History of the Nebraska Unicameral."

v. Lancaster County Nebraska Republican Party, "Primary Elections," www.lcgop.com/news/primary-elections/ (accessed August 9, 2012).

vi. Nebraska Democratic Party, "Candidates," www.nebraskademocrats.org/candidates (accessed October 10, 2012).

vii. Nebraska Legislature, "History of the Nebraska Unicameral."

viii. Ibid.

legislative caucuses attempt to structure votes on bills and amendments among the caucus members and other sympathetic members of the legislature to ensure passage. Most of this structuring of votes is done simply through face-to-face meetings with other members of the legislature, speeches on the floor of the legislature, or questions raised during floor debates, rather than through formal meetings, organization, etc. The Rural Caucus was very active in the 2011 session on water resource legislation and timber theft bills.[34] Because these issues were vital to members from rural West Texas and the Piney Woods of East Texas, members of the Rural Caucus spoke often to other Republican and Democratic legislators from urban and suburban areas regarding the importance of the bills and their impact on rural Texas. The Texas Veteran's Caucus was able to get a bill passed to have a memorial, funded by private donations, erected on the grounds of the state capitol. The Mexican American Legislative Caucus and the Texas Legislative Black Caucus have some influence over legislation as well. During the 2011 session, at least seventeen of these special legislative caucuses met.

The overall impact of a special legislative caucus varies considerably by the type of caucus and can depend on the issues involved and perhaps the lack of importance of a particular issue to members of the majority party in each chamber. When an issue is considered highly important to the majority party, the special legislative caucus may have less influence on it. Thus, the success of the Rural Caucus may reflect the relative unimportance of timber theft to the Republican majority. Although the issue is extremely important to Democrats and Republicans from rural areas of the state, the Republican majority had little political capital invested in this issue. As a result, the Rural Caucus could be more influential in passing legislation that served the interests of rural Texas better. The special legislative caucuses may be less important to the work of the Texas Senate because of its smaller size.[35] With only thirty-one members, senators are more likely to know each other and the key issues that are important to each other, regardless of party affiliation.

Special legislative caucuses may be formally organized and registered with the Texas Ethics Commission or may be simply informal meetings of members of the legislature. One study of the Texas Legislative Black Caucus (TLBC), which is more formally organized, suggests that the caucus enjoys a high degree of **cohesion**, meaning its members—or members of a political party or special legislative caucus generally—vote together on a bill or resolution. During the 1980s and 1990s, when the TLBC membership voted together as a bloc, the caucus was able to influence legislation related to the group's shared interests.[36] This degree of cohesion suggests that some of the special legislative caucuses play a significant role in

| TABLE 4.1 | Special Legislative Caucuses in the 2011 Texas Legislature |
|---|---|

| **Ideological Caucuses** |
|---|
| House Progressive Caucus |
| Legislative Study Group Caucus |
| Policy Study Group |
| Tea Party Caucus |
| **Minority and Women's Caucuses** |
| Mexican American Legislative Caucus |
| Texas Legislative Black Caucus |
| Texas Women's Political Caucus |
| Women's Health Caucus |
| **Issue Caucuses** |
| Community College Caucus |
| House Environmental Caucus |
| Legislative Air Quality Caucus |
| Rural Caucus |
| Texas Carbon Management Caucus |
| Texas High Speed Rail Caucus |
| Texas House Farm-to-Table Caucus |
| Texas Tourism Caucus |
| Texas Veteran's Caucus |
| Texas-21 Transportation Caucus |

**Source:** Compiled by the authors from information provided via e-mail by Matthew Burgin, campaign manager for Chuck Hopson, 2012.

**Cohesion**
unity within a group; in politics, when members of a political party or special legislative caucus vote together on a bill or resolution.

the legislative process. The TLBC is one of a handful of special legislative caucuses with a formal chair to oversee meetings and a staff member or two to assist the chair and the members of the caucus. In addition, the TLBC works to raise awareness of issues, bills, and amendments in the general public through press releases, letters to state agencies, and similar activities.[37]

Special legislative caucuses provide an indirect means to influence policy. In contrast to political party caucuses, the special legislative caucuses lack a formal role in the legislative process. They do not directly control appointments of members to committees. They also do not form the organizational basis of choosing chamber leadership. In addition, special legislative caucuses lack the ability to discipline members for voting against the caucus position. Thus, they are often left with secondary strategies, such as giving speeches and lobbying other members of the legislature, to get what they want. The influence of a special caucus varies tremendously by the type of special caucus, degree of organization, and issues addressed by the caucus. The influence and significance varies significantly over time as well, depending on the dynamics of a session and the individual issues addressed in a session.

## Committees

A more formal form of organization that exerts direct influence over legislation is the **committee** system. Like the U.S. Congress, the Texas Legislature utilizes a committee system to assist the legislature in accomplishing its work. The presence of committees allows, among other things, a division of labor so that bills may be reviewed in detail before being considered by the entire chamber. Three broad types of committees exist in the Texas Legislature: standing committees, statutory committees, and special committees.

### Standing Committees

The **standing committee** is the most important type of committee in the Texas Legislature. Each and every bill introduced into the legislature must pass through at least one of the standing committees and in some cases two or more of them. Thus, the work of standing committees is very important to which bills become laws and what each bill contains. Standing committees are created through the standing rules that govern the processes and procedures that the chamber operates under during the session. Although standing committees are officially re-created each session, standing committees are considered permanent committees because each standing committee typically exists across sessions and elections to the legislature. Standing committees are also chamber exclusive—that is, each standing committee is associated with a specific chamber of the legislature and is made up of members from only that chamber. In the Texas Senate, the standing committees in the 83rd Legislature ranged in membership from five senators to fifteen. The thirty-eight Texas House standing committees during that session contained between five and twenty-eight members (see Table 4.2).

Standing committees exist for the purpose of helping a chamber perform its duties and ensure that bills become laws. Some standing committees are substantive standing committees. These committees are so named because they directly handle bills

**Committee**
a formally organized group of legislators that assists the legislature in accomplishing its work, allowing a division of labor and an in-depth review of an issue or a bill before review by the entire chamber.

**Standing committee**
a permanent, chamber-specific formal work group that typically exists across sessions and across elections.

and resolutions before the legislature. They are able to change the wording of a bill and to make amendments to a bill. Thus, the substantive standing committees control the substance of what the legislature passes into law. These committees are functionally divided, meaning each committee handles bills in a specific area of policy, such as transportation or higher education. However, some substantive standing committees will consider every bill introduced. For example, every bill in the Texas House of Representatives that involves spending tax revenue, regardless of the specific policy area, must pass through the Appropriations Committee. The Texas House Ways and Means Committee handles every bill involving changes in tax law, the rate of taxation, and the types of taxes levied. Therefore, a bill that deals with higher education finance will pass through two substantive standing committees: Higher Education and Appropriations.

Another type of standing committee is the procedural standing committee. These committees focus on the organizational aspects of how the legislative process works. Some procedural standing committees handle calendars and determine when a bill will be debated. Others handle rules, or the terms of debate, associated with a bill. Some procedural committees review House organization and administration. Thus, a bill on higher education finance would pass through the two substantive standing committees above plus the Calendars Committee and possibly the Rules and Resolutions Committee for a total of four standing committees. Procedural committees in Texas House of Representatives during the 2013 session included the Calendars, General Investigation and Ethics, House Administration, Local and Consent Calendars, Redistricting, and the Rules and Resolutions committees.

Every member of the Texas House of Representatives sits on two or three standing committees, and Texas Senate members sit on at least four. The appointment process for members of the standing committees varies between the Texas House and Texas Senate. As mentioned above, the lieutenant governor appoints the members of the standing committees in the Texas Senate. In the Texas House, the process is a bit more complicated. Seats on standing committees are assigned based upon seniority for the first committee assignment, while the second (or third) committee assignment is made at the discretion of the Speaker of the House. In addition, members of procedural standing committees in the Texas House are appointed only on the basis of seniority. Prior to the start of each session of the legislature, members of the Texas House list on a note card the standing committee assignment that they prefer. These note cards are submitted to the Speaker of the House, who reviews the cards and then makes the assignments.

The membership of the committees has undergone tremendous transition over the past few decades. Prior to the 1980s, so few Republicans were in either chamber of the legislature that placing them on every standing committee proved difficult. As Republicans gained strength in the Texas House, those who courted favor with a Democratic Speaker often found themselves receiving favorable positions on committees. In the 1980s and 1990s, Republicans often were overrepresented in committees and even chaired a number of standing committees.[38]

This situation stands in sharp contrast to the party-oriented system of the U.S. Congress and many state legislatures, in which committee seats are divided so that the

## TABLE 4.2 Standing Committees in the 83rd Texas Legislature

| Texas House of Representatives | | Texas Senate |
|---|---|---|
| Agriculture and Livestock | Insurance | Administration |
| Appropriations | International Trade and Intergovernmental Affairs | Agriculture and Rural Affairs |
| Business and Industry | Investment and Financial Services | Business and Commerce |
| Calendars | Judiciary and Civil Jurisprudence | Criminal Justice |
| Corrections | Land and Resource Management | Economic Development |
| County Affairs | Licensing and Administrative Procedures | Education |
| Criminal Jurisprudence | Local and Consent Calendars | Finance |
| Culture, Recreation, and Tourism | Natural Resources | Government Organization |
| Defense and Veterans' Affairs | Pensions | Health and Human Services |
| Economic and Small Business Development | Public Education | Higher Education |
| Elections | Public Health | Intergovernmental Relations |
| Energy Resources | Redistricting | Jurisprudence |
| Environmental Regulation | Rules and Resolutions | Natural Resources |
| General Investigating and Ethics | Special Purpose Districts | Nominations |
| Government Efficiency and Reform | State Affairs | Open Government |
| Higher Education | Technology | State Affairs |
| Homeland Security and Public Safety | Transportation | Transportation |
| House Administration | Urban Affairs | Veteran Affairs and Military Installations |
| Human Services | Ways and Means | |

**Sources:** Texas House of Representatives, "House Committees," www.house.state.tx.us/committees/ (accessed July 22, 2014); The Senate of Texas, "Committees of the 83rd Legislature," www.senate.state.tx.us/75r/senate/Commit.htm (accessed July 22, 2014).

party makeup of the committee mirrors the overall strength of the party in the chamber; the majority party is guaranteed a majority of seats on every standing committee, and the majority party holds all of the committee chairs. The control of committee membership and chairs ensures the majority party a degree of control over the legislative process since every bill passes through at least one standing committee.

Beginning in the 1990s, committee assignments began to shift in the Texas House toward a more party-centered model similar to that of the U.S. Congress. However, this transition is incomplete at best because the Speaker of the Texas House retains power over many committee assignments and makes bipartisan appointments to reward supporters. After the Republicans became the majority party in 2003, the trend of overrepresenting the minority party on certain committees by the Speaker continued. Several committees during the 81st Texas Legislature, which met in 2009, contained a majority of Democratic members, despite Republican control over the legislature. Criticism of Joe Straus's leadership of the Texas House led to changes in this practice. Republicans had a majority of the seats on all of the standing committees in the Texas House in the 2011 session. Republicans also held a majority of the seats on all of the standing committees in the Texas House during that session. However, in 2013, Straus allowed three standing committees to have Democratic majorities, and fourteen committees were chaired by Democrats.

Similarly, the Texas Senate often has standing committees chaired by the minority party, a tradition that dates back to the era of overwhelming Democratic control over the chamber prior to the 2000s. In 2011, Lieutenant Governor Dewhurst appointed Democrats to chair eight standing committees despite a Republican majority in the chamber. During the 2013 session, the minority-party Democrats chaired five committees. During that session, one committee of the Texas Senate had a Democratic majority on the committee as well.

### Standing Committee Organization and Functions

Presiding over each standing committee is a committee chair. Committee chairs in Texas are quite powerful. The chair sets the agenda for the committee, determining the order in which bills sent to the committee are considered. The chair also establishes the length of debate and the amendment process for each bill. As a result, the committee chair may schedule bills that he or she supports early in the legislative session to ensure that they are considered first by the committee. Likewise, the committee chair may move bills that she or he does not support to the end of the committee's calendar, effectively ensuring that the committee runs out of time before those bills are considered. The committee chair also decides other aspects of the agenda, such as the time devoted to hearings and oversight of the executive branch and its agencies. This power over the agenda and the flow of legislation in and out of the committee gives the chair of a standing committee tremendous control over the legislative process.

Members of the tax-writing House Appropriations Committee gather on the floor of the Texas House of Representatives for an impromptu meeting in Austin, Texas.

AP Photo/Harry Cabluck

Standing committees perform several important functions for the legislature, including the marking up and amending of bills. An **amendment** is a formal change to a bill made during the committee process. **Markup** is the process by which a committee goes line-by-line through a bill to make changes without formal amendments.

Because a committee is not required to report every bill to the whole chamber, committees may kill a bill. In other words, a bill sent to a standing committee may never be returned to the whole chamber for a final vote. By not sending a bill to the whole chamber, the standing committee in effect ensures the bill does not become a law. There are two ways in which a standing committee can kill a bill. First, a majority of the members on the committee can vote against it. As a result, the bill dies in committee and does not return to the whole chamber. In addition, a bill may be placed toward the end of the committee's schedule for the legislative session. If the committee runs out of time for the legislative session and fails to act on the bill before the session ends, the bill dies in committee. This ability to kill a bill makes standing committees very powerful. While this power in the standing committees of the Texas Legislature is consistent with that in the U.S. Congress and other state legislatures, it is fairly unique among non-American legislatures. For example, this ability to kill a bill in committee is not typically found in France, Britain, Japan, or Canada, regardless of the level of government, national or regional.

Another function of standing committees in Texas is to conduct **oversight** of the executive branch agencies. Oversight occurs when the legislature reviews policies and decisions of the executive branch to make sure that the executive branch is following the intentions of the legislature. Because some laws passed by the legislature provide only general guidelines to the executive branch, the specific agency that carries out the law often has discretion to determine exactly how to implement the law. For example, the state legislature in 2005 passed a law requiring state universities in Texas to set the maximum number of hours required for a bachelor's degree at 120.[39] Most degree programs at Texas public universities required more than 120 hours. To make these changes, systems, such as the University of Texas system, and independent state universities, such as Midwestern State University, developed plans to reduce the hours required for degrees to 120. The standing committees responsible for higher education in the state legislature reviewed progress toward the 120-hour degree program every two years during the regular session of the legislature, until universities were in compliance.

New administrative regulations are also subject to review by standing committees. For example, if the Texas Department of Parks and Wildlife decides to impose a user fee of $5 on everyone who goes fishing at a state park, it is up to the legislature, if it so chooses, to review this decision the next time it meets in regular session. However, the standing committees lack the power to effect changes in new regulations and can only issue advisory opinions,[40] which executive agencies take seriously. Keeping the legislature satisfied avoids having the committee, or the legislature, develop new laws to replace administrative regulations.

Committees have the authority to hold hearings when acting on legislation and overseeing the executive. These are meetings at which experts, invited guests, organized interests, officials from other branches, officials from other levels of government, and private citizens are allowed to address the committee about issues before it.

The work of standing committees in all of these functions is enhanced by the research and writing of reports done by the committees' professional staffs. To assist the members of the standing committee in their work, each standing committee, regardless of its size, retains a permanent staff of up to six people in the Texas House and up to fifteen people in the Texas Senate. A committee's staff helps with research on bills, with the organization of committee meetings, and with other tasks essential to the smooth operation of the committee. In addition to a professional research staff, each committee is also given a clerical staff.

Individual members of the Texas House may also use the services of the House Research Organization, while senators can access the Senate Research Center. These offices help research issues, draft legislation, and provide information to members of the legislature. The Legislative Reference Library also provides resources for members of the legislature, committees, and committee staff to use when researching and writing bills.

Standing committees are allowed to create subcommittees in order to provide greater efficiency and division of labor. The Appropriations Committee in the Texas House contained five subcommittees during the 2013 session. Each of these subcommittees handled bills associated with the state budget based upon specific areas of the budget and specific policy areas. The Economic and Small Business Development Committee formed a subcommittee on manufacturing. Likewise, the Finance Committee and the Economic Development Committee each created subcommittees to aid their work.

### Statutory Committees

Statutory committees are those mandated by laws passed by the Texas Legislature. The Legislative Budget Board (LBB) and the Legislative Audit Committee are both statutory committees. Created in 1949, the LBB is tasked with developing the initial state budget for the Texas Legislature to consider. Since 1973, the board has also been charged with estimating the fiscal impact of every bill or resolution being considered by the Texas Legislature that has a budgetary impact. An amendment to the Texas Constitution (1876) added in 1978 limits the biennial growth of the state budget and empowers the LBB to establish the limit. During the interim when the legislature is in session, the LBB works with the governor to monitor the implementation of the state budget and make recommendations to state agencies about their spending. The board consists of the lieutenant governor, the Speaker of the Texas House, four senators, and four representatives. Senators and representatives must include the chairs of finance and budget committees in each chamber.

The Legislative Audit Committee consists of the lieutenant governor, the Speaker of the Texas House, the chairs of budget and finance standing committees from each chamber, and at least one other senator. The committee oversees the State Auditor's Office and hires the auditor. The primary function of the committee is to review state agency compliance with state laws and policies that address how state funds are used. For example, the committee investigates if contracts for outside services, such as office equipment purchases, are correctly conducted or if reimbursement expenses for official state travel are correctly handled.

# TEXAS (VS) NEW SOUTH WALES

New South Wales is one of the states in the country of Australia. Like the United States, Australia has a federal system of government, and, like in the United States, most Australian states have bicameral state legislatures. The New South Wales legislature is called the New South Wales Parliament and consists of a lower house called the Legislative Assembly and an upper house called the Legislative Council. However, the legislative process in New South Wales differs in several ways from that of the Texas Legislature.

Because New South Wales relies on a parliamentary system of government in which the key executive branch members are also members of the legislature, the legislative process is dominated by the executive. Bills introduced to the state parliament by members of the executive are called government public bills, and these bills are given priority in the legislature. Other bills introduced by the rest of the parliament are called private member bills. These bills are only considered after the government bills have been voted on by both houses.[i]

A second difference is the fact that during the first reading of a bill in either chamber, a member of the executive cabinet gives a speech on the purpose of the bill. Thus, if the bill is about road and highway construction, the head of Transport for NSW, the New South Wales department of transportation, is the person who gives the speech about the bill. Remember this person also sits in one of the two houses of the state parliament as an elected member of the legislature.[ii]

Reconciling differences in the versions of a bill passed by each house differs considerably in New South Wales. Recall that in Texas, like most U.S. states, a bill passed by the Texas Senate that differs from the version passed by the Texas House of Representatives will have its differences resolved by a conference committee consisting of members of both chambers. The conference committee produces a version of the bill that is sent to each house for consideration without amendment. If both houses agree to the version produced by the conference committee, the reconciled version is sent

to the governor to sign. In New South Wales, when the Legislative Assembly and the Legislative Council pass different versions of the same bill, one of four things may happen. First, the two chambers may send messages back and forth to each other until agreement is reached or one of the chambers decides to set the bill aside.[iii] Second, if both houses wish, the two chambers may meet together in a joint session in order to reconcile the bill. A third option is for the Legislative Assembly to submit the bill to the voters of New South Wales to pass it into law through a statewide referendum. This option is used when the first and second options fail. Finally, if the bill involves ordinary expenses as part of the state budget, the Legislative Assembly may pass the bill again and then send the bill directly to the governor for signing into law.[iv]

## THINKING Critically

★ What is the advantage of having a member of the executive branch explain the importance or significance of a bill during the legislative process?

★ Are there disadvantages to having a member of the executive present during discussion of a bill before the legislature?

★ Are the methods of reconciling a bill passed in different forms in the New South Wales Parliament an improvement over the process used in the Texas Legislature? Why or why not?

---

i. Parliament of New South Wales, "Legislative Process Explained" www.parliament.nsw.gov.au/prod/web/common.nsf/key/LegislativeProcessExplained (accessed September 18, 2014).

ii. Ibid.

iii. Ibid.

iv. Ibid.

## Special Committees

Special committees are created by the Texas Legislature, by an individual chamber of the legislature, or by a presiding officer to accomplish specific types of goals or to serve specific purposes. Several types of special committees exist. Creation of the special committees occurs through a few different types of processes, unique to each type of special committee. However, many political scientists and politicians often consider each of the types of special committees to be distinct, separate categories, in part to provide comparison with the U.S. Congress and with other state legislatures.

### Special Committees: Conference Committees

One type of special committee is necessary because the Texas Legislature contains two chambers. Bills may be passed in different versions in each chamber simply because the two chambers are different in their membership. As a result, actions in their respective standing committees and throughout floor debate will produce changes to each bill unique to that chamber. When a bill passes both houses in different versions as a result of these actions, a single version must be agreed to by both houses before the bill goes to the governor. If the bill begins in the House of Representatives, and if the Senate amends the House version of the bill, then the bill returns to the House as amended by the Senate. If the House agrees to the Senate's amendments, then the bill goes to the governor to be signed into law. If the House rejects one or more of the Senate's amendments, the bill goes to a conference committee. If the bill begins in the Senate, the process is reversed.

A **conference committee** is created to reconcile the differences in the Texas Senate and Texas House versions of a bill. These committees are formed when both chambers agree to form the committee. Conference committees contain ten members, five from the Texas House and five from the Texas Senate. Normally, some of the members of the standing committees who considered the original bill serve on the conference committee that reconciles it. The conference committee meets on a limited basis to reconcile the differences on a bill. After producing a single, reconciled version of the bill, the committee disbands. However, to send the reconciled version of the bill to both chambers of the legislature, at least three members of the conference committee from the Texas Senate and at least three members from the Texas House must agree to the reconciled version of the bill. The bill is then reintroduced to both chambers for consideration. Each chamber must then vote on the reconciled version of the bill without additional amendments and changes. If the reconciled version passes both houses of the legislature, the bill is sent to the governor to sign.

While the conference committee process used by the Texas Legislature mirrors the process of the U.S. Congress, other bicameral legislatures in the world do not use such a process. In Canada, when the Canadian House of Commons and Canadian Senate pass a bill in different forms, the bill is shuttled back and forth between the chambers until the two houses reach agreement. This process was adopted in Canada based upon the British Parliament, where a bill is shuttled back and forth between the British House of Commons and British House of Lords. However, Canada's constitution allows for another option unavailable in Britain. If the Canadian House of Commons and Canadian Senate are deadlocked and unable to come to a complete reconciliation on the bill, the prime minister of Canada may temporarily add up to eight members of the Canadian Senate to break the deadlock. In France, U.S.-style conference committees may be used, or a bill may shuttle back and forth between the National Assembly and French Senate, like in Canada and Great Britain. Also, the president of France has a third option. He or she may seize the bill, rewrite the bill to his or her liking, and reintroduce the bill to the French National Assembly. The National Assembly may simply vote for or against the bill. If the bill passes the National Assembly, the president signs the bill into law. The French Senate is left out of the process.

**Conference committee**
an official legislative work group that meets on a limited basis to reconcile the different versions of a bill that has passed in the Texas House and Senate.

### Special Committees: Select Committee

Another type of special committee is the **select committee**. These committees are normally temporary ones created by either the lieutenant governor for Texas Senate select committees or the Speaker of the Texas House for House select committees. If the lieutenant governor and Speaker create a select committee containing members of both the Texas Senate and Texas House, then the committee is called a joint committee. Regardless of the makeup of the membership, these committees exist for a special purpose. Once the reason for the creation of the committee is resolved or settled, then the committee normally disbands. During the 2013 session of the 83rd Texas Legislature, the lieutenant governor created two select committees for the Senate: one for transportation funding and expenditures and one for redistricting. The former reviewed the methods of financing roads currently used in Texas as well as current and future expectations regarding state highway construction. The second select committee met to resolve issues surrounding the redistricting of the Texas Legislature and other entities, as discussed in Chapter 3.

The Speaker of the Texas House formed three select committees during the 83rd Legislature. One examined the impact of legislation passed by the U.S. Congress on policies and revenue in Texas. Another produced recommendations to reform criminal justice procedures in the state courts. Finally, a select committee was created to investigate the operations and financial transactions of all state executive and judicial branch agencies to promote greater transparency in the state government. During the special session of the legislature that met in June 2013, a select committee was created to address issues surrounding the completion of the redistricting process for the Texas Legislature and other entities. While the Texas Senate also had a similar committee, the two committees were distinct and separate, unique to each chamber.

One joint committee existed during the 2013 legislature's regular session. This committee examined the structure and function of Texas higher education for ways to increase efficiency and promote accountability by the state's public community colleges and universities. The committee also examined how to make policies and activities in Texas higher education more transparent to the public.

### Special Committees: Interim Committee

A final type of committee in the Texas Legislature is the **interim committee**. Interim committees are important because the legislature does not meet each year. During periods when the legislature is not in session, interim committees may be created to provide oversight of the executive branch and to monitor public policy. Typically, interim committees mirror the division of duties and responsibilities used by the standing committees. These committees are often chamber exclusive and are temporary, existing only until the next session of the Texas Legislature. The lieutenant governor and Speaker of the Texas House may agree to create a joint interim committee that contains members of both chambers. Normally, an interim committee studies specific problems or conducts research into specific issues as instructed by the Speaker of the House or lieutenant governor. Its findings can be used to shape new bills when the legislature convenes for its next regular session.

After the 2013 regular session and the related special sessions, Speaker of the House Straus issued a number of instructions to interim committees. For example, the Higher Education Committee was to develop recommendations on the use of technology as a method of educating more students through Massive Open Online Courses (MOOCs) and was to research other ways to reduce the costs of higher education and educate more students. In addition, the Public Education Committee was tasked with monitoring the state's new student assessment system.[41] In addition, a number of interim select committees were empowered with specific activities beyond the ordinary tasks assigned to the interim standing committees. One reviewed the state's child welfare system, while another examined the economic incentives the state allows to encourage businesses to locate in Texas and for state-based businesses to develop and expand. A third interim select committee researched the impact on the state budget of support operations that Texas provides to ensure security along the Texas-Mexico border.

Among the interim committees of the Texas Senate, the Criminal Justice Committee was charged with reviewing the state's specialized courts that deal with juvenile cases, and the Health and Human Services Committee was charged with identifying ways to provide cost-effective health care to the poor in Texas using market-based, private health care providers, not the state's Medicare/Medicaid system.[42]

## WINNERS AND LOSERS

**P**arty caucuses, special legislative caucuses, and committee organization have a significant and increasingly important impact on the Texas Legislature. The committee organization, especially the standing committees, has historically proved to be a place for individual legislators to influence bills by offering amendments, changing the language of bills, and even killing bills in committee. Likewise, interim committee work allows legislators to influence state policy and politics while the legislature is not in session, and conference committees offer legislators an opportunity to develop a final version of a bill that most likely will pass into law. Because both the lieutenant governor and the Speaker of the Texas House have power over these committees through appointment of members, referring bills to standing committees, issuing charges to the interim committees, and the like, the committee structure and organization reinforce the powers of the presiding officers of each chamber. This reinforcing, to the extent that it continues today, reflects a tradition in Texas politics. In this sense, the presiding officers of each chamber are winners.

In contrast, party caucuses and special legislative caucuses may offer an alternative to the power of the presiding officers. Party caucuses, although relatively new, are becoming increasingly important to the legislature. For the majority party, the party caucus offers a mechanism to control more directly the content of bills and amendments. For the minority party, the party caucus works as a mechanism to get its message to the public through public relations and awareness campaigns. The minority party, due to its smaller size, obviously has less influence than the majority party.

The transformation of the Texas Legislature associated with the creation of party caucuses is making the majority party, the Republicans, the winners as long as the party remains cohesive within each chamber. That the Democrats are reduced to public relations and awareness campaigns places them at a distinct disadvantage. Democrats are clearly the losers in the new arrangement of Texas politics. Whether in the long term the rise of party caucuses means an end to the bipartisan, Speaker-centered nature of the workings of the Texas House of Representatives or to the workings of the Texas Senate remains uncertain. Because the leadership of party caucuses and the leadership style of the lieutenant governor and Speaker influence the role and function of the political parties and the extent of bipartisanship, winners and losers vary over time depending on this factor as well.

Special legislative caucuses are also important in the legislative process. Because they provide opportunities for members of the legislature to network on common interests, these caucuses offer a chance to work outside the normal committee system and away from the presiding officers of both chambers of the legislature. Special legislative caucuses also provide a springboard for amendments and other changes to legislation. As a result, these caucuses may work against the presiding officers and may offer an alternative to the rising power and influence of the party caucus system. However, their likelihood to be winners or losers depends on the degree of party cohesion and the style of chamber leadership.

★ Why are the Speaker of the Texas House and lieutenant governor such powerful figures in Texas politics?

★ Has the shift in Texas from Democratic Party control over the Texas Legislature to Republican Party control changed how the legislature functions in ways that impact how well legislators are able to represent the interests of their constituents?

★ How significant a role does the party caucus leader play in the ability of the party caucus to influence legislation effectively?

## LEGISLATIVE PROCESS

A primary function of the Texas Legislature is making new laws and updating existing ones. Therefore, the legislative process, or how a bill becomes a law, is an important part of the legislature. While this process is often considered relatively mundane and ordinary, several nuances of the process in Texas are quite unique.

**Bills** are the product of a number of sources. Some legislators are policy entrepreneurs who enjoy researching and writing bills to solve problems or address issues of concern to them and their constituents. Interest groups or other organized interests often develop model legislation for members of the legislature to review. In some cases, these model bills heavily influence bills that members of the legislature write. Agencies of Texas government, such as the Texas Department of Transportation or Texas Coordinating Board for Higher Education, suggest possible bills to the legislature. Most bills originate in the Texas Legislative Council, a professionally staffed arm

**Bill**
a proposed new law or change to existing law brought before a legislative chamber by a legislative member.

of the legislature. However, the creation of the Republican policy chair in the Texas House of Representatives reflects a new, party-centered source for bills.

## Introducing Bills in the Legislature

For a bill to become a law, it must be **introduced** by a member of the chamber in which it is to be considered. Because a bill must pass both houses of the Texas Legislature, the author of a bill will often seek out members of both chambers to help co-sponsor it. Thus, if the bill originates outside of the legislature itself, the organized interest or government agency seeks out a member of the legislature to sponsor or co-sponsor the bill. In addition, sponsoring or co-sponsoring a bill allows a member of the legislature to take credit for helping the bill to become a law, if it does become a law. Such **credit claiming** helps reinforce the idea that the legislator is hard at work promoting the interests of his or her district. In the end, credit claiming assists the legislator in getting reelected because the legislator may point to a list of bills that he or she made sure became law, thus helping to do what the people in the district wanted.

Each time the legislature meets for its regular session, thousands of bills are filed and introduced into the legislature. In the 83rd Legislature's regular session in 2013, a total of 10,630 bills and resolutions were introduced. About 55 percent of the items introduced were bills; the remaining 45 percent were resolutions. Of those bills and resolutions, 5,909 were passed by the legislature. Most of the items that were passed were resolutions; only 24.3 percent, or 1,437 of the total, were bills. Bills passed by the legislature are almost always signed into law by the governor. Of the bills passed by the 83rd Legislature, only twenty-six were vetoed by the governor.

Bills may be prefiled before the start of each legislative session, meaning that the bill may be sent to the chamber in which it will be introduced prior to the start of the legislative session. Most states allow prefiling of bills, with the notable exceptions of Michigan, North Carolina, and Wisconsin. In Texas, any new bill may be introduced up to sixty calendar days after the start of the legislative session. Note that "calendar days" means actual days, not just days that the legislature is meeting. Calendar days include weekends and holidays. To introduce a bill after the sixtieth day requires the agreement of 80 percent of the members of the chamber present.

Any bill dealing with the state budget must be considered by the Texas House of Representatives first. Budget bills must be introduced by the thirtieth day after the legislative session opens. Any bill that impacts the state budget must include the cost involved, a projection of future costs, the source of revenue, and the impact on local governments.[43] Texas also requires statements about the impact of the bill on the equalized public education funding formula and on criminal justice policy. These last two provisions are unique to Texas.

## Introducing Resolutions in the Legislature

In addition to bills, members of the legislature may introduce resolutions. A **resolution** expresses the opinion of the legislature on an issue or changes the organizational structure of the legislature. Three types of resolutions exist: a simple resolution, a concurrent resolution, and a joint resolution. A **simple resolution** addresses organizational

**Introduce [a bill]**
to officially bring a bill before a legislative chamber for the first time. Introducing a bill is the first step in the formal legislative process.

**Credit claiming**
the advantage derived from incumbents' ability to point to positive outcomes for which they are responsible.

**Resolution**
a legislative act that expresses the opinion of the legislature on an issue or changes the organizational structure of the legislature.

**Simple resolution**
a legislative act that addresses organizational issues; may be limited to a single house.

issues, such as changing the number of standing committees or altering the powers of committee chairs. These resolutions may be limited to a single house of the legislature. A **concurrent resolution** expresses the opinion of the legislature and requires passage in both houses. For example, the legislature may pass a resolution asking the U.S. Congress to change a policy. A resolution may also cover seemingly trivial matters, such as commending the University of Texas football team for winning the Cotton Bowl or the Texas A&M women's golf team for winning a conference championship. A **joint resolution** is particularly important because this legislative act, when passed by both chambers, proposes amendments to the Texas Constitution. Those amendments are then sent to the voters for approval at the next election.

## Legislation in Committee

When a bill or resolution is introduced into a chamber, it is assigned a number by the secretary of the Texas Senate or the chief clerk of the Texas House. The number indicates the chamber in which the legislation originated and the order that it was introduced. For example, HR 10 indicates the tenth resolution introduced into the Texas House, while SB 351 is the 351st bill introduced into the Texas Senate.

After legislation is introduced, it is assigned to a standing committee (see Infographic on pp. 140–141). In the Texas Senate, bills are referred to committee by the president of the Senate, the lieutenant governor. Bills in the Texas House are referred to committee by the Speaker of the House. Normally, bills are referred to the standing committee with jurisdiction over the policy area. Yet the Speaker and lieutenant governor have the power to send a bill to any standing committee in their respective chambers that they choose. In the Texas House, if the sponsor of a bill believes the Speaker has unfairly assigned the bill to a committee to kill the bill, the sponsor may ask for a so-called Jim Hogg Committee. When a majority of the Texas House votes in favor of the Jim Hogg Committee, the standing committee meets in front of the entire House to consider the bill.[44]

To assist in their work, a handful of standing committees in both chambers of the Texas Legislature contain subcommittees. A subcommittee may conduct a detailed examination of the bill or resolution and report to the whole committee before the final committee vote is taken. Subcommittees have the same powers as their related standing committee to amend or kill a bill.

### Calendars in the Texas House

After a series of public hearings, debates, markup sessions, and amendments, the standing committee takes a final vote on the bill. If the committee reports favorably on it, the bill returns to the entire membership of the chamber for consideration. In the Texas House, the bill then goes to one of a few special standing committees. These are procedural committees. For bills with statewide implications, the bill goes to the Calendars Committee. The Calendars Committee places each bill that it receives on the chamber's schedule, determining when it will be considered and specifying how long the bill will be debated. The Calendars Committee assigns the bill to one of several different calendars. In the Texas House, at least seven different calendars exist (see Table 4.3). These calendars are arranged in order from most important to least important. Bills on more important calendars are considered first, with bills on less important calendars handled if time remains during the legislative session. If a bill affects only a specific county, city, or other local government, it is sent to the Local and Consent Calendars Committee rather than the Calendars Committee. This standing committee determines when local and consent bills are considered by the whole Texas House and how long a bill is to be debated. The Rules and Resolutions Standing Committee performs a similar function for memorials and other resolutions.

Regardless of whether a bill is assigned to one of the seven calendars by the Calendars Committee or the Local and Consent Calendars Committee, any bill or resolution may be shifted by the Texas House to a more important (or faster) calendar by a two-thirds vote. Because the Texas House has the ability to move a bill to a different calendar than the one assigned by one of the calendar-oriented committees, the exact calendar a bill is assigned to is not as important as one might expect.

### Calendars in the Texas Senate

The calendar committees is one of the key differences between the Texas Senate and the Texas House. In the Texas Senate, there is no special calendar committee and only one calendar exists, with bills listed in the order they were formally introduced. However, the Texas Senate almost never considers bills in this order. Instead, it has developed a trick that allows senators to change the order of consideration. The first bill introduced each session is known as a **blocking bill**, or stopper—a bill that is introduced not to be passed but merely to hold a place at the top of the Texas Senate calendar. This bill prevents bills below it on the calendar from being considered. Like the Texas House

**Blocking bill**
a bill regularly introduced in the Texas Senate to serve as a placeholder at the top of the Senate calendar; sometimes called a stopper.

---

**TABLE 4.3** **Calendars in the Texas House of Representatives (Most Important to Least Important)**

| Calendar | Purpose |
| --- | --- |
| Emergency | Emergency bills; also used for taxation and appropriation bills |
| Major State | Important bills with statewide impact |
| Constitutional Amendments | Amendments to the Texas Constitution |
| General State | Bills with statewide impact deemed less important than those designated "Major State" |
| Local, Consent, and Resolution | Bills involving activities of specific counties, cities, and other governments; noncontroversial resolutions |
| Resolution | Votes in which the Texas House offers an opinion on some topic but passes no bill on it |
| Congratulatory and Memorial | House resolution expressing gratitude or thanks to some person or recognition of some event, but no bills passed on the matter |

**Source:** Compiled by the authors from data available at Texas House of Representatives, House Calendars, www.house.state.tx.us/help/calendar/ (accessed August 29, 2014).

# HOW TEXAS GOVERNMENT WORKS

## Lawmaking

**Idea for bill from:**

**A person**

**A state legislator**

**An interim committee**

**An organized interest**

### Legislation Introduced

*Legislation may be introduced as early as 60 days prior to session.*

**First Reading**
Referral to committee

### Committee Work

Bills can originate in either the House or the Senate

**First Reading**
Referral to committee

An approved House bill with amendments is printed and sent to the Senate for consideration.

**Committee Work**

**House Bill on Senate Floor**

### House Bill Sent to The Senate

Tagging

Public Hearings

Debate and Amendment

Committee Report

Placed on Senate Calendar

**A majority vote of committee membership is required.**

Senate amendments to House bills go to the House for approval

*House concurs with amendments*

*Reconciled in conference committee*

**A senator may filibuster and hold the floor for an unlimited debate.**

**Second Reading**

Debate and Amendment

Vote

**Third Reading**

Vote

*Enrollment*

**A tie vote or failure to gain a simple majority**

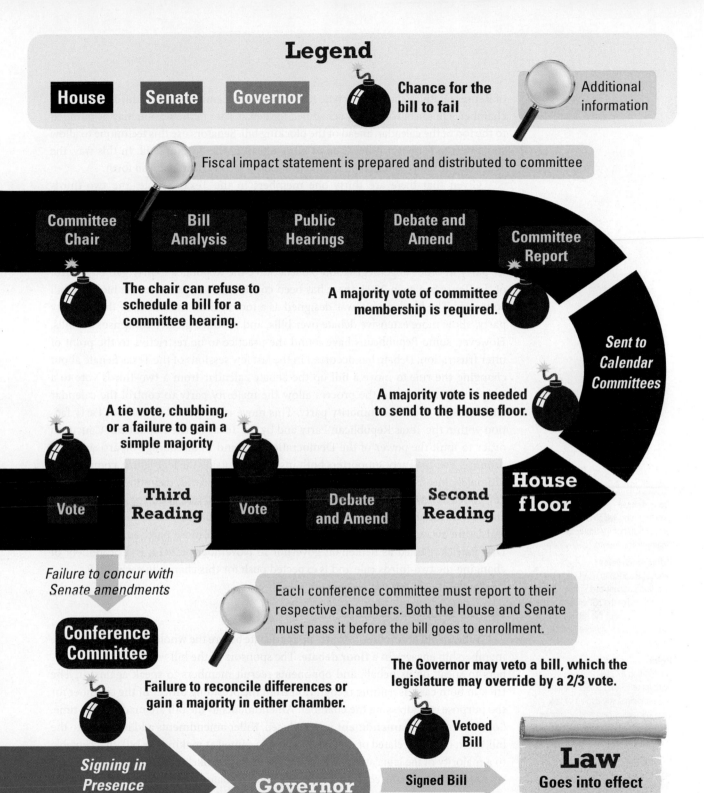

## Legend

**House** **Senate** **Governor** | Chance for the bill to fail | Additional information

Fiscal impact statement is prepared and distributed to committee

**Committee Chair** **Bill Analysis** **Public Hearings** **Debate and Amend** **Committee Report**

**Sent to Calendar Committees**

The chair can refuse to schedule a bill for a committee hearing.

A majority vote of committee membership is required.

A majority vote is needed to send to the House floor.

A tie vote, chubbing, or a failure to gain a simple majority

**Vote** **Third Reading** **Vote** **Debate and Amend** **Second Reading** **House floor**

Failure to concur with Senate amendments

**Conference Committee**

Each conference committee must report to their respective chambers. Both the House and Senate must pass it before the bill goes to enrollment.

Failure to reconcile differences or gain a majority in either chamber.

The Governor may veto a bill, which the legislature may override by a 2/3 vote.

**Vetoed Bill**

**Signing in Presence of House** **Governor** Signed Bill / Unsigned Bill

## Law
Goes into effect after 90 days unless otherwise stipulated.

**Sources:** Adapted from Texas Co-Op Magazine, "Infographic: How a Bill Becomes a Law," http://sbisdlegislative.blogspot.com/2013/04/infographic-how-bill-becomes-law.html. Original figure designed by MikeWirthArt.com & Suzanne Cooper-Guasco, Ph.D and © Texas Co-op Power/Texas Electric Cooperatives.

of Representatives, the Texas Senate may adjust the calendar by a two-thirds vote of the chamber. Thus, a bill originally scheduled for debate later in the session may be bumped to the top of the calendar, ahead of the blocking bill. Senators use this technique to allow some bills to leap over others and to jump ahead of the blocking bill. In this way, the Texas Senate chooses which bills to consider first, second, third, and so forth.

Given that there are thirty-one members in the Texas Senate, the two-thirds requirement means that any eleven members can effectively prevent a bill from being moved to the floor for debate. This situation gives the minority party the potential to threaten any bill, because the minority usually holds at least eleven seats in the Texas Senate. As such, the majority party must regularly consider the opinion of the minority party in order to get legislation passed. Since the Republican Party gained control of the Texas Senate in 2003, there has been considerable debate over the blocking bill approach. The blocking bill was designed as a tool to limit the power of the majority party, allow more extensive debate over bills, and produce greater consensus on bills. However, some Republicans have found the practice to be restrictive to the point of utter frustration. Debate has occurred in the last few sessions of the Texas Senate about changing the rule to move a bill up the Senate calendar from a two-thirds vote to a simple majority, and in the process allow the majority party to control the calendar without input from the minority party. This move is supported by the Tea Party faction within the Texas Republican Party and by the Texas Senate Republican Caucus in order to limit the power of the Democratic Party and to discourage bipartisan compromise. For Tea Party supporters both inside and outside the legislature, compromise ultimately means giving up their ideals and view of the world, including surrendering key policies and desired outcomes. This issue is certain to return during the 2015 regular session. Changing the two-thirds rule would undoubtedly continue to move the legislature away from the norm of bipartisanship into a more partisan environment. Dan Patrick, elected as lieutenant governor in November of 2014, is a proponent of changing the two-thirds rule and is expected push for this change in early 2015.

## Debate in the Legislature

When a bill or resolution comes up for debate before the whole chamber, the entire membership engages in a **floor debate**. The sponsors of the bill will arrange for members to speak on its behalf, and opponents recruit members to speak against it. The trick in both cases is gaining recognition from the presiding officer of the chamber for the purpose of addressing the chamber. Amendments to the bill are made at this time. Sometimes a **killer amendment** is introduced. Killer amendments add language to the bill, often on an unrelated or controversial topic, aimed at making the bill unacceptable to a majority of the legislature, which will then be more likely to vote against it.

At any time during committee action or floor debate, a member may attach a rider to an appropriations bill. A **rider** is an addition to the bill that deals with an unrelated subject, usually changing some aspect of an existing law or public policy. A rider may also call for the spending of money. Riders often spend money or create programs in a specific member's district. Riders are common in many state legislatures and in the U.S. Congress. In Texas, a rider may be a **closed rider**, or one that is not made public until

**Floor debate**
period during which a bill is brought up before the entire chamber for debate.

**Killer amendment**
language added to a bill on an unrelated or controversial topic in order to make the bill unacceptable to the majority of the legislature, which will then be more likely to vote against it.

**Rider**
an addition to a bill that deals with an unrelated subject, such as changing some aspect of law or public policy or spending money or creating programs in a specific member's district.

**Closed rider**
a rider that is not made public until after the legislature has voted on the bill; it is made public either when the bill goes to conference committee for reconciliation or when the governor prepares to sign the bill into law.

after the legislature has voted on the bill. Riders are revealed when a bill goes to a conference committee for reconciliation or when the governor gets ready to sign the bill into law.

After the floor debate, members of the chamber vote on the various amendments and then on the final version of the bill. This vote is the second reading of the bill (the first reading occurred when the bill was introduced to the chamber). In the Texas Senate, the time of debate is unlimited, so any member may speak indefinitely on the bill. Sometimes, a member of the Senate engages in a **filibuster**, which is an effort to kill a bill by engaging in prolonged debate and refusing to yield the floor to another member. This stalling tactic serves to prevent a vote from being taken. A filibuster is ended by a majority vote of the Texas Senate. Because debate time is limited in the Texas House, a filibuster cannot occur in that chamber. However, at times members of the House engage in lengthy debate over bills that are not controversial. This action is generally employed late in the legislative session and is used to prevent the Texas House from beginning debate on a more controversial issue or bill. This technique of delaying action on a bill to prevent the consideration of another bill is called **chubbing**. The representative engaged in chubbing may or may not be in favor of the current bill but is trying to block consideration of the next bill on the Texas House calendar. The filibuster in the Texas Senate and chubbing in the Texas House are important tools employed by the minority party in its effort to influence the legislative process and prevent the majority party from railroading bills through the legislature.

Another tool employed by the minority party to influence voting is the **quorum**. Texas Senate rules require that two-thirds of the membership be present to take a vote. Because there are only thirty-one senators, two-thirds of the membership is equal to twenty-one members. Therefore, any eleven senators may prevent business from being conducted if they absent themselves from the chamber. Again, this need for a quorum prods members of the Senate to consider the opinion of the minority party. Prior to the 1990s, the two-thirds rule allowed the handful of Republicans in the Texas Senate to join with a small number of Democrats to block legislation. Between 1993 and 2002, Republicans had enough seats to use the two-thirds rule in their favor to compel the majority Democratic Party to alter legislation; Democrats, for their part, were often frustrated by this need to accommodate Republican concerns. When Democrats became the minority party in the Texas Senate following the 2002 election, they too quickly

Lieutenant Governor David Dewhurst and Senate parliamentarian Karina Davis oversee debate during the first called special session in 2013.

**Filibuster**
an effort to kill a bill by engaging in unlimited debate and refusing to yield the floor to another member, ultimately preventing a vote on the bill.

**Chubbing**
the act of delaying action on the current bill before the Texas House of Representatives to prevent action on an upcoming bill.

**Quorum**
the minimum number of members in a legislative body who need to be present for the body to conduct business; in the Texas Senate, a quorum is twenty-one members. In the Texas House of Representatives, a quorum is 100 members.

The Texas Senate chamber contains the original walnut desks purchased in 1888. The paintings on the wall behind the lieutenant governor's desk depict key figures in Texas political history, with Stephen F. Austin's painting in the center.

discovered the advantages of the two-thirds rule. Discussion occurred after 2003 among the Republican Party as to whether the quorum rule needed to be abolished or changed to again limit the power of the minority party. As mentioned previously, this debate continues within the Republican Party, with the Tea Party faction arguing for the end of the two-thirds quorum rule.

## Voting on Passage

After the chamber vote, a third reading takes place just prior to the final vote on the bill. While numerous votes are cast, there are, broadly speaking, two types of votes that occur in the Texas Legislature. In general, voting processes are similar in both houses of the legislature. Votes may be either a voice vote or a roll call vote. A voice vote occurs when the presiding officer asks verbally for those members in favor of the bill or amendment to call out "aye," then asks for those members opposed to call out "nay." For these voice votes, the presiding officer simply announces whether the bill or amendment passes. If the presiding officer is uncertain of the result, the officer calls for a roll call vote. In addition, a member of the chamber who questions the outcome of the voice vote may call for a roll call vote. Normally, the presiding officer agrees to allow the roll call vote to occur. Typically, any important vote will be conducted as a **roll call vote**. In the Texas House, roll call votes are recorded electronically; in the Texas Senate all votes are voice votes. In the case of a roll call vote in the Texas Senate, each senator's name is called, and the senator's vote, whether "aye" or "nay," is written down. In the case of all roll call votes, each member votes separately. Each vote is then recorded, creating a permanent record of how each member voted. Some roll call votes may be conducted on paper ballots.

Sometimes legislators cannot be present for votes on the floor of the legislature. In these cases, the casting of "ghost" votes—essentially having another legislator cast a vote for the missing member—is common practice. Although members of the legislature are supposed to be present when they cast votes, sometimes the clerk of the chamber is unaware that a particular member is not present. In these circumstances, legislators arrange for other members to cast votes for them. In April 2007, Rep. Mike Krusee (R–Williamson County) attended a conference in London even as he cast some thirty votes on the floor of the House in Austin. Reportedly, Rep. Marc Veasey (D–Fort Worth) punched in votes for Krusee.[45] This practice continued into the 2013 session.

**Roll call vote**
a form of voting for which a permanent record of each member's vote is created; used for more important votes.

## The Killer Bees

No story better reflects the eccentric politics created by the rules of the Texas Legislature than the story of the Killer Bees. The Bees emerged in May 1970 during a battle over whether Texas should have a separate presidential primary in 1980. One side, supported by former lieutenant governor Bill Hobby, favored a separate primary so that conservative Democrats could cast a vote in a Republican presidential primary for Ronald Reagan or former Texas governor John Connally on March 11 and then return to the Democratic Party in May to outvote the liberals in the primary for other offices. The other side wanted a single primary that would force conservative Democrats to choose a party. Hobby nicknamed some of the liberal legislators who resisted his agenda in the legislature the "Killer Bees," because he said he never knew where they would strike next. Opponents of the separate primary were worked into a frenzy when Hobby slipped the primary into an innocuous election bill that had already passed the Texas House and was coming before the Texas Senate. This would have allowed him to get around the two-thirds vote required to pass most bills. With ten days left in the legislative session, the Bees had grown to twelve members, but they knew that they lacked the two-thirds majority required to block passage. However, they also realized that the Senate would lack a quorum and couldn't pass any more bills if all twelve of them refused to attend.

The Killer Bees took flight and disappeared from the legislature. Law enforcement was sent to round them up while the rest of the senators found themselves unable to leave the Senate as Hobby kept them in the capitol building. For five days the Bees evaded authorities, although nine of them were hiding in an apartment just over two miles from the capitol building. The Texas Rangers nearly caught Senator Gene Jones after he left the Austin hideout because of claustrophobia. When lawmen arrived at Jones's new hideout, they mistakenly arrested his brother when he answered the door while Senator Jones jumped the back fence.

Although Texans might not have usually sided with the liberal-leaning Bees, there was little sympathy for the political interests behind the bill for a separate primary, and Texans and the nation found themselves caught up in the spectacle of the small band of Bees eluding a statewide manhunt and foiling the powerful forces aligned against them. Eventually, Hobby relented, inviting the Bees back to the Senate after abandoning his maneuvers on behalf of the bill. While the saga of the Killer Bees reads like a surreal adventure, it highlights the problem with the Texas Senate's requirement that a bill be passed with two-thirds of the vote, a threshold that is high enough to allow a determined and creative minority to resist change.

Once a bill has passed one chamber of the legislature, it goes to the other chamber for consideration. Again, bills dealing with taxation and spending must start out in the Texas House of Representatives before going to the Texas Senate. All other bills may start out in either chamber before going on to the other. As noted above, once both chambers have passed a bill in identical form, the bill goes to the governor for signing. If the House and Senate have passed different versions of the same bill, then the bill first goes to a conference committee for reconciliation. The conference committee may attach several amendments or may rewrite the bill. The recommendation of the conference committee is sent back to both chambers of the Texas Legislature in the form of a report. Each chamber may accept the changes to the bill, reject the changes to the bill, or send the bill back to the conference committee. If both chambers accept the changes, the bill has passed. If the bill fails to pass either chamber or if the conference committee cannot reconcile the differences, the bill dies. If a bill has not been passed by the legislature before the end of the session, the bill dies, as bills do not carry over to another legislative session. Twenty-four states, though not Texas, allow some form of carryover.[46] After a bill is sent to the governor, he or she must sign the bill into law or veto it. If the governor does not sign the bill into law and the legislature is still in session, after ten days it automatically becomes law.

### The Governor's Veto Power

While the governor possesses the power to veto legislation, this power is limited. For all bills but those dealing with spending, the governor must veto or accept the entire bill. The governor may use a **line-item veto**, or a selective veto of some parts of a bill, on spending bills only. An override of the governor's veto is possible only by a two-thirds vote of each house of the state legislature. If the legislature ends its session, the governor has twenty days to veto the bill; otherwise, the bill becomes law. Ninety days after the legislature ends its session, any law enacted becomes effective unless the bill contains an **emergency clause**, which makes a bill effective immediately upon being signed into law.

### Trends in Legislative Activity

Given the relatively short period for the Texas Legislature to conduct its business, just 140 days every two years, the legislature's time is at a premium while in session. However, for approximately the first month, the legislature's work on the budget and major state bills is focused on action in the standing committees, with very little floor action on bills and amendments to bills. Since both chambers are waiting for bills to be introduced and for standing committees to finish their work on the bills that have been introduced, much of the activity on the floor of the legislature is on resolutions, especially those that congratulate individuals or groups for some achievement. These resolutions typically speed through the legislative process, including the standing committees, because they are normally noncontroversial. Also, remember that most bills are introduced in the first sixty days of the session since after the sixtieth day, any bill introduced requires 80 percent of the chamber to agree to consider it. As a result of these provisions, the more serious work of the legislature begins after the sixtieth day of the legislative session.

As the size and scope of state government has increased, so has the activity of the Texas Legislature. The last two decades offer some interesting insights into the level of activity of legislators. Since 1991, the total number of bills and resolutions introduced in the Texas Legislature has increased from around 7,000 items per session to well over 10,000. In addition, the total number of items that the legislature has passed has increased. However, the total number of bills passed by the Texas Legislature peaked during the 76th and 77th sessions, with recent sessions passing a few hundred fewer bills each regular session. In recent years, the number of resolutions passed by the legislature has grown faster than the number of bills passed.

What has changed in the setting of the legislature that might influence the number of resolutions and bills that it passes? Perhaps the answer lies in the rise of the party caucuses in both chambers. The creation of these caucuses has resulted in an environment in which the majority party is able to focus the attention of its members on specific bills to pass, to develop amendments to bills, to recruit speakers for floor debate, and to encourage party caucus members to vote as a block. Such structuring of the vote through a more party-centered model has allowed the legislature to pass more bills and resolutions.

What may be more telling is the balance between bills and resolutions introduced and the balance between bills and resolutions passed by the Texas Legislature. As shown in Figure 4.1, the percentage of bills introduced during the regular session has varied from 64.7 percent of all items in 1997 to 55.2 percent in 2013. However, the balance remains relatively stable over time, with the ratio of bills to resolutions introduced remaining fairly consistent. What really appears to have changed is the balance between resolutions approved by the Texas Legislature and bills approved. Since 1991, while the number of items passed has increased, as shown in Figure 4.2, the percentage of those items that were bills has changed. Figure 4.3 shows that 30.2 percent of all items passed by the legislature in 1991 were bills, while the remainder were resolutions. That percentage rose in the late 1990s but has fallen in recent sessions of the legislature to reach a new low in the 2013 regular session. In 2013, fewer than one in four items passed by the legislature was a bill, and just over three of every four items was a resolution. Although the legislature in recent years has passed resolutions covering substantive issues, such as amending the Texas Constitution or health care reform, most of the resolutions passed by the legislature are simply to congratulate individuals and groups for some achievement. The increase in the number of resolutions may simply reflect a greater number of congratulations passed by the legislature.

Even during a special session of the legislature, the workload may be staggering. In 2013, the first special session saw 568 items introduced, 130 bills of which were bills (22.9 percent). Only three bills were passed into law, but the legislature

## FIGURE 4.1 Balance of Items Introduced in the Texas Legislature, 1991–2013

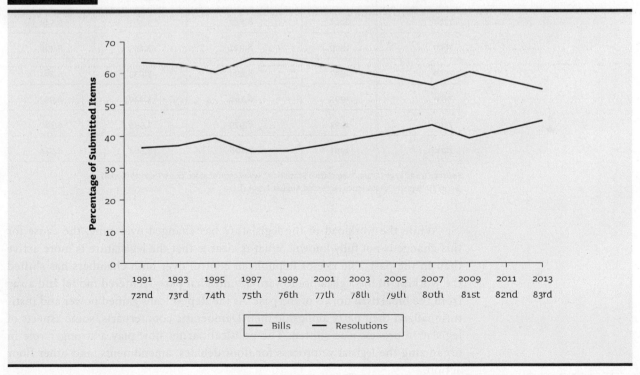

*Source:* Texas Legislature, "Legislative Statistics," www.capitol.state.tx.us/Reports/Report.aspx?ID=legislativestatistics (accessed August 4, 2014).

managed to pass 409 resolutions, which meant that bills represented less than 1 percent of what the Texas Legislature accomplished during its first session. During the second special session, 444 items were introduced, ninety-nine of which were bills (22.3 percent). The legislature passed two bills and 314 resolutions. The final, third special session featured forty-five bills and thirty-four resolutions introduced. Although the ratio of bills to resolutions is much higher than in the earlier special sessions, the legislature passed only one bill but managed to pass thirty-one of the thirty-four resolutions.

**TABLE 4.4** **Bills and Resolutions Considered by the Texas Legislature, 1991–2013**

| Session | Year | Total Introduced | Resolutions | Bills |
|---------|------|------------------|-------------|-------|
| 83rd | 2013 | 10,630 | 4,762 | 5,868 |
| 82nd | 2011 | 10,315 | 4,519 | 5,796 |
| 81st | 2009 | 12,238 | 4,819 | 7,419 |
| 80th | 2007 | 10,990 | 4,800 | 6,190 |
| 79th | 2005 | 9,347 | 3,863 | 5,484 |
| 78th | 2003 | 9,232 | 3,640 | 5,592 |
| 77th | 2001 | 8,847 | 3,303 | 5,544 |
| 76th | 1999 | 8,921 | 3,155 | 5,766 |
| 75th | 1997 | 8,594 | 3,033 | 5,561 |
| 74th | 1995 | 8,186 | 3,229 | 4,957 |
| 73rd | 1993 | 6,979 | 2,599 | 4,380 |
| 72nd | 1991 | 7,108 | 2,584 | 4,524 |

*Source:* Texas Legislature, "Legislative Statistics," www.capitol.state.tx.us/Reports/Report .aspx?ID=legislativestatistics (accessed August 2, 2014).

While the workload of the legislature has changed over time, the cause for this change is not fully known. What is clear is that the legislature is more active than in the past. The rise of Republican control over both chambers has shifted the working of the legislature toward a somewhat party-centered model and away from the bipartisan norms of the past. As the Republicans gained power and institutionalized their party alongside their Democratic counterparts, some aspects of legislative process also shifted. The political parties now play a stronger role in organizing the legislative process for floor debates, amendments, and other floor action.

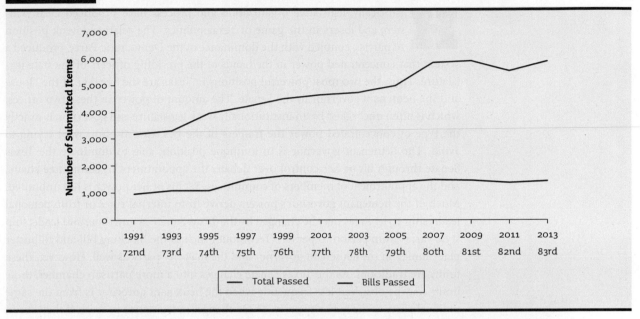

**FIGURE 4.2** Legislation Passed by the Texas Legislature, 1991–2013

*Source:* Texas Legislature, "Legislative Statistics," www.capitol.state.tx.us/Reports/Report.aspx?ID=legislativestatistics (accessed August 4, 2014).

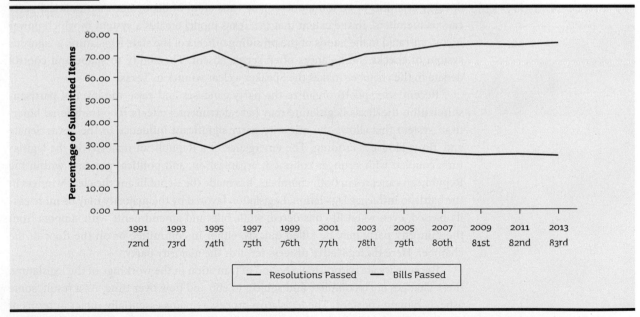

**FIGURE 4.3** Balance of Items Passed by the Texas Legislature, 1991–2013

*Source:* Texas Legislature, "Legislative Statistics," August 4, 2014, www.capitol.state.tx.us/Reports/Report.aspx?ID=legislativestatistics (accessed August 4, 2014).

# WINNERS AND LOSERS

**H**istorically, legislative organization and process have produced clear winners and losers in the game of Texas politics. The relatively weak position of parties, coupled with the dominance of the Democratic Party, produced a system that concentrated power in the hands of the presiding officers of the state legislature. Thus, the two most powerful positions in Texas are the Speaker of the House and the lieutenant governor in the Senate. The amount of power in these two offices, which is often unchecked by an institutionally weak legislature and governor, is exactly the type of concentrated power the framers of the U.S. Constitution were trying to avoid. The lieutenant governor is in a unique position, able to dominate the Texas Senate through his or her control over debate, the appointment of committee chairs, and the appointment of members of committees. Yet his or her power is not unlimited. Much of the lieutenant governor's powers derive from internal rules or from personal leadership style. Rules may be changed by the Texas Senate at any time, and leadership style varies from person to person. Techniques such as the blocking bill and filibuster place limits on the lieutenant governor and the majority party as well. However, these limits are traditions. As the Texas Senate changes into a more partisan chamber, these limits may be observed less frequently when the lieutenant governor is from the same political party as the majority party. These changes in legislative process, if they occur, will clearly benefit the majority party and harm the minority party.

The Speaker of the Texas House is arguably more powerful than the lieutenant governor and courts support from individual legislators regardless of party affiliation, rewarding supporters with favorable consideration of legislation and committee assignments. However, the Speaker's power is limited by possible revolts when the Speaker attempts to be too autocratic or runs afoul of his or her own political party caucus members. To the extent that the Texas model creates a system in which power is concentrated in the hands of the presiding officers of the state legislature, a vigorous system of checks and balances often seems absent. The ability to shape and control debate in the chamber makes the Speaker a clear winner in Texas.

Recent attempts to organize the party caucuses and raise the level of partisanship within the Texas Legislature may have detrimental effects. The traditional bipartisan system that allows the minority party significant influence in the Texas Senate and Texas House is eroding. The emergence of a Republican majority in the legislature, coupled with stronger cohesion, organization, and political pressure within the Republican caucuses in both chambers, has made the Republicans the clear winners in the battle to influence legislation. Legislation favored by the majority may be more easily passed, even when ill-considered, while bills and amendments with support from the minority party may be killed quickly, either in committee or on the floor of the chamber. Here the legislative process rewards the majority party.

Because we are witnessing a period of transition in the workings of the legislature, these changes are incomplete and subject to ebb and flow over time. As a result, some aspects remain constant. The legislative process remains essentially intact in terms of the formal steps for a bill to become a law. For example, despite threats in the Texas

Senate to abolish the need for a two-thirds vote of the chamber to move a bill to the floor or to limit the use of the filibuster, the Senate has not formally done so. In addition, the presiding officers continue to wield extensive powers over their respective chambers. Moreover, the committee structure of the Texas Legislature remains consistent with the past. Tradition trumps transition in much of this aspect of legislative process. The winners are the supporters of the existing state of affairs in the Texas Legislature.

Service in the Texas Legislature in Austin is sometimes a precursor to later service in the U.S. House of Representatives in Washington, D.C.; thus, the tradition of bipartisan cooperation in the state legislature has historically translated into a bipartisan congressional delegation from Texas in the U.S. Congress. One group of scholars has suggested that Texas's domination of leadership positions in the U.S. Congress (for example, the Speakerships of Sam Rayburn and Jim Wright in the U.S. House of Representatives and the Senate leadership of Lyndon Johnson) reflects the ability of the Texas delegation to build coalitions and get along with various factions within both parties.[47] The Texas federal delegation has long had a reputation for putting party concerns aside to cooperate in the best interests of the state. As a result, Texas has gained outsized influence in the U.S. Congress and has often received more than its share of favorable national legislation and program funding.

If partisan politics in the Texas Legislature continues to trump the need to work together to accomplish the state's business, the recent increase in partisan divisions at the state and national level may undermine legislators' abilities to get things done. Concentration of power in the hands of the presiding officers of the Texas Legislature, and the bipartisan support that results, has historically created a different set of incentives and outcomes in Austin than in Washington, D.C. In Austin, the current trajectory increasingly leaves the Democratic Party with a strategy of communication and public awareness campaigns as the primary means to get its message across. The majority party may be the winner in the short term, but status as a majority party is not guaranteed in the long term. The losers may ultimately be Texans as a whole. However, the influence of the political party is dependent on the leadership style of the presiding officer of each chamber, the cohesion in the majority party (currently the Republicans), and the style of leadership of the majority caucus leaders. Winners and losers are determined in part by these factors as well.

★ Does the difference in the process of considering a bill in the Texas House of Representatives and the Texas Senate slow down the passage of meaningful legislation?

★ How does the filibuster in the Texas Senate differ from chubbing in the Texas House of Representatives?

★ Should the Texas Senate consider reforming practices such as the filibuster and the blocking bill?

# CONCLUSION

The Texas Legislature is in a period of significant transition in terms of the role and function of political parties in legislative organization. The parties shape legislative process through control over committees, committee chairs, and floor debate. As the party caucuses in each chamber continue to organize, their ability to structure votes and communicate objectives is enhanced. New media is beginning to assist both parties in their tasks within the Texas Legislature. The days of bipartisanship may be ending as the realities of a more partisan legislature emerge. In addition, the pattern of legislative activity is changing. More bills and resolutions are introduced each session, and the balance between bills and resolutions adopted by the legislature is shifting toward a higher percentage of resolutions being passed.

However, certain traditions continue. The legislative process itself remains quite similar to the days of Democratic Party dominance in the nineteenth and twentieth centuries. Both chambers retain unique processes that profoundly shape how a bill becomes a law. The Texas Senate continues to use blocking bills, quorum calls, and filibusters, while the Texas House maintains its multiple calendars, utilizes chubbing, and has a more elaborate committee structure. Despite the rise of party caucuses and partisanship in the Texas Legislature, both chambers continue the concentration of power in the hands of their respective presiding officers. In some sense, Texas is reflecting the changes in the national political scene as well. The U.S. Congress is more partisan than in the past, and politics has become more contentious in Washington, D.C. Additionally, other southern states have also seen a shift from Democratic dominance over the executive and legislative branches to Republican dominance. While Texas has lagged in this shift compared to states such as North Carolina, the transformation of party control over the Texas Legislature leads our neighbors in Arkansas. Ultimately, changes in legislatures are often slow to occur, and many decades may be required to shift key aspects of the legislature. Texas is certainly no exception to this.

for CQ Press

Sharpen your skills with **SAGE edge** at **edge.sagepub.com/collier4e**. SAGE edge for **students** provides a personalized approach to help you accomplish your coursework goals in an easy-to-use learning environment.

## KEY TERMS

amendment (p. 130)

bill (p. 136)

blocking bill (p. 139)

chubbing (p. 143)

closed rider (p. 142)

cohesion (p. 125)

committee (p. 126)

concurrent resolution (p. 138)

conference committee (p. 133)

credit claiming (p. 137)

emergency clause (p. 146)

filibuster (p. 143)

floor debate (p. 142)

floor leader (p. 120)

ideological caucus (p. 123)

interim committee (p. 134)

introduce [a bill] (p. 137)

issue caucus (p. 123)

joint resolution (p. 138)

killer amendment (p. 142)

Legislative Budget Board (LBB) (p. 116)

lieutenant governor (p. 115)

line-item veto (p. 146)

markup (p. 130)

minority and women's caucuses (p. 123)

oversight (p. 130)

party caucus chair (p. 120)

party legislative caucus (p. 118)

president pro tempore (p. 115)

quorum (p. 143)

resolution (p. 137)

rider (p. 142)

roll call vote (p. 144)

select committee (p. 134)

simple resolution (p. 137)

Speaker of the House (p. 116)

Speaker pro tempore (p. 117)

special legislative caucus (p. 122)

standing committee (p. 126)

structuring the vote (p. 117)

## CORE ASSESSMENT

1. Does the increase in partisanship put the minority party at a bigger disadvantage when it comes to influencing legislation?

2. Looking at the data in Figures 4.2, 4.3, and 4.4, explain the overall trends in bills and resolutions in the Texas Legislature. What would you predict for the 2015 session based upon what you see?

3. How do legislators balance the need to legislate on behalf of their constituents, the demands of their political party caucus, and the desire to work for the common good of all Texans?

4. What role do you play in helping your legislator balance the demands of the need to keep constituents happy, the need to support the party caucus, and the desire to work for the common good of all Texans?

# 5 TEXAS GOVERNORS

Texas politics have undergone significant change in the last decade. With new governor Greg Abbott in the governor's mansion, it is worthwhile to reflect on how the political landscape has altered. Rick Perry changed the Texas political system in significant ways; it is also true that politics in Texas has undergone significant change in the last few years in spite of Perry. His legacy includes long-standing policies that are designed to be pro-business and socially conservative. Perry's most significant contributions include the wooing of businesses to the state, deep spending cuts, and the expansion of gubernatorial power. Interestingly, Perry's departure may mark the end of Texas's brand of conservatism that has so long defined the state. As Tea Party candidates unseat traditional conservatives and Greg Abbott comes out of Perry's shadow, Texas appears poised to move further to the right.

Perry's economic record was, rightly, his best achievement. He spent his time in office making Texas an attractive choice for businesses, advocating for low taxes and financial incentives and offering very little government regulation. In the wake of the 2008–2012 recession, Texas outperformed other states, generating a third of new jobs nationally while experiencing lower unemployment rates. In addition to his pro-business policies, Perry embraced fiscal conservatism, including deep cuts to education and social spending across the state. By the time he left office, Texas had the largest percentage of uninsured and an education system burdened by larger classes and lower teacher salaries. Perry also embodied traditional social conservative positions: he was consistently pro-life (he advocated mandatory ultrasounds for women seeking an abortion, and during his tenure more than fifty women's health clinics closed their doors), anti–gay marriage, and pro–death penalty (he oversaw the execution of more people than any other governor in U.S. history).

Perry's policies can hardly be discussed without mentioning his unparalleled tenure. As Chapter 2 details, the Texas Constitution purposely crafted the position of governor as relatively weak; originally, Texas governors served only two-year terms to ensure no one stayed too long. Texans, long distrustful of government in general and executives in particular, historically preferred constant change in the governor's mansion. The governor's power was kept in check by short terms with regular

Ben Philpott, KUT-FM

Former Texas governor Rick Perry left a significant legacy in his wake, including a brand of conservatism that has made Texas unique. U.S. senator Ted Cruz and current governor Greg Abbott (left and right in foreground) may represent a shift in that conservatism that takes the state further to the right.

turnover, limited appointment capability, and powerful leaders in the legislature. Rick Perry's fourteen-year tenure didn't just defy the long-standing norm of Texas politics, it changed the rules at almost every level, leading some to call him America's "last feudal King."[1] In 2014, Perry chose not to seek reelection, creating the opportunity for his handpicked successor, Greg Abbott, to take the reins. As Abbott gets comfortable in the governor's mansion, the state of the Texas executive is dramatically different than when Perry first came to office.

Perry's long tenure enabled him to use appointments to fill the state's bureaucracy with people who shared his political goals and supported him publicly. His unprecedented ability to shore up political support while suppressing dissent created a state that, by and large, played on Team Perry. Previous governors had to work with a bureaucracy that was at least partially appointed by their predecessors and had to rely on consensus-building rather than loyalty when working with the legislature. Under Perry, the bureaucracy that was designed to be run by commissions and boards independently "has evolved into a cabinet form of government, more or less, with the governor in complete control of every state agency. Government in Texas has become a Monopoly board on which every square is controlled by the governor's office."[2] Texas's governors have historically been limited in their ability to pursue policy initiatives, yet Perry realized legislative success in part by declaring his priorities emergency legislation and calling special sessions to focus on them. With Abbott now governor, the question is, will Abbott's close political ties with Perry translate into an extension of Perry's political influence, or will we see a return to the limited executive power outlined by the state's constitution?

Perhaps the most interesting aspect of Perry's legacy is the rise of the Tea Party in the state. Perry's last year in office saw his popularity ratings consistently behind

U.S. senator and Tea Party favorite Ted Cruz. In 2013, Cruz defeated Perry's choice for the U.S. Senate, David Dewhurst. In what was perhaps a nod to Cruz's popularity, Governor Abbott and Lieutenant Governor Dan Patrick vowed to undo many of Perry's signature policies, including giving in-state tuition to immigrants and using the Texas Enterprise Fund to lure businesses to the state.[3] Patrick has also advocated refunding the Texas Rainy Day Fund to taxpayers.[4] As Abbott seeks to make his mark as governor, the questions of executive power and Texas conservatism loom large.

In this chapter, we will examine the Texas governorship, including the formal and informal qualifications of the office. We will then examine what the Texas Constitution says about the governor's office, including gubernatorial terms, the line of succession, and procedures for impeachment. Finally, we review the powers of the Texas governor, assessing the extent to which the governorship of Texas is institutionally weak and contrasting the constitutional powers of the office with Perry's use of power.

## Chapter Objectives

★ Describe how the role of the governor developed in Texas.

★ Identify the formal powers of the Texas governor and in what ways the Texas governor may be considered weak.

★ Explain how the governor can use informal powers to achieve a legislative agenda.

★ Assess who wins and who loses under Texas's style of executive.

## THE OFFICE OF THE GOVERNOR

Texans distrust executive authority. This distrust stems in part from the American colonists' experiences under the British king and the vast powers exercised by colonial governors. The result was that early on in America, most states created relatively weak executives and preferred to vest power in the legislative branch. Texas was no exception. Distrust of governors in Texas was reinforced by Texans' experience under Mexican president Antonio Lopéz de Santa Anna. Indeed, throughout the state's history, Texans have distrusted government in general and—as governors are the most visible manifestation of state authority—governors in particular. This attitude was amplified by what occurred in Texas after the Civil War, when military rule gave way to Reconstruction rule that featured a relatively strong governor and a perceived "illegitimate" government. The subsequent Texas Constitution of 1876 deliberately weakened the executive, granting the governor little formal power, shortening the governor's term to two years, allowing the governor to make relatively few appointments, and instituting other elected executives that rivaled the governor's power.

As the state has grown and become more complex, the governor's formal power has increased to some degree; nevertheless, the office has failed to keep pace with the demands of modern Texas. The legislature, for example, has granted the governor more appointment power as it has created a growing number of minor state agencies and commissions. The governor's salary, which was notably decreased by the 1876 constitution, is now fairly competitive. And the governor's term was eventually increased from two to four years, affording governors and citizens alike a break between elections. In addition, Texas governors have become increasingly astute at employing informal powers. Texas's size and geographical position create relatively unique opportunities for its governor. For example, Texas's international border with Mexico has allowed the state's governors to participate in national policymaking, as Governor Bush did with the North American Free Trade Agreement and Governor Perry with immigration policy. The national focus on border issues has helped strengthen the Texas governorship and raise its profile. In addition, the highly visible role Texas played in the aftermaths of Hurricanes Katrina, Rita, and Ike garnered national media attention. The power of the Texas governor has grown both formally and informally, even as Texans' preference for limited government remains entrenched.

The governor of Texas tends to be a national political figure simply by virtue of governing such a large state. Although the Texas Constitution vests relatively few formal powers in the governor, as we shall see, governors who are skilled politicians can successfully utilize informal powers and become pivotal political figures. Often the pinnacle of a politician's career, a governorship is highly visible and can serve as a stepping stone to appointments to state and federal posts and election to national office, including the presidency itself. For example, former governor Preston Smith served as chair of what is now the Higher Education Coordinating Board, and, after his term as governor, Price Daniel was selected by President Lyndon B. Johnson to head the Office of Emergency Preparedness and was later appointed to the Supreme Court of Texas. Daniel, who had already served the state in a variety of elected and appointed offices, has held more high offices than anyone else in Texas history.[5] After serving as governor of the state, John Connally, who famously survived bullet wounds received when John F. Kennedy was assassinated in Dallas, became secretary of the treasury during Richard Nixon's administration. Pappy O'Daniel resigned the governorship to become a U.S. senator. Most notable, of course, is George W. Bush, who left the governor's office to assume the presidency of the United States. Other governors, such as Bill Clements and Ann Richards, chose not to seek further elected office after vacating the governor's mansion.

## Qualifications

The Texas Constitution specifies three requirements to be governor in the state. The governor must be at least thirty years of age, have resided at least five years in the state of Texas, and be a U.S. citizen. (Table 5.1 compares these requirements against those for the U.S. presidency and for governors in other states.) The governor of the state is further restricted from holding any other job or receiving outside compensation, a restriction notably absent from the state's legislature. Specifically, the Texas Constitution states that

**TABLE 5.1**  **Terms and Qualifications of Elected Chief Executives**

| Constitutional Provisions | Texas Governor | U.S. President | Other States |
|---|---|---|---|
| Age | 30 years | 35 years | 33 states set minimum age at 30; Oklahoma is the only state with a minimum age higher than 30 |
| Residence | 5 years | 14 years | 5 years or less in 34 states |
| Terms | 4 years | 4 years (limited to 2 terms of office or 10 years) | 48 states establish 4-year term, but 36 states limit the number of consecutive terms |

**Source:** Audrey S. Wall, ed., *The Book of the States*, vol. 44 (Lexington, Ky.: Council of State Governments, 2012).

the Governor elected at the general election in 1974, and thereafter, shall be installed on the first Tuesday after the organization of the Legislature, or as soon thereafter as practicable, and shall hold his office for the term of four years, or until his successor shall be duly installed. He shall be at least thirty years of age, a citizen of the United States, and shall have resided in this State at least five years immediately preceding his election. (Amended Nov. 7, 1972.)[6]

During the time he holds the office of Governor, he shall not hold any other office: civil, military or corporate; nor shall he practice any profession, and receive compensation, reward, fee, or the promise thereof for the same; nor receive any salary, reward or compensation or the promise thereof from any person or corporation, for any service rendered or performed during the time he is Governor, or to be thereafter rendered or performed.[7]

Beyond the constitutional requirements, Texas governors have tended to share other common characteristics. Since 1876, most governors in Texas have been white, Protestant, wealthy men. As Table 5.2 shows, the vast majority of modern governors have had some higher education—mostly in law—and most Texas governors have also had some military experience, ranging from service in the U.S. Army or Navy to service in the Texas National Guard or Texas Air Guard. Although the myth of the Texas rancher or Texas oilman is often used to tap into the Texas legend during gubernatorial campaigns, few modern governors actually have such experience. Notable exceptions include Dolph Briscoe, who was a wealthy cattleman and horse trader, and Clements and Bush, who made fortunes in oil.

Modern governors of Texas have also, by and large, had previous political experience. Many of the state's governors have risen from the ranks of other Texas offices, including the Texas Legislature, the Railroad Commission of Texas, and often the lieutenant governor's office. Others held national offices prior to becoming governor of the Lone Star State. Notable examples include Bill Clements, who had been deputy U.S. secretary of defense, and John Connally, who ascended to the governorship after serving as the secretary of the navy in the Kennedy administration.

TABLE 5.2 **Texts Governors since 1876**

| Governor | Party | Term | Military Experience | Occupation | Vetoes |
|---|---|---|---|---|---|
| Richard B. Hubbard | Democrat | 1876–1879 | Confederate Army | Lawyer | 0 |
| Oran M. Roberts | Democrat | 1879–1883 | Confederate Army | Lawyer/Educator | 13 |
| John Ireland | Democrat | 1883–1887 | Confederate Army | Lawyer | 10 |
| Lawrence Sul Ross | Democrat | 1887–1891 | Confederate Army | Farmer/Soldier | 7 |
| James S. Hogg | Democrat | 1891–1895 | None | Lawyer/Educator | 21 |
| Charles A. Culberson | Democrat | 1895–1899 | None | Lawyer | 33 |
| Joseph D. Sayers | Democrat | 1899–1903 | Confederate Army | Lawyer | 41 |
| Samuel Lanham | Democrat | 1903–1907 | Confederate Army | Lawyer | 32 |
| Thomas M. Campbell | Democrat | 1907–1911 | None | Lawyer/Railroad executive | 32 |
| Oscar B. Colquitt | Democrat | 1911–1915 | None | Lawyer/Editor | 60 |
| James E. Ferguson | Democrat | 1915–1917 | None | Banker/Lawyer/Farmer | 29 |
| William P. Hobby | Democrat | 1917–1921 | None | Editor | 19 |
| Pat M. Neff | Democrat | 1921–1925 | None | Lawyer/Educator | 58 |
| Miriam A. Ferguson | Democrat | 1925–1927 | None | Housewife | 30 |
| Dan Moody | Democrat | 1927–1931 | TX National Guard in WWI | Lawyer | 101 |
| Ross Sterling | Democrat | 1931–1933 | None | President of Mobil Oil | 7 |
| Miriam A. Ferguson | Democrat | 1933–1935 | None | Housewife | 24 |
| James V. Allred | Democrat | 1935–1939 | U.S. Navy in WWI | Lawyer | 48 |
| W. Lee O'Daniel | Democrat | 1939–1941 | None | Businessperson/Salesperson | 48 |
| Coke Stevenson | Democrat | 1941–1947 | None | Lawyer/Banker/Rancher | 56 |

*(Continued)*

**TABLE 5.2**   (Continued)

| Governor | Party | Term | Military Experience | Occupation | Vetoes |
|---|---|---|---|---|---|
| Beauford Jester | Democrat | 1947–1949 | U.S. Army in WWI | Lawyer | 19 |
| Allan Shivers | Democrat | 1949–1957 | U.S. Army in WWII | Lawyer | 76 |
| Price Daniel | Democrat | 1957–1963 | U.S. Army in WWII | Lawyer/Educator/Rancher | 42 |
| John Connally | Democrat | 1963–1969 | U.S. Navy Reserve in WWII | Lawyer/Rancher | 103 |
| Preston Smith | Democrat | 1969–1973 | None | Businessperson | 92 |
| Dolph Briscoe | Democrat | 1973–1979 | U.S. Army in WWII | Rancher/Banker | 72 |
| Bill Clements | Republican | 1979–1983 | None | Oilman | 78 |
| Mark White | Democrat | 1983–1987 | TX National Guard | Lawyer | 95 |
| Bill Clements | Republican | 1987–1991 | None | Oilman | 112 |
| Ann Richards | Democrat | 1991–1995 | None | Teacher/Campaigner | 62 |
| George W. Bush | Republican | 1995–2000 | TX Air National Guard | Oilman/Businessperson | 95 |
| Rick Perry | Republican | 2000–2014 | U.S. Air Force | Farmer/Rancher | 300 |
| Greg Abbott | Republican | 2015– | None | Lawyer | — |

**Source:** Compiled by the authors using data from University of Texas at Austin, Liberal Arts Instructional Technology Services, http://texaspolitics.laits.utexas.edu/html/exec/governors/index.html (accessed August 30, 2014); Legislative Reference Library of Texas.

Although Texas governors often have other political experience, many view the Texas governorship as the pinnacle of their career. In fact, recent research suggests that the governor's job is the best job in politics, even during times of economic hardship.[8] Alan Rosenthal argues that governors, unlike other officeholders, are singular decision makers who can lay claim to accomplishments and who are more likely to be listened to. After serving as U.S. senator, Price Daniel famously declared he would "rather be governor of Texas than the president of the United States"[9] and returned to Texas to run for governor. President George W. Bush called Governor Perry from the White House to let him know that governing Texas was the best job in the world.[10]

Texans have occasionally expressed a willingness to elect governors with no political experience. While inexperienced gubernatorial candidates can tap into Texans' distrust of government, it is a larger-than-life personality that helps make up for lack of experience in public service. James "Pa" Ferguson, for example, had no political experience when he was elected governor in 1914. His popularity was based less on political skill and more on his self-styled image as "Farmer Jim" who represented tenant farmers and poor workers across the state. He also impressed audiences by quoting Shakespeare, Jefferson, or Hamilton whenever the opportunity presented itself.[11]

Equally colorful—and perhaps equally ineffectual—was Governor Wilbert Lee "Pappy" O'Daniel. O'Daniel worked at a flour mill and hosted a weekly radio show during which he sold flour; featured his band, the Light Crust Doughboys; and expressed his opinions. O'Daniel's platform promised to block a state sales tax, end capital punishment, and institute a state pension for elderly Texans. Despite his lack of experience, his popularity on the radio helped him win the governor's office—twice—and afterward a U.S. congressional seat. O'Daniel was highly popular as a radio personality; he inspired a character in the Coen brothers' movie *O Brother, Where Art Thou?* As governor, however, he proved unproductive, delivering none of his campaign promises.

Inexperience does not always equate with ineffectiveness, however. In 1994, George W. Bush ran for governor with no prior experience in office. Bush did have the benefit of name recognition from his father's presidency and enjoyed a conservative reputation in an overwhelmingly conservative state. As governor, Bush was known for his ability to forge bipartisan coalitions. He successfully supported several education initiatives and state tax cuts and was a relatively popular governor.

One of the most consistent traits of Texas governors throughout the state's history is their conservative bent—and their Democratic Party affiliation. Nothing is more ingrained in Texas legend than the Democrats' hold on the state, which, until recently, had been nearly absolute. The state has had only three Republican governors since 1876, beginning with Bill Clements, who finally broke the Democrats' century-long winning streak in 1978. The dissolution of the Democratic Party monopoly is one of the most significant changes experienced by the state in recent years. The change is particularly noteworthy because it brought with it an almost complete reversal in party affiliation. Democratic Party dominance has given way to Republican Party control, and the recent trend of electing Republican governors will likely continue in the near future. Although the party identification in Texas has changed, Texans have long displayed a preference for conservative governments and limited social policy, regardless of party affiliation.

Ironically, relatively few early Texas governors were born in the state. Since statehood, just twenty-two out of forty-seven governors, or 47 percent, have been native born. Indeed, Texas's first native-born governor was the state's twentieth, James Stephen "Jim" Hogg, elected in 1890. Hogg was a Democrat who brought progressivism to the state. Texans appreciated him for protecting the interests of ordinary people rather than those of big business. Hogg also earned his place in Texas folklore by famously naming his only daughter "Ima." The myth that he named a second daughter "Ura" persists today, though in fact no such person existed. Modern governors have been much more likely to be born in Texas, although Pappy O'Daniel and George W. Bush are both notable exceptions.

Although nearly all of the state's governors have been white men, Texas has also had two women governors. In 1924, Miriam A. "Ma" Ferguson became the first female governor of Texas and the second female governor in the country, being sworn in just two weeks after Wyoming's Nellie T. Ross. After Pa Ferguson had been impeached and prevented from holding office in the state, Ma Ferguson ran as a proxy for her husband, using the campaign slogan "two governors for the price of one." Ironically, Pa Ferguson had actively opposed women's suffrage, arguing that a woman's place was

AP Photo/David Breslauer

As governor of Texas, Ann Richards reflected both new and old Texas, embracing the transformation of the state while remaining rooted in its traditions. She challenged the historical male dominance of state offices as Texas's "good ole boys" loosened their generations-old grip on state governance. Although she changed the way things were done, Richards proved equally fluent in the language and symbols of traditional Texas.

Richards moved up quickly in the ranks of state politics. After teaching junior high school social studies while raising her family, she entered government in 1976, winning a seat on the Travis County Commissioners Court. Richards fit easily into the small-town image revered in Texas, often proclaiming proudly that her father came from a town called Bugtussle and her mother from one called Hogjaw. In 1982, she won election as state treasurer and became the first woman elected to statewide office in Texas in fifty years.

She campaigned for the governor's office in 1990, calling for a "new" Texas that would offer opportunities to more residents. In the end, she won a hard-fought battle, besting West Texas rancher Clayton Williams. While in office, Richards worked aggressively to bring more women and minorities into state government. She made clear that women could find a place in Texas politics, advising them in patently Texas style, "Let me tell you, sisters, seeing dried egg on a plate in the morning is a lot dirtier than anything I've had to deal with in politics."[i] She appointed the first black regent to the University of Texas Board of Regents and brought more black, Hispanic, and female officers into the ranks of the legendary Texas Rangers.

Richards proved to be just as colorful as her predecessors. She once quipped, "Let me tell you that I am the only child of a very rough-talking father. So don't be embarrassed about your language. I've either heard it or I can top it."[ii] Like many of the men who came before her, Richards also had flaws, including a battle with alcoholism that ended in rehab and a strained marriage that ended in divorce.

She demonstrated repeatedly that women could be tough on crime, dramatically increasing the size of the Texas prison system and limiting the number of prisoners granted parole. She also championed education and environmental causes. Richards looked to modernize the way in which departments were administered and led the state in insurance reform and ethics reform.

While her tongue was sharp, her language was folksy. Richards' style won her a national following when she delivered the keynote address at the 1988 Democratic National Convention. Complaining about George H. W. Bush, the Republican Party's presidential candidate, Richards suggested the Democrats would expose his shortcomings, or, as she put it, "We're going to tell how the cow ate the cabbage."

Richards championed political activism, saying, "Sometimes it's serendipitous. Good things happen accidentally. But they're not going to happen unless well-meaning people give of their time and their lives to do that."[iii] One of her legacies is the Ann Richards School for Young Women Leaders, a school focused on giving girls the education and confidence necessary to serve as leaders in their communities. Richards preached feminism, informing the audience at the 1988 Democratic National Convention that "if you give us the chance, we can perform. After all, Ginger Rogers did everything that Fred Astaire did. She just did it backwards and in high heels."

Beaten by George W. Bush in her bid for reelection, Richards remained in the spotlight, making frequent media appearances and working as a political consultant. Asked what she would have done if she had known she would serve only one term, Richards remarked, "Oh, I probably would have raised more hell."[iv]

Richards died of esophageal cancer on September 13, 2006. Governor Rick Perry's eulogy summed up her already legendary status. "Ann Richards," he said, "was the epitome of Texas politics: a figure larger than life who had a gift for captivating the public with her great wit."[v] Richards embodied change in a state that has held fast to tradition. She embraced the traditions of the state more than many of the good ole boys, all the while challenging the state's limited role for women and minorities.

i. Mimi Swartz, "Ann Richards: How Perfection Led to Failure," *Texas Monthly*, October 1990, 60.

ii. Ann Richards with Peter Knobler, *Straight from the Heart: My Life in Politics and Other Places* (New York: Simon & Schuster, 1989), 165.

iii. "Political People and Their Moves," *Texas Weekly*, www.texastribune.org/texas-weekly/vol-23/no-12/people/ (accessed August 30, 2014).

iv. "Former Texas Governor Ann Richards Dies," *USA Today*, September 14, 2006, http://usatoday30.usatoday.com/news/nation/2006-09-13-richards-obit_x.htm (accessed August 30, 2014).

v. "Political People and Their Moves."

in the home. Thus, the women's suffrage movement opposed Ma Ferguson's election though she went on to appoint Texas's first female secretary of state, Emma C. Meharg. Ma Ferguson's administration opposed the Ku Klux Klan (she passed an anti-mask law that the courts subsequently overturned), contested prohibition laws, and called for fiscally conservative economic policy. However, Ma Ferguson's administration is perhaps best known for accusations of widespread corruption. During her administration, more than 2,000 pardons were granted, leaving the impression that pardons were for sale under the Fergusons. Ma claimed that most of the pardons were given to liquor law violators who were not really criminals, but in fact hundreds of pardons were granted to violent felons as well.[12] Ma lost her bid for reelection in the next two gubernatorial races but was elected governor again in 1932, becoming the first governor in Texas to serve two nonconsecutive terms.

More recently, Ann Richards was elected governor of Texas in 1990. Richards personified the iconic Texas image: cowboy boots, straight talk, and a reputation for being tough. She had previous experience on the Travis County Commissioners Court and as the Texas state treasurer. A former teacher, Governor Richards decentralized education policy, encouraged economic growth, and promoted women and minorities during her administration. In contrast to Ma Ferguson,

Miriam "Ma" Ferguson served as the first female governor of Texas and was the second woman in the country to assume a governorship.

Richards became a symbol of women's progress in the state, famously displaying a t-shirt of the state capitol with the caption "a woman's place is in the dome."

Although Hispanics have increasingly added their voices to the state's dialog and are both the largest and fastest-growing minority in Texas, the state has yet to elect a Hispanic governor. In 2002, wealthy oil tycoon Tony Sanchez made an unsuccessful bid for the governor's office, spending a reported $59 million of his own money.[13] Although Sanchez lost to Rick Perry, many observers saw Sanchez's campaign as a test of whether the Democratic Party could tap Hispanic voters to loosen the grip of the Republican Party on the state.[14]

## Terms

The Texas Constitution of 1876 originally established a relatively short term of just two years for the governor. A preference for short terms, usually one or two years, was common in early American state politics, reflecting a distrust of executive power carried over from the colonial era. Early on, most governors in Texas were elected to two terms, serving a total of four years. In 1972, the Texas Constitution was amended to increase the governor's term to four years. Despite the fact that Texas has no term limits, few governors have been elected to two terms since that time. Dolph Briscoe served six years after he was initially elected to a two-year term, which began in 1973, before the amendment took effect, and was reelected to a second term under the new rules. Governors elected after Briscoe won only a single four-year term until George W. Bush. Bush was the first governor to be elected to a second four-year term, although he resigned in 2000 to become president after having been governor for only six years. While Texans have shown a consistent preference for regular turnover of their governors, everything changed with Rick Perry. Lt. Gov. Rick Perry finished out Bush's term and then ran successful bids for reelection in 2002 and 2006. In 2010, Governor Perry, already the longest-serving governor in Texas, won a third term, serving as governor for an unprecedented fourteen years.

Obviously, the longer a governor serves, the more likely that governor will successfully pass his or her own political agenda. That Texas has four-year terms with no term limits is a potential source of power for its governors. The constitutional design of the governorship staggers appointments over gubernatorial terms in order to limit the impact of any single governor. However, since Perry was in office for so long, he was able to appoint every appointive office in the state; not surprisingly, this afforded him a broad base of loyalty to his administration. He also worked with legislators long enough to cultivate strong supporters in the Texas Legislature.

## Succession

If a governor is unable to fulfill his or her term, the Texas Constitution outlines an explicit line of **succession**. If the governor resigns, is impeached and convicted, or dies while in office, the lieutenant governor succeeds to the governorship. After the lieutenant governor, the line of succession goes next to the president pro tempore of the Texas Senate, then to the Speaker of the Texas House, then to the attorney general. Thus, after the 2000 presidential election, when George W. Bush resigned the governorship to assume the presidency, Lt. Gov. Rick Perry assumed the office, and the Texas Senate elected Bill Ratliff as the new lieutenant governor. Ratliff became the first lieutenant governor in the history of the state to be selected by the Texas Senate rather than winning the position in a statewide election.

When the governor is out of the state, the lieutenant governor is acting governor. Thus, when George W. Bush was running for president, Rick Perry gained considerable hands-on experience in the governor's office. Similarly, Perry's unsuccessful 2012 presidential bid cost Texans an additional $32,000 in pay to Dewhurst, the lieutenant governor at the time. By custom, both the governor and the lieutenant governor arrange to be out of the state at least one day during their terms, allowing the president pro tempore of the Senate to act as governor for the day.

## Compensation

Originally, the 1876 constitution specified the governor's salary, which meant that a pay raise required a constitutional amendment approved by a majority of voters. In 1954, however, the constitution was amended to allow the Texas Legislature to set the governor's salary. Currently, the Texas governor is paid $150,000, which puts the state

**Succession**
a set order, usually spelled out in the constitution, denoting which officeholder takes over when the sitting governor resigns, dies, or is impeached.

above the average of $134,390 for all governors.[15] Pennsylvania has the highest-paid governor, with a salary of $187,818; Maine's governor receives the lowest salary, at $70,000. The governor of Tennessee returns his salary to the state, while Alabama's governor refuses to accept his salary until that state's unemployment rate drops. Michigan's governor collects only $1.00 of his salary, Florida's governor collects $0.12, and governors in Kentucky, New York, and Vermont have voluntarily reduced their salaries.[16] Ironically, governors are paid well below the average $1.64 million annual salary of major college coaches, who receive the largest salaries among state employees.[17] That gap is even larger in Texas; the University of Texas paid Coach Charlie Strong over $9 million in 2014. Governor Perry drew criticism in January 2012 when he officially "retired" and began to draw on his state pension, which amounted to $92,000 a year in addition to his $150,000 governor's salary.[18] Perry was able to do this under the state's rule of eighty, which allows individuals to begin collecting their state retirement when their age and years of service collectively total eighty years.

Compensation for the Texas governor includes several perks in addition to salary. He or she is allocated a travel allowance and use of a state limousine, state helicopter, and state airplane. All fifty states provide an automobile for their governor, but only thirty-nine provide a state airplane and twenty-three provide a state helicopter.[19] The governor also has a staff (a few of whom earn more than the governor) to help coordinate the office, as well as drivers, pilots, chefs, housekeepers, and stewards. Depending on the governor, the staff can number anywhere from 200 to over 300 people. In addition, Texas maintains a governor's mansion around the corner from the capitol. The governor of Texas is also given a security detail for his or her protection, and if the governor runs for the U.S. presidency, taxpayer money covers the security costs. As governor, George W. Bush spent $3.9 million for security when he ran for the presidency in 2000.[20] Likewise, Perry's failed presidential bid in 2012 cost Texas taxpayers an additional $3.7 million in security.[21]

Most governors also receive free housing, although, according to the Council of State Governments, Arizona, Massachusetts, Rhode Island, and Vermont do not provide a governor's residence. In 2007, Perry moved out of the governor's mansion so that it could undergo renovation. The following year the mansion was severely damaged by a fire, most probably caused by arson. Perry was criticized in 2010 when he asked state agencies to cut spending by 10 percent even as he spent $10,000 a month in state funds on a rented residence.[22] In July 2012, four years after the initial fire, restoration of the governor's mansion was complete, costing an estimated $25 million ($3.5 million of which was comprised of public donations).[23]

## Impeachment

The Texas Constitution vests the power of **impeachment** in the Texas Legislature. According to the constitution, the legislature can impeach the governor, the lieutenant governor, attorney general, commissioner of the General Land Office, and comptroller, as well as the judges of the Supreme Court of Texas, Court of Appeals, and District Court. In order to impeach the governor, the Texas House of Representatives must approve the articles of impeachment (similar to a grand jury indictment) by a simple

**Impeachment**
formal procedure to remove an elected official from office for misdeeds; passage of the articles of impeachment by the Texas House merely suggests that there is sufficient evidence for a trial, which is then conducted by the Texas Senate.

majority. Impeachment by the Texas House merely suggests that there is enough evidence to proceed with a trial. Impeachments are then tried in the Texas Senate where conviction requires a two-thirds vote. While the Texas Constitution outlines a clear procedure for impeaching the governor, it is silent on what constitutes an impeachable offense.

Pa Ferguson remains the only governor in the state's history to be impeached and removed from office. Ferguson, whose education was limited to the sixth grade, balked when the University of Texas Board of Regents refused to let him handpick university presidents or fire university professors who had opposed his governorship. When asked why he wanted to fire the professors, Governor Ferguson famously quipped, "I am governor of Texas, I don't have to give any reasons."[24] To indicate his disapproval with the board, Ferguson vetoed the university's appropriations. Up to this point, only six American governors had been impeached, and five of those were Reconstruction era governors in the South.[25] Nonetheless, the Texas Legislature voted to impeach and remove Ferguson for misappropriation of public funds, and he was subsequently barred from holding a state office again. In spite of that, Ferguson continued to exert significant influence on politics in the state. The day before the impeachment verdict was announced, Ferguson resigned as governor. He would later claim that this made the impeachment verdict obsolete. Amazingly, in 1924, despite his conviction, Ferguson again ran for governor of the state, although an appellate court upheld his prohibition from holding state office. Even this was not enough to prevent Ferguson's influence, as he subsequently convinced his wife Miriam to run for governor in his place.

## POWERS OF THE GOVERNOR

The office of Texas governor is formally weak, and the position's strength often depends on the officeholder's ability to generate support informally for a policy agenda. In general, strong governors are granted significant appointment power, exert considerable control over the state's budget, and exercise substantial power to veto legislation. In Texas, appointment power is limited and the state budget is dominated by the Legislative Budget Board. The Texas governor's limited enumerated powers in the 1876 constitution can be traced to the governorship of E. J. Davis and in particular to the belief that Davis's Reconstruction government did not represent most Texans' preferences. The lack of formal powers in the constitution also reflects a very real preference among Texans for limited government—a preference that continues to be prevalent today.

### Executive Roles

According to the Texas Constitution, the governor of the state "shall cause the laws to be faithfully executed and shall conduct, in person, or in such manner as shall be prescribed by law, all intercourse and business of the State with other States and with the United States."[26] This means the governor must work with the state bureaucracy to administer the laws passed by the state legislature. The success of the governor in guiding the bureaucracy is directly tied to his or her **appointment power**, or ability to

**Appointment power**
the ability to determine who will occupy key positions within the bureaucracy.

# HOW TEXAS GOVERNMENT WORKS

# The Powers of the Governor

### Executive Role

**Appointment power**: As one part of the plural executive, the Texas governor has limited appointment powers; many posts are independently elected; the longer a governor is in office the more impact this power has.

**Patronage**: rewarding supporters with appointments; a longer-serving governor has more of this power.

**Removal power:** the governor must have two-thirds support from the Texas Senate to remove appointees.

**Budget power**: 27 states give the governor sole responsibility for drafting a budget; in Texas, the Legislative Budget Board dominates the process.

### Legislative Role

**State of the State address** provides the governor with an opportunity to influence the legislative agenda.

**Call a special session**: 36 states allow only legislators or the legislature's presiding officers to call a special session; Texas governors can use special sessions to force the legislature to address his or her proposals.

**Veto power:** The governor must sign or veto a bill within 10 days and has line-item veto authority; the legislature rarely musters the two-thirds vote needed to overturn a veto.

### Judicial Role

**Pardons**: A 1936 constitutional amendment took pardon power away from the governor, who must now have the majority support from the Board of Pardons and Parole before granting clemency.

### Military Role

**Commander-in-chief** of the Texas National Guard and Texas State Guard.

### Ceremonial Roles

**Crisis manager:** How governors handle crises can correspond with their degree of constituent support.

determine who will occupy key posts. A bureaucracy led by gubernatorial appointees will be much more responsive to the governor's policy goals than one that is elected independently of the governor and has its own policy agenda to pursue. In Texas, the governor's appointment powers have traditionally been limited, although they have increased in recent years. The Texas governor's appointment power is a paradox created by continual revision of the 1876 constitution. On the one hand, the governor is part of a **plural executive**, sharing administrative powers with other officials that are elected independent of the governor's office. Their independence means that often members of the plural executive are not interested in working toward the governor's goals. Since they serve based on popular election rather than gubernatorial appointment, members of the plural executive may have their own policy goals and will often work against each other. They can even represent opposing parties, making the executive more fragmented and less unified than one in which the governor appoints other executive members.

On the other hand, while the governor has little influence over the most important statewide officials, Texas has gradually given the governor more control over thousands of minor appointees in the executive branch. Gubernatorial appointees usually share the governor's basic political philosophies and tend to be loyal to the governor. Governors can also make appointments based on patronage. **Patronage** is the act of rewarding political supporters with public jobs, such as appointments. Perry was very generous with his use of patronage to reward supporters to his campaign. Approximately one-third of Perry's appointees had made campaign donations, contributing on average $3,769; Perry had received an additional $3 million from his appointees' employers.[27] As governor, Perry earned a reputation for appointing big donors to university regent positions. The *Texas Tribune* reports that about half of the regents appointed by Perry donated money to his campaign, with the average contribution being $64,000.[28] In addition, two Texas Tech regents have alleged that Perry's office pressured them to resign once they announced that they were supporting Kay Bailey Hutchison in her failed attempt to win the Republican primary in 2010.[29] Perry was not unique in his use of patronage, as previous Texas governors have also used high-level appointments to reward supporters. Former governor George W. Bush also appointed some of his most generous contributors to the University of Texas Board of Regents.[30] The use of political jobs to reward appointees is one of the most visible and effective tools that the governor has to increase the odds of realizing his or her political agenda.

The governor's single most significant appointment is that of secretary of state, although the governor also appoints other important positions, including the adjutant general, health and human services commissioner, and the state education commissioner. The governor will make approximately 3,000 appointments over a four-year term. The governor's appointment of board members typically occurs where the legislature has specifically granted the governor that power. The members of two boards, the Railroad Commission of Texas and the Texas State Board of Education, were originally appointed by the governor but are today elected. The governor can also appoint members to fill elected positions that are vacated before the holder's term has expired.

**Plural executive**
an executive branch in which the functions have been divided among several, mostly elected, officeholders rather than residing in a single person, the governor.

**Patronage**
when individuals who supported a candidate for public office are rewarded with public jobs, appointments, and government contracts.

In 2014, Attorney General Greg Abbott became the first new governor of Texas in fourteen years, succeeding Rick Perry. After a victory speech in Austin, Abbott acknowledges his crowd of supporters.

The governor's appointment power is limited by the staggered terms of those serving on the board. Typically, members of Texas boards or commissions serve staggered, six-year terms that overlap the governor's term. This means that a governor will not have appointed a majority of any board or commission until the end of his or her first term. However, governors who can successfully obtain a second term will eventually appoint all of the members of the boards and commissions in the state. Thus, the longer the tenure of the governor, the more effective the governor's appointment power will be in achieving the governor's policy goals. The unprecedented tenure of Perry meant that he was the first governor in Texas history to go through the entire appointment cycle two times during his time in office.

The Texas Constitution mandates that all gubernatorial appointments be approved by a two-thirds vote in the Texas Senate. This is a stricter requirement than that of presidential appointments, which are approved with only a simple majority vote in the U.S. Senate.[31] Since the Texas Legislature is in session only 140 days biennially, often it is necessary to fill a position while the Texas Senate is not in session. In such cases, the governor can make a provisional appointment, but such **recess appointments** require Texas Senate approval within ten days of the next session. The Texas Senate also maintains a custom called **senatorial courtesy**. Any appointee must have the approval of his or her own state senator in order to obtain the support of the Senate. If the appointee's senator does not support the appointment, then the Texas Senate will not consent to it.

**Recess appointment**
a gubernatorial appointment made while the Texas Senate is not in session; requires Texas Senate approval within ten days of the next legislative session.

**Senatorial courtesy**
the informal requirement that a gubernatorial appointee have approval of her or his own state senator in order to obtain support within the Texas Senate.

**Revolving door**
the phenomenon of legislators and members of the executive branch moving easily from government office to lucrative positions with lobbying firms.

**Removal power**
the power of the governor to remove an appointee; in Texas, the governor may remove his or her own appointees with the consent of two-thirds of the Texas Senate.

**Budget power**
the executive's ability to exert influence on the state's budget process.

**Legislative role**
the executive's role in influencing the state's legislative agenda.

**State of the state address**
the constitutional requirement that the governor address the state legislature about the condition of the state; the state of the state address occurs at the beginning of each legislative session and at the end of the governor's term.

Gubernatorial appointment power contributes to the so-called **revolving door** phenomenon (see Chapter 11). The revolving door refers to the movement of individuals from government jobs to highly paid lobbying jobs. Texas does not require a waiting period between leaving a government job and taking a lobbying position, unlike the national government and the thirty states that require a break of up to two years between a government position and a lobbying position. Texas does have a law prohibiting heads of state agencies and commissioners from lobbying their former agencies for two years, though they are permitted to lobby other governmental agencies during that time.

Finally, with the appointment power comes the **removal power**. A governor's appointees are able to exercise much greater autonomy if the governor lacks the power to remove them from their posts subsequent to their appointment. In Texas today, the governor can remove his or her own appointees but is required to obtain two-thirds support of the Texas Senate to do so.

In addition to appointment and removal powers, a governor's ability to influence both the legislature and the bureaucracy is significantly influenced by the gubernatorial **budget power**. In a strong executive model, such as that of the national government, the executive exerts considerable influence on the budget by proposing the budget that the legislature will consider. Twenty-seven states give their governors sole responsibility for drafting the state's budget.[32] However, in Texas, the governor's budgetary powers are notably weak. In 1949, the Texas Legislature created the Legislative Budget Board (LBB) to seize budgetary power from the executive branch. Since then, the LBB, co-chaired by the lieutenant governor and the Speaker of the House, has dominated the budgeting process. While the governor may still prepare his or her own budget, recent governors have viewed this as a waste of time since the legislature favors its own budget and typically ignores the governor's version. During the 82nd legislative session, Perry attempted to reassert gubernatorial influence of the budgeting process by asking members of the Texas Legislature to sign a budget compact. At a time when the Texas budget shortfall was estimated at $27 billion, and the previous legislature had already made deep cuts in education and social services, Perry's budget compact was a declaration of conservative values and thus largely supported by Texas Republicans. The compact called on legislators to promise to oppose tax increases, limit the use of Texas's Rainy Day Fund, and balance the budget with spending cuts. Although Texas Democrats felt the budget cuts were too deep, Perry's ability to successfully shape the state's budget was a significant legislative success.

The governor does exert some power over the budget through the line-item veto (discussed below), which allows him or her to strike out particular lines in an appropriations bill without vetoing the entire bill. However, even this power is limited in Texas, where a significant portion of the budget each year is earmarked for specific purposes and therefore cannot be vetoed.

## Legislative Roles

The governor plays an important **legislative role** in the state. The governor can directly influence the state's legislative agenda through the **state of the state address**. According to the Texas Constitution, the governor will inform the legislature of the condition of the state at the beginning of each legislative session and at the end of his or her term. Thus, at the beginning of the 82nd legislative session, Perry urged Texas legislators to eliminate four state agencies (including the Texas Historical Commission) and combine other agencies so that Texas would go from twenty-one to eleven state agencies. He further advocated the requirement of a sonogram before a woman could get an abortion, the expansion of virtual schools, and the adoption of an outcomes-based higher education funding system. Perry's address to the 83rd Legislature, his last state of the state address, was less ambitious, avoiding controversial topics such as abortion and immigration. Instead, Perry called for a focus on infrastructure, support of charter schools, and investment in Texas's water projects. The state of the state address can act as an important means of gubernatorial influence on the legislative agenda.

As governor, Perry's legislative strategy often relied on declaring his legislative priorities emergency legislative items. Generally, the Texas Legislature can introduce new legislation in the first sixty days but cannot vote on that legislation until after sixty days. However, the Texas Constitution (Article 3, Section 5) provides an exception for "such emergency matters as may be submitted by the Governor in special messages to the Legislature." **Emergency legislation** can be introduced in the first thirty days and voted on immediately after that. The constitution is silent on what constitutes an emergency, which has meant that, in practical terms, an emergency is anything the governor declares it to be. Since Texas has relatively short legislative sessions, the timing of the introduction of legislation can be critical to its success or failure. For example, in the 81st legislative session, Republicans introduced a voter identification bill that Texas Democrats were able to kill by slowing down consideration of legislation ahead of that bill. Thus, at the beginning of the 82nd Legislature, Perry designated voter ID legislation, a bill requiring a sonogram before an abortion, "loser pay" laws designed to decrease frivolous lawsuits, and three other bills as emergency legislation. The ability to declare proposed legislation an emergency and therefore move it up on the legislature's agenda significantly increases the likelihood that the legislation will become law.

Although they lack specific policymaking power, governors in Texas often issue **executive orders** to pursue policy objectives. Although the power to issue executive orders is not enumerated in the state constitution, governors have often issued them to advance their agenda by directing state agencies or creating specific committees or task forces to address a particular policy. For instance, as governor, George W. Bush issued executive orders to create a committee to promote adoption, a task force on illegal gambling, and a citizens' committee on tax relief.

Governor Perry also issued a number of executive orders, though he was often criticized for using them to increase the power of the governor and to circumvent the legislature. In one instance, he issued an executive order to shorten the time required for coal power permits. A state district judge later ruled that Perry lacked the authority to shorten the hearing time.[33] Perry's most controversial executive order would have required that all sixth-grade girls in Texas public schools receive the human papillomavirus (HPV) vaccine, which is designed to decrease the rates of cervical cancer. The order also provided an option for parents to opt out of the vaccine. Both liberal and conservative Texans across the state opposed what they viewed as the governor's power

**Emergency legislation**
a designation by the governor that allows proposed legislation to be moved to the beginning of the legislative session and be voted on during the first sixty days of the session.

**Executive order**
orders issued by the executive to direct existing agencies or create new committees or task forces in order to address a particular policy area.

grab. Eventually, the legislature passed a bill that prevented the vaccine from being required for school enrollment.

An important legislative function is the governor's power to call the legislature into **special session** "on extraordinary occasions." According to the constitution, the governor may convene a special session for thirty days and determine the agenda for the session. This process stands in contrast to thirty-six states that allow the members of the legislature or the legislature and its presiding officers to call a special session. Thirty-seven states allow the legislature to determine the topic of the session, including some states that require the governor to call the legislature into session. Thirty-three states place no limit on the length of special sessions.

Because the governor has sole discretion over the agenda of a special session, Texas's governors have used these sessions to force the legislature to address the governor's legislative proposals. In 2003, for example, Perry called three special sessions after the Texas Legislature had failed to redistrict the state during the regular session. At the end of the 82nd Legislature, Perry called a special session to finalize the budget, but he included several additional policy priorities that he had not been able to get passed during the regular legislative session. Perry's strategy for the special session was to pass legislation in series, rather than all at once.[34] This special session gave Perry a significant advantage in getting his preferred legislation passed. That advantage stems from the fact that the governor alone has control over the agenda in the special session. In addition, the Republican supermajority in the Texas Senate would have an easier time passing legislation that was a priority to its party since Lieutenant Governor Dewhurst announced that the chamber would not operate by the traditional two-thirds voting rules used during the regular session but would instead require a simple majority. Perry acknowledged that the special session gave him a tactical advantage, stating that "we work with a different set of rules during a special session."[35] During his tenure, Perry called twelve special sessions, whereas Bush did not call any as governor. The special session remains an effective source of power for a governor, although one that comes at a price. Texans pay approximately $1 million additional tax dollars for each thirty-day session, and governors who use this tool too often risk angering voters.

The governor in Texas possesses a variety of tools that ensure his or her influence on legislation. One of the most important of these tools is the **veto power**. Legislation passed by the legislature can be signed or vetoed by the governor within ten days. If the governor does neither, the legislation will automatically become law. If the governor chooses to veto legislation, the Texas Legislature needs a two-thirds vote in both houses in order to override the veto. Vetoes rarely achieve the two-thirds support necessary to be overridden. The last time the legislature successfully overrode a governor's veto in Texas was in 1979. In Texas, the governor's veto power is buttressed by the short legislative session, in which most bills are passed at the end of the 140 days. Passing bills late in the legislative session increases the likelihood that the legislature will no longer be in session when the veto occurs. After the legislative session is adjourned, the governor gets an additional twenty days to act on all bills still under consideration. A **post-adjournment veto**, or a veto that occurs after the legislature has adjourned, is absolute as there is no way for the legislature to overturn it.

**Special session**
meetings of a legislature that occur outside the regular legislative session; in Texas, special sessions are called by the governor and last for thirty days.

**Veto power**
the formal power of the executive to reject bills that have been passed by the legislature; in Texas, a veto can be overridden only by a two-thirds vote in both houses.

**Post-adjournment veto**
a veto that occurs after the legislature has adjourned, leaving the legislature unable to overturn it.

The veto is one of the most important sources of legislative influence for the Texas governor. In order to avoid a veto, the governor's position on any proposed legislation theoretically would be taken into account during the writing of the bill. This makes the true impact of the veto power difficult to assess. For example, as governor, George W. Bush actively worked with the legislature during the session rather than relying on the veto to exert his influence on the state's policy. It is important to note, however, that a governor who vetoes a considerable amount of legislation runs the risk of being perceived as weak; a large number of vetoes indicates that a governor did not exert sufficient influence on proposed legislation earlier in the legislative process.[36] A governor who successfully used the threat of a veto to gain legislative compromise without actually having to veto legislation is doubtless more powerful than a governor who had to actually resort to the veto.

As governor, Perry vetoed more legislation than any previous governor and made regular use of the post-adjournment veto. Perry vetoed an average of forty-three bills a session, considerably more than the average of thirty-one bills for Governors Bush and Richards. Moreover, on Father's Day in 2001, in what has been dubbed the "Father's Day massacre," Perry vetoed a record eighty-three bills in a single legislative session, more than any other governor in Texas history. Because these were post-adjournment vetoes, the legislature could not overturn them.

In an interesting turn, Perry was indicted in his last months in office for his use of a veto. When Travis County district attorney and Democrat Rosemary Lehmberg was convicted of driving while under the influence, Perry threatened to veto funding for the state's public integrity unit if she didn't resign. When Lehmberg refused, Perry made good on his promise and vetoed the funding. While Perry can publicly call for politicians to resign, and he can legally veto funding, the question is, can he use his veto as part of a quid pro quo? A Republican judge and a conservative special prosecutor found there was enough evidence to warrant a trial.

The Texas governor has also been granted line-item veto authority on appropriations bills. The **line-item veto** allows the governor to veto a specific line or lines out of an appropriations bill without vetoing the entire bill. The Texas governor is one of thirty-four governors in the country given this power over appropriations bills. Another nine governors are given the power to line-item veto any bill.[37]

> **Line-item veto**
> the ability of the executive to selectively veto only some parts of a bill; in Texas available only on spending bills.

## Judicial Roles

The framers of the Texas Constitution of 1876 sought to limit the power of the governor by making all state- and county-level judges elected rather than appointed posts. In spite of this, the governor of Texas often makes a significant number of judicial appointments to fill vacancies in between elections, subject to senatorial approval. These appointments can be a significant source of gubernatorial influence over the judiciary, since the vast majority of incumbent judges in Texas win reelection.

In addition, the 1876 constitution originally granted the governor the authority to "grant reprieves, commutations of punishment and pardons."[38] This power was curbed after Ma and Pa Ferguson were accused of abusing it by selling pardons. In 1936, a constitutional amendment created the Board of Pardons and Paroles, which

AP Photo/Mike Fuentes

One of the governor's roles is that of crisis manager. During his time in office, Rick Perry oversaw many crises in the state, including a plant explosion in West, Texas, in 2013 that killed fifteen people.

was authorized to recommend **pardons** in the state. Today, the governor can grant clemency or mercy only with the recommendation of a majority of this board. The governor exercises some influence over the board as members are appointed by the governor with senatorial approval. While the governor is not bound to follow the board's recommendations and grant clemency, he or she can grant no clemency absent the board's recommendation. The governor can also independently grant a one-time, thirty-day stay of execution in death penalty cases.

## Other Roles

The Texas governor fulfills many formal and informal roles. The governor performs a variety of what might otherwise be viewed as **ceremonial duties**. Because the governor is the state's most visible officeholder, the carrying out of ceremonial roles can in fact be an important source of power for the politically savvy governor. Since the September 11, 2001, attacks, the governor's role as **crisis manager** has also become increasingly important.[39] How a governor handles crises increasingly corresponds with his or her degree of constituent support. For instance, most Texans had a positive view of Governor Perry's handling of Hurricane Katrina. Perry's policies were generous to evacuees (offering temporary housing and opening Texas's public schools to them) and also fiercely protective of Texas (obtaining reimbursement from the federal government for the costs). Indeed, in a poll taken in the months following Hurricanes Katrina and Rita, Perry's approval rating increased by ten percentage points, and Texans polled indicated that "they felt like [Perry] was compassionate for those who were displaced and that he fought to make sure Texas did not get stuck for the cost."[40] Similarly, the explosion at a fertilizer plant in West, Texas, gave the governor national attention. But although these highly visible ceremonial and crisis manager roles can be critical sources of power, particularly for a charismatic governor, traditional sources of power for the governor continue to revolve around his or her executive and legislative roles.

## Military Roles

Finally, the governor of Texas is commander in chief of the Texas National Guard and the Texas State Guard. The governor appoints the adjutant general to command these units. The Texas National Guard remains under the governor's

**Pardon**
an executive grant of release from a sentence or punishment in a criminal case; in Texas, the governor can only grant a pardon upon the recommendation of the state's Board of Pardons and Paroles.

**Ceremonial duty**
an appearance made by the governor as the most visible state officeholder that can function as a source of power; includes appearances at events and the performance of ceremonial functions.

**Crisis manager**
the responsibility to act as a policymaker, coordinator of resources, and point person in the wake of natural and man-made disasters.

control unless it is being used for national service. Many members of the Texas National Guard have served in Iraq and Afghanistan recently under the direction of the president. If the Texas National Guard is unavailable, the Texas State Guard can be called into action for state emergencies, as it was during Hurricanes Katrina and Rita. Perry recently called up Texas National Guard troops to control the influx of undocumented children at the Texas border, at an estimated cost of $12 billion a month.

In 2006, the U.S. Congress restricted a governor's power over National Guard troops during natural disasters. During the chaos following Hurricane Katrina, President George W. Bush sought federal control over guardsmen in Louisiana, but Louisiana governor Kathleen Blanco refused to hand over power.[41] Prior to 2006, governors had sole control of the National Guard during a crisis within their state, though the president could take command of the guard for national service and domestically in times of insurrection. After Katrina, Congress expanded the president's domestic power and now allows the president to take control of troops

## MAP 5.1  Governors' Institutional Powers

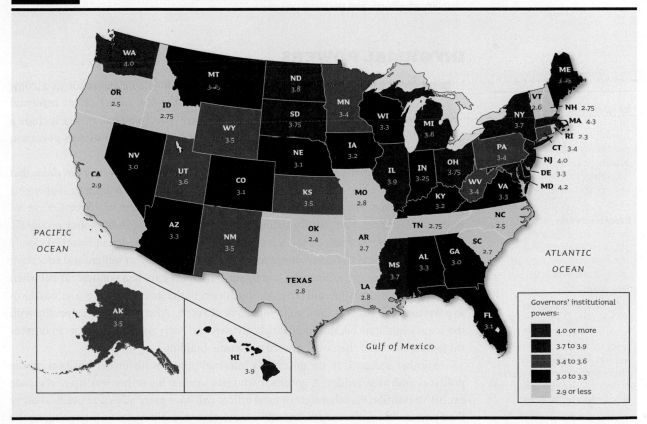

**Source:** Map based on data found in "Governors and the Executive Branch," in *Politics in the American States: A Comparative Analysis*, 10th ed., eds. Virginia Gray, Russell L. Hanson, and Thad Kousser (Washington, D.C.: CQ Press, 2010), table 7-4.

during "natural disaster, epidemic, or other serious public health emergency, terrorist attack or incident" if the president determines that state authorities "are incapable of maintaining public order."[42] Not surprisingly, all fifty state governors objected to this expansion of federal power.

### Texas Governor: Weak?

Most analyses suggest that the Texas governorship is an institutionally weak position. Scholar Thad Beyle created an index of institutional power that takes into account the extent to which a state's executive is plural; the governor's ability to serve additional terms; the degree of appointment power, control of budget, and veto power wielded by the governor; and whether or not the governor's party controls the legislature. Based on these criteria, the governorship in Texas is indeed constitutionally weak compared to other states' executives. The Texas governor's institutional power score is 2.8 on a 5-point scale; thirty-six of the fifty states have governors with more institutional powers than Texas[43] (see Map 5.1). On the other hand, because Texas is such a large, visible state, the governor has the potential to significantly expand his or her power through informal sources. In Texas, it is often the case that "personality transcends policy."[44] Thus, in spite of the lack of vigorous institutional powers, Texas governors have often managed to become a presence in national politics through visibility, charisma, and personal power.

## INFORMAL POWERS

As we have already pointed out, the ability of the Texas governor to accomplish a legislative agenda will depend in large part on her or his **informal power**. Four important attributes of informal, or personal, power include a governor's electoral mandate, political ambition ladder, personal future as governor, and performance ratings.[45]

The greater the electoral victory of a governor, the more the governor can claim that his or her agenda has a **popular mandate**. The legislature is less willing to challenge a popular governor. Thus, when more than two-thirds of the voters voted for George W. Bush as governor in 1998, the legislature was inclined to work with his policy proposals. During his first term, Bush earned a reputation as a bipartisan leader and worked closely with the Speaker and the lieutenant governor to pass legislation on welfare and education reform. In contrast, governors who win by small margins have less political capital when dealing with the legislature and other administrators in the state. Perry won a second term as governor with support from only 39 percent of voters. After this, his relationship with the Texas Legislature became increasingly divisive, and Perry sought to veto or circumvent the legislature rather than work toward consensus-building.

Another indicator of the governor's informal power is his or her position on the **political ambition ladder**. A governor who has worked his or her way up to the state executive position via other state or local offices will have more allies and political savvy than an individual whose first state office is the governorship and who is learning on the job.[46] Allan Shivers, a popular Democratic governor, was elected to the Texas Senate and later elected lieutenant governor prior to becoming governor. Shivers was a successful

**Informal power**
an attribute of personal power based on factors such as electoral mandate, political ambition ladder, personal future as governor, and performance ratings rather than on constitutionally enumerated powers.

**Popular mandate**
the claim that a newly elected official's legislative agenda is the will of the people based on a high margin of victory in a general election.

**Political ambition ladder**
the manner in which a political figure has come up through the ranks, working through various levels of state governmental offices and positions on the way to the top position; climbing several levels on the ladder can increase a politician's contacts, allies, and political savvy.

governor, creating the Legislative Council and the Legislative Budget Board, as well as improving education and roads in the state. He is perhaps best known for supporting Texas's claims to Texas tideland by backing Republican presidential candidate Dwight D. Eisenhower, who helped Texas maintain control of its offshore natural resources.

A third indicator of personal power is the governor's personal future as governor. Governors who have the ability to run again or who are at the beginning of their terms have more ability to influence other branches and offices than those governors who are approaching the end of their gubernatorial career.[47] Absent term limits, governors in Texas have the potential to hold office for a significant period of time, amassing political allies and making all important appointments in the state.

A final aspect of the governor's personal power is based on his or her performance ratings. A governor whose public approves of his or her performance will have greater political capital—and thus a greater ability to influence others in the political process.[48] After his reelection, Perry's approval ratings remained low (averaging 40 percent), indicating a limited power base.

Beyle's 2007 rating gives the Texas governor a score of 3.8 on a 5-point scale of personal power ratings, a score that falls just below the mean of 3.9. Only fifteen state governors currently have lower personal power ratings than the Texas governor. Measures of informal power will vary over time and between governors, but it is a good indicator of the importance of informal powers to the governor of Texas.

Personal power in Texas has always been somewhat different than that in other states. As noted in Chapter 1, V. O. Key argues that the size of Texas means personal politics frequently gives way to legendary personalities. Texas governors in particular have often been elected for their larger-than-life personalities rather than their ability to lead.

Perry makes a particularly interesting case for Beyle's index of gubernatorial power. Due to the frustration with E. J. Davis's administration, the framers of the Texas Constitution deliberately created an institutionally weak governor, originally setting a short term and granting limited appointment power. Even as the length of the governor's term and number of positions he or she can appoint have increased, the Texas governor remains constitutionally and comparatively weak. Yet Perry's political savvy, combined with his unprecedented tenure in the governor's mansion, created a political powerhouse who was quite effective at realizing his goals. In 2010, Perry defeated Senator Kay Bailey Hutchison in the primary and went on to win the governor's race with 55 percent of the vote. While Perry's approval ratings were never particularly high in the state, he maintained relatively consistent approval from his party's base. Though his approval ratings plummeted to their lowest point as his presidential campaign collapsed, it would be foolish to count Perry out, as he has resurrected his image before. His perceived heavy-handed HPV vaccine mandate and the attempt to create a Trans-Texas Corridor were particularly unpopular within the Republican Party, yet his ability to survive the political fallout helped earn him the moniker the "Teflon Governor." On the other hand, Perry's position as the party leader within Texas was undermined as additional challengers, notably Ted Cruz, rose in popularity. Perry's last year in office was increasingly marked with growing challenges from the right as "in a predictable but ironic twist of fate, the conservative forces that Perry has nurtured in the Texas GOP have fueled the rise of politicians more stringently conservative than Perry himself."[49]

Perry began as a member of the Texas House and was elected agriculture commissioner before being elected lieutenant governor. His rise as a Tea Party favorite and his failed presidential bid in 2012 have continued to shape his ambition, and Perry has hinted at future bids for the presidency. His political experiences, along with his national ambitions, have contributed to create a savvy politician.

## WINNERS AND LOSERS

The creation of an executive who is both vigorous enough to lead the state and act as a check on the legislature but is not so powerful as to promote tyrannical tendencies is difficult. The political culture in Texas continues to support the idea that executive power should be relatively limited. However, the potential cost of a weakened executive branch is the lack of a check on the legislative branch—and Texas, with its institutionally weak governor, has traditionally maintained few checks on its legislative branch. By not making the governor responsible for the budget, Texans lose direct accountability. By denying the governor significant appointment power, Texans stymie the governor's ability to coordinate policy and ensure that laws are executed. In general, Texas's fragmented executive branch leaves a government often working at cross purposes while the state's citizens pick up the tab. The cost is not only taxes for inefficiency in government but also a loss of accountability, as few Texans truly know who is in control of any particular process.

A governor who lacks formal power, however, will generally attempt to gain power by other means. When there is a vacuum created by a lack of executive authority and a part-time legislature, a crafty politician can successfully step in. As Perry's influence began to wane, he launched an all-out strategy designed to increase the governor's power. Perry's refusal to make most appointments while the legislature was in session denied the Texas Senate their check on gubernatorial appointments. His use of executive orders also indicated a desire to pass preferred policies while circumventing the legislative process. Perry's extensive use of post-adjournment vetoes, often without attempting to inform the legislature that he opposed a bill until he actually vetoed it, subverted the traditional negotiation process between the legislature and the executive. Moreover, fourteen years of Perry in the governor's mansion meant that he not only increased his power while in office but shaped new norms for gubernatorial leadership in Austin. The extent to which Perry's expansion of executive power in the state was confined to Rick Perry or could translate into a more general expansion of gubernatorial power remains to be seen.

★ In what ways does the Texas Constitution create an institutionally weak governor? How could the constitution be changed to increase the power of the governor?

★ How has the current governor increased his power?

★ What does Thad Beyle's index of power suggest about the Texas governor?

★ Why should Texans care if the governor is institutionally weak or unsurpassed in his or her strength?

# TEXAS (VS) LOUISIANA

Strong, interesting personalities have often dominated the governor's office in Texas. Sam Houston, Ma and Pa Ferguson, Pappy O'Daniel, and Ann Richards all left their mark on Texas politics. A neighbor to the east, Louisiana, is not without its own brand of larger-than-life politicians. Louisiana's first governor, William C. C. Claiborne (1812–1816), was known for his attempts to arrest the notorious pirate Jean Lafitte, a popular figure who attained Robin Hood status in the state. Claiborne went so far as to offer his own money as a bounty for Lafitte's capture, an act which allegedly prompted Lafitte to place a bounty on the governor's head. The twentieth century also saw its share of colorful figures who dominated the Louisiana state capitol building in Baton Rouge. Jimmy Davis ran for governor in the 1940s and again in the 1960s. He was known for taking out his guitar at campaign stops and singing the song "You Are My Sunshine," which he is credited with having written. Edwin Edwards, who served several terms in the 1970s through the early 1990s, was noted for piling up various indictments in federal court on racketeering charges, some related to his frequent visits to Las Vegas and other world-famous gambling locations. Probably the best-known Louisiana politician is Huey Long, the Populist governor and "share the wealth" advocate who was assassinated in the state capitol building in 1935.

Lesser known both inside and outside Louisiana is Oscar K. Allen, also known as "O. K. Allen." Allen was a schoolteacher from rural Winn Parish who served in several local elected offices and the Louisiana Senate. In the Senate, Governor Huey Long picked Allen to be the Democratic Party floor leader. Long also appointed Allen chair of the State Highway Commission. In these capacities, Allen served in both the executive and legislative branches of government simultaneously. When Long was elected to the U.S. Senate, he handpicked Allen as his successor. The subsequent election of Allen as governor surprised no one in Louisiana. More startling was Allen's own willingness to acknowledge Long as the source of his power. Long openly directed Allen's agenda as governor, making almost daily telephone calls to instruct Allen on what to do.[i] Even the special session of the Louisiana Legislature in 1935 that Long was observing when he was assassinated was formally called by Governor Allen per Long's instructions.

Why does Louisiana produce personality-driven politics in the same way as Texas? While the outcome may be the same, the sources are actually different. Texas's geography and weak party system contribute to its personality-driven style of governance. Noted scholar V. O. Key suggested that Louisiana's brand of governance is based upon the tight control of elites over the political system, which serves to produce populist backlash.[ii] Key suggested that Louisiana voters have long been faced with a choice of "outsiders" who use charismatic appeals to the masses to court their votes and then amass political power versus "insiders" who offer a reform agenda to undo the agenda of the populists.

## THINKING *Critically*

★ Why are Texas governors often larger-than-life figures?

★ Are Louisiana's governors similar to Texas's governors? Why or why not?

★ How does this type of candidate affect how you vote?

★ Do you feel more connected to interesting personalities? Or are you more interested in campaign issues?

i. Office of the Secretary of the State, "Louisiana Governors: 1877–Present: Oscar K. Allen," www.sos.la.gov/HistoricalResources/AboutLouisiana/LouisianaGovernors1877-Present/Pages/OscarKAllen.aspx (accessed August 30, 2014).

ii. V. O. Key, *Southern Politics in State and Nation* (New York: Knopf, 1949), 156–182.

# CONCLUSION

Texas today faces the paradox of an institutionally weak governor's office yet a legislature and state agencies that are now accustomed to an unparalled powerhouse as governor. The complicated nature of the Texas executive makes it difficult for Texans to know who to hold accountable. The lack of term limits has resulted in a governor with relatively unchecked power, which is inconsistent with Texans' preference for limited government. When the formal structure lags too far behind the needs of the state, enterprising politicians will step in, allowing constraints on power to be left to day-to-day partisan politics rather than to a clear system of checks and balances. The ambiguities of the current system leave politicians scrambling to grab power and make deals. In Texas, the people have continued to resist an overall change in the formal powers granted to the governor even as the state has continued to change and face increasingly complex problems. Texans remain content to allow their political institutions to evolve rather than address a wholesale change in institutional design.

**SAGE edge** for CQ Press

Sharpen your skills with **SAGE edge** at **edge.sagepub.com/collier4e. SAGE edge for students** provides a personalized approach to help you accomplish your coursework goals in an easy-to-use learning environment.

## KEY TERMS

appointment power (p. 166)

budget power (p. 170)

ceremonial duty (p. 174)

crisis manager (p. 174)

emergency legislation (p. 171)

executive order (p. 171)

impeachment (p. 165)

informal power (p. 176)

legislative role (p. 170)

line-item veto (p. 173)

pardon (p. 174)

patronage (p. 168)

plural executive (p. 168)

political ambition ladder (p. 176)

popular mandate (p. 176)

post-adjournment veto (p. 172)

recess appointment (p. 169)

removal power (p. 170)

revolving door (p. 170)

senatorial courtesy (p. 169)

special session (p. 172)

state of the state address (p. 170)

succession (p. 164)

veto power (p. 172)

## CORE ASSESSMENT

1. To what extent are citizens responsible for paying attention to an executive's use of patronage?

2. What are the costs and benefits of having no term limits in Texas? How did Perry's long tenure affect state policy?

3. Should Texas create more balance between its executive and legislative branches? Why or why not?

# THE PLURAL EXECUTIVE AND BUREAUCRACY IN TEXAS

Imagine driving the 2,600-plus miles from the U.S.–Mexico border, beginning at Laredo, McAllen, or Brownsville in Texas, and continuing to the border crossing between the United States and Canada in downtown Detroit, Michigan, without ever changing roads or highways, and possibly even without changing lanes. The Interstate Highway 69 (I-69) project offers such an opportunity. As a result of the significant levels of trade between Canada, Mexico, and the United States associated with the North American Free Trade Agreement (NAFTA), the I-69 project is a major priority of the U.S. Department of Transportation and the Texas Department of Transportation. The highway spans around 900 miles in Texas alone. Some of the highway's route will require upgrades to existing roadways, such as U.S. 59 and U.S. 77 in Texas, while other parts will require new roadways to be built. The Texas segment of the route begins in Laredo as I-69W, McAllen as I-69C, and Brownsville as I-69E. These three highways converge near Corpus Christi to form I-69. Interestingly, this division of the interstate into three segments of the same route is fairly unique in the U.S. interstate highway system. Only two other similar segmentations exist, both on I-35. One of these involves the I-35W and I-35E routes in the Dallas-Fort Worth area, while the other segmentation is in Minnesota. Normally, in such cases, one of the segments is normally designated the main route, such as I-69 or I-35, while the others are connector routes with a three-digit number, such as I-569 or I-335. From Corpus Christi, I-69 will travels through Houston and into East Texas. Northeast of Nacogdoches, I-69 will cross into Louisiana, circling east of Shreveport before crossing into Arkansas, then running around Memphis, Tennessee, and travelling into Kentucky. In Indiana, the highway will connect to the existing I-69 that runs from Indianapolis to Detroit. From just north of Nacogdoches, a connector route labeled I-369 will continue to Texarkana. As of the summer of 2014, over 180 miles of the project had been completed and signed as I-69. Texas had also received approval to add the interstate quality roadway along the Rio Grande from Brownsville to Laredo to the interstate highway system as I-2.

The I-69 project is important to both the United States and Texas governments because trade with our NAFTA partners in 2013 accounted for $1.14 trillion, surpassing U.S. trade with both China and the European Union. In fact, at $634 billion in

NORTH
INTERSTATE TEXAS 69
77
Sinton

Officials from the Texas Department of Transportation and others attend the unveiling of a directional sign for I-69, a multilane highway that is part of the U.S. Interstate Highway System. When completed, I-69 will stretch from South Texas all the way to Detroit, Michigan, and will provide a direct transportation link between some of the largest border crossings in North America.

2013, U.S. trade with Canada alone exceeds trade with China, while Mexico is the third-largest trading partner of the United States in any given year. In 2013, $546 billion in goods and services passed between the United States and Mexico.[1] Unlike China, with which the United States does not have a free trade agreement, trade with our NAFTA partners is more balanced, with exports and imports from each country being nearly equal. As for I-69's significance, one in every four dollars of U.S. trade with Canada crosses the border at Detroit, Michigan, and the three U.S.–Mexico border crossings associated with the I-69 project account for around one in three dollars.[2]

Former governor Perry made the project a high priority of his administration after the 2003 failed proposals for the Trans-Texas Corridor. The highway is expected to take decades to complete and to cost around $16 billion dollars.[3] The project is being championed in part by lobbying efforts of local government officials from towns along the I-69 route who see the benefits to their communities in terms of economic development. These officials and former officials have formed an organized interest called Alliance for I-69 Texas to provide positive news and information about the highway and to raise awareness of the project. Other advocates include Harris County judge Ed Emmett and Texas Senate Transportation Committee chair Robert Nichols (R–Jacksonville).[4] Within the U.S. Congress, members who represent states and communities along the I-69 route have formed a special caucus to lobby fellow members for funding priority for the project.[5]

Opposition to the road exists, however. Farmers and ranchers along the route have raised concerns about the land acquisition needed to upgrade existing roads or build new roads for the highway.[6] Groups opposed to private-public partnerships for government services, advocates of limited rights of eminent domain, and other organized interests, such as Texans Uniting for Reform and Freedom, have taken up the cause of trying to block or limit the impact of the highway.

In response, the Texas Department of Transportation (TxDOT) has developed social media sites on Facebook and other outlets to advocate for I-69, used focus groups in affected communities, and created local citizen committees to promote the advantages of I-69. These activities also help the TxDOT get community input into decisions about how to build the road, including the decision to develop the three different segments in South Texas or the question of whether to upgrade the existing U.S. 59 routes around Lufkin and Nacogdoches or to build new roadways.

This story illustrates an important point about state government. While we most often think of governors, legislatures, and courts when we think of state government, Texas, like other states, has a government that consists of many other institutions and structures. Some of these institutions and offices, such as the Texas attorney general, are accountable directly to the citizens of Texas, and others, such as the TxDOT, are indirectly accountable. The TxDOT, like many other state agencies, is operated by individuals appointed by the governor. Therefore, the citizens of Texas lack direct control of the agency. Only through our selection of a governor every four years are we able to influence some parts of the state government, such as the TxDOT. However, opposition to a department's agenda ultimately may lead elected officials to bow to public opinion and voter demands to change policy. Thus, the TxDOT may find citizens' groups, open meetings, and other processes useful in overcoming citizen opposition to the department's agenda.

In this chapter, we will review the makeup of the Texas executive branch, including five of the six statewide, directly elected offices. We will also examine an important appointed official, the Texas secretary of state. We examine the organization, roles, and functions of important state agencies, including the TxDOT, the Texas Department of State Health Services, the Railroad Commission of Texas, the Texas State Board of Education, and the Public Utility Commission of Texas. The chapter concludes with a review of the administrative operation of Texas state agencies and an examination of the accountability of the bureaucracy to the wider public.

## Chapter Objectives

★ Summarize how the Texas executive branch is organized.

★ Identify the roles of Texas boards and commissions.

★ Explain the measures in place for bureaucratic accountability.

★ Assess who wins and who loses under Texas's plural executive structure.

# THE PLURAL EXECUTIVE

The Texas executive branch consists of six offices that are chosen directly by the voters of the state. While the governor is the most recognized and familiar of these offices, the other five exert significant political and administrative power over the state government. These other five are the lieutenant governor, the attorney general, the comptroller of public accounts, the commissioner of agriculture, and the commissioner of the General Land Office. In addition, the secretary of state is an important, but unelected, officer in the Texas executive branch.

Because Texas has six statewide-elected offices, the Texas executive branch is typically called a plural executive. Each of these offices is elected independently of the governor, meaning that each elected member of the executive branch is chosen separately from the others. The election of one member of the executive is not dependent on the election of the others. In other words, the election of these officials is not on a single slate. The voter casts separate votes for each office. This approach contrasts to the U.S. executive branch, in which the U.S. president and U.S. vice president are chosen jointly as one selection or vote. Likewise, eight states in the United States, including Florida and Ohio, elect the governor and lieutenant governor jointly.

Each member of the Texas executive is directly accountable to the voters of Texas, not to the governor or to each other. An advantage to the **plural executive** is that Texans have more direct control over each of the six members of the plural executive. This approach is widely used in other states, though those states vary in the number of directly elected offices in the state executive branch. For example, Maryland and New Jersey only elect two statewide offices: the governor and the lieutenant governor. In contrast, North Carolina and North Dakota elect ten offices, including positions such as the state auditor, secretary of state, head of the labor department, and head of the insurance department. While electing a large number of the executive branch may seem a bit overwhelming, a distinct disadvantage occurs in a plural executive system such as Texas's. Because each office is independently elected, each may legitimately claim a direct mandate from the people for their political agenda. After all, the people chose them directly. The disadvantage of the plural executive is the lack of accountability to a single head executive, such as the governor. Thus, various parts of the executive branch may engage in contradictory activities. For example, a controversy developed in 2011 regarding whether or not Amazon.com was supposed to charge sales taxes on its sales in Texas. Governor Perry initially opposed such taxes, while Comptroller of Public Accounts Susan Combs vocalized her support for them.[7] The governor's claim to a mandate to set a political and policy agenda in Texas is often rebuffed by other members of the Texas plural executive. Moreover, the governor may sometimes be blamed by the voters of Texas for actions of other members of the executive who are beyond the governor's control.

In the U.S. government, the president meets with his Cabinet, which consists of the heads of the key government departments and the vice president. While their frequency and topics vary, Cabinet meetings allow the president to discuss issues and policies with key leaders in the U.S. executive branch and to coordinate policies. At

**Plural executive**
an executive branch in which the functions have been divided among several, mostly elected, officeholders rather than residing in a single person, the governor.

the state level, despite the use of plural executive systems that lack accountability to the governor, many states also maintain some form of a cabinet. In those states that formally and constitutionally require a cabinet to meet, the governor may have the power to decide when and how often this occurs. In other states, the cabinet is required to meet weekly, monthly, or at least once a quarter based upon the state's constitution or statutory law. Texas is one of only seven states without a formal executive cabinet.[8] Thus, in Texas, not only are the other executive offices not accountable to the governor, the other leaders of the executive branch do not even have to meet with the governor individually or collectively, nor do they have to meet with each other. This approach significantly limits the power of the governor over the executive branch.

## Lieutenant Governor

The office of the **lieutenant governor** is often considered one of most powerful positions in Texas. The lieutenant governor is elected by voters statewide every four years, with no term limits. Most states, including Texas, elect the governor and the lieutenant governor in the same year. Despite this, the governor and lieutenant governor are elected as separate and distinct offices. If the position of lieutenant governor becomes vacant, the Texas Senate elects from its membership a person to serve as the lieutenant governor until the next election. The lieutenant governor is the presiding officer of the Texas Senate, and he or she exerts great influence on both the debates and the bills that reach the floor in that chamber. Although this position is mainly legislative in nature (as discussed in Chapter 4), it is also constitutionally granted some executive authority. The primary executive function of the lieutenant governor is to assume the governorship temporarily when the governor is out of the state or permanently if the governor is impeached, resigns, or dies in office. In terms of executive powers, the lieutenant governor exerts considerable influence on the state's budget. The lieutenant governor co-chairs the Legislative Budget Board (with the Speaker of the Texas House) and appoints the senatorial members of that board. Unlike the governor and other members of the Texas executive, the lieutenant governor is not well compensated, receiving a salary that is the same as other members of the Texas Legislature: $7,200 per year.[9]

To be lieutenant governor in Texas, a person must be at least thirty years of age, a U.S. citizen, and a resident of Texas for at least five years. While the lieutenant governor possesses a few constitutional powers, the position is relatively weak constitutionally, as discussed in Chapter 4. The real power of the lieutenant governor comes from his or her leadership style and persuasive abilities as the presiding officer of the Texas Senate. From 2002 until January of 2015, Republican David Dewhurst served as lieutenant governor. Dewhurst had stepped his way into the lieutenant governor position by serving as land commissioner, another statewide elected office. As lieutenant governor, Dewhurst pushed through Jessica's Law, which provides for tough penalties for sexual predators. He also championed a significant property tax increase and worked to help pass B-on-Time legislation, which provides Texas college students with zero-interest forgivable loans if they maintain a B average and graduate on time. Dewhurst became an increasingly controversial leader throughout his time in office. His fellow senators complained about his leadership style, and in 2007 *Texas Monthly* magazine broke with tradition

**Lieutenant governor**
the presiding officer of the Texas Senate, elected directly by the voters. Also serves as a member of the Texas executive branch and assumes the duties of the governor when the governor is out of state, dies in office, resigns from office, or is impeached.

when it included holders of leadership positions (including the governor, the Speaker, and Dewhurst) in its list of top ten worst legislators. Dewhurst had aspirations for higher office, and in 2012 he ran for the U.S. Senate against Ted Cruz but lost in the Republican primary. Dewhurst also is rumored to have wanted to become governor. However, Rick Perry's long tenure in office prevented Dewhurst from seeking that office. After the loss in 2012 to Cruz, Dewhurst attempted to maintain his position as lieutenant governor, running for reelection in 2014. In a four-candidate race for the Republican nomination, Dewhurst lost to Dan Patrick, a member of the Texas Senate from suburban Houston. Patrick, a Tea Party–style Republican, painted Dewhurst as a moderate Republican who was out of touch with Texas conservative voters. After decades in office, Dewhurst's political career appeared to be waning. Patrick ultimately faced fellow Texas state senator Leticia Van de Putte, a Democrat from San Antonio. For the first time in Texas history, a Hispanic woman had a chance to win the lieutenant governorship. Details on this election campaign can be found at the beginning of Chapter 9.

In November 2014, Patrick won the election decisively, defeating Van Der Putte with over 58% of the vote. Patrick quickly began to set his priorities in the Senate for the 2015 session of the legislature. He pushed for the repeal of the two-thirds rule and announced that few if any Democrats would chair committees. In the area of legislation, Patrick announced a desire to see a reduction in property taxes, with a shift to sales taxes to make up the difference. He also supported repeal of the Texas DREAM Act.

## Attorney General

The constitution requires the **attorney general** to "represent the State in all suits and pleas in the Supreme Court of the State in which the State may be a party."[10] This means that the main function of the attorney general is to serve as legal representation for the state in court. Texas's first constitution provided for the appointment of the attorney general, but subsequent constitutions, including the current one, stipulated that the attorney general be elected. Today, the attorney general in Texas is elected in off-year elections to a four-year term, with no term limits. Like Texas, most states elect their attorney general, with only twelve states continuing to appoint the office. The salary of the attorney general in Texas is $150,000 per year.[11]

The attorney general's office is involved in a wide range of issues, including pursuing deadbeat dads for unpaid child support, protecting the elderly population of Texas from false consumer and insurance schemes, collecting delinquent state taxes (as it did from Enron in 2005), and recovering fraudulent Medicare and Medicaid payments, to name just a few. The attorney general is also charged with ensuring that corporations in Texas comply with state and federal laws. Thus, in 1894, the attorney general sued John D. Rockefeller's Standard Oil Company and its subsidiary, Waters-Pierce, for antitrust violations. The attorney general successfully made his case, and these companies were barred from doing business in Texas.[12]

One of the most important functions of the attorney general is to issue advisory opinions to the governor's office, the legislature, and other state agencies. These opinions offer a legal interpretation of the Texas Constitution, a state law passed by the Texas Legislature, or an executive order from the governor. For example, in 2007, Governor Perry issued an executive order requiring that all girls receive the HPV immunization

**Attorney general**
chief legal advisor for the state who represents the state in courts and issues advisory opinions on legal matters to the governor, legislature, and other state agencies.

## TABLE 6.1 Texas's Plural Executive

### Governor of Texas

- Acts as chief executive of the state; is elected by the voters every four years; no term limits.
- Makes policy recommendations to state lawmakers.
- Appoints the secretary of state and members of the state bureaucracy. The governor also appoints individuals to fill vacancies in elected offices between elections.
- Exercises constitutional and statutory duties of the governor, including
  - signing or vetoing bills passed by the legislature
  - serving as commander in chief of the state's military forces
  - convening special sessions of the legislature
  - delivering a state of the state address
  - proposing a biennial budget
  - executing line-item veto on budget approved by the legislature
  - granting reprieves and commutations of punishment and pardons upon the recommendation of the Board of Pardons and Paroles
  - declaring special elections to fill vacancies in certain elected offices
  - coordinating policy and resources during a crisis

### Lieutenant Governor

- Elected by voters statewide every four years; no term limits.
- Acts as presiding officer of the Texas Senate.
- Acts as governor temporarily when the governor is out of the state or assumes the governorship if the governor is impeached, resigns, or dies in office.
- Co-chairs the Legislative Budget Board (with the Speaker of the Texas House) and appoints the senatorial members of that board.

### Attorney General

- Elected by voters statewide every four years; no term limits.
- Serves as legal representation for the state in court.
- Ensures that corporations in Texas comply with state and federal laws.

- Collects unpaid child support and delinquent state taxes.
- Issues advisory opinions to the governor's office, the legislature, or other state agencies.

### Comptroller of Public Accounts

- Elected for four-year terms as the state's accountant, auditor, and tax collector.
- Collects a variety of state taxes and fees.
- Manages and invests state funds.
- Estimates the amount of revenue the state will generate each year.

### Agriculture Commissioner

- Elected by voters statewide every four years; no term limits.
- Heads the Texas Department of Agriculture and implements all agriculture law.
- Inspects the accuracy of market scales and gas pumps, regulates the use of pesticides, and regulates the quality of agriculture products.
- Promotes agriculture throughout the state.

### Land Commissioner

- Elected by voters statewide every four years; no term limits.
- Heads the General Land Office and administers the state's public lands.
- Makes low-interest loans available to veterans.
- Oversees the Permanent School Fund, a major source of revenue for the state.

### Secretary of State

- Appointed by the governor, with Texas Senate confirmation, to a four-year term.
- Serves as state record keeper.
- Maintains a list of lobbyist and campaign contributions, issues corporate charters, certifies notaries public, and keeps the official state seal.
- Administers elections, including conducting voter registration drives and certifying election results.
- Acts as chief administrator for the Texas Border and Mexican Affairs Division.
- Designated as the chief international protocol officer who receives international delegations.

**Source:** Compiled by the authors using information from the governor's office at www.governor.state.tx.us/about/duties (accessed September 5, 2014).

before entering the sixth grade. State senator Jane Nelson disagreed with the governor's mandate and met with Greg Abbott, then the attorney general, who issued an opinion that the governor's HPV order was merely a suggestion and not legally binding. This opinion meant that the medical community was not bound to follow the executive order. Another important task of the attorney general is to appoint the solicitor general. The solicitor general and his or her staff are the key lawyers for Texas who actually argue appellate cases before state and U.S. courts.

Once a request for a legal opinion has been received, the attorney general's office conducts extensive research into the issue, relevant laws, and constitutional provisions. Much of this work is conducted by a group of assistant attorneys general and their staff as the Opinion Committee. The committee may also ask individuals and groups that might be affected by the opinion to offer their perspectives, and the public may comment on these issues by submitting briefs. Most opinions are completed within 180 days of the initial request.[13] Once issued, the opinions of the attorney general are rarely challenged and typically carry the weight of law. One recent opinion was a ruling that a school official may carry a concealed weapon on public school property if the board of trustees of the school district has granted the official permission to carry the weapon. Another involved the proper method of calculating a county court judge's salary under the Texas Local Government Code.

Republican Dan Stewart speaks to a crowd of supporters on election night in 2014. Stewart, elected lieutenant governor in a heated race against Democrat Leticia Van De Putte, credits his staunch conservatism with winning Texas voters, including Hispanics.

Smiley N. Pool/©Houston Chronicle. Used with permission

Elected in 2002, Greg Abbott served as attorney general until January of 2015 when he became the state's governor. Prior to becoming attorney general, Abbott had been a judge on the Supreme Court of Texas. Several attorneys general have later become Texas governor, including Jim Hogg, Dan Moody, and Mark White. As attorney general, Abbott stressed family and traditional values. He established the Cyber Crimes Unit, which is used to arrest Internet predators, and the Fugitive Unit, which aims to arrest sex offenders who violate their parole. In 2005, Abbott successfully defended the display of the Ten Commandments at the state capitol building before the U.S.

Supreme Court. Abbott, who has not been shy about his desire for higher office, gained national attention when in 2010 he joined attorneys general from thirteen other states in a lawsuit opposing the national health care bill. He also authored an *amicus curiae* brief, signed by twenty-eight other attorneys general, which urged the 7th Circuit U.S. Court of Appeals to strike down a lower court order declaring the National Day of Prayer unconstitutional.

In November 2014, voters of Texas elected Ken Paxton to the position of attorney general. Paxton is a graduate of Baylor University and the University of Virginia School of Law. In 2002, he was elected to the Texas House of Representatives where he served for ten years. Paxton then served briefly in the Texas Senate from 2013–2014, representing parts of Collin County, including Frisco, Allen, and McKinney. Paxton's Tea Party leanings have included an attempt to unseat incumbent Speaker of the Texas House Joe Straus. Paxton has been a vocal critic of Straus's attempts to build bipartisan relations with the minority Democratic Party in the chamber. His tenure in office is likely to carry forward much of the agenda of Greg Abbott, including opposition to same-sex marriage, defense of pro-life legislation passed by the Texas Legislature, and staunch defenses of perceived encroachment on state powers by the U.S. national government.

## Comptroller of Public Accounts

**Comptroller of public accounts** collects fees and taxes, invests state funds, estimates revenue, and oversees payments by the state for goods and services.

Elected to a four-year term, the Texas **comptroller of public accounts** is the state's accountant, auditor, and tax collector. The comptroller is responsible for collecting a variety of taxes, including the state's sales tax (the largest source of state revenue), fuel tax, franchise tax, alcohol tax, cigarette tax, and hotel tax, to name a few. The comptroller also collects certain fees for the state, including higher education fees, vehicle registration fees, and professional fees. In addition, a 1995 constitutional amendment abolished the office of the treasurer and moved responsibility for managing and investing state funds to the comptroller's office. This action places Texas at odds with the practice in most states, in which a separate state treasurer and state comptroller exist. The state treasurer or equivalent is elected in thirty-eight states. Qualifications for the position vary tremendously, especially in terms of the minimum age to hold the position. Some states, such as Vermont, lack a minimum age for their state treasurer, while Florida and New Mexico represent the other end of the spectrum with a requirement that the officeholder be at least thirty years of age. In Texas, the comptroller must be at least eighteen years old. The comptroller must also be a citizen of the United States and a resident of the state, which are qualifications consistent with other states. In states with a separate treasurer, the office is usually required by the state constitution, as is the practice in Texas with the comptroller.[14] The comptroller makes a base salary of $150,000 per year.[15]

The practices of qualification and selection applied to most state comptroller positions are often quite different. Most state comptroller offices are defined by statutory law passed by the state legislature, not mandated by the state constitution. Texas is only one of fourteen states with an elected comptroller. In terms of qualifications for office, sixteen states require the comptroller to have some sort of specialized education or qualification for the position. For example, Alabama requires the comptroller to have a bachelor's degree, while other states, such as Rhode Island, place the additional requirement of being a certified public accountant (CPA). In Mississippi, the comptroller is expected to have at least ten years of professional experience in order to hold the position. Texas does not place any such qualifications on the comptroller.[16] This lack of professional qualification may reflect the fact that Texas's officeholder serves as both the comptroller and the treasurer. Since state treasurers across the United States are typically elected, the qualifications are often less stringent and reflect the longer constitutional basis of the position. In addition, university degree requirements and professional certifications are products of twentieth-century ideas about the professionalization of some government offices and agencies related to the rise of managerial science and public administration. These approaches to government management occurred after the writing of the Texas Constitution. While the merger of the two positions is a more recent development, the intent of the amendment to the Texas Constitution was to streamline state government in order to reduce its size and cost, not to focus on the qualification and training of officeholders.

In Texas, the most significant aspect of the comptroller's job involves estimating the amount of revenue the state will generate each year. This estimate is critical for the development of the state budget by the Texas Legislature. Since the legislature meets once every two years and must pass a budget to last until it meets again in regular session, these estimates give the comptroller significant power over the state budget. Moreover, the legislature is prohibited from exceeding the comptroller's estimations unless four-fifths of both houses approve appropriations that exceed the estimates. Thus, the comptroller exercises a great deal of influence on the state's budget.

This influence can put the comptroller in an unpopular position in the state. Legislators and the governor, often motivated to spend as much money as they can get away with, prefer generous estimates. The comptroller holds the job based in part on making accurate estimates and therefore not creating debt for the state. This tension was behind the 2003 battle between Comptroller Carole Keeton-Strayhorn and the Texas Legislature. Strayhorn, the state's first female comptroller, rankled the governor and the state legislature when she informed them that they faced a $9 billion budget shortfall. The feud between Strayhorn and the legislature culminated in legislation that transferred the comptroller's authority over two programs to the Legislative Budget Board.[17] Strayhorn's insult-trading public brawl with Governor Perry culminated with her run against him for governor in the 2006 election.

In 2006, Susan Combs, who had previously been the agriculture commissioner, was elected comptroller. As comptroller, Combs has sought to make finances in the state more transparent by creating a Web site where citizens can track how money is spent in the state. Her office also transferred hearings on tax disputes to another office in an effort to create a means of settling such disputes independent of the comptroller's office.

Reelected to the position in 2010, Combs was responsible for informing the Texas Legislature of the status of the state's financial picture entering the 2011 regular legislative session. The ongoing economic downturn meant that state revenues, especially sales taxes, lagged significantly behind, with an anticipated shortfall of $20 billion dollars.[18] That figure grew to $27 billion as the legislature began to work on the state budget, requiring significant cuts to state spending. A revised estimate of revenue was able to reduce that figure by $1.2 billion.[19] In August 2012, Combs was again warning the legislature there would be shortfalls in revenue compared to possible spending when the legislature convened in January of 2013 for its biennial session.[20] The European fiscal crisis and the sluggish U.S. national economy were continuing to strain revenue.

After the 2013 legislative session, Combs announced her intention to retire, thereby not seeking reelection in 2014. Republican Glenn Hegar defeated three other candidates in the Republican primaries to face Democrat Mike Collier in the general election. Hegar's victory over Collier allowed Hegar to assume the comptroller position in January 2015. Prior to becoming comptroller, Hegar was elected from the Katy suburbs of Harris County to the Texas House of Representatives in 2002, and in 2006 voters elected him to the Texas Senate to represent all or parts of twenty counties in central and south central Texas. Hegar has law degrees from St. Mary's University and the University of Arkansas and is a self-styled conservative who defends gun ownership and advocates pro-life positions. He lists his occupation as a farmer and is the sixth generation to live on the family land.

## Agriculture Commissioner

The agriculture commissioner is head of the Texas Department of Agriculture, which implements all agriculture laws in the state. Unlike the office of the governor or lieutenant governor, the agriculture commissioner is not a constitutionally required position. Instead, the position, like the department that the commissioner leads, exists because the Texas Legislature passed a law creating it in its current format. As a result, the position, its method of selection, and term in office may be changed by the Texas Legislature at any time at its discretion. Currently, the commissioner is directly elected by voters in Texas for a four-year term in office. The commissioner of agriculture receives a base salary of $137,500.[21]

For most Texans, the most common encounter with the agricultural department occurs at the gas station. Under Texas law, the department is responsible for weights and measures, including annual inspections of each and every gas pump in the state. These inspections ensure Texans that one gallon of gas pumped at the gas station is in fact one gallon. The department also measures scales used in the food industry and retail price scanners to ensure accuracy in these devices. In recent years, the department has been given the power to certify organically grown meats, fruits, and vegetables.

The department is also charged with promoting Texas products through the "Go Texan" branded campaign,[22] protecting agricultural products from harmful pests and diseases, and offering financial assistance to farmers and ranchers in times of economic hardship or natural disaster. In addition, it provides low-interest loans to farmers to start new farms.

The Texas Department of Agriculture administers school nutrition programs in conjunction with programs operated by the U.S. government. The department also carries out a number of functions related to rural development and economic growth. For example, it offers grant programs to rural communities to build infrastructure, such as parks and roads. In a related set of activities, the department administers the Texas Certified Retirement Community Program to help local communities attract and keep retirees, a huge population growth opportunity given the aging of the American population. The department also assists rural areas in acquiring broadband communication services and advocates policies at the state and national levels to benefit Texas farming and ranching interests.

The office of agriculture commissioner is critical to the department because the commissioner may use the position to help shape and mold policy to serve his or her interests. For example, in 2003, Commissioner Susan Combs created the Square Meals program designed to educate children about healthy eating habits; this program is critical in light of the growing problem of obesity and related health disorders in young children. About this time, the commissioner also changed policies to begin limiting access to sodas and candy in Texas schools.

The commissioner's office is often an important rung on the Texas political ambition ladder. After serving three terms as a state legislator, Rick Perry was successfully elected commissioner of agriculture. Perry served two terms before running for lieutenant governor, a position he held until Governor George W. Bush resigned to move to the White House. When Perry vacated the office, Susan Combs became the first woman in the state to hold the position of agriculture commissioner. Combs held the position for two terms before successfully running for comptroller. The current agriculture commissioner, Todd Staples, served as a state representative and state senator prior to his election as agriculture commissioner in 2006. He was reelected in 2010 to the position. In 2014, Staples announced his intention to run for lieutenant governor, leaving the commissioner's position at the end of his term in January 2015. Staples ultimately lost in the Republican primary to Dan Patrick.

Sid Miller won the Republican nomination for agriculture commissioner in 2014 in a very tight, five-candidate race that required a runoff between Miller and Tom Merritt. In an unusual primary for Democrats in recent years, a three-candidate race for agriculture commissioner featured former independent candidate for governor and self-styled Jewish cowboy Kinky Friedman. While Friedman lost in a Democratic runoff to Jim Hogan, Republican Sid Miller won the general election over Hogan. Miller, who has a degree from Tarleton State University, is a former member of the Texas House of Representatives from Stephenville in Erath County. Miller has been active on the rodeo circuit and was named "World Champion of Calf Roping" by the U.S. Calf Roping Association.

## Land Commissioner

Perhaps unique among the fifty U.S. states is the Texas **commissioner of the General Land Office**. To be elected land commissioner, a candidate must be eighteen years old, a citizen of the United States, and a resident of Texas. The land commissioner receives a salary of $137,500 per year. The office and related agency are among the oldest in Texas. At the time of independence from Mexico, the Republic of Texas created the office to manage public land, provide maps and land surveys, and to raise money through land grants to finance the Texas Revolution.[23] When Texas joined the United States in 1845, the U.S. Congress would not take over the public debts that the Republic of Texas owed to its creditors. As a result, Texas kept its debt, but it was also allowed to keep its public lands. These public lands included tidelands out to three marine leagues from the shore, unlike other states that border the Gulf of Mexico. Today, the land commissioner manages just over 13 million acres of land.

Proceeds from the sale of state lands and revenue from the extraction of minerals and other resources from state lands go to the **Permanent School Fund**. The management of this fund was the primary responsibility of the land commissioner for decades. Money in the Permanent School Fund is used to build and maintain public schools in Texas. As of August 2013, the fund contained over $29 billion in assets and had distributed almost $1.3 billion to Texas schools in 2013 alone. In addition, the fund guaranteed over $55 billion in bonds issued by Texas public school districts.[24]

The land commissioner has historically been charged with supervising mineral leases. Yet the scope of the commissioner's duties has expanded over time. For example the discovery of oil and natural gas in Texas increased the revenue stream into the Permanent School Fund. In addition, the office defended an attempt by the U.S. government to take over the tidelands of Texas. One duty added to the office is to ensure the quality of life for impoverished and disabled veterans in Texas. As a result, the General Land Office makes low-interest loans available to veterans in the state to purchase land and homes. The office also maintains state cemeteries and skilled-care facilities for Texas veterans. These tasks are assigned to an agency of the office called the Veterans Land Board.

The land office also consists of a number of other offices and agencies that help the land commissioner with the tasks assigned to this executive office. Day-to-day operations are managed by the chief clerk, whose office dates back to the creation of the General Land Office and the commissioner's position in 1836. The School Land Board provides governance for the Permanent School Fund and coordinates disbursements with the Texas Education Agency. The Coast Coordination Advisory Board coordinates coastal policies and activities with local and U.S. governments in coastal areas. A series of boards manage leases of state property owned by the Texas Parks and Wildlife Department, Texas Department of Criminal Justice, and various public universities. Conservation programs in rural areas are managed by the Texas Farm and Ranch Lands Conservation Council.

In recent years, the office has been given at least shared responsibility of ensuring environmental protection of public lands, such as the state's beaches. After the *Exxon Valdez* oil spill in Alaska, the land office was charged with developing a program to prevent a similar incident in Texas. Now when an oil spill occurs, the land office oversees the state's response to the disaster, as happened with the Deepwater Horizon spill in 2010.

The General Land Office recently began harvesting another natural resource—wind. The vast plains of West Texas produce a lot of wind, and Texas has built large banks of wind turbines in the area. In 2006, Texas surpassed California to become the nation's leader in wind production.[25] In 2007, Commissioner Jerry Patterson added offshore wind leases to Texas's already profitable offshore oil industry. Texas has begun leasing wind rights in the Gulf Coast, which will generate millions of dollars for the state over the life of the leases. Reflecting the General Land Office's traditional role as income generator for the state, Patterson boasted that "the future of offshore wind power in the [United States] is right here in Texas, and the Land Office is open for business."[26] Patterson is the sort of larger-than-life character that political scientist V. O. Key suggested would emerge in Texas politics; he flies a 1944 World War II–era plane, chews tobacco, and reportedly carries a gun in his boot. Patterson's term as land commissioner was marked by controversy. He was accused of selling Texas's public lands, including an attempt to sell the Christmas Mountains in West Texas.

Rather than seek a fourth term in office, Patterson attempted to run for lieutenant governor, but he lost in the initial Republican primary to Dan Patrick. A two-candidate race for the Republican nomination for land commissioner saw the return to Texas politics of a familiar name: George Bush. George P. Bush, son of former Florida governor Jeb Bush and nephew of former U.S. president and Texas governor George W. Bush, won the Republican primary in the initial round, thereby avoiding a runoff. Bush easily defeated his Democratic opponent in the November election. Bush's mother is a naturalized U.S. citizen from Mexico, Columba Garnicia Gallo. He graduated from Rice University and the University Texas School of Law. After law school, Bush served in the U.S. Naval Reserve, including service in Afghanistan, and as a partner in a capital equity and real estate investment firm. Bush is a founder of Hispanic Republicans for Texas, a political action committee dedicated to electing Hispanic Republicans to office.

## Secretary of State

The Texas Constitution specifically created the office of **secretary of state**. Unlike the other key offices in the Texas executive branch, which are elected, the Texas secretary of state is appointed by the governor with Senate confirmation to a four-year term. This appointment process places Texas at odds with the normal practice throughout the United States. Most states elect their secretary of state to ensure the position is directly accountable to the voters; in three states, the secretary is chosen by the state legislature.[27] Texas is only one of eight states that have a secretary appointed by the governor. The Texas secretary of state receives a base salary of $125,880 per year.[28]

Traditionally, the function of the secretary of state is that of state record keeper for the executive branch, chief protocol officer, and foreign affairs chief. This function was given to the office under the Republic of Texas Constitution after independence in 1836. At that time, President Sam Houston appointed Stephen F. Austin as the first Texas secretary of state. Unfortunately, Austin died of pneumonia only three months after taking office.[29] After statehood, the roles of protocol officer and foreign affairs chief were removed from the position. In addition to record keeping, the position eventually received new duties and responsibilities as the size and scope of state

**Secretary of state**
this position is responsible for business licensing and regulation and also administrates and supervises elections; also serves as the chief protocol officer of Texas.

government increased. One of the most important sets of records that the secretary of state's office maintains is related to elections. The office is responsible for administering the Texas Elections Code, keeping statewide voter registration lists, certifying voting systems and equipment, and maintaining registration lists of candidates and political parties. The office also oversees Project V.O.T.E. (Voters of Tomorrow through Education), which is designed to teach school-aged children about the process and importance of voting. [30] The requirement that the secretary of state serve as the chief election officer in Texas is consistent with the practice in thirty-nine of the states.

The office is also responsible for keeping records concerning banking and other business activities. All legal corporations, including businesses, must file with the office, and in return each business receives a charter or license to operate in Texas. This duty also extends to nonprofit and charitable organizations operating in the state of Texas. The secretary's office also certifies all notaries public and keeps the official state seal. Any registered trade names that a company uses or any registered trademarks are filed with the secretary of state's office. The *Texas Register*, a weekly update of all rules, regulations, meetings, opinions, and proclamations associated with official state business, is published in the secretary's office. Again, these practices are consistent with the office of secretary of state in most states.

Recent governors have expanded the job of the secretary of state through executive orders, adding three roles to the office. First, the secretary of state is now the chief administrator for the Texas Border and Mexican Affairs Division, which is charged with overseeing border issues and Mexican-Texas relations. The secretary has also been designated the chief international protocol officer; in this capacity, he or she receives international delegations. In 2010, Governor Perry added a third role, appointing Hope Andrade, the secretary at that time, as the Texas census ambassador. In this role, the secretary was charged with promoting participation in the 2010 census. Note that some of these roles restore earlier functions of the office from the time of the Republic of Texas.

Given the long history of the position, it is not surprising perhaps that many holders of the office have gone on to hold other political positions. Three secretaries later became governor of the state, while another three became lieutenant governor. Six secretaries of state were later elected attorney general. In addition, the office has been somewhat more diverse than other state executive offices. This office was one of the first to feature a woman in a highly visible state position after Ma Ferguson appointed Emma C. Meharg as the first female secretary of state. A leader in the women's suffrage movement in Texas, Jane McCallum holds the distinction as being the longest-serving secretary; she served from January 1927 until 1933. In January 2014, Governor Perry appointed Nandita Berry as the 109th secretary of state; she is the first Indian American to serve in a major statewide office. Berry served until January 2015, when Carlos Cascos's term in office began as a result of his appointment by Governor Gregg Abbot.

AP Photo/Brad Doherty/The Brownsville Herald

Shortly after the November 2014 election, Governor elect Greg Abbot named Carlos Cascos, Cameron County Judge, to be the 110th secretary of state. Cameron, a certified CPA and long-time resident of the Rio Grande Valley, has significant experience in government and public finance.

# BOARDS AND COMMISSIONS

The Texas **bureaucracy** is a complex system of elected and appointed officials working in conjunction with a wide range of boards and agencies. There are close to 300 boards and commissions in the state; some are specified in the constitution, such as the Board of Paroles and Pensions, but most, such as the Department of Agriculture, have been created by the legislature. Depending on the political mood and particular needs during the period when a board or commission was created, the membership, size, and autonomy of these entities vary greatly. Some boards are elected, providing them a good deal of autonomy from the rest of the executive branch; others are appointed and therefore obligated to the governor or the legislative leadership that appointed them. Six of the most important state agencies are the Texas Department of Transportation (TxDOT), the Texas Department of State Health Services, the Texas Department of Criminal Justice, the Railroad Commission of Texas, the Texas State Board of Education, and the Public Utility Commission of Texas.

## Texas Department of Transportation

One of the best-known agencies of Texas government is the Texas Department of Transportation. This agency is responsible for overseeing the construction and maintenance of state highways and roads, as well as federal interstate highways and roadways within the borders of Texas. Like other state agencies, the TxDOT is governed by a commission, in this case the Texas Transportation Commission. The commission members are appointed by the governor and confirmed by the Texas Senate. The commission plans and makes policies for the location, construction, and maintenance of roads. The commission also develops a statewide transportation plan that integrates road, rail, and water traffic, and it awards state contracts for the building and maintenance of state and federal highways in Texas. Finally, the commission is charged with developing public mass transportation in the state.[31]

The committee relies on a strategic plan developed with input from communities and citizens across the state to assist it in its work. Much of the work on roads across Texas involves local improvements or new routes; these projects must fit into the strategic plan and must compete with jobs from across the state to receive funding. Such projects include improvements to the I-35 corridor throughout Texas, improvements to I-20 from the Dallas-Fort Worth Metroplex to the Louisiana border, and, of course, completion of the I-69 project. However, the strategic plan goes beyond listing specific road projects and their priorities for the department. For example, the 2015–2019 plan emphasizes the implementation of informational technology to improve commute times in urban areas, sets goals for worker safety, addresses methods to improve community and citizen involvement in department decisions, and sets benchmarks to measure the performance of the department.[32] The department also oversees construction and improvement of the state's rail network. This area of policy includes possible high speed rail connections between San Antonio, Houston, and the DFW Metroplex and improvements to freight rail, especially from the Rio Grande valley to the Oklahoma border.

All transportation projects funded and directed by the TxDOT go through a similar process. First, the project is proposed, then an open comment time occurs. During this time, the TxDOT may hold open meetings, or hearings, at which citizens, organized interests, and others may offer suggestions to improve the project or voice criticism of it. In the latter case, the goal may be to prevent the project from moving forward. Some of these meetings may occur in the communities that the project is going to affect. For example, meetings in affected communities have been held with regard to the proposed upgrades to several existing highways to transform them into I-69.

Road and rail construction funding comes from a variety of sources, including the federal government. Depending on the road, up to 80 percent of construction or maintenance costs may come from the U.S. government. Other funding comes from project-specific funding as a rider attached to a bill passed by the Texas Legislature, from the general state budget, from fuel taxes, and from the sale of public bonds.

In order to balance local priorities with state and national needs, the department divides the state into four broad regions. The regions are further divided into districts of around ten to twenty counties. There are twenty-five of these districts across Texas. Each one has an office whose staff is responsible for overseeing all TxDOT projects in that district. The department is headed by an executive director appointed by commission. The executive director oversees the day-to-day operations of the department. In many ways, the director is really in charge of the TxDOT since the Texas Transportation Commission meets only a few times a year, mostly to provide overall guidance for the department. The director is assisted by an executive staff that includes separate agencies for legal affairs, engineering, planning, finance, communications, and administration. Some of the department's road and highway budget is distributed to each district for district-level construction projects.

Figure 6.1 illustrates the structure of the TxDOT, which is typical of the structure of various state departments and agencies. Most departments have a legal affairs office to handle legal issues, such as challenges to decisions and policies of the department, and to handle contracts with outside, private companies that provide services to the department. In the case of the TxDOT, the legal affairs office has additional responsibilities. It handles the acquisition of land for the construction of new roads and highways and manages contracts for the planning, building, and maintaining of those roadways.

The finance division is a division common to many Texas agencies as well. It handles the accounting of the department, including making payments to contractors and vendors and dealing with payments received by the TxDOT for its services and work. The administration division handles day-to-day operations, human resources issues, and logistics for meetings and conferences sponsored by the TxDOT. The communications division handles public relations for the department and communicates information to the public about the safety and conditions of Texas roads. This division also deals with letting the public know about upcoming projects and construction. The TxDOT has some divisions that are unique to it. These include the engineering and planning offices. These divisions deal with how Texas develops new roads and highways, from project proposal through construction, and eventually manage long-term maintenance of the roadways.

A chief of staff assists the director in administration of the office. Reporting to the chief of staff are two other important officials. One of these officials, the state legislative

## FIGURE 6.1 Texas Department of Transportation Organizational Chart

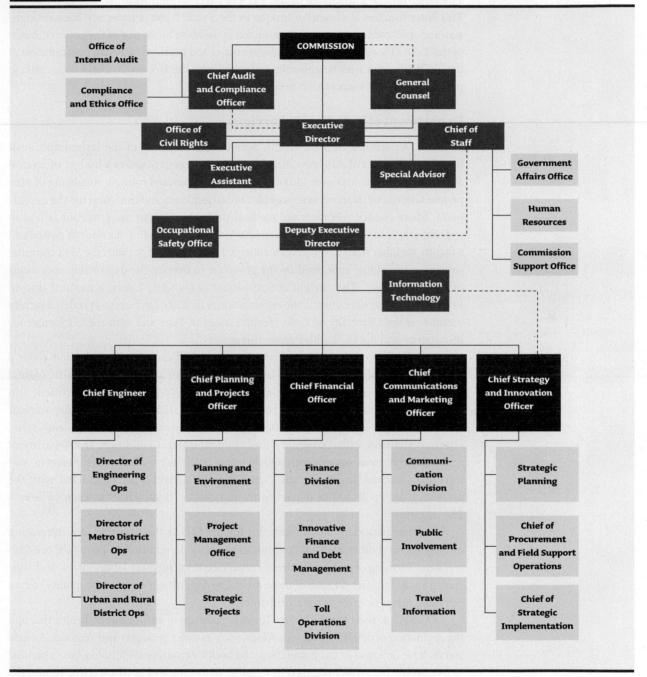

**Source:** Texas Department of Transportation, effective November 17, 2014, www.txdot.gov/inside-txdot/administration/org-chart.html.

affairs officer, ensures that TxDOT priorities are communicated to the Texas Legislature. The other official is in charge of the TxDOT's relationship with the U.S. government. This latter function is somewhat unique to the TxDOT and is necessary because highway and road construction is not conducted in isolation to the rest of the country. Much of the TxDOT's work is linked to interstate travel and traffic. As a result, coordination of the TxDOT's work with neighboring states and with the U.S. government is essential to provide seamless transportation networks nationwide.

## Department of State Health Services

The Department of State Health Services (SHS) is one of the largest and most important agencies of state government. The department oversees a budget of around $2.5 billion and employs over 11,000 people.[33] An appointed council, consisting of nine people selected by the governor, provides broad guidance and direction for the department. Many council members are medical professionals, but the governor is free to appoint others to the council as well. In 2014, the council included a church pastor and a faculty member from a community college. The council works with the SHS commissioner, an individual appointed by the governor to oversee the day-to-day operations of the department. The current commissioner is David L. Lakey, a medical doctor. Prior to assuming his duties as the commissioner in 2005, Dr. Lakey served as a faculty member at the University of Texas Health Center in Tyler and with the UT Center for Biosecurity and Public Health Preparedness.

The department is organized into a series of offices and divisions that cover a wide range of health-related issues, including consumer affairs, border health, mental health, and emergency preparedness. Like other state agencies, the department also contains offices that deal with personnel issues and with finances. The department also collects vital statistics on the health of Texans, including birth and death rates, abortion statistics, infant mortality, and child fatalities. In addition, the department maintains databases on epidemiological issues, such as rates of cancer, diabetes, and infectious diseases among Texans. Some of these activities are conducted with the assistance of county health departments and county clerk offices in each of Texas's 254 counties.

Another important area of concern for the SHS is the licensing and overseeing of hospitals and other medical facilities in the state. In addition to hospitals, the SHS regulates birthing centers, outpatient surgery centers, medical laboratories, and substance abuse facilities. In each of these areas, the department ensures the quality of care provided meets or exceeds state guidelines.

The SHS is also charged by the Texas Legislature to ensure public health through the regulation of drugs and various foods, such as dairy products and seafood. As new trends have emerged in the population, the health department's mission has expanded to overseeing businesses engaged in tanning, tattooing, and body piercing. Again, the goal here is to ensure those who access the services provided by these businesses may be certain that the risk to personal health is minimized.

Finally, an important task assigned to the SHS is the oversight of licensing for some important professions in Texas. This oversight is to ensure that those who

# TEXAS VS GEORGIA

Interstate Highway 75 (I-75) stretches for 400 miles in Georgia from the south central part of the state's border with Florida to the northwest border with Tennessee near Chattanooga. Currently, the highway is at least six lanes, three in each direction, throughout the state. Only one road in the entire state of Georgia is a tollway: Georgia Highway 400 (GA 400), which runs from central Atlanta to the northeast, ending near the town of Dahlonega. The decisions to make I-75 six lanes and to make GA 400 a tollway were made by the Georgia State Transportation Board, the equivalent of the Texas Transportation Commission.

The Georgia State Transportation Board is selected by the state legislature and is required by law to consist of one person from each of Georgia's congressional districts. Thus, as the number of representatives from Georgia in the U.S. House of Representatives changes due to reapportionment every ten years, so does the state's transportation board. After the 2010 census, Georgia was given an additional seat in the U.S House of Representatives, and, as a result, the Georgia State Transportation Board was also enlarged by one. In 2014, the board had thirteen members. In contrast, the Texas Transportation Commission consists of five members, appointed by the governor for six-year terms. If Texas followed the Georgia model, then Texas's commission would consist of thirty-six members.

In Georgia, the entire state legislature does not choose the entire board. Instead, members of the state legislature divide into small groups based on the thirteen congressional districts. All members of the state legislature from a congressional district select one member of the state transportation board. Each board member serves a five-year term.[i] Once elected, the Georgia State Transportation Board selects one of its members to be the chair, and another member is selected as the vice chair. The chair and vice chair serve one-year, renewable terms. In Texas, the governor appoints one member of the Texas Transportation Commission as the chair of the commission.

The Georgia board serves a similar function to its Texas equivalent. The board in Georgia hires a commissioner to oversee the Georgia Department of Transportation (GDOT). The board also designates which roads are part of the state highway system, approves long-range transportation plans, oversees administration of construction contracts, and authorizes lease agreements.[ii]

## THINKING Critically

★ What is the advantage to having the governor appoint the State Board of Transportation, as is the case in Texas?

★ What is the advantage to the system used in Georgia, which is based upon congressional districts?

★ To what extent does Georgia violate the principle of separation of powers?

★ How would gerrymandering congressional districts in Georgia shape or change transportation policy?

---

i. Georgia Department of Transportation, "State Transportation Board," www.dot.ga.gov/aboutgeorgiadot/board/pages/default.aspx (accessed September 19, 2014).

ii. Ibid.

---

practice these professions meet the minimum qualifications for their jobs, engage in ongoing training, and maintain the ethical standards of their professions. Some of the professions that SHS oversees the licensing for include athletic trainers, social workers, EMS technicians, midwives, opticians, social workers, and speech pathologists. In many cases, the SHS works with professional organizations, universities and colleges, and vocation training programs to coordinate the licensing programs.

## Railroad Commission of Texas

The Railroad Commission of Texas was created by Governor Hogg to regulate the railroads, decrease corruption, and protect the state's large agrarian population from crooked railroad practices. The commission was the first regulatory agency in the state and one of the most important commissions in the state's history. It is comprised of

## Railroad Commission of Texas

AP Photo

One of the legends of Texas government is the Railroad Commission of Texas. While the commission is the oldest regulatory agency in Texas and one of the few elected regulatory agencies in the nation, today the commission fails to live up to its name. In November 1890, Texas voters approved an amendment to the Texas Constitution that empowered the legislature to create an agency to regulate railroads. While the state had initially encouraged the railroads, by the 1890s many Texans, especially farmers, had grown to resent them. The Texas Traffic Association, an organization made up of the major railroads, set the rates, and, due to poor roads and unnavigable rivers, Texas farmers had no real alternatives

for shipping goods. In 1891, the legislature followed up by establishing the Railroad Commission of Texas. Initially, commissioners were appointed by the governor. However, voters in 1894 approved an amendment making the commissioners officials who were elected to six-year terms. Since that time, the Railroad Commission has had the unique designation of being a regulatory agency headed by elected officials.

Attorney General James Stephen Hogg had made the call for the creation of a railroad commission the centerpiece of his campaign for governor. The railroads labeled Hogg "communistic," but his reforms proved popular and his election represented the first stirrings of a populist

reform movement in Texas. The creation of the Railroad Commission was proclaimed to be a way of producing fair competition, but in its actual workings, the commission was used more to restrict out-of-state railroads and protect Texas-based businesses from international competitors.

In the 1920s, the Railroad Commission was given responsibility for regulating motor carriers in addition to railroads. However, the responsibility for motor carriers ended in 1994 when trucking was deregulated and responsibility for trucking safety moved to the Texas Department of Transportation (TxDOT).

Today, about three-quarters of the commission's efforts are focused on regulating oil and natural gas exploration and production. The Railroad Commission also oversees natural gas and hazardous liquids pipeline operations, natural gas utilities, LP gas service, and coal and uranium mining.

In 2005, the commission's responsibility for rail safety was transferred to the TxDOT, the last step in removing the railroads from the responsibility of the Railroad Commission. While the commission retains the distinction of being the state's oldest regulatory agency, nothing remains of its original mission and the Railroad Commission of Texas no longer regulates railroads.

three members, each independently elected in a statewide contest. The members serve overlapping six-year terms, with one member reelected every two years. By custom, the chair rotates every two years and is the member who is in the last two years of his or her term. Originally created to regulate railroads, the commission's mandate has expanded over time to include regulation of the oil and gas industry, protection of the environment, and promotion of alternative energy sources. There have long been charges that oil and gas interest groups exert too much influence over the commissioners, and the commission struggles with a reputation for emphasizing protection of the oil and gas industry at the expense of environmental protection.

One of the more recent activities of the Railroad Commission has been distributing part of Texas's share of the American Recovery and Reinvestment Act of 2009, often called the Stimulus Package. This act, passed by the U.S. Congress and signed into law by President Obama, attempted to stimulate the U.S. economy following the 2008 meltdown of the U.S. housing market and the related economic recession that followed. The Railroad Commission of Texas was allocated over $16 billion in stimulus money. Over $3 billion of this was allocated to purchase alternative-fuel vehicles for the state government in Texas. This figure includes the purchase of propane-fueled vehicles and the building of fueling stations for those vehicles. Another $12 billion was allocated for additional vehicle purchases by the state and local governments of non-propane, alternative-fuel vehicles, as well as for public awareness campaigns.

The Railroad Commission selects an executive director and other key staff, including a chief financial officer. The commission is organized into several agencies that oversee specific areas of energy policy, such as alternative energy, natural gas services, and oil and gas. In addition, as in other state commissions and departments, there is a legal affairs office, a human resources office, and an information technology office.

## Texas Department of Criminal Justice

The Texas Department of Criminal Justice oversees the state's prisons, jails, and other correctional facilities. It also supervises processes for offenders released from prison, on parole, or on mandatory suspension. A nine-member board is in charge of the department. This board is appointed by the governor for staggered, six-year terms. The board hires the executive director of the department, sets rules and policies that guide the agency, and serves as the board of trustees for the Windham School District, the school district created by the state to handle the education of juvenile offenders.

The department consists of five key divisions that report directly to the board. The divisions are the office of the inspector general, the Windham School District, the internal audit division, the office of the state counsel for offenders, and the ombudsman. The executive director also directly reports to the board and heads the other work of the department,

AP Photo/David Boe

Amtrak, the U.S. national passenger train service, links communities across Texas to the rest of the country. A high-speed passenger service from Houston to Dallas–Fort Worth, completed either by Amtrak or some other agency, would allow travel between the two major metropolitan areas in less than three hours.

including the control of correctional facilities, parole, and victim services. The director also controls offices that carry out routine activities common to all state agencies, such as a human resources office for hiring of staff and information technology. Like other states, Texas attempts to help integrate prisoners into normal life after prison, and the department maintains a prison labor operation that teaches inmates skills associated with manufacturing and industry through its Texas Correctional Industries (TCI). Products made by prisoners through TCI, such as desks and tables, may be used by public universities or other state agencies.

Also associated with the department is the Texas Board of Pardons and Paroles. This board is appointed by the governor to determine which prisoners are due to be released on parole, determine the conditions of parole, determine if parole is to be suspended, and recommend cases of clemency to the governor.

## State Board of Education

**Elected board**
a directly elected board, such as the Railroad Commission of Texas, that oversees a specific department of Texas government.

The State Board of Education is another example of an **elected board**, like the Railroad Commission. The State Board of Education is composed of fifteen members, each elected from single-member districts. The education board's main jobs include approving state curriculum and textbooks, determining passing scores for state educational testing, and managing the Permanent School Fund. The board is led by a commissioner of education who is appointed by the governor, with Texas Senate approval, from a list of candidates supplied by the board. The board and its commissioner administer the Texas Education Agency (TEA), the state's primary and secondary education department. The TEA develops curriculum standards, administers state testing requirements, and accredits and rates schools in the state. The TEA also distributes state and U.S. government funds to public schools across Texas, which is discussed further in Chapter 14.

In May 2010, the Texas State Board of Education made national news when it adopted new social studies curriculum standards. These new standards questioned the basis for the separation of church and state, stressed the Christian background of the founding fathers, and emphasized states' rights as a cause of the Civil War. Because Texas is such a large textbook market and publishers accordingly tailor their textbooks to its standards, the board's actions have stirred controversy, as Texas's new standards will likely translate into textbook changes across the nation. The board was also criticized for removing references to Thomas Jefferson from state-approved history textbooks. The board, and Texas itself, became the focus of jokes by a number of television personalities, including comedian Jon Stewart on *The Daily Show*. Some, but not all, criticism was misinformed. Some of Thomas Jefferson's contributions to American political thought were eliminated or reduced, especially where his thoughts duplicated the English philosopher John Locke, but the board retained references to Jefferson's influences over our country as president and his writing of the Declaration of Independence.

The Texas Educational Agency contains a number of offices and units to assist in its work. Key units include standards and programs, educator leadership, assessment and accountability, accreditation and school improvement, and grants and compliance. In addition to the commissioner, the agency is led by a chief deputy of education, a deputy commissioner for policy and programs, and a deputy commissioner for finance and administration. Like other agencies of state government, there is a chief financial officer, a human resources office, and an ombudsman office.

## Public Utility Commission of Texas

The Public Utility Commission of Texas (PUC) is an example of an **appointed regulatory commission** in the state. The commission is made up of three members, each appointed by the governor, with Senate approval, for overlapping, six-year terms. The commissioners oversee the electric and telecommunications industries in Texas. The commission focuses on protecting customers from unreasonable rates from electric and telecommunication companies and on promoting competition in wholesale and retail markets. The scope of its work expanded in 1996 with the Federal Telecommunication Act, which ended local monopolies in telephone service, allowing national long-distance companies to offer local telephone service. Prior to this act, companies such as AT&T that offered long-distance service could not offer local phone service. Long-distance service was assumed to be a market-driven industry, with many different companies offering service throughout the United States or in specific regions and states. Local telephone service was provided by a single company, which was granted a monopoly in exchange for providing service throughout the local area, whether the service was profitable or not. This approach ensured local telephone service to rural areas and small towns. However, the advent of new technologies, including the development and spread of cellular telephone service, as well as computers and digital communication, shifted the dynamics of long-distance and local telephone service, allowing for competition in both. The act also paved the way for cell phone, local, and long-distance telephone service, cable television, and other forms of communication to be provided by the same company.

**Appointed regulatory commission**
an agency of the state government whose members oversee a specific department of state government, are appointed by the governor, and are confirmed by the Texas Senate.

**TABLE 6.2** **Staff Size for Major State Government Functions**

| Function | Employees | Percentage |
|---|---|---|
| Higher education | 126,190 | 39.7% |
| Criminal justice, corrections | 44,785 | 14.1% |
| Public welfare | 23,032 | 7.2% |
| Transportation | 14,225 | 4.5% |
| Parks, wildlife, etc. | 11,059 | 3.5% |
| State finance | 9,395 | 3.0% |
| State police | 6,553 | 2.1% |
| State courts and justice | 5,729 | 1.8% |
| Other education | 4,970 | 1.6% |

**Source:** Audrey S. Wall, ed., *Book of the States*, vol. 44 (Lexington, Ky.: Council of State Governments, 2012), 471–472, table 8.5. Reprinted with permission of The Council of State Governments.

# TEXAS (VS) BAVARIA

Texas and the German state of Bavaria share a number of characteristics. For example, similar to Texas's status as the second-largest U.S. state by area and population, Bavaria has the second-largest population in Germany and is the single largest German state by area. Throughout most of its history, Bavaria's state government has been dominated by a single political party, the Christian Social Union (CSU). Since the creation of the modern Federal Republic of Germany and the current state of Bavaria after World War II, the CSU has won all but two elections to the state legislative body, the Landtag. Texas has experienced its share of single-party dominance as well. Bavarians speak a unique dialect of German that natives of Berlin or Frankfurt find difficult to understand, just as Texans are known for their unique accents and phraseology in American English. In addition, Bavaria is among the most religiously observant and socially conservative of the German states. This places Bavarians at odds with their fellow Germans on a regular basis and helps to generate a sense of Bavarian independence and strong state identity. Much like Austin is known for its left-leaning, Democratic Party politics that are often at odds with the state government, the Bavarian capital city of Munich is dominated by the left-of-center Social Democratic Party. The Texas-Bavaria comparison is apparently known in

## Texas Government Departments versus State Bavarian Ministries

| Texas Government Departments | | Bavarian State Ministries |
|---|---|---|
| Department of Agriculture | Department of Insurance | Ministry of the Interior |
| Attorney General/Department of Justice | General Land Office | Ministry of Education and Culture |
| State Auditor | Department of Licensing and Regulation | Ministry of Finance |
| Department of Banking | Department of Parks and Wildlife | Ministry of Economic Affairs, Infrastructure, Transport, and Technology |
| Comptroller of Public Accounts | Department of Public Safety | Ministry of Environment and Health |
| Department of Criminal Justice | Public Utilities Commission | Ministry of Labor, Social Affairs, Family, and Women |
| Texas Educational Agency | Railroad Commission | Ministry of Justice and Consumer Protection |
| Commission on Environmental Quality | Department of Rural Affairs | Ministry of Science, Research, and Art |
| Texas Ethics Commission | Secretary of State | Ministry of Food, Agriculture, and Forestry |
| Department of Family and Protective Services | Sunset Advisory Commission | Ministry of Federal and European Affairs |
| Department of State Health Services | Department of Transportation | |
| Texas Higher Education Coordinating Board | Workforce Commission | |
| Department of Housing and Community Affairs | | |

*Sources:* Compiled by authors from Bayerische Staatsregiergun, "Political Life: The Bavarian State Chancellery and the Bavarian State Ministries," www.bayern.de/Contact-.596/index.htm (accessed September 5, 2014); Texas.gov (accessed September 5, 2014).

Germany. Anecdotally, one of the authors of this textbook recently took some of his students on a study abroad program to Germany, and representatives of the Bavarian state executive branch made several of these direct comparisons during a presentation. Similar sentiments were expressed by representatives of the Hessen state government in their capital city of Weisbaden and by a university professor at the University of Leipzig.

Unlike the United States, including Texas, where state organization and election of the executive branch differs significantly from the national government, all German states possess a state government structure that mirrors the structure of the national government. In Bavaria, the state government is a parliamentary system in which voters directly elect the state's Landtag. The members of the Landtag choose the minister-president and cabinet. These people typically come from the largest political party in the Landtag. The minister-president and cabinet serve as the executive branch and supervise the various departments and agencies of the state government.

The German state government is organized into ten different departments. Each department has an area of responsibility over particular policies and activities of the state government. Some of these departments are unsurprising, such as the Ministry of Education and Culture, which supervises the state's school system. The Ministry of Finance corresponds to the Comptroller of Public Accounts in Texas. The Ministry of the Interior combines activities of state police, fire protection, and disaster preparedness. Some of the departments reflect combinations of activities that Texans may find odd, such as the Ministry of Labor, Social Affairs, Family, and Women. Others are unique to the German political system, such as the Ministry of Federal and European Affairs. This department manages relations with the German national government in Berlin. Because Germany is one of the twenty-seven members of the European Union, the department also manages Bavaria's interactions with that organization's institutions.

## THINKING *Critically*

★ What advantage does Germany possess by having all state governments mirror the structure of the national government?

★ What advantages exist to the U.S. approach, in which states may vary the selection of their executive branches?

★ What ministries of the Bavarian government are most interesting to you? Why?

★ If you were to create a state government agency in Texas that most reflected something uniquely Texas, what would the agency be?

Success in the telephone market led the state government, including the Public Utilities Commission, to examine whether the same was possible in electrical markets. The Texas Legislature passed deregulation in 2001, allowing competition in electrical markets. Prior to this bill, the state of Texas, like other states, assumed that electricity production and transmission was too costly to be a functioning market. This assumption led to the creation of monopolies granted to companies to operate in specific areas and communities in Texas. For example, Texas Power and Light, a forerunner of TXU Energy, was given the exclusive right to provide electricity in north central Texas. After 2001, companies were allowed to compete for the right to sell electricity to customers throughout Texas, so companies such as TXU began doing business with private businesses, government agencies, and residential customers throughout the state. TXU was able to enter areas that other monopolies, such as Entergy Corporation, had controlled in southeastern parts of Texas, while companies such as Entergy were able to sell in areas where TXU once held a monopoly. The assumption was that rates would fall and power companies would have an incentive to come up with ways to lower costs to consumers. However, an exception in the law was granted for rural areas in which a user-owned electrical cooperative provided power. In these areas, the cooperatives retained their monopoly. Currently, the Public Utilities Commission regulates the rates that electrical utilities charge customers and ensures that competition occurs in electrical markets throughout Texas.

The Public Utilities Commission hires an executive director to run the agency. The agency is divided into two units: (1) Administration and (2) Oversight and Regulation. Each of these units contains several subdivisions. For example, Oversight and Regulation contains offices that oversee competition, regulation enforcement, and consumer protection. The Administration, Operations, and Fund Management unit contains offices that handle the fiscal operations of the commission, general legal affairs, relations with other state agencies, and human resources.

## Staffing the State Government

The State of Texas employs over 360,000 Texans to staff the various state boards, agencies, and commissions. This figure includes individuals working directly for the governor, the Texas Legislature, and public universities and colleges throughout the state. Approximately 40 percent of these employees—the largest share—works for Texas's public universities. The next largest category is corrections, or those working in law enforcement agencies and prisons. This area accounts for 14 percent of state employees.

To staff these and other state agencies, Texas uses a mixture of the **patronage system** and the merit system. The patronage system, sometimes called the spoils system, allows individuals to give jobs as political favors, which means that people receive government jobs based upon who they know and the connection they have to a powerful political figure. Most patronage positions in Texas government are appointed by the governor himself and total around 3,000 positions. As mentioned in Chapter 5, the governor possesses significant appointment power and is able to use this power to shape key agencies of state government. Other key members of the Texas executive branch possess similar powers for some positions within their department. Within some state agencies, the board or commission that heads the agency may also possess some freedom to choose who works in key jobs within that agency. Thus, securing a government job is dependent upon who you know, not whether you are qualified for the job. The principle also applies to giving promotions and raises and to increases in job duties.

An advantage to the patronage system is the ability of an executive to shape and model the executive branch to his or her liking. In addition, jobs may be given as political rewards to one's loyal supporters during an election campaign. Finally, the patronage system encourages accountability to officials directly elected by the people.

In contrast, a **merit-based civil service system** gives individuals a government job based upon qualifications and merit. The merit system attempts to depoliticize the bureaucracy. First, merit system employees are supposed to be neutral in the services that they provide to the public. This means that government workers are not supposed to treat friends or relatives differently from others. Second, government agencies are hierarchical, with a clear chain of command from entry-level workers up to the head of the agency. Third, there is a division of labor. Certain tasks are assigned to specific individuals to perform, while other tasks are done by other workers. Fourth, the employees follow standard operating procedures. Guidelines and rules govern how employees carry out their jobs, standardizing routine decisions and limiting the power

**Patronage system**
when individuals who supported a candidate for public office are rewarded with public jobs and appointments and government contracts.

**Merit-based civil service system**
a system in which people receive government jobs based upon a set of qualifications and formal training; job promotion and pay raises are based upon job performance.

# HOW TEXAS GOVERNMENT WORKS

# A State Employment Comparison

## Percent of State Government Employees Working in Key Sectors

## Higher Education

| | |
|---|---|
| California | 38.5% |
| Colorado | 52.6% |
| Florida | 29.4% |
| Michigan | 51.0% |
| Texas | 39.7% |

## Corrections

| | |
|---|---|
| California | 15.0% |
| Colorado | 10.3% |
| Florida | 16.6% |
| Michigan | 10.4% |
| Texas | 14.1% |

## Highways

| | |
|---|---|
| California | 5.1% |
| Colorado | 4.4% |
| Florida | 4.1% |
| Michigan | 2.0% |
| Texas | 4.5% |

## State Police

| | |
|---|---|
| California | 2.9% |
| Colorado | 2.1% |
| Florida | 2.4% |
| Michigan | 1.8% |
| Texas | 2.1% |

## Public Welfare

| | |
|---|---|
| California | 0.1% |
| Colorado | 3.3% |
| Florida | 5.4% |
| Michigan | 7.4% |
| Texas | 7.2% |

## General Administration

| | |
|---|---|
| California | 6.8% |
| Colorado | 2.4% |
| Florida | 4.8% |
| Michigan | 4.0% |
| Texas | 3.0% |

## State Health & Hospitals

| | |
|---|---|
| California | 10.1% |
| Colorado | 7.4% |
| Florida | 2.1% |
| Michigan | 12.9% |
| Texas | 9.9% |

## Natural Resources

| | |
|---|---|
| California | 3.7% |
| Colorado | 3.5% |
| Florida | 5.3% |
| Michigan | 4.0% |
| Texas | 4.0% |

Source: Audrey S. Wall, Table 8.5 State Government Employment (Full-Time Equivalent) for Selected Functions, By States, 2010, Book of the States, vol. 44 (Lexington, KY: Council of State Governments, 2012): p. 471.

of employees to make decisions on their own. Note that the merit system is often also used in the private sector by business and companies. Walmart and McDonald's both operate using these principles.

The merit system in public service (government agencies) means that government workers are not dependent on who is currently holding office and will not lose their jobs when someone new is elected to office. Supporters of the merit system point out that this system allows the government to be staffed by experts in their jobs who are free to operate government agencies with a focus on efficiency and professionalism. Furthermore, the creation of merit systems at the national and state levels was associated with the rise of public administration and managerial sciences as new approaches to workplace efficiency. Interestingly, the Texas Government Code limits the merit system only to state agencies that are required by U.S. government law or regulation to use such a system.[34] However, the sheer size of U.S. government grants, cost-sharing programs, and other activities means that much of the Texas government is staffed by a merit system.

## BUREAUCRATIC ACCOUNTABILITY

As we have seen, the bureaucracy of Texas is a complex and diverse array of agency heads, board members, and commissioners that may be elected or appointed to their posts. Executive control of the bureaucracy is tenuous at best. As a result, several tools have evolved in Texas that aid the executive in exerting this control.

Texas utilizes so-called **sunshine laws**, or laws designed to make government transparent and accessible to the people. One such law, the Texas Public Information Act, grants citizens access to government records in the state. Similarly, the Texas Open Meetings Act generally requires governmental bodies to notify the public of the time, date, and nature of scheduled meetings and to open those meetings to the public. City council members from smaller cities have challenged the constitutionality of this requirement in federal court since for a small council it may mean that two people cannot discuss city business in private. When he was attorney general, Greg Abbott adamantly defended the Open Meetings Act. Sunshine laws received a significant boost in November 2007 when Texas voters overwhelmingly passed an amendment that requires both houses of the Texas Legislature to record the final vote on a bill and make that vote available on the Internet.

In addition, the state enacted a **sunset review process** (see Figure 6.2) to assess all of the statutory boards and commissions in the state. The Sunset Advisory Commission was created by the Texas Legislature in 1977 to review the effectiveness of agencies. The commission is made up of twelve members; five are from the Texas House, appointed by the Speaker of the House, and five are from the Texas Senate, appointed by the lieutenant governor. The other two members are public members, one appointed by the Speaker and one by the lieutenant governor.

The sunset review process requires most governmental commissions or agencies to be reviewed every twelve years. The commission examines a self-evaluation report submitted by the agency under review, as well as developing its own reports

**Sunshine laws**
laws designed to make government transparent and accessible.

**Sunset review process**
a formal assessment of the effectiveness of all statutory boards, commissions, and state agencies.

FIGURE 6.2 Sunset Review Process

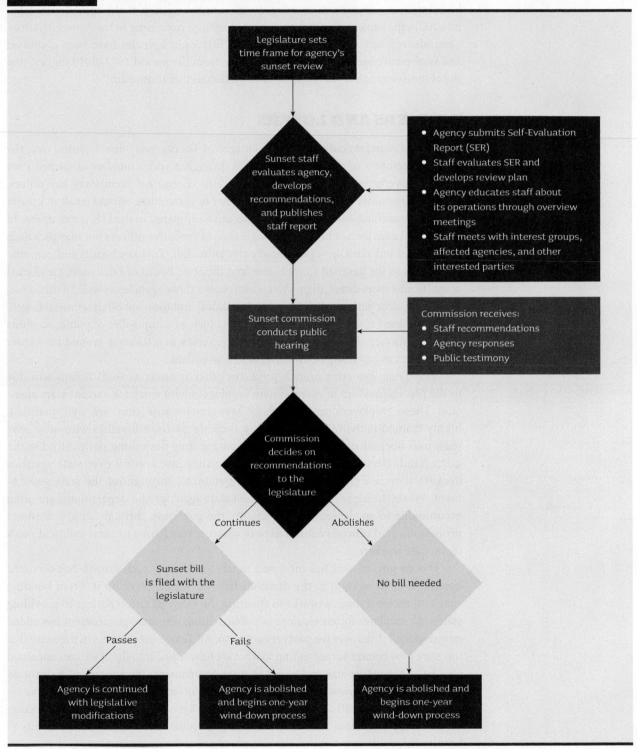

**Source:** Sunset Advisory Commission, "Sunset in Texas," January 2012, www.sunset.state.tx.us/suntx.pdf (accessed September 21, 2012).

and holding a public hearing. The commission can then recommend that an agency be continued, reorganized, or merged with another agency. If the commission takes no action, the sun automatically sets on that agency. According to the Sunset Advisory Commission's estimates, since its inception fifty-eight agencies have been abolished and twelve have been consolidated. Estimates from the period 1982–2013 suggest that the commission has saved the state $945 million in that time span.[35]

## WINNERS AND LOSERS

The plural executive offers the citizens of Texas greater direct control over the members of the executive branch through a wider number of elected state government officials. Texans' ability to choose for themselves key offices, such as the attorney general and commissioner of agriculture, should result in greater democratic accountability of the Texas executive compared to the U.S. government. In addition, Texans are not bound to a single slate of executive officers but may pick each officeholder individually, regardless of party affiliation. That key boards and commissions, such as the Railroad Commission and the State Board of Education, are elected offers Texans more direct, democratic control over those agencies as well. In this sense, Texans are clear winners. Politicians with political ambition are often winners as well. Practice gained running for statewide offices, such as comptroller of public accounts or commissioner of the General Land Office, serves as a training ground for higher offices, such as governor, U.S. senator, or U.S. president.

The Texas executive branch produces other winners as well. Texans win due to the professionalism of merit system employees who work for various state agencies. These employees work in these agencies because they are well-qualified, highly trained individuals, not because they are partisan loyalists who only have their jobs because of whom they know or what they have done politically. On the other hand, elected officials are losers when they lose control over state agencies because they lack the ability to appoint personnel throughout the state government. While the highest positions in most state agencies and departments are often accountable to an elected official, usually the governor, through an appointment process, elected officials cannot expect absolute obedience to their political goals from state workers.

If state government has increased in size and scope, such growth has occurred because it is responding to the demands that we Texans place on it. From building state and national road networks to ensuring the safety of tattoo parlors to providing statewide standards for curriculum in public schools, the state government has added new responsibilities over the past century or so. All Texans are winners in the sense that our state government is responding to what we have asked it to do. If we are concerned about the expanding size and scope of state government, the sunset review process allows for regular review of all state agencies and offers an opportunity for Texans— through our elected officials—to determine which agencies are outdated and unnecessary. Thus, the potential for a runaway state government is tempered by our ability to terminate specific agencies through this process.

However, our state executive branch produces losers in some other ways. Rather than creating an institutional structure in which an energetic legislature and executive each possesses enough power to check the other, the Texas system creates an institutional arrangement designed to keep the executive weak. As a result, members of the executive branch are often at odds with each other on key issues and policies. Paradoxically, voters have greater control over the executive, yet face an executive branch that lacks an efficient, streamlined operation. The myriad of state agencies, boards, committees, and departments seems daunting at times. Each part seems to have its own agenda, leaving Texans confused and concerned about what the state is actually doing.

★ What contradictions are apparent in the growth of state government and Texas's traditions of independence and small government?

★ How much do Texans benefit from the services the state provides?

★ Does the plural executive effectively give Texans more of a say in their government?

## CONCLUSION

The current structure of the Texas executive was created over a hundred years ago in a state that was far less complex than the one of today. It derives from a political preference for a weak executive that is a legacy of both colonial Americans' dislike of centralized power and a desire to make the executive branch more accountable to the citizens of the state. The growth of state government since the Texas Constitution of 1876 was adopted has brought new administrative agencies and organizations. Texans now find that their notion of small government is at odds with the practice of state government. Boards and commissions now regulate public utilities, supervise public health and safety, oversee public education, and control a host of additional services. These agencies were the result of public demands for government action in areas that mattered to us Texans. In addition, the advent of a merit system for organizing the state government, where implemented, results in a more professional staff in state government but one that is less eager or less dependent on pleasing the politicians of the day.

for CQ Press

Sharpen your skills with **SAGE edge** at **edge.sagepub.com/collier4e**. SAGE edge for **students** provides a personalized approach to help you accomplish your coursework goals in an easy-to-use learning environment.

appointed regulatory commission (p. 205)

attorney general (p. 187)

bureaucracy (p. 197)

commissioner of the General Land Office (p. 194)

comptroller of public accounts (p. 190)

elected board (p. 204)

lieutenant governor (p. 186)

merit-based civil service system (p. 208)

patronage system (p. 208)

Permanent School Fund (p. 194)

plural executive (p. 185)

secretary of state (p. 195)

sunset review process (p. 210)

sunshine laws (p. 210)

# CORE ASSESSMENT

1. What are the advantages and disadvantages to the plural executive system used in Texas and other states to organize the executive branch?

2. Evaluate the advantages and disadvantages of having elected boards to oversee some Texas agencies, such as the State Board of Education and the Railroad Commission.

3. In what ways do you contribute to the needs and demands for more roads and highways in Texas? Under what circumstances would you be willing to take public transportation?

# 7 TEXAS JUDICIAL SYSTEM

**W**allace Jefferson, one of the most respected judges in the country, resigned as chief justice of the Supreme Court of Texas in October 2013. Jefferson was the descendent of a slave (owned by a judge) who served two terms on the Waco City Council after the Civil War. After earning a degree in political philosophy, Jefferson earned his law degree from the University of Texas. Jefferson, who was appointed to the Supreme Court of Texas by Governor Perry in 2001, became the first African American to serve on the state's highest civil court. A few years later, he became the first African American chief justice of the Supreme Court of Texas. When he resigned, Jefferson left an impressive record behind. He often spoke of justice for all, advocating increased legal assistance for poor and middle-class families and the protection of children. Jefferson worried that "the courthouse door is closed to many who have lost their jobs, veterans and women who struggle with physical abuse."[1] He also promoted increased access to and transparency of the court. Due to Jefferson's leadership, Supreme Court of Texas documents and live Webcasts of arguments before the court are now posted online. Jefferson's greatest legacy, however, may well be the reform he never saw.

As chief justice, Jefferson continually advocated for the elimination of partisan races in Texas judicial contests. Many of his speeches focused on the corrosive influence of money in judicial elections. As Jefferson told the 81st Legislature in his state of the judiciary address in 2009, "Sadly, we have now become accustomed to judicial races in which the primary determinants of victory are not the flaws of the incumbent or qualities of the challenger, but political affiliation and money."[2] Although Jefferson continually had to compete in those partisan elections, he was well aware of the way judicial elections worked in Texas, once stating,

> You don't know who I am. I don't blame you. I have been on the statewide ballot three times, in 2002, 2006 and 2008. I was elected each time by impressive margins. Yet a July 2008 statewide poll found that 86 percent of the electorate "never heard of" me. I won because Texans voted for Rick Perry, Kay Bailey Hutchison and John McCain.[3]

© Bob Daemmrich/Corbis

Jefferson was reelected not because Texans were familiar with his record but because of Texans' reliance on straight-ticket partisan voting. And, according to Jefferson, "a justice system based on Democratic or Republican judging is a system that cannot be trusted."[4]

Jefferson has long advocated the elimination of partisan elections and the adoption of a merit system of judicial selection. There are different types of merit systems, but they all generally involve some sort of appointment process, often accompanied by retention elections. The advantage is that these systems remove partisan labels, partisan pandering, and regular campaigning from the judicial process. The result is a system of judicial selection that is more likely to appear impartial. For Jefferson, "A system that cannot provide equal access to justice, that does not protect the endangered and the vulnerable; a system that permits politics to take precedence over merit; and one that allows the innocent to remain behind bars" is badly in need of reform.[5] Nonetheless, Texans' deep-seated distrust of government has long translated into an unwillingness to fix the system, even if it is badly broken.

In this chapter, we begin by outlining the structure of the Texas judiciary. This structure is central to a consideration of justice in Texas as the system reflects ad hoc changes rather than a cohesive system of justice. Next we examine the different levels of courts in the state, explore the costs and benefits of electing judges in Texas, and consider alternative forms of judicial selection. The chapter concludes with a discussion of the criminal justice system in the state.

## Chapter Objectives

★ Describe how Texas court jurisdiction fits under the structure of judicial federalism.

★ Identify the different types of local trial courts.

★ Explain the three types of county-level trial courts.

★ Describe the role and hierarchy of appellate courts.

★ Explain the process of judicial selection in Texas.

★ Discuss the issues of representation within the Texas judiciary.

★ Identify problems with the Texas judiciary and give alternative means of judicial selection.

★ Describe the Texas criminal justice system.

★ Assess who wins and who loses under the current Texas court system.

## JUDICIAL FEDERALISM AND TEXAS COURTS

**Judicial federalism**
a system in which judicial authority is shared between levels of government.

The American court system is based on **judicial federalism**, in which judicial authority is shared between levels of government. The U.S. Constitution gives the national Congress the authority to create a supreme court and the lower federal courts. The U.S. Supreme Court's jurisdiction is spelled out in the Constitution and includes issues of constitutional law, treaties, and cases involving ambassadors and public ministers, among others. At the same time, the states created their own court systems for their respective state and local levels of government. Questions of local or state law, as well as questions regarding a state's constitution, are heard in the appropriate local- or state-level court. This means that in the United States we have a dual system of jurisprudence, in which questions of federal or constitutional law are heard in the national judicial system and questions of state law are heard in the state judicial system. The vast majority of cases are heard at the state level. The Texas judicial system is one of the largest, most complex in the country, and determining which court will hear which case is far from straightforward. The Texas Constitution says this about the state's court system:

> The judicial power of this State shall be vested in one Supreme Court, in one Court of Criminal Appeals, in Courts of Appeals, in District Courts, in County Courts, in Commissioners Courts, in Courts of Justices of the Peace, and in such other courts as may be provided by law.
>
> The Legislature may establish such other courts as it may deem necessary and prescribe the jurisdiction and organization thereof, and may conform the jurisdiction of the district and other inferior courts thereto.[6]

The resulting court system in Texas shown in How Texas Government Works on page 224, is a highly complex, confusing, and muddled one. The state constitution establishes two high courts, other appellate courts, district courts, commissioners courts, and justice of the peace courts. It also empowers the state legislature to establish other courts. Over the years, the legislature has created various municipal courts, the county courts at law, probate courts, and a variety of specialized courts that include drug, youth, and veterans courts. Courts in Texas are divided by their jurisdiction, their origin, and their geographical coverage. A court's **jurisdiction** refers to its sphere of authority. One issue of authority concerns whether a case is at the original or appellate stage. Courts with **original jurisdiction** hear the initial cases. Typically, courts of original jurisdiction hear evidence and establish the record of the case. Courts with **appellate jurisdiction** hear appeals of cases for which a decision has previously been rendered by a lower court. Rather than hearing new evidence, appellate courts are restricted to reviewing the court record from the original trial and determining whether specific points of law or procedure were applied correctly. In addition, courts are sometimes given **exclusive jurisdiction**, meaning a particular level of court has the sole right to hear a specific type of case.

A second issue of jurisdiction distinguishes whether a case is a criminal case or a civil one. In a **criminal case**, the state charges an individual with violating the law. In a **civil case**, an aggrieved party sues for damages based on claims that he or she has been wronged by another individual. In Texas, the lower-level courts (the municipal courts, justice of the peace courts, and county courts) are limited to handling the least serious criminal and civil cases. By contrast, the most serious criminal charges, called felonies, and civil suits over a certain dollar amount are heard in district- or state-level courts.

A third issue of jurisdiction concerns geographical coverage. Jurisdiction in the Texas lower courts is based on the geographical municipality, precinct, or county where the court is located. There are 458 district- or state-level courts in the state, ninety-eight of which overlap more than one county. The geographic jurisdiction of district courts therefore often overlaps with county courts. Conversely, in larger counties, such as Harris and Dallas Counties, there may be more than one district court. The state is further divided into fourteen appellate districts. The two highest courts, the Supreme Court of Texas and the Texas Court of Criminal Appeals, serve the entire state. These distinctions often become confused because, depending on the population of a city or county, courts have evolved to serve different functions and often have overlapping jurisdiction. Since the legislature can create courts with particular jurisdiction to meet the needs of diverse communities in the state, to ascertain the jurisdiction of a particular court in the state of Texas it is often necessary to look at the actual legislation that created that district.

Courts in Texas are further distinguished by their origin. Courts in Texas are either specified in the constitution or created by the state legislature. The Texas Constitution specifically provides for justice of the peace courts, county courts, district courts, and appellate courts, including the two highest courts. The state legislature is left to determine the exact number of courts. In addition, the legislature can create other levels of courts. As such, the legislature creates all municipal courts, statutory county courts, and probate courts.

**Jurisdiction**
the court's sphere of authority.

**Original jurisdiction**
the authority to hear the initial case; the evidence and the case record are established in this court.

**Appellate jurisdiction**
the authority to hear an appeal from a lower court that has already rendered a decision; an appellate court reviews the court record from the original trial and does not hear new evidence.

**Exclusive jurisdiction**
a particular court given the sole right to hear a specific type of case.

**Criminal case**
a case in which an individual is charged by the state with violating the law and the state brings the suit.

**Civil case**
a case in which an aggrieved party sues for damages claiming that he or she has been wronged by another individual.

# TEXAS VS KANSAS

While the Texas court system is multi-layered and complex as a result of the many different types of courts and courts with concurrent jurisdiction, the court system in Kansas is much less challenging to understand. For example, the Kansas court system contains only four types of courts: municipal, district, a court of appeal, and a supreme court. Compare this to Texas with its municipal courts, justice of the peace courts, county courts, district courts, fourteen courts of appeal, and two supreme courts. Unlike in Texas, courts in Kansas typically have exclusive jurisdiction over cases. Thus, jurisdiction in Kansas's court system is much more straightforward than that of Texas.

The lowest level of court in Kansas is the municipal court. Like Texas, municipal courts in Kansas exist to try cases arising from violations of city ordinances, such as traffic violations. These courts lack juries to assist in deciding the cases. There are over 370 such courts in Kansas, compared to 926 in Texas. At the next level are district courts, which serve as original jurisdiction courts for violations of state law, both civil and criminal. District courts in Kansas have exclusive jurisdiction over cases involving minors and domestic relations, even when they arise under municipal ordinances, and they hear appeals from municipal courts. Cases at the district level are typically heard by a jury. There are thirty-one district courts, each covering one or more counties in Kansas. Approximately 250 judges serve these courts. District courts in Texas have original jurisdiction over divorces, land title claims, slander, and contested elections. Compared to Kansas, however, their jurisdiction is much less clear, since they have concurrent jurisdiction with both justice of the peace courts and county courts and their jurisdiction can vary depending on what other courts are in the area.

The next level of court in Kansas is the court of appeals. Unlike Texas, which has fourteen courts of appeal that hear cases from lower courts in specific geographic areas of Texas, Kansas has a single court that hears appeals from all district courts across the state. The only cases that this court does not hear are cases involving the death penalty and other major felonies. As in Texas, these cases are appealed from the district court directly to the state's highest court. Significant questions of rights of citizens and powers of the state government are appealed directly from the district court to the Kansas Supreme Court as well. A total of fourteen judges sit on

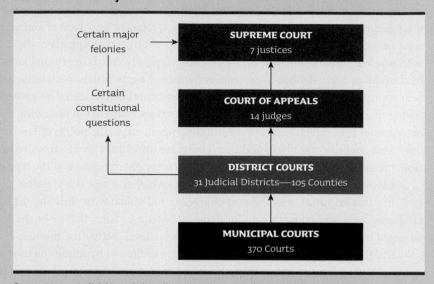

## Kansas Court System

- Certain major felonies →
- Certain constitutional questions

**SUPREME COURT**
7 justices

**COURT OF APPEALS**
14 judges

**DISTRICT COURTS**
31 Judicial Districts—105 Counties

**MUNICIPAL COURTS**
370 Courts

**Source:** Kansas Judicial Branch, http://www.kscourts.org/pdf/ctchart.pdf (accessed July 2, 2014).

the Kansas Court of Appeals, hearing cases in panels that are usually comprised of three judges.

Unlike the Texas system, which has separate top courts for civil and criminal appeals, Kansas has a single supreme court. The Kansas Supreme Court hears both civil and criminal appeals from the Kansas Court of Appeals as well as death penalty cases appealed from district court. The court contains seven justices who sit en banc, meaning all seven justices sit for all cases that the court hears. The court also hears appeals on decisions made by administrative agencies of the state. For example, a decision by the Kansas Department of Health to deny a child from a low-income family access to the state's insurance program would be appealed to the Kansas Supreme Court.

The figure in this box shows the organizational structure of the Kansas court system. Compare this box with how Texas Government Works on page 224, which illustrates the complexity of the Texas court system.

## THINKING *Critically*

★ What advantages exist to the simplistic structure of the Kansas court system?

★ What disadvantages exist to the complex structure of the Texas court system?

★ Is Texas better served by having two high courts, or is Kansas better served by having a single supreme court?

The end result is a judicial system that is ill-defined, confusing, costly, and inefficient. Jurisdiction is often unclear as district courts overlap in many counties in Texas. The state court system is even more confusing since courts often have overlapping original jurisdiction, called **concurrent jurisdiction**. The distinction between original and appellate jurisdiction is also blurred in Texas since lower-level courts often do not keep official records, meaning that the appellate court has to treat a case as if it were new. Further, the Texas Legislature can create courts to serve specific functions and often does so on an ad hoc basis.

## LOCAL TRIAL COURTS

t the local level there are two types of trial courts, each with limited jurisdiction: the municipal courts and justice of the peace courts.

### Municipal Courts

Municipal courts are courts created by the state legislature for cities in Texas. There are currently 926 municipal courts in the state, with larger cities often having more than one municipal court. Municipal courts have original and exclusive jurisdiction over violations of municipal ordinances—those that typically deal with zoning requirements, fire safety, litter laws, noise violations, traffic, or zoning laws. Municipal courts can impose fines of up to $2,000 for violations of municipal ordinances. In addition, municipal courts have jurisdiction over class C misdemeanors (criminal matters punishable by a fine of $500 or less, with no possible jail time). This is an example of concurrent jurisdiction, since justice of the peace courts also have jurisdiction over class C misdemeanors. Typically, if an officer of the city issues the citation, then the case is heard in municipal court; citations issued by county officers (such as sheriffs) are heard in the justice of the peace court. Municipal courts generally have no civil jurisdiction except in cases involving owners of dangerous dogs. By custom, the municipal courts also perform **magistrate functions**. As magistrates, municipal courts can issue search and arrest warrants, conduct preliminary hearings, and set bail for more serious crimes. The magistrate functions allow municipal courts to help decrease the workload of higher-level courts. Today, the vast majority of the cases heard in municipal courts, approximately 73 percent, deal with traffic or parking violations.[7]

Appeals from municipal courts are typically heard in county-level courts. If the municipal court is a court of record, then the county-level court exercises appellate jurisdiction. However, most municipal courts, 84 percent, are not courts of record, meaning no official transcript is recorded in cases that are brought before them.[8] Absent an official record, appeals from municipal courts are heard **de novo**, or with a new trial, in county-level courts.

Municipal judges are typically appointed by city councils to two-year terms. The city council also determines the salary for municipal judges, which varies substantially throughout the state. When the state legislature passes statutes creating municipal courts of record, the statutes require that the judges presiding over those courts be

**Concurrent jurisdiction**
a system in which different levels of courts have overlapping jurisdiction or authority to try the same type of case.

**Magistrate functions**
the authority to conduct the preliminary procedures in criminal cases, including issuing search and arrest warrants, conducting preliminary hearings, and setting bail for more serious crimes.

**De novo**
to hear an appeal with a new trial in the absence of an official case record.

licensed attorneys in the state of Texas. Since most municipal courts are not courts of record, however, most municipalities do not require their judges to be attorneys. In the absence of specific requirements, only 68 percent of all municipal judges graduated college and only 59 percent are licensed attorneys.[9]

### Justice of the Peace Courts

Counties are divided into precincts, and justice of the peace courts, or JP courts, are precinct-level courts. The number of judicial precincts in a county depends on the size of the county's population. Currently, there are 817 JP courts. The constitution provides that each county have between one and eight justice of the peace courts:

> Justice of the peace courts shall have original jurisdiction in criminal matters of misdemeanor cases punishable by fine only, exclusive jurisdiction in civil matters where the amount in controversy is two hundred dollars or less, and such other jurisdiction as may be provided by law. Justices of the peace shall be ex officio notaries public.[10]

Like municipal courts, JP courts are courts of original jurisdiction only. Civil jurisdiction of JP courts extends to cases that involve $10,000 or less. This jurisdiction is concurrent with county and district courts in cases involving amounts of $200 to $10,000. The JP court has nearly exclusive jurisdiction in civil cases involving less than $200. The criminal jurisdiction extends to class C misdemeanor cases, concurrent with municipal courts. Approximately 85 percent of all JP court cases are criminal cases, and 64 percent of these are traffic cases.[11]

The presiding officials of JP courts perform marriages, act as notaries public, and serve as magistrates for higher courts. JP courts also serve as small claims courts. One of the more interesting responsibilities of the justice of the peace is to act as coroner in counties without medical examiners. The job of the coroner is to determine cause of death, even though justices do not generally have any medical training. JP courts are not courts of record, so any appeals are heard de novo in the county courts.

Justices of the peace, like other Texas judges, are elected in partisan elections to four-year terms. Lack of educational requirements is one of the most consistent criticisms of JP courts. There are no formal qualifications for JP judges. In 2013, the *Annual Statistical Report for the Texas Judiciary* reported that 94 percent of JP judges graduated from high school, 32 percent graduated from college, and a mere 9 percent graduated from law school.[12] Salaries vary significantly by county and are set by the county commissioners court.

## COUNTY-LEVEL TRIAL COURTS

Trial courts are courts where evidence is introduced, testimony is presented, and a verdict is rendered. The trial-level court is generally where the original case record is established. At the county level, there are three types of trial courts: constitutional county courts, county courts at law, and statutory probate courts.

## Judge Roy Bean

Roy Bean, a legend of the Texas judiciary, reflects the lax nature of frontier justice in Texas and the state's fondness for amateur justice. Born in Kentucky in 1825, Bean had no formal education that prepared him for service as a judge. However, Pecos County needed a judge, one that would allow the Texas Rangers to clean up the area without having to make a 400-mile round trip to the nearest courthouse and jail. Thus, for lack of a better choice, Roy Bean became a Texas judge on August 2, 1882.

Prior to serving as a judge, Bean's legal experience had been on the other side of the bench and cell door. After fleeing legal trouble in several states, Bean settled briefly in San Diego, California, where his brother was mayor. In 1852, he was arrested and charged with assault with intent to murder for participating in a duel over a woman. He eventually escaped from jail, allegedly using a knife smuggled inside some tamales to dig himself out. After relocating to San Gabriel, California, Bean became involved in another duel in 1854, killing a romantic rival.

This time, he didn't appear before a court; instead, he narrowly escaped lynching by his victim's friends.

Bean supplemented his judicial earnings by running a bar called Jersey Lilly, named for Lillie Langtry, a British actress with whom Bean was obsessed. (Contrary to rumor, Langtry, Texas, was not named after her. The city, originally named Eagle Nest, was renamed in honor of George Langtry, an area railroad engineer.)

While occasionally voted out of office, Bean mostly held onto the position of judge until his retirement in 1902. Despite his lack of training and his possession of only one law book, Bean's justice was creative. Because he lacked a jail, he favored setting fines over requiring jail time when sentencing. Horse thieves were generally released after payment of a fine if the horses were returned. When a man died after falling off a bridge, Bean discovered that the man had been carrying forty dollars and a concealed pistol. He fined the man forty dollars for

carrying a concealed weapon and used the money to pay for his funeral expenses.

Bean's legal and bartending careers complimented each other nicely; Bean required that jurors buy drinks at his saloon during every judicial recess. His most famous venture came in 1896 when he organized a world championship boxing title match. Since boxing matches were illegal in Texas, Judge Bean arranged for Bob Fitzsimmons and Peter Maher to box on an island in the Rio Grande. While the fight lasted less than two minutes, word of the match and its promoter spread throughout the United States.

Portraying himself as the "law west of the Pecos," Judge Roy Bean epitomized Texas justice in its infancy. He died in 1903, but his legacy continues to shape the town of Langtry. In 1939, the State of Texas purchased Bean's Jersey Lilly, making it the centerpiece of Langtry's Old West tourism business, and it has had over 1 million visitors to date.

## Constitutional County Courts

The constitution mandates a county-level court in each of the 254 counties in the state; these courts are sometimes referred to as constitutional county courts. The constitution states that

> there shall be established in each county in this State a County Court, which shall be a court of record; and there shall be elected in each county, by the qualified voters, a County Judge, who shall be well informed in the law of the State; shall be a conservator of the peace, and shall hold his office for four years, and until his successor shall be elected and qualified.[13]

Constitutional county courts exercise exclusive and original jurisdiction over misdemeanors where fines can exceed $500 and jail time can be imposed (class A and class B misdemeanors). Original civil jurisdiction extends to cases involving amounts from $200

# Texas State Court Structure

**State's Highest Appellate Courts**

## Supreme Court
### (1 court – 9 justices)

*Statewide Jurisdiction*

- Final appellate jurisdiction in civil cases and juvenile cases.

## Court of Criminal Appeals
### (1 court – 9 justices)

*Statewide Jurisdiction*

- Final appellate jurisdiction in criminal cases.

**Civil Appeals**

**Criminal Appeals**

**Death Sentence Appeals**

**State's Intermediate Appellate Courts**

## Courts of Appeals
### (14 courts – 80 justices)

*Regional Jurisdiction*

- Intermediate appeals from trial courts in their respective courts of appeals districts.

**County-Level Appeals**

**State's Trial Courts of General and Special Jurisdiction**

## District Courts
### (458 courts – 458 judges)

**360 districts containing one county and 98 districts containing more than one county.**

*Jurisdiction*

- Original jurisdiction in civil actions over $200*, divorce, title to land, contested elections.
- Original jurisdiction in felony criminal matters.
- Juvenile matters.
- 13 district courts are designated criminal district courts; some others are directed to give preference to certain specialized areas.

*The dollar amount is currently unclear.

Source: Texas Courts Online, "Court Structure of Texas," September 1, 2014, www.txcourts.gov/media/654201/Court-Structure-Chart-for-publication9_1_14b.pdf (accessed November 5, 2014).

# Texas Local Court Structure

## County-Level Courts
### (510 courts – 510 judges)

County Trial Courts of Limited Jurisdiction

### Constitutional County Courts
**(254 courts)**
**(one court in each county)**

***Jurisdiction***

- Original jurisdiction in civil actions between $200 and $10,000.
- Probate (contested matters may be transferred to District Court).
- Exclusive original jurisdiction over misdemeanors with fines greater than $500 or jail sentence.
- Juvenile matters.
- Appeals de novo from lower courts or on the record from municipal courts of record.

### Statutory County Courts
**(238 courts)**
**(established in 88 counties)**

***Jurisdiction***

- All civil, criminal, original, and appellate actions prescribed by law for constitutional county courts.
- Jurisdiction over civil matters up to $200,000 (some courts may have higher maximum jurisdiction amount).

### Statutory Probate Courts
**(18 courts)**
**(established in 10 counties)**

***Jurisdiction***

- Limited primarily to probate matters.

## Justice Courts[1]
### (817 courts – 817 judges)

**(Established in precincts within each county)**

***Jurisdiction***

- Civil actions of not more than $10,000.
- Small claims.
- Criminal misdemeanors punishable by fine only (no confinement).
- Magistrate functions.

## Municipal Courts[2]
### (926 cities – 1,288 judges)

***Jurisdiction***

- Criminal misdemeanors punishable by fine only (no confinement).
- Exclusive original jurisdiction over municipal ordinance criminal cases.[3]
- Limited civil jurisdiction.
- Magistrate functions.

Local Trial Courts of Limited Jurisdiction

1. All justice courts and most municipal courts are not courts of record. Appeals from these courts are by trial de novo in the county-level courts, and in some instances in the district courts.

2. Some municipal courts are courts of record–appeals from those courts are taken on the record to the county-level courts.

3. An offense that arises under a municipal ordinance is punishable by a fine not to exceed: (1) $2,000 for ordinances that govern fire safety, zoning, and public health or (2) $500 for all others.

to $10,000 and is concurrent with JP courts and district courts. These courts can also exercise probate jurisdiction, including cases involving guardianship, uncontested wills, and determination of mental competency. Constitutional county courts also possess appellate jurisdiction over cases from either the JP or municipal courts. Appeals from these courts are by and large de novo, which increases the workload of the state court system.

Most of the cases heard in constitutional county courts are criminal cases (65 percent), with another 19 percent of the cases dealing with probate issues. Since the workload of JP and municipal courts is, for the most part, traffic related, and county-level courts tend to be overworked, lawyers often use a strategy of appealing traffic offenses in an attempt to get these cases dismissed. Often traffic appeals are not a priority in an overworked county-level court. Constitutional county courts are required to be courts of record.

The constitution requires county judges to be "well informed of the law," which has been interpreted to mean that they do not have to have law degrees. In 2013, the Office of Court Administration reported that 65 percent of county judges had graduated from college and 14 percent had graduated from law school.[14] In addition to judicial responsibilities, the county judge exercises administrative duties over the county government. In larger counties, the county judge often works exclusively on administrative duties and acts as a judge in name only. In those counties, the legislature creates additional county-level courts, called county courts at law, for judicial duties. County judges are elected in partisan elections to four-year terms. Their salaries vary by county and are set by the county commissioners.

### County Courts at Law and Statutory Probate Courts

Statutory courts, also called county courts at law, are so called because they are created by legislative statute rather than by the constitution. In larger counties where the constitutional courts are occupied with administration of the county, the legislature establishes statutory courts to handle judicial responsibilities. There are 238 statutory county courts, concentrated in larger counties. Jurisdiction of these courts varies greatly according to the statute, but is generally consistent with part or all of the constitutional county courts. However, civil jurisdiction in county courts at law extends to controversies up to $200,000, which is concurrent with district courts. When the legislature creates a statutory court it can confer civil, criminal, or probate jurisdiction, or all of these, on that court. Like constitutional county courts, statutory courts are courts of record. Statutory judges are elected in partisan elections to four-year terms. They are required to be trained in the law, and all of these judges have law degrees.[15]

## DISTRICT COURTS (STATE-LEVEL TRIAL COURTS)

State-level trial courts in Texas are called district courts. Every county in the state is served by at least one district court, while more populated areas often have several. There are 458 total district courts in the state. According to the Texas Constitution, district court jurisdiction is exclusive, appellate, and original jurisdiction of all actions, proceedings, and remedies, except in cases where exclusive, appellate, or original jurisdiction may be conferred by this Constitution or other law on some other court, tribunal, or administrative body.[16]

Thus, the jurisdiction of district courts can vary according to the jurisdiction of other courts in a particular area. In some areas of the state, there are family district courts, criminal district courts, or civil district courts. Generally, though, district courts are granted civil jurisdiction in cases involving $200 or more[17] (concurrent with JP and county courts). District courts exercise original jurisdiction over divorces, land title claims, slander, and contested elections. Their original criminal jurisdiction includes all felony cases. They also have jurisdiction over misdemeanors when the case involves a government official. In larger metropolitan areas, these courts often specialize in just one of these areas. Appeals from district courts are heard at the courts of appeals, with the exception of death penalty cases, which go directly to the Texas Court of Criminal Appeals.

A judge in the district courts must be at least twenty-five years of age, a resident of Texas, and a U.S. citizen. In addition, the judge must be a licensed attorney with at least four years' experience as either an attorney or a judge. District judges are elected in partisan elections to four-year terms.

## APPELLATE COURTS

The Texas judiciary has two levels of appellate courts. Initial appeals are heard at the courts of appeals. After the initial appeal, cases can be appealed to one of the state's two highest courts. Texas is one of only two states with two high courts (the other is Oklahoma). The Supreme Court of Texas hears final appeals in civil cases, and the Texas Court of Criminal Appeals hears final appeals in criminal cases. Appellate judges must be at least thirty-five years of age, residents of the state, and U.S. citizens. An appellate judge is also required to have at least ten years' experience as a lawyer or a judge and be a licensed attorney. Judges are elected in partisan elections for six-year terms.

Appellate courts hear cases from lower courts based on the evidence and testimony presented at the original trial. Appellate courts hear no new evidence or new witnesses. Instead, judges make their decisions based on a review of the written record from the trial, as well as from written briefs and oral arguments by attorneys arguing legal or procedural points. Upon reviewing the written briefs and oral testimony, appellate courts can **affirm**, or uphold, the lower court's decision or **reverse** part or all of it. In addition, appellate courts can **remand** the case, or send it back to the lower court, typically with instructions from the appellate court.

All appellate courts in Texas decide cases with a majority vote. The appellate court may then issue an opinion or written explanation of the decision. A **majority opinion** represents the official decision and the reasoning behind that decision. A **concurring opinion** can be written by justices who agree with the decision but disagree with the reasoning of the majority. Justices who disagree with the decision in a case can write

**Affirm**
appellate court upholds the lower court's decision.

**Reverse**
appellate court rejects the lower court's decision.

**Remand**
appellate court sends the case back to the lower court to be reexamined.

**Majority opinion**
the official decision and reasoning of the appellate court.

**Concurring opinion**
an opinion written by a justice who agrees with the decision but not with the reasoning of the court.

a **dissenting opinion**. A **per curiam opinion** is an opinion of the court as a whole without individual judges signing the opinion.

## Courts of Appeals (Intermediate Appellate Courts)

The state is divided into fourteen districts with a court of appeal in each district. Each court of appeal has between three and thirteen judges, including one chief justice. With the exception of death penalty cases, all civil and criminal appeals from the county and district courts are initially heard in the courts of appeals. Typically an appeal is heard by a panel of three judges, although they can be heard **en banc,** meaning by the entire court. A panel of judges, rather than a single judge, is traditionally used in appeals courts since there are no juries. Including more than one judge provides some limits on the power of individual judges. The case is decided by a majority vote of the judges. The court can affirm, reverse, or modify a lower court's decision, or it can remand the case to the trial court for reconsideration. Civil cases heard by a court of appeals can be appealed to the Supreme Court of Texas, while criminal cases can be appealed to the Texas Court of Criminal Appeals.

## Texas's Highest Appellate Courts: The Court of Criminal Appeals and the Supreme Court

Texas has two high courts to hear appeals from the courts of appeals: the Supreme Court of Texas, for final civil appeals, and the Texas Court of Criminal Appeals, for final criminal appeals, including automatic appeals in death penalty cases.

### Texas Court of Criminal Appeals

The Texas Court of Criminal Appeals is the state's highest court for criminal appeals. Like other appellate courts, the Texas Court of Criminal Appeals hears no new evidence and is limited to reviewing the trial record and briefs filed by the lawyers in the case. The court consists of nine judges, including a presiding judge. The court can hear appeals in panels of three judges, though most cases are heard en banc. Cases are decided by majority vote. While the court has some discretionary authority over the cases it hears, the vast majority of its caseload is comprised of cases that receive mandatory review. In 2013, 77 percent of all the cases heard by the court were mandatory. **Writs of habeas corpus** for felony convicts make up the majority of the mandatory caseload. Appeals in death penalty cases are also mandatory for the court, and the court typically considers such cases en banc. Although arguably the most important job of

Texas Court of Criminal Appeals

The Texas Court of Criminal Appeals, headed by presiding judge Sharon Keller (front, center), is the court of last resort for criminal cases in the state.

the Texas Court of Criminal Appeals, death penalty cases comprised only 5.4 percent of appeals in 2013. That year, the court heard eleven death penalty cases, affirming all of them. This court is also the final court of appeals for questions involving state law and the state constitution. However, cases involving questions of federal law or the U.S. Constitution can ultimately be appealed to the U.S. Supreme Court.

### Supreme Court of Texas

The Supreme Court of Texas is the highest court in the state for civil cases. It consists of eight justices, plus one chief justice. If the Supreme Court chooses to review a case from the lower courts, that case is decided by majority vote. The Supreme Court also makes procedural rules for lower courts, approves law schools in the state, and appoints members of the Board of Legal Examiners. It monitors the caseload of the fourteen appellate courts and can move cases between those courts to equalize the caseload. Like the Texas Court of Criminal Appeals, the cases from the Supreme Court of Texas can be appealed to the U.S. Supreme Court if they concern issues of federal law or the U.S. Constitution.

## JUDICIAL SELECTION

One of the more controversial aspects of the Texas judicial system is the selection process for judges. With the exception of most municipal judges, judges in Texas are elected in partisan contests. In order to become a judge, candidates have to raise enough money to win the election. Once on the bench, judges need to continue raising money for reelection. Texas is one of only eight states that select judges for their highest courts with partisan elections, and it is one of only eight states that choose their appellate judges with partisan elections.[18]

The argument for the direct election of judges is rooted in democracy. The people are theoretically retaining political influence since they elect the judges. This is consistent with the political culture in Texas that tends to distrust government and wants to keep choice at the individual level. Unfortunately, there are several impediments to actual popular influence on judicial elections. Foremost, Texans are faced with a long ballot that features almost every major office in the state. In addition to choosing the country's president and the state's national congressional delegation, Texans elect members of the plural executive and other bureaucratic offices, members of the state legislature, and a wide range of judicial offices in the state. For instance, in 2010, Texas's biggest county, Harris County, had "the largest ballot in the country," which featured eighty-eight races.[19] In that election, every single race was contested, including some involving third-party candidates. One of the main reasons for the length of the ballot was the election of judges, as judicial races made up 81 percent of the Harris County ballot.[20] The democratic charge for the average Texan can be literally overwhelming, and the issues in judicial selection are often relatively subtle. The result is that most Texans simply do not pay much attention to judicial campaigns. Rather than voting based on judicial competency, voting in judicial elections often amounts to little more than voting on the basis of partisan labels, image, or name recognition.

## Raul A. Gonzalez Jr.

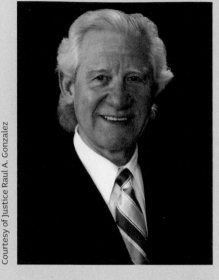

Courtesy of Justice Raul A. Gonzalez

Raul A. Gonzalez Jr. rose from picking crops alongside his parents to serving on the state's highest court. Along the way, he earned a reputation as a hard-working judge who was never afraid to speak his mind. Whether picking crops or serving on the Supreme Court of Texas, Gonzalez was determined to do whatever it took to achieve success, once stating, "I've got big hands and a big drive to succeed."[i]

Born in 1940, Gonzalez grew up in Weslaco, Texas, near the Mexican border.

After graduating from the University of Texas in 1963, he earned a law degree at the University of Houston in 1966. Gonzalez first became a judge in 1978, and over the course of his career won the support of both Republican and Democratic governors. Governor Dolph Briscoe appointed him to fill a vacancy in the 103rd District Court shortly after he first took the bench. Gonzalez was soon appointed associate justice on the Thirteenth Court of Appeals by Governor Bill Clements in 1981, becoming the first Hispanic to serve in that role. One year later he won election to a four-year term in the same position, but before it could be completed, Governor Mark White in 1984 appointed him to the Supreme Court of Texas, and Gonzalez made history by becoming the court's first Hispanic member. This also led him to become the first Hispanic elected for statewide office in Texas in 1986.

Gonzalez's focus and determination paid off in 1994 when he was challenged in the Democratic primary by Rene Haas, a well-funded challenger backed by powerful trial lawyers groups. While Gonzalez eventually won the nomination and reelection, the race was one of the most expensive judicial races in the state's history, with almost $4.5 million spent by both sides. Like many veterans of the state's highest court, Gonzales is uneasy with the expensive, partisan races that the state uses to elect judges.

Gonzalez's service on the court was more than a symbolic victory for Hispanics. As one historian of the court noted, "Not merely a Latino in surname, Gonzalez's life embodied the struggle of Mexican Americans."[ii] The court had a justice who understood the general challenges of being Hispanic in Texas. As a child he had labored in the fields with his family. As the son of parents born in Mexico, Gonzalez understood the plight of immigrants as they found their way in a new country. Gonzalez brought more than a Hispanic surname to the court, he brought a broad understanding of the needs and challenges of a population moving from the fields of south Texas to the highest posts in the state's justice system.

i. Robert B. Gilbreath and D. Todd Smith, "An Interview with Former Justice Raul A. Gonzalez," *The Appellate Advocate*, 2004, www.hptylaw.com/media/article/24_rob .pdf, 25.

ii. James L. Haley, *The Texas Supreme Court: A Narrative History, 1836–1986* (Austin: University of Texas Press, 2013), Kindle edition, 214.

**Straight-ticket voting**
the practice of selecting all the candidates for office who are running under a party label simply by checking off a single box marked with the party label.

One of the most important outcomes of requiring Texans to elect so many positions in the state is the tendency for many to vote along party lines or even utilize **straight-ticket voting**. Texas is one of fifteen states that allow straight-ticket voting in the election of state officers. The problem is that party labels are less meaningful in judicial races as compared to other political contests, and they can have substantively different meanings than party labels in other political campaigns. For instance, Republicans tend to favor businesses and defendants in civil trials, whereas Democrats are more likely to side with plaintiffs. A watch group called Court Watch estimates that between 2000 and 2010, the Republican-dominated Supreme Court of Texas ruled in favor of corporate interests or government agencies 74 percent of the time.[21] The Supreme Court has become progressively more anti-plaintiff in recent years, overturning jury decisions in 74 percent of the cases.[22] Thus, one unintended consequence of straight-ticket voting has been a significant contraction of individual rights in the state—rights most conservative Texans still vigorously seek to protect.

Texans, faced with a long ballot and limited knowledge of judicial credentials, often rely on **name recognition** when deciding who to vote for and vote on names that they recognize or even names that simply sound respectable. In judicial campaigns in particular, name recognition can produce unintended consequences since voters tend to be the least familiar with judicial races. In one study, Dallas County voters repeatedly recognized the name of only one in eight district judges.[23] This tendency has produced some particularly peculiar effects in a state where most judicial candidates are unknown to the voters. One of the most visible examples of the power of a name in judicial campaigns is Don Yarbrough. Yarbrough successfully ran for the Supreme Court of Texas in 1976, claiming God wanted him to do so. Yarbrough ran against a respected judge who was endorsed by the Texas State Bar; he also had a number of suits pending in court (including charges of business fraud) and was facing disbarment proceedings by the Texas State Bar Association. Most observers agree that Yarbrough was elected largely because voters confused him with another man, Don Yarborough, who had mounted several unsuccessful bids for governor. Others may have confused him with progressive Ralph Yarborough, who represented Texas in the U.S. Senate. Eventually, after being indicted for a felony and facing impeachment proceedings, Yarbrough resigned and fled the country.

On the other hand, democratic selection of judges has been hampered by a tendency for judicial candidates to run unopposed. This is exacerbated by the long campaign season, which creates disincentives to oppose incumbents. According to retired Supreme Court of Texas chief justice Thomas Phillips, the

> filing deadline is a year before you take office if you win, and so a lot of lawyers feel like they really don't want to be running against the judge—it's not going to be the best way to attract business for a year. So most of our rural judges, literally a majority, have never been opposed.[24]

The long ballot and the tendency for candidates to run unopposed means the perception of popular control on the judiciary remains largely a myth. Moreover, the

The 2010 Houston ballot was one of the longest in the state. A long ballot creates a high democratic cost as citizens are overwhelmed with all of the offices they have to elect.

**Name recognition**
making a voting choice based on familiarity with or previous recognition of a candidate's name

Judicial campaign signs line the side of the road. Most judges in the state of Texas are elected.

**Incumbency advantage**
the advantage enjoyed by the incumbent candidate, or current officeholder, in elections; the advantage is based on greater visibility, a proven record of public service, and often better access to resources.

**incumbency advantage** in Texas is especially robust. In fact, most incumbents run unopposed since they tend to win reelection. This tendency undermines the effectiveness of popular control on the judiciary.

## Judicial Appointment

Although judicial selection in Texas technically occurs with partisan elections, a large number of judges initially reach the bench through appointment. The constitution provides that the governor can appoint judges to fill vacancies on district and appellate courts, including Texas's highest courts. These gubernatorial appointments must be confirmed by the Texas Senate. In 2013, 38 percent of district or appellate judges originally assumed office by gubernatorial appointment. The fact that the governor ends up making judicial appointments in a system that purports to leave the choice of judges up to the voters is an important aspect of the judicial election system in Texas since a significant number of the judges chosen by the governor may run unopposed in future elections in which voters essentially rubberstamp the governor's choice. The Supreme Court of Texas illustrates the impact of interim gubernatorial appointments. Although the state's highest civil court is technically elected, six of the nine current justices originally reached it by gubernatorial appointment.

In his long tenure in office, Perry appointed more judges to the Supreme Court of Texas than any previous governor. In 2012, Perry turned heads when he appointed his former chief of staff, Jeffrey Boyd, to the state's high court. Boyd had no judicial experience prior to this appointment. In making judicial appointments, Perry consistently appointed pro-business justices. Perry's appointments were diverse (he appointed four racial minorities and two women), but three had no previous experience as a judge.[25] The governor and his supporters argued that a business-friendly environment would help the Texas economy and that he chose judges who would apply the law but not write law. Critics charge that Perry's appointments have favored big-business interests over individual rights in Texas.

## Judicial Removal

There are three primary means of removing judges in Texas. The most common means is for the voters to not reelect a judge in the next election. In addition, the constitution grants the Supreme Court of Texas the power to remove district judges for incompetence, official misconduct, or negligence. Judges can also be impeached by the Texas House and tried in the Texas Senate, with a two-thirds vote necessary in each house.

Moreover, a 1965 amendment to the state's constitution established the Commission on Judicial Conduct. The commission consists of one member from each of the following court levels (municipal, JP, county court at law, constitutional county, district, and appellate), two lawyers appointed by the state bar, and five citizens appointed by the governor who are neither attorneys nor judges. The thirteen-member commission investigates allegations of judicial misconduct. According to the Texas Constitution, judicial misconduct includes

> willful or persistent violation of rules promulgated by the Supreme Court of Texas, incompetence in performing the duties of the office, willful violation of the Code of Judicial Conduct, or willful or persistent conduct that is clearly inconsistent with the proper performance of his duties or casts public discredit upon the judiciary or administration of justice.[26]

The question of judicial fairness in Texas is not a trivial one as judges in the state have been cited for cleaning their guns or sleeping during trials. If the commission finds a judge guilty of misconduct, it can issue a public or private censure or warning, issue an official reprimand, order additional information, or make a recommendation that the judge be removed from office.

Of the 1,103 cases disposed of by the Commission on Judicial Conduct in 2013, 48 percent evidenced no judicial misconduct.[27] Some level of discipline, including public sanction, additional education, or suspension, was ordered in thirty of the cases. In five cases the judges agreed to voluntarily resign to avoid disciplinary action. Perhaps most troubling is that the vast majority of cases brought before the commission are dismissed without any public record—96 percent between 2008 and 2011.[28] The nature of the commission's work was significantly altered in 2012 when the commission refused to cooperate with a Sunset Advisory Commission audit. The Commission on Judicial Conduct claimed that its proceedings were confidential, even to state auditors. As attorney general, Greg Abbott issued an opinion upholding the idea that the commission can act with complete confidentiality.

# TEXAS JUDGES

**H**istorically, the Texas judiciary, like other elected positions, was dominated by Democrats. Since the late 1980s, however, Republicans have dominated, holding all statewide appellate posts. In addition, judges in Texas today come largely from upper-middle-class families. Recall that microcosm theory (introduced in Chapter 3) stipulates that true representation occurs only when the makeup of a society's institutions mirrors the makeup of the society as a whole. Although women account for about half of the Texas population, the vast majority of judges in the state are men. In terms of the lower courts, female judges constitute 36 percent of municipal and JP judges, 10 percent of constitutional county court judges, and 31 percent of statutory court judges. Women do not fare much better in state-level courts, composing 30 percent of district judges and 43 percent of appellate judges. In the state's highest courts, females currently comprise 22 percent of the Supreme Court of Texas and 55 percent of the Texas Court of Criminal Appeals.

The racial distribution of the courts is even more troublesome, particularly given the overwhelmingly low representation of both Hispanics and African Americans in the judicial system (see Figure 7.1). Although African Americans comprise about 12 percent of the state's population, African American judges remain relatively rare in lower-level courts in the state, ranging from less than 1/2 percent of constitutional county court judges to 5 percent of municipal judges. African American representation on state-level courts is also uneven, comprising a mere 5 percent of district judges, 1 percent of appellate judges, and 11 percent of Supreme Court of Texas judges. There are currently no African Americans on the Texas Court of Criminal Appeals. Hispanics make up approximately 38 percent of the state's population, but their representation in the Texas judiciary remains well below this figure. Hispanic representation on lower-level courts ranges from a paltry 8 percent on constitutional county courts to 19 percent on statutory county courts. Hispanics comprise 16 percent of the judges at the district level and 15 percent at the appellate level. There is currently one Hispanic on both of the state's high courts, comprising 16 percent each. For Asian and Native American groups in the state, representation in the court system is nearly nonexistent.

The issue of minority representation in Texas remains a major concern, and the manner in which judges are selected is a starting point for critics of the system. Some minorities charge that partisan elections and the dominance of the Republican Party in the state make it difficult for minorities to get elected. According to this perspective, merely removing party labels from the ballot would increase the likelihood that a minority candidate would be elected to the judiciary.

© Bob Daemmrich / Alamy

Justice Darlene Byrne, of the Family Court at Law, handles a child custody case in her courtroom Austin, Texas.

**FIGURE 7.1** **Racial Representation of Justices and Judges in Texas, 2013**

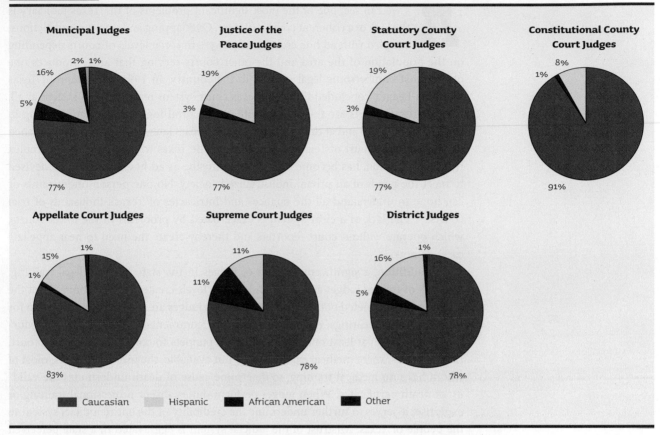

**Source:** Compiled by the authors from the *Annual Statistical Report for the Texas Judiciary*, 2013.

The nature of judicial districts may also prove to be an important impediment to minority representation in the state. Large counties in particular often treat the county as one district and then elect quite a few judges from that district as a whole. Minorities contend that using an **at-large election** system to select district and county judges makes it less likely that minorities will win. (See Chapter 12 for more information on at-large elections.)

Proponents of **cumulative voting** contend that it would benefit minority candidates. Cumulative voting allows voters to take the total number of positions in a district and divide their votes for those positions among a few candidates or even give all of those votes to a single candidate. For example, in Harris County, which has fifty-nine judges, a voter could vote for fifty-nine candidates, or vote fifty-nine times for one candidate. This system allows voters to concentrate all of their votes in a district on one or two candidates, increasing the likelihood that a minority candidate will be elected. (See Chapter 12 for a discussion of cumulative voting.)

**At-large election**
an election in which a city or county is treated as a single district and candidates are elected from the entire district as a whole.

**Cumulative voting**
a system that allows voters to take the total number of positions to be selected in a district and concentrate their votes among one or a few candidates.

# PROBLEMS WITH THE TEXAS JUDICIARY

As we can see, one of the most significant problems of the Texas judiciary is the lack of a coherent court structure. Overlapping and unclear jurisdictions, coupled with ad hoc creation of powers in some levels of courts depending on the population of the area and the other courts serving that area, produces one of the most cumbersome legal systems in the country. In 1991, the nonprofit Texas Research League concluded that the "Texas court system really is not a system at all. Indeed, Texas' courts are fragmented without a central focus and are going along in their own direction and at their own pace."[29] Two years later, a commission established by the Supreme Court of Texas concluded that "the Texas trial court system, complex from its inception, has become ever more confusing as ad hoc responses are devised to meet the needs of an urban, industrialized society. No one person understands or can hope to understand all the nuances and intricacies of Texas's thousands of trial courts."[30] The lack of a clear system is exacerbated by problems in the lower courts, which operate without court reporters and thereby create the need to hear appellate cases de novo.

In addition, a significant number of judges in the state have no legal training. The lack of trained judges at the city and county levels creates real questions about the quality of justice meted out across the state. Texas judges are infamous in the nation for sleeping during hearings, making inappropriate comments, cleaning their guns during trials, and, in at least one case, using sock puppets to communicate to the court. In rural areas where medical examiners are not available, the use of JP judges, most of whom have no medical training, to determine cause of death undermines the validity of death certificates. When judges perform duties absent professional training or expertise, it serves to further undermine the credibility of the entire judicial system to the people of Texas. Mistrust of the judicial system is aggravated in a state perceived to sell justice.

Perhaps even more detrimental is the need for judicial candidates to raise campaign funds to compete for judicial positions. This opens the Texas judiciary up to potential influence by campaign donors. Since the average Texan doesn't pay attention to judicial races, special interests, big business, and attorneys are the primary contributors to judicial contests. Inappropriate influence is likely to be greatest in Supreme Court of Texas races where campaign costs typically exceed $1 million. In 2006, Texans for Public Justice reported that a little over half (51 percent) of the contributions to the candidates for the 2006 Supreme Court of Texas race were donated by attorneys and law firms. According to its report, "Leading contributors to high-court candidates include some of the court's busiest litigators, including Vinson & Elkins ($95,000) and Fulbright & Jaworski ($50,412)."[31] Big business in Texas also actively supports judicial candidates. In the 2006 Supreme Court race, the largest donors after law firms were "Texans for Lawsuit Reform PAC ($75,000), HillCo PAC ($40,000), and the Texas Medical Association ($26,037) . . . [who] have a vested interest in the court interpreting tort, labor, and environmental laws in favor of business—even when such rulings come at the expense of consumers, workers, or communities."[32] The need to raise substantial sums of money to compete in a judicial race in the state opens judges up to undue influence, or at the very least the potential for such influence. The result is the perception, if not the reality, that the judicial system in Texas protects business at the expense of the individual.

One of the most visible recent cases of influence is that of Supreme Court justice Nathan Hecht. Hecht incurred extensive legal fees when he appealed a public reprimand from the State Commission on Judicial Conduct. In order to pay his legal debt, he received so-called late-train donations, or donations provided after the election, from several law firms and business groups. Texas Watch, a nonpartisan group, reported that seventeen parties who had each contributed at least $5,000 to Hecht subsequently brought cases before the Supreme Court of Texas. Hecht's vote on the court sided with his donors 89 percent of the time.[33]

The perception of justice for sale in Texas remains strong throughout the state and the country. National media often cover the more explicit appearances of injustice in Texas, including most notably in a segment produced by the investigative television news program *60 Minutes* in the late 1980s and again in the late 1990s. More recently, a PBS *Frontline* special report tackled the issue. Still, there has been little momentum within the state to change the selection process of judges. One successful reform is the 1995 Judicial Campaign Fairness Act. The purpose of the act is to limit contributions of individual donors to no more than $5,000 per election for statewide judicial campaigns. The primary election and general election are treated as separate elections, meaning that an individual can contribute up to $5,000 to a candidate in each election. PAC (the fund-raising arms for interest groups) contributions (including contributions from law firms) are limited to $30,000 per election for judicial candidates. Additionally, candidates are prevented from receiving more than $300,000 total from PACs. However, a candidate's participation in the limits set by the Judicial Campaign Fairness Act is voluntary. Any candidate who consents to these voluntary limits can advertise their compliance in their campaign materials and television ads.

## ALTERNATIVE SYSTEMS OF JUDICIAL SELECTION: APPOINTMENT AND MERIT

variety of alternative judicial selection processes are used throughout the country. Two of the most widely used are lifetime appointment of judges and a merit system.

### *Appointment*

At the national level, undue influence of the federal judiciary is stymied by lifetime appointment of judges. The advantage of appointing judges rather than electing them is that the judiciary can remain independent and free from political pressure. Three states use this model, allowing the governor to appoint state judges. Another two states allow the state legislature to appoint judges to appellate courts, including the states' supreme courts.

### Merit System

One alternative to electing judges in partisan elections is use of a merit system to select judges. Sometimes referred to as the Missouri Plan, the merit system is seen as a happy medium between electing and appointing judges. This system relies on a panel of experts in an attempt to balance the need for judicial independence with the accountability associated with electing judges. The panel of experts typically includes judges, lawyers, legal scholars, and sometimes ordinary citizens who are charged with reviewing potential candidates and developing a list of potential judicial nominees. The governor then nominates judicial candidates from the list. Once on the bench, the judges face periodic retention elections and are able to keep their jobs as long as a majority of voters approve. A retention election allows voters to vote to retain or remove a judge without the competition that would make campaigning, and thus fund-raising, necessary. Moreover, recent research shows that using the merit system to select a state's judicial candidates is more likely to result in minority and female judges than other methods of judicial selection.[34]

Although the United States has long embraced the necessity of an independent judiciary, and many Texans support changing the current process in the state, the businesses and professions that benefit most from the current system continue to forcefully—and effectively—oppose change. Proposals to abandon partisan elections have "passed the State Senate four times . . . it's never been allowed to have a vote in committee much less on the floor of the House of Representatives, and that's due to the power of political parties."[35] For now, there appears to be sufficient political opposition to thwart the adoption of a merit-based judicial selection system.

## CRIMINAL JUSTICE IN TEXAS

Texas political culture tends to favor politicians who are tough on crime and thus a criminal justice system that metes out swift and severe punishment. Criminal cases deal with individuals charged with violating criminal laws or committing crimes that, although there may be a victim, are technically crimes against the state. The **prosecutor** in a criminal case is the lawyer who represents the government. The **criminal defendant** is the person charged with committing a crime. In criminal cases, a twelve-member **grand jury** determines whether there is enough evidence to warrant a trial, unless the defendant waives his or her right to a grand jury. If nine of the twelve jurors on the grand jury agree that there is sufficient evidence to warrant a trial, the grand jury issues an **indictment**. An indictment is issued in the form of a true bill, which details the defendant and the alleged crime, formally charges the individual with the crime, and initiates the case. If the grand jury determines there is not enough evidence to warrant a trial, the grand jury returns no bill, there is no trial, and the accused goes free.

Criminal law ranges from traffic violations to robbery, sexual assault, or murder. The criminal justice system in Texas is based on a graded penal code in which harsher punishments are awarded for more serious crimes and for repeat offenders (see Table 7.1). Lower-level criminal violations, such as public intoxication or resisting arrest, are referred

**Prosecutor**
a lawyer who represents the government and brings a case in criminal trials.

**Criminal defendant**
a person charged with committing a crime.

**Grand jury**
a panel of twelve jurors that reviews evidence, determines whether there is sufficient evidence to bring a trial, and issues an indictment.

**Indictment**
a document (in the form of a true bill) issued by a grand jury that indicates there is enough evidence to warrant a trial.

# TEXAS (VS) MISSOURI

In 1940, Missouri took the radical step of moving from partisan elections for state judges to the Nonpartisan Retention Plan, often called the Missouri Plan. Under the Missouri Plan, an independent commission nominates three candidates to fill a vacancy on a court. The governor chooses one of the three candidates to serve on the court. After one year on the court, the judge faces a retention election in which voters decide if the judge remains on the court or must step down. After the initial election, the judge faces another retention election every four, eight, or twelve years, depending on the court. All judges must retire at the age of seventy.

Missouri uses this system for state courts of appeals and the Supreme Court of Missouri. Courts in Clay, Jackson, St. Louis, and Platte Counties, as well as courts in the city of St. Louis, use the retention election system. Many other local courts in Missouri use partisan elections for selecting judges. Twelve states have adopted the Missouri Plan, and a few others, such as Florida, use a modified version of it. Texas uses partisan elections for staffing all state and most local courts.

Proponents of the Missouri Plan claim the use of independent commissions to nominate judges shifts the focus of judicial selection to finding better-quality judges. The use of a retention election allows the public to have a periodic say on whether a judge remains in office, providing a degree of democratic accountability.

Opponents of the system point toward the fact that most judges are retained election after election, in effect creating a lifetime appointment. No Supreme Court of Missouri or appeals court judge has ever lost a retention election and been voted out of office. One study found that over a thirty-year period, only 1.3 percent of judges lost a retention election. Based on these results, critics question the point of the retention elections.

## THINKING *Critically*

★ Do you think the Missouri Plan offers advantages that the partisan system of electing judges used in Texas lacks?

★ Does the low rate of rejecting judges in Missouri undermine the Missouri Plan?

★ How do you think a plan similar to the Missouri Plan would affect the Texas court system and Texas politics?

★ Would you favor adopting such a plan?

---

to as misdemeanors. The severity of misdemeanors is distinguished in Texas law by three classes, with class C misdemeanors being the least severe and class A misdemeanors representing the most serious. Misdemeanors are typically nonviolent crimes and involve fines or prison sentences of less than a year. Felonies are more severe criminal offenses, such as sexual assault or murder, and involve harsher punishments. The capital felony is the most serious and comes with a possible death sentence. First degree, second degree, third degree, and state jail felonies comprise the lesser felonies, distinguished by the seriousness of the crime. The Texas penal code also provides for **enhanced penalties** in which repeat offenders can be charged with the next higher degree or class on their second offense. So, for example, a person arrested for driving while intoxicated (DWI) would be charged with a class B misdemeanor, whereas a person arrested for a second DWI could be charged with a class A misdemeanor.

According to Texas law, the defendant has a right to a jury trial, although that right can be waived in all criminal cases except death penalty cases. The trial jury, or **petit jury**, determines whether or not an individual is guilty. Petit juries are guaranteed in criminal cases and may also be used in civil cases if requested by either party. In the criminal case, the defendant enters a plea of either guilty, not guilty, or nolo contendere

**Enhanced penalties**
penal code provision that allows repeat offenders to be charged with a higher-degree offense on subsequent convictions.

**Petit jury**
a trial jury; jurors attend a trial, listen to evidence, and determine whether a defendant is innocent or guilty.

## TABLE 7.1  Texas Penal Code: Offenses with Graded Penalties

| Offense Level | Examples | Maximum Punishment | Court with Original Jurisdiction |
|---|---|---|---|
| Capital felony | Capital murder; murder of a child | State execution or life in prison without parole | District court; automatic appeal to Texas Court of Criminal Appeals |
| First degree felony | Murder (except under the influence of sudden passion); aggravated sexual assault; theft of $200,000 or more | Life in prison and $10,000 fine | District court |
| Second degree felony | Manslaughter; aggravated kidnapping; theft of more than $100,000 but less than $200,000 | Imprisonment for 2 to 20 years and $10,000 fine | District court |
| Third degree felony | Kidnapping; child abandonment; terrorist threat; theft of more than $20,000 but less than $100,000 | Imprisonment for 2 to 10 years and $10,000 fine | District court |
| State jail felony (fourth degree felony) | Criminally negligent homicide; dog fighting; theft of more than $1,500 but less than $20,000 | Imprisonment for 180 days to 2 years and $10,000 fine | District court |
| Class A misdemeanor | Online impersonation; possession of marijuana (more than 2 oz. but less than 4 oz.); attending a dog fight; theft of more than $500 but less than $1,500 | Confinement in jail for 1 year and $4,000 fine | Constitutional county court/ county court at law |
| Class B misdemeanor | Driving while intoxicated; indecent exposure; possession of marijuana (2 oz. or less); theft of more than $50 but less than $500 | Confinement in jail for 180 days and $2,000 fine | Constitutional county court/ county court at law |
| Class C misdemeanor | Public intoxication; possession of alcohol in automobile; theft of less than $20 | $500 fine | Justice of the peace court/ municipal court |

**Source:** Data from Office of the Attorney General, "Penal Code Offenses by Punishment Range: Including Updates from the 83rd Legislative Session," April 2014, www.oag.state.tx.us/AG_Publications/pdfs/penalcode.pdf (accessed July, 7, 2014).

(literally, no contest). The prosecutor will present the state's case by entering evidence and witnesses into the official record. The defendant can challenge the evidence and testimony. The accused is presumed innocent, and the state must prove that the individual is guilty. In order to determine guilt, the burden of proof in a criminal trial is based on whether the state has submitted sufficient evidence to prove the guilt of the accused

**beyond a reasonable doubt**. Texas requires a unanimous verdict in criminal cases. If an individual is found guilty in a criminal case, the punishment can include fines paid to the government, imprisonment, or, in certain cases, the death penalty. If found guilty, convicted criminals can appeal the conviction to the appellate courts, with the exception of death penalty cases, which are automatically reviewed by the Texas Court of Criminal Appeals.

Civil cases, by contrast, involve disputes between individuals. The **plaintiff** in a civil case claims to have been wronged by another party, the **civil defendant**. Civil law cases often involve breach of contract and other contractual disputes, but they also include family law issues, such as divorce, neglect, custody, or probate questions. Civil cases also include tort cases claiming personal injury or property damage. Civil cases can be tried by a jury or, if both parties agree, can simply be decided by the judge. The burden of proof for civil cases is based on a much lower standard than for criminal cases. To win a civil case, a plaintiff merely has to show through a **preponderance of evidence** that the defendant is likely to be guilty. Whereas criminal cases may result in jail time, plaintiffs in civil cases may ask the court to redress the grievance or award monetary damages. **Compensatory damages** are monetary awards designed to compensate the injured party for items such as medical bills incurred or lost income due to missed work. If the court wants to send a message, it may also award **punitive damages**, which are typically larger monetary awards intended to punish the defendant. Like in criminal cases, decisions in civil cases can be appealed to the appellate courts.

## WINNERS AND LOSERS

The Texas judiciary is fraught with impediments to justice for the average Texan. The system is overly complex and unnecessarily confusing, making it difficult for most Texans to understand. In addition, the large number of judges elected in the state creates an excessive cost to the average voter. As a result, it is not surprising that democratic mechanisms to protect individuals in the state provide very little protection in practice. Ironically, Texans resist change in the judiciary largely because they distrust government and want to guard their individual rights, such as the right to choose judges. But more often than not, that right buckles under the weight of the system's complexity and the regular onslaught of judicial campaigning. Texans are simply overwhelmed by the number of public officials they must elect. Texans—fiercely protective of their independence and their influence on government—in the end relinquish their authority over judicial selection to big donors in judicial campaigns. And it is those big donors, mostly business and law firms, that reap the benefits and continue to dominate the Texas judiciary. Because these groups remain ever attentive to their own interests, individual Texans lose. While Texas juries often rule in favor of those who have suffered individual harm or face losing their property at the hands of business interests in the state, judges often do not. The state's almost wholly appointed Supreme Court consistently overturns jury verdicts in favor of big businesses at the expense of individual rights.

Minorities also lose. Minorities hold few judicial posts in a state that is tough on crime, has one of the largest prison populations in the country, and is rarely

**Beyond a reasonable doubt**
the standard burden of proof necessary to find a defendant guilty in a criminal trial; the defendant is presumed innocent.

**Plaintiff**
the party claiming to have been wronged that is bringing a civil suit.

**Civil defendant**
the party alleged to have committed the wrong at issue in a civil suit.

**Preponderance of evidence**
the burden of proof in a civil case, which is lower than that in a criminal case; the plaintiff must show merely that the defendant is likely to have committed the wrong.

**Compensatory damages**
monetary damages designed to compensate the injured party.

**Punitive damages**
larger monetary awards designed to punish the defendant and, perhaps, send a message to the larger society.

sympathetic to appeals. The judicial system in Texas remains dominated by middle- and upper-middle-class white males, even though the state's demographic makeup continues to diversify. The current system of electing judges, particularly in partisan elections, ensures that minorities will continue to be underrepresented in Texas. The perception that the Texas judicial system is unjust endures for good reason: the prevailing system harms all Texans.

★ Does the high number of judicial seats that citizens are asked to vote for have a chilling effect on an informed electorate?

★ How is the partisan election of Texas's judges a potential disadvantage for the state's judiciary and citizens?

★ Given the expense of judicial elections and lack of diversity in judges' backgrounds, should reforms of the state judicial system be considered? What changes would you propose?

## CONCLUSION

Justice in Texas is a complicated affair. The judicial system is complex and confusing, and jurisdiction is often unclear. The lack of lower-level courts of record often requires cases that are appealed to be tried as if new. While Texans proclaim a strong desire for justice, in fact the current judicial system rarely satisfies. In order to develop a more responsive judicial system, Texans may need to reevaluate how their preferences are represented in the current system. For instance, the preference of voters to retain control of judicial selection via the long ballot entails a high cost. The overwhelming job of selecting nearly all of the judges in the state comes with very little payoff. More generally, Texans' resistance to change means that the state's judiciary, like other of its institutions, evolves in a piecemeal manner. The result is a system that in many ways no longer makes sense for the state.

for CQ Press

Sharpen your skills with **SAGE edge** at **edge.sagepub.com/collier4e**. **SAGE edge for students** provides a personalized approach to help you accomplish your coursework goals in an easy-to-use learning environment.

## KEY TERMS

affirm (p. 227)

appellate jurisdiction (p. 219)

at-large election (p. 235)

beyond a reasonable doubt (p. 241)

civil case (p. 219)

civil defendant (p. 241)

compensatory damages (p. 241)

concurrent jurisdiction (p. 221)

concurring opinion (p. 227)

criminal case (p. 219)

criminal defendant (p. 238)

cumulative voting (p. 235)

de novo (p. 221)

dissenting opinion (p. 228)

en banc (p. 228)

enhanced penalties (p. 239)

exclusive jurisdiction (p. 219)

grand jury (p. 238)

incumbency advantage (p. 232)

indictment (p. 238)

judicial federalism (p. 218)

jurisdiction (p. 219)

magistrate functions (p. 221)

majority opinion (p. 227)

name recognition (p. 231)

original jurisdiction (p. 219)

per curiam opinion (p. 228)

petit jury (p. 239)

plaintiff (p. 241)

preponderance of evidence (p. 241)

prosecutor (p. 238)

punitive damages (p. 241)

remand (p. 227)

reverse (p. 227)

straight-ticket voting (p. 230)

writ of habeas corpus (p. 228)

## CORE ASSESSMENT

1. If Texans continue to prefer judicial elections, does that imply an individual responsibility to participate in those elections?

2. How might Texas get more minorities in judicial posts? To what extent does minority representation in the state judiciary matter?

3. How does electing judges with limited qualifications affect justice in Texas?

# 8 TEXAS-SIZED JUSTICE

Texans hold pretty strong opinions about justice. If you break the law in this state, Texans want to see you punished. They have little patience for the rights of criminal defendants or the discomfort associated with incarceration. Most Texans feel that if you were found guilty of a crime, your sentence is your just punishment and it ought to be downright uncomfortable. So talking about prison conditions in Texas is a tricky business; in fact, state politicians prefer not to. Many across Texas want the conditions to be disagreeable. It is difficult, then, to find conditions bad enough that Texas politicians have the political will to address them. Recently, the heat in Texas prisons has been capturing national attention. After a particularly hot summer, nine prisoners died in Texas prisons in 2011 alone. At least fourteen prisoners have died from the heat since 2007.

One of those prisoners was Larry McCollum. Larry was an affable guy who wrote a bad check. He was convicted of forgery and sentenced to eleven months in prison. After serving one month of his sentence, he was transferred to the Hutchins unit in Dallas. Since Larry was new to this facility, he did not yet have his prison identification, which meant he couldn't buy a fan from the prison commissary. It also meant that when prison officials were passing out water to help prisoners cope with the extreme heat, he hadn't yet bought a cup. Three days after arriving, Larry had a seizure and went into a coma. By the time he got to the hospital, his temperature read 109.4 degrees. Larry died a few days later, and his autopsy indicated that his death was from "living in a hot environment without air conditioning." Two weeks after Larry died, Alexander Togonidze, forty-four, and Michael David Martone, fifty-seven, died at two different units in Texas. The following week, Kenneth James, fifty-two, died. All were heat-related deaths.

Only twenty-one of Texas' 111 prisons are fully air conditioned. The remaining units may have air conditioning in some common rooms, but generally not in the

AP Photo/Mayra Beltran, Houston Chronicle

The Texas prison system is facing legal actions and criticisms after several inmates died because of the hot temperatures in prisons. The attitude of some Texans, however, is that criminals do not deserve "comforts" such as air conditioning.

prisoners' living quarters. While many Texans also don't have air conditioning, the difference is when prisoners are in their cells, they have no way to escape the extreme heat. Prison cells often have no ventilation and therefore act like ovens in very high temperatures. Prison records indicate that these prisons can reach up to 150 degrees with the heat index. While the state requires its county jails to be kept below 85 degrees, the state's prisons have no such requirement. Larry's daughter, along with other prisoners and relatives, is suing the state with support from the Texas Correctional Officer's union. They assert that such prison conditions amount to cruel and unusual punishment. As the lawsuit works its way through the court system, it brings to the fore for most Texans an uncomfortable truth: Texas prison conditions may go beyond reasonable punishment. And Texans may have to pay to improve conditions across the state.

In this chapter, in order to explore the nature of justice in Texas, we will start by discussing the political culture in the state regarding justice and how that culture translates into policies. Next we will explore some of those policy results from the lens of justice. Specifically, we examine incarceration in Texas, privatization of prisons, and rights of the accused. We will then explore the effect of tort reform on issues of justice and conclude the chapter with a discussion of the death penalty.

## JUSTICE IN TEXAS

Texas has a reputation of being tough on crime, and most Texans prefer it that way. Even before Texas was independent, keeping the peace along the frontier was fraught with danger. Comanches, Wichitas, Caddos, and other native tribes faced loss of land and bison as Anglo settlements increased rapidly. The frontier with Mexico was marked by continuous fights over Texas, particularly along the Texas-Mexico border. Life on the frontier was hard, and settlers suffered their share of horse and cattle theft and stagecoach robberies. Settlements in Texas lacked much in the way of formal law enforcement. Instead, Texans learned early on to fend for themselves, a way of life referred to as frontier justice. It is not surprising, then, that the political culture that developed in Texas is one that is tough on crime and romanticizes vigilante justice. The belief that people should be able to take care of problems on their own persists in modern-day Texas. Public opinion and juries in the state tend to be sympathetic to people who take the law into their own hands to protect their families and belongings and shoot trespassers on their property. Texans still by and large retain a distrust of government and a belief that sometimes for justice to prevail, individuals have to act. As a lobbyist for the Texas District and County Attorneys Association recently put it, "There's an unwritten rule in Texas courthouses: It ain't against the law to kill a son of a bitch."[1] The resulting political culture has clear implications on the policies of the state, including widespread support for permissive gun laws, the castle doctrine, and the death penalty. Texans also enact tough and unyielding laws, criminalizing more behaviors than other states. A tendency persists to assume the accused are likely guilty, and Texans tend to be weary of complaints about prison conditions or a prisoner's access to health care. The result is that Texas today has one of the largest incarceration rates in the country and the world.

# INCARCERATION IN TEXAS

**E**verything is bigger in Texas, including the prison system. Several things contribute to the Texas-sized prison system. First, U.S. culture supports high **incarceration rates**. According to the International Center for Prison Studies, the United States currently holds more prisoners than any other country in the world.[2] America imprisons more of its citizens than any other country in absolute terms and (tied with Seychelles for first) when population is controlled for. The United States contains around 4 percent of the world's population, yet holds 25 percent of the world's prisoners.[3] Currently, Texas has the fifth-highest per capita incarceration rate in the country, with 154,000 persons in prison. As of 2012, the Texas prison incarceration rate was 601 inmates per 100,000 residents.[4] If Texas were a country, it would rank fourth in incarceration rates, above Iran, China, and Russia.[5] Texas further has 400,000 people on probation in the state and another 100,000 on parole. As mentioned above, the Texas political culture continues to demand politicians and policies that are tough on crime. The result is Texas policies that tend to criminalize more types of behavior and favor tougher sentences than policies of other states. In addition, in the last two decades, the state's population has increased, and stiffer immigration and drug laws have combined with this growth to produce a glut of potential prisoners.

> **Incarceration rate**
> a calculation of how many prisoners a state has per 100,000 people, which controls for population size.

One of the most significant changes to the Texas prison system was the national movement to adopt stiffer drug laws in the 1970s and 1980s. At the national level, President Richard Nixon declared a war on drugs, created the national Drug Enforcement Agency, and called for a national policy to address drugs in the United States. States followed suit, most notably New York, which under Governor Nelson Rockefeller adopted automatic stiff penalties for possession of small amounts of drugs. Texas's preference to be tough on crime meant that the state was eager to follow suit. The Texas Legislature adopted stiffer antidrug laws, harsher penalties for possession, and stricter guidelines for probation and parole.[6] The war on drugs directly led to a proliferation of people incarcerated in the state.

As several states have recently legalized marijuana possession, decriminalization or even legalization of marijuana is increasingly being viewed as an option in Texas. Currently, possession of even a small amount of marijuana in the state is illegal. The costs to the Texas taxpayer are significant. Texans spend an estimated $378,820 a day for arrests and incarceration due to drug possession.[7] Moreover, Texans are increasingly in favor of some form of decriminalization. In a 2014 *Texas Tribune* poll, 28 percent of Texans favored legalization for medicinal purposes, 32 percent favored legalization for small amounts, and another 17 percent supported legalization of any amount of marijuana.[8] Only 23 percent opposed legalization under any circumstance, which suggests that Texans, like the rest of the country, may be on the road to legalization. Even staunch conservative Rick Perry suggested the state should move toward decriminalization. The costs associated with criminalizing marijuana possession are significant as the state continues to grapple with deep budget cuts across the board.

## The Texas Rangers

*©Bettmann/Corbis*

The iconic Texas Rangers vividly illustrate the power of a state's legends both inside and beyond its own borders. The Texas Rangers have become a defining symbol of law enforcement, originally galloping through serials such as *The Lone Ranger*. They were featured in early radio and television programs and in the movies, where they were played by western stars such as Roy Rogers, Gene Autry, and Tex Ritter. Long after the early western stars rode off into the sunset, the Texas Rangers have continued to capture the imagination of viewers across the country on shows such as *Walker, Texas Ranger* and in movies such as *Man of the House*, starring Chuck Norris and Tommy Lee Jones.

The Rangers can trace their origins back to Stephen F. Austin, who first referred to the citizens asked to protect his settlements as "rangers" because they had to range over the countryside. The Rangers became an official extension of the temporary government of Texas in 1835 when they were called upon to protect the frontier during the Texas Revolution.

While they have been generally revered, the Rangers' image has suffered from time to time. When Sam Houston wanted to move the state's capital out of

Austin, the two Rangers who went to Austin to retrieve the archives met resistance from the local citizens and returned with their horses' manes and tails shaved. In 1918, Governor William P. Hobby allegedly used the Rangers to suppress voter turnout for James Ferguson in South Texas during that year's Democratic primary. During the 1932 election, the Texas Rangers made the mistake of backing Governor Ross Sterling. When Miriam "Ma" Ferguson won office, she retaliated by firing the entire force of forty-eight Rangers and replacing them with 2,300 "special" Rangers, many of whom were criminals. The legislature responded by authorizing the hiring of just thirty-two Rangers, leaving Texas virtually unprotected as Bonnie Parker and Clyde Barrow (the infamous Bonnie and Clyde) roamed the state robbing banks. The Rangers' image was further tainted when they were accused of being instruments of discrimination and intimidation used against Tejanos. Captain Leander McNelly, whose tactics included piling the bodies of dead Mexican rustlers in the Brownsville town square, made the Rangers particularly unpopular among Tejanos in the 1870s.

The Rangers' image today combines independence with law and order—qualities

on which all Texans can agree. While the details of the story vary, a common tale depicting the Rangers' uncanny abilities involves citizens of a town who called for a company of Rangers to stop a prize fight. When the local people arrived at the train station to greet the twenty Rangers they had anticipated would be needed to quell the expected riot, they were disappointed to see just one Ranger get off the train: legendary Ranger captain Bill McDonald. When the citizens' disappointment over the arrival of only a single Ranger became evident, McDonald responded by saying, "Hell! Ain't I enough? There's only one prize-fight!"[i] Since that time, "One riot, one Ranger" has been a common slogan associated with the Rangers.

Today, the Texas Rangers are a highly professional and modern law enforcement organization that has been part of the Department of Public Safety since 1935. Perhaps less colorful than many of their predecessors—and their television and cinema image—today's Rangers are trained to meet the demands of a high-tech state. The Rangers include 144 commissioned officers, twenty-four non-commissioned administrative support personnel, a forensic artist, and a fiscal analyst. Rangers assist local law enforcement with criminal investigations, help with the suppression of major disturbances, and conduct special investigations. While twenty-first-century Texas Rangers may look little like their predecessors, they still abide by the creed set down by Captain McDonald: "No man in the wrong can stand up against a fellow that's in the right and keeps on a-comin."[ii]

---

i. Texas Department of Public Safety, "Silver Stars and Six Guns," www.txdps.state.tx.us/TexasRangers/silverstars.htm (accessed September 1, 2014).

ii. Ibid.

## Shift to Rehabilitation

At the start of the 2007 legislative session, Texas was faced with the need for over 17,000 new prison beds, which would cost $1.6 billion by 2012. State representative Jerry Madden (R–Richardson) and state senator John Whitmire (D–Austin) proposed a shift in the Texas approach. Their proposal moved away from Texas's traditional approach of punishment and toward **rehabilitation**, advocating the allocation of resources to alternative types of treatment and correction. In that year, the legislature allocated money for 8,000 treatment beds, which gave judges the option of putting certain types of offenders in much-needed drug, alcohol, and mental health treatment facilities rather than in prison.[9] A majority of those in Texas prisons are nonviolent offenders, and the new approach opened up halfway houses and created specialty courts, such as drug courts and veterans courts, which replaced a long prison stay with mandatory treatment. The new approach also gives the courts leeway in dealing with technical probation violations, which traditionally come with mandatory imprisonment. An individual put on probation, either after serving time or in lieu of serving time, can have that probation revoked if he or she is charged with a new offense or for a technical violation. A technical violation could include missing a meeting with the assigned parole officer, failing to pay a parole fee, or failing a drug test. The underlying idea of the change in approach is that expensive prison stays should be reserved for violent criminals rather than those with substance abuse problems. Rather than focusing on punishment, the shift toward rehabilitation is designed to reduce **recidivism**, or a return to crime after release from prison. The Texas mantra of being tough on crime is being replaced with the idea of being smart on crime.

The shift from punishment-focused criminal justice to a focus on rehabilitation came at a time when Texas was facing budget shortfalls and an ever-expanding prison population. The traditional approach of building more prisons, while popular, has been costly to the state over the years. The proposal of Madden and Whitmire cost the state a $241 million investment in alternative treatment courts and facilities rather than $1.6 billion in new prisons.[10] This policy position, untenable just a decade ago, is now seen as fiscally responsible. As Madden put it, "One thing we have in prison: they get free room, free board and free healthcare, at the public's expense. And if we put them out there as a person who has a job and working and living with their family, they may end up paying taxes."[11]

The change in approach has already saved Texans millions of dollars at a time when the legislature is looking for places to cut money. It costs Texas roughly $18,000 a year to imprison someone, not including medical expenses. While housing a felon costs about $47 a day, probation costs only $1.24 a day, supervised probation costs $3.74 a day, and treatment facilities range from $5.56 to $47 a day.[12] The trend in Texas is consistent with national statistics, which show that twenty-six states saw their prison populations decline in 2009.[13] Texas has made other changes to decrease its spending on criminal justice during the severe budget shortfalls in recent years. In 2011, Texas prisons stopped serving lunch on the weekends, estimating that serving two meals a day instead of three would help save the state $2.8 million. That same year, Texas ended the tradition of granting last meal requests to individuals about to be executed. The state legislature also voted to close a state prison for the first time in the state's history.

**Rehabilitation**
an approach to criminal justice that focuses on therapy or education in order to reform criminal behavior.

**Recidivism**
a former inmate's resumption of criminal activity after his or her release from prison.

# TEXAS AND THE FED ON *Marijuana*

Texans favor a justice system that's tough on crime, and social conservatives have long warned against the potential dangers of marijuana use. Yet one of the current significant trends across the country is a move away from the criminalization of marijuana. About one-third of states have decriminalized marijuana, meaning possession is now treated as a minor offense involving a small fine. Another four states, Colorado, Alaska, Oregon, and Washington, along with the District of Columbia, have legalized marijuana. When these states first chose to legalize marijuana, it created an interesting paradox since possession of the substance was still against federal law. Since then, however, the federal government has said it will only prosecute possession in those states if it is tied to other criminal activity or involves minors in possession. More recently, President Obama referred to marijuana policy as a state's rights issue.

The choice to incarcerate people for possession and use of marijuana entails significant costs to Texas. It cost Texans an estimated $378,820 a day to incarcerate people for simple drug possession.[i] While Texas law no longer deems it a felony to possess even a small amount of marijuana, state law can still seem draconian. Jacob Lavoro made national headlines in 2014 when he was arrested for making a batch of pot brownies. Although Lavoro used 2.5 grams of THC in his brownies, the Texas teen was originally charged for the entire weight of the brownies—one and a half pounds—which carried with it a maximum punishment of life in prison.

The most significant change in Texas law to date came in 2006 when the state's legislature passed a law allowing local police to issue a citation and court date for possession without mandatory arrest. While cities such as Austin have decreased initial arrests, Dallas has continued to employ mandatory arrest for possession. In the 83rd legislative session, the state's legislature considered, but did not pass, changing marijuana possession to a class C misdemeanor. This change would have meant that Texans found guilty of possession would face a fine but not imprisonment. Although more Texans are embracing the notion of decriminalization, social conservatives still vehemently oppose any move toward legalization. Former governor Perry had suggested he would support decriminalization, but Governor Abbott has clearly stated that he favors existing drug laws and prefers focusing on compliance. Both Perry and Abbott, however, agree that marijuana laws are issues for states to decide.

★ To what extent should local governments have authority over marijuana laws?

★ Given the costs of incarceration, is the state of Texas fiscally irresponsible in continuing to criminalize marijuana use? Explain your answer.

★ How likely do you think it is that marijuana will be decriminalized or legalized in Texas in the next decade?

★ How does the federal government's authority over security clash with state governments' power over marijuana laws?

i. "High Time for Texas to Decriminalize Marijuana," *Daily Texan*, January 30, 2014, www.dailytexanonline.com/opinion/2014/01/30/high-time-for-texas-to-decriminalize-marijuana (accessed August 20, 2014).

Unfortunately, even with the move to emphasize rehabilitation, the Legislative Budget Board estimates that the Texas prison population will only continue to decline until 2014, then it will once again begin to rise.

## Prison Conditions

The political culture in Texas tends to be largely unsympathetic to the conditions inside the state's prisons. Texas has long had the reputation as having one of the toughest prison systems in the country. A 1972 case filed on behalf of Texas prisoners represented a second change that enlarged the prison system. In *Ruiz v. Estelle*, Texas prisoner David Ruiz filed a handwritten suit against the director of the Department of

Corrections, William Estelle, claiming that conditions in the Texas prison constituted cruel and unusual punishment. Ruiz alleged harsh conditions that included lack of adequate medical care, overcrowded conditions, and insufficient security. At that time, Texas prisons were undermanned and prison staff often relied on prisoners to keep other prisoners in line. Judge William Wayne Justice eventually ruled that conditions in Texas prisons were unconstitutional and ordered federal oversight of Texas prisons for the next two decades. The *Ruiz* decision ushered in the most broad sweeping prison reforms to date. One of the state's responses to this federal intervention was to spend the 1980s building prisons. At the time *Ruiz* was filed, Texas had eighteen prisons. Today there are 111 prisons in the state. The prison population ballooned, however, and Texas could not build prisons fast enough.

For decades, prisoners in the state have complained about lack of timely medical care. As the state faced a budget crisis in recent years, the 82nd Texas Legislature cut spending on prisoner health care by $75 million. At the same time, health care costs have been rising, both in general and for Texas prisons, particularly as the prison population is graying. Elderly prisoners, who make up 8 percent of the prison population, take 30 percent of the health care budget. This has led some in Texas to advocate releasing them. The chair of the Texas Senate Committee on Criminal Justice, John Whitmire, argued that "in times of fiscal concern, we're spending $1 million or more on inmates who can't get out of bed or are really sick individuals. It's just nuts."[14] Nonetheless, the Texas Board of Pardons and Paroles has so far been reluctant to consider this option for most aging prisoners.

Another long-term complaint has been the lack of air conditioning in most Texas prisons. Of Texas's 111 state prisons, only twenty-one of them are completely air conditioned. Most prisons in Texas do not have air conditioning in the cells. That means that prisoners are held in their cells, even when the temperature reaches triple digits, without windows and without any means of escaping the heat. Prison officials' records indicate that the heat index in prisons can top 150 degrees in the summer, which is dangerous for both the prisoners and the prison staff. After four inmates died of heat-related illnesses in 2011, a 2012 lawsuit was filed in federal courts arguing that the conditions are inhumane. A study by the University of Texas Law School's Human Rights Clinic agreed, arguing that these conditions, which have led to at least fourteen deaths since 2007, constitute cruel and unusual punishment.[15] In 2014, the

As the state with the most populous prison population, Texas grapples with the problem of overcrowding and has sought to address the issue through various means, including prison privatization. Texas has more private prisons than any other state.

state installed coolers in seven of its prisons, though state officials continue to reject the assertion that heat in the prisons poses a threat to inmates.

Texas prisons have also received national attention for having some of the highest instances of prison rape in the country. Although compiling good data on prison rape is notoriously difficult, as inmates are often threatened if they report rape, Texas had five of the ten prisons with the highest instances of prison rape, according to a U.S. Bureau of Justice survey.[16] The Texas Department of Criminal Justice points out that official rape complaints for the same year were actually much lower than the Bureau of Justice estimated. While issues such as food, medical care, air conditioning, and rape all raise concerns about cruel and inhumane treatment within Texas prisons, Texans and Texas lawmakers generally remain unsympathetic. For Texans, justice is black and white, and people who break the law get what they deserve. Most Texans also know hardship and believe that prisoners should have an uncomfortable life. The prevailing attitude in the state is that a prisoner's three square meals and access to television and a college education does not amount to punishment.

## Privatization of Prisons

One way Texas has tried to deal with its increasing prison population is by embracing the **private prison** option. In the 1990s, Texas firmly got on board the privatization movement, and it currently leads the country in utilizing privately run prisons, housing about 18,000 of its 154,000 prison beds in private facilities.[17] In addition, private prisons based in Texas often have contracts with other states, meaning violent criminals from those states are transferred to Texas. Defenders of privately owned prisons argue the costs for the state are significantly lower than state- or locally run facilities. They often point to jobs created by private prisons, which are built in rural areas of the state. Opponents point to the poor conditions, underpaid and poorly trained guards, and high-profile scandals involving the largest private prison corporations. Because these prisons are motivated by profit, providing adequate facilities and services to the prisoners often takes a back seat to the bottom line. Moreover, research suggests that the few jobs created by a private prison facility are outweighed by negative job growth, as private prisons have actually impeded economic growth overall.[18] In addition, critics contend that inmates moved to private facilities from other states and faced with the poor conditions at the private prisons are often more likely to be clinically depressed and are less likely to have access to family or other visitors, making rehabilitation more difficult and recidivism more likely. The state's choice to allow construction and use of private prisons means that Texas is increasingly choosing to take on other states' and the national government's prisoners.

Several high-profile scandals have drawn attention to these private facilities. For example, the GEO Group, Inc., prison company was fired in 2007 by the Texas Youth Commission (TYC) for squalid conditions after one prisoner (transferred from Idaho) committed suicide.[19] Shortly after the suicide, Idaho corrections officials visited the facility and concluded it was the worst correctional facility and that it was incapable

**Private prison**
a private, for-profit prison corporation that staffs and runs prison facilities in a state.

## Chicken Ranch

Some Texas legends are more interesting than others. A few have been told and retold again and again. However, only one has made it to Broadway and the big screen as a musical.

The Chicken Ranch in La Grange was one of the state's worst-kept secrets for decades. Operating in Fayette County, about halfway between Austin and Houston, the Chicken Ranch was said to be the oldest continuously running brothel in the nation, with roots going back to 1844 when Texas was a republic.[i] The "Chicken Ranch" label was earned during the Great Depression, when cash was in short supply and a little creative marketing led to a "one chicken for one screw" policy. The chickens provided food for the staff, and the madam brought in a little extra cash by selling surplus chickens and eggs. With the chickens wandering around the house, the place became known as the Chicken Ranch, and the name endured long after the "poultry standard" ended.

The occupants of the Chicken Ranch maintained good relations with the people of La Grange by paying their taxes, shopping with local merchants, giving generously to local charities, and working closely with local law enforcement to make sure that their clientele caused no trouble to the town. The ranch allegedly did a big business, drawing young men from nearby military bases and from Texas A&M. It was said that some fans even celebrated their team's victory at the Chicken Ranch after the Texas versus Texas A&M game on Thanksgiving Day.

In the summer of 1973, television reporter Marvin Zindler discovered the story of the Chicken Ranch and took to the airwaves of Houston to warn citizens. Zindler surprised Governor Dolph Briscoe on camera during an interview with the news that there was a house of prostitution operating in La Grange. Zindler offered up the testimony from his young camera man, who assured the governor that he had visited the Chicken Ranch the previous evening and that his personal experience confirmed that there was a brothel operating there. When Zindler asked the governor what he was going to do, Briscoe replied, "Marvin, we are going to close it up."[ii]

After the interview, Briscoe realized that while he had just promised to close a brothel, the governor of Texas had no authority to do so because this was a local matter in which state police lacked authority. Initially, Briscoe and Attorney General John Hill discussed the possibility of stationing state police nearby to record the license plates of clients so they could be shared with Austin newspapers. However, Briscoe worried that legislators would be drawn into the scandal, since, as Larry L. King wrote, "many of [them] could have driven to the Chicken Farm without headlights even in a midnight rainstorm."[iii]

The state asked local sheriff Jim Flournoy to shut down the ranch. Sheriff Flournoy declined because his office and the rest of the community had a friendly relationship with the ranch that went back decades. In fact, the sheriff claimed that he had a stack of petitions from local residents demanding that the Chicken Ranch remain open. Eventually, Briscoe provided the local sheriff with the political cover he needed by issuing an order that the ranch be closed, and on August 2, 1973, the sheriff closed the ranch and ended the run of the Chicken Ranch.

Unfortunately for Briscoe and others who wanted to put the fiasco behind them, Larry L. King wrote an article about the Chicken Ranch for *Playboy* magazine that eventually brought the ranch back to life on Broadway in 1978 in a musical titled *The Best Little Whorehouse in Texas*. The show was wildly popular, and even Briscoe snuck in to catch a performance in London where he thought he could enjoy the show without being recognized—but he was identified during intermission by other Texans catching the show. The Chicken Ranch's legend grew again after Hollywood took up the case, casting Burt Reynolds as the sheriff and Dolly Parton as the madam in a movie based on the musical.

i. Walter F. Pilcher, "Chicken Ranch," Handbook of Texas Online, www.tshaonline.org/handbook/online/articles/ysc01 (accessed September 2, 2014). Published by the Texas State Historical Association.

ii. Dolph Briscoe, as quoted in Don Carleton, *Dolph Briscoe: My Life in Texas Ranching and Politics* (Austin, Tex.: Center for American History, 2008), 220.

iii. Larry L. King, "The Best Little Whorehouse in Texas," *Playboy*, April 1974, www.newlinetheatre.com/playboy.html (accessed September 2, 2014).

of being repaired or corrected. In spite of chronic questions regarding the conditions in these private jails, a *Dallas Morning News* study found "only a few instances of TYC not renewing contracts because of poor performance" and no cases where the TYC had fined for-profit contractors for problems, though it has the authority to assess such fines.[20]

The business model of private prisons is based on continued increases in the prison population, and not surprisingly these entities have actively lobbied for longer sentences and tougher laws. Critics of what they call the prison industrial complex argue that this trend is not really about privatizing. Private prisons are still paid for by taxpayer money and are thus not actually shrinking government. Instead, they are "giving a monopoly rent to a private contractor who then goes about the same business the state would have provided."[21] One analyst has called this "faux privatization." The future of private prisons in Texas is unclear, particularly with the change in the business climate for such prisons that has accompanied the recent decrease in the prison population. This change means that a lot of companies that built new private prisons speculating on an ever-increasing prison population are now stuck with half-empty prisons. Some facilities have closed entirely.

The closure of private prisons has brought with it a new set of problems. Take the West Texas town of Littlefield. In 2000, the small town issued $10 million in bonds to build the Bill Clayton Detention Center, to be run by the GEO Group. For several years, the detention center housed prisoners from Idaho. However, after the suicide scandal, Idaho began to transfer its prisoners out of Texas. Not surprisingly, lacking customers, the GEO Group pulled out of its contract. The town of Littlefield still owed about $9 million on the now-empty facility. To pay its loan, Littlefield has had to raise fees on water and sewer usage and increase property taxes, all while its credit rating has been falling.[22] The town thought it had sold the prison in July 2012 for $6 million, but that sale fell through.

## RIGHTS OF THE ACCUSED

In the United States, our criminal justice system is rooted in the strongly held belief that people are innocent until proven guilty. This means that individuals accused of crimes have certain rights. In the Texas Constitution, many of these rights are contained in Article 1, Section 10, which states, in part, that

> in all criminal prosecutions the accused shall have a speedy public trial by an impartial jury. He shall have the right to demand the nature and cause of the accusation against him, and to have a copy thereof. He shall not be compelled to give evidence against himself, and shall have the right of being heard by himself or counsel, or both, shall be confronted by the witnesses against . . . and no person shall be held to answer for a criminal offense, unless on an indictment of a grand jury.

**Indigent defense**
the requirement that governments provide legal counsel to those charged with serious crimes who cannot afford representation.

The right of the accused to have legal counsel has long been the tradition in Texas. Long before the U.S. Supreme Court ruled in *Gideon v. Wainwright* that the Sixth Amendment to the U.S. Constitution entailed a right to counsel in criminal cases, that right was protected by the Texas constitutions. Every Texas constitution since 1836 has guaranteed the right to counsel to those who cannot afford it, a requirement called **indigent defense**.[23]

In practice, Texas political culture has not been overly supportive of the rights of the accused, and the ability to get a decent defense has varied greatly across the state. In 2001, Texas passed the Fair Defense Act, which requires minimum standards for defense lawyers, the prompt appointment of lawyers, and financial resources to hire experts and investigators in indigent cases. Each county is responsible for a plan to provide indigent defense for the accused, which most often involves judges assigning attorneys to cases on a rotating basis or based on experience. Only eighteen counties have permanent public defender offices.

Texas political culture remains tough on crime, and Texans by and large believe in swift justice. The emphasis in the state on individual responsibility means that if you find yourself on the wrong side of the law, Texans are unlikely to be sympathetic. Texans distrust government in most policy areas but exhibit a high degree of trust in the state when it comes to meting out justice. This culture has resulted in more criminalized behavior and thus higher incarceration rates than other states. The fiscal cost has also been high. Recent moves away from punishment and toward rehabilitation appeal to the fiscally conservative Texan but run counter to our sense of justice and retribution. Recent moves by the legislature allow drug abuse and mental health cases to be treated as public health concerns rather than as criminal acts, but the extent to which these moves will be embraced by judges, juries, and the average Texan remains to be seen.

## LAW AND PUNISHMENT

What happens when Texas's ideas of rugged individualism and "pull yourself up by your bootstraps" attitude meet its keen sense of right and wrong? Individual responsibility has always been central to Texans' strong sense of justice. Yet, as a state, we struggle with how to balance protecting individual rights against preventing the behavior of individuals who might take advantage of the system. As we will see, when Texans' sense of right and wrong collides with the rights of individuals, the rights of individuals often lose. Justice remains highly valued and sometimes requires harsh punishment. Texans feel justified in using lethal force to protect their homes, which is the ultimate manifestation of frontier justice. They also prefer the use of capital punishment as the most efficient means of retribution for the most serious crimes. The movement toward tort reform represents a desire to avoid frivolous lawsuits that upset Texas's sense of justice. Texas justice seems harsh to observers outside the state, but to most Texans, the punishment fits the crime.

### Tort Reform

One of the biggest changes in justice in Texas occurred as a result of changes in tort law. Tort law allows individuals who have been wronged due to negligence or malpractice to sue for damages. The idea of tort law is to protect individuals against companies, government, or other individuals' wrongful action that results in injury. The difficulty in tort law is to balance the needs of individuals who are wrongfully injured

**Tort**
a wrongful act by a person that results in injury to another person or property in civil law.

against frivolous lawsuits that cost business, and in turn consumers, a lot of money. In the 1980s, Texas saw a surge of malpractice suits with large settlements, including a dramatic rise in medical malpractice, which drove up malpractice insurance rates for doctors in the state. This led to a decrease in the number of doctors in the state, and, by 2003, Texas ranked forty-fourth out of the fifty states in the ratio of doctors to citizens.

Tort reform in Texas began with legislation in 1987 and again in 1995 that imposed limits on the amount of damages litigants could collect. In 2003, the Texas Legislature passed the most sweeping tort reform legislation, limiting the amount of noneconomic damages (i.e., pain and suffering) in civil suits to $250,000 for a physician or hospital. The goal was to stop frivolous lawsuits. Supporters of the law said the limit would lead to less lawsuits and lower insurance costs for doctors. Those lower costs would be passed on to the average Texan. Opponents of tort reform argued that the $250,000 cap would also discourage genuine claims and deny Texans their constitutional right to a jury trial. Since the Supreme Court of Texas had previously ruled that such limits were unconstitutional, the same legislative session approved a constitutional amendment allowing the legislature to set such limits.

In 2011, the Texas Legislature passed additional tort reform, the so-called **loser pay law**, which requires certain litigants who lose their lawsuit to pay the legal costs of the person who was sued. Litigants will also have to pay if they turn down a settlement offer and the final jury award is less than the settlement amount offered. This law further permits the Supreme Court of Texas to establish guidelines for judges to dismiss what appear to be frivolous lawsuits (under $100,000) earlier in the process, to avoid the costly trial. The law allows for a motion to dismiss the lawsuit at the beginning of the process, and if the judge grants that motion, the plaintiff will have to pay the fees associated with the lawsuit.

The effects of tort reform in the state are particularly important given the reputation of the state's highest civil court for favoring corporate interests over individual consumers and small businesses. One study by the group Texas Watch looked at 624 cases between 2000 and 2010.[24] It found that the Supreme Court of Texas ruled in favor of corporations and governments 74 percent of the time. Perhaps more troubling has been the Supreme Court's tendency to overturn jury verdicts, which it has done 74 percent of the time since 2004. As juries remain one of the most direct forms of democracy in the United States, it is disturbing that Texas law and Supreme Court decisions are rendering juries irrelevant.

For Texans, juries awarding millions of dollars and people suing over everything just rankles us. Texans also have a keen sense of fairness and believe that they should be able to get a fair trial if they are the victim of an egregious act. The balance between these two values is difficult. Texans tend to bristle at the idea that someone can sue McDonalds for millions

**Loser pay law**
Texas law that requires litigants to pay those they sued if they lose their lawsuits in certain cases.

HOSPITAL MEDICAL ERRORS KILL 98,000 AMERICANS EACH YEAR. -- HEARST NEWS INVESTIGATION

Seattlepi/David Horsey

for serving coffee that is too hot. On the other hand, Texans have a right to seek redress in court when they are wronged due to negligence. In 2008, when twenty-five-year-old Vanessa Samudio was struck by a police car traveling at 80 mph with no lights or sirens, she suffered permanent brain damage.[25] Samudio's medical bills were significantly more than the $250,000 cap. Unfortunately, since the 2003 reform, even Texans with legitimate claims have a difficult time even getting an attorney to agree to take their case. This is particularly true of those on limited incomes, such as the elderly, who have little means to pay for legal services absent an award. To make the case that someone got cancer because of a company's negligence or that malpractice in the nursing home led to a senior's death, expert witnesses and assessments that cost money will be needed in addition to legal fees.

Since the passage of this reform, results have been mixed. Proponents of tort reform argue that it has largely ended frivolous lawsuits, helped create a business-friendly environment, stemmed the tide of lost physicians, and decreased the cost of medical malpractice insurance. From this perspective, the average Texan would benefit from easier access to physicians and lower costs for medical services (since physicians would pay less for malpractice insurance). Critics of tort reform, on the other hand, say these benefits have never been realized. In particular, claims that Texas has seen an increase in the number of doctors do not take into account population growth. According to the Texas Department of State Health Services statistics, the number of physicians per capita actually grew at a faster rate between 1996 and 2002 than it has since the 2003 reforms.[26] In addition, a University of Texas study found no evidence that health care costs had declined after 2003, even after accounting for the average increase in those costs compared to all other states. Moreover, Texans who are the victims of negligence or malpractice face much higher costs seeking compensation, and, even if awarded, that compensation will be limited while the costs associated with their injuries may not be. The threat of paying the other side's legal fees will further be a deterrent to poorer Texans in seeking compensation. Clearly, Texas will continue to struggle with the balance between individual rights and decreasing frivolous lawsuits for the foreseeable future.

## Castle Doctrine

Consistent with Texas's culture of frontier justice, since 2007 the state has had a fairly permissive **castle doctrine** (Texas's version of the stand-your-ground doctrine). The castle doctrine derives from English common law and is based on the idea that deadly force is sometimes necessary to defend your castle. In 1973, the Texas Legislature passed a law that deadly force could be used so long as a reasonable person would not have retreated. However, in 1995, and more recently in 2007, the legislature broadened the castle doctrine and removed the duty to retreat. According to the Texas Penal Code (Section 9.01), use of deadly force is permitted in one's home, vehicle, place of work, and anywhere "a person has a right to be present." The law presumes the *reasonableness* of the use of deadly force. Previously, the law in Texas required a person faced with imminent danger to retreat, if possible. The new law no longer requires an individual to retreat so long as he or she does not provoke the person and is not engaged in criminal activity above a class C misdemeanor, which is the least severe criminal category. Now you can use deadly force in Texas to protect yourself or your property.

**Castle doctrine**
Texas law that allows the use of deadly force to defend your home, or "castle."

The castle doctrine remains largely popular in Texas, yet questions remain. For instance, shortly after Texas passed the 2007 law, Texan Joe Horn called 911 because someone was breaking into his neighbor's house. Although he was told by the dispatcher to stay inside, Horn was familiar with the new law and told the dispatcher, "The laws have been changed . . . since September the first, and I have a right to protect myself." Horn said, "I ain't gonna let them get away with this shit. I'm sorry, this ain't right, buddy. . . . They got a bag of loot. . . . Here it goes buddy, you hear the shotgun clicking and I'm going."[27] Horn shot the two men seconds before the police arrived. Under the new castle doctrine, Horn was not arrested nor was he indicted by a grand jury, even though he had to leave his house to defend his neighbor's castle. Proponents of the castle doctrine argue that homeowners have the right to defend themselves and that the castle doctrine is fundamental to that right. Critics of the law charge that individuals now have the right to shoot to kill someone in instances where even the police do not and that it threatens the presumption of innocence. When James Green was shot and killed after accidently entering the wrong house (he thought it was his friend's house), the homeowner who killed him was not charged under the castle law. When a twenty-four-year-old stole the tip jar (containing around $20) from a taco truck, the owner ran after him and killed him while he tried to flee. Under the castle doctrine, the killing was ruled a justifiable homicide. Indeed the castle doctrine raises significant questions about presumption of innocence and when use of force is necessary. A recent Texas A&M study found that states that passed castle doctrines saw an increase in the number of justifiable homicides, murder, and manslaughter rates while realizing no deterrent effect.[28] Texans will continue to grapple with the appropriate balance between protection and the taking of a life.

## Capital Punishment

In 1923, Texas adopted the electric chair (referred to as "Old Sparky") as the state's official method for carrying out **capital punishment**. Prior to the 1920s, hanging was the preferred method of state execution. In 1972, the U.S. Supreme Court ruled that the imposition of capital punishment amounted to "cruel and unusual punishment" since its selective application violated due process.[29] Up to that point, Texas had electrocuted 361 people. Following the Court's ruling, some states, including Texas, began to change their procedures to make them less arbitrary. The most significant change was the adoption of a two-stage process: first, guilt or innocence is decided, then, where a guilty verdict has been pronounced, appropriate punishment is decided separately. By the time Texas implemented its new procedures for imposing the death penalty, lethal injection had become its official means of execution.

The state may implement the death penalty if a person is found guilty of the murder of a public safety officer, firefighter, correctional employee, or a child under the age of six, or if the person is found guilty of multiple murders. Other actions that may invoke capital punishment include committing murder during a kidnapping, burglary, robbery, sexual assault, arson, or prison escape; committing murder for payment; or murdering a prison inmate serving a life sentence for murder, kidnapping, aggravated

**Capital punishment**
also known as the death penalty; refers to when the state puts an individual to death for certain crimes.

sexual assault, or robbery. The decision to implement the death penalty occurs at the local level. The district attorney must seek the death penalty, and the jury determines whether or not the death penalty is warranted in the punishment phase of the trial. In Texas, application of the death penalty is not consistent across the state. Instead, the largest urban centers account for the lion's share of death penalty cases, with approximately 23 percent of all such cases since 1976 occurring in Harris County and another 10 percent in Dallas County. Only four counties—Harris, Dallas, Tarrant, and Bexar— have accounted for around 46 percent of all executions in the state since the death penalty was reinstated.

The U.S. Supreme Court has recognized some significant limits on the death penalty. In 2002, the Court ruled in *Atkins v. Virginia* that it is unconstitutional for the state to execute defendants who are mentally retarded.[30] In spite of that Court ruling, in 2012, Texas executed Marvin Wilson, who had an IQ of sixty-one, well below the cutoff point of seventy for mental retardation.[31] In response to *Atkins v. Virginia*, the Texas Court of Criminal Appeals (CCA) had previously ruled that since mental retardation is subjective, it would add its own criteria. Among those criteria was the consideration of two questions: "Did the commission of that offense require forethought, planning, and complex execution of purpose?" and "Has the person formulated plans and carried them through, or is his conduct impulsive?" Based on the Texas interpretation of the *Atkins* decision, Marvin Wilson's execution went through, despite a national outcry. A few years after *Atkins*, in *Roper v. Simmons*,[32] the U.S. Supreme Court further ruled that juveniles could no longer be subject to the death penalty.

Texas stands at a crossroads with regard to death penalty convictions. On the one hand, Texas continues to favor and utilize the death penalty more than other states and most other countries in the world. Between 1982 and July 2014, Texas executed 515 individuals using lethal injection. Texas executes far more people than any other state in the United States and has carried out almost 37 percent of all executions in the country since 1976. The next two states are Oklahoma with 111 executions and Virginia with 110 executions. Most executions in the United States occur in the South. These executions account for approximately 82 percent of all executions in the country since 1976. Texas not only leads the nation in executions but also consistently ranks among the top ten countries worldwide in them (see How Texas Government Works, page 260).

On the other hand, Texas's use of the death penalty has decreased in recent years and is becoming less popular across the country. Eighteen states have abolished the death penalty, with a third of those instances occurring since 2007. Internationally, the death penalty has also become increasingly unpopular. Currently, 140 countries ban the death penalty, including all Western industrialized countries except the United States. In Europe, opposition to the death penalty has become so potent that European countries now refuse to sell correctional facilities in the United States the drugs used in lethal injection. While Texas is still a leader in the use of the death penalty, and no state politician would campaign on the abolition of it, the rate of executions in the state has decreased in recent years.

# Justice and the Death Penalty

## Texas Compared: Countries with the Highest Number of Confirmed Executions, 2013

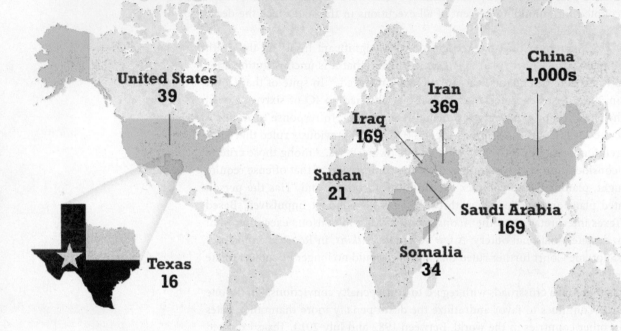

United States
39

China
1,000s

Iran
369

Iraq
169

Sudan
21

Saudi Arabia
169

Somalia
34

Texas
16

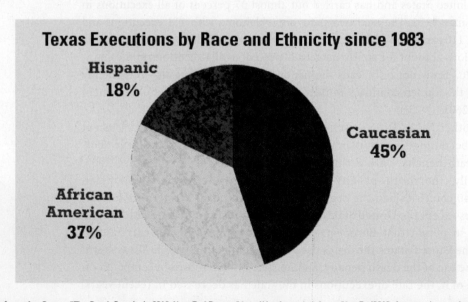

### Texas Executions by Race and Ethnicity since 1983

Hispanic
18%

Caucasian
45%

African
American
37%

Sources: Death Penalty Information Center, "The Death Penalty in 2013: Year End Report," http://deathpenaltyinfo.org/YearEnd2013; Amnesty International, "Death Sentences and Executions 2013," www.amnesty.org/en/library/asset/ACT50/001/2014/en/652ac5b3-3979-43e2-b1a1-6c4919c7a518/act500012014en.pdf.

Texas's use of the death penalty peaked in the 2000s, with an average of twenty-five executions a year, but has since declined, with an average of about fourteen since 2010. In fact Figure 8.1 shows a steady decline in the use of the death penalty. Of course, Texas still has 274 people on death row, so the state will continue to lead the country in executions for the foreseeable future. However, there has also been a marked decline in the number of capital punishment sentences being handed out across the state. Since 2010, Texas has sentenced an average of around eight people a year to death row, compared to twenty-one a year in the 2000s and thirty-four a year in the 1990s.

Although the number of executions in Texas has decreased in recent years, consistent with the rest of the United States, Texas continues to lead the country in state executions. Why does Texas execute significantly more people than other states? Texans have a strong sense of right and wrong and are deeply attached to the idea of the death penalty as a deserved punishment. Whereas other states that use the death penalty may see it as a necessary evil, Texas culture embraces the state's right to execute its citizens for the violation of certain laws. Texans' attachment to the death penalty remains as strong as their attachment to guns. Frontier Texans were often left to secure their own towns—indeed they preferred it that way, suspicious as they were of governmental interference. Imposition of the death penalty is viewed as a right, one in keeping with Texans' sense that there are no gray areas: right is right, and wrong is wrong. This attitude still prevails throughout most of the state. It can be found among Texans sitting on juries, among Texans sitting on the Texas Court of Criminal Appeals, and among

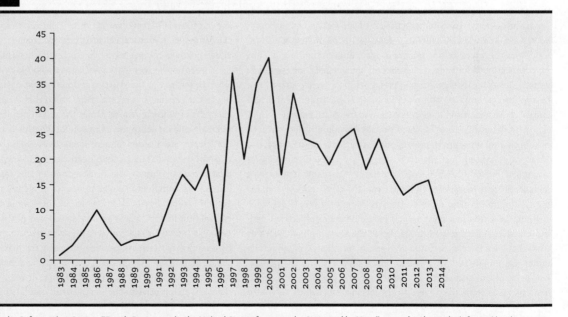

**FIGURE 8.1**  **Executions in Texas since 1983**

**Source:** Death Penalty Information Center, "Death Sentences in the United States from 1977 by State and by Year," www.deathpenaltyinfo.org/death-sentences-united-states-1977-2008 (accessed August 14, 2014).

# TEXAS (VS) CALIFORNIA

The death penalty, or capital punishment, is a controversial topic. Attitudes and orientations toward it reflect deeper values associated with the political culture of a society. Within the United States, various states have adopted different constitutional provisions and statutory laws regarding the death penalty. While both Texas and California carry the penalty, they offer differing perspectives on the issue.

Texas permits use of the death penalty, and specific language in the state constitution spells out the process for appeals. The Texas Penal Code permits capital punishment in cases of capital murder, including murder of on-duty public safety officers, intentional murder of another person, hiring another person to commit a murder, and the murder of individuals under age six, among others.

In contrast, California's state constitution prohibits forms of punishment that are "cruel or unusual." In 1972, California became the first state in the country to ban the death penalty when the justices on the California Supreme Court ruled that capital punishment met the cruel or unusual criteria. The state's voters, however, disagreed; later that year, the death penalty was restored to the California Constitution by constitutional referendum.

A key difference between the two states is that Texas regularly carries out the death penalty as a punishment while California does not. However, even though Texas has executed more persons than California since 1976, California has actually sentenced more people to death as the punishment for a crime. Several explanations exist for this difference in the rates of execution over time. First, prior to 1976, Texas and California each had executed over 700 individuals. Although both states reinstated the death penalty at approximately the same time, Texas began executing prisoners again in 1983. California did not execute a prisoner until 1992. Simply put, since reinstating the death penalty, Texas has been executing prisoners for a decade longer.[i] The reason for this involves the markedly differing natures of the two states' court systems in their orientation to the death penalty.

The California court system focuses on minimizing error to ensure that an innocent person is not put to death. In contrast, the Texas court system focuses on a speedy process and in so doing accepts a higher possible rate of error. As a result, California's appeals process requires both more time and more money be spent on it.[ii] The states also differ in their funding of a public defender system. California has a statewide public defender office that represents some death row inmates; Texas relies on pro bono work or contracts with local or regional lawyers. In addition, California falls under the jurisdiction of the U.S. Ninth Circuit Court of Appeals, whose Democratic-appointed majority is more likely to accept death penalty cases from the states in its jurisdiction, which serves to

## Executions before and after 1976

| | California | Texas |
|---|---|---|
| Total inmates on death row, 2013 | 742 | 278 |
| Executions in 2013 | 0 | 9 |
| Executions before 1976 | 709 | 755 |
| Executions since 1976 | 13 | 515 |
| Females executed since 1976 | 0 | 4 |

**Sources:** Death Penalty Information Center, State by State Database, 2014, www.deathpenaltyinfo.org/state_by_state (accessed July 15, 2014); Texas Department of Criminal Justice, "Executions: December 7, 1982, through August 20, 2012," September 21, 2012, www.tdcj.state.tx.us/death_row/dr_executions_by_year.html (accessed September 20, 2014).

delay the carrying out of a sentence. The same cannot be said of the U.S. Fifth Circuit Court of Appeals that oversees Texas.[iii]

Finally, in California, the death penalty's true purpose may be to serve as a symbol, one charged with acknowledging the seriousness of an offense in order to deter crime or express society's distaste for an act. In this case, the death penalty is not really designed as a punishment since the individual sentenced to death will not actually be put to death quickly. Instead, convicted prisoners are far more likely to live out the rest of their lives in prison. Contrast this with Texas where the death penalty is most certainly intended to deter crime—the convicted prisoner in Texas sentenced to death will be put to death.

Debate over the death penalty in California resurfaced recently when the state was faced with a serious budget crisis and began looking to cut expenses. A recent study found that it costs California an extra $125 million a year to retain the death penalty rather than to put everyone on death row in prison for life; this is in addition to $95 million per year needed for additional staff.[iv] On top of this, the state currently needs to build a new "death house" to keep up with its large death row population; the construction of this facility would cost another $400 million.[v] Finally, the costs of a capital murder trial in California typically run over $1.9 million, three times the cost of a noncapital murder trial.[vi] Cost estimates in Texas place its figure at $1.2 million.[vii] In short, in California today it is the economic costs incurred by retention of the death penalty, including the higher trial costs and the need to update the system, that is driving debate about the utility of capital punishment. In spite of that, in 2013, California voters defeated an initiative to abolish the death penalty in their state.

Texans serving on the Texas Board of Pardons and Paroles. As a former Smith County district attorney put it,

> The death penalty in Texas is primarily a function of the fact that it is in our law. We have conservative jurors and district attorneys run for election and so it's very important that DAs . . . [who come up for reelections] make decisions on cases that are consistent with the feelings of their constituents.[33]

Support for the death penalty in the state remains strong. While national polls indicate that 60 percent of Americans support the death penalty, a recent *Texas Tribune* poll indicates that 71 percent of Texans continue to do so.[34] As DNA evidence has increasingly revealed that innocent people in the United States have been put to death, national support for the death penalty has waned. More recently, budget crises have motivated some states to abolish the death penalty due to the expense associated with it. Texans not only continue to favor the death penalty at higher rates than the rest of the country, they do so despite that fact that only 51 percent of them believe the practice of it is applied fairly.[35]

Texans' preference for the death penalty remains so strong that often the actions of Texas courts seem downright odd to the rest of the country. In one infamous case, a panel of three judges from the Fifth Circuit Court of Appeals upheld a death penalty sentence even though the defendant's attorney had slept through portions of the trial. The panel ruled that since they could not determine whether the attorney had slept through critical parts of the trial, there was no basis to overturn the conviction. Although the full Fifth Circuit Court later overturned this ruling, the initial ruling is indicative of prevalent attitudes toward justice in Texas. Texas again made national news when, in 2007, the U.S. Supreme Court announced it would consider for the first time since 1972 whether the death penalty constituted cruel and unusual punishment. Michael Richard was scheduled to be executed in

A young man sits in his cell on death row at the Ellis Unit prison in Huntsville, Texas. Texas currently leads the country in number of executions.

Texas that same day, and his lawyers scrambled to put together a request to stop his execution until the Court made its ruling on the constitutionality of lethal injection. Richard's attorneys were working on their appeal late in the day when their printer malfunctioned. The attorneys called the Texas Court of Criminal Appeals, the highest criminal court in the state, and requested that the court stay open an extra twenty minutes so they could file the appeal. Texas courts have stayed open in the past to hear last-minute appeals, and three judges were at the appeals court in anticipation of a last-minute filing. In spite of that, presiding judge Sharon Keller reportedly told the attorneys that the Texas Court of Criminal Appeals "close[d] at 5:00."[36] Michael Richard was executed that day.

Texans favor retribution, and the death penalty is viewed as the fitting punishment for the crime of murder. Proponents of the death penalty in the state and elsewhere argue that it acts as a deterrent on crime. This argument is consistent with Texans' preference for politicians and courts in Texas to be tough on crime. However, opponents point out that states without the death penalty have lower murder rates than states that use it. One study by the *New York Times* concluded that ten of the twelve states without the death penalty have murder rates that are lower than the national average, whereas half the states with the death penalty have murder rates that are higher than the average.[37]

Critics of the death penalty continue to emphasize that minorities disproportionately receive the death penalty. In July 2014, the Texas Department of Criminal Justice reported that since 1983, 45 percent of executed prisoners have been white, 37 percent African American, and 18 percent Hispanic. (See How Texas Government Works: Justice and the Death Penalty.) Texas has also executed four of the fourteen women executed in the United States since 1976. Moreover, opponents point out the added expense of death penalty cases, which involve automatic appeals to the state's high court, among other things. The average time spent on death row is slightly over ten years, although the longest time spent there was twenty-four years. In 1992, a *Dallas Morning News* study estimated that taxpayers pay $2.3 million for the average death penalty case in Texas, compared to $750,000 to imprison someone in a single cell at the highest level of security for forty years.[38] This higher cost comes in every case, even those in which the death penalty only *might* be imposed. The cost of the death penalty, coupled with the comparatively large number of executions in the state each year, places a significant burden on Texas's taxpayers.

## WINNERS AND LOSERS

In many ways, Texans' preference for a tough approach to crime, demands for justice, and ardent support of the death penalty sets them apart from the rest of the country. Texans believe the punishment must fit the crime and that the death penalty represents the ultimate symbol of justice. However, these political preferences come at a high cost to the average Texan. Money spent on imprisonment rather than rehabilitation means that Texas's high imprisonment rates translate to significantly higher taxes in the state. Embracing the privatization of prisons also entails significant costs. When these for-profit centers experience high-profile breakouts, it is local and state law officials who conduct statewide searches for the escaped convicts—and it is Texas's taxpayers who pick up the cost. Although private prisons are often cited for poor conditions, Texas has yet to impose fines on these facilities. Texans are also willingly taking on other states' criminal populations, and Texas leads the way in building private prisons intended to house both its own prisoners and those of other states. However, the move by the Texas Legislature toward rehabilitation rather than punishment may help Texans become winners. As incarceration rates have leveled and over $1 billion have been saved, the increased focus on rehabilitation for nonviolent criminals clearly makes taxpayers winners.

Texans win and lose with the death penalty. Although it is increasingly unpopular nationwide, in Texas the death penalty is revered. On the one hand, Texans, in persisting with their policy preference for justice and retribution, "win" in terms of leading the country in number of executions carried out. On the other hand, Texans pay the high costs associated with ensuring that potential death penalty cases follow due process. In appropriating to themselves this cost—one that is significantly higher than the cost of life imprisonment—Texans lose.

★ Are the traditional Texan views on justice worth the burden to taxpayers? Is the shift to rehabilitation a good one for the state?

★ Do concerns that Texas has executed innocent people make you reconsider your views on the death penalty? Why or why not?

★ Are for-profit prisons, paid for by taxpayers but run by for-profit entities, good for Texas?

★ Is taking on violent criminal populations from other states worrisome or worth the risk?

## CONCLUSION

Justice in Texas is a complicated affair. The political culture in the state favors policies that are tough on crime, and Texans trust other Texans even more than the judicial system to mete out punishment. The state's prevailing culture often puts it at odds with the rest of the country, and Texans pay a significant price for their preferences. In the coming years, the state's prison population will once again start to climb, and Texans will have to ask themselves if it is worth it to continue to criminalize so many behaviors. Many countries, and other states, have begun to view drug use as a public health issue rather than a criminal one. The move toward rehabilitation represents a sea change for justice in the state. As future budget and population pressures increase, Texas will have to decide if that sea change is more or less important than its long-standing views of justice on the frontier.

for CQ Press

Sharpen your skills with **SAGE edge** at **edge.sagepub.com/collier4e**. **SAGE edge for students** provides a personalized approach to help you accomplish your coursework goals in an easy-to-use learning environment.

## KEY TERMS

capital punishment (p. 258)

castle doctrine (p. 257)

incarceration rate (p. 247)

indigent defense (p. 254)

loser pay law (p. 256)

private prison (p. 252)

recidivism (p. 249)

rehabilitation (p. 249)

tort (p. 255)

## CORE ASSESSMENT

1. What, if any, should be the limits on an individual's ability to defend his or her home, or "castle"?

2. How can we balance individual rights to seek grievances when a person is wronged against

the cost to society associated with frivolous lawsuits?

3. The death penalty is in line with the preferences of Texans. What are the various costs associated with the death penalty?

# CAMPAIGNS AND ELECTIONS, TEXAS STYLE

The 2014 campaign to elect the lieutenant governor in Texas presented voters with an interesting choice of candidates, reflecting ongoing transformations in Texas politics. The Republican candidate, Dan Patrick, emerged from a four-candidate race for the Republican nomination during the primaries. Patrick brings a degree of charisma associated with his talk radio show and from running a chain of sports bars in the Houston area. He most recently served in the Texas State Senate, representing part of Houston and unincorporated Harris County, and is associated with the Tea Party wing of the Texas Republican Party. He is known for his strong ideological stands on issues, his unwillingness to compromise, and his questioning of any role or influence of Democrats over bills and laws passed by the Texas Legislature.

Patrick's Democratic challenger in the general election was Leticia Van de Putte, a pharmacist by training and profession, and a ninth-generation Tejano. Van de Putte faced no challengers for the Democratic nomination. She is often also a charismatic figure; during attempts by Republicans to impose a redistricting of the Texas Legislature in 2003, Van de Putte was one of several Texas senators who fled to Albuquerque, New Mexico, to prevent the Senate from having a quorum to conduct business. She even appeared in an episode of Comedy Central's *The Daily Show with Jon Stewart* and addressed the issue.

Each campaign tried to frame the election in ways they believed resonated with their key base of supporters. For Patrick, the primary focus was on two main themes: border security and immigration. He bashed Democrats and Republicans in Washington, D.C., for perceived failures in keeping the border secure and stopping the flow of illegal immigrants into the United States. He called for action by the state, including the use of state law enforcement agencies to supplement U.S. Border Patrol agents.[1] He also blamed policies of President Barack Obama for creating a situation in which large numbers of children from Central and South America attempted to immigrate to the country, again often illegally, and without any adult escort or supervision. However, such appeals do not play well among the ever-increasing Hispanic population of voters. Hispanics tend to favor pathways for illegals to obtain U.S. citizenship rather than detention and deportation.[2] Patrick claims his message is not anti-Hispanic, but one of law and order. As a result, he notes the need to treat the unescorted children differently from what he deems criminal elements and gangs attempting unauthorized entry into the United States.[3] It is worth noting that Patrick's claims of the size of the influx of unaccompanied children that attempted to enter the United States have been

© Alyssa Banata

©Marjorie Kamys Cotera

shown to be an exaggeration.[4] To smooth over his positions on immigration so that Hispanics, who are a growing and important component of the electorate, might find him more acceptable, Patrick has emphasized a second theme—family values and defense of the traditional family[5]—which often resonates among the religiously observant, socially conservative elements within the Hispanic community.

Leticia Van de Putte developed a broader set of themes for her campaign. While she has discussed issues ranging from funding for public education to equal pay for women, much of her focus has been on Patrick himself and his record as it contrasts with hers. She has spoken about building bipartisanship, increasing state funds for roads, and limiting the role of high-stakes testing in public education.[6] On the immigration issue, Van de Putte focuses on the humanitarian issues involved with aiding unaccompanied children and the need for action by the federal government to solve the problem.[7] Part of the momentum that Van de Putte's campaign experienced came from enthusiasm surrounding Wendy Davis's campaign for governor. Both candidates appeared to be the strongest Democratic candidates for statewide office in over a decade, and both attracted national attention from Democratic leaders and supporters. In fact, some analysis indicated Van de Putte's contest with Patrick was the race to watch.[8] Speculation even centered on whether voters would split-ticket vote, choosing Republican candidate Greg Abbott for governor while voting for Van de Putte for lieutenant governor.[9]

Money is often a key indicator of enthusiasm and support for a candidate, and Patrick initially received significant financial support in the run-up to the Republican primary. Donations tapered off, however, especially after he secured the nomination. Van de Putte's emergence as a possible contender for office allowed her to raise more than $2 million by the end of June 30, 2014, outpacing Patrick in the months following the primaries. Overall, however, Patrick's carryover from the primary phase still left him with an estimate of over $4 million.[10]

Ultimately, the 2014 election for lieutenant governor illustrates both the tradition and the transformation of Texas politics. On the tradition side, Republican dominance since the late 1990s, like that of Democratic dominance prior to that period, ensured that Republican candidates for statewide office faced less competition from the opposition party in the election. In addition, campaign finance tends to favor the dominant party. Democrats faced an uphill battle in terms of convincing the electorate to vote for them, finding viable candidates to run for office, and funding campaigns to win office. In contrast, Patrick's need to emphasize family values, to clarify his concerns over unauthorized immigrants, and to assure Hispanics that his message was not "anti-Hispanic" represents a transformation of Texas politics that is occurring as the demographics of the state and the electorate change. That Van de Putte is a Hispanic and a woman also illustrates this demographic change.

In this chapter, we will review the history of voter registration and voter qualifications. Discussion will focus on the expansion of voting rights to African Americans, Hispanics, women, members of the armed forces, and younger voters. In the case of African Americans and Hispanics, attention is paid to the challenges of securing voting rights in the face of legal and social barriers and to the need for action by the U.S. government to rectify this situation in light of popular opinion among the white majority in Texas during the 1950s and 1960s. We will also place Texas in context with the wider American South. We then turn our attention to the various types of elections—primaries, general elections, and direct democracy elections—before discussing the ways people in Texas can vote, including early voting and electronic voting. The rates of voter registration and electoral participation are examined, and we include a discussion of the demographics of who votes in Texas elections. The chapter concludes with a discussion of campaigns in Texas, from how candidates and political parties get on the ballot in Texas to styles of campaigning, trends in campaigning, and the campaign finance system. Throughout the chapter, we will study the attempts to maintain tradition in Texas while a fundamental transformation of the electoral landscape is occurring.

## Chapter Objectives

★ Summarize the role and requirements of voting.

★ Discuss the barriers to minorities' voting rights in Texas.

★ Assess who wins and who loses when voting barriers exist.

★ Describe the different types of elections held in Texas.

★ Explain the trends and implications of voter turnout in Texas elections.

★ Discuss the role of electoral competition in Texas politics.

★ Explain the impact campaign finance has on Texas elections.

★ Assess who wins and who loses when Texas elections receive low voter turnout.

# DEMOCRACY, REPRESENTATION, AND ELECTIONS IN TEXAS

Democracy and representative government imply mechanisms for citizens to make decisions about how to govern themselves directly or through agents chosen to represent them in the various branches and levels of government. At the heart of American and Texas government is the electoral system, which includes various types of elections, processes to determine who may vote, processes to determine who may run as a candidate for office, activities associated with campaigning to win an election contest, and the system of paying for electoral contests.

The health of a democracy hinges on electoral competition. Electoral competition is the interaction between candidates, voters, electoral systems, political parties, and organized interests. A system of fair competition, access to the ballot box, and free elections are essential to democratic, representative government. Campaigns must be meaningful, offering candidates, political parties, and organized interests an opportunity to provide information on their ideologies, issue positions, and prescriptions for action to the electorate. Participation in the electoral process must be free of coercion and intimidation while simultaneously allowing free expression of voter preferences. It must also ensure that the number participating in the electoral process is maximized to ensure no systematic bias in who is participating and who is not. When some voices are heard but others stifled, when some voices are allowed to participate while others are not, the result is a distorted image of what is wanted and needed. The outcome of the election, the decisions made by the government branches so elected, and the legitimacy of the political system are distorted.

## Voter Qualifications and Registration

Access to the voting booth is a vital issue in a democracy. The rules of who may vote, how they vote, and under what conditions they vote significantly impact the legitimacy of the government and its responsiveness to the people. Thus, voting rights and qualifications are essential to determining who gets what, when, and how. For example, if voting rights are denied to a group of people based upon their race, candidates running for office might ignore the issues and concerns of people of that race.

At the Constitutional Convention of 1787, the framers of the U.S. Constitution largely left to state governments the conduct of elections. Article I, Section 4 left the "Times, Places and Manner of holding Elections for Senators and Representatives" to the states. As a result, states determine who is qualified to vote in an election, how potential voters register to vote, how candidates and parties get onto a ballot, and what types of voting equipment are used to collect and count votes. This tradition remains at the basis of the constitutional order in the United States. However, since the Civil War (1861–1865), states have faced some degree of national oversight, first through a series of amendments to the U.S. Constitution and later through U.S. Supreme Court decisions. National supervision of elections became even more prominent during the civil rights era of the 1950s and 1960s when the U.S. government attempted to rectify past discrimination in the area of voting rights. This supervision gave several national government agencies, such as the U.S. Department of Justice, greater power over state election processes and began a transformation to include new voices in the electoral process.

Prior to the civil rights era, the state of Texas attempted to deny African Americans the right to vote through a variety of laws and practices. Candidates often ignored issues of concern to African Americans, such as the condition of African Americans' schools and crime in their neighborhoods. As a result, government policy made upgrading schools in white communities or addressing crime in white areas the priority. This attempt to deny minorities a voice is a tradition of white dominance over Texas.

Because state governments in the United States are responsible for voter registration, there are fifty different sets of voter registration processes, procedures, and qualifications. For example, North Dakota lacks any formal voter registration process. On Election Day, a voter simply shows a driver's license or state identification card indicating that he or she lives in the state and community in order to vote. Eight states, including Minnesota, Iowa, and Wisconsin, allow same-day voter registration, meaning if a person is qualified to vote, then that person may register to vote and vote in an election on the same day. A few states, such as Rhode Island, allow same-day registration but limit the election contests in which the voter may participate. For example, in some cases the voter may only vote in the U.S. national election for president.

Voter registration in Texas is a bit more complicated. To register to vote, a person must be a citizen of the United States, be at least eighteen years of age, and have resided in Texas for at least thirty days. To vote in a county or other local government election, the thirty-day residency requirement applies, even if a voter is already a resident of Texas. So, a voter who moves from San Antonio to Amarillo must live in Amarillo for at least thirty days before voting in an Amarillo city election. If a voter owns property in several locations within Texas, the voter chooses which address serves as his or her primary residence for the purpose of voting.[11]

To register to vote, a voter registration form must be completed. The form is available from county voter registration offices or online from the Texas secretary of state. The completed form must be submitted in person or by regular mail to the voter registration office in the county in which the voter resides. Electronic submissions are not allowed. Since 1993, residents of Texas may register to vote when applying for a driver's license or when renewing a license. This development occurred when the U.S. Congress passed the National Voter Registration Act, more popularly known as the **Motor Voter Act**. As an election nears, some local civic organizations, such as the League of Women Voters or a university's student government association, often hold voter registration drives to get more people registered to vote. Those interested in registering to vote fill out the form and return it by mail, or the civic organization returns all of the cards to the county elections office. Some public libraries and schools make voter registration forms available. Regardless of how a person registers to vote, the form must be submitted to the county voter registration office no later than thirty days before an election.

In addition to age and residency requirements, Texas maintains other qualifications to vote. Individuals determined by a court to be partially or totally mentally incapacitated may be denied the right to vote. Likewise, convicted felons over the age of eighteen are stripped of the right to vote until they have completed their sentence, including any required parole or probation.[12] This limitation reflects the traditionalistic political

**Motor Voter Act**
the National Voter Registration Act, which allows citizens to register to vote when applying for or renewing their driver's license.

culture of Texas, which emphasizes the need to punish criminals and the idea that the rights of citizenship are not automatic.

Texas is one of fifteen states to require registration at least thirty days before an election. Under the Voting Rights Act of 1965 passed by the U.S. Congress, this time limit of thirty days is the maximum a state may impose between the end of the registration period and the actual election. As discussed above, states vary in time a voter may register before an election. The U.S. government, while limiting how far out a state may require a resident register to vote, still allows states significant control over the exact time frame for registering to vote.

Since 1972, Texas has maintained a permanent list of voters. The maintenance of the voter registration list is the responsibility of county governments. In most of Texas's counties, the responsibility is retained by the county tax assessor, a relic of the pre–civil rights era when the tax assessor was responsible for collecting poll taxes as a prerequisite to voting. Having the same office collect the poll tax and maintain voting records made sense. Other counties have shifted this responsibility to the county clerk's office. Because the county clerk is responsible for keeping other records, such as birth records and marriage licenses, placing voter registration in that office makes sense also. Finally, some counties have created a separate county elections office that, in addition to other duties discussed below, maintains the voter registration list.

## VOTING RIGHTS IN TEXAS

Under the Republic of Texas Constitution, the right to vote in Texas elections extended only to white males. In fact, no free person of African descent was permitted to reside permanently in the Republic of Texas without the consent of the Texas Congress. The status of Hispanics varied across Texas and over time. In some localities, Hispanics were considered to be white, which allowed them to register to vote and cast ballots in an election. In other localities, Hispanics were considered to be nonwhite and therefore not entitled to vote. Women, Native Americans, and African Americans were denied **suffrage**, or the legal right to vote. The Texas Constitution of 1845, adopted when Texas joined the United States, continued to deny access to voting to these groups. The Civil War and its aftermath spurred an increased role for the national government in state election processes, primarily in securing to African American males the right to vote through the Fifteenth Amendment. The expansion of the role of the national government in the area of voting rights continued into the twentieth century with the addition of women's suffrage and the passage of voting rights legislation during the civil rights era.

**Suffrage**
the legal right to vote.

### Legal Barriers to Voting in Post-Reconstruction Texas

After the U.S. Civil War, the U.S. Constitution was amended to include the Thirteenth, Fourteenth, and Fifteenth Amendments. The Fifteenth Amendment specifically requires that state governments ensure the right to vote regardless of race or prior status as a slave. Here we see the first steps by the national government to regulate voting rights of all Americans and to transform the electoral landscape by ensuring equal rights for all to vote. With the end of military occupation of the southern states and the end of Reconstruction in 1876, states such as Texas officially maintained the right of African Americans to vote even as they imposed a series of barriers to effectively bar former slaves from actually exercising that right. The exact barriers used varied by state, but collectively states in the South used five types of barriers to prohibit African Americans from voting. A **grandfather clause** prohibited them from voting by restricting the right to vote to those whose grandfathers had the right to vote. Given that most African Americans in the American South were former slaves, as were their fathers and grandfathers, they were barred from voting. While important in several states, including Louisiana, Texas never used the grandfather clause. Another technique was the **literacy test**, a test of the prospective voter's ability to read and understand aspects of American government. The poor state of public education in African American communities throughout the South from the end of Reconstruction into the 1950s ensured that many African Americans were denied the right to vote. In some communities, African Americans were given different, harder tests than whites. Unlike other southern states, such as Alabama, Texas never used the literacy test.

A third legal barrier instituted to prevent African Americans from voting was the **poll tax**, an annual tax that had to be paid before one was allowed to vote. In Texas, the poll tax proved to be an important barrier. The Constitution of 1869 permitted the use of poll taxes as a method of funding public education in Texas. Our current state constitution, adopted in 1876, also permitted the Texas Legislature to impose poll taxes on Texans.[13] The state imposed a rate of $1.50 per voter annually, while counties could impose a tax of up to $0.25 on each voter. Since most African Americans in Texas earned relatively lower incomes compared to whites, African Americans faced the choice between purchasing basic necessities versus participating in politics. Further, these taxes had to be paid well in advance, so that anyone who wanted to vote had to save up to pay the tax, and these taxes were often levied in the spring, long before most people thought about the general election in November.

The poll tax prevented many poor whites from voting as well. Disenfranchising poor, rural, white voters served a useful purpose: diluting the strength of the Populist Party. The Democratic Party feared the growing challenge of the Populist Party, which was based in farmer and labor movements throughout the United States and directly challenged wealthy interests in Texas politics. Populists focused on the economic plight of poor, small- and medium-sized family farms and sought to shift the race-based politics of the Civil War, Reconstruction, and post-Reconstruction eras to a class-based politics in which the lower and middle classes could effectively vie with the upper classes for political power. As such, the poll tax served the Democratic Party well: African Americans and potential Populist voters were eliminated from voting, and, consistent with Texas's traditional political culture, it was the "better" elements of society that were given the right to rule. The poll tax was instrumental in allowing the Democratic Party in Texas to stave off any serious challenge to its supremacy and maintain its status as the majority party for decades. Racial appeals by traditional Democrats continued into the late 1940s and beyond. For example, Governor Allan Shivers in 1948 complained of "creeping socialism" by the national Democratic Party

**Grandfather clause**
the granting of voting rights only to those citizens whose grandfathers had the right to vote; used to bar African Americans from voting in the South after the end of Reconstruction. Used in other southern states but not used in Texas.

**Literacy test**
a test of a prospective voter's ability to read and understand aspects of American government; used to bar African Americans from voting in many parts of the post-Reconstruction South, but not used in Texas.

**Poll tax**
an annual tax that had to be paid before one was allowed to vote; used in Texas.

leadership and the need for "moral regeneration" or a "spiritual awakening" to prevent integration of the races.[14] He relied upon similar themes to confront integration of public schools in the 1950s as well.

Another important technique for disenfranchising African American voters in the southern states was the **white primary**. Essentially, participation in primary elections to nominate candidates for office was restricted to members of the party only, and membership in the party was limited to white voters. Because the primary election determined the Democratic Party nominee for the general election, and because the primary was restricted to white voters, the white primary guaranteed that parties and candidates responded only to issues of concern in the white population.

Finally, many African Americans faced intimidation and violence when attempting to register to vote or when attempting to cast a vote on Election Day. While these methods of deterrence were not legal barriers, such as the white primary or grandfather clause, the threat and use of violence by the white majority caused many African Americans to disengage from the electoral process.

Among the states that used the white primary, Texas was unusual in that its use of such a primary occurred because of state law. All other states implementing the white primary did so as a matter of party rules or custom rather than law.[15] This legal use of the white primary in Texas became a key barrier to prevent African Americans from voting in our state.

Finally, violence and intimidation were also used in Texas to discourage African Americans and, at times, Hispanics from voting. The use of these techniques against Hispanics also set Texas apart from other southern states. However, the extent to which violence and intimidation were used to suppress voting varied by county and over time. In addition, the effect in Texas may have been less than in other southern states.

## Eliminating Barriers to Voting for African Americans

Ultimately, the removal of barriers to voting gave the national government significant control over state voter registration processes, and in so doing took power away from the states. This nationalization of voter registration occurred because elected officials in southern states refused to ensure African Americans' equal rights, including the right to vote. The assumption of control by the national government was a necessary step on the road to equality. Restoration of voting rights for African Americans occurred through court cases and legislation passed by the U.S. Congress.

The grandfather clause was eliminated when the U.S. Supreme Court issued its ruling in *Guinn v. United States* (1919). To eliminate this barrier, the Court relied on the **equal protection clause** of the Fourteenth Amendment to the U.S. Constitution. This clause of the Constitution requires that state laws and state constitutions treat all citizens the same. Because the grandfather clause treated African Americans, whose grandfathers clearly did not have the right to vote, differently from whites, it violated the idea that the law must treat all citizens the same. The literacy test used in other states as an important barrier to voting was removed by the passage of the Voting Rights Act of 1965 (VRA). This act is also important for other reasons that are discussed later in this section.

**White primary**
the attempt by the Democratic Party in Texas and other southern states to limit the voting in party primaries only to party members; in Texas, this practice was codified in state law.

**Equal protection clause**
clause of the Fourteenth Amendment to the U.S. Constitution requiring that state laws and state constitutions treat all citizens the same.

POLL TAX RECEIPT
STATE OF TEXAS

ORIGINAL       ROLL____ PAGE____ LINE____

**1954**       COUNTY OF WOOD       № 2154
PRECINCT       WARD____ DATE 1/31   19 55
NUMBER

RECEIVED OF Ulman H. Bruner
ADDRESS 406 Giles st Mineola       R.F.D.

| AGE | LENGTH OF RESIDENCE | | | CITIZEN | NATIVE-BORN | BORN IN (STATE OR FOREIGN COUNTRY) |
| | STATE | COUNTY | CITY | | NATURALIZED | Teacher |
| YEARS | YEARS | YEARS | YEARS | SEX | MALE | OCCUPATION |
| 44 | 44 | 3 | 3 | | FEMALE | |
| | | | | RACE | WHITE | PAID BY |
| | | | | | COLORED | Self |

AGENT

THE SUM OF    ONE AND 75/100 DOLLARS    IN PAYMENT OF POLL TAX FOR THE YEAR SHOWN ABOVE.
THE SAID TAXPAYER BEING DULY SWORN BY ME SAYS THAT THE ABOVE IS CORRECT, ALL OF WHICH I CERTIFY.

BY Jim Honeywell DEPUTY.    I. A. Denton
ASSESSOR AND COLLECTOR OF TAXES

BENNETT DALLAS, TEX.

POLL TAX RECEIPT
STATE OF TEXAS

ORIGINAL       ROLL____ PAGE____ LINE____

**1954**       COUNTY OF WOOD       № 2155
PRECINCT       WARD____ DATE 1-31   19 55
NUMBER

RECEIVED OF Vera L. Bruner
ADDRESS 406 Giles St. Mineola       R.F.D.

| AGE | LENGTH OF RESIDENCE | | | CITIZEN | NATIVE-BORN | BORN IN (STATE OR FOREIGN COUNTRY) |
| | STATE | COUNTY | CITY | | NATURALIZED | Ark. |
| YEARS | YEARS | YEARS | YEARS | SEX | MALE | OCCUPATION |
| 42 | 42 | 3 | 3 | | FEMALE | Housewife |
| | | | | RACE | WHITE | PAID BY |
| | | | | | COLORED | |

AGENT

THE SUM OF    ONE AND 75/100 DOLLARS    IN PAYMENT OF POLL TAX FOR THE YEAR SHOWN ABOVE.
THE SAID TAXPAYER BEING DULY SWORN BY ME SAYS THAT THE ABOVE IS CORRECT, ALL OF WHICH I CERTIFY.

BY Jim Honeywell DEPUTY.    I. A. Denton
ASSESSOR AND COLLECTOR OF TAXES

The poll tax was used to deny the right to vote to many African Americans in Texas. This poll tax receipt from Wood County in 1955 shows that the poll tax had been paid in full by a white couple, thereby allowing them to vote in upcoming elections.

Eliminating the poll tax proved to be more complicated. The poll tax in national elections was eliminated by the Twenty-fourth Amendment to the U.S. Constitution in 1964. However, states assumed that state and local elections, which clearly did not involve the national government, remained solely the domain of state law. Payment of the poll tax continued to be required for state and local elections for another year. Then, in *Harper v. Virginia Board of Elections* (1966), the U.S. Supreme Court struck down the poll tax in Virginia state and local elections as a violation of the equal protection clause of the Fourteenth Amendment to the U.S. Constitution.[16]

Challenging the white primary also initially proved difficult, especially in Texas. In the Texas-based case *Nixon v. Herndon* (1924),[17] the U.S. Supreme Court invalidated the white primary where required or sanctioned by state law. In response, the Texas Democratic Party declared itself a "private organization" and therefore exempt from the standards of equity applied to elections run by the state. Twenty years later, the Court threw out the white primary in *Smith v. Allwright* (1944).[18] The Court declared that the vital function of nominating candidates for office meant that political parties were public organizations. Not accepting of this decision, the Democratic Party in Fort Bend County attempted a "Jaybird" pre-primary in which only whites cast informal votes to consolidate support behind a single candidate who all whites would then back in the official primary. Seeing through this attempt at coordination and control, the U.S. Supreme Court outlawed the practice in *Terry v. Adams* (1953).[19] One estimate suggests that removing the poll tax and white primary had the immediate impact of allowing as many as 200,000 African Americans in Texas to vote.[20]

After decades of wrangling with a host of discriminatory practices, the U.S. Congress passed the **Voting Rights Act of 1965 (VRA)**. The VRA barred any "qualification or prerequisite to voting, or standard, practice, or procedure" that served to deny or abridge the right of a citizen to vote based on race or color. The law's broad language was a response to states whose practices discriminated against black citizens. Many of these practices remained in effect until the courts struck them down. Under the VRA, a state that was found to have a pattern of discrimination against a group was required to get "pre-clearance" before instituting new procedures or practices that could also have the effect of discriminating against minorities. This provision included changes in polling locations, dates for elections, qualifications for voting, and district lines drawn for state legislatures and local governments, such as city councils, county commissions, and school boards. Another provision of the VRA addressed the issue of violence and intimidation when African Americans attempted to register to vote or to cast their votes on Election Day. The VRA required the U.S. government to send election monitors into areas with a history of discrimination. The monitors, who were employees of the U.S. Department of Justice, would report any harassment or activities used to intimidate African Americans to local government officials and to state government authorities. If these local and state officials refused to stop the violence and/or intimidation, they could be charged with a federal crime for failing to enforce the VRA and could be prosecuted in federal court.

While most of the provisions of the VRA remain in force, critics have raised concerns about the pre-clearance provision, particularly the question of how long a state or local government is subject to such pre-clearance. A section of the VRA does allow local governments, but not states, to apply for an exemption to the pre-clearance provision based upon the percentage of the minority population registered to vote and percentage that votes in elections. In *Northwest Austin Municipal Utility District #1 v. Holder* (2009), the U.S. Supreme Court affirmed the right of local governments to

**Voting Rights Act of 1965 (VRA)**
a federal statute that eliminated literacy tests as a qualification to vote, greatly increasing African Americans' access to the ballot box.

apply for an exemption.[21] A few years later, the Court declared the entire pre-clearance process to be unconstitutional in *Shelby County, AL v. Holder* (2013)[22] in part because enforcement of the pre-clearance provisions relied upon data and practices from the 1960s, not from current information.

## Hispanics and Voting Rights

The history of voting rights for Hispanics in Texas is a complex story. In the days of the Republic of Texas and early statehood, some discrimination against Hispanics existed but not to the extent faced by African Americans.[23] Texans of Mexican descent had an uncertain political status in a state that reserved voting for white citizens but did not define "white." In 1897, a federal district court affirmed the civil rights of Texas Mexicans to vote after Richard Rodríguez challenged the claim that he did not qualify for citizenship since he was not "a white person, nor an African, nor of African descent, and [was] therefore not capable of becoming an American citizen."[24]

The extent of discrimination against Hispanics is somewhat uncertain, as illustrated in the contrast between the impact of the poll tax compared to the white primary. The poll tax did disenfranchise many Hispanics, just as it did poor whites and African Americans, because so many Tejanos were involved in the kind of subsistence farming and ranching that might feed their family but did not produce much cash. Therefore, the removal of the poll tax in national and state elections provided an opportunity for more Hispanics to register to vote. However, scholars debate the impact of the white primary on Hispanic voting. In some counties, Hispanics were apparently allowed to vote in the white primary when they formed an important base of support for the Democratic Party, as they did in southern parts of Texas. As evidence of this, some scholars note that along the Mexican border many local elected officials were Hispanic. Yet some scholars assert that the white primary did prohibit Hispanic voters.[25]

Although the Voting Rights Act of 1965 originally applied only to attempts to disenfranchise African American voters, the renewal of the act in 1975 extended its protection to Hispanic voters in states or counties with a history of low levels of Hispanics voting, where elections were conducted only in English, or where more than 5 percent of the voting-age population was part of a language minority.[26] States such as Texas and California are required to provide bilingual ballots that encourage Hispanic voters who are citizens to participate in elections. A provision for a bilingual ballot has also been applied to benefit Native Americans in Alaska, California, Oklahoma, New Mexico, and South Dakota. Asian Americans also are covered by this provision in selected counties across the United States.

One source of the disenfranchisement of Hispanics appears to have been economic harassment. Whites boycotted Hispanic businesses, linked bank loans to support for white candidates in elections, and fired Hispanics who engaged in political campaigns. In addressing discrimination against Hispanics voting in Bexar County, the U.S. Supreme Court identified the sources of discrimination to be primarily economic, educational, and linguistic in nature, rather than the result of law.[27] However, the use of economic and other tools to disenfranchise Hispanics varied by county.[28] Thus, rather than the formal and legal barriers that African Americans faced, the primary barriers to voting for Hispanics were intimidation tactics.

The expansion of voting rights to African Americans and Hispanics ushered in a transformation of the Texas electorate to be more inclusive of all residents of Texas. However, the recent issue of voter fraud, or concerns about possible voter fraud, has led to a wave of states passing voter identification laws. These laws require that a voter present some form of voter identification or other document on Election Day as he or she goes to the polls. Proponents of these laws state that they are necessary to ensure that only the registered voter actually casts the vote, rather than someone attempting to impersonate the voter. They claim such fraud could shift election outcomes, causing the winner—a person supported by actual registered voters—to lose to a candidate who wins as a result of support from unregistered voters. Often, unauthorized immigrants are identified as a potential source of fraudulent voters. Opponents of the identification requirement point to the lack of evidence that unauthorized immigrants vote or that the number of fraudulent ballots is sufficiently large enough to change election outcomes. They also point out that the law exempts mail-in ballots, which can be another source of voter fraud. In addition, voter ID opponents raise the issue of the intimidation of minority voters.[29] Another concern is the impact on minorities, especially those with low incomes, since such a law requires a state identification card or a state driver's license in order to vote. Racial and ethnic minorities are often less likely to possess either of these forms of identification because they cost money.[30] Thus, the requirement that a voter present a state-issued photo identification becomes a tax akin to a poll tax, which was one of the techniques used in Texas and other states to prevent African Americans from voting in the past.

Republicans began introducing these voter identification laws in the 2009 session of the Texas Legislature. By the 2011 session, they were able to successfully pass a bill addressing this issue, and Governor Rick Perry signed it into law. The bill that become law requires a voter to show one of several forms of ID when he or she votes in an election: a state-issued driver's license, a state identification card, a military ID, a concealed handgun license, a passport, or a state-issued election identification certificate. The last option can be issued upon the request of a registered voter free of charge.[31] Because the law passed prior to the U.S. Supreme Court decision in *Shelby County, AL v. Holder* (2013), it was subject to pre-clearance as discussed above. U.S. attorney general Eric Holder denied pre-clearance of the law in March 2012, stating that Texas failed to show that the law did not deny or limit the rights to vote on the basis of race.[32] Holder called the law essentially a poll tax.[33] In August 2012, a federal district court in Washington, D.C., struck down the Texas voter ID law, calling it racially discriminatory. Texas attorney general Greg Abbott planned to appeal the law all the way to the U.S. Supreme Court, noting that the highest court had approved a similar law in Georgia, where the state promised to provide free voter ID cards.[34] A similar law in Indiana was also upheld by federal courts. Ultimately, the U.S. Supreme Court's decision in *Shelby County, AL v. Holder* (2013) had the immediate effect of allowing Texas to implement the new voter identification law. Now, citizens and voting rights advocacy groups must file lawsuits to test whether the voter identification law is in effect a poll tax and thus illegal. Prior to the November 2014 elections, a U.S. district court judge in Corpus Christi threw out the voter ID law just nine days before the start of early voting. However, the U.S. Fifth Circuit Court in New Orleans overruled the district court a few days later, allowing the voter ID law to be in effect for the 2014 elections.

## Voting Rights for Women, Members of the Armed Forces, and Younger Voters

Texas proved slightly more progressive in its extension of voting rights to women. The Wyoming Territory in 1869 was the first area of the United States to grant women the right to vote. Women's suffrage in Wyoming survived the transition to statehood in 1890, making Wyoming the first state in which women could vote. In 1893, Colorado became the first state in which a state legislature granted women the right to vote. The Texas Legislature first considered the issue of women's suffrage in 1915, and by 1918 it had authorized women, or at least white women, to vote in primary elections. In all of these cases, women possessed the right to vote in some or all state and local government elections but not in elections for the U.S. national government. Two years later, in 1920, the Nineteenth Amendment to the U.S. Constitution gave women the right to vote in federal elections. Texas also proved somewhat forward-thinking by being the first state in the Old South—and the ninth in the nation—to ratify the Nineteenth Amendment. Ultimately, the United States was one of the first countries to grant women the right to vote in national elections, following in the footsteps of Great Britain, which had granted women suffrage in 1919, and other former British colonies, such as New Zealand (1893) and Australia (1901).

Historically, members of the U.S. military and their families were denied the right to vote in some states if they were not residents of that state prior to joining the military. In Texas, a provision of the original 1876 state constitution prohibited voting by all "soldiers, marines and seamen, employed in the service of the army or navy of the United States." Because residency is a requirement to vote, members of the military were effectively denied the right during a tour of duty because they were large populations considered to be transient that could overwhelm local voters. In 1965, the U.S. Supreme Court ruled in *Carrington v. Rash* (1965) that while states can impose reasonable residency requirements for voting, it cannot deny someone the right to vote because he or she is a member of the armed services. It said that members of the military who have established residency and intend to make the state their permanent home must be allowed to vote.[35] Members of the military and their families were then allowed to establish residency like any other person moving to Texas and exercise the right to vote in state and local elections.

A further extension of voting rights concerned young adults. The right to vote was associated with being an adult—historically defined as having attained the age of twenty-one. However, in 1971, the Twenty-sixth Amendment to the U.S. Constitution lowered the minimum voting age to eighteen in federal elections. States quickly followed suit, lowering the minimum voting age to eighteen for state and local elections. This extension of voting rights stemmed in part from U.S. involvement in Vietnam. Young men of this era were fighting—and losing their lives—for their country in the Vietnam War but were unable to vote in national or state elections. The discrepancy between being able to die for one's country and not being able to participate in the selection of one's political leaders struck many as wrong, spurring ratification of the Twenty-sixth Amendment.

The voting rights of college students represents an issue related to both the youth of these students and their transient nature. Today, Texas state law guarantees college students the right to choose where they will vote if the student spends weeks or months in different locations each year, including the community in which he or she attends college.[36] In the past, state and local governments attempted to prevent college students from registering to vote where they attended school if that location was different from their parent's residence. Since most votes in Texas occur on a weekday during the school year, students often find that voting in the community where they attend college is easier than returning home to vote. The argument against the participation of college students in local elections was similar to that against members of the military: they were viewed as large numbers of transient rather than permanent members of the community. However, because college students use local government services, such as roads, and pay local taxes, such as sales taxes, they often do have an interest in the politics of the community in which they attend school. In addition, once a student votes in an election, he or she is more likely to vote in future elections. Thus, by allowing students to vote in the community where they attend college, a lifelong pattern of voting is encouraged.

The objection to college students' voting may evidence a deeper distrust. Some area residents view them as outsiders who might displace local political elites and change local ordinances in the community. In fact, attempts to prevent an early voting location on the campus of Stephen F. Austin State University (SFASU) in the 2008 general election were argued in these very terms by members of the community and by some members of the Nacogdoches County Commissioners Court. Despite the tremendous success of early voting in the 2008 presidential election, similar arguments led to a 4 to 1 vote against early voting at SFASU in the 2010 general election, including the governor's election. In any case, when students go off to college they have the right to choose whether to vote at their permanent home address or at their college address, but they must choose one or the other.

An interesting quirk regarding the rights of voters in Texas centers on the conduct of the voter on Election Day. With the exceptions of treason, felony, or disturbing the peace, voters in Texas are exempt from arrest while going to or returning from voting.[37]

The history of voting rights in Texas appears to be periodic attempts to restrict the right to vote to only the "right" kinds of voters: white and, at times, Hispanic males with better education and more money. The Democratic Party of the post-Reconstruction era sought to maintain its power base by writing the "rules of the game" to exclude African Americans and to prevent the state government from responding to the demands of all citizens. As a result, state politics and policy reflected primarily the wishes of those able to vote, rather than those of all the citizens of Texas. Only after the civil rights era of the 1950s and 1960s took root did significant numbers of poorer whites and African Americans gain access to the ballot box, transforming Texas politics as the electorate became more inclusive. Efforts to include women, members of the military, and young voters in the election process proved less controversial. More recently, legal attempts to include Hispanics in Texas politics more completely—as voters, candidates, and elected officials—have proved increasingly effective.

## WINNERS AND LOSERS

The expansion of voting rights is a clear example of transition in Texas as the right to vote has broadened significantly over the course of the state's history. A state founded on an electorate of only white males now, with few exceptions, allows citizens age eighteen and older from all demographic groups to participate fully in the electoral process. However, the past establishment attempted to prevent disenfranchised groups, such as Hispanics and African Americans, from voting to maintain the tradition of white dominance in Texas politics. It was largely through the actions of the national government that Texas was forced to change its election rules and practices to be more inclusive. Texas has in turn significantly altered. As a result, the dynamics of state politics, which now force consideration of issues that matter to all of the state's citizens, have changed as well.

The expansion of the national government's powers in the area of voting rights occurred because elected officials in many states, including Texas, openly engaged in legal, political, and social strategies to deny specific groups of individuals the right to participate in elections. Ultimately, the elected officials were reflecting the attitudes and beliefs of the majority white population at the time. The authors of the U.S. Constitution worried that the tyranny of the British monarchy would be replaced by the tyranny of a majority willing to use its electoral strength to diminish or strip away the rights of others. Here the tyranny of the majority, as expressed in the past by state government and its policies, demonstrated the need for the separation of powers and checks and balances built into our system of federalism. State governments controlled by passionate majorities who desire to take away the rights of others can have their powers checked by the national government. At the same time, the constitutional design also allows the state governments to attempt to check the powers of the national government when federal power goes too far. Recent action by the U.S. Supreme Court invalidating preclearance provisions has opened the door for popular majorities to impose restrictions on voting rights paramount to poll taxes through voter identification laws.

★ Who wins and who loses with voter ID legislation in Texas? Why might such a requirement be a good idea? What are its disadvantages?

★ Why are voting rights essential in a representative democracy?

★ Do old barriers to voting, such as the poll tax and white primary, continue to affect Texas politics?

★ Was the federal government correct in taking action to remove the barriers to voting that African Americans and Hispanics faced in Texas in the past?

## TYPES OF ELECTIONS IN TEXAS

**Primary election**
intraparty election in which candidates compete to determine who will win the party's nomination in the general election.

Voters can participate in several types of elections. **Primary elections** are essentially intraparty elections. In these elections, candidates compete to represent a particular political party in a general election. Thus, the winner of a

## Landslide Lyndon

Today, visitors to the Lyndon B. Johnson Presidential Museum in Austin can watch a mechanical figure of the former president lean on a split-rail fence and spin yarns about Texas. Johnson occupies a unique position in that he has both starred in and recounted many Texas legends.

The career of Lyndon Baines Johnson saw his rise from a teacher in a poor school in Pearsall, Texas, to president of the United States. When "Pappy" O'Daniel, in what one newspaper called the "most constructive act" of his career, retired from the U.S. Senate, the battle to succeed him pitted Johnson against former governor Coke Robert Stevenson. Stevenson was considered unbeatable by some, but Johnson won the endorsement of many of the state's newspapers and "Ma" Ferguson, who remembered that Johnson attended the funeral of her husband while Stevenson skipped the service. Johnson concentrated on the large urban areas and zipped around the state campaigning via helicopter while Stevenson was content to drive around in an old Plymouth.

Stevenson finished first in the primary, easily besting Johnson by a vote of 477,077 to 405,617. However, lacking the majority needed to win the nomination, the two candidates faced off in a runoff election. Official returns from the runoff took three days to compile before the Texas

Election Board announced that Stevenson had won by 362 votes. However, "late returns" were still coming in, including what would become the legendary Box 13 from Alice, Texas, which belatedly revealed 203 uncounted ballots, 202 of them for Johnson. Upon further examination, the poll lists showed that Box 13's voters had signed in and voted in alphabetical order and in identical handwriting. Amended returns gave Johnson a margin of eighty-seven votes statewide and the nickname of "Landslide Lyndon."

The State Democratic Executive Committee had the final word on the primary returns and voted 29 to 28 to certify the Johnson victory. While some of Johnson's critics have pointed to evidence of voter fraud in Alice, others point out that there was evidence of similar vote fraud on behalf of Stevenson in East Texas. As T. R. Fehrenbach concluded in his classic history of Texas, "Johnson's men had not defrauded Stevenson, but successfully outfrauded him."[i]

While Johnson's leadership of the nation as it tackled landmark civil rights legislation, including the Civil Rights Act of 1964 and the Voting Rights Act of 1965,

Lyndon Baines Johnson Library and Museum

have given him a well-deserved place in history, it's worth remembering that Johnson, like many other leaders of his time, came to power under the wing of powerful party bosses and sometimes won high office by taking the low road.

_____

i.   T. R. Fehrenbach, *Lone Star: A History of Texas and the Texans*, updated ed. (Cambridge, Mass.: Da Capo Press, 2000), 659.

primary "wins" the party's nomination and a place on the ballot in the general election. A primary election may be a **direct primary**, in which the winning candidate automatically receives the party nomination, or it may be an **indirect primary** or **preference primary**. In an indirect primary, voters elect delegates to a party convention. Delegates are pledged to support a specific candidate seeking the party nomination. At the convention, the delegates vote among the various candidates. The winner receives the party nomination. In a preference primary, voters indicate their choice of candidate to hold office, but the actual selection is left to the political party elites.

**Direct primary**
a primary election in which the winning candidate directly receives the party nomination.

**Indirect primary**
a primary election in which voters elect delegates to a party convention; delegates are pledged to support a specific candidate seeking the party nomination.

### Primary Elections versus General Elections

The winner of a political party's primary next moves on to compete in the **general election** as that party's candidate. General elections see candidates from two or more political parties vie for elected office. These elections are interparty elections in which voters choose among several candidates representing different political parties and independent candidates. The winner of the general election wins office, for example, as governor, member of the state legislature, or judge.

In Texas, primary elections, in most instances, are direct primaries. Political parties use direct primaries to nominate candidates for all state offices, plus the U.S. House of Representatives and the U.S. Senate. In the presidential primaries, Texas and many other states use an indirect primary to nominate candidates. An alternative to the indirect primary is the caucus. In some states, parties are allowed to pick how their delegates are selected. In Texas, the two major parties must use a primary election. In 2008, however, the Texas Democratic Party adopted an unusual system, called the "Texas Two-Step," to select delegates to the party's national convention, which is responsible for nominating the party's presidential candidate. The Texas Two-Step involved a traditional preference, or indirect, primary held in early March. The preference primary was used to choose 126 delegates for the national convention. However, an additional sixty-seven delegates were selected through a caucus system that began at the precinct level on the evening of the primary. These caucuses essentially were precinct conventions. Over 3,000 delegates chosen at the precinct level moved on to county-level caucuses, which in turn chose delegates to district-level caucuses. Finally, results were aggregated at the state convention where those final sixty-seven delegates for the national convention were selected. This process took several months to complete. The Democrats used a similar system in 2012 but eliminated the precinct-level conventions, relying on county-level caucuses only. Republicans selected their delegates using a preference primary only. Details on the caucus system are found in the Texas versus Iowa Box in Chapter 10.

Three types of primaries exist: closed primaries, open primaries, and blanket or wide-open primaries. A **closed primary** restricts the voters who participate in the primary to party loyalists. Typically, prior to the primary, often when registering to vote, each individual voter must declare or list a party affiliation. At the primary, when a voter shows up to cast a ballot, the voter's name is checked against a list of registered party supporters. Obviously, this approach limits the number of voters in the primary to those willing to specify a party affiliation, thereby excluding independent voters and those affiliated with another political party. An advantage of the closed primary is the fact that candidates who win the party nomination more closely reflect the beliefs and ideas of the party faithful. On the flip side, candidates may not reflect the beliefs of the entire electorate because independent voters and supporters of other political parties are excluded from voting. A closed, enforced primary ensures that only the registered party supporters vote in the primary. However, some states and localities use a closed, unenforced primary. In this case, although voters register with a specific party affiliation, at the actual primary election a voter's name is not checked against a list of registered party supporters. A voter may therefore be registered with the Democratic Party

**Preference primary**
a primary election in which voters indicate their choice to hold office, but the actual selection is left to the political party elites.

**General election**
an interparty election in which candidates from two or more political parties and independent candidates compete for actual political office.

**Closed primary**
an electoral contest restricted to party loyalists that excludes supporters of other political parties and independent voters.

but vote in the Republican Party primary, or vice versa. In states with closed primaries, political parties may hold their primaries on different days.

In an **open primary**, a voter is not required to declare a party affiliation. At the primary, the voter requests a specific party's ballot. The ballot contains only those candidates from the party that the voter requested. Once a voter participates in a specific party's primary, he or she is prohibited, usually by law, from participating in another party's primary. Like with closed primaries, in some states the parties may hold their open primaries on different days. Independent voters often prefer the open primary because they are allowed to participate in at least one party's primary. Moreover, cross-party voting often occurs because Republicans may vote in the Democratic Party primary and vice versa. Of course, if a Republican chooses to vote in the Democratic primary, that voter is then barred from participating in the Republican primary. Also, open primaries are more subject to manipulation. For example, if a Democratic Party candidate is running unopposed in the Democratic primary, party officials may encourage Democratic voters to show up for the Republican primary and help the most extreme or easiest-to-defeat candidate win the Republican nomination. Republicans may likewise engage in the same behavior in a Democratic primary.

A few states use the **blanket or wide-open primary**. In this system, voters do not register a party affiliation. At the primary, voters receive ballot papers containing the names of all candidates from all political parties running for office. Voters still may choose only one candidate per office, not one candidate per political party. In the partisan blanket primary, the Democratic Party candidate with the most votes moves on to the general election as the Democratic nominee, and the Republican candidate with the most votes competes in the general election as the Republican nominee. The same results hold true for any and all other parties holding primary elections. The states of Alaska and California required use of the partisan blanket primary until the U.S. Supreme Court in *California Democratic Party v. Jones* (2000) upheld the right of political parties to choose their own primary system, holding that the First Amendment's right to association took precedence.[38] From 1935 until 2004, the state of Washington also used the partisan blanket primary.

Louisiana pioneered the use of the nonpartisan blanket primary. This system is a bit different from the partisan blanket primary system. In Louisiana, the top two candidates, regardless of party affiliation, move on to the general election. In the 1970s and 1980s, a common outcome of the primary saw two Democrats competing in the general election, with no Republicans on the ballot. Another unusual aspect of Louisiana's system is the fact that if a candidate wins a majority of the vote in the primary election, the candidate wins the office and no general election ensues. In effect, the primary becomes a general election. Note that Louisiana only uses this primary system for state and local elections. In 2004, voters in Washington adopted an amendment to the state constitution to change their partisan system to a nonpartisan blanket primary like Louisiana's. More recently, California voters moved in opposition to the U.S. Supreme Court ruling in *California Democratic Party v. Jones* (2000) when they approved Proposition 14, also called the Top Two Candidates Open

**Open primary**
an electoral contest in which voters are not required to declare a party affiliation to participate but must request a specific party's ballot at the primary; voters are subsequently barred from participating in the other party's primary.

**Blanket or wide-open primary**
a primary in which voters do not register party affiliations and receive ballot papers containing the names of all candidates from all political parties running for office; usually voters may choose only one candidate per office rather than one candidate per political party.

# TEXAS VS OREGON

While Texas serves as a pioneer in early voting, Oregon followed a different path in encouraging voter turnout by allowing vote by mail. In the vote-by-mail system, the state of Oregon mails a ballot to every registered voter about two weeks before the election. At their leisure, voters mark the ballot and mail the ballot back in a special envelope. A voter may also deliver the ballot by hand to designated locations throughout the state.

Historically, states allowed voters to receive a ballot early and mail it back only for absentee voting. Absentee voting required that the voter provide a legitimate reason for not being in the community on Election Day in order to cast an early ballot. In 1981, Oregon allowed limited experiments with mail-in ballots for all voters in local elections. In December 1995, the state extended the process to party primaries. By 1998, all elections in Oregon utilized the vote-by-mail system. One review of the research on the impact of voting by mail suggests that voter turnout increases between 5 to 10 percent over traditional in-person voting.[i]

The table to the right presents some statistics comparing turnout in Texas to turnout in Oregon since voting by mail became a statewide process in 1998.

## THINKING Critically

★ What is vote by mail?

★ How is the vote-by-mail system similar to early voting in Texas?

★ Do you think a vote-by-mail system would help boost voter turnout in Texas?

★ Have you ever voted with early voting in Texas?

★ Would you be more likely to vote if you could vote by mail?

---

i. Paul Gronke and Peter Miller, "Voting by Mail and Turnout: A Replication and Extension," paper presented at the Annual Meeting of the American Political Science Association, Chicago, Illinois, August 20, 2007.

## Voter Turnout in Oregon and Texas

| Election | Oregon Turnout | Texas Turnout |
|---|---|---|
| 2000 Presidential election | 65% | 44% |
| 2002 November general election | 51% | 29% |
| 2004 Presidential election | 71% | 46% |
| 2006 November general election | 52% | 26% |
| 2008 Presidential election | 66% | 46% |
| 2010 November general election | 52% | 27% |
| 2012 Presidential election | 59% | 43% |

**Sources:** Texas Secretary of State, "Turnout and Voter Registration Figures (1970–Current)," 2012, www.sos.state.tx.us/elections/historical/70-92.shtml; Oregon Secretary of State, "Statistical Summary 2010 General Election," 2010, www.oregonvotes.gov/doc/history/nov22010/g2010stats.pdf; Oregon Secretary of State, "Statistical Summary 2008 General Election," 2008, www.oregonvotes.gov/doc/history/nov42008/g08stats.pdf; Oregon Secretary of State, "Statistic Summary 2006 General Election," 2006, www.oregonvotes.gov/doc/history/nov72006/g06stats.pdf; Oregon Secretary of State, "Statistical Summary 2004 General Election," 2004, www.oregonvotes.gov/doc/history/nov22004/g04stats.pdf; Oregon Secretary of State, "Statistical Summary 2002 General Election," 2002, www.oregonvotes.gov/doc/history/nov52002/g02stats.pdf; Oregon Secretary of State, "Statistical Summary 2000 General Election," 2000, www.oregonvotes.gov/doc/history/nov72000/genstats.pdf (all Web sites accessed on September 8, 2014); some calculations made by authors.

---

Primary Act and Voter-Nominated Offices, in June 2010. This ballot measure amends the California Constitution to require the use of the nonpartisan blanket primary in state and many local elections. To get around the ruling in the *Jones* case from 2000, the state of California now considers the nomination of candidates through the primary process a voter-led process, not a function of the political parties.[39] In doing so, the ability of political parties to control the nomination process is stripped from them. A legal challenge to the new system failed in federal district court in late 2010, and the system was first used in California's June 2012 primaries. Thus, California has adopted the nonpartisan blanket primary of Louisiana. Similarly, after Washington State adopted the nonpartisan blanket primary in 2004, a 2008 U.S. Supreme Court case upheld its use in that state.

Currently, Texas's primary system is technically a closed one, as required by state law. In practice, however, Texas's system is considered semi-open.[40] The designation semi-open is appropriate because, as in an open primary, voters in Texas do not have to declare a party affiliation when registering to vote. However, the system becomes functionally closed on the day of the primary election because when a voter requests a specific party's ballot at the primary, this information is recorded and in some counties even stamped on voter registration cards at the time. For the next year, the voters cannot change party affiliation and vote in the regular primary or runoff primary of another party. If the next primary occurs within one year, a voter is forced to vote in the same party's primary as before. If the voter requests another party's primary ballot, he or she is still given the ballot for the party from the earlier primary. Electronic record keeping has enhanced the ability of local election officials and party election monitors to enforce this provision.

Another interesting requirement in Texas is that the winner of a political party's primary election must receive a majority of the vote—50 percent plus one additional vote—in the primary election. If the leading candidate does not receive a majority in the initial primary election, a **runoff election** is held a month later between the first- and second-place candidates in that party's initial primary election. In this way, the Texas primary system becomes essentially a single-member district majority (SMDM) election system, as described in Chapter 3. In the case of primaries, the use of SMDM means that the winner receives the right to run as the political party's candidate in the general election. Simply put, candidates must receive a majority of the political party's primary votes, not just the most votes.

The history of primaries in Texas is riddled with political manipulation to produce certain outcomes. In an effort to stave off defection to the Republican Party as national Democratic Party leaders began to emphasize civil rights legislation in the 1950s, election reforms in 1951–1952 allowed **cross-filing**. In cross-filing, a candidate may run simultaneously as a Democratic candidate and as a Republican, essentially competing in both parties' primaries.[41] This tactic allowed Democrats to maintain control of the Republican Party as it held its first presidential primary election in Texas. Democratic voters were able to cross over to support Republican candidate Dwight Eisenhower for U.S. president, all the while ensuring that state and local candidates who won the Republican primary were also loyal Democrats. Republicans labeled these Democratic voters "One-Day Republicans."[42] This practice seems unusual, but as recently as 1948 Texas Republicans approached prominent Democrats, including candidates for governor, and requested that they run as Republicans.[43] Note that some states today allow a related practice called electoral fusion, in which more than one party nominates the same candidate in the general election and the candidate carries both party labels on the election ballot.

**Runoff election**
a type of election in SMDM that is held when an election fails to yield a clear majority winner in the initial balloting; the runoff is limited to the top two vote-getters from the initial election, ensuring a majority win.

**Cross-filing**
a system that allows a candidate to run simultaneously as a Democratic and a Republican candidate, essentially competing in both parties' primaries.

## Direct Democracy Elections

A final type of election is the direct democracy election, which emerged during the era of the Progressive reforms. At the state level, three of the Progressive Party's ideas associated with direct democracy and voter input into the decision-making process have been adopted: the referendum, the initiative, and the recall. Opening the political system through direct democracy elections was promoted by Progressives in the early twentieth century as a method to break the power of organized interests, labor unions, and big business and return the power of the average citizen-voter.

Normally, a law is passed by having the state legislature approve a bill; the bill is then signed by the governor to become a law. In a referendum, the state legislature proposes a new law and places it on an election ballot. At the next election, citizens vote statewide to determine whether the new law is adopted or rejected. Thirty-one states use the referendum for approving new laws.[44] Texas lacks this referendum process to enact laws. Another use of the referendum, as discussed in Chapter 2, is to approve formal amendments to a state constitution. In this instance, a state legislature submits the amendment to the voters of the state for approval. Forty-nine states, including Texas, require that amendments to the state's constitution be approved by voters through this second use of referenda.

Another way to get citizens directly involved in lawmaking is the initiative. An initiative takes shape when citizens propose a new law by writing it out and then collecting the signatures of registered voters who support the law on an initiative petition form. When a set number of registered voters, which varies by state, has signed the form, the form is submitted to the state's chief elections officer for certification. Once certified, the proposed new law is placed on an election ballot for voters statewide to accept or reject. Sometimes the initiative petition is called simply a proposition. Like the referendum, states use the initiative petition to propose new laws or to amend the state constitution. Twenty-four states allow the initiative petition,[45] but Texas is not one of them.

The recall petition serves as a method for removing a sitting elected official before his or her term of office has finished. The recall operates in a manner similar to a petition: A specified number of signatures is collected on a petition calling for immediate removal of an elected official from office. Once enough signatures have been gathered, the petition is submitted to the state's chief elections officer for certification. Following the certification, voters at the next election determine whether the official remains in office. Eighteen states allow the recall petition for elected officials. Texas does not. However, local officials in Texas may be recalled in some cities and other local governments depending on the locality's plan of government and the Texas Local Government Code. The limited use of direct democracy elections reflects two realities of Texas politics. First, the Texas Constitution of 1876 predated the rise of the Progressive movement and its championing of direct democracy. Yet the lack of citizen and voter inclusion maintains the Texas tradition of limiting political input by those deemed less important by political elites.

# HOW TEXAS GOVERNMENT WORKS

## Voter Turnout

*Texas has the second largest Hispanic eligible voter population with 4.2 million. Voter turnout in the 2008 and 2010 elections fell below the national average.*

### Population and Electorate in the United States and Texas

| | Total Population | Total Eligible Voter Population | Percent Eligible Voter Population | Percent Who Cast Ballot in: 2008 Election* | 2010 Election* |
|---|---|---|---|---|---|
| **United States** | 309,350,000 | 214,972,000 | 69.5% | 53.3% | 37.0% |
| **Texas** | 25,257,000 | 15,856,000 | 62.8% | 46.1% | 26.0% |

## Characteristics of Eligible Voters

### Age

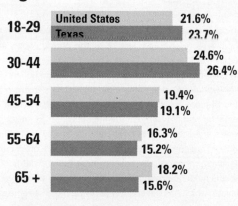

| | United States | Texas |
|---|---|---|
| 18-29 | 21.6% | 23.7% |
| 30-44 | 24.6% | 26.4% |
| 45-54 | 19.4% | 19.1% |
| 55-64 | 16.3% | 15.2% |
| 65 + | 18.2% | 15.6% |

### Gender

| | United States | Texas |
|---|---|---|
| Male | 48.2% | 48.6% |
| Female | 51.8% | 51.4% |

### Type of Citizen

| | United States | Texas |
|---|---|---|
| By Birth | 92.2% | 91.9% |
| Naturalized | 7.8% | 8.1% |

Source: Pew Hispanic Center, "Latinos in the 2012 Election: Texas," October 1, 2012, www.pewhispanic.org/files/2012/10/TX-election-factsheet.pdf.
* United States Census Bureau, Elections: Voting-Age Population and Voter Participation, Table 398: Resident Population of Voting Age and Percent Casting Votes--States,"
The 2012 Statistical Abstract, www.census.gov/compendia/statab/cats/elections/voting-age_population_and_voter_participation.html.

# TEXAS ⓋⓈ LOUISIANA

The nonpartisan blanket primary system used in Louisiana often seems attractive to voters from outside the state. The system differs from the closed primary by allowing independent and third-party voters to participate in the primary election because voters do not need to register a political party affiliation. In addition, the nonpartisan blanket primary differs from the traditional open primary in that voters do not have to choose a specific political party's primary in which to participate. Instead, a registered voter simply arrives at the polling place on Election Day and receives a ballot with all of the candidates from all of the political parties with all offices to be chosen listed. Here, voters can maximize cross-party voting by, for example, choosing a Republican for president, a Democrat for U.S. senator, a Libertarian for U.S. House of Representatives, and so forth. This ability to cross-party vote by office, which is impossible in other types of primaries because the ballot contains only candidates from a specific political party, is attractive to many voters. Since all registered voters may participate in the primary, proponents maintain that the system should produce more centrist or moderate candidates. This ability to produce such candidates was important in the California campaign to adopt the nonpartisan blanket primary.[i] After all, by restricting the ballot to registered party supporters, the closed primary essentially limits participation to conservative or right-of-center voters in the Republican primary and liberal or left-of-center voters in the Democratic primary. Independent voters are forced to choose a side or stay at home.

Does the nonpartisan blanket primary in Louisiana produce centrist or moderate candidates that reflect the views of the entire electorate rather than those of a smaller number of partisan voters? Fortunately, evidence is readily available in the form of elections results from Louisiana. In fact, results from Louisiana's elections for governor suggest that Louisiana's primary system does not necessarily produce centrist or moderate officeholders. For example, in 1991, the centrist incumbent governor Buddy Roemer, a one-time Democrat who became a Republican, received 27 percent of the vote to finish third in a twelve-candidate field. Roemer's third-place finish meant he was eliminated. In second place, with 32 percent of the vote, was David Duke.[ii] Duke, a former member of the state legislature and once grand wizard of the Knights of the Ku Klux Klan, was clearly more extremist than Roemer. Edwin Edwards, a former state governor who had been indicted and tried several times for a variety of violations of federal racketeering laws, finished in first place with 34 percent of the vote. Edwards and Duke moved on to the general election in November. Edwards defeated Duke with 61 percent of the vote.

Courtesy Louisiana Secretary of State Tom Schedler

Another example is the 1987 gubernatorial election. In that race, Edwin Edwards received 28 percent of the primary vote, and Buddy Roemer, then a Democrat, received 33 percent. While Roemer went on to become governor, third place in the primary went to Robert Livingston, the only Republican candidate, who received 18 percent of the vote.[iii] The fourth-place finish of W. J. "Billy" Tauzin, at the time a conservative Democrat and now a moderate Republican, is interesting because Tauzin was arguably more centrist than either Edwards or Livingston. The evidence suggests that centrist candidates are often crowded out in Louisiana's primary system by more extreme candidates. Simply put, centrist and moderate candidates, if sufficient in number, can split the middle vote, which has the effect of allowing more extreme candidates to get just enough votes to move on to the general election.

Note in both of the above cases the top two candidates did not receive a majority of the votes within their political party. What mattered was finishing in one of the top two positions. Hypothetically, a six-candidate race in which the candidates evenly split the votes could produce a result in which the top two candidates move on to the general election having received no more than 16 or 17 percent of the vote. Compare this with Texas's semi-open system in which the Republican and Democratic candidates moving on to the general election must have received a majority of the votes in their respective political party's primary.

The 2007 election of Louisiana's current governor, Bobby Jindal, illustrates another interesting feature of the state's primary system. (A sample ballot from the 2007 blanket primary election for governor is pictured above.) Jindal received 54 percent of the vote in the primary election. Under Louisiana's system, by winning a majority of the vote, Jindal automatically became governor. A general election for governor was not needed. Yet no other Republican candidates ran that year, while five Democratic candidates, one Libertarian, and four other candidates did. Democratic fracturing in the wake of embattled incumbent Democrat Kathleen Blanco's decision not to run for reelection handed the Republicans control of the governorship at the primary. Of course, with 54 percent of the vote, Jindal legitimately represented the majority of Louisiana voters at the time.

**THINKING** *Critically*

★ What are the advantages to Louisiana's nonpartisan blanket primary?

★ Why do you think people in California or Texas might be attracted to this system?

★ What are the advantages to Texas's current semi-open system? (See text for details on Texas's system.)

★ Which system do you prefer?

i. John Howard, "Voters Approve Prop. 14, 'Open Primary,'" *Sacramento Capitol Weekly*, June 8, 2010, http://capitolweekly.net/voters-approve-prop-14-open-primary/ (accessed September 27, 2014).

ii. Louisiana Secretary of State, "Election Results," http://electionresults.sos.louisiana.gov/graphical# (accessed August 10, 2010).

iii. Ibid.

## Too Much Democracy?

In Texas's general elections, voters are confronted with the long ballot, one Progressive era reform adopted by Texas that made as many state and local offices as possible subject to direct election by the voters. The long ballot is so called because it is just that—long. A long ballot may contain choices for all of the following: the governor, the lieutenant governor, the comptroller of public accounts, the commissioner of the General Land Office, the commissioner of agriculture, the attorney general, a state senator, a state representative, a member of the U.S. House of Representatives, a U.S. senator, members of the Railroad Commission of Texas, members of the Texas Board of Education, a justice of the peace, county commissioners, county tax assessors, a mayor, members of the city council, city judges, county judges, and state court judges (including district court, appeals court, and the two high courts). All of this is quite an undertaking.

The sheer number of elected offices and candidates running for office means that voters are often overwhelmed at the polling place. One result is that voters tend to vote for the offices that appear higher on the ballot, while ignoring and leaving blank offices that are farther down. When doing so, voters typically vote for the most "important" offices, such as the U.S. president, state governor, or U.S. senator, and leave "lesser" offices at the county and local levels blank. This phenomenon is called **roll off**.[46] For example, in 2010, the total number of votes cast for the statewide race for governor equaled almost 45,000 more than the total number of votes cast for lieutenant governor, a difference of 0.9 percent. More dramatic results occurred down the ballot. There were over 1 million fewer votes, or approximately 20 percent fewer votes, for comptroller of public accounts compared with the vote for governor. Similar trends occur during presidential elections. In 2012, over 95,000 fewer votes were cast for U.S. senator compared to the number of votes cast for U.S. president—a difference of approximately 1.1 percent. Farther down the ballot, over 1,925,000 fewer votes were cast for Place 2 on the Supreme Court of Texas compared with the votes for U.S. president—a difference of 24.2 percent. In that 2012 election, voters also filled positions on the Texas

**Roll off**
process in which voters mark off only the "more important" offices on a lengthy ballot—usually national or statewide offices—and leave the county or local office choices blank.

Court of Criminal Appeals, the state's highest criminal appeals court; the total number of votes varied by 1.6 million between the three positions. Over 21 percent of voters rolled off the ballot between selecting a candidate for the presiding judge position and the third position to be elected to the court.

Another effect of the long ballot is **party-line voting**, also known as straight-ticket voting (see Chapter 5). Party-line voting occurs when a voter selects candidates on the basis of his or her party affiliation; that is, the voter records a vote for all Democratic candidates or all Republican candidates. In this way, the voter avoids having to make tough decisions on an office-by-office or candidate-by-candidate basis.

The advantage of the long ballot is, of course, greater accountability of elected officials to the voters in the state, county, city, or other agency of state government. However, the long ballot, if used as intended by the Progressives, requires that voters ignore partisanship as a guide to selecting a candidate in the election. Instead, voters are expected to be well informed about all candidates and issues in the election, selecting wisely the most qualified candidate or the candidate with views closest to the voter's. Such expectations may be unrealistic given the sheer number of races to be decided on a lengthy ballot. Voters may tend to rely on heuristics, or "short cuts," to aid them in making their choices.[47] Short cuts include use of party labels,[48] name recognition, and ideology. Overall, the increase in the number of elected offices contributes to voter fatigue and raises the costs of voting. The unintended consequence is fewer voters turning out on Election Day.

## VOTING, VOTER REGISTRATION, AND TURNOUT

National elections are required by federal law to be held on the first Tuesday following the first Monday in November. State and local elections in Texas are also typically held on a Tuesday, and polls are open from 7:00 a.m. to 7:00 p.m. While these hours might seem extensive, in fact, for many people who work from 8:00 a.m. until 5:00 p.m., with time needed for commuting to and from work, these hours may not be enough. To help Texans turn out to vote, Texas began in 1988 to experiment with **advanced or early voting**, which allows a voter to cast a ballot before an election without giving a specific reason. Historically, to cast a ballot before Election Day a voter had to qualify for an absentee ballot by documenting a specific reason for being absent on Election Day: for example, being on vacation, being on a business trip, or being away at college. In early voting, the local elections administrator opens polling to voters during specified times and days in the weeks leading up to the election. In Texas, early voting days include weekends. Voting is made easier and occurs at the leisure of the voter, who can now avoid a hectic workday scramble to get to the voting booth before it closes on Election Day. Texas was an early adopter of such voting; its experiences and those of a handful of other states led to the expansion of early voting nationwide, and many states now have some form of it. As shown in Figure 9.1, early voting has become quite popular in Texas, especially in presidential election years. In 2014, more than 2.5 million Texans took advantage of early voting, down slightly from the 2010 statewide, midterm elections.

**Party-line voting**
process in which voters select candidates by their party affiliation.

**Advanced or early voting**
a voting system that allows a voter to cast a ballot before an election without giving a specific reason, thus making voting more convenient for the voter.

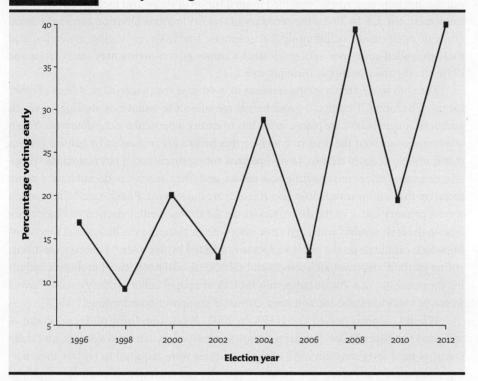

**FIGURE 9.1** **Early Voting in Texas, 1996–2012**

*Percentage voting early* (y-axis)

*Election year* (x-axis): 1996, 1998, 2000, 2002, 2004, 2006, 2008, 2010, 2012

*Source:* Compiled by the authors based on data available from the Texas Secretary of State, "Early Voting Information," www.sos.state.tx.us/elections/historical/earlyvotinginfo.shtml (accessed September 8, 2014).

## Electronic Voting in Texas

Not only do the state and federal government want to make it easier for voters to get to the polls, they want to ensure that the votes cast are accurately counted. In the wake of the 2000 presidential election, which saw a large number of irregularities in the state of Florida, Congress acted to create a single national standard for election procedures for presidential and congressional elections by passing the **Help America Vote Act (HAVA)** in 2002. Ultimately, many states and local governments began adapting procedures for nonfederal elections to comply with the HAVA simply because those elections are often held simultaneously with federal elections. Therefore, the act has had the effect of standardizing procedures for all elections to office—federal, state, and local—and in so doing has given the national government a degree of control in states' election affairs.

The HAVA mandates that all polling stations utilize electronic voting equipment and have at least one voting booth that is accessible for those with a disability. It also requires that state and local voting officials conduct educational activities and equipment demonstrations to allow voters to become familiar with the electronic voting equipment. While the act does not specify the exact equipment to be used, standards

**Help America Vote Act (HAVA)**
federal statute enacted after the 2000 presidential election to effectively standardize election procedures.

have nevertheless been set for the equipment. Congress, recognizing the expense of purchasing new equipment, provided limited funds to states and local governments to implement the act. In Texas, the secretary of state's Elections Division certified several types of equipment, including optical scanners, touch-screen voting machines, and dial-controlled computer voting (eSlates). County governments may select from one of four companies to supply the equipment.

The shift to electronic voting is meant to overcome the perceived problems of other forms of balloting. Traditional paper ballots are subject to ballot-box stuffing, in which additional paper ballots are placed in the box to ensure a particular candidate wins. When questions arise about the final vote totals, paper ballots are recounted by hand, a process that is not particularly reliable. Lever-operated voting machines, if not maintained properly, can cause errors in tabulating vote results, and these machines do not have a paper record of the vote for comparison later if results are questioned. Punch-card ballots, which were a primary cause of the difficulties in the 2000 presidential election in Florida, are among the least reliable, with high error rates both in counting the ballots and determining which candidate on the ballot was actually selected by the voter.[49] However, electronic voting methods, such as touch screens and eSlates, are also not without problems, including the possibility of software tampering, the lack of a paper ballot to verify results,[50] errors in saving votes to a database, and voter distrust of computer-based voting.[51]

When Congress passed the HAVA in 2002, about one-third of Texas's counties still used the paper ballot. Fourteen counties employed punch-card systems, and three counties used lever machines. All of these counties were required to replace their voting equipment with electronic systems. In 2000, the majority of counties employed optical scanners. With optical scanners, a voter marks a ballot, the ballot is scanned, and the results are added by the scanner's software to the database. Although optical scanners were allowed to continue under the HAVA, counties using them were still mandated to have at least one eSlate or touch-screen system available at each polling place for those with disabilities. The passage of the HAVA, then, meant that almost all of Texas's 254 counties needed to upgrade their equipment, with a substantial proportion of them needing to replace their equipment entirely.[52]

The cost of these upgrades has been high. Estimates from the Texas secretary of state's office suggest that more than $170 million was needed to comply with the HAVA.[53] Funds were made available to counties from the state based upon a formula that included the number of voting precincts and the voting-age-eligible population. Loving County, the smallest in population, with only fifty-four age-eligible voters at the time, received $27,000 in 2003 and $40,000 in 2004. Implementation of the HAVA in Harris County, with its almost 2.5 million voters, cost over $6 million in 2003 and $12 million in 2004. In the trade-off between ensuring the accuracy of the vote and the need to fund elections, Congress chose ensuring accuracy but passed most of the cost onto states and local governments. The limited funds provided by Congress were nowhere near the total cost to states and local governments to purchase the new voting equipment. Again, the role of the national government in promoting change in Texas elections becomes evident. The transition to electronic voting resulted from laws passed by the U.S. Congress.

## Contemporary Voter Registration and Turnout

The measures discussed above are all directed at making voting easier. The health of democracy is often measured, correctly or incorrectly, by using participation in elections as a benchmark. To some extent, this approach makes sense because efforts at civic education often stress voting as the "best" or "most important" form of having one's voice heard. The denial of the right to vote to African Americans has placed additional focus on exercising one's right to vote. Finally, elections are essential to concepts of modern representative democracy, thus turnout is important to ensuring representation.

Figure 9.2 tracks the rate of voter registration from 1970–2014 among the age-eligible population in the state of Texas. Beginning in 1974 and continuing into the 1990s, the rate of registration remained relatively stable, hovering in the low- to mid-60 percent range for most of the period. Registration peaked during presidential elections. From a high of 71.2 percent in the wake of the Watergate scandal in 1976, participation trended downward, reaching 70 percent in 1984. In 1994, the trend was toward higher rates of voter registration, leveling off in the low 80-percent range by the mid-2000s. Why did voter registration spike in the mid- to late 1990s? One important explanation is the impact of the 1993 Motor Voter Act. In addition, the implementation of online voter registration forms made access to registration easier for many potential new voters, leading to potentially higher registration rates. The advent of some new technologies, such as computerized databases, and better training of local election officials influenced the rates of voter registration as well. However, in recent years, voter registration has declined, falling by 2010 to about 70 percent. This trend may only reflect the improved ability to update and purge voter registration records. By 2014, the rate of registration increased slightly to 74.1 percent.

Another important consideration during elections is **voter turnout**. In Texas, voter turnout, or the number of people actually casting ballots in an election, resembles trends from across the United States. Voter turnout tends to be higher in presidential election years than in off-year, mid-term elections. Moreover, special elections and local elections tend to have very low levels of voter turnout.

Voter turnout is calculated one of two ways: as the percentage of ballots cast in the election based upon (1) the total number of registered voters or (2) the total population

Voters in San Antonio wait in line to cast their ballots. Long waits are more common in presidential elections, when voter turnout is higher, than in midterm elections, primaries, or special elections.

**Voter turnout**
the number of people casting ballots in a given election.

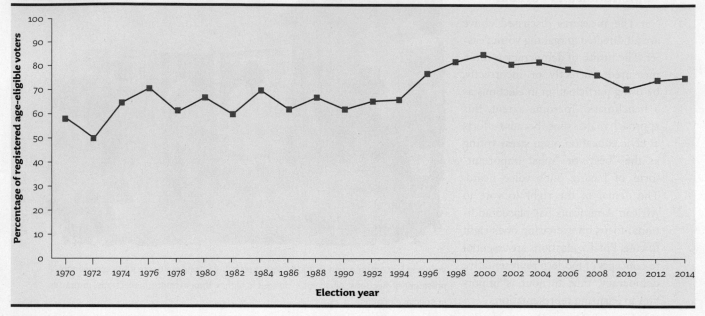

## FIGURE 9.2   Rate of Voter Registration, 1970–2014

*Source:* Compiled by the authors based on data from the Texas Secretary of State, "Turnout and Voter Registration Figures (1970–Current)," www.sos.state.tx.us/elections/historical/70-92.shtml (accessed September 8, 2014).

aged eighteen and over (the voting-age-eligible population). Often, government officials like to report turnout based on the first method, in part because rates of turnout are inflated when using it. Obviously, the total number of registered voters is normally lower than the total number of people who are of eligible voting age.

This issue of using registered voters or the age-eligible population to determine turnout is important when comparing voter turnout rates over time or across states. States sometimes change the eligibility requirements; for example, southern states, such as Texas, have clearly manipulated registration requirements to exclude African Americans, as discussed earlier. Also, registration processes and voter eligibility vary from state to state. North Dakota, as noted earlier, lacks any form of registration, so that anyone showing up on Election Day with a valid state driver's license or other proof of residency is allowed to vote. In neighboring Minnesota, voters are allowed to register to vote up to and on Election Day. These differences produce variations in the percentage of the age-eligible population that is registered to vote.

Thus, the more accurate figure, especially for comparison purposes, is to use the total population eighteen and over (the voting-age-eligible population). In general, voter turnout among the age-eligible population hovers in the 40 to 50 percent range for presidential elections but declines to the high 20- or low 30-percent range for midterm, off-year elections. Recent elections have adhered to these trends. In 2012, 58.4 percent of registered voters and 43.6 percent of age-eligible voters turned out for the election.[54] Interestingly, the gap between turnout among the age-eligible population and actual registered voters narrowed between 1992 and 2004. This narrowing of the gap between turnout and age-eligible population reflects the trend toward increased voter registration, whether as a result of the Motor Voter Act, ease of online registration, improvements in database management, or some other cause. Since 2004, the gap has grown wider again.

What about voter turnout in special elections? Figure 9.3 shows the trends in voter turnout in special elections in Texas since 1977. With the exceptions of the May and June elections of 1993, all other special statewide elections since 1977 concerned amendments to the Texas Constitution. In general, voter turnout in special elections is quite low, never reaching higher than 35 percent of registered voters or 20 percent of age-eligible voters. Two of the three most recent special elections, in 2003 and 2005, saw slight increases in the rate of turnout compared to earlier elections. In subsequent special elections in 2007 and 2009, the rate of voter turnout fell to around 5 percent. In 2013, 6.1 percent of age eligible voters cast ballots in the special election to amend the state constitution.

## FIGURE 9.3 Turnout in Texas Special Elections, 1977–2013

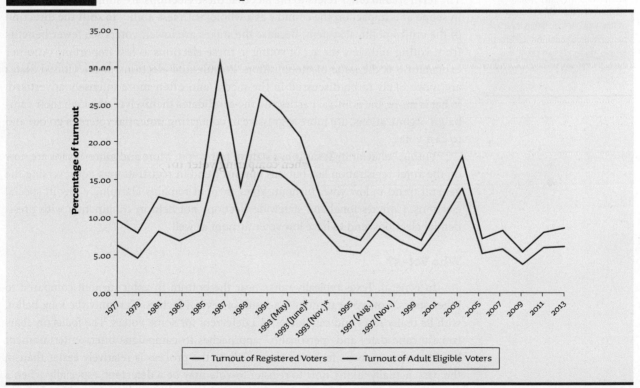

**Source:** Compiled by the authors from data available from the Texas Secretary of State, "Election Results," www.sos.state.tx.us/elections/historical/index .shtml (accessed September 8, 2014).

**Note:** The June 1993 election was a runoff for the U.S. Senate, a constitutional election occurred in November 1993.

The 2005 special election involved a series of constitutional amendments, including a controversial proposal involving the definition of marriage. This amendment energized social conservatives who supported the language of the amendment, which limited marriage to a union between a man and a woman. However, many opponents, including gay and lesbian organizations, were also mobilized to vote to prevent passage of the amendment. Their efforts failed, however, and the amendment passed with 76.3 percent of the vote. The controversial nature of this amendment explains in part the increase in voter turnout that year. Normally, the amendments are largely noncontroversial, often technical changes to the Texas Constitution. As a result, turnout is low. The 2013 election was an example of this, with nine amendments on the ballot, including the elimination of the state medical board, adding exemptions to state ad valorem taxes, and creating a state water implementation fund.

So why is voter turnout typically higher for presidential elections than for midterm elections for governor, members of the U.S. House of Representatives, and the state legislature, and why do mid-term elections in turn have higher voter turnouts than special elections? One answer lies in what scholars who compare elections across different countries refer to as **second-order elections**.[55] Second-order elections are elections for offices other than the national executive in presidential systems like the United States' or the national legislature in parliamentary systems like Great Britain's. The term *second order* refers to the fact that these elections are simply less important in scope and impact on the country as a whole, with less ability to shift the direction of the entire political system. Because the stakes are lower, voters see fewer benefits from voting and view the act of voting in these elections as less important. Another explanation is the issue of mobilization. Presidential elections in the United States are more likely to be discussed in the media and often more intensely advertised. What is more, the political parties and the candidates themselves, through their campaign organizations, are more aggressive in contacting potential voters to go out and to cast votes.

Voting behavior in Texas is in a state of transition. More and more Texans are now on the voter registration list, but this upward trend in registration is not reversing the general trend in low voter turnout. Voter turnout remains alarmingly low in special elections. Congressional and statewide elections not held in conjunction with presidential elections tend to have low voter turnout as well.

**Second-order elections** elections for offices below the national executive level in countries with presidential systems like the United States' or the national legislature level in parliamentary countries like Great Britain; generally viewed as less important in scope and impact on a country.

### Who Votes?

In general, Texas typically ranks near the bottom in voter turnout compared to other states. Low voter turnout is a result of several factors. Certainly the long ballot, with its many races and candidates, is a deterrent for some voters. The focus on charismatic candidates and "personality" approaches to campaigns offers entertainment but little serious focus for some voters. While the process is relatively easier than in the past, actually taking time to register to vote may be a deterrent, especially when a potential voter realizes that the list of registered voters is used by state and local courts to call people for jury duty. Lower turnout is also a result of Texas's traditionalistic political culture, which tends to cast a negative view on politics and political life in

## TABLE 9.1 Voter Turnout Rates across Demographic Groups in the 2012 Presidential Election

| Characteristic | Texas | United States | Minnesota | Hawaii |
|---|---|---|---|---|
| **Sex** | | | | |
| Men | 43.4% | 54.4% | 68.9% | 45.7% |
| Women | 49.2% | 58.5% | 72.0% | 49.1% |
| **Race/Ethnicity** | | | | |
| White, non-Hispanic | 59.8% | 63.0% | 74.0% | 67.6% |
| African American | 61.1% | 62.0% | 49.2% | N/A |
| Asian | 23.8% | 31.3% | 56.2% | 43.7% |
| Hispanic | 27.7% | 31.8% | 32.5% | 31.4% |
| **Age** | | | | |
| 18–24 | 22.5% | 38.0% | 57.0% | 22.1% |
| 25–44 | 37.8% | 49.5% | 63.8% | 36.6% |
| 45–64 | 55.6% | 63.4% | 76.6% | 57.0% |
| 65–74 | 69.9% | 71.1% | 81.5% | 59.1% |
| 75+ | 68.1% | 67.9% | 79.2% | 63.4% |

**Sources:** U.S. Census Bureau, *Current Population Survey*, "Reported Voting and Registration by Sex, Race, and Hispanic Origin, for States, November 2012," table 4b, www.census.gov/hhes/www/socdemo/voting/publications/p20/2012/Table04b.xls (accessed September 8, 2014); U.S. Census Bureau, "Reported Voting and Registration of the Total Voting-Age Population, by Age, for States: November 2012," table 4c, www.census.gov/hhes/www/socdemo/voting/publications/p20/2012/Table04c.xls (accessed September 8, 2014).

**Note:** N/A = Not available.

general; the state's strain of extreme individualism can make voting seem more of a chore than a right to be exercised. Finally, the relatively weak organizational nature of Texas's political parties limits their ability to mobilize voters. We will return to this theme in Chapter 10.

The rate of turnout in Texas is not consistent across demographic groupings such as race/ethnicity, gender, and age. To illustrate these differences, the 2012 presidential election provides an example of the patterns of turnout in an election in Texas. Table 9.1 provides comparisons between Texas, the U.S. average, Minnesota, and Hawaii. Minnesota had the highest turnout in 2012, and Texas had the lowest.

Note the differences in the rates of voter turnout between various demographic groups. For example, men are less likely to vote than women at the national level. That trend holds in each of the three states in the comparison. Non-Hispanic whites typically voted more than other ethnic groups. These trends are consistent with national trends on turnout by gender and ethnic group. However, the presence of Barack Obama on the presidential ballot energized the African American community, and many communities and states saw significant gains in African American voter turnout in 2008 and 2012.

Throughout the United States and in Texas, voter turnout varies considerably by age group. The youngest voters, ages 18–24, consistently vote at levels much below the national or state average. While some improvement occurs in the 25–44 age bracket, the highest rates of voting occur among those over the age of 45, especially among those in the 65–74 age bracket. The trends in the 2012 election were consistent with prior presidential elections. These differences in turnout by age level are important. Older Americans' propensity to vote leads candidates and parties to address disproportionately the concerns of older voters relative to those of younger voters.

Low voter turnout has consequences for Texas politics. Assuming there are differences in the policy preferences, party identifications, and other characteristics of voting behavior between the various ethnic groups, low voter turnout among African American and Hispanic voters in Texas means that fewer government decisions reflect these groups' beliefs. Similarly, government decision makers are less responsive to the concerns of younger voters because, as a group, younger voters tend to vote less. In addition, lower turnout among various ethnic groups reduces the likelihood that minority candidates are elected to office. As a result, the system is less representative of the population as a whole.

## ELECTORAL COMPETITION IN TEXAS ELECTIONS

As emphasized at the beginning of this chapter, who gets on the ballot is an important aspect of elections. Elections imply choice and, ideally, ideological diversity as well as demographic variety among the candidates. Everyone running for office in the state of Texas must be a resident of Texas and of the relevant election district. A candidate must also be registered to vote. Beyond these requirements, getting on the ballot as a candidate results from one of two processes: nomination by a political party or qualifying as an independent candidate.

For candidates running with a party nomination, the candidate gets on the ballot either by competing in and winning a primary election or being selected from a party convention. Political parties that won 20 percent or more of the vote in the last governor's election must hold primary elections. To qualify for the primary election, a candidate must pay a filing fee. The filing fee varies from $5,000 for a candidate for U.S. senator to $300 for candidates for the state board of education. In lieu of paying the filing fee, candidates may qualify for a party primary by filing a petition with a set number of signatures from registered voters. This number varies from 5,000 signatures to the number of signatures equivalent to 2 percent of the vote in the governor's election in the state, county, or election district. If a political party receives 5 percent or more of the vote, but less than 20 percent, the party may use a primary election or nominating convention to place candidates on the general election ballot. However, the filing fee requirements remain in place. Parties with less than 5 percent of the vote in the most recent governor's election must first register with the secretary of state's office by collecting the signatures of registered voters who support the party. A party must secure enough signatures to equal 1 percent of the total votes for all candidates for governor at the last election.

An **independent candidate**, a candidate running for office without a political party affiliation or nomination, must submit an application for a place on the general election ballot. In addition, the candidate must gather signatures of registered voters willing to sign a petition that the candidate's name should appear on the ballot. The number of signatures needed varies from 1 to 5 percent of the total votes for all candidates for governor at the last election. If the independent candidate is running for a countywide office, the candidate needs to collect 1 to 5 percent of the total votes for governor in that county. Because they lack a party affiliation, independent candidates do not compete in primary elections in Texas. In fact, independent candidates cannot declare their intention to run for office until after primary elections are over and cannot have voters who participated in the primary elections sign the petition form that puts them on the ballot. Write-in candidates qualify by either paying a filing fee or, like independent candidates, completing a nomination petition. Once a candidate decides to run for a party nomination either by party primary or party convention, he or she cannot run as an independent candidate in the general election.

Even as Texas maintains its tradition of ballot access for major-party candidates, independent candidates, and write-in candidates, another tradition endures in the state, one whereby rules and procedures are used to make access to the ballot for minor-party candidates more challenging. The rule requiring minor parties to constantly reapply to have their party name and label on the ballot based upon statewide totals in the governor's election clearly favors the established Democratic and Republican parties. The hurdles put in place by Texas's ballot-access rules and procedures reflect the traditional political culture that dominates much of the state: a desire to keep the "wrong" kinds of candidates and political parties off the ballot. Denying access to the ballot to these candidates and political parties minimizes challenges to existing political elites and ensures the tradition of Democratic and Republican domination of state politics. Of course, periodically, a political party such as the Libertarians or Greens does qualify automatically for access to the ballot.

Of course, getting on the ballot is only an early step in the electoral process, and merely holding an election to fill an office does not equate to democratic, representative government. Many authoritarian and totalitarian political systems often hold elections in order to create the illusion of democratic legitimacy. Truly democratic elections require some degree of real choice. A ballot with only one candidate hardly offers a choice. More importantly, the choice must be between viable alternatives. In other words, elections imply not just a choice between A and B but that both A and B have some possibility of actually winning the race.[56] This concept of two or more choices, each with some possibility of winning—or what is called electoral competition—is important for another reason. Electoral competition has been linked to higher rates of voter turnout.[57] Does Texas meet this standard of democratic elections? If not, what can be done to create a truly competitive Texas democracy?

In 1998, Republicans won control of the Texas Senate, and in 2002 they won control of both houses of the Texas Legislature for the first time since 1876. By 2006, Republicans controlled all six statewide elected offices and both houses of the Texas Legislature, and they dominated other statewide elected offices, such as both of the state's high courts, the Railroad Commission of Texas, and the Texas Board of Education. This domination continued through the 2014 election, during which the Democrats were unable to beat the Republicans in any statewide race. As we will see in the next chapter, the Democrats have not been able to compete effectively for statewide offices, and there are many legislative districts where only one party has a candidate in the race. Clearly, our parties are not providing Texans with competitive races in many cases.

In most elections in which an **incumbent**, or current officeholder, is running, the incumbent possesses a significant advantage over his or her challengers. The incumbent, by virtue of already holding office, is well known to voters. The advantage of having voters be familiar with the identity of a candidate is called name recognition. Name recognition is also enhanced by media coverage of the incumbent's activities, speeches, and public appearances before and during the election campaign. Of course, challengers with previous experience in other elected positions will also have a degree of name recognition.

Incumbents are also advantaged by having an existing record of positions on issues, both from previous elections and in the context of decisions made while in office. This advantage is known as **position taking**. For executive branch offices, position taking taps into an incumbent's record of accomplishments, including programs created or abolished, new initiatives created, and so forth. In the legislature, incumbents are advantaged by having a record of votes on specific bills and resolutions. The legislator's position is therefore known based upon his or her voting record in the legislature. Presumably the incumbent has attractive positions to some of the voters, otherwise he or she would not likely have been elected in the first place.

Another positive aspect of incumbency is the ability to engage in **credit claiming**. Credit claiming occurs when an incumbent points out positive outcomes for which he or she is responsible. Credit claiming could include obtaining state funding for new buildings at a local community college or state university, sponsoring a bill that changed the penalties for underage consumption of alcoholic beverages, or taking a stand against perceived runaway spending by the legislature.

In elections to a legislature such as the Texas Legislature or U.S. Congress, incumbents are also favored by **casework**, or solving problems for the people back home. However, the most important advantage of incumbency may be the advantage that an incumbent possesses in raising money for an election campaign. Incumbents typically raise much more money than non-incumbents during an election cycle. Organized interests, knowing the advantages that the incumbent has, contribute willingly to his or her reelection campaign to remain in good standing or court new relationships with the incumbent.

Finally, incumbents often find it much easier to raise money since lobbyists and the organized interests they represent will use fund-raising as an opportunity to gain access to elected officials. Special interest groups are especially fond of legislators who hold important positions in leadership or on committees, and these incumbents can use the money to enhance the other advantages of incumbency that they possess.

**Incumbent**
the current officeholder.

**Position taking**
an incumbent's advantage in having an existing record of positions on issues, both from previous elections and in the context of decisions made while in office.

**Credit claiming**
the advantage derived from incumbents' ability to point to positive outcomes for which they are responsible.

**Casework**
the process of solving problems for constituents.

## Campaigns in Texas History

Election campaigns in Texas have regularly been the stuff of legends, starting in the era of the Republic of Texas. While running for his second term as president of Texas, Sam Houston was attacked by Vice President David Burnet, who described Houston as a drunken coward who failed to fight the Mexican Army before San Jacinto and possessed "beastly intemperance and other vices degrading to humanity."[58] Houston responded by calling Burnet a hog thief. When Burnet became enraged and challenged Houston to a duel, Houston laughed off the challenge, in part, because he "never fought down hill."[59]

After statehood, this trend continued. In his 1857 run for the governorship, Houston gave speeches, sometimes with an antislavery message, that ranged from two to four hours. When pro-secession candidates attacked him, Houston responded by telling his audience that one candidate had left a political career in Arkansas because of a banking fraud scandal and that the other had killed two men in South Carolina before coming to Texas.

Race has been an issue in many Texas campaigns. However, the races under attack have not always been the same ones. Playing off the distrust of Germans that resulted from World War I, opponents of James Ferguson claimed that the improper loans that had led to Ferguson's impeachment were from the kaiser of Germany. Ferguson retorted that William P. Hobby, his opponent, had put "full-blooded Germans" in key government positions. When another of Ferguson's opponents claimed to be a solid prohibitionist but belonged to the Houston Club for its literary pursuits, Ferguson publicized the club's recent spending, which included $10,483 for liquor but only $112 for books.[60]

The U.S. Civil War as a political issue still lingered as late as 1912. Governor Oscar B. Colquitt struggled in his reelection bid because he had criticized the state textbook board after it rejected a history book because it contained a photograph of Abraham Lincoln. Many Texans also flocked to see Colquitt's opponent, William Ramsay, who played upon southern sentiments in his speeches and had bands play "Dixie" during campaign events.

Radio and television have played a role in Texas, as they have in other states. Wilbert Lee "Pappy" O'Daniel used his radio show to launch his campaign for governor. The years since have seen the broadcast media of radio and television become the central tool of candidate's campaigns. While candidates still travel the state and personally interact with voters, the battles of advertising and of efforts to get covered by news organizations have become the primary concern of campaigns. While O'Daniel made the most of the new technology of radio, his campaign platform (the Ten Commandments) and his motto (the Golden Rule) were decidedly ancient. He cashed in on these sentiments by sending his children through the audience to gather contributions.[61]

## Campaigns in Texas Today

Today's campaigns are modern, featuring high-tech use of the Internet and other media. In the 2006 gubernatorial election, independent candidate Kinky Friedman used the Internet to show Texans his "Kinkytoons" commercials that portrayed what the defenders of the Alamo would have done if led by today's parties. While not as colorful as Friedman, the other independent candidate, Carole Strayhorn, took to the television airwaves to paint herself as "one tough grandma." Trying to live up to the larger-than-life legacy of earlier Texas politicians, Democrat Chris Bell appeared in an ad as a giant figure looming over Texas landmarks such as the capitol building and the Alamo. The larger-than-life Texas campaign is alive and well.

In general, campaigns in Texas are very much like those in the rest of the nation. The state's large size does require that candidates come up with more cash and produce more style. To run a campaign in Texas means to advertise in not a handful of media markets, but around twenty separate television markets. Major metropolitan areas such as Austin, Dallas-Fort Worth, Houston, and San Antonio have a local newspaper that dominates the market, but these papers lack significant circulation outside their cities. Compare this to neighboring Arkansas, where the Little Rock television market covers almost all of the state. To campaign in Arkansas, one only needs to run ads in five or six television markets. In addition, the *Arkansas Democrat-Gazette*, based in Little Rock, circulates widely across the entire state. Texas voters also remain connected to the legends of Texas history, meaning that candidates will continue to use icons such as the Alamo and the cowboy heritage. Ironically, campaigns embrace the larger changes in the state by adopting new technologies, such as the Internet, to transmit these time-tested messages of traditional Texas mythology.

### The Costs of Campaigns in Texas

What do the millions spent on campaigns buy candidates in Texas? For decades, most campaigns have spent most of their budget on advertising. Getting candidates' names and messages in front of the voters has taken a variety of forms, with campaigns using mail, newspapers, radio, and television to reach voters. However, the ways of reaching Texas voters are as diverse as Texans themselves. In 2010, Rick Perry spent over $22 million on his reelection campaign, while challenger Bill White spent over $18 million. While the exact form of advertising each candidate used cannot be discerned from the reports the candidates filed with the Texas Ethics Commission, we can see that Rick Perry spent about $17.7 million (about 80 percent of his spending) on advertising, and Bill White spent about $14.9 million (about 83 percent).[62] In 2010, Rick Perry spent $225,000 on a NASCAR sponsorship, while Bill White's campaign spent $128,000 placing biographical inserts into 272 newspapers.[63] Campaign spending increased dramatically as Texans began to watch more and more television.

Because candidates are given several months to submit and revise campaign spending reports with the Texas Ethics Commission, the total amounts spent during the 2014 elections in Texas will not be known until well into 2015. While those totals are not available as of this edition, expectations are that spending for 2014 will feature significant contributions for governor and lieutenant governor. By September of 2014, Greg Abbott had reported over $21.9 million in contributions, while Wendy Davis reported over $3.8 million. Also, David Dewhurst reported over $10.2 million in his unsuccessful bid for reelection, which ended in his loss to Patrick in the Republican primary.

## Campaigns and the Media

The future of campaigning could look very different. The rise of digital media, coupled with massive databases and social media, has already shifted the priorities of campaigns, and campaign consultants are closely watching these trends to see how much they transform the process. Traditionally, campaigns spent a lot of their money getting their message to voters. This generally meant buying as much advertising space in newspapers or time on radio or television as possible in hopes that their message will reach the public. Today, citizens can use social media sites, such as Facebook, Twitter, or Tumblr, to spread messages they like. This means that campaigns can now spend more time and effort on producing different messages and leave the task of spreading that message to supporters. The traditional media strategy was to take what the campaign thought would be its most popular ad and put it on the air over and over again in hopes that it would eventually reach the right audience members and catch them when they were paying attention. Today, campaigns produce a variety of commercials, share them through YouTube or Facebook, and then hope that you pass along to your friends the ad that you most like. This technique fits Texans, with their big personalities and often unique messages, very well.

While television remains an important source of entertainment and information for Texans, it operated in a very different fashion just a few decades ago. First, television is no longer dominated by the big three networks. There was a time when Americans had only three choices for the evening news and prime-time entertainment: ABC, CBS, and NBC. Today, there are many more choices, which creates both challenges and opportunities for campaigns. On the one hand, candidates can no longer find one place where they can reach a large audience since the viewing audience is scattered over the wide range of broadcast and cable options. On the other hand, the shows we pick may help smart campaigns target specific audiences. Most obviously, conservatives watch Fox News, while liberals favor MSNBC. Beyond that, cable channels such as Lifetime target women, while Spike targets men. This allows a campaign interested in talking specifically to a certain group of people to find the right audience.

Additionally, television has changed thanks to the rise of cable television and addressable cable boxes. Cable companies can now target ads to specific neighborhoods and will soon be able to target specific homes. This means that in a few years, you and the people next door could be watching the same television show at the same time but see different

Gubernatorial candidate Greg Abbott speaks to supporters during a campaign rally in 2014. Abbott campaigned to succeed Rick Perry as the next Texas governor and won the election.

commercials during the break. These ads would be targeted based on databases that political campaigns and commercial marketing companies build based on information they gather on the magazines you buy, the church you attend, the car you drive, and a host of other information that firms have been gathering on you. These data-mining operations operate in a very similar way to the advertising on Facebook. One issue for campaigns is the significant rise of on-demand television platforms, such as Netflix and Hulu, as well as DVR recording, all of which allow viewers to avoid traditional TV advertising by candidates. In response, campaigns are attempting to find new approaches to get their message to voters through emerging technologies and new forms of communication.

Candidates have shifted emphasis in recent years, moving away from traditional yard signs and large billboard displays toward new media outlets, such as digital ads on Facebook, Yahoo, and popular news media Web sites, such as FoxNews.com and CNN.com.

We may see Texas political ads move from television to computers to handheld devices within the span of a single generation. While most campaigns will probably continue to make some use of traditional campaign items, such as bumper stickers, yard signs, lapel buttons, and balloons, it may be possible to win office using only digital advertising through Facebook, YouTube, and whatever comes next. Thus, new media seem to be transforming the method of campaigning, but whether the style and substance are changing is yet to be seen.

## CAMPAIGN FINANCE IN TEXAS

Inevitably, the discussion of elections turns to the issue of money. Campaign finance is important because without money candidates and political parties have trouble getting out their message, and voters have a difficult time gathering information and making decisions about which candidate they will vote for. Money also provides essentials for election campaigns, such as television and radio advertising and travel throughout the state or election district. It also pays for office space, telephones, Web sites, public opinion polls, and campaign staff.

The issue of campaign finance is important to a discussion of the health of American democracy, voter participation, and outcomes of elections. In a large, diverse state such as Texas, a well-funded campaign is often viewed as crucial. However, the sources of campaign money raise important concerns, such as who is giving money to candidates and what those candidates may be doing in return. When an organization gives a candidate a contribution, it is typically doing so with the expectation that the candidate will at least listen to the group's concerns. The issue of campaign finance also raises the question of whether organized interests "buy" favorable legislation, court rulings, and executive decisions.

### Regulating Campaign Finance

Because money matters, the issue of free speech comes to the forefront of the debate. On the one hand, campaign contributions are a form of political speech because by contributing to a candidate's campaign, individual citizens or interest groups are expressing their political position. On the other hand, the cost of modern campaigns virtually guarantees that those with more money to contribute are "heard" more often, regardless of the opinions of the entire electorate or even a majority of voters. The issue of money in elections also raises serious concerns about potential quid pro quo—that is, organized interests receiving favorable laws as a result of campaign contributions.

On January 30, 1976, the U.S. Supreme Court in *Buckley v. Valeo* struck down limitations on expenditures on the grounds that "it is clear that a primary effect of these expenditure limitations is to restrict the quantity of campaign speech by individuals, groups and candidates. The restrictions . . . limit political expression at the core of our electoral process and of First Amendment freedoms."[64] While the Court struck down limits on how much campaigns could spend, it upheld limitations on contributions because they safeguard the integrity of the electoral process and, according to the Court, "expenditure ceilings impose significantly more severe restrictions on protected freedom of political expression and association that do its limitations on financial contributions."[65] The court extended the protection of free speech to unions and corporations in *Citizens United v. Federal Election Commission* (2010),[66] and, as we will see in Chapter 11, this opened up many interesting new channels of money.

While the court's protection of the right to spend money on behalf of a person's views was a victory for free speech, it contributed to some inequalities that concern some reformers. For example, the Court has ruled that limiting what an individual contributes to his or her own campaign violates the First Amendment of the U.S. Constitution. This means that while the government might limit how much an individual gives to another person's campaign, wealthy candidates can spend unlimited amounts of money from their own accounts. For example, David Dewhurst put about $19 million of his own money into his failed candidacy for the U.S. Senate in 2012. Likewise, what an individual or organized interest spends on their own, independent of a candidate's campaign, cannot be limited. Thus, if money is equal to speech, then those with more money have more freedom of speech, thus limiting the rights of those without money.

Some countries, such as Germany, have addressed this issue by providing **public financing** of elections. Essentially, the government covers the costs of campaigning by providing subsidies to parties and candidates or by providing a reimbursement for campaign costs. Thus, parties and candidates do not have to raise money for the campaign from private citizens or organized interests, such as labor unions, special interest groups, or corporations. A public finance system is in contrast to the reliance on **private financing**. Private financing occurs when individual citizens, interest groups, labor unions, or corporations make donations to candidates and political parties to cover the cost of an election.

The United States possesses a mixture of systems, with most elections privately financed. An exception is the U.S. presidential election, which features some public financing. Presidential candidates can qualify for federal matching funds during the presidential primary season as long as they accept federal spending limits. Similarly, the presidential nominees of the two major parties can receive large lump-sum grants

**Public financing**
a system of campaign financing in which the government covers the cost of elections for political parties or candidates.

**Private financing**
a system of campaign financing in which citizens, interest groups, labor unions, and corporations donate funds to cover the cost of elections for political parties or candidates.

($91 million in 2012) to pay for their campaigns provided that they do not accept other funds. While these grants are attractive, candidates have recently declined them so that they can spend as much as they can raise. For example, in 2008, Barack Obama declined the federal general election grant of $84 million and eventually raised and spent about $294 million. Federal campaign finance law uses these funds as incentives to get presidential candidates to voluntarily accept the campaign spending limit that the court ruled would be unconstitutional if required by law.

Campaign finance laws in the United States tend to emphasize reporting the sources of campaign finance, the size of donations, and the patterns of candidate spending rather than limiting campaign spending. The idea is that voters can hold candidates accountable for excessive spending or accepting money from unsavory donors if those candidates have to publicly disclose this information. The responsibility for collecting this information and providing it to the public rests for state elections with the Texas Ethics Commission. Candidates are required to file reports with the commission every month once they begin to campaign. After an election, a final report must be filed within three months of the election. The Texas Ethics Commission maintains a searchable database for citizens on its Web site, www.ethics.state.tx.us.

To provide context, Canadian campaign finance laws were largely modeled on U.S. laws and experiences. While Canada also focuses on disclosure, it chooses to emphasize spending limits rather than donation limits. In Canada, political parties, organized interests, and individual candidates may collect as many donations and as large of donations as they can. However, all campaign spending is limited. Maximum limits in national election campaigns are set based upon a formula that considers the size of the electorate in each single-member district for the lower house of the Canadian Parliament, the rate of inflation since the last election, and the performance of officially registered parties and independent candidates in the last election. These limits apply to national political parties, individual candidates, and organized interests. Several of Canada's provinces, such as Ontario, have replicated the national campaign finance laws for provincial elections.

## Contribution Disclosure

All state and local elections in Texas are privately financed, and Texas state law places few restrictions on how much can be given. In Texas, there is an emphasis on **disclosure**. Disclosure is the idea that each candidate reports who has contributed money to the campaign and how much has been contributed by an individual or group. Texas does not place limits on how much an individual, interest group, labor union, or corporation may contribute. However, candidates must disclose the source of any contribution over $50. Texas election law does prohibit members of the legislature and most statewide officers from accepting political contributions during a period beginning thirty days before a regular legislative session convenes and ending twenty days after final adjournment. These officials are allowed to accept contributions during a special session but must file a special report within thirty days of the end of the session. Candidates cannot accept contributions from labor organizations or corporations. However, as we'll see in the next chapter, labor unions and corporations can spend

**Disclosure**
the reporting of who contributes money to a campaign and how much is contributed by an individual or corporation.

their own funds advocating for candidates and issues as long as they act independently of the candidate's official campaign.

Political action committees from within the state are allowed to give as much as they want. However, the law mandates that a political action committee (PAC) have at least ten contributors before it makes a political contribution. Political organizations outside the state are limited to a $500 contribution unless they provide documentation listing every donor who gave $100 or more to the organization in the previous twelve months. While some Texans wonder about the wisdom of allowing out-of-state political action committees to give any money to Texas political campaigns, having a mailing address from outside Texas does not mean that the committee does not represent citizens of the state, as many Texans support national organizations, such as the National Rifle Association. Similarly, the designation of "in state" only means that the group has filed for organization under Texas law, and such a group could receive large amounts of funds that originated outside of Texas.

## Judicial Campaign Contributions

Because state and local judges are elected in Texas, judicial elections are also covered by campaign finance laws. Texans hope that their judges will be as impartial as possible, and to alleviate fears that justice in Texas can be "bought" through campaign contributions, additional regulations limit the size of all contributions made to a candidate's campaign to get elected as a judge. The limits on individual donors depend on the size of the judicial district and range from $1,000 for judicial districts with a population of 250,000 or less to $5,000 for judicial districts with a population of 1 million or more; individual donors to candidates for statewide judicial offices are limited to $5,000 as well. Law firms may contribute up to six times the individual limits, but individual members of the law firm are limited to $50 contributions. Similarly, statewide candidates may accept only $300,000 from PACs.

Judicial candidates may also opt to accept voluntary spending limits. Like contribution limits, the voluntary limit for a judicial office is based on the size of the judicial district. For example, the limit begins at $100,000 for districts that have less than 250,000 people and eventually rises to $500,000 for districts with more than 1 million people. The contribution limit for statewide office is $2 million. Candidates accepting these limits enjoy an unusual reward—if their opponent exceeds the expenditure limits, the candidate is no longer subject to limits on contributions and expenditures. While the law has been considered a success by some, a 2012 race for a state district court in Marshall saw challenger Brad Morin reject the voluntary limits when he entered the race. This rejection left some reformers concerned because they had hoped that pressure from voters and rival candidates would be enough to nudge judicial candidates into accepting the voluntary limits.[67]

## Campaign Spending

Since final data on the 2014 election regarding campaign finance is not available until well into 2015, we will use the 2010 election to illustrate the role of money

## TABLE 9.2 Campaign Spending for Candidates in the 2010 Texas Gubernatorial Election

| Candidate (Party Affiliation) | Amount Raised | Amount Spent | Votes Received | Money Spent Per Vote |
|---|---|---|---|---|
| Rick Perry (Republican) | $49,479,069.15 | $46,393,982.92 | 2,737,481 | $16.95 |
| Bill White (Democrat) | $26,298,865.37 | $24,807,297.91 | 2,106,395 | $11.78 |

**Source:** Texas Ethics Commission, www.ethics.state.tx.us/ (accessed September 25, 2012); authors' calculations.

in Texas elections. The National Institute on Money in State Politics estimated that Texas candidates raised $234 million in that election cycle.[68] As Table 9.2 illustrates, Rick Perry and Bill White spent about $71 million over the primaries and general election, with the campaigns of the two candidates spending an average of $14.70 for every vote. This doesn't include the $14.5 million spent by Kay Bailey Hutchison and the $10.6 million spent by Farouk Shami in their attempts to win their party's nomination.

The candidates competing for the sixteen seats in the Texas Senate up for election in 2010 spent $11 million. Candidates for the Texas House spent over $78 million. That amount may seem modest for 150 House races, but many of those races were not competitive and the price was much higher in some districts. Stefani Carter and Dan Branch each spent about $1.4 million in their election victories. However, the biggest spender in the House in 2010 was Speaker Joe Straus, who spent over $5.2 million holding onto his seat in San Antonio. Meanwhile, Patrick Rose spent $1.3 million in a losing bid to retain his seat in the House.

The sources of contributions reveal a great deal about who is concerned with Texas politics and is able to invest heavily in it. As might be expected, the oil and gas industry contributes large sums of money. Across all races and candidates, oil and gas companies gave over $16.2 million in 2010. The only other industry to give more was lawyers/lobbyists, who gave $22.9 million. This may be misleading since most of the lobbyists work to represent industries other than the law, and money from oil and gas or other categories was likely funneled through their lobbyists. As he often is, Bob J. Perry, the owner of a large home construction firm, was the state's largest individual contributor to the campaigns of others (although Farouk Shami spent over $9.6 million of his own money in his bid for the Democratic nomination for governor). Perry contributed almost $3 million on his own to various candidates for office and gave another $2.1 million with his wife, Doylene. Texans for Lawsuit Reform, a lawyer/lobbyist organization that advocates for lawsuit reform and is widely acknowledged to have a huge impact on the issue, donated $5.7 million.[69]

## WINNERS AND LOSERS

Politics involves decisions about who gets what, and thus it is not surprising that those groups that participate in politics are more likely to be the winners in a state's distribution of resources. In theory, the strength of a democracy lies in the ability of all citizens to exert pressure on the political system. When representative democracies are working, public policy reflects compromises that take into account the needs of a wide range of groups in society. Historically, differences in participation were created by institutional barriers to voting, ranging from the outright denial of suffrage to some groups to obstacles such as white primaries and poll taxes designed to stifle a particular group's participation. Removing these barriers to voting has occurred slowly and often as a result of federal imposition of election standards.

Unfortunately, in spite of the enfranchisement of minority groups in the state, minority participation in the electoral process remains significantly lower than white participation. Asian and Hispanic groups in particular exhibit extremely low levels of voting participation. Minorities will continue to struggle to make their voices heard as long as they keep their distance from the voting booth. Texas is one of the most diverse states in America, but this is not reflected in its voting patterns.

Voter turnout is also significantly lower among certain age groups. College-age voters are the least likely to show up at the polls and, therefore, the least likely to be represented by state policies. Because policies in Texas often ignore the needs of college-age voters, in times of budget crisis, college students are often the first group that legislators target. The deregulation of tuition at state universities and Governor Perry's veto of appropriations for state community colleges are just two recent examples of such targeting. Groups in the state who remain apathetic about voting will continue to be the first sacrificed in times of budget cuts.

Finally, the long ballot in Texas exerts a palpable cost by increasing voter apathy throughout the state. Ironically, Texans resist changes to the election system, preferring to keep many of the most important public offices elected because of their distrust of government. Elected officials are theoretically more accountable to the people. Yet, in any given election, most Texans are not exercising the option to have a say in who wins that election. In some instances, voters face noncompetitive elections at the level of the state legislature. The result is that average Texans are becoming increasingly disconnected from the political process.

* Which type of primary (open, closed, wide open) do you prefer? Why?
* Are restrictions to campaign contributions and spending necessary?
* Do large contributors have undue influence on Texas politics?
* Is the U.S. Supreme Court correct in declaring campaign contributions to be free speech? Why or why not?

# CONCLUSION

Texas elections, like all election systems, are designed to produce certain types of outcomes. Historically, election rules and voting rights were designed to disenfranchise African American voters and, to a lesser extent, poor, rural, white voters. The rules historically were also designed to allow the Democratic Party to maintain control over the election system. Thus, until the 1960s white elites and the Democratic Party were clearly the winners of the electoral game. The transition of Texas politics toward inclusion of minorities and women occurred in large part through the actions of the national government in securing voting rights for disenfranchised groups, especially African Americans and Hispanics. By increasing the national government's role, a second transition was spurred: Congress and the U.S. Supreme Court moved into the area of elections by establishing over time a set of standards that all states must follow in the conduct of national, state, and local elections. The mandated use of electronic voting equipment is the latest example of this transition.

The emergence of the Republican Party in the 1960s altered Texas politics, bringing greater electoral competition in the state for the first time since the end of the Reconstruction era. However, while electoral competition has certainly increased in high-level elections, such as those for the U.S. House of Representatives and the U.S. Senate, the emergence of the Republican Party has not necessarily produced increased electoral competition at the level of the state legislature. Periods of alteration between Republican and Democratic dominance of statewide elected offices in the executive branch and various commissions have been recently replaced by Republican dominance. The absence of electoral competition in some elections, combined with voter apathy and disengagement by certain demographic groups, means that the true winners in Texas legislative politics may be those who contribute the money that finances the election campaigns. Candidates who are well financed do quite well. The organized interests that donate to campaigns expect some form of return for their efforts to fund the winner's campaign. We will explore the influence of these organized interests and the role of the political parties in this financing system more thoroughly in the next chapter.

## KEY TERMS

advanced or early voting (p. 292)

blanket or wide-open primary (p. 285)

casework (p. 302)

closed primary (p. 284)

credit claiming (p. 302)

cross-filing (p. 287)

direct primary (p. 283)

disclosure (p. 308)

equal protection clause (p. 275)

general election (p. 284)

grandfather clause (p. 274)

Help America Vote Act (HAVA) (p. 293)

incumbent (p. 302)

independent candidate (p. 301)

indirect primary (p. 283)

literacy test (p. 274)

Motor Voter Act (p. 272)

open primary (p. 285)

party-line voting (p. 292)

poll tax (p. 274)

position taking (p. 302)

preference primary (p. 284)

primary election (p. 282)

private financing (p. 307)

public financing (p. 307)

roll off (p. 291)

runoff election (p. 287)

second-order elections (p. 298)

suffrage (p. 273)

voter turnout (p. 295)

Voting Rights Act of 1965 (VRA) (p. 277)

white primary (p. 275)

## CORE ASSESSMENT

1. Do the differences in voter turnout across Texas's demographic groups, such as age and ethnicity, matter in the state's politics?

2. For strategic purposes, states often prefer to report voter turnout based on total number of registered voters rather than voting-age population. In reviewing the information in this chapter, how different are those numbers for Texas? What are the implications of reporting voter turnout using each method of calculation?

3. How important is it to ensure the maximum ability of all groups in society to register and vote in elections?

4. What effects occur in our political system if you vote or fail to vote in an election?

# 10 POLITICAL PARTIES

I t's relatively easy to count votes on Election Day or members of the legislature when it convenes and declare that the Republicans are in control of Texas government. It's much harder to say who is in control of the Republicans.

The divisions within the party were evident as Republicans gathered for their 2014 party convention. Although the party already appeared almost certain to keep its hold on every statewide office and a majority of the seats in the Texas Legislature, many Republicans were not content to celebrate and wanted to make absolutely clear what their vision of the party looked like. Unfortunately, they disagreed on what that was.

Every party has it quarrels over issues. Despite the fact that they had control over both the White House and Congress, the war in Vietnam and the civil rights movement divided national Democrats so much in 1968 that riots erupted in the streets outside their national convention in Chicago. While today's Texas Republican Party conflict is not as dramatic, it reflects the same underlying dynamic: once your party gains control over government, people will work harder to control the party. This is one of the paradoxes of political parties—the more successful the party is on Election Day, the more intense the battle within the party. After all, there's much less at stake when you're trying to set the course of a party unlikely to win election. While Texas Republicans have enjoyed the success brought by the influx of people and energy associated with the Tea Party movement, these new Republicans do not always agree with the more traditional "establishment" Republicans.

Over the years, hundreds of planks (policy positions) have been crammed into the platform as hosts of interests within the Republican Party sought the official embrace of their favorite issues. The 2014 platform included a variety of planks that left most Republicans wondering if they were really worth inclusion. For example, the platform included calls for the freedom to raise and promote exotic livestock and for the full diplomatic recognition of Taiwan. The platform also called for the return of the Confederate Widow's Plaque to the Supreme Court of Texas building and the right of Texans to opt-out of "smart meters" used by electric companies. The platform weighed in at forty pages and over 14,000 words. Not to be outdone, the 2014 Texas Democratic platform offered up more than 28,000 words of advice for the state, spread out over sixty-two pages.

A Kilgore Rangerette poses for a photo with an elephant decked out in patriotic wear at the American Airlines Center in Dallas. Members of the Republican National Committee visited the site in 2014 while scouting for a 2016 convention locale.

All these platform planks may mean there is something for everyone. It may also mean there is probably something against everyone. Most partisans (the few who actually read the platform) might agree with most of what they read. However, it seems likely that even those partisans can point to things in the platform they don't like. For example, the Texas Democratic Party's advocacy of the decriminalization of marijuana at the state and federal levels irritated many older Democrats. And younger Republicans were restless with their party's embrace of "reparative therapy" as a treatment for homosexuality.

If putting together a party platform is a political minefield, why put down more mines than you have to? Why don't the parties slim down their platforms? The answer is that, like mines, party platform planks are as risky to remove as they are to install. Also, part of the answer is that the old resists change brought by the new. Many young Republicans came away from the convention unhappy with the party's stand on same-sex marriage and medical marijuana. The convention, however, was controlled by older Republicans who sought to defend what they saw as traditional Texas values. The Texas Republican Party, like the state itself, is enduring growing pains.

The disagreements within the Texas parties don't just reflect the natural conflict between old and new. These debates also relate to the conflicting views on the function of parties. Some party members view the platform as a pure statement of principle that should closely reflect the views at the heart of the party. For these people, the platform is an opportunity to articulate a strong political ideology, distinct from other parties. For many, the Republican label carries with it certain views that the party must adhere to regardless of the consequences in the general election. Other party members view the platform as part of a strategy for winning elections. These Republicans worry about the impact of an immigration policy that could alienate Hispanic voters in a state with a rising Hispanic population. Other Republicans worry that their party's stands on marijuana and same-sex marriage will chase libertarian-leaning young conservatives away. For these Republicans, the platform is an opportunity to protect the electoral health of the party in the future—even if it means a few compromises to the spirit of the party today.

In this chapter, we will look at political parties and their contribution to the practice of democracy in Texas. Political parties remain unpopular but important partners in state politics. While political parties can help citizens enter into the political process, we will see that the parties are finding it increasingly difficult to engage citizens, and they often fail to fully represent the citizens of the state.

## Chapter Objectives

★ Explain the main functions of political parties.

★ Describe the roles of political parties and the consequences of weak parties.

★ Discuss how state and local parties in Texas have changed over time.

★ Assess who wins and who loses when political parties represent citizens of the state.

## THE DEVELOPMENT OF POLITICAL PARTIES IN TEXAS

While the battle between political parties has often served as the premier vehicle for competition in U.S. politics, Texans have rarely enjoyed the benefits of a truly competitive party system. Early Texans were not strangers to political parties, but they initially shunned them. Sam Houston had been a close political ally of Andrew Jackson, whose patronage system did much to build the early Democratic Party in the United States. Despite his Democratic roots, however, Houston generally avoided party labels in his Texas campaigns, and the state's earliest elections were dominated by personalities rather than parties.

Ironically, just as political parties were taking root in Texas, the national Whig Party collapsed in the mid-1850s. Its replacement, the Republican Party, held antislavery positions that ensured it found little support in the state. The American or Know-Nothing Party, an anti-immigration party, aggressively cultivated Texans, forcing the Democratic Party to become fully organized in Texas for the first time in 1854.[1] Even as the Democratic Party was beginning to take hold in the state, the divisions that would culminate in the Civil War separated Texans into pro-union and secessionist factions and blotted out any chance of Republicans winning statewide office. The bitterness that followed Reconstruction was directed toward the Republican Party, allowing the Democratic Party to dominate the state for decades. The biggest challenges to the Democrats came from the Greenback Party in the 1870s and 1880s and the Populists or People's Party in the 1880s and 1890s.

The Populist Party, backed largely by small farmers looking to democratize the economic system, favored programs such as a graduated income tax, an eight-hour workday, and government control of railroads. The Populists made the greatest gains in the American Midwest, but the party shared a common cause with the Farmer's Alliance (itself an outgrowth of the Grange movement) that had organized in Lampasas, Texas, in the mid-1870s.[2] Texas's Populist Party built on the foundation of the fundamentalist churches, an especially important social network in early Texas and one of the few that brought farm families together. Farmers thus often linked religious themes with their desire for relief from economic pressures.[3] Before fading from the Texas scene, the Populists won 44 percent of the vote for J. C. Kearby, their candidate in the 1896 election. Kearby ran with the support of the Republicans, who had not fielded their own candidate that year. Populists' call for government ownership of the railroads and limits on land ownership by corporations was decidedly at odds with the pro-business Republican Party. Eventually, the partnerships with the Republicans and other groups took their toll, undermining the consistency of the Populist Party's ideological foundations. Meanwhile, some of their more popular ideas were appropriated by Democratic politicians, such as Governor Jim Hogg, who won the favor of many Texas farmers by taking on the railroads.

The next challenge to the Texas Democratic Party emerged from the Progressives, a formidable force for reform in much of the country. Because Texas's Progressives lacked the targets for reform that energized the party nationally, such as corrupt, big-city party machines and unfavorable economic policies, they turned instead to cultural issues, such as alcohol prohibition.[4]

Texas had a few local party machines through which local party officials could dispense **patronage**, such as offering government jobs, contracts, and other favors to party loyalists to perpetuate their power. George Parr's political machine ran Duval County in South Texas for thirty years after Parr inherited it from his father, Archer. By working closely with poor Hispanics and getting to know them, Parr earned their loyalty and their votes. He built a political and economic empire founded on money taken from businesses and government accounts. Parr's ability to deliver votes to friendly candidates made him a kingmaker in Texas; Parr was responsible for pushing local election officials to find the questionable votes that secured Lyndon Johnson's Democratic primary victory in the 1948 U.S. Senate campaign.

George Parr wasn't the first Texas official involved in creative ballot counting. In 1869, citizens in Navarro County were unable to cast their votes after the county's registrar absconded with the registration lists before the election. In the same year, Milam County ballots were never counted, and in Hill County an official took the ballots to another jurisdiction to count, with results that surprised many Hill County voters.[5] While Texas needed the reforms championed by the Progressive movement, changes were slow to come.

**Patronage**
when individuals who supported a candidate for public office are rewarded with public jobs, appointments, and government contracts.

# TEXAS (VS) NEW YORK

In November of 2006, voters in Texas and in New York participated in elections for one of their U.S. senators. Texas voters selected from three candidates: a Republican, a Democrat, and a Libertarian. In New York, voters selected from among candidates from nine different political parties. One key difference between the two elections was the fact that in New York three political parties selected and listed the same candidate for U.S. senator: Hillary Clinton. She was the candidate for the Democratic Party, the Independence Party, and the Working Families Party. Her primary opponent, John Spencer, ran as the Republican Party candidate and as the Conservative Party candidate. In New York, the ballot is laid out so every party and candidate appears separately. As a result, Hillary Clinton's name appeared on the ballot three times and John Spencer's name appeared twice.

The practice of two or more parties legally running the same candidate for office is called electoral fusion. Electoral fusion is allowed in a handful of states, including New York. While electoral fusion was once practiced in Texas as a means of protecting Democratic dominance, it is now illegal.

The practice of electoral fusion allowed voters to support Hillary Clinton or John Spencer without voting for either of the two major parties. In addition, during the campaign, both Clinton and Spencer had to address issues of concern not only for their respective party's base of voters but also for the additional parties that gave them a nomination.

## U.S. Senate Election in New York, 2006

| Candidate | Percentage of Votes | Party |
|---|---|---|
| Hillary Rodham Clinton | 57.4% | Democratic |
| John Spencer | 25.8% | Republican |
| John Spencer | 3.8% | Conservative |
| Hillary Rodham Clinton | 3.4% | Independence |
| Hillary Rodham Clinton | 3.2% | Working Families |
| Howie Hawkins | 1.2% | Green |
| Jeffrey T. Russell | 0.4% | Libertarian |
| Roger Calero | 0.1% | Socialist Workers |
| William Van Auken | 0.1% | Socialist Equity |

**Source:** New York State Board of Elections, "U.S. Senate Election Returns Nov. 7, 2006," www.elections.ny.gov/NYSBOE/elections/2006/general/2006_ussen.pdf (accessed September 3, 2014); some calculations by authors.

## THINKING *Critically*

★ What is electoral fusion?

★ How does electoral fusion allow third parties to participate in an election?

★ How does electoral fusion legitimize voting for third parties?

★ Why did Texas Democrats support electoral fusion in the past?

★ Why did the practice become illegal in Texas?

---

In general, the Progressives found themselves caught up in the prohibition movement because promoting political reform and banishing alcohol were seen as tools for building a better society. As with the Populists, churches played an important role, and evangelicals and women's groups were drawn to the Progressive cause.[6] Also like the Populists, the Progressives saw much of their agenda absorbed by the Democrats.

The Republican Party in Texas slowly developed in the early twentieth century, with Herbert Hoover carrying the state in 1928 only to suffer a major setback during the Great Depression, a disaster that many Texans blamed on President Hoover and the Republican Party. While the depression and World War II hurt Republicans seeking statewide office, Texans slowly warmed to Republican presidential candidates. In 1952, the Texas Democratic Party officially supported Republican candidate Dwight D. Eisenhower, and, for the second time in Texas's history, a Republican presidential candidate carried the state. Texas Democrats avoided the Republican tide that swept across the state in 1952, however, when every Democratic nominee for statewide office except one cross-filed for positions on the ballot as both a Democrat and a Republican under the provisions of a 1951 law.

Political supporters turn out for a San Antonio fund-raiser for President Barack Obama. Political participation in fund-raisers and other campaign- and election-related activities remains low in Texas and throughout the United States.

© James Southers/Alamy

While the Democratic Party would eventually lead the nation in civil rights, from Reconstruction until the 1960s it often supported segregation and racism in Texas and elsewhere in the South. African Americans were barred from participating in Democratic primaries, and the party created special white primaries as a matter of law in Texas and as a matter of practice in other southern states. Since the Democratic Party enjoyed a virtual monopoly in statewide general elections, African Americans were effectively shut out of any meaningful role in elections. Democratic governor James "Pa" Ferguson proclaimed, "A negro has no business whatever taking part in the political affairs of the Democratic Party, the white man's party."[7] Eventually, the civil rights issue split the Democratic Party of Texas, a breakup common throughout the southern states.

In the latter part of the twentieth century, Texas starred in the transition that saw southern states turn away from the Democratic Party and embrace the Republican Party. The Republicans finally broke the Democrats' dominance in 1961, and they won statewide office for the first time since Reconstruction when Republican John Tower won the U.S. Senate seat vacated by the election of Democrat Lyndon Johnson to the vice presidency. The Republicans did not win the Texas governorship until 1978 when William Clements won a surprise victory. By 2000, Democrats were unable to effectively challenge Republicans for any statewide office. Thus, in less than forty years, Texas went from being a state dominated by the Democratic Party to one dominated by the Republican Party. Exit polls from the 2014 election for governor revealed that 38 percent of Texas voters identified themselves as Republicans, 27 percent as Democrats, and 35 percent as independents. Similar transitions have occurred throughout the South, but the trend really began with Texas. Texas is often considered the least "southern" of the southern states[8] and as such is something of a trend leader in southern development. The "Texafication" of American politics includes an emphasis on low taxes; high-tech, industry-embracing policies; and limited spending on social welfare.[9] Republicans throughout the region and nation have capitalized in part on the success of Texas Republicans.

Domination of a state by one party is not always the case in American politics. After the 2014 elections, eighteen states had divided governments, with a governor faced with at least one house of the state legislature in the hands of the opposition party. Among the other states, seven had both the legislature and governor's mansions in the hands of Democrats, while in the other twenty-three they were in the hands of Republicans.

## Parties, Competition, and Voter Participation

A general election ballot offers voters a choice, preferably one between viable alternatives. In other words, elections imply not just a choice between A and B but that both A and B have some possibility of actually winning the race.[10] This concept of two or more choices, each with some possibility of winning—or what is called electoral competition—is important for another reason. Electoral competition has been linked to higher rates of voter turnout,[11] and in Texas, the choice between viable alternatives is not always on the ballot.

The dominance of one party in Texas does not necessarily mean that there is no competition. A common joke has been that Texas only has one party but has enough conflict for six. For much of the state's history, its political battles were fought during the process of nominating Democratic candidates. With Republicans unable to mount a serious challenge, Texas politicians understood that the winner of the Democratic nominating primary was effectively the election winner. Today, the dominant parties are the opposite, but the dilemma is the same and the battles to win the primary are often the most hotly contested.

Few voters take part in the primaries of either major party. For example, the 2014 primaries that selected candidates for governor, lieutenant governor, and other statewide elected officials saw only 3.0 percent of Texans voting in the Democratic primary and 7.2 percent voting in the Republican primary. Spurred in part by the presidential primaries, turnout was slightly higher in 2012, when 3.2 percent of Texans voted in the Democratic primary, and another 7.9 percent voted in the Republican primary. In contrast, turnout for the Democratic primaries during the 1970s—when that party dominated—was generally between 15 percent and 19 percent. As Figure 10.1 shows, in the 1970s less than 5 percent of Texans took part in the Republican primaries, a matter of little consequence since Republican gubernatorial candidates were seen as having little chance of winning office. However, since that time, the stature of the Republican Party has grown tremendously, even though participation rates in the party's primaries have not increased dramatically. It appears that the GOP hasn't grown into its new boots as far as voter electoral participation is concerned, and, alongside the Democrats, it is left to contend with the troubling trend of reduced voter participation. With just 7.2 percent of eligible citizens selecting the Republican nominees who won statewide offices in November 2014, it is fair to say that the parties have not succeeded in creating the broad participation that ensures that all Texans' voices are heard in Austin.

One of the ways of judging how much electoral competition exists is to look at how often voters even have a choice between the two major party candidates. Even if a party has little success in a district, having a candidate on the ballot at least offers voters a

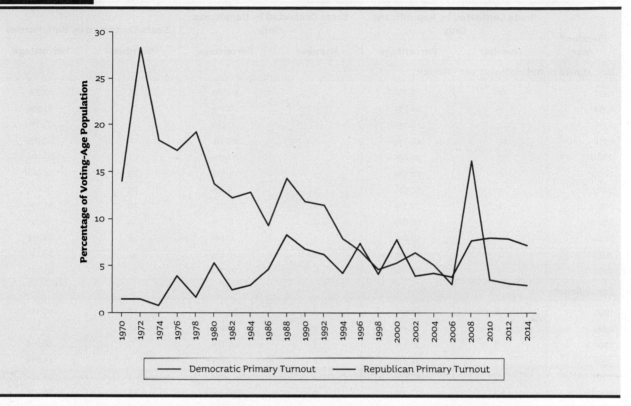

*Source:* Texas Secretary of State, "Turnout and Voter Registration Figures (1970–Current)," www.sos.state.tx.us/elections/historical/70 92.shtml (accessed July 3, 2014).

choice in November. Candidates from minor parties have never done well in Texas and currently do not seem likely to threaten major party candidates.

As Table 10.1 indicates, in 2014 voters had a choice in less than two-thirds of U.S. House races in Texas. That year about 19 percent of House races included no Democratic candidate and almost 17 percent had no Republican candidate. Thus, in a state dominated by the Republican Party, the Republicans gave up on one in five races.

Elections to the state legislature are even less competitive. In Texas Senate elections, very rarely are more than half of the seats competitive in the sense of having both major parties with candidates on the ballot. From 1992 until 2014, the general trend was declining competition between the two parties. In a good year, half of the races were competitive.

Texas House of Representatives elections tend to be one-party races. In 2014, Democrats were unable to field a candidate in 40 percent of the Texas House races, and Republicans were unable to field a candidate in 30 percent. That left only 30 percent (forty-five races) with candidates from both the major parties on the ballot, meaning that less than one in three Texas House races included candidates from both major parties.

## TABLE 10.1 Party Competition in Texas Elections, 1992–2014

| Election/ Year | Seats Contested by Republicans Only | | Seats Contested by Democrats Only | | Seats Contested by Both Parties | |
|---|---|---|---|---|---|---|
| | Number | Percentage | Number | Percentage | Number | Percentage |
| **U.S. House of Representatives (Texas)** | | | | | | |
| 1992 | 2 | 6.7% | 3 | 10.0% | 25 | 83.3% |
| 1994 | 5 | 16.7% | 0 | 0.0% | 25 | 83.3% |
| 1996 | 2 | 6.7% | 0 | 0.0% | 28 | 93.3% |
| 1998 | 5 | 16.7% | 7 | 23.3% | 18 | 60.0% |
| 2000 | 3 | 10.0% | 6 | 20.0% | 21 | 70.0% |
| 2002 | 4 | 12.5% | 5 | 15.6% | 23 | 71.9% |
| 2004 | 4 | 12.5% | 3 | 9.4% | 25 | 78.0% |
| 2006 | 1 | 3.1% | 5 | 15.6% | 26 | 81.3% |
| 2008 | 6 | 18.8% | 2 | 6.3% | 24 | 75.0% |
| 2010 | 6 | 18.8% | 0 | 0.0% | 26 | 81.3% |
| 2012 | 4 | 11.1% | 2 | 2.8% | 31 | 86.1% |
| 2014 | 7 | 19.4% | 6 | 16.7% | 23 | 63.9% |
| **Texas Senate** | | | | | | |
| 1992 | 4 | 12.9% | 9 | 29.0% | 18 | 58.1% |
| 1994 | 6 | 19.4% | 9 | 29.0% | 16 | 51.6% |
| 1996 | 5 | 33.3% | 3 | 20.0% | 7 | 46.7% |
| 1998 | 5 | 31.3% | 4 | 25.0% | 7 | 43.8% |
| 2000 | 6 | 40.0% | 4 | 26.7% | 5 | 33.3% |
| 2002 | 10 | 32.3% | 9 | 29.3% | 12 | 38.7% |
| 2004 | 6 | 40.0% | 5 | 33.3% | 4 | 26.7% |
| 2006 | 7 | 43.8% | 2 | 12.5% | 7 | 43.8% |
| 2008 | 5 | 33.3% | 4 | 26.7% | 6 | 40.0% |
| 2010 | 8 | 50.0% | 0 | 0.0% | 8 | 50.0% |
| 2012 | 13 | 41.9% | 4 | 12.9% | 14 | 45.2% |
| 2014 | 6 | 40.0% | 1 | 6.7% | 8 | 53.3% |
| **Texas House of Representatives** | | | | | | |
| 1992 | 36 | 24.0% | 61 | 40.7% | 53 | 35.3% |
| 1994 | 37 | 24.7% | 62 | 41.3% | 51 | 34.0% |
| 1996 | 49 | 32.6% | 43 | 28.7% | 58 | 38.7% |
| 1998 | 53 | 35.3% | 44 | 29.3% | 53 | 35.3% |
| 2000 | 53 | 35.3% | 57 | 38.0% | 40 | 26.7% |
| 2002 | 48 | 32.0% | 35 | 23.3% | 67 | 44.7% |
| 2004 | 51 | 34.0% | 39 | 26.0% | 60 | 40.0% |
| 2006 | 37 | 24.7% | 43 | 28.6% | 70 | 46.7% |
| 2008 | 37 | 24.7% | 39 | 26.0% | 74 | 49.3% |
| 2010 | 54 | 36.0% | 38 | 25.3% | 58 | 38.7% |
| 2012 | 64 | 42.7% | 34 | 22.7% | 52 | 34.7% |
| 2014 | 60 | 40.0% | 45 | 30.0% | 45 | 30.0% |

**Source:** Compiled by the authors from data available from the Texas Secretary of State, "1992–Current Election History," http://elections.sos.state.tx.us/elchist.exe (accessed July 3, 2014).

Third parties, such as the Libertarians or Greens, could field candidates and bring more competition to some elections. Getting on the ballot, however, is a huge hurdle, and candidates of these parties do not often present a real challenge to those of the major parties. The 2008 election, in which the Libertarian Party fielded thirty-nine candidates for the Texas House of Representatives, illustrates this situation. Libertarian candidates averaged about 7.5 percent of the vote in the districts they contested. The best performances by Libertarians occurred in races in which one of the two major parties failed to nominate a candidate. For example, in the 45th District, which includes Blanco and Hays Counties in Central Texas, the Libertarian candidate received 27 percent of the vote, providing the only opposition to the Republican incumbent, Jason Issac.

While you might consider the number of noncompetitive elections of little concern, consider that the 2014 election was widely anticipated as a good year for Republican candidates. With President Obama's popularity dropping during his second term and statewide Republicans expected to win every race, prospects were high for Texas Republicans. Yet in six congressional districts and forty-five Texas House districts, the Texas Republican Party could not field a viable candidate. If voters did not have a candidate to support in a year as promising as 2014, when could they expect to have a chance in those races? It's easy to see why some voters might feel discouraged.

One method of assessing party competition across all fifty states is to develop a measure that takes into account the patterns of competition across gubernatorial elections, percentages of state legislature seats won by parties, the length of time the governorship and legislature are controlled by each party, and the proportion of time the parties divide control over state government. This method is called the Ranney Index. Calculated for 2007–2011, the Ranney Index places Texas in the category of one-party Republican control. Texas, which was considered a competitive state just over a decade ago, has become one of the least competitive states (see Table 10.2).

Ultimately, Texas may see Republican domination decline as the state's demographics change. However, the Democratic Party has had increasing difficulties finding candidates to run for some offices, and Texans have had to rely on competition within the nominating process of the Republican Party to produce quality candidates for statewide office.

## POLITICAL PARTIES IN TEXAS

Texas history has often strained traditional definitions of political parties. One classic definition of a political party comes from eighteenth-century British political philosopher Edmund Burke, who described a party as people "united for promoting by their joint endeavors the national interest, upon some particular principle in which they are all agreed."[12] As we've seen, Texas at times experiences almost as much fighting within its parties as between them, straining the application of the traditional definition of parties to Texas politics. For example, while today's Republican Party can be labeled a conservative party, Republicans frequently clash on the meaning of conservatism, as conflict over issues such as immigration and education divide

## TABLE 10.2 Party Competition in U.S. States

| State | Ranney Party Control Index | Rank: Most Democratic to Most Republican | State | Ranney Party Control Index | Rank: Most Democratic to Most Republican |
|---|---|---|---|---|---|
| **Modified One-Party Democrat** | | | Mississippi | 0.500 | 27 |
| Massachusetts | 0.758 | 1 | Nevada | 0.484 | 28 |
| West Virginia | 0.722 | 2 | Pennsylvania | 0.475 | 29 |
| Arkansas | 0.717 | 3 | Michigan | 0.470 | 30 |
| Hawaii | 0.717 | 4 | Louisiana | 0.437 | 31 |
| Maryland | 0.701 | 5 | Virginia | 0.435 | 32 |
| **Two-Party Competition** | | | Ohio | 0.426 | 33 |
| Washington | 0.644 | 6 | Tennessee | 0.413 | 34 |
| Delaware | 0.640 | 7 | Oklahoma | 0.377 | 35 |
| New Mexico | 0.621 | 8 | Indiana | 0.371 | 36 |
| Rhode Island | 0.620 | 9 | Missouri | 0.370 | 37 |
| New York | 0.620 | 10 | **Modified One-Party Republican** | | |
| Colorado | 0.620 | 11 | Arizona | 0.339 | 38 |
| Illinois | 0.615 | 12 | South Carolina | 0.324 | 39 |
| New Hampshire | 0.609 | 13 | Alaska | 0.324 | 40 |
| Oregon | 0.605 | 14 | Texas | 0.311 | 41 |
| North Carolina | 0.602 | 15 | Georgia | 0.304 | 42 |
| Connecticut | 0.602 | 16 | Kansas | 0.295 | 43 |
| New Jersey | 0.589 | 17 | Florida | 0.292 | 44 |
| Iowa | 0.588 | 18 | South Dakota | 0.263 | 45 |
| Vermont | 0.583 | 19 | Nebraska | 0.261 | 46 |
| California | 0.579 | 20 | North Dakota | 0.248 | 47 |
| Minnesota | 0.551 | 21 | Wyoming | 0.246 | 48 |
| Montana | 0.540 | 22 | Utah | 0.199 | 49 |
| Wisconsin | 0.532 | 23 | Idaho | 0.194 | 50 |
| Maine | 0.523 | 24 | *50-state average* | 0.486 | |
| Kentucky | 0.523 | 25 | | | |
| Alabama | 0.512 | 26 | | | |

**Source:** Modified from Virginia Gray, Russell Hanson, and Thad Kousser, eds., *Politics in the American States: A Comparative Analysis* (Washington, D.C.: CQ Press, 2013), 88.

**Note:** The Ranney Index runs from 0 to 1, with 0 indicating complete domination of the state governorship and legislature by Republicans and 1 indicating complete control by Democrats.

Texans who claim the conservative label. Further complicating matters, as we will see later in this chapter, the Texas Republican Party disagrees with the national Republican Party on several issues.

The realities of the **political party** in Texas are best captured by Leon Epstein's definition of a party as "any group, however loosely organized, seeking to elect governmental office-holders under a given label."[13] While this definition does not meet everyone's hopes for the function of a party, it does match the realities of Texas's parties historically and distinguishes parties from interest groups by noting that parties nominate candidates for office under their label while interest groups do not.

Texas provides an interesting case for examining the role that many political scientists want parties to play. Some scholars want politics to meet the standards of the **responsible party model** of politics, in which each party holds firmly to a consistent, coherent set of policies and has an ideology clearly distinct from the other parties. The virtue of responsible parties is that they provide voters with clear choices and firm positions the parties are pledged to honor if elected. In contrast, political scientist Anthony Downs has described an **electoral competition model** in which parties move to the center of the political spectrum as they attempt to win votes, sacrificing the more purely ideological positions preferred by the proponents of the responsible party model. In this view, the political parties are more pragmatic than ideological and are ready to shift their issue stands from year to year in order to win office. Like American political parties in general, parties in Texas do not match either model perfectly. In fact, as we saw at the beginning of the chapter, Texans sometimes disagree about which model they prefer.

**Political party**
any group, however loosely organized, seeking to elect governmental officeholders under a given label.

**Responsible party model**
the view that each party should hold firmly to a clear and consistent set of policies with a coherent ideology distinct from that of other parties in order to present voters with clear choices.

**Electoral competition model**
the view that parties make a pragmatic move to the center of the political spectrum as they attempt to win votes, sacrificing the more purely ideological positions.

## Party Loyalty and Identification

If you had to summarize the relationship between Texans and their political parties, you'd have to conclude, "it's complicated." While Texans may be independent in some ways, many can be fiercely loyal to their parties. Texans, after all, elected nothing but Democrats to statewide office for almost a hundred years after Reconstruction, and a century of loyalty has to count for something.

Today, Texans vote loyally for their new favorite party, the Republicans. In the 2014 election, the lowest percentage of the vote won by a statewide Republican candidate was Lt. Governor Dan Patrick's 57.9 percent, and in some statewide races the Democrats did not even put up a candidate. John McCain carried Texas with 55 percent of the vote in 2008 and Mitt Romney won 57 percent of the vote in 2012.

When asked where they place themselves on the ideological spectrum, from extremely liberal to extremely conservative, most Texans placed themselves on the conservative end of the spectrum, with 47 percent describing themselves as either extremely conservative, somewhat conservative, or leaning conservative (see Figure 10.2). However, in a 2014 poll, 47 percent of Texans said that they usually think of themselves as Republicans, 43 percent thought of themselves as Democrats, and 10 percent considered themselves independent. Public opinion polls have often suggested that the balance between the two parties in Texas is much closer than it appears in election outcomes, and it seems that many Texans call themselves Democrats or independents but vote Republican in elections.

**Political Ideology and Party Identification in Texas, 2014**

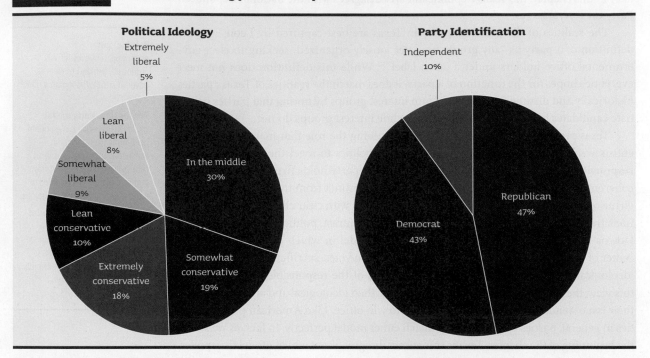

**Source:** University of Texas/*Texas Tribune*, "Texas Statewide Survey of 1,200 Adults, May 30 to June 8, 2014," http://s3.amazonaws.com/static.texastribune .org/media/documents/uttt-jun2014-summary-all.pdf (accessed July 18, 2014).

The relationship between a voter and his or her party is almost always complicated. While party identification is the best predictor of how someone will vote, some of the earliest survey research in political science has shown that party identification is as much a way of seeing the world as it is a choice that citizens make. A voter's choice of candidates is shaped by his or her perception of campaigns and other events, but these perceptions are shaped by the voter's party identification.[14] Members of a political party can be resistant to changes to their partisanship because they see the world through Republican or Democratic lenses that lead them to discount or completely ignore information coming from the other party. Changes to media, such as the growth of social networking sites like Facebook, have only further enabled this tendency, and citizens today can spend much of their lives never encountering information that might change their party identification. Texans seem locked into political parties, despite the fact that so many harbor concerns about their divisive role in American politics and their inability to produce effective leadership in government. Thus, the political parties continue to control elections even as they fail to win the hearts and minds of most citizens.

## Functions of Parties

State and local parties have a variety of important roles in a representative democracy. The most obvious is the nomination of party candidates. Since the distinguishing characteristic of a party is electing candidates under its label, selecting nominees is a central function of the state and local parties. *Slating*, or putting together a list of candidates for all positions, is often seen as an important role of state and local parties as they assemble teams of candidates ready to bring their party's ideas into a variety of offices.

Related to getting candidates on the ballot and elected is the need to seek out the right candidates. Thus, one of the most important functions of state and local parties is recruitment. As each party attempts to build a winning team, it seeks out the most politically talented individuals for the next generation of politics. Precinct and county party leaders must be alert to the presence of individuals with the talent to take themselves and their party to victory in an election. Before he was president, George W. Bush was a Texas governor urged by state Republicans (and some Democrats) to run for president. Before that, he was a businessman urged into state politics by local Republican leaders.

The next step for state and local parties is to support their candidates. Both state parties provide logistical support for party candidates. Some of the support is financial, with parties providing cash contributions as well as advertising and similar support. The parties also provide training for candidates and their campaign staffs. This has become an increasingly important function of state parties as candidates have had to move beyond basic campaigning and embrace polling, Web site usage, and social networking. One party leader said, "I see the party organization as a sort of quartermaster corps, delivering services that achieve economies of scale."[15]

One function that is rapidly expanding may define modern parties: fund-raising. Headlines about presidential involvement in fund-raising in the 1990s clouded the fact that much of the fund-raising being done was actually sending money into state party accounts. Fund-raising and spending in campaigns had shifted to the states because federal campaign finance laws restrict how much individuals can give to the national parties. State parties in general faced few such restrictions and thus found themselves the recipients of the big checks their national parties could not legally accept. However, the McCain-Feingold Act (also known as the Bipartisan Campaign Reform Act of 2000) closed this loophole in campaign finance law. While fund-raising remains an area of controversy, the parties must raise funds to promote their agendas or help their candidates, and they thus remain locked in a competition in which they try to raise more money than the other parties.

Another function is mobilizing voters. Through phone banks, door-to-door canvassing, mailings, and advertising, the parties reach out to voters and encourage them to go to the polls. Of course, a party is most likely to reach out to those voters who will support that party's candidates. However, democracy in general can benefit from healthy competition if both parties reach out to voters and increase turnout in general.

Parties can also be an important tool for representation. Texas's one-party nature has often meant its general elections were not competitive, and the redistricting process described in Chapter 3 divided the state even further by creating districts that are either heavily Republican or heavily Democratic. This means that many Texans live in districts in which it is unlikely that their party will be able to effectively compete. As a consequence, some citizens see themselves as part of a **chronic minority**, a group destined to rarely win an election or achieve majority status. Such citizens see

**Chronic minority**
a group that rarely wins elections or achieves majority status and thus sees few reasons to become actively engaged in politics.

few reasons to become actively engaged in politics and have little hope that their views will be reflected by their representatives in Austin. Parties can offer some hope that such views will be heard, even if these views are channeled through an elected official from another area of the state. For example, Democrats in areas that find themselves represented by Republicans in the Texas House and Senate may hope that Democrats from other parts of the state will give voice to their concerns and advance their causes.

The ultimate function of political parties is control of government since the point of winning elections is getting party candidates into office. In some ways, this function goes against the constitutional order, because our system of checks and balances and separation of powers is intended to keep any one faction from having too much influence. However, parties are elected so they will have influence and get things done, and their ability to coordinate the efforts of officials across the branches of government can be an important tool in creating the kind of leadership a state in transition needs.

## The Consequences of Weak Parties

The scholar V. O. Key observed that Texas's geographic size makes it hard for well-formed political networks to function. Without closely knit political networks, it has been harder for parties to maintain enduring political organizations across the broad geographic expanse of the state. Those parties that were able to build organizations often did so through dramatic appeals to the public that were generally short-lived and created a political coalition based more on personality than policy goals. For example, it was his skills as a flour salesman rather than dependence on a well-ordered political machine that brought Wilbert Lee "Pappy" O'Daniel into the governorship. In contrast, other southern states saw the rise of personal political machines, such as the Longs in Louisiana, that spanned several generations.

With no well-organized party organization to provide resistance, political outsiders have often found their way into the Texas governor's mansion. In the absence of a well-established political order, working through the system has less value, and a political newcomer's dramatic appeal can more easily win the election. While the early twentieth century saw the success of some lively outsiders, such as James E. "Pa" Ferguson and Pappy O'Daniel, more recent elections have seen the rise of political newcomers, such as William Clements and George W. Bush, leading the Republican revival in the state.

Changes in the national politics have weakened Texas parties further. Early in U.S. history, the lack of communication and the decentralized nature of American government meant that the national parties looked something like a collection of state and local party bosses. They gathered at each party's national conventions to bargain their way to the selection of a presidential candidate for the party, a process that often took several days and repeated ballots.

Several changes combined to alter the nature of the parties and the role of local party leaders. First, the creation of party primaries took control of the nomination from party leaders and gave it to voters in party primaries. Later, the rising power of the national government naturally shifted attention from state parties to the national interest groups and parties that grappled with these issues in the White House and on Capitol Hill. Later, the rise of media campaigns made candidates more reliant on the

# HOW TEXAS GOVERNMENT WORKS

## Party Organization

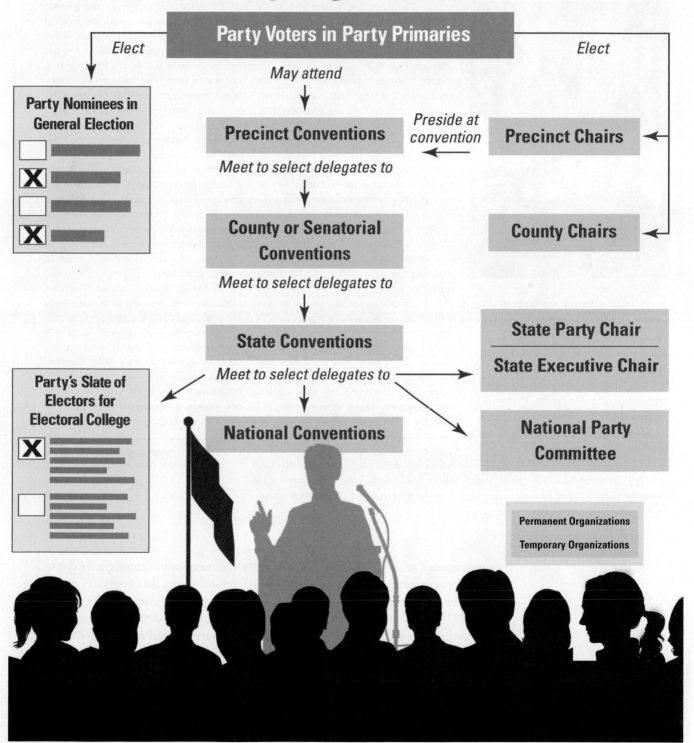

**Party Voters in Party Primaries**

*Elect* *Elect*

*May attend*

**Party Nominees in General Election**

**Precinct Conventions**

*Preside at convention*

**Precinct Chairs**

*Meet to select delegates to*

**County or Senatorial Conventions**

**County Chairs**

*Meet to select delegates to*

**State Conventions**

**State Party Chair**

**State Executive Chair**

*Meet to select delegates to*

**Party's Slate of Electors for Electoral College**

**National Conventions**

**National Party Committee**

Permanent Organizations

Temporary Organizations

## Pappy O'Daniel

ND-41-A004-01, Austin History Center, Austin Public Library

As we've noted, Texas's size has given an advantage to characters flamboyant enough to grab the voters' attention across the state. One of Texas's legendary governors, "Pass the Biscuits, Pappy" O'Daniel (pictured, left, with Harry Akin) is a fine example of the ability of a colorful outsider to push aside established party leaders and land on top of the state's power structure.

Wilbert Lee O'Daniel was born in Ohio but moved to Texas in 1925. As sales manager for a flour mill, O'Daniel became well known as the host of a radio show featuring music from Bob Wills and Milton Brown's band, The Light Crust Doughboys. The show opened with someone saying, "Pass the Biscuits, Pappy." It mixed inspirational stories with music, including songs that O'Daniel penned with titles such as "The Boy Who Never Got Too Big to Comb His Mother's Hair." In 1938, purportedly spurred by listener letters urging him to run for governor (although others suggest that wealthy business interests and a public relations expert had done the real urging), O'Daniel declared his candidacy, proclaiming the Ten Commandments as his platform and the Golden Rule as his motto. O'Daniel won the Democratic nomination without a runoff and, facing no real opposition, won the general election with 97 percent of the vote.

An estimated 100,000 people packed into Memorial Stadium in Austin to witness his inauguration, but O'Daniel quickly exhibited his lack of political skill by proposing a thinly disguised sales tax, making numerous questionable appointments, and forgetting his only specific campaign promise—a $30-a-month pension for every Texan over sixty-five. By the time of his reelection campaign, he was opposed by almost every newspaper in the state, with the *Dallas Morning News* proclaiming, "The highest office in the state has been the laughingstock of the United States for a year and a half."[i] Voters nevertheless returned O'Daniel to office, but he accomplished little in his second term beyond positioning himself for a move to the U.S. Senate by appointing Andrew Jackson Houston, Sam Houston's only surviving son, to fill a vacancy left after Sen. Morris Sheppard died in April 1941. Houston, the oldest man to serve in the U.S. Senate to that point, died the next year, leaving O'Daniel without an incumbent to worry about in the special election. O'Daniel's only serious primary challenger was a young ex-congressman named Lyndon Baines Johnson. Johnson led through much of the ballot counting, but late returns from rural districts gave O'Daniel the victory, leaving Johnson to await another day.

While O'Daniel's colorful character effectively swept Johnson aside in the Texas primary, it did nothing to endear him to the Washington establishment. O'Daniel's down-home, colorful stylings won him few victories in the nation's capital. His public appeal made him a legend in Texas, but O'Daniel's leadership did little to leave any real legacy of accomplishment, either in Austin or Washington, D.C.

---

i.  Randolph B. Campbell, *Gone to Texas* (New York: Oxford University Press, 2004), 394.

money needed to air ads than on the local party volunteers who campaigned door to door. Most recently, political power has followed the shifting tracks of political money that came with changes to campaign finance rules. The 2010 U.S. Supreme Court decision in *Citizens United v. Federal Election Commission* and other changes mean that union, corporate, and other funds can be used to purchase political advertising directly without the need of political middlemen, such as political parties.

Rather than giving money to the broad party organization, states are seeing more and more money going into legislative campaign committees, which are fund-raising committees that raise money from individuals and interest groups and then distribute it to candidates at the national political party level. While these committees can help members of a party win election, they may weaken the influence of the state party because these groups need not support the party's agenda and may represent one particular faction of the party at the expense of others. For example, while Citizens for Lawsuit Reform gives millions of dollars directly to Republican candidates and generally agrees with the Republican Party, its ability to contribute or spend money independently rather than through the party means that it does not have to work with party leaders. Party leaders can still exert influence under these new campaign laws, but the challenges they face continue to grow as organized interests have fewer reasons to work with them.

## PARTY ORGANIZATIONS

Because of the role they play in the practice of democracy in the state, the organization and functioning of political parties is subject to some regulation by the state. The U.S. Supreme Court has ruled that state law can regulate the internal affairs of political parties only if it is "necessary to ensure that elections are orderly, fair, and honest."[16] Texas state law still places restrictions on the selection, composition, rules, and meeting dates of the state and local political party committees. In fact, Texas is rated a "heavy regulator," with some of the most extensive laws governing the state's parties.[17]

Political parties in the United States are composed of both temporary and permanent organizations. The **temporary party organizations** are gatherings of ordinary party members through primaries and in meetings known as caucuses and conventions. The **permanent party organizations** are the party officials selected by the temporary organizations to conduct the business of the party in between primaries, caucuses, and conventions.

While the temporary nature of party conventions may make them seem less important, like any democratic organization, America's political parties draw their legitimacy from the participation of citizens. As such, a political party is a **grassroots organization**, or a group in which power and decision making reside with average citizens. This relationship makes these gatherings of party members the foundation upon which the party claims legitimacy.

Citizens' participation in Texas's two major parties begins at the local level through primaries, which are elections in which ordinary citizens vote to choose the candidates that will represent a party on the ballot in the general election (See "How Texas Government Works" graphic on page 329). Primaries have been part of Texas elections since the Terrell Election Law in 1905 mandated that major political parties use primaries to select their nominees. Prior to that, parties were free to make their nominations however they pleased, with nominees usually being chosen by nominating conventions composed of party leaders without input from average citizens. Progressives promoted primaries as a means to take the choice of candidates away from political bosses meeting behind the scenes and expand participation to ordinary citizens.

Current Texas law requires that the major parties (those that received 20 percent or more of the vote for governor in the last election) use primaries to choose their

**Temporary party organizations**
gatherings of ordinary party members, such as primaries, caucuses, and conventions.

**Permanent party organizations**
the party officials selected by the temporary organizations to conduct party business between the primaries, caucuses, and conventions.

**Grassroots organization**
a group in which power and decision making reside with average citizens; the participation of average citizens is the foundation upon which these groups' legitimacy rests.

candidates for office. Parties whose candidate for governor received between 2 percent and 20 percent of the vote in the last election have a choice between nominating candidates by convention or by primary. Parties whose gubernatorial candidates received less than 2 percent of the vote must use conventions because of the costs involved in holding primaries. Primaries require separate voting booths for each party in every precinct in the state. To control costs, minor political parties, such as the Libertarian Party, typically choose conventions when given the option of primaries.

For decades, the major political parties operated their primaries as they pleased, claiming along the way that their private status allowed them to set their own restrictions—including barring black voters. Until 1972, political parties paid for primaries, relying on hefty candidate filing fees to fund these elections.

As noted in Chapter 9, Texas party primaries are technically closed primaries with only party members allowed to vote. In practice, Texas primaries are much more accessible and function as semi-open primaries in which any voter may participate without having previously registered a party affiliation. When Texans vote in a party's primary, their voter registration cards are stamped with the name of that party. Under state law, this "affiliates" citizens with a specific party for an entire year and thus makes them ineligible to participate in any other party's primary that year. While this affiliation does make them a member of the party for that year in some sense of the word, this affiliation does not obligate them to contribute to, vote for, or support in any way that party's candidates. By law, a party affiliation expires at the end of each voting year; before the primaries in the next set of elections two years later, all voters receive new registration cards with no party affiliation, leaving them free to vote in whichever primary they choose. The impact of affiliating with a party by voting in its primary is that the citizen is excluded from participating in the nominating process of other parties or independent candidates. In addition, Texas's "sore loser law" prohibits someone from voting or running in the primary of one party and later running for office under the label of another party in the same year. In 2012, two Democratic candidates in Angelina County were disqualified from the November ballot because they had cast votes in the Republican primary that year.

In states with more restrictive closed primaries, citizens face a deadline before which they must declare their party affiliation; this can be as much as eleven months before the primary in which they wish to participate. One advantage of such strict rules is that they ensure that the people who vote in the primaries are "real" party members. A disadvantage is that voters who are excluded from the party's primary by such rules may feel less inclined to get behind the party's candidates. Thus, parties have to balance between maintaining some sense of ideological purity by excluding people who may not share their views and the need to be inclusive and bring in as many voters as possible.

The flexibility of Texas's primary voting system can create its own set of problems. For generations, many conservative Texans continued to vote in the Democratic primary since they could often nominate like-minded conservatives as Democrats and see them elected in November. Meanwhile, other conservatives sought to make the Republican Party more viable. Today, Democrats face a similar dilemma. Many vote in the Republican primary hoping to make that party's nominee as moderate as possible. Others will seek out the nominee who will most embarrass the Republican Party.

Under state law, a political party's nominee must receive a majority of the total number of votes in the primary. Races that generate competition from three or more candidates raise the possibility that no nominee will get the required majority, necessitating a **runoff primary** in which the top two finishers from the first primary face off. This was the case in the May 27, 2012, primary for the U.S. Senate when David Dewhurst won 44.6 percent of the vote, Ted Cruz won 34.2 percent, and seven other candidates divided up the rest of the vote. With neither candidate having a majority, Dewhurst and Cruz then faced off in a runoff primary on July 31. Ted Cruz won with 56.8 percent of the vote.

The parties may also include nonbinding referendum items on their primary ballot. For example, in 2012, the Republican Party included referendum items on school choice, health care, federal spending, and public prayer. These items generally serve little purpose other than as symbolic statements designed to rally voters around shared goals. The lowest level of support among the 2012 items was 75.5 percent of Republican primary voters casting their vote for the proposition that stated "the Texas Legislature should redraw the court-imposed lines for Congress and State legislative districts in its upcoming session in order to remedy inequities." Meanwhile, Texas Democrats were approving their party's support for casino gambling, affordable college tuition and in-state tuition, and a change in legal status for illegal immigrants who became college graduates or joined the military.

## Local Parties

Party primaries also elect local party officers. In Texas, party members in each voting precinct elect by a majority vote a **precinct chair** and in a countywide vote select a **county chair**. These officers are responsible for managing the local affairs of their party for the next two years. To be eligible to be a county or precinct chair of a political party, a person must only be a qualified voter and not hold or be a candidate for any elective federal, state, or county office. To make participation as easy as possible, state law provides that a candidate for county chair or precinct chair not be required to pay a fee in order to get on the primary ballot.

At the county level, each party has a county executive committee composed of a county chair and the precinct chair from each precinct in the county. This committee is the permanent committee that oversees the party's organization, fund-raising, and campaigning within the county. There is often little competition for these positions, and they sometimes go vacant because most Texans are content to leave the business of politics to others. However, in some

**Runoff primary**
a primary that occurs if no nominee receives the required majority of the votes in the primary; the top two finishers face off in a second primary to determine the nominee for the general election.

**Precinct chair; County chair**
a precinct chair is selected by party members in each voting precinct by majority vote; a county chair is selected by countywide vote. These party officials are responsible for managing the local affairs of their party for the next two years.

U.S. senator Ted Cruz speaks to delegates at the Texas GOP Convention in Fort Worth, Texas, in 2014. The Tea Party favorite's popularity may signal a shift to a stronger conservatism in the state.

© Rex C. Curry/AP/Corbis

areas, conservative Christian groups have aggressively sought to win those positions in the Republican Party as a means of exerting more influence over party affairs, a strategy that has contributed to their success in gaining control of the Republican Party statewide. The success of conservative Christian political forces in Texas illustrates that big political victories are often built upon many small efforts.

While these local officials still have some influence, their role has diminished over the last century. The power of local party officials to select political candidates and select delegates to state and national conventions was lost as the parties became more democratic through the introduction of primaries. In addition, when campaigns relied on the labors of individuals going door to door and communicating one-on-one with voters, the local party officials were one of the few organizations positioned to mobilize the necessary human resources. Today, campaigns are increasingly in the hands of media-savvy campaign specialists and require less human effort and more cash to pay for advertising on television and radio and technical know-how to establish an effective presence on the Internet. Candidates now use direct mail, the Internet, and other techniques to raise money without working through local party leaders. Although these local party officials may still enjoy some political clout, their influence must be based on providing campaigning or fund-raising skills since they no longer control patronage positions.

On the same day as the primary voting, the parties hold precinct-level meetings, or **conventions** (in much of the nation these meetings are called **caucuses** when conducted at the local level), in which party members meet to conduct a range of party business. Primary conventions are temporary organizations in the party structure that convene on the day of the primary election between 7:00 p.m. and 9:00 p.m., usually in the same location as the primary election. Sometimes, Republicans and Democrats hold their precinct conventions in different rooms in the same building, often the same school, church, fire station, or other building that hosted voting earlier that day. State law requires that a written notice at the polling place provide to primary voters the date, hour, and place for convening the precinct convention.

While these meetings are open only to party members, recall that party affiliation in Texas requires only showing up for the primary and requesting the party ballot. Thus, citizens in Texas can choose their party the day of the primary election and return in the evening to attend their party's caucuses. Minor parties that do not use primaries to nominate candidates obviously cannot require that citizens vote in their primary to participate in their party's convention. In these cases, a citizen wishing to participate in the convention of a party that has not held a primary may affiliate with that party simply by taking an oath prescribed by law: "I swear that I have not voted in a primary election or participated in a convention of another party during this voting year. I hereby affiliate myself with the _____ Party."

Precinct conventions are used to elect **delegates** (and alternates) who will attend the party's conventions held later at the county level or Texas senatorial district level. The number of delegates a precinct is allotted is based on how many members of the party voted in that precinct in that election. While selecting those party members to represent the precinct at future conventions is the primary function of the precinct conventions, attendees may also vote on resolutions related to political issues, especially those on which citizens want their party to take an official stand.

**Conventions (caucuses)**
meetings at which party members participate in a range of party business.

**Delegates**
party members elected to attend their party's conventions that are held later at the county level or the Texas senatorial district level.

On the third Saturday after the primary election, each of the major parties holds its **county or senatorial district convention**. A county convention is held in a county if the county is not situated in more than one state senatorial district. If a county is in more than one state senatorial district, a senatorial district convention is held in each part of the county that is in a different senatorial district. These conventions select delegates to the statewide convention and deal with other party business.

## State Parties

Texas's political parties hold their state conventions biennially in June. The convention includes delegates selected by the county or senatorial district conventions, although nominees for or holders of state or national government offices are entitled to attend the state convention of their party, but they may not vote in the convention unless they have been selected to serve as delegates by their county or senatorial district through the usual process.

While the state conventions are temporary party organizations, meeting over a few days every two years, they are important events because state parties really only take form when the parties' members gather in state conventions at this time. For example, state law requires that party rules must be approved by the party's state convention. While gathered, each state convention writes and approves their **party platform**, the document that officially spells out the issue stands of the party. Each issue position of the party platform is referred to as a **plank**. (See Table 10.3 for excerpts from the 2014 platforms for the Texas Republican and Democratic parties.)

While often the subject of dramatic debates, party platforms are largely symbolic documents with no binding effect on the candidates or officeholders of the party. While the 2014 Texas Republican platform included a brief section on enforcement, it provided that "every Republican is responsible for implementing this platform."[18] This actually means that no party officer or committee has authority to enforce the platform. Further, there has been no enforcement of the platform's call for party candidates to indicate their positions on platform planks and to make such information available on the party Web site. While some party members may want to enforce such standards, the basic party structure in Texas gives the party's officers no real control over who declares himself or herself a Republican or Democrat.

Texas's parties, like most of those in the South, are relatively weak. For example, Texas's party leaders do not make pre-primary endorsements, a practice more common in the Northeast and Midwest. The permanent officers of the parties do hold some authority, yet they are often rivaled by elected officials from their party. While the head of the Republican Party is selected by the state Republican convention, Governor Greg Abbott can rightfully claim that he reflects the wishes of the Republican voters statewide. Thus, the label of "party leader" is much more subjective than the official party organization charts would suggest.

Each party's leaders are selected by the state conventions. Delegates elect a **state party chair** and **executive committee** to carry on the activities of the party between state conventions. By law, each party's state executive committee consists of one man and one woman from each state senatorial district. In addition, each state committee's chair and

**County or senatorial district convention**
a convention in which delegates to the statewide convention are selected; held on the third Saturday after the primary election.

**Party platform**
the document that officially spells out the issue stands of a party; written and approved at the party conventions.

**Plank**
an individual issue position of the party platform.

**State party chair**
individual selected at the state party convention to head the state executive committee; state law mandates that if the chair is a man, a woman must be the vice chair, or vice versa.

**Executive committee**
this group, selected at the state party convention, carries on the activities of the party between party conventions; by law, the committee consists of sixty-two members—one man and one woman from each of the state's thirty-one senatorial districts.

## TABLE 10.3 Comparison of 2014 Texas Party Platforms

| Issue | 2014 Texas Republican Party Platform | 2014 Texas Democratic Party Platform |
|---|---|---|
| Abortion | "Until our final goal of total constitutional rights for the unborn child is achieved, we support laws that restrict and regulate abortion...." | "Texas Democrats...trust the women of Texas to make personal and responsible decisions about when and whether to bear children." |
| Bilingual education | "We encourage non-English speaking students to transition to English within three years." | "Texas should...reject efforts to destroy bilingual education." |
| Capital punishment | "Properly applied capital punishment is legitimate, is an effective deterrent, and should be swift and unencumbered." | "[T]o promote public confidence and fairness in the Texas Criminal Justice system, Texas Democrats call for...legislation that would abolish the death penalty...and replace it with the punishment of life in prison without parole." |
| Drugs | "We oppose legalization of illicit and synthetic drugs. We support an effective abstinence-based educational program for children." | "Texas Democrats urge...the passage of legislation to decriminalize the possession of marijuana and regulate its use, production, and sale as is done with tobacco and alcohol." |
| Higher education | "Since data is clear that additional money does not translate into educational achievement, and higher education costs are out of control, we support reducing taxpayer funding to all levels of education institutions." | "To offer affordable access to higher education, we support...restoration of formula contact hour funding to the level prior to Republican cuts, adjusted for inflation and student growth." |
| Homosexuality | "Homosexuality must not be presented as an acceptable alternative lifestyle, in public policy, nor should family be redefined to include homosexual couples....We recognize the legitimacy and efficacy of counseling, which offers reparative therapy and treatment for those patients seeking healing and wholeness from their homosexual lifestyle." | "Texas Democrats call for the immediate repeal of the Texas Defense of Marriage Act and the Texas Constitutional Marriage Amendment and oppose other attempts to deny the freedom to marry to loving same-sex couples....We recognize and applaud the many unions and businesses whose standard contracts prohibit LGBTQ employment discrimination." |
| Immigration | Texas Republicans support ending in-state tuition for illegal immigrants. | "We strongly oppose...any effort to repeal in-state tuition benefits to Texas undocumented students." |
| Minimum wage | "We believe the Minimum Wage Law should be repealed." | "We believe the minimum wage must be raised, enforced, and applied meaningfully across-the-board to restore lost purchasing power for all workers." |
| Right to bear arms | "We oppose the monitoring of gun ownership, the taxation and regulation of guns, ammunition, and gun magazines. We collectively urge the legislature to pass 'constitutional carry' legislation, whereby law-abiding citizens that possess firearms can legally exercise their God-given right to carry that firearm as well." | "Texas Democrats support just and smart policies, including: requiring that all persons who sell guns of any kind through employment at a gun manufacturer or through a FFL Dealer pass a Brady background check; strengthening programs designed to trace crime gun purchases to shut down unscrupulous firearms dealers; removing restrictions on the ability of local, state, and federal law enforcement to access important gun trace information...." |

**Sources:** Excerpted from the 2014 Texas Democratic Party Platform, http://txdemocrats.bytrilogy.com/pdf/2-Platform.pdf (accessed September 3, 2014) and from the 2014 Republican Party of Texas Platform, www.texasgop.org/wp-content/uploads/2014/06/2014-Platform-Final.pdf (accessed September 3, 2014).

vice chair positions must include some combination of a man and a woman—either the chair must be a man and the vice chair a woman, or vice versa. Texas's state party executive committee is typical of state party committees, if there is such a thing as a typical state party committee. As one text points out, "So great are the differences between these committees from state to state—in membership selection, size, and function—that it is difficult to generalize about them."[19]

## Nominating Presidential Candidates

In addition to conducting the business of the state parties, the state party conventions in presidential election years must also select the parties' delegates to the national party convention and the representatives to the parties' national committee, as well as the slate of electors who will be available to serve in the Electoral College.

Today, state law requires that major parties in Texas hold presidential "preference primaries" in presidential election years, in conjunction with their regular primaries. Texans may use this primary to express their preference for one of the candidates on the ballot, or they may vote "uncommitted" if the rules of their party allow such a vote. While holding these primaries at the same time as the nominating primaries for other offices makes some sense by consolidating voting dates, it presents a dilemma in national politics as many states attempt to move their primaries earlier in the year to garner as much attention as possible from presidential candidates. Texas, which held its primaries in June for many years, moved its primary date up to early March in 1988 and joined the ranks of "Super Tuesday" primaries, so named because many of the large states held their party primaries on that Tuesday. In 2007, in response to moves by other states to hold their primaries even earlier, the Texas Legislature considered moving its primary to February to avoid being left to vote on presidential nominations after a candidate had already won enough state and local votes to lock up the nomination. In 2008, Texas Republicans and Democrats cast their votes on March 4, by which date about two-thirds of the states had already voted. In 2012, the party primaries were originally scheduled for March 6. However, legal challenges to redistricting delayed the state's primaries until districts could be finalized and candidates were given some time to enter the race and begin to meet voters. Ultimately, the 2012 primaries were moved back to May 29—well after the parties' choices of presidential nominees were clear.

The problem for Texas is that many citizens prefer to nominate their candidates a little closer to Election Day. Moving up the nominating process earlier in the year only extends an already-long campaign season. Some states hold separate presidential primaries at different times from the primaries used to select other offices. Other states, such as Kansas and Iowa, have opted not to hold a presidential primary in their state and rely on a caucus instead.

Texas's presidential primary has not always been binding. When voters filed through the voting booths during the day to vote in the primary, the number of delegates that their favorite candidate was allocated was decided by party members who attended the precinct conventions that evening and other conventions later in the spring. Today, while the party conventions select which individuals will be sent to the party's national convention as delegates, the allocation of these delegates

between the competing candidates for president is determined by party rules, which use results from the presidential preference primary to allocate candidates on a districtwide or statewide basis. Currently, state law requires that at least 75 percent of delegates representing the state at the party's national convention be allocated based on the votes in the presidential primaries. However, the law does not dictate exactly how the parties use the results of primary voting in allocating those delegates. For example, the Republicans have an elaborate system of allocating delegates using the vote counts at the congressional district and statewide levels. A candidate who receives more than 50 percent of the votes within a congressional district is entitled to all of the delegates to the Republican convention from that district. When no candidate gets 50 percent, the delegates are divided between those candidates who received more than 20 percent of the vote.

In 2008, Texas came under scrutiny for its system of delegate allocation because candidate Hillary Clinton won the popular vote in the state's Democratic presidential primary but did not win the majority of the 228 delegates Texas sent to the Democratic National Convention. The controversy resulted from Texas's complicated allocation process. **Allocation** refers to how many of the state's delegates will attend the national convention pledged to vote for a specific candidate or attend as undecided. Because the Texas Democratic Party wants to encourage participation in all stages of the nominating process, delegates are actually allocated in three ways: (1) allocation based on primary day votes, (2) allocation based on convention attendance, and (3) unpledged superdelegates.

The contest between Barack Obama and Hillary Clinton in the 2008 Texas Democratic primary provides a good illustration of the complexities of the current

**Allocation**
the process by which party rules designate how many of the state's delegates to the national party convention will be pledged to vote for a specific candidate or will attend as undecided.

system. Of Texas's 228 delegates in 2008, only 126 (or 56 percent) were allocated based on the votes cast by Democrats in the primary on March 4. However, it's not as simple as counting up the votes statewide. Delegates are actually allocated to a candidate based on the proportion of votes they receive within each of the state's thirty-one Texas Senate districts (candidates who get less than 15 percent of the vote in the district get no delegates). So, on primary election night, what looks like a statewide competition is actually thirty-one separate competitions.

Not all Senate districts are equal in the eyes of the Democratic Party because while all the districts have about the same number of Texans in them, they don't all have the same number of Democrats. Based on Democratic voter turnout in past elections, districts may select anywhere from two delegates (District 31 in West Texas) to eight delegates (District 14 in Austin).

Another sixty-seven of the state's 228 delegates (29 percent) are allocated to a candidate based on how many Democrats showed up at the party's precinct-level conventions and signed in for their favorite candidate. Thus, attending the precinct convention after voting in the primary is like casting a second vote for your candidate. The system has earned the nickname the "Texas Two-Step," which makes it sound more fun than voters actually find it to be.

While the Texas process has been criticized, Texas Democrats voted at the 2010 state convention to retain the Texas Two-Step. Why would they do this? Remember, the parties do things other than nominate presidential candidates. If the parties give voters something kind of fun and interesting to do at the party convention (such as support a favorite candidate), they stand a better chance of roping voters into attending to the other, more mundane business of the party (for example, establishing rules and debating the party's platform). It's a kind of political bait-and-switch that can pay off because getting voters involved in the party makes them more likely to support their candidate.

The often-overlooked third leg of the Texas Two-Step rests on unpledged superdelegates. Superdelegates are elected officials and party leaders who get invited to the national convention without going through the selection process required of ordinary Democrats. While this may be unfair in many regards, it is designed to connect the state's leading Democrats with the presidential nominating process. In fact, both parties have superdelegates, although the Democrats invite more of them to their national convention.

The lack of strict national party rules for counting delegates reflects the independence of the state parties and the nature of American political parties. In 2011, for example, many states ignored the national parties' threats to exert more control by reducing the number of delegates of those states that had violated party rules and went ahead and moved their presidential primaries to dates earlier than those allowed by national party rules. The states considered the attention they received from the candidates and national media worth the risk that the national parties would follow through with the threatened sanctions.

## The State Parties and the National Parties

Although citizens generally consider parties to be consistent across all levels of government, there are actually significant differences between the expressed opinions

# TEXAS (VS) IOWA

While most states require parties to hold primaries to nominate candidates for the general election, Iowa uses a system of caucuses. The word *caucus* allegedly comes from a Native American word for a meeting between tribal leaders.[i] The Iowa caucus system developed in the late 1800s within political parties as a method of selecting delegates to political party conventions. The Iowa Caucuses operate similarly to a closed primary in that the participants must be registered with a political party. This process effectively limits the Republican caucuses only to Republicans and the Democratic caucuses only to Democrats.

On the night of the Iowa Caucuses, participants gather in over 2,000 local, precinct-level meetings. Historically, these meetings occurred in the homes of local party activists, creating a feeling of neighborliness among participants. In recent years, the meetings have occurred at a local school, library, or church, or at a similar place. To some extent, the caucuses still take on the flavor of a giant precinct party.

The two major parties have slightly different rules concerning how the caucus proceeds. For the Republican Party, the caucus consists of participants dropping the name of a candidate in a hat. Results are then tabulated. At a separate meeting, participants choose delegates to attend a state convention where the official nomination of party candidates for the general election takes place. At the Democratic caucus, participants break into groups based upon which candidate they support. Note that "undecided" is an acceptable grouping. If any group consists of less than 15 percent of the total number of participants, then those group members must realign with another group. Participants then lobby and persuade members of the other groups or the groups with less than 15 percent to change their preference. When all remaining groups supporting a candidate are above 15 percent of the total participants at that location, delegates to the party county convention are allocated based upon the size of the groups. Here is a comparison of the results of the party caucuses since 1972 when the Iowa Caucuses gained their reputation as a presidential bellwether and grabbed the attention of candidates and the nation alike.

By tradition, the Iowa Caucuses are the first caucuses held in the United States. Because winning, or at least doing well or "better than expected," in an Iowa Caucus creates momentum for a candidate's campaign and encourages financial support from donors, the Iowa Caucuses are very important to candidates running for U.S. president. For example, Rick Santorum's narrow win in the 2012 Republican Iowa Caucus gave his campaign a boost that helped him be seen as one of the primary challengers to Mitt Romney. Because so much attention is paid to Iowa's caucus results, critics suggest that Iowa carries too much weight in presidential elections, especially considering the state's relatively small and homogenous population.

While turnout for Texas primaries is quite low, the turnout rates for the Iowa Caucuses appear to be increasing. However, turnout for

## Results of the Iowa Caucuses since 1972

| Year | Democratic Party Iowa Caucus Winner | National Party Nominee | Republican Party Iowa Caucus Winner | National Party Nominee |
|------|-------------------------------------|------------------------|-------------------------------------|------------------------|
| 2012 | Barack Obama | Barack Obama | Rick Santorum | Mitt Romney |
| 2008 | Barack Obama | Barack Obama | Mike Huckabee | John McCain |
| 2004 | John Kerry | John Kerry | George W. Bush | George W. Bush |
| 2000 | Al Gore | Al Gore | George W. Bush | George W. Bush |
| 1996 | Bill Clinton | Bill Clinton | Bob Dole | Bob Dole |
| 1992 | Tom Harkin | Bill Clinton | George H. W. Bush | George H. W. Bush |
| 1988 | Richard Gephardt | Michael Dukakis | Bob Dole | George H. W. Bush |
| 1984 | Walter Mondale | Walter Mondale | Ronald Reagan | Ronald Reagan |
| 1980 | Jimmy Carter | Jimmy Carter | George H. W. Bush | Ronald Reagan |
| 1976 | Uncommitted | Jimmy Carter | Gerald Ford | Gerald Ford |
| 1972 | Edmund Muskie | George McGovern | Richard Nixon | Richard Nixon |

**Source:** Compiled from "Caucus History: Past Years' Results," *Des Moines Register*, http://caucuses.desmoinesregister.com/caucus-history-past-years-results/ (accessed September 3, 2014).

the Iowa Caucuses is harder to determine simply because, in contrast to closed primaries, lists of registered Democratic or Republican voters do not exist. Estimates of participation in the Democratic caucuses indicate that the percentage of the population that participates in the caucuses is increasing over time.[ii]

## THINKING *Critically*

★ Have you ever voted in a primary in Texas? Why or why not?

★ Would you be more likely to participate in the Texas presidential primaries if they occurred earlier in the nomination process or if the candidates campaigned more actively in the state?

★ What do you think the advantages or disadvantages of a system such as the Iowa Caucuses would be if Texas changed to that system?

i. "Frequently Asked Caucus Questions," *Des Moines Register*, www.desmoines register.com (accessed November 5, 2007).

ii. Ibid.

of the parties. Because American parties are grassroots organizations in which power flows from the bottom up, the national parties are not able to impose their views on the state parties. Texas political parties vividly illustrate the inability of the national parties to control party members. For example, for years the national Democratic Party championed civil rights while some of the conservative Democrats who controlled the Texas Democratic Party vigorously opposed civil rights legislation. More recently, the Texas Republican Party platform has consistently "demanded" the elimination of presidential authority to issue executive orders and the repeal of all previous executive orders, despite the fact that the executive order was used frequently by George W. Bush and other Republican presidents.

The national party conventions have come to be dominated by the campaign organization of the presidential candidates rather than by the state parties. Because delegates to the national convention are selected based on attachment to national presidential candidates rather than service in the local party, the local party's role has been diminished. This undermines some of the representational role of parties as local concerns disappear into the shadow of national politics.

State and local parties in the United States are in a precarious position. While local party leaders remain important actors in recruiting party candidates and building the parties at the local level, the rise of mass media and candidate-centered campaigns has taken away some of the local parties' most important functions as vehicles for raising money and getting candidates' messages out. Some have called state and local parties "Mom-and-Pop Shops in the Information Age,"[20] and as citizens make more use of television and the Internet to learn about candidates, local parties may find less to do. This represents one way in which changes in the state may permanently transform the way the parties operate and who in the parties holds significant power.

## WINNERS AND LOSERS

Although the primaries and conventions may technically be open to any eligible voters willing to declare themselves members of a party, Texans generally seem increasingly uninterested in participating in the business of parties. In March 2014, only 7.2 percent of Texans went to the polls to choose between the Republican nominees for office; only 3 percent voted in the Democratic primary. With just over 10 percent of eligible Texans voting in the primaries that year, how representative are the nominees of the two major parties? V. O. Key argued that "over the long run, the have-nots lose in a disorganized politics."[21] According to Key, when there are no strong parties, no one has the incentive and ability to mobilize disorganized interests. Without well-organized parties, some citizens will remain disorganized and their interests diffuse. Organization is especially important to anyone wishing to promote serious reform since reform efforts require battling an entrenched status quo.

Domination by one party complicates matters. Without groups to mobilize the masses, there is no policy debate, leaving voters less informed and the meaning of election victories less clear. Without an ongoing agenda, party labels are much less meaningful, and differences between parties are more difficult for voters to discern. This means that new Texans looking to take their place in politics and old Texans interested in reforming the system will both need to be well organized as they promote change. This lesson applies most particularly to Hispanics as they increasingly attempt to exert influence in Texas politics and to Republicans as they seek to remove institutional barriers to their political rise.

Ironically, while Texans value their independent nature, independent Texans suffer the most in this setting. While these voters could legally show up and vote in either the Republican or Democratic primary, doing so might imply a level of support for the party that they are uncomfortable with. Additionally, the strong partisans that dominate voting in Texas primaries may be creating choices too extreme for the tastes of independent Texans. Thus, such voters may stay home during the primary and then find themselves equally uncomfortable with the choices they have in the general election.

★ What elements in the Texas political process inhibit voters from participating more widely in state politics?

★ How have changes in national politics impacted Texas's state politics? Are these changes for the better? Why or why not?

★ How does strong partisan ideology serve to weaken Texas's political parties?

## CONCLUSION

The importance of parties in Texas is not in dispute, but their place in Texans' hearts and their contribution to competitive elections is less certain. V. O. Key, who defined much of our understanding of Texas and southern politics, noted, "As institutions, parties enjoy a general disrepute, but most of the democratic world finds them indispensable as instruments of self-government, as means for the organization and expression of competing viewpoints on public policy."[22]

They may express frustration and proclaim their political independence, but the citizens of Texas have proved unswervingly loyal to first the Democratic Party and now the Republican Party. Despite their disdain and doubts, Texans continually turn to these political institutions, ensuring them a place in the future of Texas politics.

for CQ Press

Sharpen your skills with **SAGE edge** at **edge.sagepub.com/collier4e. SAGE edge for students** provides a personalized approach to help you accomplish your coursework goals in an easy-to-use learning environment.

## KEY TERMS

allocation (p. 338)

chronic minority (p. 327)

conventions (caucuses) (p. 334)

county chair (p. 333)

county or senatorial district convention (p. 335)

delegates (p. 334)

electoral competition model (p. 325)

executive committee (p. 335)

grassroots organization (p. 331)

party platform (p. 335)

patronage (p. 317)

permanent party organizations (p. 331)

plank (p. 335)

political party (p. 325)

precinct chair (p. 333)

responsible party model (p. 325)

runoff primary (p. 333)

state party chair (p. 335)

temporary party organizations (p. 331)

## CORE ASSESSMENT

1. Is it the responsibility of the political parties to better represent those who are not taking part in party primaries and caucuses, or is it the responsibility of citizens to become more engaged and change the parties to better represent them?

2. Should the state of Texas make it easier for people to form new parties and get them on the ballot?

3. Will political parties remain relevant in Texas? Are there other ways people can work together to advance shared political views?

# 11 ORGANIZED INTERESTS

There was a time when the televised discussion of campaign finance law was left to a small collection of specialized lawyers and scholars earnestly debating the impact of different types of political action committees (PACs) late at night on C-SPAN. However, recent court decisions about the free-speech rights of corporations and the huge dollar amounts behind the fund-raising of so-called super PACs have turned the loopholes in campaign finance laws into fodder for lively debate and satire.

Stephen Colbert, star of Comedy Central's *The Colbert Report*, saw opportunity in the elaborate facades crafted from the loopholes in America's campaign finance laws. In a brilliant bit of political theatre, Colbert, aided by Trevor Potter, former chair of the Federal Election Commission and general counsel to John McCain's presidential campaigns, sat before a national television audience and created the Colbert Super PAC: Americans for a Better Tomorrow, Tomorrow. Next, they fashioned the Colbert Super PAC SSH Institute ("ssh" as in "hush") from the depths of Internal Revenue code, creating a 501(c)(4) non-profit organization the legal status of which made it exempt from the campaign finance laws requiring the disclosure of donors. Because the primary function of Colbert's new institute was not electioneering, it was not subject to campaign finance laws. Colbert's fans could give as much money as they wanted, and their donations would remain secret during the election. Colbert claimed that the primary mission of his organization was educational and that it would dedicate itself to educating citizens to the fact that gay people cause earthquakes. The Colbert Super PAC SSH Institute can run issue or advocacy ads as long as it doesn't specifically advocate for the election of specific candidates. Further, the organization can turn around and take the funds raised from secret donors and donate the money to Americans for a Better Tomorrow, Tomorrow, reporting only the institute's name as "donor" and thus shielding the identity of the original contributors.

Colbert was having fun running circles around the campaign finance laws, and Americans realized that if the "Colbert Nation" could conspire to subvert the campaign finance system in front of a basic cable audience, it would be easy for a well-financed interest to buy some democracy behind the scenes. Colbert let others in on the fun when he offered a "Super Fun PAC" kit for $99 that included directions on how one might start his or her own super PAC. This helped college students and others to start

Bill Clark/CQ Roll Call Group/Getty Images

their own super PACs, including Texans for a Better Tomorrow, Tomorrow; Cats for a Better Tomorrow, Tomorrow; Howard Stern Fans for a Baba Booey Better Tomorrow, Tomorrow; Penn Staters for a Better Tomorrow, Tomorrow; and Bears for a Bearable Tomorrow.

Colbert's antics brought the nation's attention back to a serious question that had hung over the political system from its creation: Can we really control special interests? If Stephen Colbert could circumvent the law for fun in his spare time, couldn't other organized political interests easily do the same?

In Texas, the power of such groups is clear as Texans for Fiscal Responsibility, a 501(c)(4) nonprofit corporation; Empower Texans Foundation, a 501(c)(3) nonprofit organization; and the Empower Texans PAC work together to advance their agenda of economic and political liberty by nominating only conservative Republicans and defeating Democrats at the polls.[1] Texans are also major contributors to national PACs such as Club for Growth, and Texas candidates such as Ted Cruz have been major beneficiaries of the support for Club for Growth and other conservative organizations.

Colbert was rekindling James Madison's worries about the "mischiefs of faction" from the debates during the ratification of the U.S. Constitution. Madison claimed in *Federalist* No. 10 that one of the most important advantages of the proposed Constitution was the new system's ability "to break and control the violence of faction."[2] Madison knew that the freedoms essential to democracy would continue to nourish faction. He acknowledged that factions could "clog the administration" and "convulse the society." Still, Madison believed that a system of carefully designed separation of powers and checks and balances would limit the ability of powerful factions to win control of government and strip away the rights of others.

In this chapter, we will look at the impact that organized interests and the money they provide has on the practice of democracy in Texas. Lurking in the shadows of the three branches of Texas government, organized interests remain indistinct but important players in state politics. While organized interests can help bring citizens into the political process and provide important issue information to voters or legislators, we will see that they often fail to adequately represent the citizens of the state and can become a hindrance to state government's ability to keep pace with change.

## Chapter Objectives

★ Describe the role of organized interests in Texas.

★ Identify the ways in which organized interests seek to influence policy.

★ Assess who wins and who loses when organized interests are involved in Texas politics.

## ORGANIZED INTERESTS IN TEXAS POLITICS

Organized interests step into some of the vacuum left by the lack of party competition discussed in the previous chapter. With Republicans winning every statewide election since 1994, as Democrats did a few decades earlier, some of the state's political battles have moved from between the parties to between interest groups. These battles are played out publicly in the primary election battles of candidates and privately in the struggle for control of the legislative process. Some organized interests have done well working with members of both parties, while others have worked consistently with just one party.

In this text we use the term *organized interest* for what many textbooks, journalists, and citizens would refer to as *special interests* or *interest groups*. Many, if not most, of the forces tugging at the political system today are not the large membership organizations that we generally think of as interest *groups*.[3] Many important players in politics are individual citizens or businesses rather than groups. Nowhere is this more evident than in Texas, where many individual businesses, such as AT&T and TXU Energy, spend millions of dollars lobbying the Texas Legislature without benefit of joining a group, and where some individual citizens, such as James Leininger, pour millions of dollars into issues such as public school vouchers.

An **organized interest** is any organization that attempts to influence public policy decisions. *Organization* in this sense does not mean a collection of individuals.[4] Instead, organization reflects the direction of systematic efforts aimed at influencing the political process. Thus, *organized interest* sometimes refers to the systematic efforts of an individual. In addition, it should be clear that many of the organizations in politics represent corporations, not individuals. For example, the Chamber of Commerce, a very important group at the state and federal level, is a collection of businesses, not individual citizens.

Our definition is well suited for some of the key issues in this chapter. As we will see, many interests in the state may be special, but they are not organized and will not have a meaningful impact on the state's politics. In fact, one of our key arguments is that the failure of some interests to organize is fundamental to understanding who wins and who loses in Texas politics.

Organized interests in Texas benefit from the part-time nature of Texas government. Legislators meeting during the frantic 140-day legislative session find themselves moving through legislation quickly and needing help to sort out the issues. With little professional staff available, lawmakers become more reliant on the kind of information and assistance lobbyists dish out. The part-time commissioners who head bureaucratic agencies provide another entry point for interests' influence in the state. As governors look for citizens to occupy the boards that oversee so much of the Texas bureaucracy, they are likely to turn to wealthy donors—especially those with a connection to the policy area being regulated.

## Interest Group Formation

A variety of factors play into Texans' decisions to join interest groups. Some of Texas's early organized interests were held together by the provision of **solidarity benefits**, which are social interactions that individuals enjoy from joining a group and from working together for a common cause. Texas's size shaped its politics from its earliest days, as the Patrons of Husbandry, more commonly known as the Grange, formed in 1867, largely to escape rural isolation and address the educational and social needs of the farmers who found themselves widely dispersed across the Texas plains. Over time, the Grange became more engaged in economic matters and farmer protests. By 1875, the Grange had more than 1,000 lodges in Texas, claiming over 40,000 members in a state with about 250,000 voters.[5] When the Grange faded, it was replaced by the Farmers' Alliance, which got its start in 1877 as an attempt by farmers to sell their goods without intermediaries. While modern Texans may not be as isolated as their ancestors, they may still join a group to make new friends, find a little romance, or simply enjoy the sense of connection that is gained when working alongside others with similar interests.

**Organized interest**
an individual, group of people, or group of businesses that organizes its efforts to influence public policy.

**Solidarity benefits**
the social interactions that individuals enjoy from joining a group and from working together for a common cause.

## James Leininger

Dr. James Leininger is a man on a mission to transform education in Texas and is an example of how organized interests can seek to influence state policy. Leininger began his journey to become the state's leading advocate of school vouchers over twenty years ago when he discovered that some of the employees of his very successful hospital bed company were functionally illiterate despite having high school diplomas. Initially, he tried to help by personally sponsoring a mentoring program. When his mentoring program failed to produce change, Leininger became interested in vouchers, which are certificates given to parents that can used to pay for education for their children at the school of their choice as a means of allowing students to find their way into better schools. He began by offering scholarships to help poor students pay the $3,000 needed to attend public schools in other districts or private schools. Over the years, students in his

privately funded scholarship program have enjoyed a 100 percent graduation rate and 95 percent have gone on to college.

In 1993, Leininger began working with the Texas Legislature to create a state-funded voucher system. In the years since, he has backed voucher-friendly candidates and worked directly with the legislature. In the 2006 election, he pumped over $5 million into campaigns, backing Republican candidates who favored vouchers. In five races, Leininger backed Republican challengers to the Republican incumbents in that party's primary, in one race accounting for 96 percent of a candidate's campaign funds. While the flood of money was alarming to some, Leininger's massive spending generally failed to be effective. Despite spending about $2.5 million in five Republican primary races, three of the five candidates that Leininger backed failed to unseat the incumbent.

In 2007, Leininger announced that he would be ending his privately financed voucher program for 2,000 students and urged the legislature to approve a state-funded system. While he has ended his own program, Leininger plans on continuing to support pro-voucher candidates and a statewide voucher program in Texas.

While Leininger has not won approval for vouchers, he has been attacked for his efforts to change public schools in Texas. Leininger attributes the bad press coverage he has received to misunderstanding and misrepresentation of the voucher issue. However, some of the concerns emerge from the natural worries that people have about one person playing such a large role in an election. Either way, James Leininger has demonstrated the potential for one person to take political action on his or her own.

The advantage of organizing political interests on preexisting social networks is evident today. In modern Texas, churches, already homes to groups of people connected through religious communion, are particularly effective at mobilizing their members for political action. The large impact of conservative Christians on the state stems from groups such as the Texas Christian Coalition, the Texas Restoration Project, the Texas Eagle Forum, and the American Family Association of Texas tapping into the social networks already built by churches.

Another motivation for group membership is the **expressive benefits** individuals enjoy by taking action to express their views. Many individuals and groups protest even in the face of widespread antipathy or hostility. While this behavior may seem irrational at some level, so is yelling at the television during sporting events—a behavior that is not limited to Texans. Thus, Texans may want National Rifle Association (NRA) stickers on their vehicles or American Civil Liberties Union cards in their wallets as a way of expressing themselves in a political system that seems too large to notice them very often.

According to **disturbance theory**, organized interests have become more numerous as society has changed. As society and the economy develop, becoming more complex and diverse, new interests emerge. These new interests begin to voice their

**Expressive benefits**
benefits that arise from taking action to express one's views; motivates group membership.

**Disturbance theory**
a theory of group formation that states that as societies become more complex and more diverse, new interests emerge to voice their concerns, prompting established interests to mobilize to protect the status quo.

concerns, which leads to the mobilization of established interests that seek to protect themselves from the challenges posed by the emerging interests.[6] This theory helps to explain the rise in the number of organized interests active in politics in conjunction with the ongoing transformation of the state.

One of the challenges to getting people to join political groups is the free-rider problem. The **free-rider problem** occurs in the case of citizens who do not contribute to the efforts of a group even though they enjoy the results of those efforts. The problem arises because groups labor for **collective goods**, which are benefits that, once provided, go to everyone and cannot be effectively denied to others, even those who did not contribute to the effort. Those who do not organize or work to advance their interest still enjoy as many benefits as those who do. The dilemma of the free-rider problem is that citizens will see little point in making an individual contribution to political efforts since their individual contribution is small and the work will go on without them. For example, all students may enjoy lower tuition, better facilities, and similar benefits from group action even if they do not belong to any student-oriented group or contribute to student organizations in any way.

The free-rider problem is common in politics as well as in the rest of life. Government itself is a partial solution to the free-rider problem. It creates rules and compels citizens to share the burden of the advancement of a common good. Government partially solves the free-rider problem by jailing citizens who refuse to pay taxes or abide by common rules. College students are familiar with their own free-rider problem: roommates who eat groceries that another roommate paid for or who don't do their share of cleaning chores.

Two things can happen when Texans prefer to leave politics to others and fail to get involved. First, nothing gets done. When only a few people who take an interest in an issue become active, their impact will be minimal. Second, when only a narrow slice of interested citizens becomes involved, the few who do take action may poorly represent the views of others. In a process known as unraveling, a relatively small number of people take over an organization and define its goals in a way that drives away more moderate members. As moderate members fall away, the group becomes increasingly radical, driving away still more of those moderates until the organization no longer reflects the views of the majority of those interested in the issue.

Given these problems, what keeps like-minded Texans working together? One solution to the free-rider problem is the provision of **selective incentives**, or benefits that can be given to members but effectively excluded from nonmembers. For example, the Texas State Teachers Association proudly proclaims it is "Fighting for Public Schools." However, new members are drawn into the organization with the promise of savings on services ranging from shopping to snowboarding. Current members are encouraged to log in for updates by monthly drawings for "free stuff." Similarly, while many Texans join the National Rifle Association to protect their gun rights, the NRA also offers its members an official NRA membership ID card, a choice of three magazines, $5,000 of accidental death and dismemberment coverage, and $2,500 in insurance for their firearms against theft, accidental loss, and damage. Because these kinds of benefits go only to members, they can help organizations build membership,

**Free-rider problem**
occurs when citizens who do not contribute to the efforts of a group nevertheless enjoy the results of those efforts.

**Collective goods**
benefits that, once provided, go to everyone and cannot be effectively denied to others, even those who did not contribute to the effort.

**Selective incentives**
benefits exclusively available to members of an organization.

and they are common to many of the nation's most successful interest groups. However, many observers may worry about the moral authority of groups built on free tote bags and discounted travel. For example, the American Association of Retired Persons (AARP) is known for using its political muscle to protect Social Security benefits and other programs that profit senior citizens. However, it attracted some of its estimated 38 million members with discounted travel and insurance, even though some of these members oppose AARP's position on health care reform and other important issues.

The fundamental dynamics of interest group organization often leave the citizens with the greatest needs facing the greatest barriers to getting organized. Because they lack the resources to organize members or the money needed to finance campaign contributions or professional lobbyists, some Texas citizens will remain at a disadvantage. For example, college students are impacted tremendously by decisions made by the Texas Legislature, Higher Education Coordinating Board, and other officials who control the costs and content of higher education in Texas. In contrast, administrators and regents of the schools are well represented because these schools often have their own lobbyists, and university presidents can often be found in Austin testifying before committees or meeting with members of the legislature. Students who wish to organize and be heard, however, are faced with apathy and a lack of resources on the part of their peers, which leaves them largely unorganized and in a weak position relative to other interests. As a result, it is easy for legislators to overlook students' views. Thus, in 2003, when Texas faced a budget crunch, the easiest solution for the Texas Legislature was to pass a law that allowed state schools to raise their tuitions, and Texas students learned a hard lesson about the cost of inaction.

### Types of Interests in Texas

Probably the most visible organized interests in Texas are economic interests. These organizations attempt to produce economic benefits for group members. They might be corporations working individually or collectively to lower taxes, reduce regulation, or alter some other business policy to help their bottom line. As Table 11.1 indicates, many of Texas's businesses hire lobbyists to represent them in Austin. The large dollar amounts reflected in the table often conceal the full effort of these businesses since some business leaders will lobby on behalf of their businesses without additional compensation.

Economic interests also include **labor unions**, which seek better pay or working conditions for their membership. For example, the Texas AFL-CIO spends much of its time lobbying for bread-and-butter issues such as raising the minimum wage and improving the quality of schools on behalf of about 500,000 labor union members in Texas. In a similar fashion, **professional associations**, such as the Texas State Teachers Association and the Texas Medical Association, represent the needs of professionals who are not represented by unions. Some businesses work collectively through **trade associations**, which are organizations of similar businesses working together to advance shared goals. For example, the Texas Hospitality Association (THA) is a coalition of restaurants and bars that lobbies on state laws related to how

**Labor unions**
organizations that represent the interests of working people seeking better pay and better working conditions.

**Professional associations**
organizations that represent the needs of professionals not represented by unions.

**Trade associations**
organizations of similar businesses that work together to advance shared goals.

**TABLE 11.1** Top 10 Companies or Groups Spending over $1 Million on Lobbying in Texas, 2013

| Client | Interest Group | Maximum Value of Contracts |
|---|---|---|
| AT&T Corp. | Communications | $8,225,000 |
| Energy Future Holdings Corp. | Energy/Natural Resources | $3,305,000 |
| American Electric Power | Energy/Natural Resources | $2,400,000 |
| Oncor Electric Delivery Co., LLC | Energy/Natural Resources | $2,000,000 |
| CenterPoint Energy | Energy/Natural Resources | $1,885,000 |
| TX Medical Assn. | Health | $1,470,000 |
| Linebarger Goggan Blair & Sampson | Lawyers & Lobbyists | $1,430,000 |
| TX Trial Lawyers Assn. | Lawyers & Lobbyists | $1,400,000 |
| TX Oil & Gas Assn. | Energy/Natural Resources | $1,290,000 |
| Centene Corp. (Superior Healthplan) | Health | $1,260,000 |

**Source:** Texans for Public Justice, "Austin's Oldest Profession: Texas' Top Lobby Clients and Those Who Service Them," September 11, 2014, http://info.tpj.org/reports/pdf/Oldest2013WithCover.pdf (accessed September 11, 2014).

the food and beverage service sector does business. The THA's mission statement calls for the repeal of the state law that requires distilled spirits to be purchased only from a retail store.

In contrast, **public interest groups** pursue noneconomic policies on behalf of the general public (even if not all members of the general public agree on the issues, policies, or solutions). For example, Texans for Public Justice attempts to promote better government by scrutinizing campaign finance and lobbying, while Texans for Lawsuit Reform (TLR) seeks to reduce the abuse of the legal system. Some **single-issue interest groups** might also be considered public interest groups since the issue their members are grouped around is one that impacts the public in general. For example, the Texas Right to Life Committee and the Texas Abortion and Reproductive Rights Action League focus their efforts primarily on the issue of abortion, while the Texas State Rifle Association and Texans for Gun Safety square off over gun rights.

Another type of interest is other governments, often referred to as the **intergovernmental lobby**, in which different levels of government lobby each other. As a state, Texas sits in the middle of the intergovernmental lobby, lobbying the national government and being lobbied by cities, counties, and school districts. For example, the cities of Austin and Houston spent about $1 million each on lobbying in 2013, while the Metropolitan Transportation Authority of Harris County spent about $485,000 on its own lobbying effort. In addition, the state is lobbied on behalf of state institutions,

**Public interest groups** organizations that pursue noneconomic policies on behalf of the general public, even if all members of the general public do not agree on these issues or policies.

**Single-issue interest groups** groups usually organized around one side of a single issue, such as pro-choice or anti-abortion groups.

**Intergovernmental lobby** the lobbying that occurs between different levels of government, such as between the state and national government or between local governments and the state government.

such as universities. While some of this lobbying is done on a contract basis with professional lobbyists, many institutions, such as the universities, rely on their upper administration to represent them in Austin.

Texas state government works closely with members of the U.S. Congress to maximize federal grants coming into the state. For example, questions were raised about $1.2 million that Texas had paid for lobbying contracts spanning the period between 2003 and 2007. While the idea of governments lobbying each other may sound odd, and the prospect of Texas paying millions of dollars for representation in Washington may seem wasteful, keep in mind that Texas receives about one-third of its budget—over $65 billion in the 2013–2014 biennial budget—from the national government. This means that if the state paid a lobbyist $1 million a year, and that lobbyist's efforts contributed to increasing the state's federal grants by only 1 percent, the state would receive a roughly thirtyfold return on the money it spent on the lobbyist.

## What Organized Interests Contribute to the Political Process

Organized interests in Texas play the same kind of roles that they do in other states and countries. However, given the condition of Texas's parties, some of these functions are especially important in the state.

One of the primary functions of organized interests is to provide *representation* for groups to complement the geographic representation provided by elected officials. In an essentially one-party state such as Texas, group representation may be especially important to many Texans who live in areas in which no one from their party/ideology holds office. Beyond that, Texans have interests that may be best served based on something other than the geographic representation provided by legislative districts. For example, Texas's teachers come together through groups such as the Texas State Teachers Association to work on educational issues. Public school teachers, while a small part of any one community, comprise a huge bloc of voters across the state. Likewise, farmers comprise a small percentage of the population in any one legislative district, and they have interests that are often very different from the rest of their communities. To make their voices heard, they join collectively in farmers associations that help promote their interests.

The *education* function is also very important, since many of the issues that impact Texans' lives lie beyond their everyday experiences and knowledge. Organized interests in Texas help bring attention to issues and educate citizens about what their government is doing and how it impacts their lives. For example, environmental groups draw citizens' attention to environmental issues and help them understand the scientific and technical aspects of these issues and the potential impact of the issues on their physical or economic health.

Similarly, Texans may benefit from *program monitoring*, which occurs when organized interest groups invest their efforts in keeping an eye on the many large bureaucratic agencies and small boards that do much of the work of governing in the state. The average citizen has little time to do this and may lack the expertise to track levels of pollution or deal with budget implementation issues. Organized interests serving as watchdogs may help uncover bureaucratic misbehavior in some cases and deter it in others.

Organized interests can also play an important role by providing program alternatives. In education, for example, teacher groups and other organized interests have put forward alternative reforms to public schools in Texas and helped give citizens alternatives that might never emerge from the education bureaucracy. Organized interests may not seem like the best source of reform, but in some cases they may prove more supportive of reform and innovation than bureaucrats and elected officials.

# INFLUENCING POLICY IN TEXAS THROUGH ORGANIZED INTERESTS

Organized interests utilize several strategies for influencing policy: electioneering, litigation, and lobbying. With **electioneering**, interests try to shape public policy by influencing who is elected to office. Seeking a statewide office such as governor necessitates reaching into every corner of the state, which requires lots of advertising dollars. Most candidates find that they cannot raise enough money for such a campaign from individual donors contributing small amounts; therefore, donors able to supply large amounts, such as organized interest groups, become especially important in deciding which campaigns get off the ground.

## Organized Interests' Spending on Elections

Organized interests influence elections in a variety of ways. The most visible and perhaps the most important is through spending. Individuals such as James Leininger have the resources to make large donations and through them can have a major impact. However, most individuals do not have as many financial resources as Leininger. To make their voices heard, these people contribute to campaigns as part of a group in order to bring together enough money to have an impact on the candidates. These contributions pass through interest groups—usually a **political action committee (PAC)**. PACs are essentially the fund-raising arms of organized interests set up in order to meet the requirements of state and federal campaign finance laws. During the 2009–2010 election cycle, 1,302 general purpose PACs in Texas reported expenditures of over $133 million (a 12 percent increase over the previous election cycle). Over 51 percent of that amount was spent by business PACs that poured $68 million into campaigns during the two years leading up to the 2010 election. Ideological PACs, including single-issue PACs and PACs associated with political parties, totaled about 43 percent ($58 million), while labor PACs accounted for just over 5 percent of PAC spending ($7 million).[7] Even without elections for governor and other statewide elected offices, a slightly larger number of PACs (1,364) spent $126 million in 2012, with almost $70 million (56 percent) coming from business-oriented PACs and another $47 million coming from single-issue or ideological PACs.[8]

**Electioneering**
method used by organized interests to try to shape public policy by influencing who is elected to office, especially by serving as sources of campaign funding.

**Political action committee (PAC)**
the fund raising arm of an interest group that has been organized to meet the requirements of state and federal campaign finance laws.

## The League of United Latin American Citizens

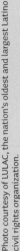

The League of United Latin American Citizens (LULAC) began in 1929 in Corpus Christi, Texas, when delegates from Alice, Austin, Brownsville, Corpus Christi, Encino, Harlingen, La Grulla, McAllen, Robstown, and San Antonio came together to lay the foundation for an organization that would bring together the various groups that had been working on the rights of Mexican Americans. While LULAC initially brought together three of the best known Hispanic groups in Texas—the Knights of America, the Sons of America, and the League of Latin American Citizens—other groups were reluctant to join. LULAC seeks to promote Hispanic pride in a society that is bilingual and bicultural. Some groups have advocated civil disobedience or even rebellion against Anglo authorities, but LULAC emphasizes assimilation into American culture and loyalty to the United States and its government. LULAC has gone so far as to make "America" its official song, English its official language, and "George Washington's Prayer" its official prayer. Further, membership is limited to native-born or naturalized citizens of Mexican American extraction, and members are required to take an oath of loyalty to the government of the United States as well as to its Constitution and laws.

LULAC's moderate approach to politics has left them disdained by some activists who deride them as "middle-class assimilationists." LULAC, which is largely composed of older, middle-class Hispanic citizens, has met resistance from much of the Anglo community throughout the organization's history. Sometimes its complaints about inequality were simply ignored. At other times, attempts to organize were met with threats at gunpoint.

The organization was especially active in the years after World War II when members returned from military service and sought to more fully participate in American life. In 1948, LULAC filed suit in the case of *Delgado v. Bastrop ISD*, which helped end segregation in the public schools. The organization also helped end the exclusion of Mexican Americans from juries and party primaries in Texas. Most recently, LULAC has been involved in lawsuits challenging redistricting in Texas that it argued reduced Hispanic representation in Congress and the Texas Legislature.

While part of the organization's work involves filing lawsuits seeking the protection of voting rights through the courts, LULAC has also created a number of its own programs. LULAC's Little Schools of the 400 project began in 1957 to teach forty-four basic English words to Hispanic preschoolers. The program became the model for Texas's Preschool Instructional Classes for Non-English Speaking Children and the federal government's Headstart program. LULAC has also helped build affordable housing for low-income families and has provided job training through forty-three employment centers in the United States. It has also worked with Fortune 500 companies to create partnerships between these companies and the Hispanic community.

While LULAC has grown to national prominence and maintains an office in Washington, D.C., its Texas roots remain strong. It has an executive office in San Antonio and a large office in El Paso that manages the organization's finances, membership materials, and group archives. Today, LULAC has more than 900 local chapters or councils that serve their communities through scholarship and other programs. It maintains an active agenda that includes a broad range of issues from foreign policy and marriage equality to energy independence. However, the group remains close to its original promise to "eradicate from our body politic all intents and tendencies to establish discrimination among our fellow-citizens on account of race, religion or social position as being contrary to the true spirit of Democracy, our Constitution and Laws."[i]

i. Cynthia E. Orozco. *No Mexicans, Women, or Dogs Allowed: The Rise of the Mexican American Civil Rights Movement* (Austin, University of Texas Press, 2009), Kindle edition, 66–67.

Texans for Lawsuit Reform (TLR) continues to be the biggest-spending PAC (independent of political parties) in Texas. In 2008, TRL spent about $4.3 million in an effort to elect legislators and judges who supported its desire to reduce the cost of nonmeritorious lawsuits. That amount increased to $6.7 million in the 2010 election cycle and $7.8 million in 2012. Of that $7.8 million, TLR gave $4.6 million directly to candidates, with 92 percent going to Republicans. A new PAC, Back to Basics PAC, spent $4.2 million in the 2010 election supporting Democratic candidates and attacking Republicans. All but $30,730 of Back to Basics' funding came from Houston attorney Steve Mostyn. The spending of the state's largest union PAC in 2012, the Fort Worth Firefighters, looks relatively small in comparison, at $804,710. In fact, that spending is smaller that the contributions of many individual donors, and the total of all union PAC spending is only slightly more than the money spent by TLR.[9]

Spending by an independent group can be an asset or a liability. For example, during the 2010 election for governor, a full-page newspaper ad paid for by Back to Basics PAC attacked Rick Perry by calling him a coward for refusing to debate Bill White. The ad was criticized as "grade-school name calling" and may have helped Perry by shifting news coverage away from his unwillingness to debate to the nature of the attacks against him.[10]

Organized interests often supplement the money they give to candidates by spending money on their own advertising or on providing materials that others can distribute. The Christian Coalition, for example, produces voter guides, brochures that list the candidates' positions on issues important to the group that members can print and distribute at their own expense. Texans for Fiscal Responsibility and Empower Texans have been especially effective with their Fiscal Responsibility Index that grades legislators on their stands on spending and business issues identified by these groups. By giving some legislators A+ grades and the "Taxpayer Champion" title and others poor or failing grades, these groups have succeeded in defining the debate much more effectively than moderate or liberal groups.

Other organized interests have launched radio and television ad campaigns backing candidates or issues. In 2010, the National Rifle Association spent $534,034 million independently in the Texas governor's race.[11] Such **independent political expenditures** have been protected by the courts because they reflect the free speech of political interests. Thus, individuals and groups can spend as much money as they can raise—as long as they do not coordinate with the candidates' campaigns. The courts have allowed limitations on contributions because they safeguard the integrity of the electoral process, but they have rejected expenditure limits because they impose more severe restrictions on freedom of political expression and association than do limitations on financial contributions.

Many people believe that politics will be dramatically transformed by the U.S. Supreme Court's ruling in *Citizens United v. Federal Election Commission*, 558 U.S. 50 (2010). In that decision, the court ruled that the First Amendment's guarantee of free speech prohibits the government from restricting independent political expenditures by corporations and unions. At the same time, the Court upheld the ban on campaign contributions by unions and corporations. Union members and

**Independent political expenditures**
spending on behalf of a candidate that is done without coordination with the candidate or his or her campaign.

corporate officers have always been allowed to make contributions as individuals, but such spending directly from union and corporation accounts had been prohibited since Congress passed the Taft-Hartley Act in 1947. This act made permanent a wartime ban on labor union contributions in federal elections and extended the ban on contributions by national banks, corporations, and unions to include a prohibition on any expenditures in connection with federal campaigns. Texas laws contained a similar prohibition. However, immediately after the *Citizens United* decision, the Texas Ethics Commission issued an advisory opinion stating that the state's ban on independent spending by corporations and unions was unenforceable in light of the decision, and, in 2011, the Texas Legislature passed a bill (HB 2359) formally removing the corporate and union ban on political expenditures from the state's election code.

The *Citizens United* decision added the deep pockets of unions and businesses to independent political expenditures, giving rise to **super PACs**. Super PACs, technically independent expenditure-only committees, may raise unlimited sums of money from corporations, unions, associations, and individuals and then spend those sums to overtly advocate for or against political candidates. A poll performed in the summer of 2012 found that only 40 percent of Americans could correctly identify the term *super PAC* and that nearly half (46 percent) did not know what the term referred to. Another 14 percent gave incorrect definitions of the term.[12]

One of the newest issues in campaign finance is dark money. **Dark money** is money spent on political activities by a nonprofit organization that does not have to report its sources of funding because of the way it is organized. Because these organizations declare themselves nonprofit (rather than political), they are organized under Internal Revenue Service rules usually associated with charities. In fact, these groups are often referred to as 501(c)(4)s and 501(c)(6)s, in reference to the specific areas of IRS code. In 2012, Governor Perry vetoed legislation that would have required these groups to report their donors. Reformers say that voters have the right to know who is behind campaign spending in state elections and that transparency is essential in order for voters to hold organized interests and candidates accountable. Those defending dark money say that donors want their privacy protected because they fear reprisals for their political activities.

The impact of super PACs and dark money has yet to be seen. On one hand, the additional money spent on these independent ads will probably have some effect since it is unlikely that such ads would be completely ineffective. Still, voters worried about elections being bought by large donors can be comforted by the reality that that spending only buys as much democracy as we allow it to, and citizens can (and do) ignore political advertising.

Perhaps a greater concern is that super PACs will have an impact on politicians seeking the support of well-financed interests. Just because these donors are not buying voters doesn't mean that they're not buying politicians. While the impact of the *Citizens United* decision may be less dramatic than some critics contend, there is no doubt that the case will provide additional avenues into elections for corporate and union money. It seems unlikely that these large donors will spend millions of dollars and not remind any candidate they helped win about those efforts.

**Super PAC**
an organized group that can raise and spend unlimited amounts of money as long as it does not coordinate with candidate campaigns.

**Dark money**
money spent on political activities by a nonprofit organization that does not have to report its sources of funding.

There is also the concern that spending by political actions committees drowns out the candidates themselves. Citizens often fail to notice the difference between advertising sponsored by candidates and that sponsored by outside groups. Further, these outside groups often favor negative ads. The Center for Responsive Politics estimated that the top fifteen independent expenditure groups spent more than $600 million nationally in the 2012 election cycle, with $520 million (86 percent) of that spent on negative ads.[13] These groups are largely unaccountable because they can move on or change their names before the next election, while candidates and elected officials are left to attempt to work with the animosities and misrepresentations left behind by such advertising.

An ad by Back to Basics PAC stirred controversy by calling then-Texas governor Rick Perry a coward.

## From Activism and Litigation to Lobbying

Organized interests may also provide other kinds of assistance to candidates, such as volunteering time to help candidates, challenging legislation in court, or seeking to influence policy through lobbying. Labor unions and other groups with large memberships may provide volunteers to help staff phone banks, campaign door to door, stuff envelopes, or provide other kinds of help with campaigns. This is one area in which student groups hold an advantage. While they seldom have enough money to make large cash contributions, student groups can provide much-needed volunteers to campaigns. Students can help work phone banks, distribute campaign brochures, put up yard signs, and perform other essential campaign work.

Sometimes organized interests turn to the courts for assistance and use litigation to advance their causes. While an individual who believes his or her rights have been violated may lack the resources to take the case to court, groups of people can band together to file lawsuits. For example, the League of United Latin American Citizens (LULAC) filed a lawsuit challenging the Texas Legislature's redistricting plan on the grounds that it violated the voting rights of the Latino community in Texas according to the 1965 Voting Rights Act. The case resulted in a 2006 U.S. Supreme Court decision, *LULAC v. Perry*, that struck down the redistricting plan; the justices cited diluted representation in violation of the Voting Rights Act.[14]

In Texas law, **lobbying** is defined as contact by telephone, telegraph, or letter with members of the legislative or executive branch to influence legislation or administrative action. This form of direct lobbying is what people generally think of when they think about how groups try to influence government. Disagreement over the exact meaning of lobbying persists. In 2014, Michael Quinn Sullivan was

**Lobbying**
direct contact with members of the legislative or executive branch to influence legislation or administrative action.

# HOW TEXAS GOVERNMENT WORKS

## Lobbying

### Who Lobbies

- Labor unions
- Professional associations
- Trade associations
- Public interest groups
- Single-issue interest groups
- Different levels of government (intergovernmental lobby) from local to federal

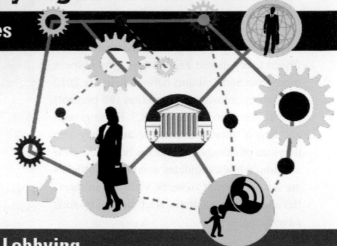

### Types of Lobbying

**Grassroots lobbying**

Groups attempt to influence legislation through public opinion, such as mobilizing group members to contact officials.

**Astroturf lobbying**

Elite spending of large sums of money to generate an appeareance of public support for their agenda.

**Grasstop lobbying**

Attempts to influence legislators through key constituents or friends of the legislators.

**Planting sod**

Tactic that transfers grassroots grown in one place to other issues.

### Examples of Lobbying Goals

**The Texas AFL-CIO wants to raise the minimum wage and increase the quality of schools.**

**The Texas Right to Life Committee focuses on abortion issues.**

**AT&T advocates for its interests in the communications industry.**

fined $10,000 for failing to register as a lobbyist in 2010 and 2011. The Texas Ethics Commission found that Sullivan had communicated directly with members of the legislature about bills being considered and thus met the legal definition of lobbying.[15] Sullivan's lawyer argued that requiring lobbyists to register is unconstitutional. In addition, he argued that Sullivan merited an exemption because his contribution to newsletters from his organization, Empower Texans, made him a journalist and not a lobbyist.

Lobbying embraces a wide range of efforts. Writing about lobbying in *Texas Monthly* in 1974, Richard West noted that "to lobby successfully requires a great deal of energy from a man who must wear many different hats. Lawyer. Educator. Entertainer. Friend and companion. And if the occasion arises, procurer."[16] For example, during the legislative session, Texans for Lawsuit Reform offers massages, manicures, and pedicures on top of the usual food and drink to the "ladies of the legislature" at their annual "Girls Night Out" event at the Four Seasons Hotel in Austin. While the legislators and staffers in attendance are not offered money, sixteen of the roughly eighteen legislators who attended in 2007 won $1,000 scholarships to be donated to the school of their choice.[17] Texas law does prohibit legislators, statewide officers other than judges, and certain political committees from accepting campaign contributions just before and just after the legislative session. For example, a moratorium on accepting contributions began December 14, 2014, and continued through the legislative session until June 21, 2015.

Legislators benefit from a cozy relationship with organized interests in a variety of subtle ways. During the legislative sessions, carts of food zip around the Texas capitol building, and legislative offices find that they can feast upon meals and snacks provided by lobbyists. In the evening, legislators and their staffers can always find receptions and dinners funded by organized interests. "How Texas Government Works: Lobbying" on the previous page illustrates the substantial investment companies put into lobbying, with many big names in Texas industry spending well over $1 million. Unfortunately, precise reports on spending on lobbying are unknown because the state only requires that Texas lobbyists report values in ranges (e.g., $100,000 to $149,999). However, it is clear that the state's top spenders invested a great deal in trying to influence the legislative session.

Lobbying is often a bipartisan affair since many of the big issues that stir the public and separate the two parties sometimes have little to with the more narrow interests of a particular industry or other special interest group. For example, according to Richard West, the Wholesale Beer Distributors of Texas worries little about the broader political leanings of a candidate. The members' interest is simple: "Does he drink an occasional beer or is he high tenor in the Baptist Church choir who denounces demon rum every Sunday? It doesn't matter if he is a Commie-Red-Pinko-Symp or worships the spirit of Joseph Goebbels. Will he vote wet or dry?"[18]

One technique is not entirely new but has been facilitated by advances in mass communication. Via **grassroots lobbying**, groups will attempt to influence legislators through public opinion. One version of grassroots lobbying is when a large group mobilizes its members to contact officials. For example, the Texas State Teachers

**Grassroots lobbying**
attempts by organized interests to influence legislators through public opinion; extension of democratic principles in which groups of citizens spontaneously mobilize to build support for a cause.

Association has members in every legislative district (plus family and friends) who can be counted on to write letters, call legislators, or attend legislative committee hearings. One of the most dramatic examples of grassroots lobbying was the thousands of people who streamed into the capitol during the special session in June of 2013 as Wendy Davis filibustered the abortion regulation bill.

One narrower version of grassroots lobbying is **grasstop lobbying**, which is an attempt to influence legislators through key constituents or friends of legislators. Rather than calling upon thousands of citizens to contact their elected officials, grasstop lobbying efforts rely on the influence of a few key citizens to sway elected officials. One example of grasstop lobbying in Texas is the use of oil and gas industry executives, who are often prominent members of their communities or large contributors to campaigns.

Grassroots lobbying is a legitimate extension of democratic principles in which groups of citizens spontaneously mobilize to build support for a cause. However, the misuse of public opinion has stirred concerns, as some groups have used negative or misleading information to advance their cause. One variation of grassroots lobbying is often described as **astroturf lobbying**. As the name implies, astroturf lobbying simulates grassroots support in an attempt to influence legislators. Often done by specialized lobbying firms, astroturf lobbying involves political elites spending large amounts of money to create the illusion of public support behind a group's agenda. Sometimes this involves large donors using phone banks to urge citizens to contact legislators based on misleading or incomplete information. In *Grassroots for Hire*, Edward Walker describes how Students for Academic Choice (SAC) mobilized students to fight rule changes to student grants and loans that would harm "single mothers, veterans, and adult students who work full time while attending school."[19] As it turned out, the SAC was sponsored and funded by the Career College Association, the leading trade association working on behalf of for-profit colleges and universities. Thus, a group whose face is ordinary students may be actually directed by large universities. Walker goes on to argue that there has been a rise in a "subsidized" public in which "select citizens are targeted and trained for participation," and he argues that this is more like "planting sod" than astroturf because these professional advocacy consultants are not creating false grassroots but transferring grassroots grown other places to their issues.[20] As was the case with the SAC, the interest behind the student needs was legitimate. However, those students would have found it much more difficult to organize and could not have traveled to Washington to meet with federal officials without the sponsorship of the group funded by the schools they attended. Lawmakers only heard from those student interests that aligned with those of the universities. This reflects the concern that those with the most resources get the most effective representation. We often think of grassroots activism as a tool that ordinary citizens use to challenge the power of government, corporations, and other powerful players. However, it is often the case that the interests of ordinary citizens are most often heard when they align with the interests of those who already enjoy the most influence.

**Grasstop lobbying**
the attempt to influence legislators through key constituents or friends.

**Astroturf lobbying**
a simulation of grassroots support, usually conducted by specialized lobbying firms; involves spending large sums of money to generate the appearance of public support to advance a group's agenda.

## Lobby Regulation

For most of its history, Texas has had little meaningful regulation of lobbying activity, which is reflected in legends such as those about poultry magnate Lonnie "Bo" Pilgrim passing out $10,000 checks on the floor of the Texas Senate in 1989. In 1957, the Lobby Registration Act required that lobbyists disclose certain activities and began the process of reform. Today, Texas law prohibits contributions from thirty days before the start of a legislative session to twenty days after the session ends.

Texas law requires that a person seeking to influence policy register as a lobbyist if he or she expends more than $500 or receives more than $1,000 in compensation in a three-month period. Because lobbyists in Texas must file reports that disclose only the range of their salaries in categories (such as "$50,000 to $99,999") rather than in precise dollar amounts, we cannot determine exactly how much they spend or receive. However, with millions of taxpayer dollars at stake, it should come as no surprise that lobbying is a well-developed industry in Austin. Texans for Public Justice estimates that 2,932 clients paid 1,704 Texas lobbyists up to $349 million during the legislative sessions in 2013. In fact, as Table 11.2 reveals, ten people managed to earn $2 million or more as lobbyists in that year.

Overseeing lobbying in Texas is the Texas Ethics Commission (TEC), created by a constitutional amendment approved by Texas voters in 1991. The TEC is composed of eight members, with no more than four members from the same party. Four of the commissioners are appointed by the governor, two by the lieutenant governor, and two by the Speaker of the Texas House.

### TABLE 11.2  Top Ten Texas Lobbyists, 2013

| Name | Maximum Value of Contracts | Number of Contracts | Political Background |
| --- | --- | --- | --- |
| Andrea McWilliams | $4,545,000 | 53 | Ex-legislative aide |
| Carol McGarah | $3,290,000 | 53 | Ex-Senate aide |
| Russell "Rusty" Kelley | $3,275,000 | 52 | Ex-Speaker aide |
| Stan Schlueter | $3,075,000 | 23 | Ex-legislator |
| Dean R. McWilliams | $3,045,000 | 34 | Ex-Senate aide |
| Randall H. Erben | $2,675,000 | 27 | Ex-Asst. secretary of state |
| Michael Toomey | $2,400,000 | 26 | Ex-legislator; ex-governor's aide |
| Mignon McGarry | $2,320,000 | 24 | Ex-Senate aide |
| Ron E. Lewis | $2,260,000 | 28 | Ex-legislator |
| Robert D. Miller | $2,125,000 | 31 | Ex-legislative aide |

**Source:** Texans for Public Justice, "Austin's Oldest Profession: Texas' Top Lobby Clients and Those Who Service Them," September 11, 2014, http://info.tpj.org/reports/pdf/Oldest2013WithCover.pdf (accessed September 11, 2014).

The Texas Constitution also gives the TEC the authority to recommend—subject to approval by the voters—the salary and per diem payments of members of the legislature, the lieutenant governor, and the Speaker of the Texas House. The legislature has given the commission legal responsibility for administering laws related to political contributions to candidates and the election of the Speaker of the House, as well as regulation of lobbyists, oversight of the personal financial disclosure reports required of state officials, and other matters related to integrity in state government. The commission meets roughly every two months and has an executive director selected by the commissioners to manage the commission's staff and daily work.

TEC rules prohibit officeholders from accepting certain gifts and track what government officials receive. Elected officials and other state employees are barred from soliciting or accepting any gift, employment, business opportunity, or other favor that might influence their official duties. Officials may accept non-cash items of less than $50 in value from a lobbyist. However, if a lobbyist provides officials with food, beverages, entertainment, lodging, transportation, etc., the lobbyist must be present at the event. Officeholders are not allowed to accept honoraria or other compensation for speaking if the invitation is related to their status as an officeholder. While travel expenses to a speech can be accepted, the officeholder may not accept any pleasure travel from a group.

## Lobbyists' Relationship with Texas Legislators

While there is some debate about how much influence these large lobbying contracts actually have, there is no doubt that the millions of dollars invested in professional lobbying will have some impact. These companies did not become large by making investments that did not produce returns. Clearly, they have reaped some reward in keeping their views before the legislature.

While there is a debate about the impact of lobbyists in Austin, there is no doubt about their visibility during the legislative session. Legislators and staff find themselves wined and dined by lobbyists, and free meals are not hard to come by during the session. The rule that lobbyists be present explains why you will often see the staff of a lobbying firm tending a table of breakfast burritos left by an interest group. Of course, winning a legislator's vote is not as easy as buying him or her a meal, and state officials consistently deny that their support can be bought with gifts, travel, or campaign donations. However,

Teachers discuss school funding, reform, and other issues with a member of the staff of State Representative Craig Eiland (D–Texas City) at the state capitol office in Austin. The Texas Classroom Teachers Association holds an annual "lobbying day" to meet with lawmakers and promote the association's interests.

AP Photo/Will Weissert

giving elected officials campaign contributions or sharing a meal with them is a means of getting access and creating a friendly connection between official and lobbyist. With so many constituents and professional lobbyists competing for a legislator's time, gaining access to the legislator or his or her staff is a fundamental part of winning influence.

Access can be promoted in a number of ways beyond traditional lobbying or campaign contributions. Former House Speaker Tom Craddick was criticized for raising over $1 million for renovation and upkeep on the Speaker's apartment in the Texas capitol building after AT&T and Dallas oilman T. Boone Pickens led the list of donors, each chipping in $250,000 for the apartment. While the money was controlled by the State Preservation Board, many people were concerned that gambling interests and other special interests were the source behind the money used for the Speaker's living quarters.

Legislators especially rely on lobbyists given the short sessions and limited staff assistance in Texas. With only 140 days in the session and a staff of only a few full-time people, legislators find themselves needing information on a wide variety of issues on very short notice. The familiar face of a lobbyist may be the easiest source of information for a hurried legislator or staff person trying to sort out complicated issues such as health care or education funding. This is one of the reasons that former officials or staffers are the more prominent and successful lobbyists. These veterans of the process are familiar with the problems of the legislators, if not the legislators themselves.

There are also lobbyists who are experts in their field. Anyone who has read through state law knows that much of the language is highly technical and involves the details of business and other practices that legislators would find difficult to master in a short period of time. Some legislative issues are extremely complex, such as the environmental impact of different types of oil and gas production or the intricacies of health care insurance. For this reason, some lobbyists are drawn from the ranks of regulatory agencies or the businesses they regulate as organized interests seek out someone who can put together a strong factual case for their cause.

Lobbying has long been a concern in Texas, and there has often been disagreement about the proper relationship between lobbyists and legislators. For example, at one time it was considered acceptable for large companies to keep legislators who were also lawyers "on retainer." In this arrangement, members of the Texas Legislature would accept payments from companies even as they deliberated over legislation impacting that company. One textbook published in 1964 matter-of-factly described this as an "especially common and possibly effective method of exerting influence" for businesses because "when a bill comes up involving the industry or business concerned, their representative is already sitting in the legislature, ready to care for the interests of his clients."[21]

The fluid movement of people between public service and lobbying enterprises concerns many Texans. This movement, known as the **revolving door**, sees legislators and members of the executive branch moving easily from government office to lobbying firms where, as former government officials, they are able to use the access they have developed through years in public service for private gain. According to the Center for Public Integrity, between the close of the 2005 legislative session and the start of the 2007 session, eight former legislators became lobbyists, helping Texas lead

**Revolving door**
the phenomenon of legislators and members of the executive branch moving easily from government office to lucrative positions with lobbying firms.

# TEXAS VS WASHINGTON

The State of Washington tackles the issue of lobbying very differently than Texas. In 2007, one ranking of attempts to regulate lobbyists and their activities placed Washington as first in the nation, while Texas ranked twelfth.[i] Among the points of comparison was the fact that in 2005, lobbyists spent over $173 million lobbying in Texas and only $37 million in Washington. In Texas, there are nine registered lobbyists with the state government for every member of the state legislature. In Washington, the ratio is six lobbyists per member of the state legislature. More telling is the fact that seventy of the lobbyists in Texas are former members of the legislature now hired to lobby their former colleagues. In Washington, only fifteen former members of the state legislature work as lobbyists.

When it comes to defining and registering lobbyists and their activities, the two states differ in a number of areas. As the table comparing Texas with Washington shows, Washington's regulatory environment provides a more detailed accounting of the activities of lobbyists who attempt to influence the state government than does that of Texas.

## THINKING *Critically*

★ Which provisions of Washington's lobbyist regulations not found in Texas do you find the most attractive?

★ How do you think such provisions would change the dynamics of money in Texas politics?

i. The Center for Public Integrity, "In Your State—Washington" and "In Your State—Texas," www.publicintegrity.org/hiredguns/iys.aspx (accessed August 11, 2010).

## Lobbying in Texas and Washington State

| Activity Regulated | Texas | Washington |
|---|---|---|
| Register if lobbying executive | Yes | Yes |
| Register if lobbying legislature | Yes | Yes |
| Minimum spent to qualify as a lobbyist | $500 | $0 |
| Must provide photo with registration form | No | Yes |
| Must report compensation | Yes | Yes |
| Must itemize all spending | No (only over $25) | Yes |
| Campaign contributions disclosed on registration form | No | Yes |
| Lobbyists' employers must file spending report | No | Yes |
| Online registration and reporting allowed | No | Yes |
| State conducts audits of lobbyist reports | No | Yes |

*Source:* Compiled by the authors from data available at The Center for Public Integrity, "Lobby Disclosure Comparisons 2003," 2007, www.publicintegrity .org/hiredguns/comparisons.aspx (accessed August 11, 2010).

the nation in lawmakers turned lobbyists, with seventy having made the transition.[22] In 2007, renewed concern developed after Governor Perry issued an executive order calling for all sixth-grade girls to receive mandatory vaccines designed to protect them from cervical cancer. While many citizens applauded the governor's enthusiasm for combating cancer, others questioned the need for mandatory vaccines, particularly after it became public knowledge that Perry's former chief of staff was now a lobbyist for the vaccine's manufacturer. As Table 11.2 illustrates, in 2013, most of the state's best-paid lobbyists had previously served as a state official or staff person. Stopping the revolving door, or even slowing it down, is politically difficult because it asks state legislators to support laws limiting their future careers. Also, limits on what officials do after their years of public service are limits on their First Amendment rights and could keep some from lobbying for causes they truly believe in or that their constituents would favor.

Some relatives of legislative leaders have found jobs as well-paid lobbyists, suggesting that interest groups are buying influence through family members. One study found that at least six well-paid lobbyists had members of their families serving in high-level positions in Texas government.[23] One member of the legislature, Jim Pitts, had a twin brother, John, who worked as a lobbyist. While the two claim to have avoided discussing issues during the legislative session, the close connection illustrates the concern of many. Although an interest in politics is often shared in families, and it would not be unusual to find several members of a family ending up in different areas of politics, these close relationships and the size of the lobbying contracts raise concerns.

## The Relationship between Organized Interests and Parties

As discussed in the previous chapter, the relationship between organized interests and parties can be troublesome. While some organized interests consistently support one party over the other, they can also highlight differences within the party and challenge the party establishment. This was vividly illustrated in the 2012 U.S. Senate nominating contest between Lt. Governor David Dewhurst and Ted Cruz. Cruz's candidacy received massive amounts of support from the Club for Growth, most of it in the form of independent expenditure ads attacking Dewhurst as "big spending and tax raising." The criticism of Dewhurst's record did not go over well with the Republican legislators and governor who had signed off on those budgets, which were now being portrayed as filled with wasteful spending.

The ability of groups such as the Club for Growth to wage a campaign independently of the party and candidate creates a challenge for the party organization, which would rather maintain control of as much of the money and campaign message as possible. The challenge is compounded when the special interest group is national and allows people from outside Texas to shape the campaign. The job of the party is to elect as many people as possible under the party's label, but the mission of an interest group may be much narrower. In contrast, the organized interest will promote commitment to its agenda regardless of how narrow that agenda or its appeal might be.

# WINNERS AND LOSERS

**Pluralist perspective**
a view of politics that argues that democracy is best practiced when citizens participate through groups; a greater number of organized interests means wider participation and a healthier democracy.

**Hyperpluralism**
a view that the system today has evolved beyond simple pluralism and is now one in which many narrow interests are represented, often at the expense of the broader public interest.

One important debate in the area of organized interests is always who wins and who loses. One perspective on this issue is the **pluralist perspective.** This perspective looks at politics as a collection of interests and argues that democracy is best practiced when citizens participate through groups. When many interests are represented, pluralists see wide participation and a healthy democracy. The leading voice of pluralism was political scientist Robert Dahl who, in his classic *Who Governs?*, concluded that no single interest dominated and that politics was open to broad participation with organized interests representing the needs of real people.[24]

Critics of pluralism disagree with the idea that the presence of a large number of interest groups means that citizens are well served; some people, they argue, will be better represented by organized interests than others. C. Wright Mills maintained that the "power elite," the wealthy and powerful interests, were better represented than ordinary citizens.[25] As one scholar colorfully suggested, "The flaw in the pluralist heaven is that the heavenly chorus sings with a strong upper-class accent."[26] Most Texans don't have enough money to contribute to an interest group or hire the lobbyists and other staff needed to build support for their agenda. There are some groups that represent poor Texans, but, ironically, these groups are generally funded and led by people who are not themselves poor. That is, poor Texans remain reliant on wealthy patrons to advocate for them.

One of the challenges to the pluralist view is that we have gone beyond simple pluralism and evolved into a system of **hyperpluralism** in which many narrow groups are represented, often at the expense of the broader public interest. For example, the National Rifle Association may effectively represent many Texans on the issue of gun ownership, but that does not mean that its members are heard on issues unrelated to the NRA's narrow focus. Hyperpluralism was given a boost with the *Citizens United* decision because now corporations and labor unions can put money directly into political advertising without working with the political parties or candidates. The rise of dark money may allow even more narrow interests to have a larger voice. As is evident from looking over the groups functioning in Texas, many businesses and groups labor in Austin on behalf of narrow interests, while very few work on behalf of citizens in general. While the two-party system may be divisive, at least it encourages the interests within each party to work together.

Some of the arguments implicating organized interests have little to do with class or party. One view is that special interests have made it impossible to get rid of a government program that is no longer needed, whether it's a social program benefiting the poor or a subsidy benefiting businesses.[27] In this argument, organized interests have been successful at protecting their own spending, even if it is at the expense of everyone else's pocketbooks. While all organized interests win in this state of affairs, they also all lose, as taxpayers remain burdened with programs that are ineffective.

The ability of some groups to effectively organize while others cannot produces clear winners and losers in the state. In Texas, businesses, and often individual businessmen and -women, have effectively organized. Once organized, the relatively loose laws governing lobbying make it easy for them to exert considerable influence in Austin. Other groups, perhaps due to apathy or a lack of money, or both, fail to effectively organize and pay a high price. For instance, the vast majority of college and university students in Texas consistently show little interest in politics. In recent years, the state of Texas has deregulated tuition, capped the number of courses students can withdraw from, and limited the number of hours Texans can enroll in before they pay out-of-state tuition. Students might well ask what kind of voice they had when these issues that are impacting them directly were being debated in the legislature.

★ Does the state's attempt to have a part-time legislature put organized interests at an advantage or disadvantage?

★ Do organized interests contribute to problems such as hyperpluralism and polarization?

★ Is there anything Texas can do to limit the impact of large campaign donors without limiting free speech?

★ How well do organized interests in Texas represent the needs of average Texans?

## CONCLUSION

Parties and organized interests can be both allies and enemies in the political process. While organized interests often support political parties, there are times when narrow interests will abandon the broader goals of the political parties and feed divisions within the parties. However, while the two political actors may at times clash, their impact on Texas politics is undeniable.

The factions that James Madison sought to muzzle with our system of checks and balances are alive and well in Texas. Like citizens of other states, Texans generally express disdain for "special interests" while enthusiastically joining their favorite groups. Whether for or against gun control, education reform, or other issues, Texans are never shy about taking sides.

Although Texans scorn these groups, few states have systems in which their lobbyists play a stronger role. The citizen government that Texans want representing them in Austin finds itself surrounded by professional lobbyists and other members of the influence industry, and the part-time nature of the legislature makes its members willing to rely to some extent on former colleagues and other lobbyists for information when facing policymaking decisions.

for CQ Press

Sharpen your skills with **SAGE edge** at **edge.sagepub.com/collier4e**. SAGE edge for **students** provides a personalized approach to help you accomplish your coursework goals in an easy-to-use learning environment.

astroturf lobbying (p. 360)

collective goods (p. 349)

dark money (p. 356)

disturbance theory (p. 348)

electioneering (p. 353)

expressive benefits (p. 348)

free-rider problem (p. 349)

grassroots lobbying (p. 359)

grasstop lobbying (p. 360)

hyperpluralism (p. 366)

independent political expenditures (p. 355)

intergovernmental lobby (p. 351)

labor unions (p. 350)

lobbying (p. 357)

organized interest (p. 347)

pluralist perspective (p. 366)

political action committee (PAC) (p. 353)

professional associations (p. 350)

public interest groups (p. 351)

revolving door (p. 363)

selective incentives (p. 349)

single-issue interest groups (p. 351)

solidarity benefits (p. 347)

super PAC (p. 356)

trade associations (p. 350)

# CORE ASSESSMENT

1. Should donations to political groups be kept confidential or be open to public disclosure? Should society do more to protect the privacy of political donors or does entering into the public discourse require putting aside some privacy?

2. Is it the responsibility of the government to listen to all citizens, or is the responsibility of citizens to ensure that they become politically active?

3. How should the state of Texas regulate professional lobbyists?

# LOCAL GOVERNMENT IN TEXAS

For many Texans, homeownership means a quiet house in a nice neighborhood in the suburbs near excellent schools and good shopping. Houses are well maintained, lawns are regularly mowed, and yards are kept free of clutter. Often neighborhood amenities, such as swimming pools, walking trails, tennis courts, clubhouses, and exercise facilities, complete the picture of the perfect place to live. These neighborhoods sometimes have homeowners associations (HOAs) that provide the amenities, and such amenities are funded through annual or monthly fees paid to the association. In addition, such neighborhoods have restrictive covenants that limit the types of fencing that can be placed in yards, prohibit parking in the streets, and provide standards for landscaping and upkeep for the homes. All of these regulations are enacted ostensibly for ensuring the value of homes in the neighborhood over time. After all, who wants to pay large sums of money for a house and pay a mortgage to a bank for decades only to have the value of the home drop over time so that when you sell the house, you get less than you paid for it?

Michael and May Clauer purchased a home in the Heritage Lakes neighborhood of Frisco, north of Dallas. The home was owned outright, and the family was not paying a mortgage to a bank. They had lived in the home for several years when Michael, a member of the National Guard, received orders to report for active duty in Iraq in 2008. Michael went off to serve our country, while May stayed in Frisco and struggled to survive without her husband. She entered a deep depression, ignoring many of her routine activities. One of those activities included paying the dues they owed to the Heritage Lakes Homeowners Association. The HOA began sending notices that the Clauers payments were overdue, and the couple took on late fees for nonpayment. After a year of nonpayment, the total amount owed came to $977.55. While May had received these notices, they remained unopened, like many other letters and notices. Then, the HOA foreclosed on the Clauers' house, selling the $300,000 home for just $3,201. The company that purchased the Clauers' home then resold it for $135,000. The new owners began eviction procedures against the Clauers to have them removed from the house.

When Michael, still serving in Iraq, received word of the foreclosure and eviction, he was shocked. The Clauers, like many Texans, were unaware that homeowners associations are able to foreclose on people's homes. To make matters worse, in Texas at the time, an HOA could foreclose on a house, seizing it from the owners, without

© Charles O'Rear/Corbis

Suburban sprawl dominates the landscape outside many medium- and large-sized cities in Texas. Decisions to allow such wide-scale development are a function of local governments, such as city and county governments. To provide services such as water, trash collection, and recycling to communities, Texas relies upon a hodgepodge of overlapping city, county, and municipal utility districts.

a court order or hearing. However, the practice of foreclosing on a person serving on active duty in the U.S. military violated federal law under the Servicemembers Civil Relief Act. This law protects people on active duty from foreclosure and other financial obligations without due process of law. In July 2010, the Clauers were given their home back. They have since sold it and moved to Virginia.[1]

Such activity might seem outrageous, but the Heritage Lakes Homeowners Association defended its actions by pointing out that all homeowners receive a copy of the HOA rules when they purchase a home in the subdivision. The foreclosure procedure is a method of allowing the HOA to handle situations in which nonpayment of dues and fines for violations of the HOA rules occur.[2] However, cases like that of the Clauers led state legislators to begin investigating the practices of homeowners associations across the state. One Houston couple reported $20,000 in fines from their HOA for having painted their house gray, a color that violated HOA rules.[3] In Colleyville, a developer wrote HOA rules so specific that the number of day lilies a homeowner could plant was regulated. Another Houston couple faced foreclosure proceedings for building an overhang in the back of their house that violated HOA rules.[4] Anecdotally, one of the authors of this textbook, while living in the Dallas area, was notified in person by a neighbor that the author's Honda Civic was "inappropriate" for the neighborhood. Another author's HOA in Nacogdoches sent out notices to homeowners indicating when front doors needed to be restained or repainted due to weathering over time, while at the same time allowing the developer to violate the HOA rules by parking a boat in his driveway. All of this action occurs in a state in which citizens heavily value private property ownership and hold a deeply entrenched belief in being allowed to do what one wants with one's own property.

During its 2011 regular session, the Texas Legislature took action to limit the power of homeowners associations. Such limits were fought heavily by the Texas Association of Builders because homebuilders and developers often are the creators of homeowners associations. These individuals design neighborhoods and entire communities to have a certain aesthetic quality. Foreclosures are rare and used only as a weapon against chronic noncompliance.[5] While not governments in the traditional sense, homeowners associations in Texas have come to exercise a degree of control over neighborhoods equivalent to or beyond that of ordinary cities and counties through traditional zoning and planning ordinances. In their efforts to maintain the property values and aesthetics of a neighborhood, HOAs are acting like governments.

In this chapter, we will review the basic foundations of the myriad of local governments in Texas, discussing the creation, powers, and organization of county government. Then we review city government, focusing on the differences between general law and home rule cities. We will also examine the functions of city governments and survey their elections processes. Finally, we will conclude with a review of other forms of local government, including public education and special districts such as municipal utility districts.

## Chapter Objectives

★ Describe what is meant by the term *local government* and how it fits in a federal system.

★ Explain Texas's one-size-fits-all approach to county government and the historical context in which it developed.

★ Identify the different types of city government and the issues they face.

★ Describe how public education and special districts serve as other forms of local government.

★ Assess who wins and who loses under the structure of Texas local government and its distribution of powers.

## LOCAL GOVERNMENT: THE BASICS

Local government involves a wide range of entities. Most often, we think of local government as referring to cities and counties. In Texas, local government also includes school districts, community college districts, municipal utility districts, water conservation districts, and airport districts, among others. Local government does not just end with water supply concerns. Numerous local governments exist to provide for public schools, junior colleges, hospitals, parks and recreation, economic development, ports, airports, libraries, and fire protection. For example, residents of the Cypress-Fairbanks area of northwest Harris County have at least eight local governments governing their lives, providing necessary services and levying taxes to fund those services. These separate and distinct local governments include the Cypress-Fairbanks Independent School District, Harris County Flood Control District, Port of Houston Authority, Harris County Hospital District, Lone Star Community College District, Harris County Education Department, Harris County Emergency Services District 9, and a municipal utility district. One reason for the large number of local governments is that Texas's counties often do not provide the same services that counties in other states provide. In the absence of strong county governments, Texans have found other ways to obtain the services they desire, in part by creating many other types of local governments.

Texas has the second-highest number of local governments of any state in the United States (see Table 12.1), ranking behind another large-population state, Illinois, and ahead of Pennsylvania and California. On one hand, large-population states may be expected to generate more local governments. However, comparing the total number of local governments to the size of the population shows that Texas has 20.5 local governments for every 100,000 residents. This ratio is lower than many other states in the region, such as Oklahoma, which has a significantly smaller population. Therefore, for a state the size of Texas, we may have fewer local governments than other states. As a result, Texans may have a lower level of public services, such as water, sewer, and trash collection, or Texas may rely on fewer governments to provide the same services that residents of other states receive.

The common characteristic of all of these local governments is that each exists as an arm of the state government. Regardless of the type of local government, all local governments are creatures of the state government, a concept known as **Dillon's Rule**. In an 1868 case before the Iowa Supreme Court, Justice John Forrest Dillon affirmed the principle that local governments have only those powers specifically granted to them by the states.[6] The U.S. Supreme Court later echoed this view. The Court ruled that states may change the powers of their cities, even if the residents living in the city do not approve.[7] By extension, this concept applies to all forms of local government within a state, including county governments and special districts.

In other words, the powers, duties, and very existence of each and every local government are determined by the state government. This legal status exists between local governments and their respective state government in every state in the country. As an illustration, during the financial crisis of 2008–2012, when several cities in Michigan

## TABLE 12.1 Units of Local Government Compared to State Population, 2012

| Number of Local Governments | | |
| --- | --- | --- |
| **State** | **Number** | **Governments Per 100,000 People** |
| **Top Five** | | |
| Illinois | 6,963 | 54.4 |
| Texas | 5,147 | 20.5 |
| Pennsylvania | 4,897 | 38.6 |
| California | 4,425 | 11.9 |
| Ohio | 3,842 | 33.4 |
| **Bottom Five** | | |
| Delaware | 339 | 37.7 |
| Nevada | 191 | 7.1 |
| Alaska | 177 | 1.5 |
| Rhode Island | 133 | 25.3 |
| Hawaii | 21 | 1.5 |
| **States Bordering Texas** | | |
| Oklahoma | 1,852 | 52.9 |
| Arkansas | 1,556 | 53.7 |
| Louisiana | 529 | 11.8 |
| New Mexico | 863 | 41.1 |

***Source:*** U.S. Census Bureau, *Census of Governments*, "Local Governments by Type and State: 2012," http://www2.census.gov/govs/cog/2012/formatted_prelim_counts_23jul2012_2.pdf, table 2 (accessed August 14, 2014); population per 100,000; calculated by authors.

**Dillon's Rule**
the principle that, regardless of the type of local government, all local governments are creatures of the state government and have only those powers specifically granted to them by the state.

found themselves in heavy debt and unable to meet their financial obligations, the state passed a law allowing the governor to take over local governments, appoint an emergency city or town manager, and suspend local, elected government. Only a vote by citizens of Michigan in a statewide referendum stopped the practice.[8]

In Texas, the constitution provides a basic framework to define the types, powers, and responsibilities of local governments in the state. Statutory laws, such as the Texas Local Government Code, Texas Education Code, Texas Utilities Code, and even the Texas Water Code, supplement the framework found in the Texas Constitution. For example, the Texas Constitution specifically grants to the Texas Legislature "the power to create counties for the convenience of the people."[9] These constitutional provisions and statutory laws go so far as to specify how local governments elect officials, which administrative offices must exist, and what types of taxes local governments may use to fund their activities.

Because there are fifty states in the United States, essentially fifty different systems of local government have developed. States diverge tremendously in the structure and functions of their local governments. As examples, Connecticut and Rhode Island lack county government in the sense that Texas and other states use it. In both of those states, counties serve primarily as a method of reporting population for the U.S. Census. Most functions that Texans associate with county government are performed in Connecticut by township governments and in Rhode Island by cities and towns. Ohio and several other states maintain township governments to provide specific services, such as snow removal and cemetery maintenance. Other states, such as Georgia, maintain countywide school districts. Arkansas allows school district boundaries to cross county lines. A number of states, such as Tennessee and Louisiana, allow cities and counties to merge into a single local government, and in Virginia some cities are independent of or outside of counties; these cities in Virginia existed prior to the creation of counties after the American Revolution.

Because local governments of all types are extensions of a state government, a second relationship necessarily exists: the relationship between local governments and the national government in Washington, D.C. This relationship is more complex. The U.S. Constitution mentions explicitly only state governments and the national government. On a legal and technical level, then, local governments do not exist in the eyes of the U.S. Constitution. In practice, however, the national government recognizes that state governments and state constitutions create local governments and that such governments exist within states. The norm is to hold state governments responsible for the policies and procedures of their local governments. For example, if local school districts are unable or unwilling to comply with a federal law or federal court decision, the U.S. government ultimately requires the state government to solve the problem. A dramatic example involved the failure in the 1970s and 1980s of the Kansas City, Missouri, public school system to integrate its schools following the U.S. Supreme Court's ruling in favor of desegregation. The federal courts went so far as to hold the Missouri state government responsible for the problem and to require the use of statewide taxes to pay for integration of Kansas City schools.[10]

A federal system of government, as described in Chapter 2, exists where the powers of government are divided between a national government and state governments, with each level of government having an independent base of power. This arrangement contrasts with a unitary system of government in which all power is centralized and other levels of government are allotted power at the discretion of the central government. The exact division of powers in a federal system may be dual federalism, in which each level has distinct and separate powers, or cooperative federalism, in which the state governments and the national government jointly carry out some tasks.

Two other arrangements within federal systems are fiscal federalism and administrative federalism. Under **fiscal federalism**, the U.S. government sets goals and objectives or develops new programs, then the national government provides financial incentives for the state governments to participate in the programs. In response, states begin to develop their own programs or change their own policies to match the goals of what the national government wants. States typically receive money from the national government to cover some of the costs of these programs. For example, if the U.S. Congress and the president believe that providing computers and Internet access to students in elementary, middle, and high schools is essential to learning in the twenty-first century, then they will fund a federal program that provides money to those states that decide to buy new computers and equip new and existing schools with Internet access according to the terms of the federal program. The money provided by the national government is matched with contributions from the state government and then given to schools for implementation. In some cases, the local government may be asked to contribute funds also. There are numerous examples of this type of program, spanning a variety of policy areas that include health care for the disabled, immunization programs for poor children, road construction, and draining and sewer system improvements, among others.

**Administrative federalism** works in a similar manner—minus financial input, however. The national government sets up guidelines for policy then expects the state governments to pay for the programs on their own without matching funds from the national government. Under administrative federalism, for example, the national government may wish to improve K–12 public education. To do so, the U.S. Department of Education may set minimum standards for student achievement for each grade level, then states are expected to bear the costs to change school curricula, including courses and subjects taught at each grade level, to meet the national standards. States may also exceed these minimal standards set by the U.S. government.

How do fiscal and administrative federalism connect to local government? In fiscal federalism, the national government provides money in the form of grants, or sums of money given to state or local governments to fund a program or policy. Usually, states allow local governments to apply to the state for a share of the money, often through a competitive process. Thus, local governments must develop the skills and staffs to write the applications, provide evidence of the need for the funds, and develop budgets. In addition, once a local government receives a grant, it must report back in detail to the state government how the money was used. Local governments become the key agents of program implementation. In terms of administrative federalism, local governments again serve as agents of implementation. However, state governments establish how best to achieve the national government's objectives, outlining an approach that is then handed to local governments to carry out. Again, in education policy, if the national

**Fiscal federalism**
use of national financial incentives to encourage policies at the state and local level.

**Administrative federalism**
the process whereby the national government sets policy guidelines then expects state governments to pay for the programs they engender without the aid of federal monies.

government sets student learning objectives, and then these objectives are adopted by the states, each state decides whether to keep those objectives at a minimum or to exceed the recommended objectives from the national government. States then bear the cost of ensuring textbooks cover all the objectives, state and national; providing assessment tools to determine if students master the objectives; training teachers and administrators in schools on the new objectives; and so forth. The state may also pass much of this cost on to local school districts, which ultimately become responsible for the day-to-day instruction and assessment of students attempting to master the objectives.

## COUNTY GOVERNMENT, TEXAS-STYLE

Texas counties vary tremendously in population, natural resources, and land areas. However, all Texas counties are structured the same way, and this structure is grounded in historical development and constitutional provisions. As a result, Texas county government exhibits a one-size-fits-all approach. The lack of variation in government structure makes Texas unusual compared to some states.

### History and Function of Counties in Texas

Local government in Texas is rooted in the old municipality system of the Mexican Republic. Under Mexican rule, Texas contained four municipalities, large areas containing a town and surrounding rural areas. Initially, the four municipalities were San Antonio, Bahia (Goliad), Nacogdoches, and Rio Grande Valley. The number of these governments increased as the population and settlements grew. When the Republic of Texas was established, twenty-three counties were created based upon these Mexican municipalities, including Nacogdoches, Bexar, and Brazos. At statehood in 1845, the county system was retained. The Confederate Constitution of 1861 created 122 counties, and the number of counties continued to increase under subsequent state constitutions. In 1931, Loving County became the last county to be established. Interestingly, the organization of Loving County marked its second era of existence. The first Loving County had originally been carved in 1893 from Reeves County as part of a get-rich-quick scheme to defraud landowners and the state of Texas by the organizers of the county. The scandal surrounding Loving County, which involved falsified county records, illegitimate elections, and low population, prompted the Texas Legislature to abolish the county in 1897. The arrival of the oil industry to western Texas later spurred its reestablishment.[11]

Texas today has 254 counties, more than any other state. Georgia is the next closest with 159 counties. Hawaii and Delaware have the fewest, with three counties each. In Texas, counties are created by laws passed by the state legislature, subject to a few limitations from the Texas Constitution. For example, new counties may not be smaller than 700 square miles, and existing counties from which a new county is created cannot be reduced to less than 700 square miles.[12] Historically, county boundaries were drawn so that a county's citizens could travel to the county courthouse and return home in a single day.[13] By population, Harris County is the largest county in Texas, with over 4.1 million people. Only two counties in the United States are larger in population: Cook

# HOW TEXAS GOVERNMENT WORKS

## Local Governments in Perspective

*Number of Local Governments by State as of 2012*

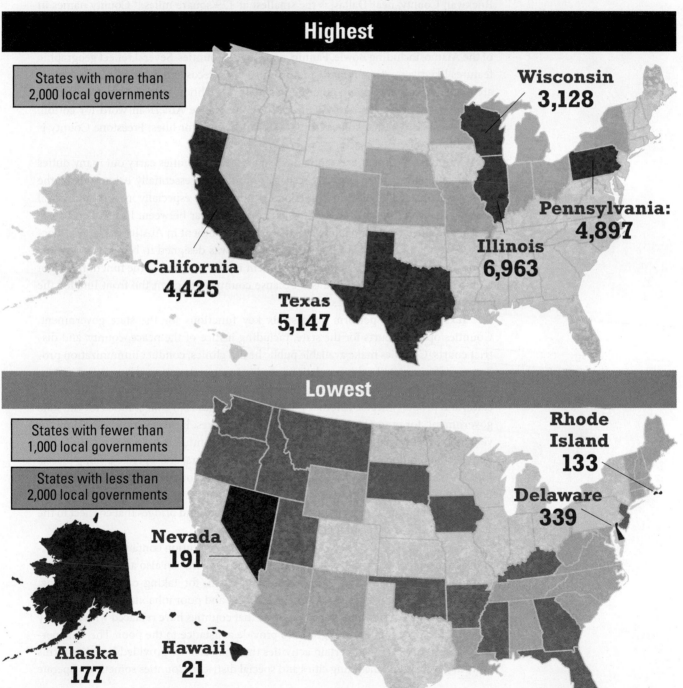

### Highest

States with more than 2,000 local governments

**Wisconsin** 3,128

**Pennsylvania:** 4,897

**Illinois** 6,963

**California** 4,425

**Texas** 5,147

### Lowest

States with fewer than 1,000 local governments

States with less than 2,000 local governments

**Rhode Island** 133

**Delaware** 339

**Nevada** 191

**Alaska** 177

**Hawaii** 21

Source: United States Census Bureau, "Individual State Descriptions: 2012," 2012 Census of Governments, issued September 2013, www2.census.gov/govs/cog/2012isd.pdf.

County, Illinois, and Los Angeles County, California. The smallest county in Texas by population is Loving County, with just eighty-two people. In addition, Loving County holds the distinction of being the smallest county in terms of population in the country as a whole. In terms of geographic area, Brewster County is the largest in Texas at 6,204 square miles, an area larger than the states of Connecticut and Rhode Island combined. Rockwall County, near Dallas, is the smallest at 129 square miles.[14] County names in Texas reflect a variety of historical and cultural influences. In addition to the county names derived from Mexican municipalities, twelve counties are named for defenders of the Alamo, including Bowie, Fannin, and Taylor Counties. Several reflect geographic features like rivers, streams, and landforms, such as Pecos and Sabine Counties. Some are named for governors and other figures in Texas politics, such as Coke County and Lamar County. Panola County is named for the Native American word for cotton, while Lampasas County comes from the Spanish word for lilies. Freestone County is named for a variety of peach.

County government is essential in Texas because counties carry out many duties for the state government. In this respect, counties are essentially extensions of the state government. The role and function of counties are especially important in rural areas of the state where cities and towns are few and far between. In the days before well-maintained roads and highways, the state government in Austin was largely inaccessible to many Texans. So, county government was designed to bring state government closer to the people. County government is also essential to the function of both administrative and fiscal federalism because counties are often the front line for the delivery of a variety of policies.

Texas's counties perform at least six key functions for the state government. Counties operate courts for the state, including justice of the peace, county, and district courts. Counties make available public health clinics, conduct immunization programs, enforce state health regulations, and inspect restaurants. They also maintain vital records for the state, including marriage licenses, death certificates, birth certificates, and property deeds. Another function of counties is to collect funds for the state government, for example, in the form of property taxes, license plate fees, and motor vehicle title fees. Counties are also responsible for conducting elections; they maintain election equipment, oversee the registration of voters, and operate polling places. Finally, counties work jointly with state government to carry out other functions. For example, counties help with law enforcement by maintaining sheriff or constable offices and operating county jails. They also build roads and bridges that connect to the state's network of roads and highways.

In a strange twist on Texas politics, the Texas Constitution contains a strong provision against imprisonment for debt. However, the constitution also allows each county to provide a "Manual Labor Poor House and Farm, for taking care of, managing, employing, and supplying the wants of its indigent and poor inhabitants."[15] This provision of the state constitution is an arcane one that counties have replaced with a variety of national, state, and local programs to provide assistance to the poor. The state permits counties to carry out certain activities that may also be provided by other forms of local government, including cities and special districts. Counties sometimes operate parks, run libraries, own airports, and manage hospitals. Services such as water, sewer, and garbage collection may also be provided through a county government.

## Governing Texas Counties

All Texas counties are governed the same way. This means that counties are controlled directly by state laws, the most important being the Texas Local Government Code. Adherence to state law means that all 254 counties in Texas have the same form of government (see Figure 12.1). Every county government is led by a **commissioners court**. This court is made up of four elected commissioners and the county judge from the county constitutional court. The selection of the commissioners and the county judge is conducted by **partisan election**—that is, an election in which each candidate's name and party affiliation are listed on the ballot. The elections for the four commissioners in every county are by the single-member district plurality (SMDP) system. (See Chapter 3 regarding the state legislature, and later in this chapter in reference to city council elections.) The county judge is elected at large by voters across the county. The members of the court, including the county judge, are elected for four-year terms. Commissioners are elected to staggered terms of office.

Each commissioner is responsible for running the county government in his or her own district. One of the primary responsibilities of a commissioner is the maintenance of roads and bridges in the district. Each commissioner determines which roads are paved and repaved, when bridges are repaired, and which company receives the contract to perform road projects in his or her district/precinct. Commissioners do not have to work collectively but may act solely in the interest of their precincts. In some counties, however, the commissioners do agree to pool resources and make these decisions about roads and bridges collectively in the interest of the whole county.

County commissioners may also collectively pass ordinances concerning the sale, possession, and consumption of alcoholic beverages. State law, however, permits residents to override the commissioners court regarding alcoholic beverage control policy. In this instance, it is the county commissioner's election district, or precinct, that determines alcohol control policy. Voters in a commissioner's district may file a petition to hold an election in the precinct to change the alcoholic beverage control policy. The election is limited to just that precinct, and any policy change affects the possession and consumption of alcoholic beverages only in that precinct. For example, at one time in East Texas's Angelina County, alcohol policy varied across the county because voters in one precinct voted to permit individuals to purchase alcohol in public places if the purchaser was an adult over age twenty-one and had also bought a private club membership. In another precinct, the sale of beverages was permitted only in restaurants and bars to those over age twenty-one who showed a valid ID. In still other parts of the county, the sale and possession of alcoholic beverages remained illegal because voters had not petitioned for a change in policy, nor had that commissioner consented to the sale of alcoholic beverages in his or her precinct.

Students of Texas politics are often confused by the term *commissioners court*, which implies a judicial function. This confusion is increased by the presence of

**Commissioners court**
the governing body for Texas counties, consisting of four elected commissioners and the judge from the county constitutional court.

**Partisan election**
a type of election in which candidates' names and party affiliations appear on the ballot.

FIGURE 12.1 **The Structure of County Government in Texas**

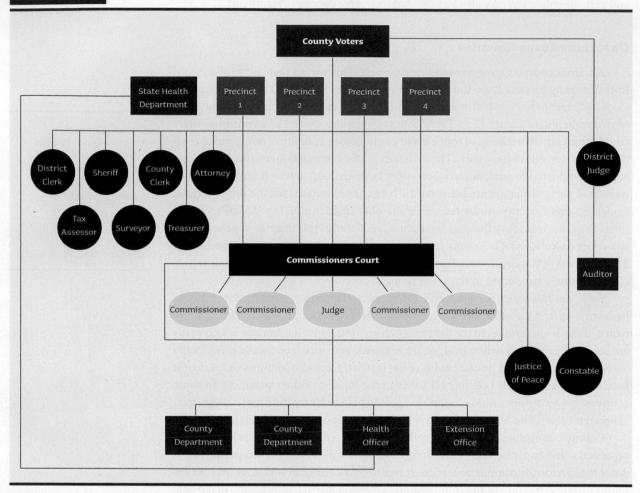

**Source:** John A. Gilmartin and Joe M. Rothe, *County Government in Texas*, issue 2, V. G. Young Institute of County Government, Texas Agricultural Extension Service, Texas A&M University, 2000.

the county constitutional court judge on the commissioners court. In fact, the commissioners court serves as a legislative body for the county rather than as a judicial body. The commissioners court passes ordinances that govern the county, determines types and rates of taxes to fund the county government, and passes the annual county budget. The commissioners court also serves as a collective executive for the county. It administers state and federal funds for local government use, oversees the various county departments and agencies, and holds final responsibility for the conduct of elections in the county. The county constitutional court judge serves as the presiding officer of the commissioners court, certifies elections, and appoints temporary replacements when a commissioner resigns.

The county constitutional court judge also serves as the justice for the county court. Thus, the role of the county judge crosses all three branches of government. The county constitutional court judge is in charge of the county budget and oversees day-to-day administration of the county, both of which are executive functions; the judge serves on the commissioners court, a legislative function, and the judge hears cases before the county court, a judicial function.

Although the Texas Constitution (1876) and its predecessors mirrored the U.S. Constitution's separation of powers at the state level, similar provisions were not included for county government. As discussed above, the structure of county government in Texas does just the opposite by giving the county judge judicial, legislative, and executive powers. In addition, few checks and balances exist to limit the power of county judges. In a state that prides itself on small and limited government, the structure of county government seems at odds with the prevailing political culture.

To assist the commissioners court, the voters elect a variety of other county officers. Typically, these officers are elected for four-year terms. Voters elect a county **sheriff** to oversee law enforcement in the county. The sheriff appoints deputy sheriffs and operates the county jail. The **county clerk** is responsible for maintaining county records, including birth and death reports and marriage licenses. In some counties, the county clerk also serves as the county elections officer and registrar of voters. The **county attorney** serves as the chief prosecuting attorney for misdemeanors in local courts, represents the county in legal activities, and offers legal advice to the county government. The county **tax assessor** collects property taxes and license plate fees, issues title certificates for cars and trucks, and, in some counties, acts as the registrar of voters and chief elections administrator. Since 1978, many counties have created a unified tax assessor district that provides property tax assessment and collection for the county and the cities and school districts in it. The county tax assessor's involvement with voter registration is a holdover from the days of the poll tax (see Chapter 9). The **justice of the peace** serves as an elected judicial officer for minor criminal and civil cases. Normally, each of the four precincts or districts of the county has a justice of the peace. The justice of the peace is assisted by a constable, also elected at the precinct level; the **constable** serves a law-enforcement capacity that includes investigating crimes and serving warrants. Large-population counties may also have deputy constables in each precinct.

Several other officers may be elected or appointed. A district clerk maintains court records for county and district courts. For larger counties, an **auditor** is appointed by the district judge to oversee county finances, a county public health officer directs local public health clinics, and a county agricultural agent assists with the needs of the farming community in rural counties. Some counties have a county elections administrator.

These officials are assisted by a host of employees that work for the various departments of the county government. From receptionists and administrative assistants to county land surveyors, counties employ thousands of Texans to perform the day-to-day operations of county government. In all but a handful of Texas counties, these jobs are essentially patronage. In a patronage system, elected officials give out government jobs to whomever the elected official wishes to have them—often loyal supporters. A person hired for a government job then serves at the wishes of the elected official and may be fired at will for any reason. Historically, under patronage, government jobs were handed out as political favors by the person who won an election. In some

**Sheriff**
the elected county official who oversees county law enforcement.

**County clerk**
the elected county official who maintains county records and in some counties oversees elections.

**County attorney**
the county official who represents the county in legal activities and offers legal advice to the county government.

**Tax assessor**
the elected county officer who collects county taxes and user fees.

**Justice of the peace**
an elected county officer who acts as a judicial officer for minor criminal and civil cases.

**Constable**
an elected county officer who acts as a judicial officer for minor criminal and civil cases; assists the justice of the peace with his or her duties

**Auditor**
a county officer appointed by the district judge to oversee county finances.

cases, the person who got a job in government service lacked any qualifications for the position. Of course, many of the men and women who work for county governments throughout Texas are competent, qualified people. They hold jobs without the protections of a **merit-based civil service system**. In a merit system, people receive government jobs based upon a formalized system of qualifications and usually have formal training for the position, including college degrees or vocational certification. Often, merit systems require an applicant to take a test or examination to determine if he or she is qualified. Individuals receive promotions and salary increases based upon a standard scale or series of performance goals. A patronage system may mimic the merit system by mandating qualifications for offices or setting minimal standards for getting a job, but the fact remains that these standards are not mandated by anything other than the decisions of county commissioners.

The Texas Local Government Code allows counties with 190,000 or more people to create a merit-based civil service system. Counties with less than 190,000 retain a patronage system. The creation of a merit system may be initiated by a vote of the county's commissioners court or by the county's voters.[16] In counties with over 500,000 people, a civil service system may be limited to the county's sheriff's department. As a result of the 2010 census, twenty-two counties in Texas qualified to implement a civil service system. A report from 2009, the most recent available, found that only nine counties in Texas had created one.[17] Harris County, the most populous county in the state, lacks a civil service system for county employees. All seven of the counties with populations large enough to establish a civil service system for the sheriff's department have done so. Thus, in Harris County, sheriff's department employees operate within a civil service system, but the rest of the county's employees do not.[18]

A civil service system for a county is administered by a **county civil service commission**. The commission is appointed by the commissioners court for a term of two years. The civil service commission develops job definitions, qualification processes, classification of employees, and requirements for promotion. Additional responsibilities of the commission include developing disciplinary procedures for employees who violate policies and procedures and constructing a grievance process to handle employee complaints.

## County Finances and Operations

To provide for day-to-day operations, counties in Texas rely on property taxes as their primary source of income. Other sources of revenue are motor vehicle license fees, service fees, and federal aid. Service fees include the costs of obtaining official documents, such as marriage licenses and birth certificates, as well as court fees required to file a case with the county court.[19] In counties without incorporated cities or transportation districts, the county may also use sales taxes to finance the county government. While county governments face an upper limit on the rate that may be assessed for property taxes, voters may agree to additional property tax rates to fund roads and bridges in the county or for additional special services that the county may provide, such as flood control. Additional services that citizens desire beyond those financed by the county budget may be funded by creating special districts to

---

**Merit-based civil service system**
a system in which people receive government jobs based upon a set of qualifications and formal training; job promotion and pay raises are based upon job performance.

**County civil service commission**
the agency administering the county's civil service system; develops job definitions, qualification processes, employee classifications, and other aspects of the system.

fund hospitals, libraries, ports, airports, and so forth. Some counties have created special districts called municipal utility districts to provide basic utilities such as water, sewers, and electrical delivery. However, such districts may be created to provide services in only parts of a county. Special districts are discussed later in this chapter.

In some counties, the county government contracts with private businesses to provide the basic services counties normally offer through their budgets and related property taxes. This process involves either **privatization** or **contract outsourcing** of government services. Often services such as trash collection and recycling are targeted for privatization and contract outsourcing. A new outsourcing trend is the building of toll roads. In some counties, a private company is contracted to build and maintain a highway for the county or state. Individuals who use the highway pay a fee to drive on the road. This fee helps to repay the private company for the cost of building the highway and for routine repairs to it. Harris, Dallas, Tarrant, Bexar, Travis, and Smith Counties all now have toll roads.

In 2009, the city of Kennedale, located near Arlington in the Dallas-Fort Worth Metroplex, decided to save money and to help balance the city's budget by eliminating its recycling program. In response, a local resident decided to create a recycling program herself. Theresa Picard created a business called America Can Recycle; she began offering to pick up recyclables from residents and local businesses for a small fee. All proceeds that the business generates are given to the Kennedale Independent School District. While this approach is not the traditional route to privatization, America Can Recycle does illustrate privatization in action.[20]

Property taxes provide the primary source of funding for county governments in Texas. However, rates of property taxes vary tremendously in the state. In addition, property taxes include two categories of taxes. Counties impose general revenue taxes to fund basic county functions, activities, and services. In addition, counties may levy additional property taxes for a specific task or function. These property taxes do not go into the county's general revenue fund, but instead go to a specific fund to pay for those activities. For example, a county might create a special property tax to fund road and bridge construction rather than rely on the funds from the general county revenue fund. Thus, property tax money from the special tax goes to a separate account to fund only road and bridge construction. Designated funds like these may be in addition to normal funds.

Law enforcement in Texas is a function of city, county, and state government. While cities such as Austin have police departments, county governments use sheriffs, justices of the peace, and constables to enforce the law. The Texas Rangers and Texas Highway Patrol serve as law enforcement agencies at the state level.

**Privatization**
a process whereby a government entity sells off assets or services to a private company that is then responsible for providing a service; for example, a school district sells its buses to a private company and then allows the company to provide transportation to schools.

**Contract outsourcing**
a process whereby a government entity contracts with a private company to perform a service that governments traditionally provide, such as a contract to collect trash and garbage.

In 2013, Midland County represented the low end of property tax rates in Texas, with rates at $0.14 per $100 of the assessed value of the property, while Duval County maintained the highest rate at $1.12 per $100. In Duval County, $0.15 per $100 of property value was assessed specifically for a special fund to pay for road and bridge construction, another $0.80 went to the county's general fund for the county budget, and $0.17 went to other designated activities, such as flood control (See Table 12.2).

In Texas, real estate is the only property that is routinely taxed for the purposes of funding local governments. Other states assess personal property taxes as well. Personal property may include recreational vehicles, furniture, electronic appliances, and animals. Some states include the cars and trucks that a family or business owns in their personal property tax assessments. In states such as Missouri and Kansas, the tax on cars and trucks can be quite substantial. For example, Greene County, Missouri, assesses cars at 33.3 percent of the assessed value of the vehicle per $100 times the local tax rate. So, a person with a $30,000 car in Greene County follows this formula to determine the tax: $30,000 (the value of the car) divided by 100, multiplied by 0.333, then multiplied by 0.7461 (the property tax rate). In 2013, the tax on the car would have been approximately $224.[21] Note that in Missouri and Kansas, cities, fire protection districts, and school districts may also levy personal property taxes as well. In Texas, while other local governments, such as school districts and cities, may levy property taxes, just like with counties in Texas, property taxes are levied only on real estate, not personal property. The use of property taxes as the primary source of funding for county government is not without controversy. For counties with high property values, the use of property taxes provides ample revenue to fund county services. The reliance on property taxes stems in part from the inability of many counties to levy sales taxes to fund local government. In addition, property taxes permit the state of Texas to avoid the imposition of income taxes, common in many states. However, property values vary tremendously across the state's counties in many rural areas without significant natural resources or economic development, lower property values might mean an inability to raise adequate revenue. In some instances, property tax rates are substantially higher in these counties to compensate for the relatively lower value of property in the county. Critics of property taxes also point out that the taxes are paid only by individuals who actually own property. If an individual does not own property, he or she does not pay taxes but still has use of public services. In some communities, 30 to 35 percent of residents do not own property and therefore enjoy services provided by counties, cities, and local governments without contributing directly to the provision of those services, though costs may be passed on to them indirectly through higher rents.

The structure of county government in Texas reflects the continuity and tradition of the state. Although the number of counties has increased, as have their populations, the Texas Constitution and statutory law prevent variation in the structure of the commissioners court and its powers. This lack of variation is true for most other county officials and their duties as well. As a result, Harris County and Loving County essentially share the same system of government, despite their tremendous difference in population and demand for government action. While Harris County's government is larger in terms of total staffing and size of budget, it basically does what Loving

## TABLE 12.2 Property Tax Rates in Texas, 2013

| County | Total Tax Rate Per $100 | General Fund | Other Provisions |
|---|---|---|---|
| **Five Highest Rates** | | | |
| Duval | $1.12 | $0.80 | $0.32 |
| Jim Hogg | $1.12 | $0.08 | $0.32 |
| Loving | $1.05 | $1.01 | $0.04 |
| Brooks | $1.03 | $0.80 | $0.23 |
| Throckmorton | $1.00 | $0.84 | $0.16 |
| **Five Lowest Rates** | | | |
| Martin | $0.23 | $0.20 | $0.03 |
| Dimmit | $0.23 | $0.00 | $0.23 |
| Upton | $0.23 | $0.23 | $0.00 |
| Karnes | $0.19 | $0.16 | $0.03 |
| Midland | $0.14 | $0.14 | $0.00 |

*Source:* Texas Comptroller of Public Accounts, "Tax Rates and Levies by County," www.window.state.tx.us/taxinfo/proptax/taxrates/ (accessed July 9, 2014).

County's government does, and in about the same way. County governments cannot adapt to the realities of their situation or the changes that occur over time. In order for counties to significantly adapt and update the uniform, single approach to county government required in Texas, the state legislature would have to either alter the Texas Local Government Code or propose amendments to the state constitution.

# CITIES

Although counties provide essential services to Texans as an extension of the state government, cities develop more directly from citizen input. In addition, the Texas Constitution and statutory laws give cities more discretion than counties to adapt to change in such areas as city organization, election system, local laws, and form of government. Given the wide divergence in population size, geographic location, and resource base among cities, the flexibility given to them better equips them to carry out local government functions in a rapidly changing state.

A city is created in Texas when the population of an area that is not already incorporated as a city reaches at least 200 people. To form a city, the residents must also define its exact boundaries and negotiate with the county regarding the services the new city government will provide versus those the county already provides to the residents. At this point, residents of the area may gather signatures of others living there who support the creation of a city. After gathering the required number of signatures—up to 10 percent of the registered voters of the proposed city—the petition is presented to the county constitutional court judge, who places the issue on the ballot at the next county election. A city may also be created when residents living within an existing city receive permission to leave it and form a new one. Once a city is created, it continues to exist even if the population drops below 200 people. Only a majority vote by the registered voters living in the city can dissolve it.

The Texas Constitution provides for two categories of status for cities: general law and home rule. A city is normally a **general law city**. In other words, the default status of cities when created is general law. The Texas Local Government Code specifies the exact forms of government, ordinance powers, and other aspects of city government. However, general law cities often find that this arrangement is too rigid to adapt to the demands of population growth, demographic change, and economic development.

Three types of general law cities exist in Texas. These are General Law Type A, General Law Type B, and General Law Type C cities. General Law Type A cities are typically larger cities that contain at least 600 residents. They must have the strong mayor form of city government discussed below; the Texas Local Government Code calls this system the aldermanic form.[22] Type A cities may choose between SMDP and at-large election systems (discussed later in the chapter) and are required to have a wider range of city officials, either appointed or elected, than the other types. For example, Type A cities must have a tax assessor, a treasurer, a city secretary, and a city attorney. Type A cities may change their form of government to a council-manager system by vote of the residents. In contrast, General Law Type B cities contain between 201 and 9,999 residents. These cities are governed by the weak mayor system described below. The city council, confusingly called the city commission in the Texas Local Government Code, must be elected using an at-large election system.[23] General Law Type C cities have between 201 and 4,999 residents. These cities are required to have a commissioner form of government/weak mayor form of government, unless in an election the residents vote to adopt the council-manager system described below.[24] The mayor and commission normally serve two-year terms in office. In addition, a Type C city must have a city clerk and a city tax assessor.

Almost a century ago, a 1912 amendment to the Texas Constitution began to give cities more flexibility by allowing some to become home rule cities. A **home rule city** is a city that has been granted greater freedom in the organization and function of its city government. A general law city with 5,000 or more people is permitted to shift to home rule. The advantages of home rule include the ability to adopt any of the three forms of city government, change the administrative structure by creating or abolishing departments, and alter systems of electing city officials without seeking the permission of the state. Home rule cities are governed by a **city charter**, subject to voter approval.[25] A city charter is a plan of government that details the structure and function of the city government. The city charter also discusses land usage within the city limits, specifies the election system for elected city officials, and details the types of **ordinances**, or laws passed by a city government, the city may enact. General law cities of all types lack a city charter and are governed directly by state law and city ordinances. Home rule cities have more freedom to pass ordinances and have some influence over land usage just outside the city boundaries. This land-usage power varies from half a mile for cities over 1,500 people to five miles for cities over 25,000. Home rule cities have greater powers of **annexation**, or the addition of areas adjacent to it into the city limits. Once a city becomes a home rule city, it retains this status even if the population falls below 5,000.

**General law city**
the default organization for Texas cities, with the exact forms of government, ordinance powers, and other aspects of city government specified in the Texas Local Government Code.

**Home rule city**
a city that has been granted greater freedom in the organization and functioning of city government; it can make structural and administrative changes without seeking permission from the state.

**City charter**
in home rule cities, a plan of government that details the structure and function of the city government; similar to a constitution.

**Ordinance**
a law enacted by a city government.

**Annexation**
a process whereby areas adjacent to a city are added to the city, thereby extending the city limits.

## Tommy Joe Vandergriff

AP Photo/City of Arlington, Texas

When Tom Vandergriff became mayor of Arlington, Texas, in 1951, the city of 7,000 residents spread over four square miles and was described by some as "the 'dash' between Dallas and Fort Worth." Only twenty-five years old when he was elected, Vandergriff might have seemed an unlikely candidate to transform his community. In his almost twenty-six years of service, however, he played a central role in the transformation of Arlington into a business, sports, entertainment, and education hub in North Texas.

One of Vandergriff's first endeavors was to help bring a $33 million General Motors auto assembly plant to Arlington. This required negotiating a deal for a 250-acre plot of land big enough to host the plant and forging an agreement for the state to build a highway to the site in order to ensure materials could be shipped in and new cars could be shipped out efficiently. The plant

opened in 1953 and by 2014 employed 4,500 workers who built about 1,140 Escalades, Tahoes, Suburbans, and Yukon sport utility vehicles daily.

To put the city on the map with regard to higher education, Vandergriff played a role in turning Arlington State College into a four-year school in 1959 and brought the school into the University of Texas system in 1965. The University of Texas at Arlington is currently designated an emerging research university, offering numerous degrees to more than 33,000 students.

Vandergriff's plans did not end there. After visiting Disneyland in the 1950s, Vandergriff decided to bring a theme park to Arlington. With his encouragement, developer Angus Wynne Jr. led the building of Six Flags Over Texas. The historically themed park opened in 1961, and in the half century since its inception it has become the anchor of one of the world's largest theme park chains, with eighteen parks spread across the United States, Mexico, and Canada. The park attracts more than 3 million visitors every year.

Vandergriff believed that making Arlington a major city also required major league baseball. In 1959, he won voter approval of a $9.5 million bond issue to construct a baseball stadium, and he set about looking for a major league baseball team. His first choice was the Houston Astros, but he was met with opposition from Astros owner Judge Roy Hofheinz, who received support from his friend, President Lyndon Johnson. The president spent more than an hour on the phone with Vandergriff, trying to convince him that Texas only had room for one major league team. The young mayor simply remarked, "I just listened."[i] And

bided his time. In 1971, Vandergriff went after the Washington Senators, but again he faced presidential opposition, this time from Richard Nixon. According to legend, Vandergriff happened to be in the office of Senators owner Bob Short when Nixon's son-in-law David Eisenshower arrived. Vandergriff hid in a closet until the man finished explaining Nixon's concerns. In the end, Vandergriff prevailed, and the team moved to Arlington in 1972, becoming the Texas Rangers.

Not everything Vandergriff touched turned to gold. After a failed venture at a marine park, which left the city in debt from millions of dollars provided in bond money, Vandergriff resigned from the Arlington City Council. He went on to serve in Congress as a Democrat from 1983 to 1985, but lost his House seat to Republican Dick Armey amid the Republican landslide behind Ronald Reagan's 1984 reelection. He returned to politics as a Republican in 1990 and was elected Tarrant County judge.

By the time of his death, Vandergriff had seen Arlington grow to a population of over 365,000 covering almost ninety-six square miles. The city sees an estimated 6.8 million visitors every year and has played host to World Series, Super Bowls, NCAA Final Four basketball games, and other major sporting events. It also entertains millions annually at Six Flags, Hurricane Harbor, and other vacation destinations.

i.   Gerry Fraley, "Presidents Were No Match for Tom Vandergriff," *Dallas Morning News*, January 2, 2011, www.dallasnews.com/sports/texas-rangers/headlines/20110102-fraley-presidents-were-no-match-for-tom-vandergriff.ece (accessed September 9, 2014).

One survey of cities conducted in 2007 found that the overwhelming majority (71.9 percent) of Texas cities are general law cities. This figure includes many cities with populations of more than 5,000. The residents of these cities have chosen to continue as general law cities despite their large size. Almost all other cities are home rule cities. A very small fraction of Texas cities—less than one-half of 1 percent, or just two cities—are classified as "other." These cities have exemptions from the general law–home rule dichotomy. Josephine in Collin County and Latexo in Houston County make up this category.

## Forms of City Government

There are three basic forms of city government in Texas: the weak mayor-council system, the strong mayor-council system, and the council-manager system (see Figures 12.2–12.4). The strong mayor-council system occurs when the voters of the city elect a mayor as the chief executive and a city council to serve as the city's legislature. Together, the mayor and city council make policy for the city, pass ordinances for lawmaking, and oversee the city's various departments.

The mayor serves as the head of the city's executive branch, develops the city budget, appoints the heads of the departments of city government, sets the agenda for the council, and serves as chief administrator of the city's departments. The mayor also serves as a representative of the city's citizens at important functions, opening businesses, speaking on behalf of a city's citizens, attending conferences with other mayors, and negotiating on behalf of the city. In many cities, the mayor may veto ordinances passed by the city council. The city council, as the legislative branch of city government, is responsible for passing ordinances; in some cities, the council may override a veto by the mayor. In addition, the council approves the city budget. In small cities, the mayor and council members may be part-time positions. In large cities, both positions may be well compensated because serving as mayor or sitting on the council is a full-time job. In Texas, the strong mayor system is sometimes called the mayor-council, mayor-commission, or mayor-aldermanic form of government.

The advantage of the strong mayor system is the concentration of power in the hands of the mayor. The mayor provides leadership on issues of the day and sets the priorities of the city. The mayor's control over the city budget and over the city's departments allows for greater harmony and efficiency in policy implementation. In addition, the strong mayor system mirrors the separation of powers between the executive and legislative branches of government found in the national government. However, the concentration of power in the hands of the mayor may lead to personality-driven politics, to the detriment of the city. The power of the mayor also reduces the influence of the city council, which is designed to be the representative branch of city government.

In contrast, the weak mayor-council system features a directly elected mayor whose powers are much more diluted relative to those of the city council. Although the mayor still oversees the day-to-day operations of the city, the mayor and city council share power over the creation and adoption of the city budget. Ordinances are jointly determined by the mayor and council. Collectively, the mayor and city council choose the heads of the various city departments and jointly oversee the city bureaucracy. In some cities, voters directly elect the heads of the various city

FIGURE 12.2 | Mayor-Council Form of City Government with a Weak Mayor

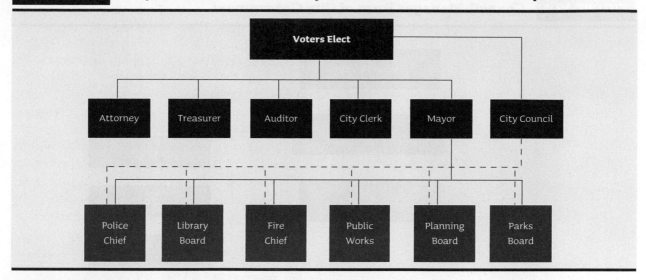

FIGURE 12.3 | Mayor-Council Form of City Government with a Strong Mayor

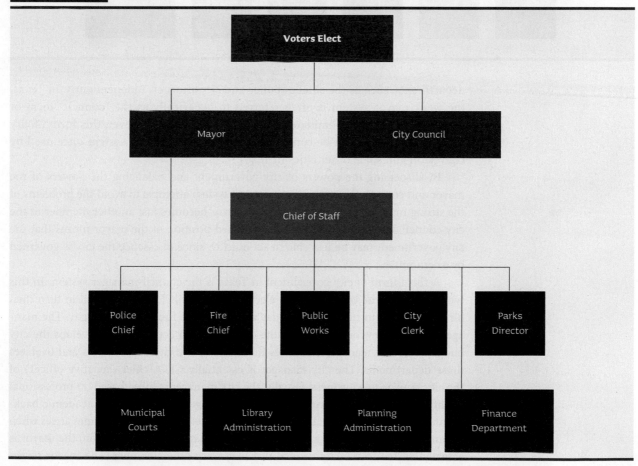

FIGURE 12.4   **Council-Manager Form of City Government**

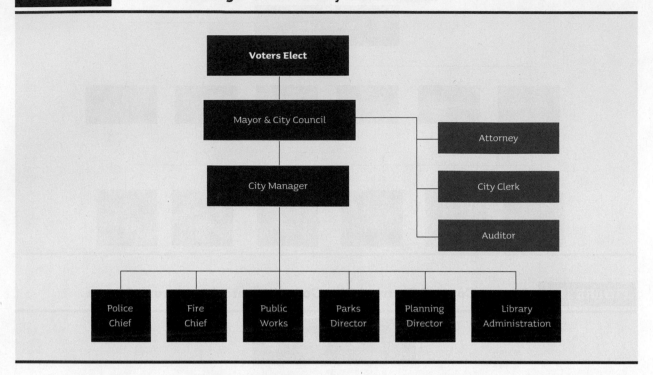

departments, such as the chief of police and city attorney, independently. In Texas, the weak mayor system is often referred to generically as the "council" form of government or the "commission" form of government. However, this form of city government should not be confused with the commissioner system once used by Galveston and some other cities in Texas.

By dispersing the powers of city government and balancing the powers of the mayor and council, the weak mayor-council system attempts to avoid the problems of the strong mayor system. Essentially, the mayor becomes just another member of the city council. On the other hand, the weakened position of the mayor means that the city government may be less able to act quickly, since in essence the city is governed by a committee.

A third form of city government in Texas is the council-manager system. In this type of system, the voters in a city elect a city council. The city council in turn then hires a manager to run the day-to-day administrative functions of the city. The manager proposes new ordinances for the city council to consider and develops the city budget. The city manager also hires the heads of the city departments and oversees those departments. The city manager is essentially CEO (chief executive officer) of the city, similar to a business. Usually, the city manager is hired based on professional qualifications, including prior experience in city government and an academic background in public administration or political science. Confusion sometimes arises when a council-manager system includes an elected "mayor." In this situation, the mayor is actually elected to the city council just like every other member. The mayor serves

# TEXAS VS OHIO

When the U.S. Congress began to address the issue of lands beyond the original thirteen states, it passed the Northwest Ordinance. In 1785, as part of that law, the territory that would become the state of Ohio was surveyed. The survey was used to set aside plots of land six miles by six miles, for a total of thirty-six square miles per plot, and each plot of land became a township.[i] Variations on this standard size were allowed when the survey encountered a natural land feature, such as Lake Erie, or a political boundary, such as the border with Pennsylvania. Each township was subdivided into sections, with one section per township set aside for public schools and four set aside as payment to veterans of the American Revolution. These townships sat as a level of governmental administration between the county government and municipal governments, such as cities and towns. The remnants of these townships are the school districts in rural parts of Ohio.[ii]

The concept of the township later became used in Ohio for another type of local government entity: the civil township. Civil townships provide a number of services to residents in Ohio, including cemetery maintenance, trash collection, road and bridge maintenance, and snow removal.[iii] These townships in Ohio are created by county governments, and all areas of the county not in a city or town are part of a township. A county's board of commissioners may divide or consolidate any township within the county. However, voters may also, through a home rule provision, consolidate or divide a township.[iv] Any new township created by voters can only include land that is not in an existing city or town. When an area of a township is incorporated, or annexed, into a city or town, the township may be dissolved. If only part of the township is incorporated, the area of the township not incorporated may consolidate with another township, or the township may continue to function within the city.

A civil township is governed by an elected board of trustees comprised of three members who serve four-year terms in office.[v] The trustees may hire an administrator to oversee day-to-day operations of the township. Trustees have the power to levy taxes to pay for township government and services,[vi] and the township may provide services above and beyond those listed above. Some additional services include demolition of derelict property, solid waste disposal, the hiring of a resident physician, the operation of airports, the development of harbors and port facilities, the provision of public libraries, and the creation of township parks. Interestingly, in Ohio, when services provided by a county government conflict with or duplicate those of a township government, by law the township continues to provide the services, while the county must stop the activities.[vii] Townships may consolidate or transfer their powers to a county government after a vote of the residents of the township.[viii]

Currently, a total of 1,308 township governments exist in Ohio. These townships account for 35 percent of all local governments in the state. In contrast, Texas lacks township governments. Services typically provided by Ohio townships are often provided in Texas by cities. If a person does not live in a city in Texas, the county government may provide such services. However, municipal utility districts (MUDs) in Texas can be created to provide these services, or individuals may contract with private companies to provide them.

## THINKING *Critically*

★ What is the advantage of creating township governments in Ohio?

★ Does this additional level of government in Ohio better serve residents? Why or why not?

★ How are municipal utility districts (MUDs) in Texas similar to townships in Ohio?

★ How do MUDs in Texas differ from townships in Ohio?

---

i. Ohio History Central, "Township," www.ohiohistorycentral.org/entry.php?rec=2190 (accessed September 9, 2014).

ii. Ohio Revised Statutes (2012), chap. 501.

iii. Ohio Revised Code (2012), chap. 503, sec. 02.

iv. Ohio Historical Society, "Township."

v. Ohio Revised Statutes (2012), chap. 505, sec. 03.

vi. Ohio Constitution (1851), art. 10, sec. 2.

vii. Ibid., art. 10, sec. 3.

viii. Ibid., art. 10, sec. 1.

---

merely as a figurehead and holds no significant power beyond that of a member of the city council. In some cities, the mayor serves as the presiding officer of the city council. Council-manager systems, sometimes called commission-manager systems, are most

AP Photo/Tony Gutierrez

The Denton city council meets to discuss a petition from residence to ban the practice of fracking for oil and natural gas within city limits. This controversy pitted homeowners and residents against each other.

common among Texas's home rule cities.

The advantage of the council-manager system is the removal of day-to-day administration of the city from the turmoil of politics. Routine decisions can be made outside partisan politics or personality politics common to the elected offices of the mayor-council system. The resulting management of city government in a council-manager system is assumed to be both more professional and more efficient than in alternative systems. However, because city managers are involved in formulating policies for the city and are charged with initiating the city budget, in practice they almost inevitably become involved in politics as well.

A final form of city government, pioneered by Galveston after the 1900 hurricane that devastated the city, contains a city council that is comprised of the heads of the various city departments. Thus, the chief of police, chief of the fire department, commissioner of streets and bridges, head of the library, etc. sit as the city's legislature to perform functions such as passing ordinances and developing the city's budget. Each department head is elected directly by voters throughout the city. One department head is chosen as the presiding officer of the city council, sometimes taking on the title of mayor. This system, favored in the early 1900s by Progressives who sought greater direct democratic control over city departments by voters, spread from Galveston across the country. However, by the 1960s, cities in Texas began reverting back to traditional mayor-council and council-manager systems.

According to a survey by the Texas Municipal League, the strong mayor-council system is more common than the weak mayor-council system in Texas. Only a handful of cities use the latter system, while nearly 40 percent of cities employ strong mayor systems. The most common system, however, is the council-manager system, which accounts for 58 percent of cities in Texas.[26]

### City Elections

The Texas state government distinguishes between general law and home rule cities with respect to the type of election system that a city uses. Home rule cities are permitted to choose from among four different election systems for elections to the city council. These cities may choose at-large, at-large by place, single-member district (SMD), or cumulative voting systems. Some cities also employ a combination of SMD and at-large systems.

The SMD system, discussed extensively in Chapter 3, occurs when the city is divided into several election districts. The number of districts equals the number of seats on the city council. Each district elects one member of the city council, so that if there are seven seats on the city council, then there are seven districts. Voters in each district cast a single vote for their most preferred candidate. In a single-member district plurality system, the candidate with the most votes in the district wins the seat on the city council. Some cities adhere to the single-member district majority system, which requires the winning candidate to win a majority of the votes, or 50 percent of the votes plus one additional vote.

In an at-large system, candidates compete for seats on the city council without reference to specific districts or seats on the council. Instead, voters are allowed to vote for as many candidates as there are seats on the council. For example, if there are seven seats on the city council and eighteen candidates running for office, each voter will vote for up to seven of the eighteen candidates. The candidates with the most votes, up to the total number of seats on the city council, win election to the council. If there are seven seats on the council, the seven candidates with the most votes of the eighteen are elected to the council.

A variation of the at-large system is the at-large by place system. In this system, candidates declare that they are running for particular positions or seats on the city council. The candidate for each seat that receives the most votes wins that seat. Thus, if there are seven seats on the city council, a candidate decides for which seat he or she is running. At the election, a voter has seven votes and chooses one candidate running for each of the seven seats. The key difference between the at-large and the at-large by place system is the fact that in the at-large by place system, candidates are grouped into different seats or "places" on the ballot. In contrast to the single-member district system, the seats or places for which candidates compete lack any connection to specific geographic areas or neighborhoods in the city.

The final system is the cumulative voting system. Like an at-large election, all candidates compete for seats on the city council without reference to specific seats, places, or districts. Voters possess a number of votes equal to the number of seats on the council. However, voters may choose to give all of their votes for the same candidate or may spread their votes among several candidates. Thus, if the city council contains seven seats, a voter may give all seven votes to the same candidate or may give three votes to one candidate and four votes to another candidate. The voter may spread the votes among as many or few candidates as the voter desires, so long as the voter casts no more votes than there are seats on the council. The candidates with the most votes, up to the number of seats on the council, win election to the city council. Again, if there are seven seats, the top seven candidates win.

Advocates of the single-member district system suggest that the direct connection between a member of the city council and the voters is an advantage. Each voter knows that a specific member of the council represents the voter's area of the city. If a problem occurs, the voter knows exactly whom to approach. Thus, government should be more responsive to citizens. Another advantage is that SMD city elections appear to increase racial and ethnic diversity among the candidates that are elected to the city council. This prospect for minority representation is an outgrowth of the Voting Rights Act of 1965 (discussed in Chapter 3). Since the 1970s, many cities in Texas have moved from at-large systems to SMD systems, including El Paso, Fort Worth, and San Antonio. However, district systems suffer from the same issues of partisan gerrymandering that occur with the state legislature and U.S. House of Representatives. In the late 1800s and early 1900s, the SMD system became associated with city-based **machine politics**, in which political organizations headed by a local party boss controlled specific seats on the city council by using city jobs, government contracts, and other giveaways. The party boss ran the city for personal power and gain.

The advantage of the at-large system is the ability of the city council to act on behalf of the entire city and to consider ordinances and policies from the perspective of the whole city, not the particularistic views of an area or neighborhood in the city. Citywide campaigns may also produce better-qualified candidates with broad-based, citywide appeal. At-large systems were also offered in the past as a method of solving the machine politics problem associated with single-member district systems. However, at-large systems have been used in Texas to suppress minority votes, especially those of African American and Hispanic voters. Very simply, the Caucasian majority histori-cally voted exclusively for white candidates, effectively overwhelming minority voters and candidates. In some cities, members of the council have consistently come from wealthy areas in town, and less well-off and minority voters have found themselves governed by officials who see or understand little about where minority voters live. In contrast, the SMD systems allow creation of majority-minority districts to boost minority representation, as discussed in Chapter 3.

Cumulative voting advocates point to the ability of voters to express intensity of preference among the candidates running for the city council. By giving three or four votes to the same candidate, a voter indicates a greater preference for that candidate than if the voter gives only one or two votes for a candidate. Another advantage is the ability to enhance minority voting by concentrating votes. If minorities concentrate their votes among one or two candidates, while whites disperse votes among several candidates, the likelihood of minority candidates winning is increased. Evidence from school board elections in Texas suggests that minority representation is enhanced under cumulative voting.[27] However, because few local governments use this system, the question remains whether or not minority representation is actually increased. Also, the concentration or dispersal of votes creates a greater possibility of spoiled ballots, especially in comparison to SMD systems. A spoiled ballot occurs when a voter mismarks a ballot in such a way as to invalidate the ballot, causing it not to be counted. In an SMD system, a voter sim-ply chooses the most preferred candidate and casts only the single vote. In cumulative voting, the voter must be careful not to cast more votes than positions to be elected. If there are six seats on the city council, accidentally casting seven votes would spoil the ballot. The ballot and the votes on the ballot would not be counted. Because a voter may give multiple votes to candidates and may spread the votes across several candidates, the likelihood of spoiled ballots increases relative to the SMD system.

**Machine politics**
a system of patronage whereby political organizations, led by a local party boss, disperse city jobs, government contracts, and other benefits to maintain control of city governance; power, once acquired, is typically used for personal gain.

Some cities attempt to have the best of both worlds by creating a hybrid of the SMD system and at-large system. Houston is an example of a city that pursues a hybrid approach. The fourteen-member city council in Houston consists of nine members elected from single-member districts and five members elected at large. A candidate chooses to either run in the district in which he or she lives or conduct a citywide campaign for an at-large seat. Proponents of this system point to the ability to balance the geographic link between a particular neighborhood or part of the city and a specific member of the city council found in the SMD system and the broader, citywide orientation of the at-large members that a hybrid system allows. In addition, ethnic and racial minorities continue to benefit from the preservation of the district system in electing minority candidates to the city council.

Election systems in city politics remain an area of change and transition in Texas. City governments, especially those that utilize home rule, are more successful than county- or state-level governments in securing more representative outcomes—for example, the election of minorities to the city council. The shift away from at-large and at-large by place systems to SMDs is indicative of this change. In some cities, experiments with hybrid systems containing both at-large and single-member district seats also demonstrate the adaptability of Texas cities. Whether cities will make additional changes to election systems based upon the recent success of cumulative voting in producing more diverse city councils and school boards remains uncertain.

## Issues in City Government

Because city government is typically the level of government closest to the people, cities address a large number of issues that will most directly and immediately affect Texas residents. Most of the streets within a city's boundaries are maintained by the city government. Cities often provide a variety of services to residents, including libraries, museums, and parks. Cities offer public health and safety services, such as police protection, fire protection, restaurant inspections, and child-care facility inspections. Many also engage in policies to attract new businesses to the community for the purposes of economic development.

Zoning and planning policies are among the most controversial issues that cities confront. Given the average Texan's attitudes toward land, including a commitment to the idea that individuals retain maximum rights to use their property as they see fit, conflicts between individual property owners and the broader needs of the city are inevitable. This desire to allow individual owners to maintain absolute control over their property is a key reason why Houston, despite being among the largest cities in the United States, has largely avoided the issue of zoning. In **zoning policy**, the city restricts what property owners may do with their property. Most often, zoning involves designating parts of a city for residential use, commercial use, and industrial use. Residential-use restrictions may include designating an area single-family housing only, limiting the number of houses that can be built per acre, or permitting apartments and condominiums only in certain areas. Commercial zoning restrictions may include specifying where large-scale shopping centers and shopping malls may be built, limiting the number of entrances or exits to businesses' parking lots, or restricting the

**Zoning policy**
policy whereby the city restricts what individuals and entities may do with their property, usually by designating certain areas of the city for industrial, commercial, or residential uses.

location of establishments that serve alcoholic beverages. Industrial zoning restrictions involve identifying where large factories, industrial plants, and high-technology firms may build their facilities. Other issues addressed by zoning policies range from the size of signage that a business may erect to regulations on how residential homes are built.

Zoning and planning often pit those seeking to develop property, build new shopping centers, or construct more houses against established neighborhoods. These battles are usually played out in local politics. Sometimes the state legislature becomes involved in conflicts over zoning and planning. In such cases, one of the sides in the battle tries to go around city government by appealing directly to the state legislature. For example, a bill introduced into the Texas Legislature in 2007 tried to restrict the ability of cities to regulate the size of lots and homes within the boundaries of the city. At issue was the building of so-called McMansions, large homes of over 3,000 square feet. Major property developers attempted to get the state legislature to enact a law to prevent cities from passing ordinances prohibiting the construction of McMansions. The bill ultimately failed because time ran out on the state legislature. Often, historic districts require that changes to buildings in the area be approved by a review board so that they conform to the historic look of the area.[28] In some instances, local zoning laws in historic areas have prevented developers from buying older homes, tearing down the homes, and building McMansions.

A recent controversy in zoning and planning involves efforts by some Texas cities to supersede or go beyond state laws, especially in the area of hydraulic fracking, often shortened simply to fracking. Hydraulic fracking is a method of using pressurized liquids to create small fractures in deep rock to allow natural gas or petroleum to migrate to a well to be pumped to the surface. While the liquid, often a brine solution of water and chemical additives, is kept at a pressure level to replace the rock formation that is fractured, the practice of fracking has become controversial for its potential contamination of ground water and other water supplies, noise pollution, spills and backflows, and possibility of causing earthquakes.

The issue of fracking prompted the city council of Dallas to go beyond state laws to limit the practice of fracking in an innovative way. Rather than directly contradict state law by prohibiting fracking, the city council used zoning and planning ordinances to limit its practice. A city ordinance was amended to prevent the drilling of a well within 1,500 feet of a residence, in effect creating a zone the size of the Dallas Cowboys' football stadium between a potential well and a residence. As a result, large areas of Dallas have become inaccessible to wells.[29] A similar ban exists in the Dallas-Fort Worth Metroplex suburb of Flower Mound.

In spring 2014, opponents of fracking began to campaign for a petition to allow residents of Denton, located north of the Metroplex, to vote in November of that year to ban fracking outright. This drive by an organized interest, the Denton Drilling Awareness Group, came after the city of Denton expanded its required zone to 1,200 feet between a residence and a proposed well. While not as restrictive as Dallas's 1,500 feet, the Denton ordinance resulted in allegations that Eagle Rock Energy had violated the law by drilling wells within city limits without permits.[30] When the petition was submitted to the city government, the city placed a temporary ban on the drilling of new wells. Voters approved a permanent ban on fracking in the November 2014 election. However, within days of the election, lawsuits challenging the ban had been filed in state courts.

## The Galveston Hurricane

By the start of the twentieth century, Galveston had become the state's leading port and one of its largest cities. By 1900, about 37,000 people lived in Galveston, and the city was often referred to as the "Queen City of the Gulf." The prosperous city enjoyed such luxuries as gas streetlights and theaters, funded by the commerce gained from being one of the nation's leading ports and from the investments flowing through its twenty-three stock companies. Until a few years earlier, it had the largest population in the state, briefly edging out San Antonio. Galveston reflected the optimism of the time. It had been hit by hurricanes in 1867 and 1875 but continued to rebuild and thrive, despite dire warnings about future storms.

The storm that hit on September 8, 1900, proved to be more powerful than any before, producing winds of 120 miles per hour and a fifteen-foot storm surge on an island whose highest point was only nine feet above sea level. The storm killed about 6,000 people and destroyed 3,600 buildings—more than half the buildings in the city.

After the devastation created by the hurricane, residents feared that Galveston would suffer the same fate as Indianola, which went from being the second-largest port in the state to obscurity after being hit by storms in 1875 and 1886. In response to the crisis, the citizens of Galveston created a new system of government designed to facilitate the rebuilding. Under the so-called Galveston Plan, the city was initially governed by five commissioners that were partly elected and partly appointed by the governor, although later the legislature modified the system to require citywide election of all commissioners. Commissioners were chosen citywide to promote cooperation across parts of the city and minimize the corruption brought by localized "bosses," who might dispense jobs in return for political support. Collectively, the commission wrote the basic policies of the city as did other city councils. However, in addition to these general duties, each commissioner administered a specific portion of the city's functions, such as safety or public works.

The city's recovery under the Galveston Plan was considered remarkable. The city constructed a seawall seven miles long and seventeen feet high. Thirty million cubic yards of sand were pumped from the Gulf of Mexico to raise the ground level of the city by seventeen feet, and the houses that survived the storm were raised and placed on new higher foundations. These preparations would help the city survive subsequent hurricanes in 1909 and 1915.

The Galveston Plan became one of the most widely adopted reforms of the Progressive era. Houston adopted the system in 1905, and, by 1917, about seventy-five Texas cities and 500 cities nationwide were using the commission form, which was embraced by reformers, including presidents Theodore Roosevelt and Woodrow Wilson.

Ironically, the Galveston Plan can no longer be found in Galveston or anywhere in Texas. The city, like many others, has adopted the council-manager form of government. Economically, Galveston lost much of its luster after Houston succeeded in dredging a ship channel that allowed it to create a port that brought railroads and ships together in a safer inland location. While Galveston's charming historic residences and buildings have kept it a popular tourist destination, the city is no longer a major commercial center. In addition, Galveston is once again facing a challenge as recent surveys have indicated that the island is gradually sinking, meaning that the city will once again have to band together to hold off the sea.

Local governments attempt to use their ordinance-making powers to protect local homeowners and reflect the public policy beliefs of the local citizens who elect them. Local voters often oppose fracking in their communities for the drawbacks listed above. However, these innovative uses of zoning and planning policies place city ordinances in conflict with state lawmakers in Austin. State lawmakers tend to reflect broader public interests, including general majority public opinion in the state. Some lawmakers support fracking because it allows local property owners to sell or lease the mineral rights to their property to a company that will drill on their property and neighboring properties. Thus, bans on fracking conflict with property ownership.[31]

(Chapter 15 addresses the economic and environmental impacts of fracking in greater detail.)

This attempt to use city ordinance-making power to supersede or move beyond state law has occurred in other policy areas as well. In immigration policy, some cities in Texas have enacted ordinances that prohibit city police and other law enforcement agencies from complying with national immigration laws related to illegals. Such sanctuary cities include Austin, Dallas, Denton, Katy, and McAllen.

Another issue related to zoning and planning is annexation. When a city wishes to expand its borders, the expansion may occur for several reasons. The residents of the area that the city plans to expand to may want to be annexed. The residents may see benefits to being within the city limits, including access to services the city provides—perhaps the city has a good police department or excellent fire protection, or maybe the city's water system is superior to that of the county.

Economic development may be spurred by annexation, making annexation an attractive prospect. The city adds new territory in order to entice new businesses to locate in the area. Similarly, cities seek to expand to prevent themselves from becoming hemmed in, surrounded by other cities. Once a city is surrounded on all sides by other cities, it is developmentally, and hence perhaps economically, limited. Population growth and economic development can then occur only within the existing city's land capacity. Cities may also annex areas to increase revenue. Newly annexed areas provide new sources of property and sales taxes. Cities especially desire to annex areas that are economically and financially well-off. In addition, the annexation of new areas allows cities to receive more money from the state and national governments. Often, funding formulas for grants are tied to a city's size. Politically, larger cities receive more seats in the state legislature as well. State law permits cities to annex up to 10 percent of their land area each year. If a city annexes less than 10 percent, then the difference may be carried over to another year. However, a city may not annex more than 30 percent of its land area in any given year.[32]

Economic development in cities may occur through means other than annexation. Attracting the right businesses into a community produces the rewards of population growth and economic growth. These results in turn may allow a city to attract even more businesses. New businesses generate new jobs and pay taxes, giving city governments more reason to welcome newcomers. To attract businesses, cities often provide incentives, such as rebates on city sales tax and reductions on property tax rates. Cities often build infrastructure for businesses as well: access roads to the business, water lines to the property, and other essentials that the business may require. On the downside, more development means more traffic to channel, more children to educate, more garbage to collect, and more services of every kind to provide.

City budgets are often a source of conflict. Budgets are generated by a variety of sources. Cities levy property taxes just like counties do. They may collect franchise fees, for example, which are fees paid by cable television, electrical power, and natural gas providers operating within the city limits. Cities also raise revenue from hotel and motel occupancy taxes and from fines from traffic tickets issued by police. They may also raise money by levying sales taxes on purchases made within the city limits. To fund special projects, such as acquiring land for parks, building city courthouses, or establishing a city museum, cities may issue **municipal bonds**, which are certificates of indebtedness. When a city issues municipal bonds, it is essentially pledging to pay back

**Municipal bond**
a certificate of indebtedness issued by a city that serves as a pledge by the city to pay back the loan over time with interest; used to raise money for services and infrastructure; may also be issued by other forms of local government, such as counties, school districts, and special districts.

a loan over time with interest. Regardless of the sources of revenue, the city must prioritize how to spend what it raises. Because revenues are limited, emphasizing the expansion of the city park system or the building of new sidewalks inevitably means less money for other projects, such as public health initiatives or erecting new streetlights.

A variety of contrasts between cities and counties exist in Texas. At a basic level, counties are the creation of the state government and exist solely to carry out specific functions the state legislature and constitution designate. Cities, in contrast, are created by citizens and residents who seek additional services from local government that counties are not able to provide. While the Texas Legislature and Texas Constitution ultimately determine what cities may or may not do, cities are established by citizens.

Another key difference is that cities, unlike counties, are allowed some flexibility in the form of government and election system they employ, which allows them a degree of transition and change to adapt to new circumstances. As Texas continues to experience high population growth rates in the early twenty-first century, the needs of citizens for more, better, and faster services require flexibility. The concentration of the state's population in metropolitan areas, including the development of massive suburbs and bedroom communities on the sites of former pine forests, farms, and ranches, has created—and continues to create—profound challenges to city and county governments. Although flexibility is most evident in home rule cities, General Law Type B cities possess a degree of flexibility as well. Because cities can collect revenue from a wider variety of sources, they can adapt to change more readily than counties. They can also exert influence on the zoning and use of land just outside their boundaries. Counties lack this ability. In fact, a city's influence may infringe on the rights of property owners outside the city limits and on the ability of counties to regulate land use within unincorporated areas of the county near the city's boundaries. Larger cities with home rule status are also freer of state control over their plan of government, the content of city ordinances, and the process of changing these arrangements.

## Homeowners Associations: Not Quite a Government, but Close

While not technically a form of government, homeowners associations exercise powers similar to cities and counties in Texas. HOAs are legally chartered institutions under Texas law. Typically, an HOA is created by a developer or builder of homes to ensure that an aesthetic look and feel to a neighborhood is maintained. HOAs also provide services to residents, such as golf courses, swimming pools, walking trails, clubhouses, and other amenities that enhance the quality of life. Some HOAs even employ their own security services to handle minor issues that arise in the neighborhood. HOAs may also be created by those who own houses or property in the neighborhood.

An HOA is usually governed by a board elected by those who own houses or vacant lots in the neighborhood. Votes are determined by the amount of land owned. If all lots are the same size throughout the neighborhood, then once the neighborhood is complete, each person will have the same vote. However, if some lots are bigger than others, votes may be allocated proportionally to the amount of land owned.

While most of the nation is shifting toward the acceptance of same-sex relationships, the state of Texas remains firmly entrenched in denying same-sex couples any recognition. The clearest example of this is the amendment to the state's constitution that declares that the state of Texas only recognizes marriage as being between a man and a woman. Although a federal judge has struck down this prohibition as unconstitutional, the U.S. Fifth Circuit Court of Appeals in New Orleans upheld the ban, signaling the need for action by the U.S. Supreme Court because other circuit courts had struck down such bans. Texas goes further than its constitution to deny same-sex couples recognition; for example, it bars them from adopting children and excludes them from inheritance law. Texas's constitutional ban is the most restrictive toward same-sex couples in the U.S.

As the federal and state governments increasingly clash over the rights of same-sex couples, the city of Houston has entered the fray. Houston recently elected the state's first openly gay mayor and became the first city to extend employment benefits to same-sex couples working for the city. This means that employees of the city who have been married in a state where same-sex marriage is allowed will now be allowed to add their partners to their health insurance and dental plan and as beneficiaries on retirement benefits. Houston mayor Annise Parker announced this decision in late 2013. She said the policy was based on the legal advice of Houston's city attorney, David Feldman, after a recent federal court overturned parts of the Defense of Marriage Act (DOMA), which allows states to decide whether or not same-sex marriages are legally recognized within their borders. Conservative groups in the state immediately launched a legal challenge to the policy. While Parker moved to have the case tried in federal courts, Greg Abbott, as attorney general, filed a brief requesting the case remain in state courts where it could be tried according to the state's laws. Interestingly, in 2001, Houston voters had amended the city charter to only provide benefits to legal spouses of employees. As DOMA continues to face challenges in federal courts, questions regarding same-sex marriage and the benefits allowed to same-sex partners in Houston and the rest of the state remain in limbo.

★ What arguments exist for local government having authority over same-sex benefits?

★ Does government—at any level—have a responsibility to provide equal access to all people on benefits and other matters? Explain your answer.

★ To what extent is the federal constitution relevant in the question of same-sex benefits? To what extent is the state constitution relevant?

To illustrate, if a neighborhood is going to cover twenty acres of land, and ten acres will be divided into one-acre lots, then each of the owners of those lots will receive one vote. If the remaining ten acres will consist of five two-acre lots, then an owner of a five-acre lot will receive two votes (one for each acre) in the homeowners association. Often, a developer or builder retains significant control over the HOA during the actual building and development process since he or she retains ownership of the land until houses are built and sold. To follow the example above, in our twenty-acre neighborhood, if all ten of the one-acre lots are sold, and none of the two-acre lots have been sold, then there would be ten people with one vote and the developer with ten votes (two votes for each of the five lots of two acres).

The HOA governing board is responsible for the upkeep of any amenities provided by the HOA, ensuring that bills are paid, and seeing that dues are large enough to cover expenses. The board also checks to make sure the rules and covenants of the HOA are followed by homeowners. If individuals fail to pay their dues or violate the rules, the HOA is legally able to rectify the situation. These remedies may include sending letters and notices, levying fines, and, in extreme cases in Texas, filing liens on homeowners, garnishing wages, or seeking foreclosures. Some HOAs have architectural committees that approve new homes, monitoring the style of the home, size of the home, number of stories, and how the home fits on the lot. Other HOAs may have the entire board act to approve new construction. These approval processes may also apply to outbuildings such as detached garages or storage units on the property, types of fencing materials used, and even plantings in flower beds.

Following the Texas Legislature's investigation of potential abuses by HOAs in 2010 and 2011, new laws were passed to reform HOA activities. Open records requirements are now in place to ensure homeowners are aware of actions and decisions by HOAs. Open meeting laws now require HOAs to hold open, public meetings that all homeowners can attend; such meetings must be publicly announced at least seventy-two hours in advance.[33] Additional requirements include the need to obtain a court order before foreclosing on a home and a prohibition of HOAs banning solar panels.[34] However, some ambiguity exists in the law still, mostly surrounding the activities of HOAs in which the developer or builder still owns at least half of the land and therefore half of the votes.[35]

## OTHER FORMS OF LOCAL GOVERNMENT

In addition to counties and cities, Texas contains a variety of other forms of local government. These include districts to handle the conduct of K–12 public education across the state. Special districts such as community college districts and municipal utility districts also complete the variety of local governments in Texas.

### Public Education as Local Government

An important function of state government is the education of its citizens. Like other state constitutions, the Texas Constitution (1876) makes specific references to education, including public schools, universities, and community colleges.[36] Texas, like other states, uses several forms of government to provide for the education of its citizens through universities, community colleges, state technical schools, elementary schools, middle schools, and high schools.

One of the local governments most familiar to Texans is the local school district. In most instances, these are referred to as independent school districts (ISDs). Basic elementary and secondary education is the responsibility of the local board of education. These boards exist at the discretion of the Texas Legislature and operate under the authority of the Texas Constitution. The Texas Education Code, a statutory law passed by the legislature and signed by the governor, provides additional guidelines for K–12 education. Most students enrolled in K–12 education in Texas attend a school that falls under the jurisdiction of one of the more than 1,000 separate independent school districts. However, a handful of public schools continue to operate under the pre-ISD system. Under the Texas Education Code, pre-existing school systems such as common schools, county schools, and municipal schools may still operate.[37] County and city governments, and the voters in these counties and cities, determine whether or not a pre-existing school should continue to stand or be converted into an ISD.

Municipal schools are owned and operated by a city government directly and educate only those students living within a city's boundaries. Similarly, a county school system occurs when a county government directly owns and operates all public schools within the county. County and municipal school districts may have an elected board of education or may have a board chosen by the county or city government.

The term *independent school district* (ISD) in Texas refers to local public school districts that are governed separately from, or independent of, any other form of local government or state government control. An ISD is governed by a board of trustees that is elected by the voters living within the boundaries of the school district. Boards are elected by at-large, at-large by place, or cumulative voting systems.[38] Members of the board serve four-year terms in office, with staggered elections so that half the board is elected every two years. The board of trustees of an ISD consists of three to seven members. To be a trustee, a candidate must reside within the school district and must be registered to vote. The boundaries of an ISD may be contained within a county, may include parts of two or more counties, and may include a city or parts of a city.

The ISD system is not unique in the United States, although the term to describe the system is. Under federalism, states are allowed to create school systems however they choose, and education policy is largely considered the domain of state governments. Two neighboring states illustrate differing approaches to education. Arkansas's school districts are similar to those of Texas. School districts are independent of local governments. In Arkansas, school district lines may cross county lines or may be contained within a single county. District lines may also be limited to a single city or include several cities. Some school districts in Arkansas are drawn based on the proximity of a road or highway to a school. In the Ozark and Ouachita Mountains, sometimes the closest school via highway or road may be in another county. Louisiana, by contrast, has countywide school districts. All public schools in a county are part of the same public school system. Most school systems are parish-wide, with just a handful of exceptions, such as the cities of Monroe, Bogalusa, Baker, Central City, and Zachary. Even in Louisiana where, with a handful of exceptions,

Completed in 2012, a new $60 million football stadium sits at Allen High School in the Dallas suburb of Allen, Texas. The decision to build such a stadium, which rivals some NCAA Division I (Football Championship Series—FCS) stadiums, was made by the board of trustees of Allen Independent School District. The stadium was built at a time when other school districts in Texas were struggling to meet their budgets, keep class sizes low, and retain good teachers. Ironically, in 2014, two years after it was completed, the stadium was declared structurally unsound. Significant cracks appeared in the concrete foundation of the stadium, requiring extensive repairs, and it could not be used for the 2014 football season.

© LM Otero/AP/Corbis

parish-wide (countywide) school systems exist, local school boards are elected separately from parish and city governments. The parish school boards make decisions independent of the parish government. To give another example, the nation's largest school system is the New York City public school district, which is owned and operated directly by the city of New York.

In Texas, the board of trustees of an ISD oversees the schools of the district by authorizing construction of schools, selling bonds to finance projects, collecting property taxes to fund operations, and providing guidelines for schools. Guidelines may include directions on the hiring of teachers and administrators, curriculum decisions, discipline policies, and budget decisions.[39] In effect, the board of trustees runs the schools in the district.

Although the ISD system is designed to give citizens local control over their schools, the state of Texas exerts control in specific areas. In particular, the state uses its power over the creation, existence, and support of school districts to enforce statewide policies. These policies include the classes that students must take, the textbooks that students use, and the structure of district budgets.[40] To this end, the Texas Constitution provides for the State Board of Education.[41] The State Board of Education consists of fifteen members elected from single-member districts across the state. A commissioner, appointed by the governor and confirmed by the Texas Senate, heads the board. The structure, function, and policy implications of the State Board of Education are discussed in Chapter 14.

## Special Districts

Special districts are created when the residents within the proposed boundary of the district petition to create one. Examples of special districts are airport authorities, library districts, municipal utility districts, and community college districts. The process is similar to the process of creating a city. In contrast to a city or county, however, a special district provides a single service or a limited number of services to the residents of the district. The creation of a special district can be complicated, depending on the type of district. Hospital districts are created by first passing an amendment to the Texas Constitution, then by the approval of voters in the proposed district. Community college districts are first authorized by the Texas Legislature. The Texas Commission on Environmental Quality approves the creation of municipal utility districts. Special districts have even been created to build and manage sports stadiums for professional sports teams in Texas, even though the primary beneficiary is a private business.

Normally, special districts are created when a county or city government is unable or unwilling to provide a service itself, or when the existing local government prefers to allow a special district to provide the service. Because counties face limits on the amount of property tax they levy, special districts allow counties to overcome this limit by essentially "farming out" new services to a special district. In some instances, residents of a county may choose to join a special district that exists in another county. In this case, the residents take a vote to join the special district, or a local government may request that the special district start providing services in the

# TEXAS VS TENNESSEE

Because local governments, like cities and counties, are created by state legislatures and state constitutions, the United States has fifty different systems of local government. Some states give a lot of responsibilities and powers to counties, while others do the same with their cities. Some states allow cities to be independent of counties. Other states allow the merger of city and county governments into a single entity. Tennessee is one such state.

In 1963, the Tennessee state government permitted the city of Nashville and surrounding Davidson County to merge. Called the Metropolitan Government, the consolidated government was intended to improve services, especially in areas of Davidson County outside of the city limits—essentially the rural areas of the county. These unincorporated areas wanted better police protection, fire and ambulance services, parks and recreation, and mass transit. Services to these areas would be uniform across the county. However, residents of rural areas did not necessarily want *all* of the services that Nashville provided to its residents and the accompanying higher level of taxes, nor did residents in the county want annexation into the city.[i] As a result, the Metropolitan Government created two different levels of service. A general services district (GSD) provides a uniform level of services throughout Davidson County at the same property tax rate regardless of location in the county. As part of the GSD, a common city-county court system and jail replaced separate city and county operations. An urban services district offers additional services to the city of Nashville and other communities that opt into the district. These include street lighting, water, refuse collection, street cleaning, and sanitation.[ii]

The Metropolitan Government is governed by the Metropolitan Council, which has forty members who are elected by a combination of single-member district plurality and at-large election systems. A Metro mayor serves as the chief executive, and a finance director oversees the budget. Decisions relating to the urban services district are made by a three-person committee whose members are part of the Metropolitan Council.[iii] Davidson County is served by a single consolidated school district. The school board is directly elected, but the school budget must be approved by the Metro mayor and finance director.

However, the merger of the city of Nashville and Davidson County is only a partial consolidation because seven other cities and towns located in Davidson County that existed prior to the merger remain independent. Communities such as Belle Meade and Goodlettsville participate in the general services district. However, the additional services of the urban services district must be provided separately or by a contract with the Metropolitan Government.[iv]

The creation of the Metropolitan Government allowed the city of Nashville and Davidson County to harmonize the level and quality of services provided to citizens in the city and county. Zoning and planning became a function of the consolidated government, forestalling competition between the city and county and producing a common approach to economic development. Economies of scale developed in the provision of services, so that many services are provided at a lower cost to taxpayers than if the city and county provided the services separately. In addition, supporters of consolidation maintain that the result has been more local government accountability and a better national image for Nashville.[v]

## THINKING *Critically*

★ How many local governments, including school districts, municipal utility districts, cities, and other special purpose districts, are there in your county?

★ Do you think the level of services varies tremendously across your county?

★ What advantages might there be if the services provided by the various local governments in your county were consolidated, as in the case of Metropolitan Nashville–Davidson County in Tennessee?

★ Are there disadvantages to city-county consolidations?

---

i. Pennsylvania Economy League of Southwestern Pennsylvania, "A Comparative Analysis of City/County Consolidations," February 7, 2007, www.alleghenyconference.org/PEL/PDFs/CityCountyConsolidationsComparativeAnalysis.pdf (accessed September 28, 2012).

ii. Ibid.

iii. Ibid., 79.

iv. Ibid.

v. Ibid.

area. Special districts are funded primarily by property taxes that residents agree to pay to provide the services. If the district crosses county lines, then arrangements are made for the tax assessors in each county to collect the taxes and transfer the funds to the district. Thus, special districts often can overcome the problems of coordinating services across multiple cities and counties. This approach is very useful in major metropolitan areas like the Dallas-Fort Worth Metroplex, for example. Some special districts are authorized by voters to issue municipal bonds, while others charge user fees for their services.

Special districts are governed by a board of usually five members. The board is often elected by voters in the district. In some instances, it is appointed, usually by the mayors, city councils, and commissioners courts operating within the district. The board oversees the regular operation of the special district, hires necessary staff and professionals, and makes policies regarding the provision of services. For example, the Port of Houston Authority is governed by an appointed board of seven members. Some members are appointed by the Harris County Commissioners Court, while others are appointed by cities within Harris County. The authority oversees the collection of public and private dock facilities along the Houston Ship Channel and monitors ship traffic on the channel and in Galveston Bay. For community colleges, its board of trustees hires the chancellor or president of the college. The board decides, within state guidelines, the degrees that will be offered and the coursework that is required. The board also enters into agreements with four-year universities to determine the transferability of courses, harmonization of degree programs, and ease of transfer to four-year institutions. It establishes pay scales for faculty and staff, qualifications to be on faculty, and rates of tuition and fees for students. In some cases, community colleges have service areas defined by a law passed by the Texas Legislature. Angelina College in East Texas has the exclusive right to operate in all or parts of thirteen East Texas counties. In contrast, Harris County contains several community college districts, including Houston Community College, Lone Star College, and San Jacinto Community College. Currently, fifty separate college districts exist in Texas. Community colleges educate over 550,000 Texans each year.

The advantage of a special district is the ability to provide services that ordinarily might not be provided. In addition, the services may be provided to promote economic development. In the case of **municipal utility districts (MUDs)**, which provide water, sewer, and similar services to individuals and businesses outside city limits, these services may entice new businesses to relocate to the area or developers to construct new homes. Again, in some instances, the special district aids in bridging disputes between cities or counties over the provision of services. However, like other local government elections, special election district elections are low-turnout events, and thus the decisions made by voters may reflect the wishes of only a few. Also, the proliferation of special districts in an area creates confusion among residents, who may not know who is responsible for what. Special districts also encourage conflict among local governments as multiple districts compete for property tax resources and pursue contradictory goals.

**Municipal utility district (MUD)**
a special district that provides water, sewer, or similar services to individuals and businesses outside city limits.

# WINNERS AND LOSERS

**A**s we have seen in previous chapters, choices about the structure of government, the distribution of powers within government and between levels of government, and how government is selected directly impact citizens. In Texas, various levels of local government provide different services and create additional tax burdens on citizens. To the extent that local government in Texas creates flexibility, citizens win. To the extent that each level of local government creates additional, obscure taxes, citizens lose.

Cities are clear winners in the state because they are relatively powerful entities that provide a significant number of government services to citizens. Home rule cities are even bigger winners. They have tremendous freedom to choose their form of government, election system, and organization of city government. However, counties are often losers. Counties, especially large-population ones, are strapped with the same form of government that all other counties in Texas possess. Little freedom exists for them to tailor their plans of government and structures to their needs.

The winners in education are often the residents of the districts. In ISDs, residents benefit by having local school boards that govern smaller areas than might otherwise occur under a countywide system. This arrangement reinforces the small-town and rural bias common in Texas political history. School boards should be more responsive to voters and parents, especially in smaller-enrollment school districts. This arrangement allows policies and programs to be tweaked to the wishes of local concerns. For example, Hudson ISD, located just outside of Lufkin in East Texas, operates the largest high school in Texas without a football team. Hudson High School is classified as an AAA school for University Interscholastic League athletic and academic competitions. However, residents are wary of the football culture of many other towns and communities of Texas, including nearby AAAAA football powerhouse Lufkin High.

Residents are also often winners with regard to special districts if they are willing to create a district and to see their property taxes raised to cover the additional services that the special district provides. In addition, residents within a city or in part of a county may elect to create the district to provide selected services to a particular area, even if the majority of residents in the entire city or county do not want those services. Thus, the creation of special districts gives Texans the freedom to choose whether to accept certain services and the corresponding taxes and to reject those services (and taxes). However, this buffet-style approach produces significant variation in the services that residents receive and results in divergent rates of property taxes across the state and even within cities and counties. Residents also find themselves subject to several local governments, a confusing array that offers little coordination of services throughout a county or metropolitan area. Moreover, the heavy use of property taxes to fund all of these services may depress property values in some parts of the state, causing significant variation in taxation levels between rural and wealthy areas of the state; it also places the burden of paying for services largely in the hands of property owners.

In addition, the funding of local government through a variety of property taxes and fees often creates a significant and obscure tax burden on citizens throughout the state. Reliance on property taxes, discussed here and in Chapter 13, overburdens citizens who live in larger metropolitan areas or rural areas where property tax rates are significantly higher to compensate for lower property values than in wealthier suburban areas. The property tax is a distinct burden on retirees, whose spending and income often decrease while property taxes remain at the same level. By amendment to the Texas Constitution, retirees are protected from increases in property tax rates. As noted above, the property tax burden is not evenly shared in local government, as individuals who do not own property utilize basic services such as emergency care or education without contributing to their cost directly. Texans may also be losers because each ISD, MUD, community college district, etc. must bear the administrative costs of operating the district, including such expenses as office space, office equipment, and staffing. Local governments in Texas ultimately raise their costs of operation to pay for these administrative expenses, passing these costs on to citizens of Texas, who pay higher taxes in the process. For example, a county-wide school district in Georgia or Louisiana requires one central office administration, not the five, six, or even nine that each school district in a county in Texas may have. Government in Texas is clearly proving unnervingly complex and, arguably, costly. In the end, the citizens of Texas lose.

★ How do counties in Texas differ from cities in their powers, duties, and responsibilities, and which do you think has more advantages?

★ Should Texas allow counties to have some form of home rule?

★ Are there more advantages or disadvantages to the single-member district election system for local governments in Texas?

★ Do the state's local governments benefit from or struggle under at-large election systems?

## CONCLUSION

Local government in Texas is a diverse set of governments. Ultimately, all local governments are dominated by the state government, which determines the powers of local governments and the organizational structure of them. Local government, in the form of cities, counties, and special districts, exists to aid the state of Texas in delivering public policies and public services in areas such as transportation, education, and public health. Citizens also create, with the permission of the state, some forms of local government, such as cities and special districts, to provide specific services that the citizens want. Texas provides little flexibility to its local governments, although cities are afforded more freedom under home rule provisions than other forms of local government. However, residents of cities of sufficient size must choose to adopt home rule status before they can take advantage of it. In the end, Texans are confronted with a set of overlapping jurisdictions providing a variety of public services and overseeing a plethora of public policies with various degrees of effectiveness.

## KEY TERMS

administrative federalism (p. 375)

annexation (p. 386)

auditor (p. 381)

city charter (p. 386)

commissioners court (p. 379)

constable (p. 381)

contract outsourcing (p. 383)

county attorney (p. 381)

county civil service commission (p. 382)

county clerk (p. 381)

Dillon's Rule (p. 373)

fiscal federalism (p. 375)

general law city (p. 386)

home rule city (p. 386)

justice of the peace (p. 381)

machine politics (p. 394)

merit-based civil service system (p. 382)

municipal bond (p. 398)

municipal utility district (MUD) (p. 405)

ordinance (p. 386)

partisan election (p. 379)

privatization (p. 383)

sheriff (p. 381)

tax assessor (p. 381)

zoning policy (p. 395)

## CORE ASSESSMENT

1. If minority representation is a concern in Texas local government, which election system would you recommend a city or school district adopt? Why?

2. What are the advantages and disadvantages of the use of municipal utility districts (MUDs) to provide services that are normally provided by cities and counties in other states?

3. How does the NIMBY ("not in my backyard") problem in local government relate to or contradict the role of personal responsibility of citizens to their neighbors?

4. How should members of local school boards balance the demands of the constituents who elected them to office with the need to provide an education for the entire community?

# 13 FISCAL POLICY

What would bring a Japanese automaker to Texas? In 2014, at least part of the answer could be found in the Texas Enterprise Fund (TEF). In April of that year, Governor Rick Perry announced that Toyota planned to relocate its North American headquarters to Plano. Perry cited a "combination of low taxes, fair courts, smart regulations and [a] world-class workforce [that] can help businesses of any size succeed and thrive" as reasons why Toyota wanted to make Texas its new home.[1] However, Perry was offering Toyota something beyond the traditional Texas fare of low taxes and minimal business regulation: $40 million in funds from the TEF. To sweeten the deal further, the city of Plano agreed to a grant of $6,750,000 and offered Toyota a 50 percent tax abatement for ten years and a 50 percent rebate on taxes for the ten years after that.

Of course, the plan to bring Toyota to Texas was not without controversies and complications. The *Houston Chronicle* wanted the details of the plan released to the public, but the governor's office cited the need to keep details of the deal confidential lest other states offer "competing incentives."[2] The state's newspapers argued that the use of public funds brought with it the public's right to scrutinize that use. The governor's office, however, did not want to show its hand until the deal was done.

Calling Texas government conservative is overly simplistic and glosses over details that make some Texans who might regard themselves as conservative uneasy. As we will see in this chapter, the way in which Texas raises and spends state money involves a lot of conflicting priorities that may or may not fit our traditional sense of liberal or conservative, Democratic or Republican. No one should confuse Texas's brand of conservatism with a government that is passive and disengaged from the state's economy. In fact, Perry and other state leaders have prided themselves on taking the lead on economic development. As of June 2014, the TEF, which bills itself as "the largest 'deal-closing' fund of its kind in the nation," has allocated $555 million.[3]

Conservative economic policy in Texas does not mean cautious. Governments, like businesses, may make investments and take risks. Putting millions of tax dollars on the table to attract new business is both activist and ambitious. As he looks toward a run for the presidency, former governor Rick Perry loves to talk about economic development. Perry tells audiences that the state's low taxes bring businesses to Texas (and, he hopes, take him to the White House). Fiscal policy in Texas has always been a topic of

In 2014, the Texas Enterprise Foundation played an integral role in luring auto manufacturer Toyota into moving its North American headquarters to Plano, bringing lucrative jobs to the state.

interest, but the state can expect even more scrutiny in the coming years. Texas has already been the subject of several books. Some books have titles such as *Texas Got It Right!* and portray Texas as the vision of all that is good and right in America,[4] while others portray the state as some kind of dystopian nightmare like in the Hunger Games—with more guns.[5] Some of these books are little more than partisan exercises designed to show particular parties and/or candidates in the best or worst possible light. The *Wall Street Journal* saw fit to challenge the state's budget in a June 2013 editorial titled "Texas Goes Sacramento: Republicans Spend Their Energy Gusher, and Then Some." If the comparison to California was not insulting enough, the *Wall Street Journal* went on to compare a Texas budget written by conservative Republicans to the product of liberal California Democrats by saying the budget was "the kind of stunt one would expect from Nancy Pelosi" and suggesting Perry veto it.[6] While the validity of the *WSJ*'s claim of an exploding Texas budget is questionable, it leaves no doubt the state's budget is being watched closely inside and outside of Texas.

In this chapter, we will describe the policymaking process and examine types of policies generally found in government, as well as some of the specific fiscal policies that emerge from the process. Policy comes to Texans through a variety of actors in the state government. Some policies result directly from the actions of the Texas Legislature as it gathers every two years to write new laws. Many policies result from executive orders and other actions of the governor or other elected executives. Others emerge from the bureaucracy as it interprets the laws enacted by the legislature. Finally, local policies result from the actions of city or county governments. Government is seldom tasked with problems that have easy solutions. As we will see in the discussion of the budget, policy solutions are difficult because Texans often do not even agree on whether or not there is a problem. Texas's government under different flags and constitutions has been struggling for generations to find solutions to the problems Texans face. However, a rapidly changing population continually redefines our old problems and generates new problems as immigration from other countries and other states continues to bring new people and new politics to Texas.

## Chapter Objectives

★ Describe the basic steps in the policymaking process.

★ Identify the different types of taxes that Texans pay.

★ Assess who wins and who loses under the Texas tax system.

★ Describe other state revenue resources, including the role of the federal government.

★ Explain the state's pay-as-you-go budgeting system.

★ Discuss how subsidies work as fiscal policy tools.

★ Assess who wins and who loses under Texas's fiscal policy.

**Policy**
the actions and activities of government.

**Agenda setting**
the stage in which policymakers prioritize the problems facing the state.

**Policy formation**
the stage in which possible solutions are developed and debated.

**Policy adoption**
the stage in which formal government action takes place.

**Policy implementation**
the stage in which the policy is carried out in state agencies.

**Policy evaluation**
the stage in which the implementation of a policy is examined to see if policy goals are being met.

**Redistributive policy**
moves benefits, usually in the form of money, from one group to another in an attempt to equalize society.

## THE POLICYMAKING PROCESS

**P**olicy, or the actions and activities of government, is the bread and butter of governance. Scholars have identified five stages in the policymaking process, which are depicted in Figure 13.1. In the **agenda setting** stage, policymakers prioritize the various problems facing the state. These policymakers may discover a problem themselves through sources ranging from their own everyday experiences to formal legislative hearings, or a problem may be brought to their attention by individual citizens, interest groups, or media reports. In the **policy formation** stage, possible solutions are developed and debated. Next, in the **policy adoption** stage, formal government action takes place with approval of the legislature or through administrative action by a member of the executive branch. After approval, policies move into the **policy implementation** stage, during which state agencies follow up on the actions of elected officials. In this stage, bureaucratic agencies develop rules and regulations that detail the guidelines for how the policy will be carried out. Finally, in the **policy evaluation** stage, government agencies, the legislature, and interest groups assess the implementation of the policy to determine if its goals are being met.

Political scientists have categorized policies into three types: redistributive, distributive, and regulatory. **Redistributive policy** moves benefits (usually in the form of money) from one group to another in an attempt to equalize society by taxing people with higher incomes to provide benefits to people with fewer resources. **Distributive policy** is similar except that it attempts to meet the needs of citizens without targeting any one group as the source of money. As a result, distributive policies are easier to implement because their costs are widely dispersed, and such policies face less opposition since no group is identified as the source of funds. **Regulatory policy** attempts to limit or control the actions of individuals or corporations. For example, businesses may face fines or other penalties as a disincentive for polluting or causing other socially undesirable outcomes. Thus, policy is at the heart of politics as the government resolves the question of who gets what from government.

## SOURCES OF STATE REVENUE: TAXES

**M**aybe the most obvious way of looking at who gets what from government is examining the money that Texas takes from its citizens (taxes) and puts into various programs (spending). While the intentions and effectiveness of the different policies the state spends money on will be discussed in Chapters 14 and 15, we need to first look at **fiscal policy**, which is how government seeks to influence the economy through taxing and spending, and **subsidies**. Fiscal policy includes policies intended to shape the health of the economy overall, as well as policies the state uses to encourage specific businesses and discourage others.

**Distributive policy**
moves benefits to meet the needs of citizens but does so without targeting any one group as the source of money.

**Regulatory policy**
attempts to limit or control the actions of individuals or corporations.

**Fiscal policy**
how government seeks to influence the economy through taxing and spending.

**Subsidy**
incentive designed to encourage the production or purchase of certain goods to stimulate or support some businesses.

### FIGURE 13.1    The Policymaking Process

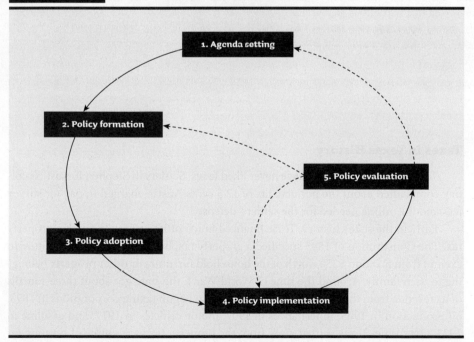

**Source:** Christine Barbour and Gerald C. Wright, *Keeping the Republic*, 4th brief ed. (Washington, D.C.: CQ Press, 2011), 475.

# TEXAS AND THE FED ON *Fiscal Federalism*

While Texans and the federal government often disagree about who has the authority over different policy issues, a related and equally contentious issue is who will pay for different policies. Texas has historically claimed sovereignty over a wide range of policy issues; it has also complained that the state gives more to the federal government than it gets. Relative to other states, Texas has not always fared as well with federal dollars as some. A study by the Tax Foundation found that in 2004 Texas ranked thirty-sixth out of fifty states on federal funds received relative to federal taxes paid by residents of the state. Overall, Texas at that time received $0.94 for every $1.00 Texans paid in federal taxes.[i] An analysis of census data by *The Economist* showed that from 1990–2009 Texans paid more in federal taxes than the federal government spent in Texas.

The gap between what some states get and what their residents pay reflects what is sometimes termed *fiscal transfers*. The reasons behind this gap are complicated because there are so many types of federal spending. Some of the gap does not reflect a transfer from one state to another so much as it does transfers from wealthy to poor communities. Puerto Rico, New Mexico, Mississippi, and West Virginia enjoy the greatest advantage, while Delaware, Minnesota, and New Jersey receive the least federal revenue compared to what their citizens pay.[ii] While some people have suggested that part of this gap results from federal hostility toward Texas, the data behind the gap they describe occurred while a Texan was in the White House.

A number of changes, including increasing military expenditures, changing demographics, and a growing number of Texans living in poverty, reveal some evidence that this trend has reversed. In recent years, Texas has received more federal money than it has paid. At the same time, Congressman Joe Barton of Texas, a frequent critic of the federal government, believes that while Texas is now getting a fair share of federal spending, the federal government attaches too many strings to the funds.[iii]

★ Should a state reasonably expect to get back in federal spending what it pays in federal taxes?

★ To what degree should the level of government that pays for policy implementation have authority over that policy issue?

---

i. Tax Foundation, "Federal Tax Burdens and Spending by State," Special Report no. 139, October 19, 2007.

ii. "America's Fiscal Union: The Red and the Black," *The Economist*, August 1, 2011, www.economist.com/blogs/dailychart/2011/08/americas-fiscal-union (accessed September 22, 2014).

iii. Sean Collins Walsh, "Texas Can No Longer Complain That It Gives More Than It Gets from Federal Government," *Dallas Morning News*, August 5, 2012, www.dallasnews.com/news/politics/headlines/20120805-texas-can-no-longer-complain-that-it-gives-more-than-it-gets-from-federal-government.ece (accessed September 22, 2014).

## Taxes in Texas History

Texans, not surprisingly, have never liked taxes. Settlers in Stephen F. Austin's colony complained about the per-acre tax of 12.5 cents Austin charged to pay for survey fees and the militia needed for the settlers' defense.[7]

Early in the state's history, Texas financed much of its activity through a property tax. The Constitution of 1845 specified a property tax, but it allowed the legislature to exempt from taxation $250 worth of the household furniture or other property belonging to each family. Around the time of World War I, the state got about three-fourths of its revenue from the property tax. Texas had also begun taxing corporations in 1893, oil production in 1905, inheritances in 1907, motor vehicles in 1917, and gasoline in 1923. Over time, Texas shifted away from the property tax as a source of revenue for state government, passing it down to local governments, who now rely on it.

## State Taxes Today

Today, Texas relies on a complicated mixture of over sixty separate taxes. Texas is one of nine states with no **income tax**, a tax calculated as a percentage of income earned in a year. Two states (New Hampshire and Tennessee) have no general income tax but do tax dividend and interest income. While the idea of avoiding income tax is appealing, Texas has demonstrated that there are many, many other ways of raising revenue for the state. As Bob Bullock quipped while he was serving as the state's comptroller, "There are only certain taxes known to civilized man, and Texas has nearly all of them, except the income tax."[8]

### General Sales Tax

In 1961, Texas implemented its first **general sales tax**, a tax imposed on goods and services, when it imposed a tax of 2 percent on many goods sold. That tax rate has increased to 6.25 percent and expanded to include more goods and services. Today, the state sales and use tax is added to certain services, retail sales, and the leases and rentals of most goods. Food products for human consumption are exempt from the sales tax unless they are candy, soft drinks, or prepared meals. In 1967, the Local Sales and Use Tax Act authorized cities to add a local tax of 1 percent on all retail sales. Today, Texas cities, counties, transit authorities, and other special-purpose districts have the option of imposing an additional local sales tax for a combined possible maximum for all state and local sales taxes of 8.25 percent. Cities are allowed a maximum of 2 percent, counties a maximum of 1.5 percent, transit authorities 1 percent, and special purpose districts 2 percent.

By 1967, the sales tax had become the largest source of tax revenue for Texas. In 2013, the state sales taxes brought in $25.9 billion, accounting for about 54 percent of Texas taxes, by far the biggest source of tax revenue for the state.

Comparing the sales taxes of the forty-five states that use a statewide sales tax is difficult because each state uses a different mixture of state and local sales taxes. In fact, thirty-eight states allow local governments to collect sales taxes. For example, the state of New York imposes a sales tax rate of only 4 percent, but counties in New York have local sales tax rates that allow them to add an additional percentage that ranges from 3 percent to 5.75 percent. Alaska has no statewide sales tax but allows as much as 5 or 6 percent in Juneau and Kodiak, respectively. Other states, such as Connecticut, have a state-level sales tax with no local add-ons. Texas's sales tax of 6.25 percent is tied for the thirteenth-highest state sales tax rate in the nation, a point behind California's sales tax of 7.25 percent. However, California does not allow as much to be added by local governments, and the average sales tax rate in Texas (8.15 percent once local add-ons are included) is slightly lower than in California (8.41 percent). The highest combined rate for state and local sales taxes is Tennessee's 9.45 percent.[9]

While the Texas sales tax covers a wide range of products and services, there are many exemptions that encourage some activities over others. Professor Lori Taylor noted in her analysis of the Texas sales taxes that Texas families are encouraged to

**Income tax**
a tax calculated as a percentage of income earned in a year.

**General sales tax**
an across-the-board tax imposed on goods and services sold within a jurisdiction.

# TEXAS (VS) NEW JERSEY

Every year, the Tax Foundation, a nonpartisan tax research group based in Washington, D.C., calculates Tax Freedom Day to illustrate what portion of the year citizens must work to pay their federal, state, and local taxes. In 2014, it estimated that the average American works about 111 days out of the year to pay his or her taxes, making Tax Freedom Day fall on April 21.

By the Tax Foundation's estimate, Tax Freedom Day comes a few days earlier (April 13) for Texans, placing Texas thirty-second among the fifty states in terms of total state taxes paid per capita. The most heavily taxed states, according to the Tax Foundation, are New Jersey and Connecticut.[i] One of the reasons for New Jersey's high taxes is that its citizens are relatively prosperous, with a median household income of $71,637, compared to Texas's median household income of $51,563 and the national average median of $53,046.[ii] Because families in Texas have lower incomes, they naturally pay lower federal income taxes than families in higher-income states, such as New Jersey and Connecticut. In addition to the federal income tax, New Jersey has a separate state income tax with six brackets and a top rate of 8.97 percent (the sixth-highest individual state income tax rate in the nation).

Overall, the highest rates of taxation are found in the Northeast, with Connecticut (#1), New Jersey (#1), New York (#3), and Massachusetts (#5) having the four highest rates in the nation. In contrast, taxes are generally lower in the South, with Alabama (#46), Tennessee (#47), Mississippi (#49), and Louisiana (#50) among the least-taxed citizens.

## THINKING Critically

★ Can you think of some advantages of living in a state with a high income tax, such as New Jersey? What might these be?

★ Can you identify problems in Texas that might be better addressed if the state had more revenue?

★ Can you think of other ways the state might raise revenue without imposing income taxes?

---

i. Kyle Pomerleau and Lyman Stone, "Tax Freedom Day 2014 is April 21, Three Days Later Than Last Year," Tax Foundation, April 7, 2014, http://taxfoundation.org/article/tax-freedom-day-2014-april-21-three-days-later-last-year (accessed May 23, 2014).

ii. U.S. Census Bureau, State Fact Sheets, www.census.gov.

---

eat at home because the prepared food served at restaurants is taxed while food to be prepared at home is not. Taylor notes that numerous exemptions are buried so deep in the tax code that we seldom notice them. For example, Texans must pay taxes on getting their dishwashers repaired but not their cars. Similarly, Texans pay a sales tax on getting their clothes washed but not on getting their car washed. Taylor goes on to conclude that "we could lower the sales tax rate by nearly a third and return revenues to current levels—simply by following the basic principles of good governance and refusing to play favorites with the tax code."[10] Thus, Taylor's analysis demonstrates how exempting some good and services from our "general" sales tax comes at a price and that taxing more good and services could allow Texas to reduce the tax rate we pay on each item without reducing what the state brings in. In addition to the general sales tax, Texas has a separate tax of 6.25 percent on the sale, rental, or lease of motor vehicles. There is also a tax of 3.25 percent on the sale of manufactured housing. These taxes bring in another $3 billion per year, or 8 percent of the state's revenue.

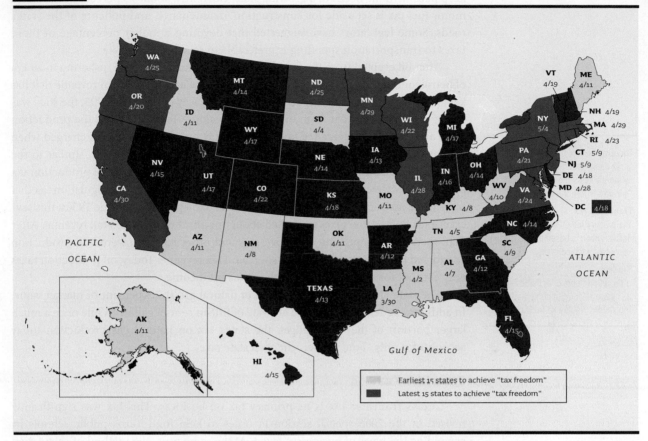

**MAP 13.1** Tax Freedom Days, 2014

Earliest 15 states to achieve "tax freedom"

Latest 15 states to achieve "tax freedom"

**Source:** Adapted from Tax Foundation, "America Celebrates Tax Freedom Day: Tax Freedom Day by State, Calendar Year 2014," http://taxfoundation.org/sites/taxfoundation.org/files/docs/Tax%20Freedom%20Day%202014%20Map_0.pg (accessed August 15, 2014). Used by permission of Tax Foundation.

## Gasoline and Severance Taxes

Texas has a separate tax on the sale of gasoline. Unlike the general sales tax that is a percentage of the cost of the product, the gasoline and diesel fuel tax charges consumers in Texas a fixed rate of twenty cents on every gallon of gasoline they buy (on top of 18.4 cents a gallon in federal taxes). Texas's gas tax rate is one of the lowest in the nation (thirty-eighth out of the fifty states and the District of Columbia), coming in at less than half of New York's 50.6 cents a gallon but much more than Alaska's eight cents a gallon. This tax generates over $3.1 billion each year, or about 8 percent of the state's tax revenue. The Texas Legislature has not raised the gasoline tax since 1992, and these funds are not keeping up with the increasing costs of building and maintaining Texas roads. In addition, the rising fuel efficiency of vehicles and the increased prominence of electric vehicles means that the ratio of miles driven to gas taxes collected continue to rise. While some legislators have taken the risk of calling for an increase in the gasoline tax to help fund the state's growing demand for roadways, Texas has increasingly turned to the toll roads discussed in Chapter 15 to keep pace with the needs of a growing state. Currently, about 75 percent of the state's motor fuel tax is set aside for construction, maintenance, and policing of the state's roads. Some legislators have suggested that devoting a higher percentage of those taxes to transportation spending is preferable to raising the tax rate.

After oil erupted from the Spindletop well on January 10, 1901, ushering in an era of petroleum, taxes on Texas's oil production became a huge source of revenue that has kept many Texans from having to pay much in the way of taxes. By 1905, the state was raking in $101,403 a year from oil production alone. Texas still taxes the production of oil and gas with a **severance tax**, which is a tax on natural resources charged when they are produced or "severed" from the earth. These severance taxes, similar to the value added tax (VAT) common in Europe, take the form of Texas's oil production tax that takes 4.6 percent of the market value of oil produced and the oil regulation tax that takes three-sixteenths of a cent from each barrel of oil produced. In the 1950s, this severance tax and related taxes generated about one-third of the state's tax revenue. After that, increased competition from overseas and other factors lowered oil production and forced the state to shift to other sources of tax revenue. Today, oil production taxes only account for about 6 percent of the state's tax income.

The state also taxes the production of natural gas at 7.5 percent of market value. In addition, liquefied gas is taxed at a rate of fifteen cents a gallon. While once a much larger portion of the state budget, the state's tax on natural gas production today accounts for only about 3.1 percent of all state taxes.

### Franchise Tax

Texas's **franchise tax** is its primary tax on business. This tax was significantly revised in the 2006 special session in order to help fund Texas public schools by expanding the types of businesses taxed. At the same time, the method of calculation of the tax was changed. Today, the franchise tax is based on the taxable margin (a variety of measures designed to approximate profit) of the company and has been labeled the margins tax by some. In fact, the franchise tax is complicated and can be based on either the net taxable capital or net taxable earned surplus of a business. In 2013, the franchise tax generated $4 billion, or about 10 percent of all state tax revenue. While Texas generally enjoys a reputation as a business-friendly state, the franchise tax has been described by one critic as "one of the most destructive taxes on corporate and small businesses in the country" because it imposes a higher burden on some industries than others.[11] One problem is that the franchise tax can be imposed on businesses even when they're not profitable.

### Sin Taxes

Like other states, Texas brings in revenue through so-called **sin taxes**, which are taxes on products or activities that some legislators want to discourage. The objects of sin taxes make inviting targets, as elected officials look for places to impose taxes on the least sympathetic products possible. Governor Milo Roberts instituted the state's first sin tax in 1879, creating a two-cent tax on each drink and a half-cent tax per beer

**Severance tax**
a tax on natural resources charged when the resources are produced or "severed" from the earth.

**Franchise tax**
the primary tax on businesses in Texas, which is based on the taxable margin of each company.

**Sin tax**
a tax on products or activities such as cigarettes or gambling that some legislators would like to discourage.

drawn. To ensure that the taxes were being paid, every saloon had to have a hand-cranked counter that rang a bell to register the tax being paid.[12] While the federal government has its own **excise tax**, which is a tax paid at the time of purchase with the cost of the tax usually included in the price of the product, on alcoholic beverages, Texas has separate tax rates on liquor, beer, wine, malt liquor, and mixed drinks. While some alcohol is taxed by volume, mixed drinks are taxed at 14 percent of sales. In 2013, Texas's taxes on alcohol totaled about $976 million. This is a small portion (2 percent) of the total state taxes as the contribution of a single product, but Texans might be surprised to realize that they drink enough to average over $6 in alcohol tax annually for every Texan of drinking age and generate almost $1 billion in tax revenue.

The rise in the state's tax on cigarettes, passed in May 2005 to help pay for schools, illustrates the complexities of the sin tax. On January 1, 2007, the state's tax on a pack of cigarettes leapt a full dollar for a total tax of $1.41 a pack, driving the cost of most packs of cigarettes to over $4 and making the state's tax much higher than in Louisiana ($.36) or Oklahoma ($1.03). Some Texans contemplated quitting smoking, an effect intended by groups such as the American Cancer Society that lobbied for the increase. Some saw the tax increase as a way of offsetting the health care costs to a state that sees over 20,000 people a year die from smoking-related illnesses. Since about half of the revenue from the tobacco tax is designated for the funding of public schools, imposition of the tax may seem an easy way to raise revenue at the expense of unpopular products. However, these taxes can be problematic. Because Louisiana's tax of thirty-six cents per pack is one of the lowest in the nation, some Texans simply cross state lines to buy their cigarettes, just as New Mexico's smokers streamed into Texas when New Mexico increased its tax by seventy cents per pack in 2003. With convenience stores claiming that cigarettes account for over one-quarter of their sales, the outflow of Texas customers results in a significant loss of revenue, depriving Texas merchants of customers and the state of Texas of taxable sales. While Texas's tobacco tax may seem high compared to its neighbors, it has not gone as far as states such as New York where cigarettes are taxed at a rate of $4.35 a pack.

The state's newest sin tax is a $5 fee for each person entering a business that provides live nude entertainment and allows consumption of alcoholic beverages. Referred to under tax policy as the fee on sexually oriented businesses, the fee has become better known as the "pole tax" (named for the tendency of strippers to utilize poles in their dancing routines). The fee has been challenged on free speech and other grounds since its enactment in 2008, but it has survived as of this writing.

The state's mixture of taxes in 2013 is spelled out in Table 13.1. As the table demonstrates, while Texas's tax rates may be low, the system is far from simple as the state looks to a wide variety of sources for its tax dollars.

## Property Taxes

While Texas's state taxes are lower than most other states, local governments impose a significant local **property tax**, which is a tax on the value of real estate that is paid by the property owner. And while the Texas Constitution forbids a statewide property tax, cities, counties, and local school districts charge property taxes that they

**Excise tax**
a tax paid at the time of purchase, with the cost of the tax included in the price of the product.

**Property tax**
a tax on the value of real estate that is paid by the property owner; used by county and local governments to fund such programs as public schools.

rely heavily on for their revenue. In 2006, the Texas Legislature reduced school property taxes by one-third. The plan traded lower school property taxes for higher taxes on businesses, smokers, and used-car purchasers. While the legislature's reform promised significantly lower property tax rates, about two-thirds of local school boards in the state opted to increase the rates after the legislature had reduced them.[13] While the increases were relatively small and within the limits created by the law, they served to reduce the size of tax cuts the legislature sought. Further, with state funding for public schools reduced by budget cuts in recent years, local school districts are even more dependent on property taxes.

These complications reflect the challenges of a mixed-funding system that leaves local school boards dependent on the state for much of their money while remaining subject to state rules on how they raise remaining revenues. Many local school

## TABLE 13.1 Texas State Taxes by Source, Fiscal Year 2013

| | 2013 Revenue | Percentage of Total Tax Revenue | Percentage of All Sources of Revenue |
|---|---|---|---|
| **Tax Collections** | | | |
| Sales tax | $25,943,807,086 | 54.3% | 26.20% |
| Motor vehicle sales/rental taxes | $3,878,379,684 | 8.1% | 3.90% |
| Motor fuels taxes | $3,221,502,038 | 6.7% | 3.30% |
| Franchise tax | $4,798,699,188 | 10.0% | 4.80% |
| Insurance taxes | $1,764,153,450 | 3.7% | 1.80% |
| Natural gas production tax | $1,495,202,962 | 3.1% | 1.50% |
| Cigarette and tobacco taxes | $1,598,089,091 | 3.3% | 1.60% |
| Alcoholic beverages taxes | $976,893,685 | 2.0% | 1.00% |
| Oil production tax | $2,990,890,113 | 6.3% | 3.00% |
| Utility taxes | $434,870,937 | 0.9% | 0.40% |
| Hotel tax | $441,131,849 | 0.9% | 0.40% |
| Other taxes | $247,719,032 | 0.5% | 0.30% |
| Total taxes | $47,781,045,666 | 100.0% | 48.20% |

**Source:** Texas Comptroller, "Revenue by Source for Fiscal Year 2013," www.window.state.tx.us/taxbud/revenue.html (accessed May 25, 2014).

**Note:** Totals may not sum due to rounding.

boards are faced with growing student populations, rising utility bills, and increasing staff costs, even as the legislature has capped available funding. Locally elected school boards are left with few alternative sources of revenue and have little choice but to raise property taxes or cut budgets.

A similar problem plagues county government in areas seeing a boom in oil and gas production. The severance tax on oil and gas goes to the state while counties must rely on property taxes that change slowly. Meanwhile, the heavy vehicle traffic that arrives with the oil and gas production plays havoc on the roads the county maintains, and the funding formulas that the state uses to distribute road maintenance funds give the counties little revenue to work with to deal with the damaged roads.

A receipt for $16.25 in state and county taxes that Thomas W. Grayson owed in 1852 for taxable property. This property included 660 acres on Salado Creek in Bexar County, two "negros," thirty-five head of cattle, one wagon, and one carriage. Ironically, freed slaves would go from being taxable property to being discriminated against with a poll tax.

In 2011, the approximately 4,000 taxing entities in Texas levied around $40.6 billion in property taxes, an increase of about 0.8 percent from the year before. About half of that ($22 billion) was levied by school districts, while cities collected about $6.8 billion and counties brought in about $6.7 billion. The remaining $5 billion in taxes were levied by a wide range of special districts.[14] As Figure 13.2 reflects, while Texans enjoy having no income tax, they make up some of the difference with a higher sales tax from the state and higher property taxes levied at the local level.

Setting property tax rates may seem like a simple process. However, the property tax is an **ad valorem tax,** a tax based on the value of property. Even if the property tax rates remain the same, governments may raise the tax paid by citizens by increasing the amount of the **appraisal,** the official estimate of a property's value. This problem is especially serious in rapidly growing areas where property values rise quickly as new residents increase the demand for housing. This creates what critics call a "stealth tax increase" as citizens see the value of their homes increase even though they are not offering their houses for sale. As Table 13.2 illustrates, large changes in taxes collected are not unusual, with property tax collection jumping 11 percent in Texas in 2008 but remaining flat in the years since.

Disagreements over appraisal values often create tension between residential property owners and the owners of commercial properties. Fairness has become an important issue in appraisals because many people feel that the process in Texas undervalues

**Ad valorem tax**
a tax based on property value, which is subject to periodic appraisals.

**Appraisal**
the official estimate of a property's value.

FIGURE 13.2    Sources of Tax Revenue: Texas and the National Average

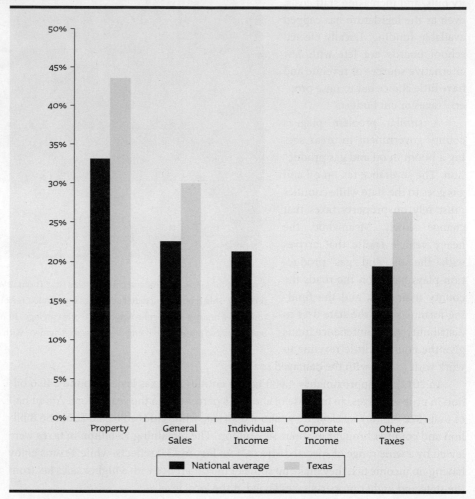

**Source:** Lyman Stone, "Facts & Figures: How Does Your State Compare?," Tax Foundation, table 8, http://taxfoundation.org/article/facts-figures-2014-how-does-your-state-compare (accessed June 4, 2014).

commercial and industrial properties, leaving homeowners to pick up more than their share. Reformers argue that the owners of large commercial properties are more likely to hire lawyers to challenge property valuations. Assessment of residential property values are relatively easy to establish based on the prices paid for the large number of homes sold each year with the price of each home publicly available. Commercial properties are often valued on the revenue that they generate from rents or other revenue that may be confidential information not available to tax assessors.

Currently, the state caps the annual increase in a home's taxable value at 10 percent. This benefits senior citizens and others living on fixed incomes who may have trouble keeping up with the taxes on their homes as property values rise. As one resident of Austin complained, "I am now paying as much in property taxes as I used to pay for my entire mortgage payment when I first bought the house in 1988."[15] Texas offers a cap on school taxes, and the Texas Constitution was amended in 2003 to allow (but not require) cities and counties to cap seniors' taxes. While this may give retired Texans some protection against rising rates, it shifts the burden for taxes to others and may present a serious problem for areas with high numbers of retirees.

## WINNERS AND LOSERS

The type of taxes Texas uses creates obvious winners and losers. A **progressive tax**, such as the federal income tax, places higher rates on people with higher incomes. A **regressive tax**, in contrast, takes a higher proportion of income from people with lower incomes than from people with higher incomes. Sales taxes are often cited as examples of regressive taxes, even though everyone pays the same tax rate on purchases. Critics of sales taxes point out that people with lower incomes tend to spend a larger share of their income on the kind of items taxed at sale. A 2013 study by the Texas comptroller's office showed that while the high-income Texans paid more in sales taxes, as a percentage of income, the lowest-income Texans paid a higher percent of their income.

Some Texans have advocated an income tax like those used by other states to shift more of the state's tax burden to people with higher incomes. While critics complain about the complexity of an income tax system with exemptions and schedules of deductions, the vast array of current state taxes is evidence that Texas has already created a complicated system without an income tax. Even some conservative legislators privately concede that replacing some of Texas's long list of taxes with a single income tax based on calculations already done for federal income taxes would actually simplify taxation in the state. However, these legislators worry that if the state does away with small taxes in favor of an income tax, nothing would prevent the state from gradually reinstating these small taxes whenever the government needed more money.

Choosing how much to tax and who to tax is a clear example of who wins and who loses. With so many taxes, it should not be surprising that almost every Texan finds something to dislike about them. And, with voters already unhappy, it is easy to see why the legislature has not been anxious to look at new taxes. When the political price of new taxes is so high, our elected officials tend to avoid updating the system altogether because changes will inevitably shift the tax burden and be seen as new taxes, even when they are designed to replace old taxes.

**Progressive tax**
a graduated tax, such as an income tax, which taxes people with higher incomes at higher rates.

**Regressive tax**
a tax that takes a higher proportion of income from people with lower incomes than from people with higher incomes.

★ Does the state's tax system place more of an undue burden on specific groups of citizens or types of businesses? How or how does it not do this?

★ Does having different levels of government taxing citizens create inequalities and confusion?

★ Is the Texas tax system too overly complicated? Why or why not?

★ Should Texas have an income tax? Why or why not?

## TABLE 13.2 Property Taxes Levied, Calendar Years 1991 to 2011 (in Millions)

| Tax Year | School District | City | County | Special District | Total Property Taxes | Percentage Increase |
|----------|-----------------|------|--------|------------------|----------------------|---------------------|
| 1991 | $7,566 | $2,304 | $1,894 | $1,460 | $13,223 | 10.9% |
| 1992 | $8,181 | $2,312 | $1,996 | $1,40 | $13,981 | 5.7% |
| 1993 | $8,682 | $2,362 | $2,177 | $1,536 | $14,757 | 5.5% |
| 1994 | $9,024 | $2,494 | $2,311 | $1,621 | $15,450 | 4.7% |
| 1995 | $9,341 | $2,597 | $2,392 | $1,628 | $15,958 | 3.3% |
| 1996 | $9,910 | $2,701 | $2,537 | $1,699 | $16,847 | 5.6% |
| 1997 | $10,395 | $2,847 | $2,658 | $1,760 | $17,660 | 4.8% |
| 1998 | $11,335 | $3,006 | $2,828 | $1,889 | $19,058 | 7.9% |
| 1999 | $12,010 | $3,248 | $2,979 | $2,041 | $20,278 | 6.4% |
| 2000 | $13,392 | $3,531 | $3,201 | $2,389 | $22,513 | 11% |
| 2001 | $15,155 | $3,885 | $3,567 | $2,704 | $25,310 | 12.4% |
| 2002 | $16,419 | $4,187 | $3,850 | $2,865 | $27,320 | 7.9% |
| 2003 | $17,264 | $4,415 | $4,122 | $3,092 | $28,893 | 5.8% |
| 2004 | $18,534 | $4,608 | $4,463 | $3,369 | $30,974 | 7.2% |
| 2005 | $20,195 | $4,902 | $4,773 | $3,610 | $33,479 | 8.1% |
| 2006 | $20,918 | $5,323 | $5,340 | $3,972 | $35,553 | 6.2% |
| 2007 | $18,874 | $5,890 | $5,837 | $4,513 | $35,115 | −1.2% |
| 2008 | $21,233 | $6,451 | $6,343 | $4,953 | $38,980 | 11% |
| 2009 | $21,780 | $6,594 | $6,527 | $5,134 | $40,034 | 2.7% |
| 2010 | $21,558 | $6,755 | $6,527 | $5,395 | $40,275 | 0.6 |
| 2011 | 22,002 | $6,810 | $6,743 | $5,039 | $40,593 | 0.8 |

*Source:* Legislative Budget Board, "Fiscal Size-Up: 2014–15 Biennium," www.lbb.state.tx.us/Documents/Publications/Fiscal_SizeUp/Fiscal_SizeUp.pdf, fig. 50 (accessed May 25, 2014).

## SOURCES OF STATE REVENUE: OTHER RESOURCES

While the taxes outlined so far generated almost $48 billion in 2013, they accounted for just over 48 percent of state revenue. This raises the question of where the state gets the rest of its money. As Table 13.3 indicates, tax revenues are only part of the funding picture.

## Federal Grants

The large share of the state budget that comes from the federal treasury might surprise many Texans. In 2013, Texas received about $32.5 billion from the federal government, which accounted for almost one-third of the state's finances. As Figure 13.3 illustrates, the share of the Texas budget coming from federal funds has increased dramatically over the last two decades. In the 1980s, federal funds accounted for less than one in four dollars in state spending, but by 2003 that rate had increased to one in three. The drop in sales tax revenue associated with the economic downturn, combined with the surge in federal spending in the stimulus program, brought the federal contribution to the state budget to over 42 percent in 2010. However, while some of the increasing federal role in the state's budget reflects the Obama administration's programs, the long-term shift reflects a growing federal role under Republican and Democratic administrations.

As the discussion of fiscal federalism in Chapter 2 illustrates, these federal monies often come with strings attached. In some cases, they pay for programs in which the state and federal government partner. The large dollar amounts account for much of state leaders' willingness to accept federal rules.

**TABLE 13.3** **Texas State Revenue by Source**

| Revenue by Source | 2013 Revenue | Percentage of All Sources of Revenue |
|---|---|---|
| Tax collections | $47,781,045,666 | 48.2% |
| Federal income | $32,530,326,029 | 32.8% |
| Licenses, fees, fines, and penalties | $7,919,704,761 | 8.0% |
| Interest and investment income | $1,182,874,186 | 1.2% |
| Net lottery proceeds | $1,893,285,121 | 1.9 % |
| Sales of goods and services | $225,926,149 | 0.2% |
| Settlements of claims | $609,960,852 | 0.6% |
| Land income | $1,325,664,892 | 1.3% |
| Contributions to employee benefits | $86,521 | 0.0% |
| Other revenue | $5,574,338,463 | 5.6% |
| **Total revenue** | **$99,043,212,641** | **100.0%** |

**Source:** Texas Comptroller, "Revenue by Source for Fiscal Year 2013," www.window.state.tx.us/taxbud/revenue .html (accessed May 25, 2014).

**Note:** Totals may not sum due to rounding.

FIGURE 13.3 **Federal Funds as a Share of Total Texas State Revenue, 1980–2013**

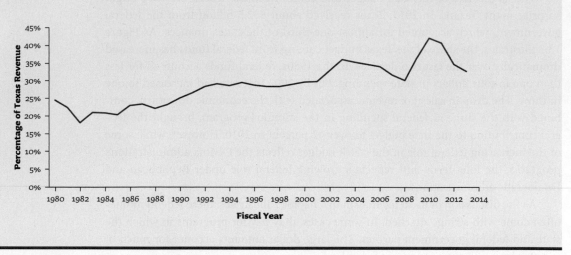

**Source:** Texas Comptroller, "Texas Net Revenue by Source: Fiscal 1978–2012," www.texastransparency.org/State_Finance/Budget_Finance/Reports/Revenue_by_Source/revenue_hist.php (accessed June 5, 2014).

### Interest, Licensing, and Lottery Funds

Rounding out the revenue picture for Texas are various funding sources that together account for about one-fifth of all state revenue. Some of this money comes from the licensing of various professions and businesses. While these fees resemble taxes on certain professions, the argument that they simply offset some of the specific expenses associated with licensing justifies counting them as something different from taxes. In addition, the state receives money from fines paid by those found guilty of traffic and other violations.

In 2013, the state received over $1.2 billion in income from returns on its bank balances and other investments. The largest source of investment income came from the state's **Permanent School Fund**, a fund set aside to finance education in Texas. The state received another $1.3 billion from income derived from land.

Texas also makes money from a state lottery. Some of the proceeds of lottery ticket sales go into the prizes, with the state and retailers dividing the rest. In 2013, about $4.4 billion in lottery tickets were sold, and about $2.8 billion in cash prizes were awarded by the state. After about $236 million in commissions and other payments to retailers and $194 million in administrative expenses, the lottery brought in almost $1.1 billion for state use. Most of that revenue ($1 billion) went to a fund to support Texas public schools, while another $5.2 million went to support the Texas Veterans Commission, and another $41.9 million went into the state's general revenue fund.[16] While unpopular with a wide variety of groups, the lottery remains a part of Texas state finances for the same reason as the other taxes and fees: no one has found a more popular way to replace the money it generates. For example, many social conservatives in the Texas Legislature find the state's profits from gambling distasteful or immoral. However, eliminating the Texas lottery would require increasing taxes or cutting popular

**Permanent School Fund**
a fund set aside to finance education in Texas; the state's largest source of investment income.

programs to offset the revenue lost. Thus, taking this revenue source off the books would be politically difficult.

## SPENDING AND BUDGETING

Texas government has not always been frugal. During the three years of Mirabeau Lamar's presidency, the government of Texas spent about $4.85 million while taking in only about $1.08 million.[17] Lamar had reversed Sam Houston's policy of cooperating with the Native American tribes, and the hostilities spawned by Lamar's desire to wipe Native Americans off the face of the state cost Texas dearly. By contrast, Houston's administration spent only about half a million dollars in the three years after Lamar's presidency.

A man picks out some lottery tickets as the store owner waits to pull them. The sale of lottery tickets has become an important but controversial source of revenue for the state of Texas.

© ZUMA Press, Inc / Alamy

As the Texas economy changes and Texans' expectations for government change, spending in Texas shifts. One of the fundamental causes of a growing state budget is a growing state population. As Table 13.4 details, Texas spends its money on a wide array of functions. While some details of the policies in these areas will be discussed in later chapters, our concern here is how overall spending is managed.

### State Budgeting

Texas has a **"pay-as-you-go" system** that requires a balanced budget and permits borrowing only under a very few circumstances. The Texas Constitution provides that state borrowing cannot exceed $200,000 unless such borrowing is needed to "repel invasion, suppress insurrection, or defend the State in war" or unless such borrowing is approved by voters. The Texas Legislature may declare an emergency, but doing so requires getting a four-fifths vote of both the Texas House and Senate before the spending limit can be exceeded.[18]

While many Texans might assume that balancing the state budget is relatively simple, the system created to ensure that the budget stays balanced has spawned some unique features in Texas government, especially in the role of the comptroller of public accounts. At the beginning of each legislative session, the Texas Constitution requires that the comptroller certify how much money will be in the state's accounts in the two years that the legislature is budgeting for. For example, when the Texas Legislature convened in January 2013, Comptroller Susan Combs reported to the legislature that "revenue collections from all sources and for all purposes should total $208.2 billion."[19] The estimate from the comptroller effectively became the ceiling for state spending that the legislature had to operate under.

**"Pay-as-you-go" system**
a fiscal discipline, adopted by Texas and many other states, that requires a balanced budget and permits borrowing only under a very few circumstances.

## TABLE 13.4　State Spending by Function, Fiscal Year 2013

| Government Function | Amount | Percent of Total |
|---|---|---|
| General government: executive departments | $2,303,450,209 | 2.5 |
| General government: legislative | 135,437,227 | 0.1 |
| General government: judicial | 270,101,181 | 0.3 |
| **Total general government** | **$2,708,988,616** | **2.9** |
| Education | $31,530,983,505 | 33.7 |
| Employee benefits | 3,478,190,888 | 3.7 |
| Health and human services | 38,735,710,434 | 41.4 |
| Public safety and corrections | 4,295,903,947 | 4.6 |
| Transportation | 7,603,809,915 | 8.1 |
| Natural resources/recreational services | 2,303,753,622 | 2.5 |
| Regulatory services | 357,731,982 | 0.4 |
| Lottery winnings paid | 661,198,706 | 0.7 |
| Debt service: interest | 1,334,549,422 | 1.4 |
| Capital outlay | 556,153,797 | 0.6 |
| Total net expenditures | $93,566,974,834 | |

**Source:** Texas Comptroller, "Texas Net Expenditures by Function—Fiscal 2013," www.window.state.tx.us/taxbud/expend.html (accessed May 29, 2014).

These provisions put the Texas comptroller in a unique—and powerful—position. As former comptroller Carole Strayhorn pointed out,

> The comptroller's office is a constitutional office; there's nothing like it in any other state. I tell the legislature what they can spend, and I certify that the budget is balanced. Unless and until I certify that budget, there is no appropriations bill, and there is nothing for the governor to line-item veto.[20]

The position of comptroller does not seem to be the kind of position to launch a political career from. After all, the job combines the dubious warmth enjoyed by being the state's tax collector with the excitement of accounting and auditing for the state. Bob Bullock, however, made his time as comptroller an important part of his rise to power. When he became comptroller in 1975, the office ran on mechanical adding machines and the most advanced piece of equipment in the office was an electric letter opener. Bullock increased the budget for his office from $16.5 million to $46 million in four years, largely by promising the governor and the legislature that for every extra dollar he was budgeted he could bring in ten more in tax revenue. When asked if he could find another $10 million so the state could buy Big Bend Ranch State Park, Bullock is said to have replied that he couldn't find $10 million for the park, but he could find $11 million for the new park and $1 million for pay raises for the Texas Rangers. Bullock increased tax collections through a combination of updated technology and aggressive auditors who became known as "Bullock's Raiders." Bullock and his auditors made some of his raids on television, a tactic that motivated other businesses owing back taxes to pay up. The process was not always smooth or genteel, and Bullock was sued by the Texas Council of Campfire Girls after he forced them to pay $13,284 in sales taxes.

The constitution allows the state to sell revenue bonds to finance activities specified in Article 3. These bonds are sold to investors and then paid back with the revenue from the services they provide. For example, Texas often issues tuition revenue bonds that may pay for new buildings on college campuses with student fees set aside to pay back the debt. At the end of the 2013 budget year, Texas had about $37.9 billion in outstanding state bonds.[21]

Then-Governor Rick Perry announced key budget principles in 2012 in preparation for the legislature passing the next two-year budget. In its last budget, the state made nearly $15 billion in budget cuts.

While the public debt in Texas is relatively low compared to other states, the debt of Texas cities has been increasing in recent years. Total debt for Texas local governments was just over $200 billion at the end of the 2013 fiscal year.[22] An analysis from the comptroller's office revealed that local government debt had more than doubled in the decade from 2001 to 2011, rising from $87.6 billion to $192 billion.[23] While the comptroller's report was somewhat critical of localities for this borrowing, it's only fair to point out that some of this borrowing resulted from efforts to keep up with explosive growth subsidized by state funds from the comptroller's office. Communities with rapid growth have trouble keeping up with this growth because their tax rates are limited and new schools, roads, and water systems are expensive.

## State Spending

While the state's constitution establishes numerous barriers to state debt, these provisions have not stopped increased state spending. Despite the fact that Texas is a conservative state, spending continues to rise. As Figure 13.4 demonstrates, spending in the state has been increasing steadily for the past thirty years. Much of this increase can be explained by inflation and the fact that the state's population has roughly doubled in the same time frame. However, Texas's government has grown dramatically under both Republicans and Democrats, and this enlargement reflects the increased demands of a growing and changing state.

FIGURE 13.4 **Trends in Spending, 1978–2013**

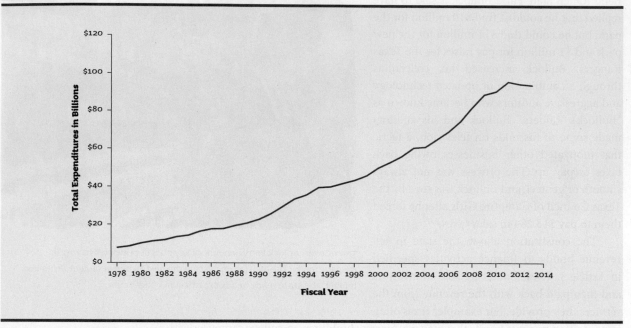

**Source:** Texas Comptroller of Public Accounts, "Texas Expenditure History by Function," www.texastransparency.org/State_Finance/Budget_Finance/Reports/Expenditures/by_Function/expend_hist.php (accessed May 29, 2014).

## The Rainy Day Fund

The Economic Stabilization Fund (ESF), often referred to as the Rainy Day Fund, was set up by a constitutional amendment approved by the voters in 1988. The ESF receives an amount equal to 75 percent of the amount of oil production tax collections in excess of 1987 levels and 75 percent of the amount of natural gas tax collections in excess of 1987 levels. The fund also receives one-half of any unused General Revenue Funds at the end of each biennial budget. In addition, the Texas Legislature may also add revenue to the fund whenever it wants.

Using the funds is much more difficult. Under certain circumstances, such as when the comptroller certifies a budget deficit, the legislature may appropriate money from the ESF with a three-fifths vote of each house. The legislature can use funds from the ESF for any purpose with a two-thirds vote of the members present in each house.

In 2011, the ESF became a major source of conflict. Advocates of using the fund argued that the economic downturn was the kind of "rainy day" that the ESF was designed to help with. Advocates of leaving the fund untouched argued that the economic downturn could continue and that the state needed the fund to protect against future budget shortfalls. In the end, the legislature used about $3.2 billion from the fund that reflected budget shortfalls carried over from the previous budget, leaving $6.3 billion in the ESF for future budget shortfalls.

The legislature has also supported use of the ESF for specific uses. In November 2013, Texas voters approved a constitutional amendment that would allow the state

# HOW TEXAS GOVERNMENT WORKS

## State Spending in Perspective

**Total State Expenditures per Capita**

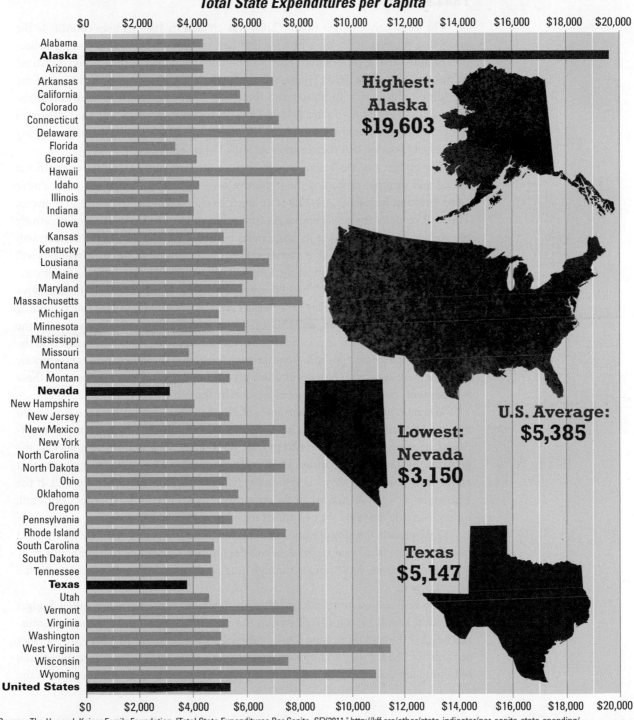

Highest:
Alaska
**$19,603**

U.S. Average:
**$5,385**

Lowest:
Nevada
**$3,150**

Texas
**$5,147**

States listed (top to bottom): Alabama, **Alaska**, Arizona, Arkansas, California, Colorado, Connecticut, Delaware, Florida, Georgia, Hawaii, Idaho, Illinois, Indiana, Iowa, Kansas, Kentucky, Lousiana, Maine, Maryland, Massachusetts, Michigan, Minnesota, Mississippi, Missouri, Montana, Montan, **Nevada**, New Hampshire, New Jersey, New Mexico, New York, North Carolina, North Dakota, Ohio, Oklahoma, Oregon, Pennsylvania, Rhode Island, South Carolina, South Dakota, Tennessee, **Texas**, Utah, Vermont, Virginia, Washington, West Virginia, Wisconsin, Wyoming, **United States**

Axis: $0, $2,000, $4,000, $6,000, $8,000, $10,000, $12,000, $14,000, $16,000, $18,000, $20,000

Source: The Henry J. Kaiser Family Foundation, "Total State Expenditures Per Capita, SFY2011," http://kff.org/other/state-indicator/per-capita-state-spending/.

to use $2 billion from the ESF to finance water projects. During the third special session of 2013, the legislature agreed to a constitutional amendment that, after being approved by voters in 2014, allowed the state to divert some oil and gas production tax revenue into the ESF for road construction and maintenance.

### The Legislative Budget Board

The Legislative Budget Board (LBB) was created in 1949 to help coordinate the budgeting process in Texas, a process that had previously been a haphazard collection of individual appropriations bills. As outlined in Chapter 4, the LBB is co-chaired by the Speaker of the Texas House and the lieutenant governor. The inclusion of the presiding officers of both houses and the chairs of key committees ensures that the LBB wields tremendous political clout. The LBB sometimes works with the Governor's Office of Budget, Planning, and Policy (GOBPP), which is responsible for developing the budget proposal that the governor submits to the legislature.

The budget process begins months before the legislature starts its work. In the spring and summer preceding the legislative session, the LBB sends out a Legislative Appropriation Request (LAR) that state agencies use to develop their budget requests. The LAR contains the performance measures that will be used to gauge how effectively the agency is accomplishing its basic mission. The LBB and the GOBPP meet with agencies to discuss their budget requests. Eventually, these appropriation requests will become the basis for the budget the LBB will propose to the legislature when it convenes the following January. The LBB also provides the legislature with the legislative budget estimates that detail how much each agency requested and how much funding it received in previous budgets. The legislature is not completely dependent on the LBB analysis. During the legislative session, the Senate Committee on Finance and the House Committee on Appropriations independently hold hearings and hear testimony from the state agencies. These committees often amend the proposed budget, and these amendments continue through consideration by the full House and Senate.

The state budget faces scrutiny even after it has been approved by the House and Senate. After the appropriations bill is passed, the comptroller must certify that sufficient revenue will be available to pay for the budget. The budget then goes to the governor for his or her signature. The Texas governor has line-item veto authority that allows him or her to remove or veto individual items in the appropriations bill. If the legislature is still in session when the governor vetoes a line in the appropriations bill, it may override the veto by a two-thirds majority vote in each house.

Once passed, the appropriations bill becomes the budget for the state for the next fiscal year. The fiscal year in Texas begins September 1, meaning that the state's budget year runs from September 1 through August 31 and does not coincide with the calendar year.

The LBB enjoys tremendous influence because it prepares the initial budget estimate that will be considered during the legislative session, and its work continues beyond the initial proposal. During the legislative session, the LBB staff provides analysis for the legislative committees involved in spending. Texas law requires each bill in the legislature to have a fiscal note prepared by the LBB staff that estimates the

**FIGURE 13.5** Texas Biennial Budget Cycle

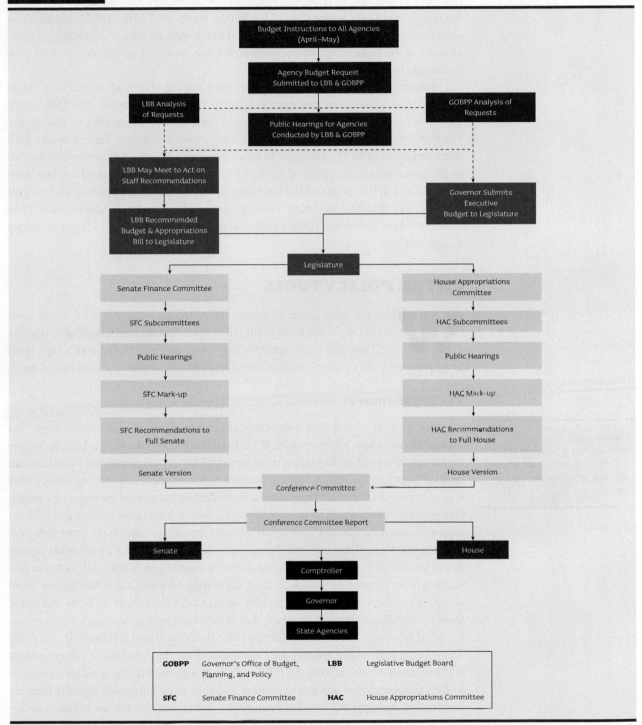

**Source:** Senate Research Center, "Budget 101: A Guide to the Budget Process in Texas," January 2011, www.senate.state.tx.us/src/pdf/Budget_101-2011.pdf, 5 (accessed May 28, 2014).

cost of the bill. Because elected officials tend to want to spend more than they have, many critics feel that the fiscal notes have become politicized and that they often ignore the true costs of bills favored by the leadership. At the end of the 2007 legislative session, Governor Perry complained that fiscal notes were no longer providing accurate pictures of the costs of legislation and warned that he would no longer sign bills with inaccurate fiscal notes.[24]

Between sessions, the LBB or the governor may recommend prohibiting a state agency from spending money appropriated to it by the legislature. The LBB or the governor may also transfer money from one state agency to another or change the purpose for which an appropriation was made. Such recommendations by the LBB must be approved by the governor in order to go into effect, while recommendations by the governor require approval by the LBB. This was the process used by state leaders in 2010 when they instructed state agencies to reduce their spending and to "give back" money that had previously been appropriated by the legislature in 2009. They did this so that the budget could remain balanced when tax revenues failed to live up to expectations.

## FISCAL POLICY TOOLS

While the basic issues of taxing and spending occupy the minds of most Texans, there are some fiscal policy tools that require special attention. As we'll see, these are especially important in Texas because although these practices were embraced by Governor Perry, many people in the state want to end them.

### Tax Expenditures

One form of subsidy that is especially difficult to measure is tax expenditures. **Tax expenditures** include any reductions in tax liabilities that result from tax benefits to particular taxpayers rather than taxpayers in general. These kinds of selective incentives can be used to encourage certain types of businesses. For example, the state of Texas grants special tax breaks to certain types of natural gas drilling because of the high costs associated with these techniques. These subsidies are different from other kinds of government support because they do not show up on a budget since they reflect taxes never collected.

The tax-free holiday celebrated annually in Texas since 1999 is a kind of tax expenditure because it exempts certain items from the sales tax each year as Texans are getting ready for the start of school. In 2014, the comptroller estimated that Texans saved about $83 million during the tax holiday weekend.[25] While these millions will never show up as dollars spent by a program, they resulted in lower government revenues and financial advantage for citizens willing to face the crowds that weekend. In 2007, the Texas Legislature added another tax free weekend for the purchase of certain energy efficient items. Research from the Tax Foundation suggests that the holidays only serve to shift shopping from one day to another and that some businesses actually increase their prices during them. The Tax Foundation also argues that the tax holidays generate additional administrative costs for small business and government and that they are supported by a few large businesses that consider them a form of free advertising.[26]

**Tax expenditure**
any reductions in tax liabilities that result from tax benefits to particular taxpayers rather than taxpayers in general.

Tax breaks for certain professions may seem the stuff of modern politics, but they are not new to Texas. In fact, the constitutions of 1845, 1861, 1866, 1869, and 1876 all authorized an income or occupational tax, but with the provision that agricultural or mechanical pursuits were exempt. Thus, we can see a preference for farm income extending back to the origins of the state.

Local governments sometimes provide tax abatements that exempt certain businesses from some of their property taxes. For example, in 2011, Fort Worth put together a package that reportedly included $13.5 million in tax breaks for Bell Helicopter as incentive for the helicopter maker to remain in the area.[27] According to another story, California chain In-N-Out Burger got its own tax break, meaning that Whataburger (a Texas institution) could be paying higher taxes to fund incentives to bring in competition.[28] Many cities offer grants and tax breaks to businesses thinking about relocating. While bringing jobs to an area might seem popular at first glance, these incentives shift the tax burden to existing businesses that may not enjoy paying the tax bill for their new neighbors. In addition, tax dollars might be used to bring in businesses that are controversial (for example, nuclear power plants).

Local governments in Texas have not always found managing growth an easy task. Communities must often scramble to keep up with the growing need for more schools, roads, and water. As Frisco school superintendent Jeremy Lyon noted, "State leaders have done an excellent job creating an environment that interests companies in moving here. What gets lost is that you need a vibrant school system to attract the families that also will move."[29]

## Subsidies

While we often think of the federal government as being much more activist than the Texas state government, the state of Texas and many of its cities are not shy about subsidizing activities they want. For example, Comptroller Susan Combs agreed to have the state pay just over $250 million over ten years to help bring Formula One racing to Texas. In both 2012 and 2013, the state paid out just over $25 million to support the United States Grand Prix, with local governments chipping in another $4 million each per year. The comptroller's office considered these subsidies important to encouraging development of a $242 million racetrack that was estimated to pump $400 million into the Texas economy.[30] The subsidies came from the state's event trust funds, which have paid out amounts ranging from the $26,856,950 provided to support the 2011 Super Bowl to the $2,727 the state paid to help bring the 2011 Little Dribblers' Basketball National Tournament to Texas. Along the way, the state of Texas paid $3,853,401 to bring the International Convention of Alcoholics Anonymous to San Antonio (with another $616,544 provided by the city) and $1,800,595 to host MegaFest 2013 (a two-day, family-oriented fellowship event), with host city Dallas chipping in another $288,096. Generally, contributions from local government must match the state's contribution by providing one dollar of local funds for every $6.25 in state funds. Funds are only available for an event that is competitively bid and involves a community competing with cities outside Texas for the right to host it.

In 2005, the Texas Legislature created the Texas Emerging Technology Fund (TETF) to support start-up companies in cutting-edge fields. Since its creation, the TETF has handed out 190 grants totaling about $425 million that are designed to create jobs and to position Texas as a leader in high-tech firms. According to the governor's office, these funds have created 1,883 jobs for Texans.[31]

It is telling that when the Future Business Leaders of America met in San Antonio in June of 2012 to prepare young people for careers in business, the organization did so with the help of $322,157 in state and local subsidies. While Texas is a conservative state, even a conservative state engages in a variety of partnerships between the public sector (government) and the private sector (businesses). This may not seem consistent with the conservative legends of Texas, but in reality the state has always had a hand in encouraging economic development. For example, after World War II, the state began construction of a farm-to-market road system designed specifically to help Texas farmers and ranchers move their products to market. The state also offers tax breaks for certain types of high-cost natural gas production to help encourage energy production.

Many college students benefit from state programs such as scholarships (awards usually based on grades or special talents) and grants (usually awarded based on financial need). For example, many students attend college in Texas with the support of TEXAS (Towards EXcellence, Access and Success). TEXAS provides grants created by the Texas Legislature to students whose families might have trouble affording college. The state also funds the Top 10 Percent Scholarship for high schools students who finished in the top 10 percent of their graduating class.

## WINNERS AND LOSERS

Texans are generally big fans of the system of free enterprise, and many think that the free market and not the government should be picking economic winners and losers. In June 2007, the Texas Legislature created the Texas Moving Image Industry Incentive Program that provides grants and tax breaks to films, television programs, commercials, and video games produced in the state in the name of creating jobs. In signing the bill, Governor Rick Perry noted neighboring Louisiana's success with a similar program and told Texans that the entertainment industry "creates jobs, builds the economy and serves as an incubator for the development of the creative arts industry."[32] In 2009, when Perry signed a revision of the law, he held the bill-signing ceremony at Robert Rodriguez's Troublemaker Studios and boasted that the law was "strengthening our state's investment in a vital industry."[33] The law, to some degree, has had its desired effect and, according to Robert Rodriguez, brought production of his new movie *Machete* to Texas.

Help for companies extends beyond the entertainment industry. In 2012, the State of Texas finalized a plan to give Apple $21 million over ten years from its Texas Enterprise Fund (TEF), while the city of Austin offered $8.6 million in grants and Travis County promised an additional grant of at least $5.4 million over 15 years.[34] This plan was expected to help bring a $304 million investment from Apple that could create more than 3,600 jobs. Anyone familiar with Apple knows that the company did not need much help in 2012.

While we often think about "winners versus losers" as pitting big companies against consumers or small businesses, there are times when the state makes winners of some companies at the expense of others. The problem is that when state and local governments give grants or tax breaks to bring a company into the area, the company's arrival does not diminish the need for government revenue. In fact, it likely increases the demand for services because the company and its employees will need additional infrastructure, such as roads. This means that existing companies must pay more taxes to make up the difference. Ironically, this can lead to a company seeing its taxes go up in order to support the arrival of competition.

Having the state picking economic winners and losers runs contrary to Texans' support for free enterprise. However, the problem is that other states are providing incentives, and failing to do the same could put Texas at a huge disadvantage in its competition with other states.

Why would a Texas governor get tangled up in the politics of movies and computers? Rick Perry was actually following a tradition of Texas governors going back to John Connally in the 1960s. Connally realized that the future of the state's economy had to be based on more than cowboys and oilmen, and he sought ways to diversify. Likewise, Perry was reaching out to lasso new jobs for Texas, which was part of his strategy of economic development.

While some businesses are greeted with fanfare and gifts, others face a more daunting reception. For example, Tesla Motors does not use traditional car dealerships to sell its cars. Shoppers may visit Tesla showrooms to view sample vehicles, but they must order their own car directly from Tesla Motors and await delivery. Texas franchise law prohibits such direct purchases and requires that consumers buy vehicles through local car dealerships. While the state's car dealers argue that this provides protection to consumers, some state leaders have said that Texas should consider abandoning laws that they describe as "antiquated." This is another example of the conflict between the new and the old in Texas, with the needs of existing dealerships protected by law.

So, in Texas politics, how free your enterprise is depends on your enterprise and how well represented it is in Austin. As we have seen, even a conservative government like Texas's is actively engaged in trying to shape the economy. Inevitably, this will lead to picking winners and losers.

★ Can Texas control spending when citizens are reluctant to see so many services cut?

★ What is an appropriate use for the state's Economic Stabilization Fund?

★ Should the state's tax system or spending be revised? How?

★ Are tax breaks useful in bringing business to Texas, or are the costs of luring business to the state too high?

# CONCLUSION

While Texans generally consider themselves conservative, their support for specific budget cuts can be less than overwhelming. A poll of Texans taken as the Texas Legislature began its work in 2011 showed very few supported cuts to public education (18 percent), pre-kindergarten classes (38 percent), or state grants to college students (27 percent). There was also little support for reducing state contributions to teacher and state employee retirement programs (32 percent); ending the children's health insurance program (13 percent); cutting payments to Medicaid providers, such as doctors and hospitals (14 percent); cutting state funding for nursing home care (10 percent); closing centers for juveniles or adults (33 percent); reducing new highway construction (37 percent); closing community colleges (24 percent); or reducing border security (15 percent).[35] Texans watched their legislature struggle to cut $15.2 billion in spending. This included $4 billion in cuts to what public schools would have received under current law. There were no easy answers, and when the legislature met again in 2013, 62 percent of Texans thought restoring cuts to public education should be the legislature's top priority.[36]

Texans will continue to face tough budget choices. As with other states, Texas expects its revenue to increase as the economy continues to recover from the recession. However, that growth may be slow, and states remain worried that growing populations and demands for services will outpace it.

While the state's leaders enjoy bragging about how many people and businesses come to Texas, they know that these newcomers will create the demand for more water, new roads, more schools, and other government services. As we saw at the beginning of the chapter, attracting new businesses sometimes involves tax breaks or other incentives, the costs of which fall on existing taxpayers. Thus, the tension between old and new Texans finds its place in the state's tax code and budget.

**for CQ Press**

Sharpen your skills with **SAGE edge** at **edge.sagepub.com/collier4e**. **SAGE edge for students** provides a personalized approach to help you accomplish your coursework goals in an easy-to-use learning environment.

## KEY TERMS

ad valorem tax (p. 421)

agenda setting (p. 412)

appraisal (p. 421)

distributive policy (p. 413)

excise tax (p. 419)

fiscal policy (p. 413)

franchise tax (p. 418)

general sales tax (p. 415)

income tax (p. 415)

"pay-as-you-go" system (p. 427)

Permanent School Fund (p. 426)

policy (p. 412)

policy adoption (p. 412)

policy evaluation (p. 412)

policy formation (p. 412)

policy implementation (p. 412)

progressive tax (p. 423)

property tax (p. 419)

redistributive policy (p. 412)

regressive tax (p. 423)

regulatory policy (p. 413)

severance tax (p. 418)

sin tax (p. 418)

subsidy (p. 413)

tax expenditure (p. 434)

## CORE ASSESSMENT

1. To what degree should individual citizens advocate taxes that promote their personal wealth and to what degree should they advocate tax policies that are the most equitable?

2. Should society use tax policy to support or punish private behavior that society considers sinful or inappropriate? Should tax policy be used to advance moral issues or should it be limited to simply generating revenue?

3. What type of tax is most effective and most fair?

# 14 EDUCATION AND SOCIAL POLICY

I f you're a student reading this textbook for a required course, your day has already been impacted by Texas education policy in a couple of ways. First, the Texas Legislature has required that you take the class by writing Section 51:301 of the Texas Education Code, which mandates the broad outline of the requirement:

> Every college and university receiving state support or state aid from public funds shall give a course of instruction in government or political science which includes consideration of the Constitution of the United States and the constitutions of the states, with special emphasis on that of Texas. This course shall have a credit value of not less than six semester hours or its equivalent.

In implementing Section 51:301, the Texas Higher Education Coordinating Board (THECB) is left to map out exactly what its content means. Over the last few years, the coordinating board has decided that a more precise set of standards is needed to make these course offerings as consistent as possible across the state's schools. Originally, schools had been free to meet the requirement however they saw fit. Some addressed it with separate U.S. and Texas politics courses. Some taught the two political systems side by side and divided the six semester hours based on concepts such as institutions or behavior. However, that created problems for students who transferred between schools and had only completed part of the requirement. Mixing and matching the widely differing approaches to teaching U.S. and Texas politics was considered to be the largest issue in college transfers in the state, and the THECB decided it was time to try to simplify things.

Of course, simplifying things in a state a big as Texas is not easy, and coming up with a plan that pleased faculty at all of the state's schools was impossible. The board formed committees, drew up a plan, and solicited feedback. While the THECB wanted to mandate separate U.S. and Texas politics courses, many of the state's schools, including some of its largest, disagreed. A coordinating board decision determined that all two-year schools would have to accept the mandate from the state, but the state's four-year schools could do as they pleased.

The wrangling over how Texas politics is taught in the state's schools reflects the kind of balancing act we see in public education and other policy issues. The state

Students await their diplomas during the graduation ceremony at Mission Community College in El Paso, Texas. Texas has about 1.3 million students in its colleges and universities.

wants to create a system of accountability because citizens want to see an educational system that is both efficient and effective. However, as we will see with the issue of standardized tests in our public schools, even if you are comfortable with the government becoming so heavily involved in something such as education, creating, measuring, and enforcing standards brings additional costs and unintended consequences. The push toward standardization also undermines the diversity of choices students face when they choose a college. After all, if all of the schools are alike, what's the point in having a choice? Oddly, a state that often advocated giving students and parents choices found it had to limit those choices in the name of efficiency.

The lack of educational diversity Texas offers is especially problematic in a state with a diverse economy that is seeking to prepare its youth to become the next generation of farmers, ranchers, software engineers, etc. Thus, the drive for control by the state can create costs and inefficiencies of its own, and citizens have to decide how much control elected officials and bureaucracy can or should have.

This chapter will assess the impact of a growing and changing population on state education policy and social policies such as welfare and health care. We first look at how the state attempts to get millions of young Texans from kindergarten to high school graduation. We then turn to a system of higher education designed to take Texans beyond a high school diploma to college degrees. Finally, we will look at how the state tries to meet the basic needs of Texans in the areas of food, shelter, and health care.

## EDURCATION POLICY

During the 2012–2013 school year, over 6.5 million Texans were in the state's educational system at some level. About 641,000 were in nursery school, preschool, or kindergarten; 1.9 million were in elementary school (grades 1–5); just over 1.1 million were in middle school (grades 6–8); and almost 1.4 million were in high school (grades 9–12) (See Table 14.1).[1] In addition, 1.4 million people were enrolled in institutions of higher education (see Figure 14.1).[2]

Education is important even to those Texans not in school because the state's educational system energizes the economy of the state by providing its businesses with the qualified workforce needed to be competitive. Also, the research conducted at the state's universities leads to innovations needed for the future. Further, the state's schools help create a society with citizens ready to engage in civic life and prepared to indulge in the rich cultural pursuits of arts, music, and literature. With education's influences being so wide, it's no surprise then that the importance of schools to the state's businesses has increased through the years. This fact was highlighted in 2007 when a new group calling itself Raise Your Hand, Texas formed with the purpose of seeking educational reforms, which it felt were needed to keep Texas economically competitive. Although the organization is chaired by a former lieutenant governor Bill Ratliff, most of the board members are current or former heads of major corporations, such as Texas Instruments, Continental Airlines, and AT&T, reflecting the ongoing interest of business in public education.

Texas's schools have become a major battleground in Texas politics because they represent an essential investment in the state's future, and citizens' desire to see such a large investment handled wisely has subjected our schools to scrutiny. Some groups, such as Raise Your Hand, Texas, worry that the standardized tests used to hold public schools accountable have discouraged students who face too many tests and teachers who feel that innovative teaching will not be rewarded. At the same time, reformers look at the rising price of education and insist that the state try to ensure that money be spent wisely.

## Public Education in Grades K–12

Political battles over public education are nothing new, predating the state and even the Republic of Texas. In fact, the authors of the Texas Declaration of Independence included in their list of grievances that Mexico had "failed to establish any public system of education, although possessed of almost boundless resources (the public domain) and, although, it is an axiom, in political science, that unless a people are educated and enlightened it is idle to expect the continuance of civil liberty, or the capacity for self-government." During his presidency, Mirabeau Lamar earned the nickname of "Father of Texas Education"[3] by championing education in the new republic and setting aside three leagues of land for each county to support elementary schools. Despite Lamar's vision, the limited value of this land, combined with Texans' reluctance to finance schools with tax dollars and the preference of many for private schools, delayed realization of a public school system until the Constitution of 1868 centralized the public schools.

The foundation of the modern public school system in Texas was laid in 1949 when the legislature passed the Gilmer-Aikin Act, named for Rep. Claud Gilmer and Sen. A. M. Aikin. This act guaranteed Texas children twelve years of school with a minimum of 175 days of instruction per year. The legislation also redesigned the state's governance of public education by replacing the nine-person appointed State Board of Education (SBOE) with commissioners elected by voters in districts. While we take this structure for granted today, it was regarded as revolutionary at the time, and Dolph Briscoe, a member of the Texas House who worked on the legislation and went on to serve as governor, recounted how the bill was attacked as "communistic."[4]

By 2013, Texas had 8,555 public schools in 1,228 school districts. These schools educated about 5 million students and employed about 327,419 teachers and another 314,765 administrators and support staff.[5] The state's school system is overseen by the Texas Education Agency (TEA), which is run by a commissioner of education appointed by the governor and the SBOE. The SBOE has grown to fifteen members elected from districts and has a chair appointed by the governor. Members of the SBOE are unpaid but reimbursed for travel and other work-related expenses. The board meets every few months and decides broad education issues, such as curriculum and standards for passing state-mandated exams.

While the idea of having an elected board of education suits Texans' desire to have control over their government, recent battles in the board have led some to question whether or not the process has become too politicized. The most visible battle involved the creation of curriculum guidelines for teachers in areas such as science and history. In 2009, the SBOE found itself embroiled in intense debate over the teaching of evolution. The next year, the board was battling over changes to the history curriculum guidelines, which, according to comedian Stephen Colbert, "decides which historical

## TABLE 14.1 Texas School Enrollment

| K–12 (2012–2013 School Year) | Enrollment |
| --- | --- |
| Early education and kindergarten | 641,480 |
| Elementary (1–5) | 1,924,168 |
| Middle (6–8) | 1,124,128 |
| High (9–12) | 1,386,064 |
| **Total K–12** | **5,075,840** |

*Source:* Texas Education Agency, "Enrollment in Texas Public Schools, 2012–13," March 2014, www.tea.state.tx.us/acctres/Enroll_2012-13.pdf (accessed June 2, 2014).

figures all of our children will be drawing mustaches and eye-patches on."[6] This debate brought Texas into the national spotlight when the SBOE voted to remove founding father Thomas Jefferson from draft guidelines of the list of political philosophies to be discussed. Eventually, Jefferson was voted back into that section, but the debate over guidelines went beyond historical figures as the board voted to remove hip-hop from the list of cultural movements. The ardency of the debate makes clear that the SBOE has become intensely involved in partisan politics and the so-called culture war. Unfortunately, this means that a few narrow issues, such as evolution, will dominate campaigns for the SBOE, while broader issues, such as the value of highly detailed guidelines, are forgotten as candidates try to score partisan points. The disdain and ridicule generated by the debate over curriculum guidelines is compounded by the fact that this debate results in dictating from Washington or Austin what teachers do in the classroom. In the end, both students and teachers may see their efforts devalued as politicians wrangle over which political philosophy gains control over the curriculum.

One of the overlooked issues involving the SBOE is its management of the Permanent School Fund (PSF). The PSF's origins go back to 1854, at which time the new state of Texas set aside $2 million from the $10 million payment it received from the United States for giving up claims to some of the land it had claimed as the Republic of Texas. The Constitution of 1876 revived the fund and granted the proceeds of the sale of certain public lands to the PSF. Since that time, money from the sales and leasing of these public lands has gone into the PSF, with the returns on the investment of the funds being made available for use in Texas public schools. In 1960, the U.S. Supreme Court recognized Texas's claim to a 10.35-mile seaward boundary of lands off its coast, and proceeds from the sale and the mineral lease rights to these lands have also helped fill the fund. The PSF was valued at about $29 billion at the end of 2013 and is the second-largest educational endowment in the country. Only interest from this fund can be spent, and the PSF has distributed over $23 billion to Texas public schools since 1960.

The SBOE's work with consultants and the staff of the Texas Education Agency that oversee the management of these funds led to ethics charges after board members were accused of receiving gifts from firms involved in the fund. Even putting aside ethics rules, the challenges the part-time SBOE faces in effectively handling the very different tasks of setting statewide education policy, constructing a curriculum for public school students, and managing billions of dollars make it unlikely that board members will be expert in everything they must do. With a wide range of tasks before them, the SBOE members must master the world of education and high finance to make sure the state gets the most out of its schools and its investments.

### Equality in Education

Texas education was further transformed by the civil rights era (which was also attacked as "communistic" by opponents), although change proved slow. Texas schools had embraced the idea of separate-but-equal schools since the Constitution of 1876, which specified that "separate schools shall be provided for the white and colored children, and impartial provision shall be made for both." This reflected the principle of "separate but equal" upheld by the U.S. Supreme Court in the 1896 decision of *Plessy v. Ferguson*.[7] While

## Neither Separate Nor Equal: Hispanics in the Education System

While the battle for equal rights has often been played out before the U.S. Supreme Court, the nature of discrimination and the ambiguous legal status of Hispanics in Texas has posed a unique set of challenges for Tejanos.

For decades, the official position of the state of Texas was that Hispanics were not a distinct race from whites and therefore did not need the equal protection for races promised in the Fourteenth Amendment. In the 1930s, about 90 percent of South Texas school districts maintained separate schools for Hispanic students and made no attempt to disguise this segregation. Many of these schools carried the official designation of "Mexican School." Although schools for African American children had some obligation to be separate but equal after the

1896 decision in *Plessy v. Ferguson*,[i] Mexican schools were generally neglected.

In *Delgado v. Bastrop Independent School District* (1948), federal district judge Ben C. Rice declared that it was unlawful and unconstitutional to segregate Hispanic American children in Texas public schools. The decision did, however, permit the segregation of students based on English proficiency. Thus, because they were judged not fluent in English, Hispanic students could still be placed in inferior schools. Of course, putting these students into crowded, inferior schools helped ensure that they did not improve their English and therefore never moved into the mainstream Anglo schools. Some Hispanic students received bad grades regardless of their actual language skills. And in some cases, students with Hispanic

surnames were placed in Mexican schools even though they spoke only English.

Eventually, in *Herminca Hernandez et al. v. Driscoll Consolidated ISD* (1957), a federal court declared the segregation of Mexican American students unconstitutional. As the case had been with racial segregation following the *Brown v. Board of Education*[ii] decisions, however, local school districts resisted change and equality has remained elusive. Supported by the League of United Latin American Citizens and other groups, parents continue to battle local school districts to guarantee a quality education for Hispanic students.

---

i.  163 U.S. 537.

ii.  347 U.S. 483 (1954); 349 U.S. 294 (1955).

---

the races remained separated, the provisions for their schools remained far from "impartial" in Texas, with many schools for nonwhite students underfunded.

The reality of equal schools remained elusive even after 1954 when the U.S. Supreme Court issued the landmark *Brown v. Board of Education*[8] decision that declared segregated public schools to be a violation of the equal protection clause of the U.S. Constitution. The Court put aside the possibility of separate facilities being equal and declared that laws separating the races were interpreted as denoting an inferiority of black children that would undermine their motivation to learn. Despite the Court's unanimous agreement in the original decision and in a follow-up decision known as *Brown II*,[9] which was handed down in 1955 and called for desegregation "with all deliberate speed," little progress was seen in Texas in the decade after the *Brown* decisions. Texas governor Allen Shivers told local school districts that he saw no need for them to change, and students in many areas remained separated by race.

More pressure came through the federal government via the Civil Rights Act of 1964 and the Elementary and Secondary Education Act of 1965. Eventually, the U.S. Department of Justice filed a lawsuit against the state of Texas that resulted in a 1970 decision by Judge William Wayne Justice, the chief judge of the U.S. District Court for the Eastern District in Tyler, to desegregate the state's public schools. The decision also gave the court authority to oversee the state's implementation of the desegregation.[10]

One of the challenges of education in a changing state is addressing the needs of students who primarily speak other languages. In 2014, the League of United Latin American Citizens (LULAC) filed a lawsuit renewing its claim that the state has failed to support programs that help students learn English. About 17 percent of the state's public school students qualify as English language learners (ELL). According to the LULAC brief, the problem goes beyond recent immigrants: "Contrary to popular belief, a majority of ELL students in secondary schools are not classified as recent immigrants and have been in U.S. schools for at least three years."[11] LULAC's court case alleges that the state has failed to maintain high enough standards for certification to teach languages and that, as a result, a majority of ELL students are not making adequate progress in English and that this is also inhibiting their success in other classes.[12]

## Funding for K–12

The state's struggles with equality have extended beyond race to include differences created by funding. Education policy in the state's public schools is especially complicated because it brings together the efforts, money, and rules of federal, state, and local governments. In the 2010–2011 school year (the last year complete financial data was available before this book went to press), Texas public schools received 43.4 percent of their budgets from the state, 11.9 percent from the federal government, and 44.7 percent from local sources. As this indicates, while federal laws such as No Child Left Behind have continued to increase federal involvement in Texas public schools, the financial responsibility for schools remains mostly with state and local officials.

Combined, federal, state, and local governments spent over $54.7 billion on Texas public schools in 2010–2011, averaging $ 11,146 per pupil.[13] Given the large investment of tax dollars, and with the future of the state's children at stake, the education issue is primed for conflict. At the same time, various political groups seeking to bring their concerns into the schools up the ante, triggering debates about emotional issues such as prayer and contraceptives, as well as other societal concerns.

The financial inequality between school districts remains one of the most vexing problems in Texas politics. While the Texas Legislature mandated a statewide curriculum in 1981 and continues to dictate most of what local schools must teach, much of the financial responsibility for these mandates remains with the local school district. In 1949, the state of Texas provided about 80 percent of funding for public schools. However, today that figure has been cut in half. This shift to local funding has left the public schools largely dependent on local property taxes, meaning that school districts located in areas with high property values have been able to provide more resources for their students, while school districts with low property values have had to get by with much less.

In 1989, the Supreme Court of Texas's unanimous decision in *Edgewood Independent School District v. Kirby*[14] forced the funding issue into the legislature when the court ruled that Texas's system violated the Texas Constitution's requirement of free and efficient schools. The court noted that two schools in Bexar County illustrated the inequity, as the Edgewood Independent School District had $38,854 in

## Mansfield High

© Bettmann/Corbis

Before the desegregation of Little Rock High School became the turning point in the desegregation of public schools in America, a similar battle was fought in Texas. Mansfield, a small town southeast of Fort. Worth, had 1,450 residents in the 1950s, about 350 of them African American. Like most southern communities, Mansfield's restaurants, churches, schools, and social functions were segregated. And, as in many southern communities, African Americans realized that the path to full citizenship and equality lead through quality schools.

The struggle for integration in Mansfield is chronicled in Robyn Duff Ladino's *Desegregating Texas Schools: Eisenhower, Shivers, and the Crisis at Mansfield High*. In an effort spawned by the Bethlehem Baptist Church and organized by the National Association for the Advancement of Colored People (NAACP), black residents began to look for ways to get the *Brown v. Board of Education* decision declaring segregated schools unconstitutional applied in Mansfield. Black parents were not interested in seeing their children receive the kind of second-rate education that would virtually assure a life as a second-class citizen. While some advocates of continuing segregation asked that the state be able to set its own timeline for ending segregation, many hardliners saw the separation of the races as a traditional value that should not be tinkered with. Governor Shivers demonstrated the uncompromising view of many segregationists when he proclaimed, "We are going to keep the system that we know is best. No law, no court, can wreck what God has made."[i]

As was often the case in Texas, opposition to desegregation was passionate and carried implied or explicit threats to students crossing the separation between the races. Some people advocated a gradual implementation of desegregation. While Mansfield High was technically open to black students, they knew attending put their lives at risk. Large crowds gathered in front of the school when it opened for registration in the fall of 1956. For several days, an effigy of a black figure hung from the flag pole in front of Mansfield High School instead of the American flag, and black students who were thinking about enrolling likely understood that the local law enforcement officers who would not remove the black figure would also not protect black students attempting to enroll at the campus beneath it. State and local officials refused to ensure the safety of black students, and those students decided that making the long bus ride into schools in Fort. Worth was safer than risking their lives at Mansfield High School.

---

i.  Robyn Duff Ladino, *Desegregating Texas Schools: Eisenhower, Shivers, and the Crisis at Mansfield High* (Austin: University of Texas Press, 1996), 38.

property taxes per student, and Alamo Heights had $570,109 in property taxes per student. After three failed special sessions of the legislature, the fourth session produced a bill to raise sales taxes one-quarter of a cent and increase taxes on cigarettes to bolster education funding. While this financing scheme did not fully satisfy the court, it did hold off further reform (thanks to court appeals by the state) until the early 1990s. In 1993, the Texas Legislature again addressed the issue by passing a law that established an equalized wealth level for schools and created a process for redistributing money between districts. This law became known as the "Robin Hood" plan because it took money from "rich" school districts and gave it to "poor" districts. For example, the Comanche Peak Nuclear Power Plant in Glen Rose provides the foundation of

Judge John Dietz, after refusing to recuse himself from the case, ruled the Texas school finance system unconstitutional in 2013. Here he questions a witness during a school finance trial.

a strong property tax base and has a relatively well-funded school district with reasonably few children. In contrast, the Edgewood school district has a large number of students coming from the kind of modestly priced starter homes often owned by young couples starting families.[15] Under the current "Robin Hood" system, districts like Glen Rose share their revenue with districts like Edgewood. Unfortunately, this has failed to fully equalize funding and has left many school districts frustrated by seeing their tax dollars go elsewhere.

During a 2006 special session of the Texas Legislature called to try to resolve the inequality, the legislature expanded the business tax in an effort to provide sufficient funding for the state's schools. However, this did not offset the accompanying cut in property taxes mandated by the legislature, and thus schools continue to have trouble making ends meet.[16]

In 2012, the state faced lawsuits representing about 600 school districts that include about three-fourths of the state's students. These lawsuits continue the argument that the state has failed to provide an adequate education and that the lack of funding from the state has forced local school boards to raise their property tax rate to the maximum allowed by the legislature, thus creating the kind of statewide property tax the Texas Constitution forbids. In February 2013, Texas district court judge John Dietz ruled, holding that the state does not adequately or efficiently fund public schools and that it has created an unconstitutional de facto property tax in shifting the burden of paying for schools to the local level. However, the judge reopened the case in response to changes to financing and standardized testing passed by the legislature in 2013. Lawyers spent much of 2014 debating who should decide the case. In the summer of 2014, Greg Abbott, then the attorney general, filed a motion that Dietz should recuse (disqualify) himself from presiding over the case. Dietz had taken the case in 2011, and, by the summer of 2014, he had heard fifteen weeks of testimony and reviewed thousands of exhibits. Dietz had compared the case to a long running soap opera in 2013 when he said, "There were 13,858 episodes of *As the World Turns*, and we are getting pretty close."[17] A whole new season began in August of 2014 when Dietz ruled the system unconstitutional.

The state's unending lawsuits associated with unequal funding are rooted in the local property taxes that schools rely on for much of their funding. Given the wide disparity in the value of property, inequity has proven hard to remove, and the state is certain to grapple with this issue well into the future.

One consequence of rising education costs is that citizens want more information about how well their tax dollars are being spent. Parents worried about their children's futures, employers concerned about quality in the workforce, and taxpayers worried about cost have all contributed to a demand for constant reevaluation of public education, and a call for reform was inevitable.

## Accountability and Reform in K–12

Texas has labored to improve the quality of its public schools through various reform movements while still addressing the need for equality. In the 1980s, a committee led by wealthy businessman H. Ross Perot pushed for reforms and saw the Texas Legislature adopt many of its recommendations in a special session in the summer of 1984. The **Education Reform Act** required that teachers and administrators take the Texas Examination of Current Administrators and Teachers (TECAT) to ensure basic competency before being recertified. Students were also tested periodically, beginning Texas's long experimentation with standardized testing, which ultimately spread across the nation during the presidency of George W. Bush. The act also included the controversial "no-pass, no-play" rule that kept students with an average below 70 in any subject from taking part in extracurricular activities. The new law also called for more funding for poor school districts that lacked resources because of the reliance on local property taxes to fund schools. Some of these reforms proved unpopular, as "no pass" sometimes meant "no play" for high school football players.

While these reforms eventually helped cost Mark White, the governor at the time, his reelection bid, some of the reforms White signed into law endured and became part of a movement toward accountability that has now become nationwide. Part of the Education Reform Act required students in odd-numbered grades to take tests in language arts and math. It also required students to pass an exam before they could receive their diploma. While these tests have occasionally changed names and subject matter, they have become a central part of the state's education policy.

Ironically, while the reform bill he signed helped end the political career of Governor White, George W. Bush continued to press for more standardized testing, and his rise to the presidency was based partly on his promise to do for the nation's schools what he had done for schools in Texas.

States, and increasingly the national government, have been demanding more accountability from local school districts, making Texas a focal point in this debate because of the state's early embrace of standardized testing. In 1990, the Texas Assessment of Academic Skills (TAAS) was implemented and used to create higher standards for state assessment before being replaced in 2003 by the Texas Assessment of Knowledge and Skills (TAKS). In spring of 2012, the State of Texas Assessments of Academic Readiness (STAAR) replaced the TAKS, and Texas high school students are now required to take separate end-of-course exams at the end of each school year in the four core subject areas: English, math, science, and social studies. Students have to score an average of 70 on the tests in each subject in order to graduate; the tests must count for 15 percent of a student's final grade in the class. For grades 3–8, the STAAR program assesses the same subjects as the TAKS did. Texas has created (and re-created) these

**Education Reform Act**
a 1984 statute that requires teachers and school administrators to take a test to assure basic competency before being recertified; students are also tested periodically to monitor progress and are required to pass an exam before being allowed to graduate.

tests to create a standard by which student progress can be tracked and schools evaluated based on that progress. The idea is that these standards create guides that citizens can use to evaluate their schools and hold them responsible.

In 2013, the legislature responded to the concerns of parents and many educators and reduced the number of state-mandated tests required to graduate from high school from fifteen to five in the core areas of biology, U.S. history, algebra I, and English I and II. Many parents felt that the number of high-stakes exams required to graduate was placing too much pressure on students. And for many critics of testing, the reforms passed in 2013 did little to deal with the heavy emphasis on test preparation over instruction. A February 2014 University of Texas/*Texas Tribune* poll found that 64 percent of respondents thought that reducing the number of standardized tests students take would be either extremely effective or somewhat effective in improving the quality of education.[18]

### Unintended Consequences

These high-stakes exams may have spawned some unintended consequences. For example, in 2012, Texans discovered that state law mandated that students who had failed one of the STAAR tests could not be admitted to the state's four-year universities. The only way students who had failed these exams could enter a four-university as a freshman was to get a high score on the ACT or the SAT (1500 out of 2400 on the SAT). While this appears not to have been the intention of any of the legislators who pushed the bill, it found its way into law and impacted thousands of students.[19] Another unintended consequence of this high-stakes testing is that it may be bringing out the worst in our teachers and administrators. Studies funded by the *Dallas Morning News* found evidence of massive amounts of cheating on the 2005 and 2006 exams. According to the newspaper's analysis, more than 50,000 students' exams showed evidence of cheating. Because schools see their ratings tied to test scores, and teachers' raises are also dependent on the scores, concerns go beyond student cheating and extend to "educator-led" cheating, in which teachers or school administrators aid students or change answers after the exam to produce higher passing rates. Evidence of cheating was three times as frequent in schools that had been underperforming—those schools where the pressure to cheat would have been greatest. For example, in one previously underperforming school district, science scores went from 23 percent below the state average to 14 percent above; evidence of cheating was found in half of the district's eleventh-grade science exams.[20] Such results were eight times more common in the eleventh-grade exams, which determine graduation, than at other grade levels. Confronted with these figures, Texas officials generally were content to call these results "anomalies" rather than proof of cheating.[21]

While the state's system of testing was intended to help citizens evaluate local schools, credibility concerns leave Texans doubting the validity and value of high-stakes tests in public schools and worrying that these tests seriously undermine the entire educational process. State officials have little incentive to follow up on the evidence of cheating, since it would undermine the validity of their measures and their claims to progress. With their federal funds and the state's reputation on the line, local and state officials have incentive to ignore evidence of cheating.

### Texas's Performance

Overall, Texas's record on public schools has been mixed. Texas has made progress on high school graduation rates. One recent report from the U.S. Department of Education found Texas tied for fourth in high school graduation rates for the 2011–2012 school year with 88 percent, compared to a national average of 80 percent.[22] Another analysis put Texas much closer to the average with an averaged freshman graduation rate of 78.9 percent, just ahead of the national average of 78.2 percent.[23] The differences between the two measures reflects the challenges both of educating Texans and of measuring our success since each tracks different sets of students and deals with transfers and other issues differently. The state's performance on other scores lags farther behind. The average SAT score for Texas students ranked forty-sixth, although some of this may have resulted from a relatively high percentage of Texas students taking the SAT (59 percent).[24] Texas students scored exactly at the national average (20.9) on the ACT exam.[25]

Protestors oppose Texas's standardized testing. Texas's tough curriculum standards in part helped fuel those of the No Child Left Behind Act, which was passed under the presidential administration of George W. Bush. While some students excel, others struggle to keep up, and the standards and accountability measures remain controversial, prompting the state to reconsider some of its policies.

John Anderson/Austin Chronicle

In some ways, it should not be surprising that Texas has struggled in educational attainment. For generations, the state's economy was largely agricultural in an era when farming and ranching usually involved little formal education. For many Texas families, the time young people spent in the classroom was a luxury they could not afford, as they needed their children to help in the fields or pastures. Further, these professions required less formal education in early Texas. Today, fewer Texans live on the farm, and the new economy demands more education than ever. Government is under greater pressure to provide graduates who are ready to tackle college or technical fields that are increasingly demanding. However, the fact that there is a need for a change does not ensure that change will occur rapidly.

### The Goals of a Public School Education

The educational reforms passed in 2013 went beyond reducing the number of standardized tests and altered the basic curriculum required of students beginning in the 2014–2015 school year. This law, frequently referred to simply as House Bill (HB) 5, addressed the fundamental issue of the goals of a public school education. Previously, all Texas high school students had to complete four years each of science, English, social studies, and math. Beginning in fall 2014, high school students began to take a foundation curriculum that includes four English credits; three credits each in science, social studies, and math; two foreign language credits; one fine arts credit; and one P.E. credit. Students add a fourth science and math credit when they select one of five diploma "endorsements" in areas including STEM (science, technology, engineering, and math); business and industry; public services; arts and the humanities; and multidisciplinary studies. For example, the public services endorsement includes courses directly related to health occupations, law enforcement, culinary arts, and hospitality. The business and industry endorsement includes courses that support construction, welding, automotive technology, and information technology. Advocates of the change say it will keep more students interested and in school and ready to enter the workforce with useful skills. Critics worry that students who fail to pursue endorsements that do not prepare them for college will find themselves locked out of a college education.

The debate over HB 5 often turned on what Texans wanted for their children. While some wanted to ensure that every student was encouraged to prepare for college, others wanted to facilitate moves into careers that might not require a college degree.

In many ways, the struggles of Texas public schools dramatically reflect the basic dilemmas of public policy. Citizens want as much efficiency as possible, and in response legislators create systems of accountability. However, accountability testing is costly and generates unintended consequences, such as cheating, which then leads to more oversight, more bureaucracy, and more expense. Despite the challenges of public education, the demands for a better-educated workforce keep the state focused on continued improvement of public schools.

## WINNERS AND LOSERS

Every Texan has a stake in the state's public school system. Parents, teachers, students, employers, and the rest of the community count on the public schools to produce quality graduates ready for the workforce and for civic life. However, Texans bring a wide range of expectations to the system, and the state has struggled to meet the demands of its growing and diverse society. Texas has been committed to attracting high-tech firms. However, these firms require the kind of highly trained workforce that can only be produced by a first-rate educational system. Texas schools struggle to meet those expectations as well as the demands that come with receiving federal and state funds. An important question is how effectively the learning encouraged by the state's standardized testing system meets up with the needs of students preparing to enter the workplace or higher education. While Texas created standardized testing to provide the impetus for improvement in public schools, some parents, students, and employers are questioning the validity of the state's testing regime and the federal government's reliance on it for funding decisions.

Some of the state's leaders have promoted the idea of school vouchers. While voucher programs can take a wide variety of forms, they center on allowing families to receive a payment, or voucher, from the state that could be used to pay for an education at whatever school they chose. Advocates of vouchers believe that allowing families to choose schools will create healthy competition that will encourage schools to improve their education in order to attract students. Opponents of vouchers worry that such a program would harm public schools by destabilizing their funding and leaving them

Education policy has traditionally been left to state and local governments. That all changed when President George W. Bush signed the **No Child Left Behind Act (NCLB)**. Under NCLB, states must develop and administer tests to all students at select grade levels in order to receive federal funding. While NCLB does not create a single national test or set of standards, it does mandate that each state test its students and demonstrate steady improvement in test scores from year to year. The essential argument behind NCLB is that schools should be held accountable for meeting basic education standards. However, critics of the law argue that NCLB has resulted in education that is geared toward teaching to the test. Frustrations with the law led most states, including Texas, to apply for waivers from the federal program.

As NCLB became increasingly unpopular, President Obama advocated the Common Core State Standards (championed by Bill Gates). Common Core is an attempt to establish consistent education standards across the country. States do not have to participate in Common Core, and so far Texas has opted out. The state legislature passed legislation in 2013 that prohibits Texas from adopting Common Core or using Common Core standards in its classrooms.

Proponents of federal education policy point to uneven education levels across states and argue that states should be held accountable for how they spend federal education dollars. Opponents argue that education and curriculum decisions should be made at a local level. From their perspective, federal management of local education results in an overly complicated policy that rarely fits the needs of the local community. When it comes to education Americans have their doubts about both the federal and their state governments. An August 2014 poll of Americans found that 56 percent thought local school boards should have the most influence over what is taught in the public schools, with 28 percent favoring state government and 15 percent preferring the federal government.[i]

While we most often hear about the struggle between the federal and state governments, tensions also exist between Texas government and local school districts beyond the high-stakes battles over school finance and standardized tests discussed elsewhere in this chapter. Many teachers and school district officials resist the large number of mandates from the state about what is taught and how it is taught. Greg Abbott campaigned for governor partly on a plan that offered "genuine local control by giving school districts operational flexibility over their schools and by empowering families to make meaningful educational choices."[ii]

★ Does the state have a responsibility to ensure access to an equal quality of education across Texas? If so, what does it mean if Texas allows its local governments greater control over schools?

★ To what extent should local governments be in control of education policy?

★ If national standards like those of No Child Left Behind and Common Core can be sidestepped by states through waivers and other exemptions, how much influence does the federal government really have over the implementation of policy at the state level?

i. Valerie J. Calderon, "Americans Wary of Federal Influence on Public Schools: Prefer Local School Boards over Federal Government, 56% to 15%," Gallup, August 20, 2014, www.gallup.com/poll/175181/americans-wary-federal-influence-public-schools.aspx (accessed August 21, 2014).

ii. "Greg Abbott's Educating Texans Plan: Governance," Texans for Greg Abbott, www.gregabbott.com/wp-content/uploads/2014/04/Greg-Abbotts-Educating-Texans-Plan-Governance.pdf (accessed June 20, 2014).

with only the neediest students. Overall, vouchers are popular among Texans, with 51 percent saying in a 2014 poll that creating a voucher program would be an effective way of improving schools.[26]

Some school choice already exists in Texas. A 1995 revision of the Texas Education Code authorized the creation of charter schools. These schools receive public funds but are set up independently of traditional public schools and have been established by entities ranging from private firms to state universities. While charter schools are subject to fewer state rules than traditional public schools, they are subject to the same

> **No Child Left Behind Act (NCLB)**
> the federal education act based on the Texas standardized testing statutes that requires schools to institute mandatory testing to track student progress and evaluates schools based on that progress.

testing and accountability standards. The idea behind providing flexibility to charter schools is to encourage innovation and efficiencies in teaching that might not emerge through the existing school structure. Currently, about forty-two states allow charter schools as an alternative to traditional public schools. In 2014, New Orleans created the nation's first all-charter system.[27]

The most popular reform among Texans is rewarding teachers. Seventy-six percent of Texans said that increasing pay of public school teachers would be extremely effective or somewhat effective at improving education. The same percentage supported providing more incentives for individuals to pick teaching as a profession.[28]

Even if Texans agree on the structure of the state's schools, finding the money for better teacher pay is and will continue to be a struggle. Texas currently ranks thirty-second in teacher pay with an average salary of $48,819, compared to a national average of $56,103.[29] Bill Hobby once wrote that "school finance reform in Texas is like a Russian novel. The story line runs across generations, the plot is complex, the prose is tedious, and everybody dies in the end."[30] While the Texas Declaration of Independence called for improved schools, how to make that a reality has puzzled Texas politicians since.

★ Are the Texas Legislature's means of funding K–12 schools adequate and equitable?

★ How much should local school districts be directed by the state and federal government?

★ How do the state's accountability measures affect the success of its schools and their students?

★ What changes do you think should be made to the state's education policy and why?

★ Should the state's public school curriculum attempt to prepare every student for college?

## Higher Education

The challenges facing higher education are as daunting as those facing the state's public schools. Not only is the state seeing its population increase, it is expected that a growing share of that population will seek to attain some kind of education beyond a high school diploma. Today, higher education in Texas brings together a wide variety of institutions seeking to serve students beyond K–12. As Figure 14.1 shows, in the fall of 2013, the state of Texas enrolled 1.33 million students in its thirty-eight public universities, fifty public community college districts, three state colleges, two independent junior colleges, four state technical colleges, nine public health-related institutions, and one independent health-related institution. In addition, Texas is home to about forty private colleges and universities with another 126,532 students. While large institutions such as the University of Texas and Texas A&M are the most visible parts of higher education in the state, the system includes a variety of other institutions with widely different goals. As the Texas economy continues to diversify, higher education must meet the demands of the global market by providing the state's citizens with the increasingly wide range of skills required to maintain competitiveness.

**FIGURE 14.1** **Higher Education Enrollment in Texas, Fall 2013**

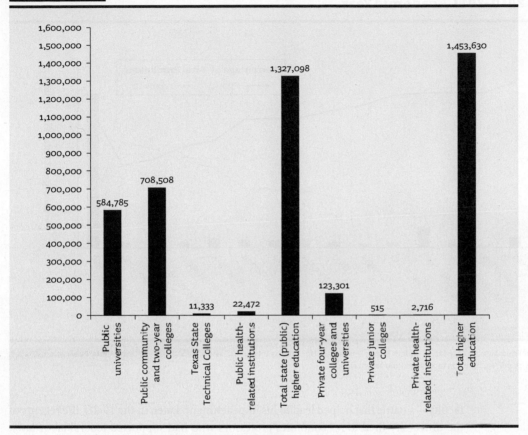

**Source:** Texas Higher Education Coordinating Board, Certified Fall 2013 Texas Higher Ed Enrollment Data, May 22, 2014, www .txhighereddata.org/index.cfm?objectid=787E6F83-DA63-ED42-BBB84792D2E35965 (accessed June 2, 2014).

Texans apparently love their state-supported universities. An analysis of the fifteen most populous states found that Texas has the highest proportion of students enrolled in public universities and the lowest proportion in private universities. As Figure 14.2 shows, in 2010–2011, over 88 percent of Texas's higher education students were in state schools, and about 12 percent attended private schools. This is less than half the national average of students attending private schools and a quarter of the rate of Massachusetts, which sent over half of its students to private schools.

The relationship between the state's politicians and the University of Texas has become a stormy one as the government subjects its universities to more and more scrutiny. Jay Mathews once commented that "K–12 education is watched as carefully as a third grader crossing the street, but higher education's claims go largely unexamined."[31] As we will see, this may have been true at some point, but the state is becoming increasingly engaged in the inner workings of its institutions of higher education. Located in Austin, right under the nose of the Texas government, the University of Texas has proved an appealing target for politicians who have sought to reach across town and squash pesky academics. Governor James Ferguson battled with the University of Texas

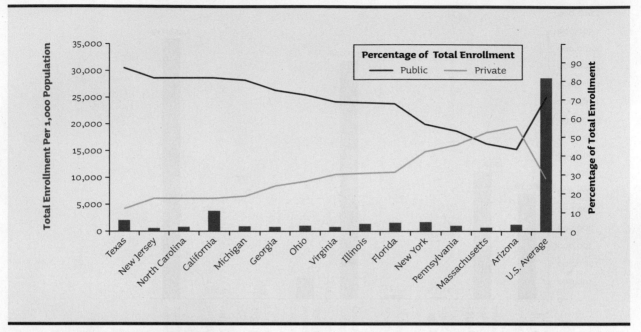

*Source:* U.S. Department of Education, in Legislative Budget Board, "Fiscal Size Up, 2014–15 Biennium," www.lbb.state.tx.us/Documents/Publications/Fiscal _SizeUp/Fiscal_SizeUp_2014-15.pdf, 63, figure 79 (accessed June 22, 2014).

faculty—a battle that helped lead to his impeachment. Later, in the 1940s, the regents of the university fired four economics professors who had supported federal labor laws, eliminated funding for social science research, and banned John Dos Passos's *U.S.A.* trilogy shortly before it won a Pulitzer Prize. The recent effort of some regents to oust UT Austin president Bill Powers and the attempt to impeach UT regent Wallace Hall demonstrate that higher education continues to be a political battleground.

If anything, the state's interest in higher education has become more serious as the state's business and political leaders have seen more need for a highly trained workforce and the cost of a college education has increased.

### Funding

**Permanent University Fund (PUF)**

an endowment funded by mineral rights and other revenue generated by 2.1 million acres of land set aside by the state; investment returns support schools in the University of Texas and Texas A&M systems.

Higher education in Texas has been aided by the **Permanent University Fund (PUF)**. The PUF was created by the Constitution of 1876, which added 1 million acres to the 1 million acres previously granted to the University of Texas. Initially, the land, spread over nineteen counties in West Texas, generated little money. Most of the value of that land was in grazing leases that netted about $40,000 in 1900. In 1923, the PUF changed dramatically when the Santa Rita well struck oil on university lands, and by 1925 the PUF fund was growing at about $2,000 every day. Today, the PUF totals about $15.9 billion and provides support for schools in the University of Texas and Texas

A&M systems. The PUF is an endowment, meaning that the principal from this account cannot be spent and that only investment returns can be used. In 2013, these payments increased to about $644 million a year, which is made available to the eighteen universities and colleges in those systems.[32] PUF funds may be used only for construction and renovation projects or for certain academic excellence programs.

Amendments to the Texas Constitution in 1984 and 1993 allowed the legislature to provide appropriations to universities, health-related institutions, and the Texas State Technical College institutions not funded by PUF funds. This Higher Education Fund (HEF) is similar to the PUF and can be used only to construct and repair campus buildings or to purchase capital equipment or library materials. The HEF was designed to provide the kind of support previously enjoyed only by schools in the University of Texas and Texas A&M systems.

### Directing Policy

Higher education policy in Texas is overseen by the Texas **Higher Education Coordinating Board (THECB)**, which is made up of nine citizens appointed by the governor for six-year terms. The governor also appoints the chair and vice chair. No board member may be employed in education or be engaged in business with the THECB. Thus, while some agencies draw largely on expertise from within related fields, the law forbids such a background in higher education policy for members of the THECB. As with other state boards, these citizens serve without pay but may be reimbursed for travel expenses incurred as part of their duties as board members. The board meets quarterly and is responsible for setting the broad direction of education policy—within the boundaries established by Texas law. For example, in October 2000, the THECB approved Closing the Gaps, a long-term plan intended to guide higher education in Texas for the next fifteen years. It proposed addressing the demands of a diverse and growing economy by adding 500,000 (later increased to 630,000) students to the rolls of higher education institutions, increasing the number of degrees awarded, and improving the quality of programs and research, all by 2015.

One of the most important functions of the board is the selection of a full-time commissioner of higher education to run the agency between the quarterly meetings of the THECB. Raymund A. Paredes, the current commissioner, was initially appointed in 2004, and he has played a visible role in the Closing the Gaps initiative and other reforms to higher education that are related to costs and accountability.

While statewide policy is set by the coordinating board, each university or university system is overseen by a board of regents. Each institution has nine regents appointed to staggered, six-year terms by the governor with the consent of the Texas Senate. Regents are volunteers who serve without pay, although they may be reimbursed for travel and other expenses. There is some disagreement about exactly what the role of regents should be. Former governor Bill Hobby has suggested that the current system ties regents more closely to politics than higher education. He points out that board members at private schools are called "trustees" and see themselves as representatives and advocates of the university. In contrast, the "regents" label implies that the boards of state universities rule over the schools as agents of the politician who appointed

**Higher Education Coordinating Board**
a group of nine people appointed by the governor for six-year terms to oversee higher education policy in Texas.

## Governor James Ferguson and the University of Texas

James E. "Pa" Ferguson came to office after the 1914 election as a champion of the small farmer. Sometimes called "Farmer Jim" (although he had been practicing law since 1897 and added insurance, real estate, and banking to his interests), he had never held office before he won the support of farmers by promising laws that limited the rent they could be charged. He also managed to win the support of anti-prohibition forces.

Ferguson's battle with the University of Texas (UT) began in 1915 when he confronted the university's president, William Battle, because Ferguson saw no reason that the university's hiring of faculty needed to be any different than his patronage hires for other state positions. Battle refused to fire six faculty members who had angered the governor. Ferguson demanded that Battle be replaced, and, when asked his reason for wanting Battle's removal, Ferguson proclaimed, "I don't have to give any reason. I am Governor of the State of Texas."[i] To make matters worse, the next year the UT Board of Regents failed to consult Ferguson before picking Robert Vinson as the university's new president, and Vinson, like Battle, then also refused to fire faculty members who irritated the governor. Ferguson warned Vinson that unless the faculty members were fired he would face "the biggest bear fight that has ever taken place in the history of the State of Texas."[ii]

Ferguson warned the legislature when it opened the 1917 session that he opposed higher education when it "bec[a]me either autocratic or aristocratic in its ways or customs." That year Ferguson vetoed virtually the entire appropriations for the University of Texas and warned the regents, "If the University cannot be maintained as a democratic university then we ought to have no University."[iii]

Ferguson's battle with the University of Texas cemented a coalition of UT alumni, prohibitionists, and supporters of women's suffrage. Ferguson had treated others the way he treated UT, once explaining his stand on women's suffrage by saying, "If those women want to suffer, I say let 'em suffer."[iv]

The Texas Senate eventually convicted Ferguson of ten charges/articles; five were related to misapplication of public funds, three dealt with his quarrel with the university, one dealt with enforcement of the state's banking laws, and one found that he had received $156,500 in currency from a source that he refused to reveal.

Ferguson resigned from office a day before his removal by the Senate and contended that, because he had resigned, his impeachment and the ban from office that accompanied it were not valid. Impeachment would have ended the careers of most politicians, but not Ferguson, who claimed that his family motto was "Never say 'die,' say 'damn!'"[v] Despite the ban from elective office that came with impeachment, Ferguson ran and lost in the 1918 Democratic primary for governor, and in 1920 he ran for U.S. president on the ticket of the "American Party" that he created. In 1924, "Pa" Ferguson ran his wife, Miriam A. Ferguson, for governor, and she won a term but failed to win reelection after questions about an exceptionally large number of pardons she issued undermined her campaign. The Fergusons, however, were not done, and Miriam was elected again in 1932. When Ferguson ran Miriam again for office in 1940, however, the Ferguson magic was long gone and the voters turned her away.

i. Randolph B. Campbell, *Gone to Texas: A History of the Lone Star State* (New York: Oxford University Press, 2003), 350–351.

ii. Ibid., 351.

iii. Ibid., 351.

iv. James L. Haley, *Passionate Nation: The Epic History of Texas* (New York: Free Press, 2006), 468.

v. Norman D. Brown, *Hood, Bonnet, and Little Brown Jug: Texas Politics, 1921–1928* (College Station: Texas A&M University Press, 1984), 97.

them.[33] In practice, regents seem to do some of both. Governor Perry's appointees to university boards often carried with them many of the governor's ideas about priorities in higher education. However, university regents have often been champions of their universities and strong advocates of the schools' interests.

In 2007, the legislature added a student regent to each board of regents. The law provides that the student regent is not an official member of the board of regents, but it gives him or her all the same powers and duties as the members of the board of regents of the system, except the student regent is not able to vote on any matter before the board or make or second any motion before the board. The selection of a student regent begins with the student government selecting five applicants from among the student body to recommend to the chancellor. The chancellor then selects two or more applicants as recommendations to the governor, who has the final choice. There has been some debate over whether the student regent should be able to vote on board matters. For some, the idea of giving the student regent a voice amounts to turning over control to a potentially untested and unreliable young person.[34] Representative Patrick Rose, who was one of the original supporters of a student regent and favors giving them a vote notes, "We've met the same opposition that I think has always defeated this idea—that only middle-aged people and senior citizens ought to be making the decisions for college students."[35] Lost in the argument is the fact that, if allowed, the student vote would only be one vote. If nothing else, student regents bring a unique perspective and an up-to-date understanding of student needs and concerns to board meetings.

### Expectations and Realities

Universities are under increasing pressure to meet state goals. One such initiative defines success by graduation rates. However, a four-year graduation rate is an outdated relic of a time when more students were full-time students. Today's students are less likely to be the full-time, unmarried, and unemployed students straight out of high school that are known as traditional students. Changing demographics, a dynamic job market, and rising tuitions have all altered who attends college and what else they do while there. Further, when a study based on ACT scores indicated that only 26 percent of the class of 2013 was ready for college, it may be unrealistic to believe that universities can turn many of these underprepared students into college graduates in four years.[36] The state's universities find themselves caught between conflicting demands. In 2010, the state's colleges and universities had to return 5 percent of their current budget and then start mapping out 10 percent in budget cuts for the coming years in case the state's budget woes continued. Compared to the 2010–2011 biennium, state support for institutions of higher education declined by $305.6 million (5 percent) for general academic institutions, $308.3 million (11.7 percent) for health-related institutions, and $53.4 million (2.7 percent) for two-year institutions. At the same time, the Texas Legislature passed a bill (HB 8) that mandated that the THECB devise funding formulas that incorporate the consideration of undergraduate student success measures. While such success-based funding is a popular notion, turning it into a formula that does not encourage grade inflation and does not turn away at-risk students is difficult—especially for a state committed to dramatically expanding the number of people in higher education.

### Access to Higher Education

With Texas's population rapidly expanding and its economy increasingly global and high tech, it becomes important to look at who has access to higher education in the state. Expanding access to higher education has been an important goal since 2000 when the state's Closing the Gap initiative was announced with the goal of adding 630,000 students to the ranks of higher education by 2015. As of 2013, the state had added almost 590,000 more students and awarded almost 237,000 degrees.[37]

Heman Marion Sweatt walks across the campus in 1950 after winning the right to attend the University of Texas School of Law.

While Texas has been seeing progress, it has been uneven at times, and the growth in higher education enrollment has leveled off in recent years. Texas, like other states, has a gender gap in education. A significantly higher percentage of Texas women (6.8 percent) were enrolled in the fall of 2013 compared to Texas men (5.2 percent). Further, the coordinating board's analysis reveals Hispanic participation continues to lag behind the state's goals and that enrollment growth of white students has slowed in recent years after a surge after 2000.[38] The state is also having trouble increasing the number of degrees awarded in science, technology, and math.[39]

In 1997, the Texas Legislature approved a law that guaranteed students in the top 10 percent of their high school class admission to any university in the state. While this allows every Texas community a chance to place its students in the most exclusive universities, critics complain that it overlooks some students from highly competitive school districts and demanding private schools. In fall 2006, 71 percent of students entered the University of Texas through the top-ten-percent rule, limiting the school's ability to bring in students from out of state or those who distinguished themselves through special abilities, such as art or music, that were not fully reflected in the student's general academic performance. In 2009, the University of Texas and its allies won their battle to modify the law that capped the number of students that the university had to accept under this rule at 75 percent of its entering class. For example, UT admitted the top 8 percent of Texas high school graduates for the fall of 2013.

Inequality in higher education has been an issue throughout the state's history. In fact, a landmark civil rights case, *Sweatt v. Painter* (1950), dealt with higher education in Texas. In that case, Heman Marion Sweatt was refused admission to the School of Law of the University of Texas on the grounds that the Texas Constitution prohibited integrated schools. Initially, the state responded to Sweatt's suit against UT president Theophilus Painter by creating a separate law school only for black students known as the Texas State University for Negroes (today the Thurgood Marshall School of Law at Texas Southern University). Sweatt continued to press his case, insisting that the school for black students was far from equal. Ultimately, the U.S. Supreme Court agreed with Sweatt that the two facilities were not equal (although the court would continue to recognize the doctrine of "separate but equal" until *Brown v. Board of Education* in 1954).

Today, legal cases deal with accusations of reverse discrimination. The Texas appellate courts specifically addressed the issue of minorities in higher education in 1996 in *Hopwood v. Texas*;[40] the courts ruled that race-based admission violated the U.S. Constitution. That standard has been loosened by subsequent U.S. Supreme Court cases, which have ruled that although race can't be the sole deciding factor, it can be used as a factor in university admissions decisions. The use of race in university admissions remains a complicated matter.

In October 2012, the U.S. Supreme Court heard oral arguments over the University of Texas's use of race in admissions. In the case of *Fisher v. the University of Texas*, Abigail Fisher alleged that she had been denied admission because she is white. The university uses race as part of its consideration of applicants who are not automatically admitted under the state's top-ten-percent rule. The breadth of concerns behind the issue were revealed by a brief supporting the university that was filed by Tom Izzo, "Tubby" Smith, Johnny Dawkins, and other NCAA Division I basketball coaches, as well as the National Association of Basketball Coaches and the Women's Basketball Coaches Association, all of whom want to ensure that diversity at universities is not isolated within the athletic department or other corners of the campus. The brief stated, "Our student-athletes, and all of the students who attend our institutions, receive the best education when they are able to interact with others within a university community that is broadly diverse across its entire scope."[41] The coaches' brief was one of over fifty such briefs filed. The Obama administration, seventeen U.S. senators, sixty-six U.S. representatives, fifteen state governments, and about 100 colleges, as well as relatives of the late Heman Marion Sweatt, have filed such similar briefs in support of the university.[42] In 2013, the U.S. Supreme Court sent the case back to the federal circuit court with the instructions to review the school's policy with a somewhat higher standard and signaling that a university's use of affirmative action in admissions is constitutional only if it is "narrowly tailored." In July 2014, the Fifth Circuit court ruled that the university's use of race was so tailored and that "to deny UT Austin its limited use of race in its search for holistic diversity would hobble the richness of the educational experience."[43]

The battle over college admissions reflects issues of representation on many dimensions. The coalition that stood behind the ten-percent rule included not just representatives of minority and border districts whose populations were the initial focus of the legislation but legislators from rural districts who also saw it as a means of ensuring that their students had an equal opportunity to be admitted to the universities they chose. However, while this coalition of interests was winning the right for its students to gain admission to the university of their choice, the cost of a university education in the state was climbing, creating another barrier to getting the education needed to find a place in the new Texas economy.

## Costs of Higher Education

The cost of higher education has become a major access issue as rising tuition and fees pose a barrier to college for many students. In 2003, the Texas Legislature deregulated tuition at state schools, allowing each campus to raise its tuition as it saw fit. Since then, colleges have responded to declining state funds for schools by turning to their students to make ends meet. By 2008, the average cost of tuition in state schools had risen 83 percent.[44]

As Table 14.2 demonstrates, in 2014 the average cost of tuition and fees at a state university in Texas was $7,986 and ranged from the $4,746 paid at Sul Ross State University Rio Grande College to the $11,806 paid at the University of Texas at Dallas. In a state where the average per capita income is only $25,809, these tuition costs are doubtlessly intimidating even when federal and state loans and grants are available.

## TABLE 14.2 Tuition and Fees at Texas Public Universities, 2014–2015

| Institution | Texas Resident | Nonresident |
| --- | --- | --- |
| **State Average** | **$7,986** | **$19,083** |
| Lamar University | $9,340 | $20,200 |
| Midwestern State University | $8,088 | $10,038 |
| Prairie View A&M University | $8,637 | $20,103 |
| Sam Houston State University | $8,932 | $19,792 |
| Stephen F. Austin State University | $8,772 | $19,632 |
| Sul Ross State University | $6,900 | $17,760 |
| Tarleton State University | $8,108 | $18,968 |
| Texas A&M International University | $7,558 | $18,652 |
| Texas A&M University | $9,242 | $26,356 |
| Texas A&M University at Galveston | $9,630 | $20,544 |
| Texas A&M University–Commerce | $6,753 | $17,504 |
| Texas A&M University–Corpus Christi | $8,287 | $19,113 |
| Texas A&M University–Kingsville | $7,434 | $18,635 |
| Texas A&M University–San Antonio | $7,313 | $17,869 |
| Texas Southern University | $7,875 | $17,454 |
| Texas State University | $9,500 | $20,360 |
| Texas Tech University | $9,608 | $20,468 |
| Texas Woman's University | $7,560 | $18,420 |
| The University of Texas at Arlington | $9,380 | $18,068 |
| The University of Texas at Austin | $9,798 | $33,842 |
| The University of Texas at Brownsville | $5,928 | $16,844 |
| The University of Texas at Dallas | $11,806 | $30,378 |
| The University of Texas at El Paso | $7,018 | $17,639 |
| The University of Texas at San Antonio | $9,082 | $19,800 |
| The University of Texas at Tyler | $7,312 | $18,172 |
| The University of Texas–Pan American | $6,134 | $17,132 |
| University of Houston | $10,331 | $24,378 |
| University of Houston–Downtown | $6,614 | $17,474 |
| University of Houston–Victoria | $6,748 | $17,608 |
| University of North Texas | $10,066 | $20,926 |
| West Texas A&M University | $7,361 | $8,312 |

**Source:** Texas Higher Education Coordinating Board, www.collegeforalltexans.com/apps/collegecosts.cfm?Type=1&Level=1 (accessed June 24, 2014).

## TABLE 14.3 Tuition and Fees at Texas Public Community Colleges, 2014–2015

| Institution | Texas Resident in District | Texas Resident Out-of-District | Nonresident |
|---|---|---|---|
| **Statewide Average** | **$2,466** | **$3,791** | **$5,400** |
| Alamo Community College | $2,008 | $5,470 | $10,660 |
| Amarillo College | $2,392 | $3,623 | $5,453 |
| Angelina College | $2,130 | $3,330 | $4,650 |
| Austin Community College | $2,490 | $7,860 | $9,870 |
| Blinn College | $2,674 | $4,082 | $6,330 |
| Central Texas College | $2,040 | $2,700 | $6,000 |
| Cisco College | $3,360 | $4,260 | $5,340 |
| Collin County Community College District | $1,220 | $2,390 | $4,190 |
| Dallas County Community College District | $1,665 | $3,015 | $4,695 |
| Del Mar College | $2,914 | $4,414 | $5,524 |
| El Paso Community College District | $2,580 | $2,580 | $4,530 |
| Galveston College | $1,900 | $2,260 | $4,150 |
| Grayson College | $2,401 | $3,541 | $5,131 |
| Houston Community College System | $1,680 | $3,384 | $3,792 |
| Kilgore College | $1,770 | $3,810 | $5,280 |
| Laredo Community College | $4,080 | $5,580 | $7,140 |
| Lone Star College System District | $1,864 | | $3,964 |
| McLennan Community College | $3,450 | $3,990 | $5,700 |
| Midland College | $2,250 | $3,660 | $4,830 |
| Navarro College | $1,035 | $1,715 | $2,460 |
| North Central Texas College | $1,800 | $3,060 | $4,770 |
| Odessa College | $2,580 | $3,900 | $5,160 |
| Panola College | $2,100 | $3,540 | $4,470 |
| Paris Junior College | $1,815 | $2,745 | $4,155 |
| San Jacinto College Central Campus | $1,750 | $3,010 | $4,600 |
| South Plains College | $2,272 | $2,800 | $3,184 |
| South Texas College | $3,300 | $3,573 | $4,440 |
| Southwest Texas Junior College | $2,618 | $4,208 | $5,108 |
| Tarrant County College District | $1,650 | | $6,150 |
| Temple College | $2,640 | $4,620 | $7,020 |
| Trinity Valley Community College | $2,220 | $3,660 | $4,500 |
| Tyler Junior College | $2,352 | $3,762 | $4,362 |
| Victoria College | $2,712 | $4,122 | $4,722 |
| Weatherford College | $2,440 | $3,760 | $5,320 |
| Wharton County Junior College | $2,750 | $4,280 | $5,240 |

*Source:* Texas Higher Education Coordinating Board, www.collegeforalltexans.com/apps/collegecosts.cfm?Type=1&Level=2 (accessed August 12, 2014).

Texas has about fifty community college districts that support about eighty-five campuses. Table 14.3 reports the costs of tuition and fees at some of the state's public community colleges. Texas public community colleges are two-year institutions that serve their communities by offering vocational, technical, and academic courses and certifications. Their tuition fees are slightly more complicated than state universities because each community district is supported by a local taxing district that supplements state funding. People living within these districts pay less in tuition and fees because their tax dollars support the college in general.

Former lieutenant governor Bill Hobby has argued that the relationship between the state and its universities has changed. "The perception that state universities are highly subsidized by tax dollars is no longer true," he said. "Such universities used to be called 'state supported.' Today, 'state-assisted' might be a better term."[45] There has even been some discussion of schools such as the University of Texas "going private" by shunning state revenue. This would save some money from the state budget, but the state would also lose control over an important component in education in the state.

The challenges to families trying to put their children through college have been compounded because the state's budget cuts to its schools were accompanied by cuts to many of the state's financial aid programs for college students. For example, the THECB's major financial aid programs were cut by 15 percent, and the Texas Grant Program was cut by 10 percent. Similarly, the Tuition Equalization Grant program was cut by 20 percent, and the B-on-Time program, which provides zero-interest loans that turn into grants for students who meet certain standards, faced a 29 percent cut. Funding for work study programs and the Texas Educational Opportunity Grants that serve students in community colleges survived without cuts, but they saw no growth to match the rise in enrollment. Thus, the state's students and schools are facing a host of challenges as more and more students pursue the limited funding available for higher education. At the same time, the state's employers are seeing a growing demand for a workforce that needs higher levels of education. With more students needing more education than ever before, the state faces the daunting task of meeting the growing needs of students and employers with a stagnant or shrinking budget.

## Accountability in Higher Education

As is the case with public schools, accountability has become a major issue in higher education. While the state's demand for accountability in higher education lags behind the systems in place in the public schools, assessment of courses and programs has become an increasingly prominent part of what universities and their faculties must do. Support for the general idea of accountability might be high, but defining what that means and how it is measured generates tremendous disagreement. For example, the state has begun to develop a system of success-based funding for schools that would allocate state funds to schools partially based on how many students graduate or meet some other standard of academic success. Even if academic success were easy to define, basing funding on such success is difficult given the different missions of the state's schools. Some institutions, such as the University of Texas, are encouraged to focus on

## TABLE 14.4　State Education Performance Measures

| Measure | Texas | Percentage National Average | Texas Ranking |
|---|---|---|---|
| Average graduation rates for public high school students | 72.5% | 73.4% | 36 |
| Percentage of public high schools offering advanced placement in the four core subject areas | 29.0% | 32.6% | 32 |
| Estimated rate of high school graduates going to college | 56.9% | 63.8% | 42 |
| In-state tuition prices at public two-year institutions by state rank | $2,049 | $3,387 | 49 |
| In-state tuition prices at public four-year institutions by state rank | $8,078 | $8,043 | 22 |
| Full-time freshman-to-sophomore retention rates at public two-year institutions | 57.8% | 59.0% | 19 |
| Full-time freshman-to-sophomore retention rates at public four-year institutions | 73.8% | 78.2% | 36 |
| Three-year graduation rates of associate degree–seeking students at public two-year colleges | 11.1% | 9.6% | 45 |
| Six-year graduation rates of bachelor's degree–seeking students at public four-year colleges | 55.3% | 49.1% | 35 |
| Adults ages 25–64 with less than a high school diploma | 18.7% | 11.3% | 1 |
| High school graduates going to college | 56.9% | 63.8% | 42 |

**Source:** The College Board, "The College Completion Agenda 2012 Progress Report," http://media.collegeboard.com/digitalServices/pdf/advocacy/policycenter/college-completion-agenda-2012-progress-report.pdf (accessed September 12, 2014).

educating the state and nation's top students; other schools open their doors to students who are less likely to graduate. There have also been initiatives aimed at making the use of funds, quality of teaching, and value of scholarly research more transparent to the community at large.

As Table 14.4 illustrates, the state's success in the classroom has been mixed compared to that of other states. While Texas has historically kept tuition relatively affordable, the state's students have not been completing their education at the same rate as their peers in other states. While our lagging rates of higher education may have been suited to the agricultural past of the Texas economy, the state's hope of becoming a leader in high technology and international business demands that Texas keep up with other states and provide the workforce that leading-edge firms need.

### Universities' Other Contributions

While teaching is a primary function of universities, the state looks to universities for other reasons as well. Universities are an important resource for knowledge. As anyone who has watched a 1950s science fiction movie knows, the first place a community turns to when it encounters the unknown is a professor at the local university. Whether the nation needs Indiana Jones to find a lost relic or a small town has to confront giant ants, the knowledge developed at universities should be a helpful resource for the community. In a more subtle way, higher education helps the state economy by developing the knowledge behind innovative ideas that can fuel new businesses or industries. For example, the Texas Emerging Technology Fund, a fund managed by the governor's office, has invested more than $177.3 million in research projects affiliated with Texas universities in the hopes that the research produced at these schools will turn into new business that will keep Texas ahead of changes in the economy.[46]

In some ways, Texas's colleges and universities are important players in the state's economic development program. The University of Texas has played an important role in making Austin a high-tech center, and Texas A&M hopes to have a similar impact on the state after winning a federal biosecurity contract worth $286 million to develop a center for researching and manufacturing drugs to respond to bioterrorism or pandemics. A&M system chancellor John Sharp called the award "one of the biggest federal grants to come to Texas since NASA was placed here some years ago."[47]

## WINNERS AND LOSERS

The value of higher education seems clear, but so do the challenges it faces. Studies continue to show that college graduates earn higher salaries. Perhaps the most compelling evidence for the state's need for higher education is the interest that business leaders in Texas have demonstrated through their support for the state's universities. While the value of education's contribution to the state's future is clear, exactly what must be done to prepare Texans for the future is not.

Texas must continue to invest wisely in education as its students prepare to compete for jobs globally. Thomas Friedman's bestselling book, *The World Is Flat*, describes how American firms and workers need to prepare for competition from global sources. Today, the competition for jobs may arrive electronically. Thanks to the Internet, citizens of far-away countries, such as India and China, may be in a position to compete for work as effectively as if they were living next door. These "digital immigrants" are already providing services for some Texas firms, ranging from technical assistance in call centers to outsourced accounting services. As the rest of the world provides college degrees for more and more of its citizens, higher education institutions in Texas need to help students to prepare to compete with these digital immigrants from all over the globe. The state's leaders will need to decide if that learning will occur in person in traditional classrooms or in massive open online courses (MOOCs) shared on handheld devices.

★ How might the disparity in access to education present challenges for the state's citizens and economy?

★ How much should the state subsidize universities?

★ Should Texas colleges and universities be held to standards similar to those used in K–12 schools? Why or why not?

★ Considering the swiftly changing nature of the economy, are Texas schools effectively preparing students for the rapidly changing workforce?

## HEALTH AND HUMAN SERVICES

**H**ealth and human services encompasses programs that help provide food, shelter, and health care to millions of Texans. In fact, Texas spends over $25 billion a year on 200 different health and human services programs and employs 48,000 state workers in those programs.[48] This fact may directly contradict one of the state's legends: the image of the rich Texan. This image has emerged because the families that run sizeable ranches or manage large oil fields make for good storytelling. The real lives of most Texans are much less glamorous than those seen on shows such as *Dallas* or the reality program *Big Rich Texas*. Many Texans in the real world live a modest, hardscrabble life. In 2014, the per capita income in Texas was $25,809, well below the national average of $28,051. A study by the Census Bureau found that just over one in three Texans lived in a poverty area, which is a census tract where 20 percent or more of the residents live at or below the poverty level.[49]

American federalism has increasingly entwined state government with national policy related to health and human services through federal-state partnerships in programs such as Temporary Assistance for Needy Families, Medicare, and Medicaid. Generally, Americans think of such policies as coming from Washington, D.C. In fact, the states play an important role in delivering many of the benefits, working in partnership with the federal government. Moreover, each state faces a unique set of challenges. In 2013, for example, Texas had one of the highest rates of poverty (16.8 percent) in the nation, well above the national average of 14.5 percent. However, while many Texans live in serious need of health care or other social services, the Texas tradition of individualism means that the state has only grudgingly provided these services on a limited basis.

### Social Welfare Programs

Social welfare programs include a wide range of ways in which the government takes a role in providing for the needs of people who cannot or will not provide for themselves. These include programs that help with shelter, food, clothing, jobs, medical aid, or assistance in old age. Sometimes these programs partner charitable organizations

**FIGURE 14.3** Poverty: Texas versus the United States, 1980–2013

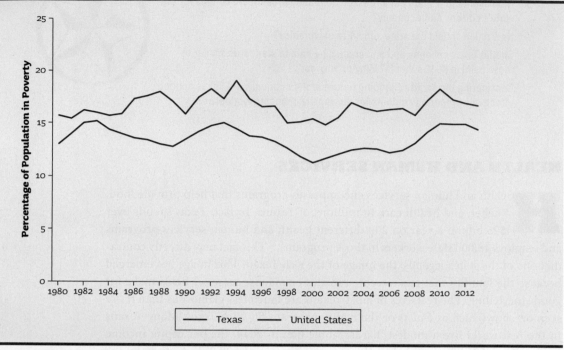

**Source:** U.S. Census Bureau, Historical Poverty Tables, "Percent of People in Poverty, by State," www.census.gov/hhes/www/poverty/data/historical/
hstpov19.xls (accessed September 22, 2014).

with government agencies. Frequently, the state finds itself working—sometimes reluctantly—with the federal government.

Texas provides assistance to some families with children under eighteen through **Temporary Assistance for Needy Families (TANF)**. Under this program, eligible households receive monthly cash payments and Medicaid benefits. TANF provides cash payments through an electronic debit card known as the Lone Star Card. Cash benefit programs are those programs in which individuals receive funds that they spend themselves.

Recipients must accept the terms of a personal responsibility agreement that requires them to stay free of alcohol or drug abuse, seek and maintain employment, ensure that children are attending school, and take part in parenting and other programs if asked. In August 2014, 39,990 Texas families were receiving TANF, including 64,475 children and 9,492 adults, with the average recipient receiving about $71 a month.[50] Families may also qualify for the **Supplemental Nutrition Assistance Program (SNAP)**, which is designed to help low-income seniors and single people, people with disabilities, and families in need buy food from local retailers. (SNAP was formerly known as food stamps.) In Texas the program is overseen by the Health and Human Services Commission and SNAP benefits are distributed using the Lone Star Card, a plastic card that functions much like a credit card, allowing individuals to

**Temporary Assistance for Needy Families (TANF)**
federal program that provides eligible households with monthly cash payments and Medicaid benefits.

**Supplemental Nutrition Assistance Program (SNAP)**
program that helps low-income seniors, people with disabilities, single people, and families in need buy food from local retailers.

purchase food directly from retailers. These benefits cannot be used for hot, ready-to-eat foods; cigarettes; alcoholic beverages; cosmetics; or paper goods. In May 2014, about 1.4 million families, including 3.3 million Texans, were receiving an average of $274 per family a month in benefits. The majority of recipients were children under eighteen (1.8 million) or seniors (224,534). While the benefits are available to adults with no children, they must work at least twenty hours a week or meet other work requirements in order to qualify. Adults without dependent children that do not meet work requirements are limited to three months of benefits in a thirty-six-month period. The benefit period can be longer for adults in a job-training program working at least twenty hours a week.

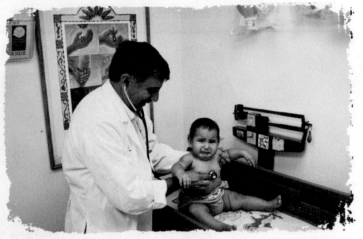

A doctor cares for a child at a health clinic in McAllen, Texas. Health and human services like Medicaid and Temporary Assistance for Needy Families are important in the state, which has one of the highest poverty rates in the nation, but social welfare programs may often be available only on a limited basis.

## Health Care

Health care has become an important issue for the state and the federal government. The state of Texas faces the challenges of rising health care costs as it deals with those who cannot afford health care and as it struggles to pay for the health insurance of its state employees. The state is also concerned with making sure that health care costs are as low as possible in Texas so that employers see the state as an affordable place to set up business. Recently, Texas has become a central battleground in the national health care debate. On one hand, former governor Perry was among the leading opponents of the Affordable Care Act (ACA) championed by President Obama, which is attempting to extend health care coverage to all Americans. On the other hand, a 2012 Gallup poll found that Texas led the nation in uninsured people with 27.6 percent uninsured—four points higher than second-place state Mississippi, where only 23.5 percent of people lack health insurance, and much higher than the national average of 17.1 percent[51] (see Map 14.1). As the state of Texas continues to resist federal solutions to the health care problem, it must consider what alternatives it can promote.

### Federal and State Programs

A variety of programs address the health care needs of Texans, and the 8,500 employees of the Texas Health and Human Services Commission (HHSC) are responsible for overseeing the state's health policies. Like many Texas agencies, the HHSC is overseen by a council of nine citizens appointed by the governor. The day-to-day operations of the commission are conducted by the executive commissioner, a professional administrator appointed by the governor, who works with the council to develop rules and policies for the commission. The HHSC holds responsibility for overseeing the state's contributions to both Medicaid and the Children's Health Insurance Program (CHIP), as well as several other smaller programs related to health care.

**MAP 14.1** **The Uninsured in America, 2012**

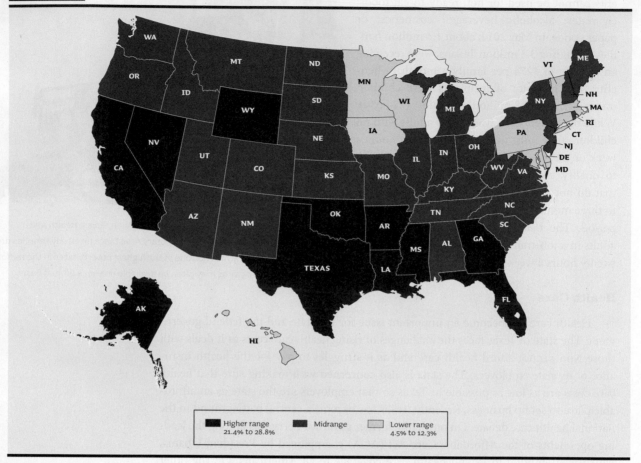

**Medicaid**
a federal program providing medical coverage for low-income people and some elderly and disabled people.

The federal **Medicaid** program provides medical coverage for people with low incomes and some elderly or disabled people. Congress created the Medicaid program in 1965, and Texas began participating in it in September 1967. Federal law requires states to cover certain groups and gives states the flexibility to cover additional groups. States share the cost of Medicaid with the federal government. In 2013, there were over 3.65 million Texans covered by Medicaid, with 2.75 million (76 percent) under nineteen years of age, 134,663 who were pregnant women, 246,421 who were aged, and another 548,591 classified as blind or disabled. The remaining 3 percent (119,524 people) of Texas Medicaid recipients are adults who qualify based on lack of income alone.[52]

Although part of the Affordable Care Act encourages states to extend Medicaid coverage to nearly all nonelderly adults with incomes at or below 138 percent of the poverty level (about $32,500 for a family of four in 2013) by offering to pay the cost of this coverage, Texas has declined to participate in this expansion. The state's fear is that while the federal government would initially pay the full cost of expanded coverage, the costs of the program might shift back to the state at some point in the future.

For those families making too much to qualify for Medicaid but not enough to afford private health insurance, the **State Children's Health Insurance Program (SCHIP)**, a federal-state program, offers the children in these families health care, including regular checkups, immunizations, prescription drugs, hospital visits, and many other health care services.[53] In April 2014, that program covered 495,187 Texas children beyond the 2.75 million children covered by Medicaid.

**Medicare** is a federal health insurance program that serves about 3.2 million Texans who average about $8,000 in benefits each year. Medicare is available to senior citizens who have worked and paid into the system for ten or more years. This means that in 2014 about 82 percent of the state's Medicare recipients were age sixty-five or over; the remainder qualified for Medicare because of disability. There are actually several components to Medicare. Part A covers in-patient hospital care, while Part B covers doctors' fees and other outpatient costs. In 2003, President George W. Bush signed legislation adding Part D, which extended Medicare coverage to provide prescription drugs.

### The Politics of Health Care

The controversy over the Affordable Care Act has often been a highly partisan debate about the power of the federal government. While that is a legitimate issue, the debate has often taken us away from fundamental issues of health care and the burdens that health care costs put on individual Texans, their employers, and the facilities that must often care for the poor and uninsured.

## WINNERS AND LOSERS

**W**hile turning down the federal money contained in the Affordable Care Act might seem like a simple answer in a conservative state such as Texas, the implications of declining the federal funds associated with expanding Medicaid under the ACA are complex. State accounts may come out ahead by not accepting the burdens that come with these funds, but county and private hospitals could come out losers because they will see patients without Medicaid or other insurance showing up in emergency rooms or experiencing stays in the hospital they cannot afford. Thus, county hospitals will see patients that they cannot turn away, but those poor patients will leave county taxpayers to pay their tab.

★ Is the potential taxpayer burden of refusing federal funds for national health care reforms worth the state insisting on its independence?

★ Have controversies over issues such as abortion and privatization hurt health care services for Texas residents?

★ How does the state reconcile its provision of health care and social welfare programs with the Texas culture of independence?

# HOW TEXAS GOVERNMENT WORKS

## Citizens in Need

### Per Capita Income

$25,809 — Texas
$28,051 — United States

### Persons below Poverty

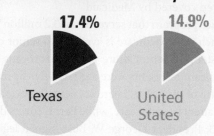

17.4% — Texas
14.9% — United States

### Persons without Health Care Insurance

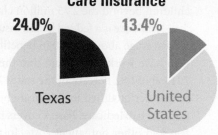

24.0% — Texas
13.4% — United States

Source: Gallup: "Arkansas, Kentucky Report Sharpest Drops in Uninsured Rate" August 4, 2014, www.gallup.com/poll/174290/arkansas-kentucky-report-sharpest-drops-uninsured-rate.aspx#1.

Source: Gallup: "Arkansas, Kentucky Report Sharpest Drops in Uninsured Rate" August 4, 2014, www.gallup.com /poll/174290/arkansas-kentucky-report-sharpest-drops- uninsured-rate.aspx#1.

## Who Pays For Human Services

*The state and federal governments both provide benefits to Texas residents in need. Who pays what share of the costs for these programs?*

### Temporary Assistance for Needy Families

Eligible households receive monthly cash payments, through the electronic debit Lone Star Card.

Texas 48%
United States 52%

Source: Center for Budget and Policy Priorities, TANF Spending Fact Sheet 2012, www.cbpp.org/- files/8-7-12tanf-factsheets/8-7-12tanf-TX.pdf.

### Medicaid

Medical coverage for people with low income, and some elderly and disabled.

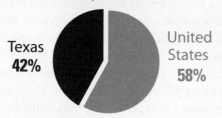

Texas 42%
United States 58%

Source: Kaiser Family Foundation, Federal Medical Assistance Percentage for Medicaid and Multiplier, FY 2015, http://kff.org/medicaid/state-indicator/federal-matcing-rate-and-multiplier/

### Medicare

Senior citizens who have paid into the system for ten years or more receive health coverage.

Texas 0%
United States 100%

### Children's Health Insurance Program
### State Children's Health Insurance Program

Families making too much to qualify for Medicaid but not enough to afford private health insurance receive coverage through this joint federal-state program.

Texas 29%
United States 71%

Source: Legislative Budget Board, "Top 100 Federal Funding Sources in the Texas State Budget, February 2013," page 21, www.lbb.state.tx.us/Federal_Funds/Other_Publications/583_Top%20100%  20Fed%20Funds%20in%20Texas.pdf.

### Supplemental Nutrition Action Plan

Texas 0%
United States 100%

While the federal government pays for all benefits, Texas pays for 50 percent of administrative costs.

Source: Texas Health and Human Services

## CONCLUSION

Texas is experiencing dramatic changes in both its education and health care policies. Texas schools struggle to keep up with educating a growing population and meeting the demands of a rapidly changing economy. With regard to health care, the state has a population that is growing and a health care system that is becoming dramatically more expensive. While both problems seem difficult to solve, neither can be ignored. Texas businesses need an educated and healthy workforce. In addition to the thorny issue of health care for those who cannot currently afford it, businesses in Texas and the rest of the country (as well as the state government itself) are also seeing the costs of insuring their employees skyrocketing.

for CQ Press

Sharpen your skills with **SAGE edge** at **edge.sagepub.com/collier4e**. **SAGE edge for students** provides a personalized approach to help you accomplish your coursework goals in an easy-to-use learning environment.

## KEY TERMS

Education Reform Act (p. 449)

Higher Education Coordinating Board (p. 457)

Medicaid (p. 470)

Medicare (p. 471)

No Child Left Behind Act (NCLB) (p. 453)

Permanent University Fund (PUF) (p. 456)

State Children's Health Insurance
    Program (SCHIP) (p. 471)

Supplemental Nutrition Assistance Program (SNAP) (p. 468)

Temporary Assistance for Needy Families (TANF) (p. 468)

## CORE ASSESSMENT

1. How much of the financial burden of higher education should fall on students?

2. How much should the state of Texas do to ensure that all its citizens have the opportunity for a quality education? How much responsibility for public schools should be left to local school boards?

3. How can the government help protect citizens from catastrophic illness while still providing incentives for individuals to be responsible for their own health care needs?

# 15 TRANSFORMING TEXAS

## Energy, Environment, Transportation, and Immigration Policies

I n 2010, Pearsall, located just southwest of San Antonio, was a quiet little town with a population of just under ten thousand. But Pearsall, which sits atop the Eagle Ford Shale, was about to become a Texas boom town. By 2012, the town had brought in 50,000 workers, and houses, restaurants, and other service industries could not be built fast enough. Investors and some entrepreneurial locals were making big money. Pearsall is just one of many sleepy small towns experiencing the economic miracle of Texas's natural gas explosion. It is the return of the Texas boom town.

About 300 miles north of Pearsall is Weatherford, Texas, where Steve Lipsky lives. Thanks to the Barnett Shale, Weatherford is also experiencing the natural gas boom. The well on Lipsky's property that supplied water to the family had been acting up. When a technician checked out the well, Lipsky was told that it was contaminated with natural gas. In fact, when the county fire marshal came out to measure the gas, Lipsky put a lighter to his fire hose and shot flames high into the air. According to the fire marshal, the hydrocarbon detector went "bonkers," reading in the explosive range.[1] After checking the Railroad Commission of Texas's Web site, Lipsky discovered that two gas wells had recently been fracked almost directly below his house.[2] Lipsky, who had been tired and nauseated for months and had suspected that he might have cancer, started to worry about the consequences of fracking. His family has been unable to drink the water from their well. The Railroad Commission's own investigation of Lipsky's well found cancer-causing benzene in levels higher than allowed. What could not be proven was that the fracking caused the natural gas and chemicals to be found in the water well.

Fifty-five miles north of Weatherford, residents in the town of Dish, Texas, faced the same problem. When the town's 225 residents started experiencing everything from nosebleeds to cancer, they blamed the fracking that had begun in 2005.[3] After his son had a particularly bad nosebleed, the town's mayor, Calvin Tillman, packed up his family and moved. The problem, according to defenders of fracking, is that finding chemicals and natural gas in water supplies around fracking does not show causality. Dish spent $15,000 on an air quality study that found elevated levels of several chemicals, including benzene,[4] but, like Lipsky, the town couldn't prove causation. In fact, scientists

A working gas wellhead sits just outside a resident's home in Dish, Texas. As methane shows up in local water supplies, people are able to light the water from their kitchen sink on fire. Critics argue that fracking releases methane and other compounds, including carcinogens, into the air and water supply, and residents worry about the potential health problems.

say it takes twenty years for solid tumors to develop as a result of exposure to these chemicals, so being able to show a link to cancer is a far-off prospect. The economic boom, by contrast, is occurring right now, and Texans all over the state are feeling, either directly or indirectly, the benefits of the economic growth. Meanwhile, critics worry about the safety of fracking and its long-term effects on air and water quality. The growing pains of the natural gas boom, it turns out, may involve more than just building houses fast enough.

In this chapter, we explore Texas policies that celebrate traditions and change. We examine Texas's rich history of oil and natural gas discoveries and how this helped shape the state's economy. We further explore the current natural gas boom, including the costs and benefits of fracking, to understand how it has shaped politics in the state. Next, we will look at the state's environmental policy, specifically with regard to air and water, and the growing field of alternative energy, as well as the state's new foray into hazardous waste disposal. The evolution of transportation policy, from railroads to roads to mass transit, will then be reviewed. We end with an examination of how Texas's immigration policy continues to shape the state.

## OIL AND GAS IN TEXAS

Nothing has done more to transform Texas than the discovery of oil. In the 1800s, Texas was a frontier state dominated by agriculture, with vast plains of land and little civilization or law enforcement in much of the state. But in the twentieth century, Texas became an oil state. Early settlers had seen the oil seeping from the ground, but they could find little use for it beyond the occasional boat repair until the American oil boom in the 1800s started in Pennsylvania and flourished in the eastern part of the country. Texas's earliest discoveries of oil, in Nacogdoches County in 1866 and in Corsicana in 1894, were relatively modest, and few people expected the state to figure in the oil boom. That changed when a well drilled at Spindletop in Beaumont struck oil. The world took notice when Lucas No. 1 erupted, shooting oil 100 feet into the air for the next nine days before finally being capped. As oil collected around the area, it caught a train on fire, creating a cloud of smoke that hovered over the city and returned to earth via a rain that ruined the paint on the houses in town.[5] Word of the discovery made its way across America, and Texas's towns were soon overrun by those wanting to strike it rich. The Texas oil rush had begun.

### Oil's Influence on Texas

As a result of the discovery of oil, Texas's population growth got a boost in the early 1900s as people flooded the state in search of oil. As we saw in Chapter 2, the 1866 Texas Constitution allowed individuals to retain the mineral rights to their lands. Some Texans suddenly found ranchland that had barely sustained their herds highly prized by oil companies. Predicting the location of oil was (and still is) an uncertain business, and many investors bought up land or mineral rights in the hope of finding oil. Initially, Texas law favored individual prospectors, called wildcatters, and discouraged large oil companies. Texas antitrust laws did not allow integrated oil companies until 1917. That meant that companies that refined, stored, and transported oil were not allowed to produce it.[6] Under these rules, many small oil companies appeared and flourished in Texas, although many more produced only dry wells and quickly went out of business. In 1901, 491 new oil companies were granted charters by the state.[7] Moreover, oil discoveries soon reached across Texas and supported a wide range of oil-related businesses, including refineries and manufacturers of drill bits and other machinery.

As many Texas oil men went from rags to riches, so did the state treasury. In 1905, the Texas Legislature passed its first tax on oil production, at 1 percent of the value. The discovery of oil led to a significant stream of income for the state. In 2011, the tax on oil production was at 4.6 percent and natural gas was taxed at 7.5 percent, amounting to $2.6 billion of the state's revenue.[8] While Texas has benefited from oil and gas, the tax code also significantly subsidizes the industry. In 2006, the state comptroller estimated that 96 percent of the state's $1.4 billion in subsidies went to the oil and gas industry.[9]

The oil boom also directly benefited the University of Texas and Texas A&M. When Texas wanted to start a university, it had little money but an abundance of land. As early as 1839, the Republic of Texas Congress set aside fifty leagues of land to establish two universities. However, the state didn't actually create any universities until the federal government offered subsidies under the Morrill Land-Grant College Act of 1862. In 1866, the Texas Legislature added a million acres of land for public universities, which facilitated the creation of a Permanent University Fund in 1876. Much of the land used to endow the fund was in West Texas and generally thought to be of little value until the discovery of oil in the Permian. In 1931, the legislature passed a law that allocated three-fourths of the fund's money to the University of Texas at Austin and the remaining one-fourth to Texas A&M University. The state's current oil and gas boom has significantly increased the value of the fund. In the 2013 fiscal year, oil and gas royalties provided $648 million to the Permanent University Fund, compared to only $279 million in the 2009 fiscal year.[10]

The Texas economy continued to be driven by the oil industry throughout the twentieth century. Oil helped move Texas from an agrarian state to an urban one. Perhaps more importantly, oil gave Texas a boom and bust economy. The Texas economy rose as the price of oil surged, and the state faltered as the price fell. Oil cushioned Texas from the worst of the Great Depression. Along the way it made (and broke) many small towns. In 1981, oil and gas made up 26.5 percent of gross state product (GSP). By the mid-1980s, the price of oil plunged to $11 a barrel, and the Texas economy fell with it. The result was significant migration out of the state and a smaller oil and gas industry.[11] Following the 1980s recession, Texas diversified its economy, and oil and gas dropped to a mere 7.4 percent of GSP by 1999. As the United States dealt with the great recession that started in 2008, record prices of oil per barrel helped soften the blow to Texas's economy. In 2008, rising prices and technological advances helped oil account for 16.5 percent of Texas's gross state product.[12] Today, oil and gas remains a significant portion of the state's economy. The technologies that facilitated the recent natural gas boom in the state (discussed below) are now being used to drill for oil in addition to natural gas, giving new life to old oil fields. The Texas economy

## Hot Oil

While Texans often think of oil producers as solid citizens who may enjoy a cozy relationship with elected officials, this hasn't always been the case. In fact, the state's relationship with oil producers has been rocky. Writing about the Texas oil industry in the 1930s, Wayne Gard declared, "Oil is the toughest baby the New Deal has tried to civilize. It is still one of the most obstreperous American industries, though it has become the third largest. It is shot through with lawlessness and with flagrant disregard for the public interest."[i]

The trouble erupted in the 1930s when a glut of oil came onto the market. During this decade, when the East Texas oil fields began producing, the surplus of oil drove down prices to a few pennies per barrel. The East Texas oil fields, which were not discovered until October 1930, were populated with 15,271 wells by 1935.[ii] To stabilize the situation, the governor asked the Railroad Commission of Texas to put together a proration plan that would force producers to cut back how much oil came from their wells. In August 1931, when producers ignored an order from the Railroad Commission to stop production, Governor Ross Sterling, himself a former chair of Humble Oil, announced East Texas oil producers were in "rebellion," declared martial law, and sent in the National Guard to shut down oil fields in Rusk and Gregg Counties.[iii]

Despite the governor's decree, many small drillers continued to operate in defiance of limits imposed by law and smuggled "hot oil" in what became known as the "hot oil wars," which continued for almost four years. Oil men created phony wells next to real wells to win the right to produce more oil. Gasoline was smuggled out of eastern Texas in oil trucks disguised as moving vans or through hidden pipelines. Some producers hired their own "rangers" to approach federal officials with both guns and cash.[iv] Illegal "moonshine" refineries sprouted to serve the hot oil market.

The federal government was eventually drawn into the battle after members of the Railroad Commission of Texas appealed to the newly elected U.S. president. Franklin Roosevelt signed an executive order in July 1933 that sent hundreds of federal agents into the field to enforce it.

Some of the lawlessness was driven by simple greed, but some oil men were pushed to the limits because they had purchased oil rights and equipment on credit. Unlike independent oil men, the large oil companies could afford to leave the oil in the ground and resume drilling when the price rebounded.

i.   Wayne Gard, "Hot Oil from Texas," *The American Mercury*, May 1935, 71.

ii.  Ibid., 73.

iii. Bryan Burrough, *The Big Rich: The Rise and Fall of the Greatest Texas Oil Fortunes* (New York: Penguin Press, 2009), 77.

iv.  Gard, "Hot Oil from Texas."

has diversified significantly, now as likely to operate in computer chips, telecommunications, and finance as in oil and gas. Yet oil remains a powerful industry as well as a powerful source of identity for the state.

The politics of oil continues to be a part of Texas politics. The United States has been trying to move away from dependence on oil from the Middle East, and in 2008 a Canadian company called TransCanada proposed a pipeline that would make importing Canadian oil easier by extending the Keystone pipeline into Texas. While the larger Keystone pipeline has not been approved yet, the section of the pipeline that will transport crude oil from Canada to Oklahoma and down to the Gulf Coast of Texas is moving forward. Supporters argue it will help stabilize the oil supply and generate construction jobs necessary to build the pipeline. Opponents contend the pipeline will create only a few, temporary jobs, the benefits of which are outweighed by environmental and property rights concerns. Along with concerns about the amount of water the pipeline will use, the pipeline has generated controversy because of the use of tar sands, which are more corrosive than conventional oil. Environmentalists worry that the tar sands make eventual leaks in the pipeline more likely, increasing the possibility of contaminating ground water along the pipeline. Several homeowners along the route refused to grant the Canadian company the right to put the pipeline through their properties, which raised interesting questions about the power of a foreign company to assert **eminent domain**. Although Texas property owners were able to get a temporary restraining order against TransCanada, in August 2012 a Lamar County Court at Law judge ruled that TransCanada did in fact have eminent domain rights to the land. The Supreme Court of Texas refused to hear the case, allowing the Canadian company to seize land from Texas farmers to complete the pipeline. The issue of eminent domain is likely to increase in importance in the near future as discoveries of natural gas lead to more pipelines being built across the state.

## The Natural Gas Boom and Fracking

Today, Texas is experiencing a second boom—the natural gas rush. The oil crisis of the 1970s created a national push to explore ways to decrease America's dependence on oil. The resulting decades of research by the U.S. Department of Energy yielded improvements in technology that have made it economically viable to extract natural gas trapped in shale formations. Hydraulic fracturing, or **fracking**, involves extracting natural gas from shale formations underground. The shale rock is fractured and injected with millions of gallons of water and chemicals that cause the natural gas to rise to the surface of the well. Although fracking has been used by the oil and gas industry for a long time, modern fracking is significantly different from traditional fracking. Advances in technology allow what is called horizontal fracking, which extends oil drilling horizontally underground. Horizontal fracking uses significantly more water and chemicals to get the natural gas deposits out of the shale. As oil became increasingly scarce and its cost rose, fracking took off across the state. The Barnett Shale led not only the state but the country in a natural gas boom.

Little in Texas politics has been more controversial than fracking, which promises economic prosperity to its proponents and environmental doom to its detractors. For proponents, fracking allows companies to access natural gas that had been previously too expensive to obtain. Fracking can be an engine for economic growth, helping to revive the natural gas industry and create jobs for Texans. Certainly the oil and gas industry has a vested economic interest in the practice of fracking. But so do Texas homeowners, many of whom have signed over the rights for a company to frack on their property in exchange for monthly royalty checks. At the height of the price of natural gas, those checks were substantial, and initially Texans didn't ask too many questions.

The economic impact on the state has been considerable. Texas accounts for almost one-third of the country's natural gas production and holds almost a quarter of the country's natural gas reserves. Texas has three large natural gas reserves: the Barnett Shale, the Eagle Ford Shale, and the Haynesville Shale. According to proponents, the natural gas boom creates jobs and economic growth across the state, including areas around the Eagle Ford Shale and in economically depressed West Texas. Advocates of fracking point to benefits beyond the state of Texas as well. Accessing natural gas reserves can help America decrease its dependence on oil and coal. Moreover, if the shale boom continues, the United States is on track to become a net

**Eminent domain**
the power of the government to take private property for public use, generally for public functions, such as roads.

**Fracking**
fracturing underground rock formations and using high-pressure injections of chemicals and water to cause natural gas to rise to the surface.

Methane's presence in local water supplies means people are able to light the water from their wells and faucets on fire. Critics argue that fracking is releasing methane and other compounds, including carcinogens, into the air and water supply.

exporter of natural gas instead of a net importer.

Texans' excitement about fracking soon changed to concern as people began to question its safety. Opponents of fracking are concerned about the damage it can do to the state's air and water quality. People are increasingly worried that fracking is releasing methane and volatile organic compounds, including cancer-causing benzene, into the air and water. Critics of fracking argue that the air quality around shale sites has significantly worsened, and cities have noticed a marked increase in smog. In 2012, the Environmental Protection Agency (EPA) appeared to agree, issuing a rule that beginning in 2015 oil and gas companies have to capture the toxic gases released while fracking. Opponents of fracking also charge that the chemicals used to extract the natural gas are contaminating the state's drinking water. These chemicals are unregulated by the government and are generally treated as a trade secret. Many believe that fracking releases methane into the water supply. A 2014 study by scientists at the University of Texas at Arlington found that the level of methane in the water in Parker County was dangerously high, measuring at 83 milligrams per liter, well beyond the federal limit of 10 milligrams per level. Moreover, this report was the first to essentially link the methane in the water to fracking; the chemical signature in the water is essentially the same levels as that of the Barnett Shale.[13]

Fracking also uses a large amount of water, estimated to be between 1 million and 5 million gallons in a five-day period. Texans began paying attention to the amount of water that oil and natural gas companies were using when the state experienced a severe drought in 2011. The city of Grand Prairie became the first to adopt water restrictions that included fracking industries. In response, Chesapeake Energy simply started bringing in water from neighboring Arlington, which angered residents there. In response to water use concerns, oil and gas companies have vowed to recycle the water they use to frack. However, a 2014 study revealed that about 92 percent of the water used in fracking is consumed rather than returned to the reservoir.[14] Not only does fracking rely on large quantities of water but oil and gas companies pay the same tax-subsidized price for water as a town's residents. Although Texans face severe water shortages across the state, the absence of state regulation on water use for fracking persists.

In addition, Texans are becoming increasingly worried about earthquakes in areas where they are not typical. In areas such as Cleburne in North Texas and Timpson in East Texas, minor earthquakes have occurred in places that historically have not had earthquakes. Beginning in 2008, Texans have seen an increase in minor earthquakes, clustered around injection sites.[15] A recent study from the University of Texas found a link between fracking and earthquakes. Critics argue these minor earthquakes are particularly problematic since gas pipelines in these areas are not required to be built to withstand earthquakes.

For Texas, a lot is on the line. The promise of an economic boom based on the oil and gas industry is the essence of the Texas cultural identity. It also is politically attractive to oil companies that have long been political powerhouses in Texas politics. Environmental stewardship in the state has often taken a back seat to economic interests. So far, state politicians have been hesitant to do anything to curb fracking. One exception came with the 82nd Legislature, which passed a law requiring oil and gas companies to disclose many of the chemicals, as well as the amount of water, used to frack a well. The effect of the law remains unclear as it does not require prior notice and many of the chemicals remain undisclosed because the industry claims they are trade secrets.

Fracking is redefining the landscape of Texas. State and local governments have been slow to regulate the practice even among growing concerns of citizens living near the state's shale wells. A notable exception is Denton, Texas. In the 2014 election, the city became the first in the state to ban fracking. Within hours of the vote, the Texas General Land Office and the Texas Oil and Gas Association sued the city. The Texas Railroad Commission office has said they will continue to issue fracking permits despite the ban.

## ENVIRONMENTAL POLICY

Given its wide, open spaces and the individualistic nature of its citizens, it is perhaps not surprising that concern about the environment has been slow to develop in Texas. Even in such a conservative state, however, there is some need for **regulation**. Regulation can be defined as government rulemaking and enforcement intended to protect citizens from harm by private firms. While federal regulations generally attract the most attention, much of the regulatory task is left to the states.

In the language of economics, government regulation protects citizens from **negative externalities**. An externality occurs when costs are imposed on someone who is not participating in a transaction. For example, a citizen who does not make, own, drive, or ride in an automobile still must live with the pollution created by cars. This is a problem in a free-enterprise system, which assumes that costs and benefits involve just those people buying and selling a product. Those people involved in a transaction express their desire for cleaner or safer products as they shop by favoring products with those qualities and avoiding those without them. An individual not taking part in a transaction has no influence on shaping the characteristics of a product through market participation, thus creating the need for government involvement. Many Texans own houses on land that others own the mineral rights to. When individuals not living on the land possess and sell the rights to drill for natural gas, for instance, many Texas homeowners have no say in the transaction. In short, if you're not buying or selling a product, you have no way of dealing with its impact on your own life without regulation.

**Regulation**
government rulemaking and enforcement intended to protect citizens from being harmed by private firms.

**Negative externality**
an unintended cost imposed on someone who did not participate in the economic transaction.

Texas has long tended to emphasize business interests over environmental protection. Twentieth-century Texas was a state defined by and large by the oil boom. The state's politics have often been dominated by oil interests. When it comes to environmental regulations, the interests of big oil coincide with the frontier attitude of keeping government small and unobtrusive. Texans prefer little regulation of business and have long been skeptical of policies designed to protect the environment. Texas politicians have tended to stress making the state friendly to big business, which prefers not to be regulated. When Rick Perry was governor and Greg Abbott was attorney general, the state became almost hostile to attempts by the federal government to protect the environment. In fact, by 2012, Abbott had sued the EPA over twenty times.

The agency in Texas responsible for protecting the state's environment is the **Texas Commission on Environmental Quality (TCEQ)**. The agency consists of three commissioners who are appointed by the governor, with Senate approval, and an executive director hired by the commissioners. The commissioners serve staggered, six-year terms. Environmental policy in Texas is also a product of federal regulations. The federal Clean Air Act and Clean Water Act, for example, set minimum pollution standards that the EPA, along with the TCEQ, must enforce.

**Texas Commission on Environmental Quality (TCEQ)** the agency that oversees state environmental policy, including air and water quality.

## TEXAS AIR QUALITY

So what does the air quality in Texas look like? On the one hand, Texas has dramatically improved its air quality in recent decades. On the other hand, the state continues to be one of the largest polluters in the country. Improvements, while remarkable, have occurred in part because Texas has been polluting at a considerably higher rate than other states. As one environmental lawyer put it, "For the most part, Texas has lowered its toxic emissions, but so has essentially every other state in the country."[16] In spite of these improvements, Texas leads the country in carbon dioxide emissions; in fact, according to the EPA, the state is responsible for more emissions than the next two states combined.[17] In response to federal regulations designed to decrease carbon emissions, Texas has sued the EPA to try to prevent the national government from regulating greenhouse gases.[18] Although air quality in most metropolitan areas in the state improved over the previous decade, many Texas cities have struggled to meet federal ozone standards. A 2014 American Lung Association study that examined air quality across the country gave nineteen Texas counties an "F" for ozone pollution and ranked Houston-The Woodlands and Dallas-Fort Worth sixth and eighth, respectively, for worst ozone pollution in the country.[19]

While environmental policy has most often been the concern of the federal government, many states have taken their own paths, even with regard to problems such as climate change that reach beyond state lines. California, for example, has for a long time aggressively pursued environmental policies that go beyond federal standards.

# TEXAS (VS) CALIFORNIA

Anyone who has watched a television game show such as *The Price Is Right* that features luxury car models being given away as prizes is familiar with the idea of California emissions standards. While the U.S. government has enacted a series of minimum standards regarding auto emissions, California has long been at the forefront of this activity, regularly creating standards that exceed those required by the federal government. Since the 1970s, California has enacted the most restrictive standards regarding the gases coming out of the exhaust pipes on cars, trucks, and other automobiles. Eleven other states have also enacted auto emission standards beyond the minimum standards set by the federal government.

Several agencies in California are involved in the regulation of auto emissions, including the California Environmental Protection Agency, the Department of Public Health, and the Department of Consumer Affairs–Bureau of Automotive Repair. Key pollutants subject to regulation include carbon dioxide, hydrocarbons, and ozone. These agencies in the past led the United States in developing additional equipment on vehicles to limit emissions, in requiring the use of unleaded gas, and in mandating routine inspections of vehicles. For example, California required the use of fuel injectors and catalytic converters long before they became standard across the United States. Current efforts by California include those to increase sales of zero-emission vehicles, to encourage the use of alternative fuels, and to boost the fuel efficiency of cars.

Opponents of California's efforts at regulation note that the result of such differing regulations is variations in automobile standards across states. This variation creates additional costs to makers of cars, which are then passed on to the people who buy cars and trucks. In the end, they argue, the U.S. government should be the appropriate level of government to regulate auto emissions.

Texas, in contrast, maintains little state legislation above and beyond the minimum standards established by the U.S. government. One of the few requirements in Texas is the imposition of annual auto emission standards in metropolitan areas such as Houston that have consistently high levels of air pollution linked to automobiles. Texas also requires all state, city, and county governments that own fifteen or more vehicles to purchase some low-emission vehicles.

## THINKING *Critically*

★ How is California a leader in the regulation of auto emissions?

★ How does California's attempt to regulate auto emissions affect the size and scope of its government?

★ Do you think that Texas and other states should set standards that are stricter than those set by the U.S. government?

★ What do you think the advantage of Texas adopting stricter emissions standards might be?

As governor and attorney general, respectively, Perry and Abbott took on the EPA and EPA standards in the state on an unprecedented scale. One of the most visible examples of this has to do with air quality. The federal Clean Air Act limits the amount of certain pollutants industries can produce from each source. In order to give businesses more flexibility, the TCEQ allowed industries in Texas to meet that limit using flexible permits. Flexible permits allow industries to meet the EPA standard by measuring their overall pollution levels across an entire facility rather than measuring at each pollution point. In 2010, the EPA ruled that flexible permits allow companies to emit pollution levels in violation of the Clean Air Act since pollutants concentrated in one area can be harmful to nearby neighborhoods. In 2014, the EPA reached a new deal with the TCEQ that allows the agency to issue conditional flexible permits. Texas also sued the EPA over regulations meant to address pollution that drifts into neighboring states. In 2014, the U.S. Supreme Court upheld EPA rules that require states to address pollution that crosses borders into other states.

## WATER AND SCARCITY

**A**s the Lone Star State has started facing severe water shortages, Texans have had to deal with new realities. In 2011, Texas experienced a severe drought that dried up lakes and rivers, causing strains in everything from cattle ranching to cotton growing. The drought meant that farmers didn't have sufficient water to keep horses or cattle, and the lack of rain sent the price of hay through the roof. Many Texas farmers sold off their cattle, and around the state stories of horses being given away at auction or abandoned on the side of the road became common. The Ogallala Aquifer, which provides water from West Texas to South Dakota, experienced the largest decline in twenty-five years as a result of this drought.[20] Towns across the state have been running dangerously low on water, many of them having to ship it in. At the beginning of 2012, Spicewood Beach became the first town in Texas to officially run out of water. In summer of 2014, an estimated twenty towns were within ninety days of running out of water. In what some are dubbing "toilet to tap," Wichita Falls announced it would become the first city in the country where half of the city's drinking water came from recycled waste water. Texas, for the first time in history, cut off water to rice farmers in the state due to low water levels. Unfortunately for the state, experts say Texas is likely to experience more droughts in the foreseeable future.

As water rights have become an increasingly salient issue, the state has had to prioritize water access. In Texas, water that is above ground is owned by the state. However, Texas water rights are based on the **rule of capture**, which comes from English common law. Rule of capture says if you own property in the state, you own the water underneath that property. Thus, unlike most other states, in Texas a landowner can use up shared underground water without any legal liability to adjacent land owners. The drought has forced the state's politicians to address water use. The 83rd Legislature moved $2 billion from the state's Rainy Day Fund into a water fund that will give loans for reservoir and dam development across the state. The current state water strategy includes a controversial plan to create a 70,000-acre reservoir in East Texas to supply water to Dallas area residents. Residents of East Texas object to what they perceive as a land grab by wealthier Dallas County. The proposal would flood an area of East Texas that has long held

> **Rule of capture**
> Texas law that says property owners own the water below their property.

AP Photo/Tony Gutierrez

Lack of water across the state hurts all Texans, including its vast farming and ranching communities. It is estimated that Texas agriculture producers lost $7.62 billion due to the drought.[21] Lack of water also affects industry directly since many Texas industries, such as oil and gas, timber, high-tech industries, and manufacturing, depend on water for their businesses. Drought conditions also threaten water quality across the state. Texas already has some of the most polluted waterways in the country. Drought conditions increase the toxicity in streams and lakes, which can be harmful to fish and aquatic life.[22]

## Private Property and Takings

One of the most pervasive legends in Texas is that of private property. Most Texans view their property as being exclusively under their own control. However, this is increasingly false.

The idea of "takings" emerges from the Fifth Amendment to the U.S. Constitution, which prohibits the taking of private property "for public use, without just compensation." Traditionally, this clause has been examined in the light of eminent domain, the power of government to take property for public use. Generally, eminent domain has been used to take private property for government use for public services, such as roads. Recently, the limits of eminent domain have been tested as the government has taken private property for public uses such as the Dallas Cowboys' new stadium in Arlington, toll roads operated by private firms, and the Keystone pipeline. In this more expansive use of power, the taking of private property is justified for general economic development that will create jobs and other advantages for the entire community. Thus, "public use" doesn't exclude private profit.

Another use of the takings label deals with the impact of regulation on the value of private property. One example of regulatory takings would be environmental regulations that place restrictions on the uses of private property designated as wetlands. These rules restricting how individuals use their property may diminish the value of the property. In this case, the government is restricting use of property to promote the general welfare, which is certainly a public concern. However, for many years the courts did not support compensating citizens for regulatory takings. Restrictions on land use are not unique to environmental regulation. Property owners in cities also face restrictions on how they use their land. For example, zoning rules prohibit building businesses in residential areas. However, environmental regulations reach outside cities to the rural areas where many people have retreated in their attempt to avoid rules imposed by government and their neighbors.

The problem of takings reflects a cost of government that frequently does not show up on the balance sheet of costs and benefits. Sometimes government regulation requires costly action, such as altering coal plants to produce less pollution, with the cost being passed along as higher utility bills. At other times, government policies restrict citizens' uses and enjoyment of their own property.

However, without some ability to extend its authority onto private property, the government would lack the ability to create and enforce meaningful rules related to the environment or public safety, since pollution and other problems don't honor property lines. Without such rules, individuals could block the flow of creeks and cut off water supplies to, or cause flooding for, other citizens. Neighborhoods could find adult businesses placed next to family homes or schools. Thus, the matter of who wins and who loses involves a balancing act in which the government must weigh the public safety against the rights of individual property owners.

family farms and timber tracts, among other things. As Texans run out of water in some cities and sell their water in others, Texans are likely to face severe water shortages for the foreseeable future.

## ALTERNATIVE ENERGY

Although the twentieth century marked Texas as an oil state, twenty-first-century Texas is thus far still finding its place. One area where Texas has thrived is wind energy. Since 2006, Texas leads the country in wind energy. According to the American Wind Energy Association, Texas has 12,355 megawatts of total wind capacity, which far outstrips California, the second-biggest wind producer with 5,829 megawatts of capacity.[23] Wind power has become increasingly popular in Texas since it allows the state to capitalize on its vast land. Windmills have emerged on now dry oil fields and struggling farms across the plains of West Texas. The increased viability of wind energy has become an engine of development in rural areas, such as in Nolan County where property values have surged in recent years thanks to wind farms.[24] In 2013, wind energy accounted for 8.3 percent of the total electricity generated in Texas.[25] Wind energy is currently more expensive than more traditional energy sources, but a 1992 federal tax incentive called the federal clean energy tax made wind development more feasible. That tax credit expired at the end of 2013, however, which will likely dampen enthusiasm for future wind development. Nonetheless, Texas is home to six of the ten largest wind farms in the country, putting it far ahead of other states. The state has also passed laws to facilitate wind development. In 2008, the Texas Legislature authorized a 3,600-mile transmission line to transmit wind power from West Texas to metropolitan areas that use the most energy, such as Dallas, Austin, and Houston. The recently completed lines are capable of transmitting 18,500 megawatts of power.

While Texas has made significant progress with wind energy, its progress in using other types of alternative energy has been more limited. As the Texas power grid strains under record heat and drought, finding alternative energy sources is extremely important. Thanks to its vast plains, Texas ranks first in solar resource potential.[26] However, although Texas leads the country in oil, natural gas, and wind production, solar development remains extremely limited in the state. Policies that have generated support for solar energy in other states are notably absent in Texas. There are no state tax incentives for solar development, and Texas is one of only a handful of states without a net-metering policy, which allows residents to sell their excess electricity back to the grid. Solar energy is much more expensive than other types of energy sources, but advocates point out that it has a considerable advantage over wind since it produces the most power on hot summer days when the energy grid experiences peak usage. As Texas looks to the future of energy, EPA rules on limiting pollution to neighboring states and policies targeted at lowering emissions will likely make coal more costly in the years to come. As the state's continued drought jeopardizes the feasibility of continued fracking, the state's investment in wind energy is likely to pay off. Nonetheless, Texas's alternative energy record remains limited: 40 percent of the state's energy still comes from natural gas and another 37 percent from coal.

## HAZARDOUS WASTE

In the spring of 2012, Texas became the first state in thirty years to open a low-level radioactive waste site. The site, located in West Texas's Andrews County, is only the fourth radioactive waste site in the country, and the first in Texas. Previously, hazardous waste from Texas's companies was shipped to Utah. Texas has the only site in the country authorized to accept the more hazardous B and C classifications of radioactive waste. The Texas site is particularly controversial since it sits atop the Ogallala Aquifer and scientists worry about the potential for it contaminating the groundwater.

During the TCEQ's own review process, scientists and engineers unanimously concluded that the dump was too close to the Ogallala Aquifer and that radioactive contamination of the aquifer was a risk. In spite of that, TCEQ's executive director at the time, Glenn Shankle, issued the permit for Waste Control Specialists to develop the

# HOW TEXAS GOVERNMENT WORKS

## Energy Use and Production

### Top 5 States in Energy Consumption per Capita, 2012

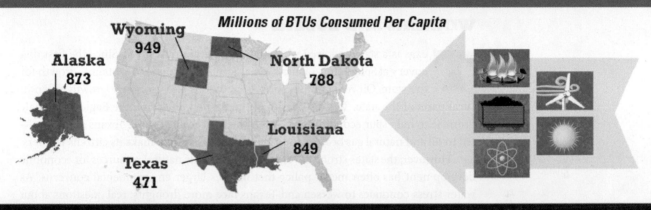

**Millions of BTUs Consumed Per Capita**

Wyoming 949
Alaska 873
North Dakota 788
Louisiana 849
Texas 471

### Top 5 States in Energy Expenditures per Capita, 2012

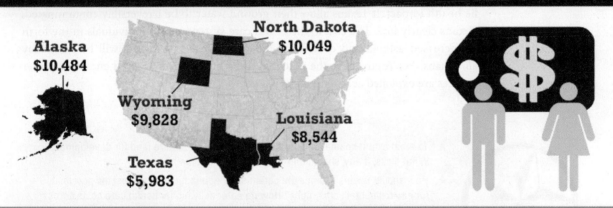

Alaska $10,484
North Dakota $10,049
Wyoming $9,828
Louisiana $8,544
Texas $5,983

### Top 5 States in Total Energy Production, 2012

**Trillions of BTUs Produced**

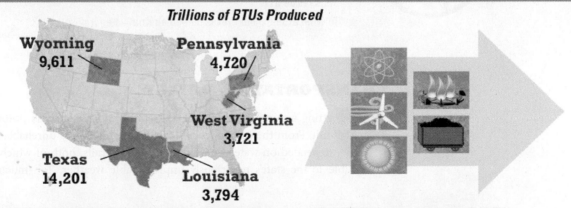

Wyoming 9,611
Pennsylvania 4,720
West Virginia 3,721
Texas 14,201
Louisiana 3,794

Source: U.S. Energy Information Administration, "Texas State Energy Profile," last updated March 27, 2014, www.eia.gov/state/?sid=TX.

site. Within a week, Shankle was hired as a lobbyist for the company. While the original deal was to accept waste only from Texas and Vermont, in 2011 the state legislature authorized the site to accept waste from thirty-six additional states. Proponents argue that rural Andrews County stands to gain considerable economic advantage from the site. Opponents worry about the potential for groundwater contamination and the danger of having a large number of trucks loaded with hazardous materials driving across the state.

## WINNERS AND LOSERS

Texas is a state endowed with abundant natural resources. Since the first discovery at Spindletop, oil has been a significant engine of economic growth for the state. Oil remains a major source of jobs and economic growth, often in rural parts of the state. The discoveries of the Barnett Shale and the Eagle Ford Shale promise to help spur economic growth for the foreseeable future. Texans are committed to oil and natural gas because the state's natural resources make its citizens winners.

However, the state's strong devotion to the use of its natural resources for economic development has often meant policy that ignores larger environmental concerns. As water stress continues to worsen and Texans face more droughts, real questions about how we use our water need to be explored. Perhaps more importantly, new technologies such as fracking cannot be pursued without consideration of the potential public health impact. If Texans allow their ground water to be irreversibly contaminated, Texans clearly lose. The cost to the health care system and to individuals in the form of increased asthma and cancers related to increased pollutants will be shared by all Texans. Yet Texans have the potential to be big winners as wind and solar power sources are exploited across the state.

★ To what extent should eminent domain be used to acquire land for development? What limits, if any, should there be on eminent domain?

★ How should Texans balance the potential for economic gain against the possibility for environmental catastrophe? How do potentially higher health care costs across the state figure into this calculation?

★ How should the state balance its pursuit of economic growth with the well-being of its residents?

★ To what extent should Texas pursue alternative energy sources?

## TRANSPORTATION POLICY

Getting around Texas during the state's early years was notoriously difficult. From the early days of the frontier, travel was unreliable since Texans depended on waterways or undeveloped trails, both of which were highly susceptible to the state's notoriously unpredictable weather. Too much rain meant muddy, impassable roads, and too little rain left waterways too shallow to be usable.[27] Road development in Texas faced serious obstacles: As it is the second-largest state, parts of which are sparsely populated, counties in Texas tended to be fairly isolated. Texas was also a relatively poor state, and Texans leaned toward fiscal conservatism. Despite these challenges, a rapidly growing state needed a means of moving its people and goods around. This was especially important to the state's farmers, who found themselves spread across the large state. Texas's transportation priorities have evolved as the state first relied mostly on railroads, then turned to roads, and is now looking to mass transit to meet the residents' transportation needs.

## Railroads

Texans initially had a complicated relationship with the railroads. The state's farmers were dependent on the railroads' ability to move produce, but the monopolies that the railroad enjoyed in most areas left the farmers at the mercy of whatever shipping rates the railroad set. In 1836, the First Congress of the Republic of Texas authorized creation of a company to build a railroad system in the state. However, the financing and engineering of this railroad proved too daunting, and the state would not see its first tracks laid until 1852 when a route was established that ran from Buffalo Bayou to the Brazos River at Richmond.[28] While rail lines connecting the state's cities developed naturally, reaching the farmers in the more remote areas of the state was not worth the financial risk, and the railroads had already grown accustomed to getting help from government as they moved west across America.

Early Texas was cash poor and land rich, so in 1854 the state authorized giving railroads 10,240 acres of land for each mile of railroad completed. In addition, numerous Texas cities began offering deals to the railroads in hopes of bringing them in, along with the prosperity and jobs they brought. Cities competed against each other, and money was often passed under the table. As we saw in Chapter 12, some towns, such as Abilene, thrived when the railroad arrived, while cities such as Buffalo Gap withered without the arrival of the railroad. Eventually, the state accepted the need to subsidize railroads if they were going to reach across Texas, and the state gave the railroad companies over 32 million acres (an area the size of Alabama).[29] Though initially slowed by the Civil War, rail development eventually took off. Texas had a mere 486 miles of track operating in 1870, but over the next two decades, the railroad added another 8,000 miles of rail connecting every city in Texas that had a population of 4,000 residents (except Brownsville).[30] Once rail lines were laid, both the railroads and the state had incentives to bring in more settlers—even if it took a little creative promotion. New citizens were lured to the "less humid" regions of West Texas, where rainfalls averaged only about fifteen inches a year and farming and ranching were difficult for Anglos schooled in the agricultural techniques of the less arid eastern United States.

In 1890, Attorney General James Stephen Hogg decided that his office was not able to keep up with the enforcement of regulations on the state's railroads. Hogg advocated for the creation of a railroad commission, making the call for the commission a centerpiece of his campaign for governor. Although the railroads labeled Hogg as "communistic," his reforms were appealing to voters, and Hogg became Texas's first native-born governor in 1891. Today, Texas's Railroad Commission focuses on regulating the oil and gas industry rather than railroads.

Modern-day Texas continues to pay the price for lack of investment in railroads, as large parts of the state remain isolated. Railroads have fundamentally changed from a transportation method primarily used for moving goods to one increasingly moving people around the state. Recent federal funds for building high-speed rails have encouraged several European firms to propose building these systems to connect major areas of the state. These proposals range from connecting Austin to Houston to a high-speed rail between East Texas and Dallas. Perhaps the plan that has generated the most enthusiasm is connecting Houston to Dallas-Fort Worth. Although enthusiasm for building traditional railroads in Texas has never been particularly strong, there seems to be growing support for some strategic high-speed rail lines across the state.

## Roads

While Texas saw some railroads built in the late 1800s, the building of roads didn't really take off for another half a century. For most of its history, Texas left road building and maintenance to fiscally strapped county governments. County governments were authorized to procure ten days of labor each year for building roads and bridges from every male citizen between the ages of eighteen and forty-five and every slave between the ages of sixteen and fifty.[31] However, as they often lacked the financial means to do so, most counties simply did not build roads. There were only a few miles of graded roadway in 1860.[32] Some roadways were little more than a mass of wagon ruts; others were mostly cow trails. The first significant movement in Texas to improve the poor roads occurred when the U.S. Congress passed the Federal Aid Road Act of 1916. Under this act, the national government matched state money with federal money to be used for building roads and bridges. In order to qualify for the federal money, states had to have a state-managed highway program. Texas, which still left road development to counties, responded in 1917 by creating the Texas Highway Department to coordinate state highway development. Though Texas was relatively slow to prioritize building roads up to this point, the new department wasted no time applying for the newly available funds. In fact, within six months, the Texas Highway Department had submitted its first request for federal money and had spent over $9 million in road construction.[33] About the same time, Texas set its first speed limits of 18 miles per hour in rural areas and 15 miles per hour in the city.[34] Texas quickly became one of the leaders in road building among states.

Early in the twentieth century, Texas built roads on an unprecedented scale. The state paved its first road in 1918, and within ten years had 18,000 miles of roadway.[35] Texas quickly surpassed other states in the miles of roads it built, and, as one historian notes, "[It] went from a horse culture to something resembling an automobile culture in one swoop."[36] In the 1940s and 1950s, Texas tripled its total miles of highways. Like the expansion of railroads, the development of roads across the state often determined the future of small towns, as cities where highways were built flourished and those bypassed by the state highway system stagnated.[37] By the 1970s, however, Texas highway development was no longer keeping up with the needs of the state. The oil crisis of the 1970s led to both inflation and more fuel-efficient vehicles, which decreased the Texas Highway Department's ability to build new roads since road development relied on a gasoline tax for a significant portion of its revenue. At the same time, the Texas population was seeing significant and unending growth. Compounding the problem, the cost of building roads has substantially increased in recent years. The Legislative Budget Board estimates that between 2002 and 2007, the cost of building roads soared, rising 62 percent in a mere five-year span.[38] Or, as one researcher put, in the past forty years Texas has seen its population increase "by 125 percent, the number of vehicles increase by 172 percent and the number of miles we drive increase by 238 percent. At the same time, the lane-miles of state-maintained roadways (our highways, farm-to-market roads primarily) have increased by only 19 percent over that same period of time."[39] Texas, which once led the country in highway development, has not kept up with the state's population growth, and the highway program has languished.

### Funding Roads

One of the most significant obstacles to an efficient road system is the ability to pay for it. Funding roads in Texas has always been a highly politicized affair. The Texas Highway Department originally relied on a vehicle registration tax for money, though it quickly shifted the funding mechanism from this registration to a gasoline tax. In 1923, the state legislature introduced the first tax on gasoline, which was one cent per gallon. Texas raised the gas tax over the years to keep up with inflation, although the last increase occurred over two decades ago. The current state gas tax, which was adopted by the Texas Legislature in 1991, is twenty cents per gallon. With inflation, the twenty-cent tax was only worth about twelve cents per gallon in 2012. The national government levies an additional 18.4 cents a gallon tax on gas. That makes the total gas tax for Texans 38.4 cents, well below the national average of 49.9 cents per gallon, and fortieth in the country, in spite of the fact that Texas maintains more miles of roads than other states.[40]

In addition to the gas tax, Texas utilizes a variety of other taxes and fees to pay for its roads and bridges. These include vehicle registration fees, title certificate fees, over-size weight permits, motor vehicle sales and use taxes, motor lubricant sales taxes, and, increasingly, tolls.[41] Different types of taxes are discussed at greater length in Chapter 13. Historically, the two greatest sources of money for building roads in Texas were the federal matching dollars and the gasoline tax. Including all taxes and fees related to transportation, the average Texan pays approximately $232 a year toward the state's transportation needs.[42]

In 1946, Texas passed the so-called **Good Roads Amendment**, which requires the lion's share of these fees be used for road construction. Specifically, Article 8, Section 7a of the Texas Constitution requires that three-fourths of all road-user fees be used for building and maintaining roads and the remaining one-fourth be used to pay for state education. The Good Roads Amendment was designed to protect money for highway funding from being spent by the Texas Legislature on other services.

Texas legislators have consistently resisted raising the gasoline tax, exacerbating the state's difficulty in creating a transportation network that keeps pace with its

**Good Roads Amendment**
state constitutional requirement that 75 percent of road-user fees be spent on building and maintaining roads and the remaining 25 percent be used for education.

urbanization and population growth. In the 1920s, Texas formally adopted a pay-as-you-go funding system for road construction, representing Texans' traditionally fiscally conservative approach to government. This meant that, unlike other states, Texas could not borrow money for road construction but had to fund roads as it built them. The pay-as-you-go funding for Texas transportation continued until 2001 when the financial strains of the state's highway department had reached a crisis point. In that year, the Texas Legislature and Texas voters amended the state's constitution to allow the state to issue bonds (borrow money) to keep up with the transportation needs of the state. By the end of 2012, the state had issued approximately $17 billion in bonds to build roads and bridges.[43]

Since eliminating the pay-as-you-go system, Texas now pays a significant portion of money each year to finance its debt burden. The Texas Department of Transportation (TxDOT) estimates that for every billion it borrows, it will have to pay $65 million in annual interest rates.[44] In less than a decade, Texas's fiscally conservative approach to building roads was history. In 2011, the Texas Legislature for the first time appropriated more money for servicing its transportation debt than it allocated for actually building roads.[45] The 83rd Legislature, in its third special session, passed legislation designed to improve the state of transportation funding in the state. The legislation requires half of the money that currently goes to the Rainy Day Fund from the state's oil and gas production tax to be diverted into a fund for transportation. Even with the current natural gas boom, this will only generate an estimated $1.2 billion a year, well short of the $4 billion a year necessary to maintain current Texas roads. This measure was approved by voters in November 2014.

### The Texas Department of Transportation

In 1991, the Texas Legislature created the Texas Department of Transportation, which combined the Texas Department of Highways with the Texas Motor Vehicle Commission and the Texas Department of Aviation. The five-member Texas Highway Commission oversees the TxDOT. The commissioners are appointed by the governor, subject to Texas Senate approval. The commissioners serve staggered, six-year terms. As of 1991, Texas law requires at least one commissioner come from a rural part of the state. The commission's job is to plan and oversee construction and maintenance of Texas highways and to develop mass transportation systems. In addition to the commission, the TxDOT employs an executive director, which until 2009 was required by law to be a professional engineer. Today, the TxDOT is comprised of around 12,000 employees and enjoys an annual budget of $18.6 billion.[46]

As Texas's population growth has continued to outpace that of the rest of the country, Texas road construction has been increasingly strained. The TxDOT has recently come under fire for being bloated and inefficient. A 2008 Texas sunset review of the TxDOT was scathing in its criticism, pointing to an atmosphere of distrust within the agency and calling for more transparency. The review specifically called for the TxDOT to undergo more frequent **sunset reviews**—every four years rather than the typical twelve-year review cycle—to assess its effectiveness. It also recommended abolishing the five-member commission and the current executive director and replacing them with

**Sunset review process**
a formal assessment of the effectiveness of all statutory boards, commissions, and state agencies.

a single commissioner. The state's legislature has largely ignored the review's recommendations. The TxDOT also saw its popularity tank as a result of the attempt by that agency, along with Governor Perry, to build the Trans-Texas Corridor. The TxDOT's reputation for mismanagement came under fire again in 2007 when it made an accounting error that caused the agency to overestimate its revenue by $1.1 billion. When the TxDOT again made news in 2012, this time for finding an extra $2 billion, state representative David Simpson concluded that "an agency that can miss a billion dollars and then find a billion dollars has got some problems."[47] Most recently the TxDOT made headlines when it announced its current plans include pulling up existing paved roads in the state and replacing them with gravel roads.

### Public-Private Partnerships

Faced with increasing populations and decreasing funds to build roads, in 2002 Governor Perry began to advocate for **public-private partnerships (PPPs)**. PPPs allow government infrastructure to be built by private investment entities seeking to profit and create alternative funding in the cash-strapped state. Texas attempted to encourage such projects when the legislature passed the 2011 Texas Public and Private Facilities Infrastructure Act to help facilitate PPPs. In the case of Texas roads, PPPs would allow private corporations to build roads and charge tolls for use of those roads. The money generated from the tolls goes to the private firm rather than state coffers. Throughout his tenure, Governor Perry was one of the most vocal advocates for privatizing toll roads.

**Public-private partnerships (PPPs)** government infrastructure built by private companies for profit.

The most ambitious example of a PPP was Perry's proposal for the Trans-Texas Corridor (TTC). The Trans-Texas Corridor was a proposed 4,000-mile network of tollways that included six passenger lanes and four commercial truck lanes. The 1,200-foot-wide corridor would also have included two high-speed rail lines, two commuter rail lines, two freight rail lines, and utility lines for water, oil, fiber optics, and natural gas. Texas's portion of the so-called NAFTA superhighway, connecting Mexico to Canada, would have cost an estimated $175 billion.

Criticisms of the TTC were swift and bipartisan. In particular, parts of the TTC were going to be outsourced to a Spanish-based firm called Cintra, which would fund portions of the TTC and then collect the tolls for those roads for the next fifty years. Texans bristled at the idea of paying a foreign-owned company for the use of roads in their state. Moreover, the TTC would be built on approximately 5,000 current acres of farmland, which the state would claim under its power of eminent domain. For Texas farmers, taking prime Texas farmland for a road that would be the width of four football fields ran afoul of their preference for small, nonintrusive government. Texans across the political spectrum vehemently opposed the plan. Although the TTC was eventually declared dead by the TxDOT, parts of the TTC remain, most notably the construction of I-69, which will connect Laredo to Texarkana via Houston to facilitate the traffic moving goods from Mexico to the rest of the country.

Although the TTC appears to be effectively dead, the use of PPP toll roads as a means to build roads in the state has flourished. Toll roads such as 121 connecting Collin County to Denton County and 130 in Austin are public-private partnerships.

The North Texas Tollway Authority (NTTA), a private company, paid $3 billion for the right to turn 121 into a tollway. The NTTA updated and extended the highway, which it renamed the Sam Rayburn Tollway. After raising rates several times, the NTTA board voted in 2009 to automatically raise rates every two years. In 2012, a driver who traveled the current length of 121 paid $3.06 ZipCash one way. So for Texans who drove the tollway to and from work five days a week, the cost was around $30 per week.

Proponents of using PPPs to build toll roads argue that it provides Texas with a means to build desperately needed roads that the state would not otherwise be able to afford. They also claim that private firms will be driven by competition and desire for profit to use new technologies and other efficiencies to provide these routes as cheaply as possible. Opponents contend that tolls amount to a back-door tax and point out that private firms are free to set their own rates and raise them at will. Critics also point out that the fifty-year contracts are too long and create monopolies rather than foster private competition. Toll roads remain politically attractive in the legislature, however, as they amount to a fee on citizens across the state while allowing Texas politicians to claim they did not raise taxes.

As stated above, private companies can raise the prices of tolls annually. For example, builders of toll roads in Central Texas announced that their rates would increase by 25 to 50 percent in January 2013, although the original proposal kept tolls at their initial levels until 2015.[48] By comparison, in the past, Texas toll roads were treated as a public good rather than a for-profit industry. For example, the Texas Turnpike Authority completed Interstate 30 as a toll road in 1957. The highway took seventeen years to pay off, and in 1977 the state took over the road and removed the toll booths. Not only have new roads increasingly been built based on a toll or user fee, but Governor Perry advocated turning roads that are paid for into toll roads, including Interstate 30. More recently, the Texas Turnpike Corporation proposed building a private toll road connecting Wylie to Greenville, which is located northeast of Dallas. Unlike PPPs, this road would be the first in the state to be owned and operated entirely by a private corporation. The potential for a wholly private toll road raises significant questions about the role of government in providing public goods, not the least of which is to what extent can the private company use eminent domain.

Texas transportation expansion faces increasing financial difficulties, and the state must start preparing for the future. As the recession continued and gas prices soared, many Texans began driving less, thus generating less state revenue for building roads. During the 1990s, Texans preferred big trucks and SUVs, which tended to be particularly fuel inefficient, but Texans have responded to increased gas prices by buying more fuel-efficient cars, which further decreases state revenue generated by the gas tax. An increase in the number of electric and hybrid vehicles will generate little or no fuel tax revenue. Clearly, Texas will have to reexamine how it is going to pay for its transportation needs. Politicians want to avoid increasing the gas tax, so utilizing toll roads and private funding are more politically attractive choices. State senator John Carona advocated indexing the gas tax to inflation, which would allow the gas tax to keep up with increased prices without politicians having to actually vote to raise taxes. However, this proposal has, predictably, been unpopular among state lawmakers. Moreover, ending the pay-as-you-go system in the state has resulted in desperately needed dollars from the existing gas tax being used to pay interest on loans rather than being applied toward building new roads. At the same time, surges in Texas's population and deteriorating infrastructure are causing an unprecedented transportation crisis in the state, and addressing transportation needs is becoming politically difficult. As Texans have begun to feel the financial pinch of the numerous toll roads emerging across the state, the popularity of those roads has plummeted. Gregg Abbott responded at the 2014 State Republican Convention with a promise to fix Texas roads without either raising taxes or adding toll roads.

## Mass Transit

While Texas is facing serious problems with regard to its highway system, the mass transit situation in the state has been slow to get off the ground. Texas recognized its need for mass transportation in the 1850s when a system of stage coaches moved people around the state. Even then, the stage coach lines made much of their profit from government contracts to carry mail.[49] Until recently, Texas has paid little attention to developing mass transit infrastructure. Only bigger urban centers have some form of light rail, and even those are relatively recent projects and remain limited. Texas didn't open its first light rail until 1996 when Dallas Area Rapid Transit (DART) opened its first line. Houston's MetroRail opened a 7.5-mile stretch in 2004, and Austin opened Capital MetroRail in 2010. Other major urban areas, including San Antonio and Corpus Christi, still do not have any light rail service. DART has expanded to operate the most miles of light rail in the United States. Senator Kay Bailey Hutchison points to DART as a model for transportation success in the country today. Other light rail systems, such as Houston's, have struggled to get off the ground and faced delays and funding issues. By 2012, MetroRail had built only one segment of its original five-line proposal and did not expect additional lines to be completed before 2014.

Texas's neglect of light rail systems significantly costs the state. When the federal government offered grants for high-speed rail as part of a 2010 stimulus package, Texas was caught unprepared. In fact, Texas received only $11 million, or 1.3 percent, of the available grant money.[50] By comparison, California received $2.5 billion of the same federal funds. In order to attract federal funds, Texas needs a statewide plan for mass transit.

Although the state was unprepared to accept federal money, some Texas cities have fared much better. DART received a $700 million federal grant in 2006 to help expand its light rail system, and in 2011, Houston received $900 million in federal grants to be paid over five years. Texas, though late to the mass transit party, is starting to catch up. In 2009, the legislature passed a bill that requires the TxDOT to develop a statewide passenger rail transportation plan and creates a rail division within the agency. Nonetheless, it will take time for Texas's mass transit infrastructure to match that of other states.

## WINNERS AND LOSERS

Texas's thriving economy, increasing urbanization, and constant population growth are creating serious stress on the state's roads and highways, with no end in sight. The state needs roads, and it is going to have to find a way to pay for those roads. Texas continues to have one of the lowest gas taxes in the country. As long as politicians see increasing the gasoline tax as politically unviable, poor road infrastructure and private, often foreign, ownership of Texas roads appear inevitable. Politicians, who like to claim they have not raised taxes, are the winners in this story. The reality, though, is that toll roads amount to what some call a hidden tax. As the state's population booms and transportation infrastructure fails to keep pace, more citizens will be paying that tax. The private companies that operate the toll roads have an incentive to continue to raise tolls, and they don't face the political backlash that politicians do. Those increased tolls do not go to pay the state's bills. Arguably, raising the gasoline tax would be better for Texans since it is not a hidden tax and would be put toward paying for collective goods. Even a significant increase of the gas tax is unlikely to be as expensive as the costs associated with regular toll road use. Texans, particularly those in large cities who increasingly face the choice of paying the tolls or spending hours in traffic, lose.

More critical for Texans is the move from a pay-as-you-go system of funding transportation to borrowing money to fund the building of roads. This move was designed to allow Texans to keep up with increased demands on roads. In reality, the state now spends much of its meager transportation budget financing its debt. As Texas now spends more on servicing the debt than on building roads, it is Texans who lose. As urbanization and population pressures continue, Texas will have to look toward expanding its transportation network, which means it will need to pay more attention to mass transit and even high-speed rail.

★ What are the costs to Texans if politicians do not raise the state's gasoline tax?

★ How does the elimination of pay-as-you-go funding requirements affect the state's ability to continue to meet its transportation needs?

★ What changes should the Texas Legislature make to reform transportation policy?

★ When weighing the pros and cons of highways, mass transit, and high-speed trains, what should Texas's transportation priorities be?

## IMMIGRATION POLICY

Texas has always been an immigrant state. Early Texas attracted immigrants from Spain and France. Mexican Texas attracted Anglos from America as well as continued European immigration. Even as Stephen F. Austin established a legal colony, other Anglos flooded into Texas illegally. For Spain, Mexico, and eventually the United States, governing early Texas depended in part on populating the vast frontier. Beginning in the early 1800s, Texas attracted a significant immigrant population of Germans, along with Poles, Czechs, Swedes, and others. In 1871, the state legislature created the Texas Bureau of Immigration in order to attract immigrants. Although that bureau did not last more than a few years, the waves of immigrants continued. Recent Texas immigrants are more likely to come from Latino or Asian countries. The state's identity has always been entrenched in the immigrant's story—the story of risking everything to come to a strange and rough land and making a life from nothing. Immigration was critical to Spain's inability to control the frontier, it was central to Texans declaring independence from Mexico, and it remains crucial to the state's current economy.

Texas unveiled the new Tejanos monument on the grounds of the capitol in Austin in 2012. The monument celebrates the contributions of Mexican and Spanish settlers to Texas.

While Texans feel a kinship to the immigrant story, they are less tolerant of undocumented immigrants, especially as the economy has worsened in recent years. High rates of unemployment lead to worries that undocumented immigrants are taking jobs. It remains unclear, however, to what extent those jobs would be filled by native Texans. For example, when the national government cracked down on the use of illegal immigrants, the Pilgrim's Pride plants in East Texas had a hard time replacing that workforce. Locals complained that the hours were long and the pay low at the chicken plant. Chicken mogul Bo Pilgrim testified that the country depends on the labor of illegal immigrants. After years of having a "Help Wanted" sign outside and being unable to fill jobs with local workers, Pilgrim's Pride in Nacogdoches eventually hired hundreds of refugees from Burma to debone chicken in its factory there. In 2006, Bo Pilgrim, along with thirty other Texas business leaders, including Texas homebuilders, hotel managers, and automobile dealers, signed an op-ed piece that argued that undocumented laborers were critical to their industries.

Still, the story of immigration in Texas remains a complicated one. Clearly immigration issues moved to the forefront of Texas concerns when the economy stagnated. In the 82nd legislative session, over forty bills were introduced that dealt with immigration issues. Those bills included the now-defunct sanctuary city legislation, an e-verify bill that required I-9 information to be electronically filed in a national database, and a bill that would have prohibited county registrars from issuing birth certificates to children born to documented or undocumented immigrants in the state. None of this legislation passed, including the sanctuary city bill, which was opposed by several police groups. Although immigration is a federal issue, the sanctuary city bill would have required local law enforcement officers to check immigration status on everyone they pulled over. By contrast, the 83rd Legislature, perhaps in acknowledgment of the rapidly changing demographics of the state, largely avoided immigration issues.

In some ways, the debate over illegal immigrants tells us more about Texas politics than immigration itself. In reality, immigration is a federal issue, and the U.S. Citizenship and Immigration Services is taking the lead in sealing the country's borders and managing the flow of legal immigrants into the country. Despite this, many state and local officials continue to make public proclamations and pass new rules. In May 2007, the town of Farmers Branch, Texas, made national headlines by passing an ordinance that would punish landlords for renting to undocumented immigrants in that city. In 2012, a federal appeals court ruled the ban unconstitutional.

### Costs and Benefits of Undocumented Workers

Some of this conflict results from differences among Texans over the costs and benefits of immigration. Other debates emerge because the costs and benefits of immigration policy fall unevenly. It is estimated that while undocumented immigrants cost the state of Texas $1.16 billion, they pay $1.58 billion in state taxes and fees. While the state enjoys a net benefit from undocumented immigrants, however, local governments often feel the pinch, paying the lion's share of costs for services such as indigent care, law enforcement, and other services that result from the presence of immigrants while bringing in only a small fraction in taxes.

An increase in government taxing and spending is not the only impact of an estimated 1.4 million undocumented immigrants in Texas. The comptroller's office estimated that the absence of those immigrants would cost the state's economy $17.7 billion.[51] The distribution of costs and benefits to the government and the private sector reflects the origins of some divisions. Clearly, many Texas cities and school districts bear a disproportionate burden from undocumented immigrants. At the same time, these workers were drawn to Texas by the promise of wages from businesses that then benefited from their labors. The forces of the free market drew these immigrants into the U.S. economy, if not into citizenship.

The fate of Cactus, Texas, after immigration raids illustrates the degree to which some businesses and local economies rely on immigrant labor. On December 12, 2006, Immigration and Custom Enforcement (ICE) officers raided the Swift meatpacking plants in Cactus, a small town of 2,639 in the Texas Panhandle, arresting 292 workers. Some of those arrested had lived and worked in Cactus over fifteen years, and their arrests left behind upset families and large numbers of job openings that Swift scrambled to fill. As these families and the community tried to patch themselves together, the plant, now woefully shorthanded, found itself offering employees who referred good job candidates a bonus of $650 for unskilled candidates and $1,500 for experienced ones.[52] As other industries that rely on immigrant labor have also found, it is often difficult to fill jobs that immigrants do.

# TEXAS AND THE FED ON *Immigration*

Traditionally, immigration policy has been viewed as the specific purview of the national government. State governments have police powers within their borders, but it has generally been the job of the U.S. Congress and the president to craft a national immigration policy. In recent years, most Americans agree that comprehensive immigration reform is needed, but what that reform should look like remains a matter of contention. Some argue that we should streamline the process for would-be immigrants and create a path to citizenship for those unauthorized immigrants who have been living in the United States for a long time. Others contend that we should tighten security on our borders and advocate such measures as increasing the number of border patrol agents, relying more on aerial drones, and building fences along the border. The latter group maintains that the national government has failed to do its job to secure the country's borders. When Texas witnessed a significant increase in unaccompanied minors showing up along its border with Mexico in the summer of 2014, the two views of immigration collided.

Rick Perry, then governor, responded to the influx of unaccompanied children by both calling for national action and mobilizing Texas's National Guard, stating that "Texas can't afford to wait for Washington to act on this crisis."[i] President Obama urged Congress to pass reform before it adjourned for the summer, but it failed to do so. Interestingly, both U.S. House Speaker John Boehner and Perry urged the president to undertake unilateral action. As Perry revealed in an interview, "I was like, Mr. President, you can deal with this. You can unilaterally direct the Department of Defense to put those troops on the border."[ii]

As the state and national government argue over what the appropriate action should be, local governments are getting in on the game. Two Texas counties (Tom Green and Galveston), along with one Texas city (League City), passed resolutions prohibiting even temporary housing of immigrants. Legal specialists declared the resolutions unenforceable, and local leaders noted that the resolutions represent their unhappiness with how the federal government has failed to address the immigration issue.[iii]

★ What responsibility does the federal government have toward immigrants?

★ Can states govern immigration policy if they believe the national government is not adequately addressing the issue? Explain your answer.

★ What authority, if any, should local governments have to deal with an influx of immigrants?

---

i. David Saleh Rauf, "State Leaders OK Plan to Increase Border Patrol," *Houston Chronicle*, June 18, 2014.

ii. "Texas Gov. Perry: Illegal Immigrant Surge a 'Humanitarian Crisis' Obama Can Stop," Fox News, July 10, 2014, www.foxnews.com/politics/2014/07/10/texas-gov-perry-illegal-immigrant-surge-humanitarian-crisis-obama-has-power-to/ (accessed September 12, 2014).

iii. Gilad Edelman and Terri Langford, "Texas Cities Pushing Back on Border Surge," *Texas Tribune*, July 21, 2014, www.texastribune.org/2014/07/21/texas-cities-pushing-back-border-surge/ (accessed September 12, 2014).

---

While the influx of people into the United States remains a federal issue, border states such as Texas bear the burden of delivering the promises made in the U.S. Constitution. One of the most important legal cases in the dispute over illegal immigration occurred in Tyler, Texas. In the 1982 case *Plyler v. Doe*,[53] the U.S. Supreme Court ruled that School Superintendent Jim Plyler could not charge undocumented immigrants residing in Tyler $1,000 in tuition to attend public schools. In the majority opinion written by Justice William Brennan, himself the son of Irish immigrants, the Court pointed out that the Fourteenth Amendment required that states provide equal protection of the law to "any person within its jurisdiction" and that the language of that amendment had been intentionally designed to protect the rights of aliens living in the United States.[54] Reflecting on the decision more than twenty years later, in 2007, Plyler remarked, "It would have been one of the worst things to happen in education—they'd cost more not being educated."[55]

Immigrants from Central America who crossed into Texas from Mexico await transportation to a U.S. Border Patrol processing center.

The realization that Texas benefits from educating its immigrant population was one of the driving forces behind the 2001 Texas Dream Act. That act allows undocumented immigrants to pay in-state tuition rates at Texas state universities if they graduated from a Texas high school, have lived in the state at least three years, and are in the process of seeking legal residence. Texas was the first state to pass a dream act, and another seventeen states have since adopted their own versions.

It became clear in the spring of 2014 that Texas and other border states were facing a larger than usual number of immigrants attempting to cross the border. The number of unaccompanied minors arriving had been steady since 2011, with a marked increase beginning in late 2013. These children are typically fleeing violence in Honduras, Guatemala, or El Salvador. Their families, who may pay $6,000 to $10,000 to so-called coyotes to transport the children to the United States, are often told their children will be allowed to stay once in the country. Texas cities scrambled to deal with the large influx of children, which reached record numbers in June 2014. Governor Perry ordered a surge on the border, authorizing the Texas Department of Public Safety to spend an additional $1.3 million a week and in July authorizing the deployment of up to 1,000 Texas National Guard troops to stop the flow of children across the border. The U.S. Congress went on summer recess without passing any measure to address the crisis. In the interim, Texas towns pulled together resources to feed, house, and educate the immigrants as they waited to be processed by national immigration.

The issue of immigration captures the state's ongoing struggle with change and the two political parties' attempts to balance the new versus the old. The political dynamic behind one side of the immigration debate was illustrated by former Republican congressman Dick Armey, for years one of the state's leading conservatives, who complained that after years of Republicans courting Hispanic voters in Texas, his party was throwing away its future on the immigration issue. As Armey articulated the issue, "Who is the genius that said, 'Now that we've identified that [the Hispanic community] is the fastest growing demographic in American, let's do everything we can to make sure we offend them?' Who is the genius that came up with that bright idea?"[56] The state's Republican Party continues to grapple with how it will reconcile immigration issues in the state. On the one hand, conservative elements within the party, who are more likely to vote in primary contests, favor stricter immigration laws. Some have suggested it was Perry's support of the state's Dream Act legislation that led to his decline in popularity in the 2012 presidential race.[57] On the other hand, Hispanics remain the fastest-growing demographic in the state. Hispanics in Texas are also more likely to support the Republican Party than Hispanics in other parts of the country.[58] The state's recent legislative session, in which legislators largely ignored immigration policy rather than take a controversial stance, reflected these opposing forces and the pending identity problem of the Texas Republican Party. How Republicans address immigration in the near future will directly impact their future viability as the dominant party in the state.

## WINNERS AND LOSERS

While some Texans worry that immigration from Mexico will transform the politics of Texas, a broader view of our history reveals that change is the Texas way of life. Native American populations were challenged by the Spanish and later the Mexican governments; those governments would, in turn, see themselves pushed out by the Anglo settlers who first moved Texas to independence and then to statehood. Texas's union with the United States was quickly undone by secession and the decision to join the Confederate States. The end of the Civil War saw Texas's return to the United States, but under very different terms imposed by the Radical Republicans, whose Reconstruction government was rooted in the North. Eventually, Reconstruction ended, leaving Texas to find its way through a century that saw more demographic than political change. During the last 125 years, Texas has seen its population explode as immigrants from all over the United States and the world have converged on the state, once again seeking the opportunity promised by the area.

With so many immigrants continuing to come to Texas, who wins? According to the state's comptroller, the Texas economy clearly benefits from immigrants who come into the state and often work low-paying jobs. Texas industry wins, as it is able to fill low-wage jobs that are often unappealing to native-born Texans. Texas's tradition of immigration and its very "pull yourself up by your bootstraps" identity forms the heart of the immigrant story. Texans also win due to the state's Dream Act since educating the immigrant population creates an even more productive workforce. Nonetheless, as local governments bear the costs from undocumented immigrants while the state government enjoys the bulk of the economic benefit from them, local governments lose in the economic calculus.

★ What are the benefits of Texas's high rate of immigration?

★ What are the costs of undocumented immigration in the state, and to what extent are those costs disproportionately shared?

★ To what extent do industries in Texas depend on undocumented workers?

## CONCLUSION

Nothing is more legendary in Texas than the state's relationship with oil. As Texas moves toward the future, its reliance on oil, coal, and natural gas will likely need to be augmented by alternative energy sources. Texas has always been blessed by its large endowment of land. The state's vast plains make it ideal for harnessing wind and solar energy, and the state has the potential to lead the country in new energy sources, much as it did with oil and gas. Texas also must increasingly look to its strained resources, such as water, as it struggles with how to be a good steward of its greatest endowment. The state's ability to deal with fundamental changes in everything from environmental policy and adequate natural resources to sufficient transportation will define its future. Texas has never stayed the same, and it remains in the enviable position of being a place where people can find numerous opportunities to better their lives. This promise of opportunities that draws one set of people to Texas today will inevitably draw others in the future, and the immigrants from Central and South America are only the latest chapter in the changes that have defined the state.

Occasionally, we become so engrossed in recounting our colorful and larger-than-life traditions that we don't notice that dramatic events such as the battle of the Alamo may have been the markers of great change, but that change has always been with us. This is not surprising. As each regime departs, it leaves behind a little of its legacy, its traditions, and its own legends. The Texas policies discussed in this chapter each display markers of these legacies and traditions while at the same time illustrating how modern demands are forcing change.

Texas's myths and legends are often stories of change. Stephen F. Austin became the "Father of Texas" by bringing new settlers to the state before he played a key role in the revolutionary movement that those settlers then brought about. The battle of the Alamo was a pivotal point in the transition from Mexican to American rule, and it immediately served as a powerful symbol that motivated the Texas army to defeat Santa Anna's army at San Jacinto.

What is especially appealing about many of Texas's legends is the degree to which we Texans all share them. Standing in the line to visit the Alamo, you will encounter people of every race. These people are drawn to the Alamo not because the battle there was between the Anglo and Mexican forces but because the battle defines a dynamic state that draws people of every race and nationality. The defenders of the Alamo took their stand *for* change rather than against it, and future generations of Texans will—each in their own way—do the same.

### for CQ Press

Sharpen your skills with **SAGE edge** at **edge.sagepub.com/collier4e**. **SAGE edge for students** provides a personalized approach to help you accomplish your coursework goals in an easy-to-use learning environment.

## KEY TERMS

eminent domain (p. 479)

fracking (p. 479)

Good Roads Amendment (p. 491)

negative externality (p. 481)

public-private partnerships (PPPs) (p. 493)

regulation (p. 481)

rule of capture (p. 484)

sunset review process (p. 492)

Texas Commission on Environmental
Quality (TCEQ) (p. 482)

## CORE ASSESSMENT

1. To what extent do you have a responsibility to protect the environment?

2. How should the state balance economic gains associated with oil and natural gas against environmental dangers and lack of water?

3. What is the optimal way for Texas to pay for roads in the future?

# APPENDIX

## DECLARATION OF INDEPENDENCE OF THE REPUBLIC OF TEXAS

### UNANIMOUS DECLARATION OF INDEPENDENCE, BY THE DELEGATES OF THE PEOPLE OF TEXAS, IN GENERAL CONVENTION, AT THE TOWN OF WASHINGTON, ON THE SECOND DAY OF MARCH, 1836

When a government has ceased to protect the lives, liberty and property of the people from whom its legitimate powers are derived, and for the advancement of whose happiness it was instituted; and so far from being a guarantee for the enjoyment of those inestimable and inalienable rights, becomes an instrument in the hands of evil rulers for their oppression; when the Federal Republican Constitution of their country, which they have sworn to support, no longer has a substantial existence, and the whole nature of their government has been forcibly changed without their consent, from a restricted federative republic, composed of sovereign states, to a consolidated central military despotism, in which every interest is disregarded but that of the army and the priesthood—both the eternal enemies of civil liberty, and the ever-ready minions of power, and the usual instruments of tyrants; When long after the spirit of the Constitution has departed, moderation is at length, so far lost, by those in power that even the semblance of freedom is removed, and the forms, themselves, of the constitution discontinued; and so far from their petitions and remonstrances being regarded, the agents who bear them are thrown into dungeons; and mercenary armies sent forth to force a new government upon them at the point of the bayonet. When in consequence of such acts of malfeasance and abdication, on the part of the government, anarchy prevails, and civil society is dissolved into its original elements: In such a crisis, the first law of nature, the right of self-preservation— the inherent and inalienable right of the people to appeal to first principles and take their political affairs into their own hands in extreme cases—enjoins it as a right towards themselves and a sacred obligation to their posterity, to abolish such government and create another in its stead, calculated to rescue them from impending dangers, and to secure their future welfare and happiness. Nations, as well as individuals, are amenable for their acts to the public opinion of mankind. A statement of a part of our grievances is, therefore, submitted to an impartial world, in justification of the hazardous but unavoidable step now taken of severing our political connection with the Mexican people, and assuming an independent attitude among the nations of the earth.

The Mexican government, by its colonization laws, invited and induced the Anglo-American population of Texas to colonize its wilderness under the pledged faith of a written constitution, that they should continue to enjoy that constitutional liberty and republican government to which they had been habituated in the land of their birth, the

United States of America. In this expectation they have been cruelly disappointed, inasmuch as the Mexican nation has acquiesced in the late changes made in the government by General Antonio Lopez de Santa Anna, who, having overturned the constitution of his country, now offers us the cruel alternative either to abandon our homes, acquired by so many privations, or submit to the most intolerable of all tyranny, the combined despotism of the sword and the priesthood.

It has sacrificed our welfare to the state of Coahuila, by which our interests have been continually depressed, through a jealous and partial course of legislation carried on at a far distant seat of government, by a hostile majority, in an unknown tongue; and this too, notwithstanding we have petitioned in the humblest terms, for the establishment of a separate state government, and have, in accordance with the provisions of the national constitution, presented the general Congress, a republican constitution which was without just cause contemptuously rejected.

It incarcerated in a dungeon, for a long time, one of our citizens, for no other cause but a zealous endeavor to procure the acceptance of our constitution and the establishment of a state government.

It has failed and refused to secure on a firm basis, the right of trial by jury; that palladium of civil liberty, and only safe guarantee for the life, liberty, and property of the citizen.

It has failed to establish any public system of education, although possessed of almost boundless resources (the public domain) and, although, it is an axiom, in political science, that unless a people are educated and enlightened it is idle to expect the continuance of civil liberty, or the capacity for self-government.

It has suffered the military commandants stationed among us to exercise arbitrary acts of oppression and tyranny; thus trampling upon the most sacred rights of the citizen and rendering the military superior to the civil power.

It has dissolved by force of arms, the state Congress of Coahuila and Texas, and obliged our representatives to fly for their lives from the seat of government; thus depriving us of the fundamental political right of representation.

It has demanded the surrender of a number of our citizens, and ordered military detachments to seize and carry them into the Interior for trial; in contempt of the civil authorities, and in defiance of the laws and constitution.

It has made piratical attacks upon our commerce; by commissioning foreign desperadoes, and authorizing them to seize our vessels, and convey the property of our citizens to far distant ports of confiscation.

It denies us the right of worshipping the Almighty according to the dictates of our own consciences, by the support of a national religion calculated to promote the temporal interests of its human functionaries rather than the glory of the true and living God.

It has demanded us to deliver up our arms; which are essential to our defense, the rightful property of freemen, and formidable only to tyrannical governments.

It has invaded our country, both by sea and by land, with intent to lay waste our territory and drive us from our homes; and has now a large mercenary army advancing to carry on against us a war of extermination.

It has, through its emissaries, incited the merciless savage, with the tomahawk and scalping knife, to massacre the inhabitants of our defenseless frontiers.

It hath been, during the whole time of our connection with it, the contemptible sport and victim of successive military revolutions and hath continually exhibited every characteristic of a weak, corrupt and tyrannical government.

These, and other grievances, were patiently borne by the people of Texas until they reached that point at which forbearance ceases to be a virtue. We then took up arms in defense of the national constitution. We appealed to our Mexican brethren for assistance. Our appeal has been made in vain. Though months have elapsed, no sympathetic

response has yet been heard from the Interior. We are, therefore, forced to the melancholy conclusion that the Mexican people have acquiesced in the destruction of their liberty, and the substitution therefor of a military government—that they are unfit to be free and incapable of self-government.

The necessity of self-preservation, therefore, now decrees our eternal political separation.

We, therefore, the delegates, with plenary powers, of the people of Texas, in solemn convention assembled, appealing to a candid world for the necessities of our condition, do

hereby resolve and DECLARE that our political connection with the Mexican nation has forever ended; and that the people of Texas do now constitute a FREE, SOVEREIGN and INDEPENDENT REPUBLIC, and are fully invested with all the rights and attributes which properly belong to the independent nations; and, conscious of the rectitude of our intentions, we fearlessly and confidently commit the issue to the decision of the Supreme Arbiter of the destinies of nations.

RICHARD ELLIS, president of the convention and Delegate from Red River.

| | | | |
|---|---|---|---|
| Charles B. Stewart | Wm B. Scates | Sam P. Carson | James Power |
| Thos Barnett | M. B. Menard | A. Briscoe | Sam Houston |
| John S. D. Byrom | A. B. Hardin | J. B. Woods | David Thomas |
| Franco Ruiz | J. W. Bunton | Jas Collinsworth | Edwd Conrad |
| J. Antonio Navarro | Thos J. Gasley | Edwin Waller | Martin Parmer |
| Jesse B. Badgett | R. M. Coleman | Asa Brigham | Edwin O. LeGrand |
| Wm D. Lacey | Sterling C. Robertson | Geo. C. Childress | Stephen W. Blount |
| William Menefee | Benj. Briggs Goodrich | Bailey Hardeman | Jas Gaines |
| Jno Fisher | G. W. Barnett | Rob. Potter | Wm Clark, Jr. |
| Mathew Caldwell | James G. Swisher | Thomas Jefferson | Sydney O. Penington |
| William Mottley | Jesse Grimes | Rusk | Wm Carrol Crawford |
| Lorenzo de Zavala | S. Rhoads Fisher | Chas. S. Taylor | Jno Turner |
| Stephen H. Everitt | John W. Moore | John S. Roberts | Test. H. S. Kimble, |
| Geo W. Smyth | John W. Bower | Robert Hamilton | Secretary |
| Elijah Stapp | Saml A. Maverick | Collin McKinney | |
| Claiborne West | from Bejar | Albert H. Latimer | |

# NOTES

## CHAPTER 1

1. Clint Skinner, *Six Flags Over Texas: Fifty Years of Entertainment* (Clint Skinner, 2011), 43

2. V. O. Key, *Southern Politics in State and Nation* (Knoxville: University of Tennessee Press, 1984), 267.

3. Ben Barnes with Lisa Dickey, *Barn Burning Barn Building: Tales of Political Life, from LBJ through George W. Bush and Beyond* (Albany, Texas: Bright Sky Press, 2006), 168.

4. John Steinbeck, *Travels with Charley: In Search of America* (New York: Bantam Books, 1961), 231.

5. Randolph B. Campbell, *Gone to Texas* (New York: Oxford University Press, 2004), 15.

6. James L. Haley, *Passionate Nation: The Epic History of Texas* (New York: Free Press, 2006), 6.

7. Campbell, *Gone to Texas,* 41.

8. Ibid., 85.

9. Ibid., 88.

10. Ibid., 80.

11. Ibid., 186.

12. Haley, *Passionate Nation,* 272.

13. Campbell, *Gone to Texas,* 207.

14. Ibid., 299.

15. Ibid., 350–351.

16. Ibid., 366.

17. Christine Barbour and Gerald C. Wright, *Keeping the Republic,* 4th brief ed. (Washington, D.C.: CQ Press, 2011), 23.

18. Daniel J. Elazar, *American Federalism: A View from the State* (New York: Thomas Y. Crowell, 1966), 86.

19. Colin Woodard, *American Nations: A History of the Eleven Rival Regional Cultures of North America* (New York: Viking, 2011).

20. Bill Bishop, *The Big Sort: Why the Clustering of Like-Minded American Is Tearing Us Apart* (New York: Houghton Mifflin Harcourt, 2009).

21. "In Texas, 31% Say State Has Right to Secede from U.S., but 75% Opt to Stay," Rasmussen Reports, April 17, 2009, www.rasmussenreports.com/public_content/politics/general_state_surveys/texas/in_texas_31_say_state_has_right_to_secede_from_u_s_but_75_opt_to_stay (accessed August 24, 2014).

22. Randolph B. Campbell, "History and Collective Memory in Texas: The Entangled Stories of the Lone Star State," in *Lone Star Pasts: Memory and History in Texas,* eds. Greg Cantrell and Elizabeth Hayes Turner (College Station: Texas A&M University Press, 2007), 278–279.

23. Campbell, *Gone to Texas,* 15.

24. T. R. Fehrenbach, *Lone Star: A History of Texas and the Texans* (Cambridge, Mass.: Da Capo Press, 2000), 24.

25. Texas State Data Center population projections.

26. United States Census Bureau, "State and County Quick Facts," http://quickfacts.census.gov/qfd/states/48000.html (accessed August 25, 2014).

27. Office of the State Demographer, "Texas State Data Center 2012 Population Projections, 2000–2010 Migration Scenario," http://osd.state.tx.us/Resources/Presentations/OSD/2014/2014_02_24_Texas_Fiscal_Officers_Academy.pptx (accessed September 3, 2014).

28. U.S. Census Bureau, "Selected Social Characteristics in the United States: 2006–2008, American Community Survey: Texas," Selected Economic Characteristics, 2012 American Community Survey 1-Year Estimates, Census Bureau, http://factfinder2.census.gov/faces/tableservices/jsf/pages/productview.xhtml?pid=ACS_12_1YR_DP02&prodType=table (accessed September 3, 2014).

29. Andrew Dugan, "Texan Hispanics Tilt Democratic, but State Likely to Stay Red," Gallup Politics, February 7, 2014, www.gallup.com/poll/167339/texan-hispanics-tilt-democratic-state-likely-stay-red.aspx (accessed August 25, 2014).

30. U.S. Census Bureau, "Texas Dominates List of Fastest-Growing Large Cities since 2010 Census," Census Bureau Reports, June 28, 2012, www.census.gov/newsroom/releases/archives/population/cb12-117.html (accessed August 25, 2014).

31. U.S. Census Bureau, "Oil and Gas Boom Driving Population Growth in the Great Plains, Census Bureau Estimates Show," Census Bureau Reports, March 14, 2013, www.census.gov/newsroom/releases/archives/population/cb13-46.html (accessed August 25, 2014).

32. University of Texas/*Texas Tribune*, Texas Statewide Survey, June 2014, http://s3.amazonaws.com/static.texastribune.org/media/documents/uttt-jun2014-summary-all.pdf (accessed August 25, 2014), 21.

33. *Texas Almanac 2012–2013* (College Station: Texas A&M Press Consortium, 2011), 17.

34. Jared Bernstein, Elizabeth McNichol, and Karen Lyons, "Pulling Apart: A State-by-State Analysis of Income Trends," Center on Budget and Policy Priorities and Economic Policy Institute, January 2006.

35. James E. Crisp, *Sleuthing the Alamo: Davy Crockett's Last Stand and Other Mysteries of the Texas Revolution* (New York: Oxford University Press, 2004), 59.

36. Anna J. Hardwicke Pennybacker, *A New History of Texas for Schools* (Tyler, Texas, 1888), 49.

37. Terrence Stutz, "Texas Won't Cover Tejanos at Alamo," *Dallas Morning News*, March 12, 2010.

## CHAPTER 2

1. David Schmudde, "Constitutional Limitations on State Taxation of Nonresident Citizens," *Law Review of Michigan State University–Detroit College of Law* (Spring 1999): 95–169.

2. Ibid., 125.

3. Becca Aaronson, "Perry Directs HHSC to Pursue Medicaid Block Grant," *Texas Tribune*, September 16, 2013.

4. *South Dakota v. Dole*, 483 U.S. 203 (1987).

5. Thomas Dye, *American Federalism: Competition among Governments* (Lexington, Mass.: Lexington Books, 1989).

6. Robert T. Garrett, "Federal Judge Voids Texas' Gay Marriage Ban, Though He Delays Order from Taking Effect Immediately," *Dallas Morning News*, February 26, 2014.

7. Rick Perry, press release, March 21, 2010, http://governor.state.tx.us/news/press-release/14396/ (accessed September 3, 2014).

8. Newt Gingrich and Rick Perry, "Let the States Lead the Way," *The Washington Post*, November 6, 2009.

9. "Attorney General Abbott: Texas and Other States Will Challenge Federal Health Care Legislation," March 21, 2010, www.oag.state.tx.us/oagNews/release.php?id= 3269 (accessed September 3, 2014).

10. "Statement by Gov. Perry on Supreme Court Ruling Regarding Obamacare," Office of the Governor Rick Perry, June 28, 2012, http://governor.state.tx.us/news/press-release/17385/ (accessed September 3, 2014).

11. Randolph B. Campbell, *Gone to Texas* (New York: Oxford University Press, 2004).

12. Ibid.

13. Ibid.

14. Ibid.

15. Ibid.

16. "83rd Legislature's Regular Session: What Happened, What Didn't," *Texas Tribune*, May 28, 2013, www.texastribune.org/2013/05/28/83rd-lege-what-happened-and-what-didnt/ (accessed August 27, 2014).

17. Ibid.

18. Texas Constitution (1836), General Provisions, sec. 10.

19. Texas Constitution (1836), General Provisions, sec. 6.

20. Texas Constitution (1876), art. 6, sec. 2.

21. Cornyn, "The Roots of the Texas Constitution."

22. Roy R. Barkley and Mark F. Odintz, eds., *The Portable Handbook of Texas* (Austin: Texas State Historical Association, 2000).

23. Campbell, *Gone to Texas*.

24. Cornyn, "The Roots of the Texas Constitution."

25. Texas Constitution (1845), art. 3, sec. 1.

26. Joe Ericson, "An Inquiry into the Sources of the Texas Constitution," PhD diss., Texas Tech University, 1957. See also Janice C. May, *The Texas State Constitution: A Reference Guide* (Westport, Conn.: Greenwood Press, 1996).

27. Campbell, *Gone to Texas*.

28. Texas Constitution (1866), art. 8, sec. 1.

29. Ericson, "An Inquiry into the Sources of the Texas Constitution."

30. May, *The Texas State Constitution*.

31. Ibid.

32. Texas Constitution (1876), art. 1, sec. 1.

33. Originally a state treasurer was also included in the plural executive, but this office was eventually dissolved.

34. Oklahoma is the only other state to have two high courts.

35. Calvert, De León, and Cantrell, *History of Texas*.

36. Only the constitutions of South Carolina, California, and Alabama have been amended more times.

37. Texas Secretary of State, "Turnout and Voter Registration Figures (1970–Current)," www.sos.state.tx.us/elections/historical/70-92.shtml (accessed September 16, 2014).

38. May, *The Texas State Constitution*.

39. Campbell, *Gone to Texas*, 371.

40. Bill Ratliff, quoted in Juan B. Elizondo Jr., "Time to Rewrite Constitution," *Austin American-Statesman*, October 28, 1999.

41. Bill Stouffer, chair of Common Cause Texas, quoted in Elizondo, "Time to Rewrite Constitution."

## CHAPTER 3

1. David Mutto, "The Brief: Texas Political News for August 14, 2013," *Texas Tribune*, August 14, 2013, www.texastribune.org/2013/08/14/brief-texas-political-news-aug-14-2013/ (accessed September 3, 2014).

2. Olivia Messer, "The Texas Legislature's Sexist Little Secret," *Texas Observer*, July 31, 2013, www.texasobserver.org/the-texas-legislatures-sexist-little-secret (accessed June 9, 2014).

3. "Editorial: Sexism in the Texas Legislature," *Dallas Morning News*, August 6, 2013, www.dallasnews.com/opinion/editorials/20130806-editorial-sexism-in-the-texas-legislature/ (accessed June 11, 2014); Carol Morgan, "Lechers in the Texas Legislature," *Lubbock Avalanche-Journal*, August 1, 2013, http://lubbockonline.com/interact/blog-post/carol-morgan/2013-08-01/lechers-texas-legislature (accessed June 11, 2014).

4. Center for American Women and Politics, Rutgers University, "Women in State Legislative Elections: 1992–2012," www.cawp.rutgers.edu/fast_facts/elections/documents/canwinleg_histst.pdf (accessed June 9, 2014).

5. Corrie MacLaggan, "Women Underrepresented in Texas Legislature," *Texas Tribune*, January 31, 2014, www.texastribune.org/2014/01/31/women-and-texas-legislature (accessed June 4, 2014).

6. Emily Ramshaw, "Despite Party Politics, HD-134 Foes Share Many Traits," *Texas Tribune*, October 15,

2012, www.texastribune
.org/2012/10/15/despite-part-politics-
hd-134-candidates-share-traits/
(accessed June 9, 2014).

7. James Madison, *Federalist* No. 51 in *The Federalist Papers*, ed. Clinton Rossiter (New York: Penguin Putnam, 1999), 288–293.

8. 369 U.S. 186 (1962).

9. 377 U.S. 533 (1964).

10. Audrey S. Wall, ed., *Book of the States*, vol. 44 (Lexington, Ky.: Council of State Governments, 2012), table 3.2.

11. Ibid.

12. Ibid.

13. Ibid.

14. Brandi Grissom et al., "Twenty Weeks in Texas in Which the Budget Held Sway," *Texas Tribune*, www.texastribune
.org/texas-legislature/82nd-legislative-
session/20-weeks-in-texas-in-which-
the-budget-held-sway/ (accessed September 5, 2014).

15. Ibid. (See footnote 18.)

16. Ibid.

17. "83rd Legislature's Regular Session: What Happened, What Didn't," *Texas Tribune*, May 28, 2013, www
.texastribune.org/2013/05/28/83rd-
lege-what-happened-and-what-didnt/
(accessed August 27, 2014).

18. Ibid.

19. National Council of State Legislatures, "NCSL Backgrounder: Full- and Part-Time Legislatures," www.ncsl
.org/?tabid=16701 (accessed August 10, 2010).

20. Ibid.

21. Texas Ethics Commission, "Commission Rules," chap. 501, para. 50.1.

22. All data for state legislative compensation from Wall, *The Book of the States*, vol. 44, 88–91, table 3.9.

23. Wall, *The Book of the States*, vol. 44, 104–109, table 3.13.

24. Peverill Squire, "Measuring State Legislative Professionalism: The Squire Index Revisited," *State Politics and Policy Quarterly* 7, no. 2 (2007): 211–227.

25. Texas State Constitution (1876), art. 3, sec. 6; art. 3, sec. 7.

26. Thomas M. Spencer, *The Legislative Process, Texas Style* (Pasadena, Tex.: San Jacinto College Press, 1981), 20–21.

27. Texas Constitution (1876), art. 3, sec. 8.

28. Wall, *The Book of the States*, vol. 44, 83–84, table 3.3.

29. Adapted from the National Conference of State Legislatures, "The Term Limited States," February 2013, www.ncsl.org/
legislatures-elections/legisdata/chart-of-
term-limits-states.aspx (accessed June 7, 2014).

30. Adapted from Kendra A. Hovey and Harold A. Hovey, *CQ's State Fact Finder* (Washington, D.C.: CQ Press, 2007), 109, table D-8; Keon Chi, ed., *The Book of the States*, vol. 36 (Lexington, Ky.: Council of State Governments, 2004), 85, table 3.4.

31. Audrey Wall, "2012 Legislative Elections," (Lexington, Ky.: Council of State Governments, 2013), available online at http://knowledgecenter.csg
.org/kc/content/2012-legislative-
elections (accessed June 7, 2014); Council of State Governments, *The Book of the States*, vol. 45, 61, table 3.4.

32. Legislative Reference Library of Texas, "81st Legislature (2009)—Statistical Profile," www.lrl.state
.tx.us/legis/profile81.html and "78th Legislature (2003)—Statistical Profile," www.lrl.state.tx.us/legis/profile78.html (both accessed August 27, 2014).

33. Peter Slevin, "After Adopting Term Limits, States Lose Female Legislators," *Washington Post*, April 22, 2007, A04.

34. Steven Smith, Jason M. Roberts, and Ryan J. Vander Wielen, *The American Congress*, 4th ed. (New York: Cambridge University Press, 2006), 26.

35. Ibid.

36. Quoted in Iain McLean, "Forms of Representation and Systems of Voting," in *Political Theory Today*, ed. David Held (Cambridge, UK: Polity Press, 1991), 173.

37. David M. Farrell, *Electoral Systems: A Comparative Introduction* (New York: Palgrave, 2001), 11.

38. Texas Constitution (1876), art. 3, sec. 2; art. 3, sec. 25.

39. Texas Legislative Council, "State and Federal Law Governing Redistricting in Texas," 2001, www.tlc.state.tx.us/
pubspol/redlaw01/redlaw01.pdf
(accessed August 28, 2014).

40. 379 U.S. 433.

41. *White v. Register*, 412 U.S. 755 (1973).

42. 478 U.S. 30.

43. Richard Matland and Deborah Brown, "District Magnitude's Effect on Female Representation in U.S. State Legislatures," *Legislative Studies Quarterly* 17 (November 1992): 462–492; Robert Darcy, Susan Welch, and Janet Clark, "Women Candidates in Single- and Multi-Member Districts: American State Legislative Races," *Social Science Quarterly* 66 (December 1985): 945–953; James King, "Single-Member Districts and the Representation of Women in American State Legislatures: The Effects of Electoral System Change," *State Politics and Policy Quarterly* 2 (June 2002): 161–175.

44. U.S. Department of the Interior, Census Office, *Report of the Population of the United States at the Eleventh Census: 1890* (Washington, D.C.: Government Printing Office, 1895), 41–42.

45. U.S. Census Bureau, "State and County Quick Facts: Nacogdoches County, Texas," 2007, http://quickfacts.census
.gov/qfd/states/48/48347.html (accessed August 27, 2014).

46. U.S. Census Bureau, "State and County Quick Facts: Dallas County, Texas," 2007, http://quickfacts.census.gov/qfd/
states/48/48113.html (accessed August 27, 2014).

47. Texas Constitution (1976), art. 3, sec. 2.

48. *Shelby County, Alabama v. Holder* (2013) 570 U.S. _____

49. 526 U.S. 541.

50. 509 U.S. 630.

51. 515 U.S. 900.

52. Ross Ramsey, "You Thought Redistricting Was about the Candidates?," *Texas Tribune*, June 15, 2012.

53. Sam Attlesey, "Panel OKs Map Favoring GOP," *Dallas Morning News*, November 29, 2001.

54. 548 U.S. 204.

55. Peggy Jones, "Did New Voting Lines Doom Incumbent East Texas Legislators?," *News Journal*, www.news-journal.com/news/local/did-new-voting-lines-doom-incumbent-east-texas-legislators/article_16361306-5135-55f5-befa-506fdf5887a6.html (accessed August 28, 2014).

56. Ross Ramsey, "Redistricting Is a Threat to West Texas Freshmen," *Texas Tribune*, December 6, 2012, www.texastribune.org/2010/12/06/redistricting-is-a-threat-to-west-texas-freshmen/ (accessed August 28, 2014).

57. Aman Batheja, "Redrawn District Creates Volatile Race for Nash," *Texas Tribune*, May 10, 2012, www.texastribune.org/2012/05/10/redrawn-district-creates-volatile-race-nash/ (accessed August 28, 2014).

58. Tim Eaton and Kate Alexander, "U.S. Supreme Court Blocks Texas Redistricting Maps," *American-Statesman*, December 9, 2011, www.statesman.com/news/news/local/us-supreme-court-blocks-texas-redistricting-maps/nRhs3/ (accessed August 28, 2014).

59. Ross Ramsey, "Redistricting Exposes a Split in the Minority Ranks," *Texas Tribune*, March 9, 2012, www.texastribune.org/2012/03/09/redistricting-exposes-split-minority-ranks/ (accessed August 28, 2014).

60. Ross Ramsey, "Redistricting, Redone by Lawmakers, Goes Back to Judges," *Texas Tribune*, July 1, 2013, www.texastribune.org/2013/07/01/redistricting-redone-lawmakers-goes-back-judges (accessed August 28, 2014).

61. Ross Ramsey, "Judges: 2014 Primaries Can Use Lege-Approved Maps," *Texas Tribune*, September 6, 2013, www.texastribune.org/2013/09/06/2014-primaries-can-proceed-judges-rule/ (accessed August 28, 2014).

## CHAPTER 4

1. Texas House of Representatives, House Journal, 83rd Legislature, Regular Session, Proceedings, 17.

2. Ross Ramsey, "Speaker Race: Simpson Praying, Hughes Staying," *Texas Weekly*, December 12, 2012, www.texastribune.org/2012/12/14/speaker-race-simpson-praying-hughes-staying/ (accessed August 28, 2014, 2014).

3. Texas House of Representatives, House Journal, 83rd Legislature, Regular Session, Proceedings, 12–17.

4. April Castro and Liz Austin Peterson, "Texas House Speaker Refuses to Step Down amid Uproar," *Arkansas Democrat-Gazette*, May 27, 2007, 7A.

5. "Speaker Fight: Legal Arguments," *Daily Sentinel* (Nacogdoches), May 27, 2007.

6. House Journal, 80th Legislature, Regular Session, Proceedings, 17–22.

7. House Journal, 81st Legislature, Regular Session, Proceedings, 8–15.

8. Ross Ramsey, "Can Warren Chisum Win a Speaker's Race?," *Texas Tribune*, September 13, 2010, www.texastribune.org/2010/09/13/can-warren-chisum-win-a-speakers-race/ (accessed August 28, 2014).

9. House Journal, 82nd Legislature, Regular Session, Proceedings, 9–16.

10. Ross Ramsey, "Straus Loses Lieutenants, and Senate Sees a Shift," *Texas Tribune*, May 30, 2012, www.texastribune.org/texas-politics/2012-legislative-election/redder-senate-bout-blues-house/ (accessed August 28, 2014).

11. Morgan Smith, Ben Philpott, and Jay Root, "Straus Opponents Out in Full Force at GOP Convention," *Texas Tribune*, June 7, 2012, www.texastribune.org/texas-politics/2012-elections/straus-opponents-find-receptive-audience-gop-conve/ (accessed August 28, 2014).

12. Thomas Morris Spencer, *The Legislative Process, Texas-Style* (San Jacinto, Calif.: San Jacinto College Press, 1981), 22–23.

13. Nancy Martorano, "Distributing Power: Exploring the Relative Powers of Presiding Officers and Committees in the State Legislative Process," paper presented at the 2004 annual meeting of the American Political Science Association, Chicago, September 2–5, reported in Keith Hamm and Gary Moncrief, "Legislative Politics in the States," in *Politics in the American States:*

*A Comparative Analysis*, 10th ed., ed. Virginia Gray, Russell Hanson, and Thad Kousser (Washington, D.C.: CQ Press, 2012).

14. Keith Hamm and Robert Harmel, "Legislative Party Development and the Speaker System: The Case of the Texas House," *Journal of Politics* 55, no. 4 (1993): 1140–1151.

15. Jeremy Warren, political communications director for Senator Rodney Ellis, telephone interview with the author, July 13, 2012.

16. Wayne Francis, *The Legislative Committee Game: A Comparative Analysis of Fifty States* (Columbus: Ohio State University Press, 1989), 45.

17. Bruce Anderson. "Electoral Competition and the Structure of State Legislatures: Organizational Complexity and Party Building," PhD diss., Rice University, 1997.

18. Hamm and Harmel, "Legislative Party Development and the Speaker System: The Case of the Texas House."

19. Jessica Farrar, member of Texas House of Representatives, telephone interview with author, August 1, 2012.

20. Ibid.

21. Chuck Hopson, member of Texas House of Representatives, telephone interview with author, July 13, 2012.

22. Ibid.

23. Naomi Gonzalez, member of Texas House of Representatives, telephone interview with author, July 19, 2012.

24. Farrar, telephone interview with author.

25. Curtis Smith, chief of staff for Texas House of Representative Terry Calanas, telephone interview with author, July 11, 2014.

26. Warren, telephone interview with author.

27. Ibid.

28. Ibid.

29. Charles W. Wiggins, Keith E. Hamm, and Charles G. Bell, "Interest Group and Party Influence Agents in the Legislative Process: A Comparative State Analysis," *Journal of Politics* 54 (1992): 82–100.

30. Travis Clardy, member of the Texas House of Representatives, personal interview with the author, July 18, 2014.

31. Audrey S. Wall, ed., *The Book of the States*, vol. 44 (Lexington, Ky.: Council of State Governments, 2012), 139–144, tables 3.11 and 3.12.

32. Farrar, telephone interview with author.

33. Gonzalez, telephone interview with author; Clardy, telephone interview with author.

34. Gonzalez, telephone interview with author; Hopson, telephone interview with author.

35. Warren, telephone interview with author.

36. Michelle G. Briscoe, "Cohesiveness and Diversity among Black Members of the Texas State Legislature," in *Politics in the New South: Representation of African Americans in Southern State Legislatures*, eds. Charles E. Menifield and Stephen D. Shaffer (Albany: State University of New York, 2005).

37. Warren, telephone interview with author.

38. Hamm and Harmel, "Legislative Party Development," 1140–1151.

39. Kathryn Birdwill, "Bill Requires Universities to Limit Credit Hours Needed to Earn Degree," *Daily Sentinel*, January 6, 2006.

40. Chi, *The Book of the States*, vol. 38, 125–130, tables 3.25 and 3.26.

41. Joe Straus, "Interim Committee Charges: Texas House of Representatives—83rd Legislature," www.house.state.tx.us/_media/pdf/interim-charges-83rd.pdf (Accessed August 1, 2014).

42. Lieutenant Governor, "83rd Session Select Interim Charges Related to Higher Education," 2014, www.ltgov.state.tx.us/docs/DHD_Interim_Charges83_HED_CJ_SAF_040814.pdf (Accessed August 3, 2014).

43. Chi, *The Book of the States*, vol. 38, 109–110, table 3.18.

44. Spencer, *The Legislative Process*, 31–32.

45. W. Gardner Selby, "It's Not Every Day a Legislator Travels Oversees while Voting in the Texas House," *Austin American-Statesman*, April 27, 2007.

46. Wall, *The Book of the States*, 151, table 3.14.

47. Anthony Champaign et al., *The Austin Boston Connection: Five Decades of House Democratic Leadership, 1937–1989* (College Station: Texas A&M University Press, 2009).

## CHAPTER 5

1. David Freed, "Rick Perry: America's Last Feudal King," *Harvard Political Review*, September 6, 2013, http://harvardpolitics.com/united-states/rick-perry-americas-last-feudal-king/ (accessed September 5, 2014).

2. Paul Burka, "Guv Story: Rick Perry's Most Important Legacy Is That He Accomplished Something That No Other Governor Was Able to Do: Completely Change How Government Works," *Texas Monthly*, July 2014, www.texasmonthly.com/story/how-rick-perry-completely-changed-texas-government (accessed July 30, 2014).

3. Will Weissert, "Texas GOP Taking Aim at Parts of Gov. Rick Perry's Legacy," *Dallas News*, June 4, 2014, www.dallasnews.com/news/politics/state-politics/20140604-texas-gop-taking-aim-at-parts-of-gov.-rick-perry-s-legacy.ece (accessed August 4, 2014).

4. Ibid.

5. Daniel Murph, *Texas Giant: The Life of Price Daniel* (Austin, Tex.: Eakin Press, 2002).

6. Texas Constitution (1876), art. 4, sec. 4.

7. Texas Constitution (1876), art. 4, sec. 6.

8. Alan Rosenthal, *The Best Job in Politics: Exploring How Governors Succeed as Policy Leaders* (Washington, D.C.: CQ Press, 2012).

9. University of Texas, The Texas Politics Project, "Governors of Texas," www.laits.utexas.edu/txp_media/html/exec/governors/24.html (accessed August 30, 2014).

10. Peter Boyer, "The Right Aims at Texas," *Newsweek*, May 29, 2011.

11. Kenneth E. Hendrickson, *The Chief Executives of Texas* (College Station: Texas A&M University Press, 1995).

12. Ibid.

13. Jim Yardley, "The 2002 Elections: Races for Governor: In Texas, Republican Who Inherited Top Job Is the Winner Outright," *New York Times*, November 6, 2002.

14. Jim Yardley, "In First, Texas Hispanic Seeks to Be Governor," *New York Times*, September 5, 2001.

15. *The Book of the States*, vol. 46 (Lexington, Ky.: Council of State Governments, 2014).

16. Ibid.

17. Erik Brady, Steve Berkowitz, and Jodi Upton, "College Football Coaches Continue to See Salary Explosion," *USA Today*, November 20, 2012. See also Erik Brady, Jodi Upton, and Steve Berkowitz, "Salaries for Football Coaches Back on Rise," *USA Today*, November 17, 2011.

18. Jay Root, "Perry 'Retires' to Boost Pay," *Texas Tribune*, December 16, 2011.

19. *The Book of the States*, vol. 46.

20. Jay Root, "Rick Perry's Taxpayer-Funded Security Costs Rise," *Texas Tribune*, December 25, 2011.

21. Associated Press, "Gov. Rick Perry's Security Bill for Presidential Run Grows," *Dallas Morning News*, July 6, 2012.

22. Jay Root, "Governor Perry's Temporary Digs Costs Texas Big Bucks," *CBS News*, May 17, 2010, www.cbsnews.com/stories/2010/05/17/national/main6491367.shtml (accessed August 30, 2014).

23. Kathy Warbelow, "Texas Spends $25 Million on Mansion as Perry Seeks Cuts," *Bloomberg News*, July 11, 2012.

24. Frederic A. Ogg, "Impeachment of Governor Ferguson," *American Political Science Review* 12, no. 1 (February 1918): 111–115.

25. Cortez A. M. Ewing, "The Impeachment of James E. Ferguson," *Political Science Quarterly* 48, no. 2 (June 1933): 184–210.

26. Texas Constitution (1876), art. 4, sec. 10.

27. Texans for Public Justice, "Governor Perry's Patronage," April 2006, http://info.tpj.org/reports/pdf/Perry%20Patronage2010.pdf (accessed August 30, 2014).

28. Matt Stiles and Brian Thevenot, "Perry's Appointed Regents Are Big Donors," *Texas Tribune*, August 24, 2010.

29. Brittany Pieper, "Another Former Tech Regent Says the Governor Pressured Their Resignation," KCBD News

Channel 11, September 12, 2009, www .kcbd.com/Global/story.asp?S=11120348 (accessed August 30, 2014).

30. Alan C. Miller, "Texas Corporate Interests Financed Bulk of Bush Races," *Los Angeles Times,* July 14, 1999.

31. Brian McCall, *The Power of the Texas Governor: Connally to Bush* (Austin: University of Texas Press, 2009).

32. *The Book of the States,* vol. 46.

33. R. G. Ratcliffe, "Court Limits Perry's Power over Agencies," *Houston Chronicle,* February 21, 2007.

34. Brandi Grissom et al., "Day One, First Called Session of the 82nd Legislature," *Texas Tribune,* May 31, 2011.

35. Ibid.

36. Margaret R. Ferguson, "Roles, Functions, and Powers of the Governors," in *The Executive Branch of State Government,* ed. Margaret R. Ferguson (Santa Barbara, Calif.: ABC-CLIO, 2006).

37. *The Book of the States,* vol. 44.

38. Texas Constitution (1876), art. 4, sec. 11.

39. Thad Beyle and Margaret Ferguson, "Governors and the Executive Branch," in *Politics in the American States: A Comparative Analysis,* 9th ed., eds. Virginia Gray and Russell L. Hanson (Washington, D.C.: CQ Press, 2008).

40. "Poll: Texas Governor Perry Job Approval up Post Hurricanes," *Fox News,* December 6, 2005, http://www .foxnews.com/story/0,2933,177867,00 .html (accessed August 30, 2014).

41. Kavan Peterson, "Governors Lose in Power Struggle over National Guard," *American City and County,* January 16, 2007, http://americancityandcounty .com/emergency-response/governors-lose-power-struggle-over-national-guard (accessed August 30, 2014).

42. Ibid.

43. Beyle and Ferguson, "Governors and the Executive Branch," table 7-5.

44. Paul Burka, quoted in McCall, *The Power of the Texas Governor.*

45. Beyle and Ferguson, "Governors and the Executive Branch," 203–204.

46. Ibid.

47. Ibid.

48. Ibid.

49. Joshua Blank and Jim Henson, "Polling Center: Does Texas Still Burn for Perry?," *Texas Tribune,* June 27, 2013.

## CHAPTER 6

1. U.S. Department of Commerce, Office of Trade and Policy Analysis, "Top U.S. Trade Partners," www.trade .gov/mas/ian/build/groups/public/@ tg_ian/documents/webcontent/ tg_ian_003364.pdf (accessed August 18, 2014).

2. U.S. Department of Transportation, "North American Transborder Freight Data," www.transborder.bts.gov/ programs/international/transborder/ TBDR_QA.html (accessed August 18, 2014); some calculation by authors.

3. Aman Batheja, "Rick Perry Calls for More Funds for I-69 Project," *Texas Tribune,* February 6, 2013, www .texastribune.org/2013/02/06/perry-calls-for-more-funds-for-i-69-project/ (accessed August 14, 2014).

4. Peggy Fikac and Dug Begley, "Interstate 69 Coming Piece by Piece," *Houston Chronicle,* www.houstonchronicle.com/ news/article/Interstate-69-coming-piece-by-piece-4257896.php (accessed August 14, 2014).

5. Alliance for I-69 Texas, "Tracking the Progress of Interstate 69 in Texas," www.i69texasalliance.com (accessed September 5, 2014).

6. Cindy Horswell, "Part of U.S. 59 Being Renamed Interstate 69," *Houston Chronicle,* www.chron.com/news/ houston-texas/article/Chunk-of-trade-corridor-designated-in-Houston-area-3747886.php (accessed August 14, 2014).

7. Barry Harrell, "Perry Vetoes Online Sales Bill, but Measure May Not Be Dead Yet," *Austin American-Statesman,* May 31, 2011, www.statesman.com/ news/news/state-regional-govt-politics/ perry-vetoes-online-sales-tax-bill-but-measure-may/nRbTh/ (accessed September 5, 2014).

8. Audrey S. Wall, ed., *The Book of the States,* vol. 44 (Lexington, Ky.: Council of State Governments, 2012), 223, table 4.6.

9. Ibid., 237–242, table 4.11.

10. Texas Constitution (1876), art. 4, sec. 22.

11. Wall, *The Book of the States,* vol. 44, 227, table 4.11.

12. Jonathan W. Singer, *Broken Trusts: The Texas Attorney General versus the Oil Industry, 1889–1909* (College Station: Texas A&M Press, 2002).

13. Texas Attorney General, "About Attorney General Opinions," www .oag.state.tx.us/opin/ (accessed September 19, 2014).

14. Wall, *Book of the States,* vol. 44, 264–265, tables 4.24 and 4.25.

15. Ibid., 237–242, table 4.11.

16. Ibid., 286–298, tables 4.30, 4.31, and 4.32.

17. HB 7 transferred the Texas Performance Review and the Texas School Performance Review to the Legislative Budget Board.

18. Helen Eriksen, "Budget Shortfall on Lawmakers' Minds as Legislative Session to Open January 11," *Houston Chronicle,* January 5, 2011, www.chron .com/default/article/Budget-shorfall-on-lawmarkers-minds-as-1688298.php (accessed August 25, 2012).

19. Peggy Fikac, "State Revenue Gets a $1.2 Billion Boost," *Houston Chronicle,* May 17, 2011, www.chron.com/news/ houston-texas/article/State-revenues-get-a-1-2-billion-boost-1693255.php (accessed September 19, 2014).

20. Peggy Fikac, "Economic News Is Good, but There's No Celebrating," August 12, 2012, *Houston Chronicle,* www.chron.com/news/fikac/article/ Economic-news-is-good-but-there-s-no-celebrating-3782933.php (accessed September 5, 2014).

21. Wall, *Book of the States,* vol. 44, 237–242, table 4.11.

22. Texas Department of Agriculture, "What Does the Texas Department of Agriculture Do?," www.texasagriculture .gov/About/WhatdoesTDAdo.apx (accessed September 5, 2014).

23. General Land Office, "History of the Texas General Land Office," www .glo.texas.gov/GLO/history-of-the-Land-Office/index.html (accessed September 5, 2014).

24. Texas Educational Agency, "Texas Permanent School Fund Annual Report—Fiscal Year Ending August 31, 2013," www.tea.state.tx.us/index4.aspx?id=2147489178&menu_id=2147483695 (accessed August 17, 2014).

25. Steven Quinn, "Texas Tops in Wind Energy Production," *USA Today,* July 25, 2006.

26. "Texas Awards Rights for Offshore Wind Farm," October 3, 2007, www.msnbc.msn.com/id/21113169/ (accessed September 5, 2014).

27. Wall, *Book of the States,* vol. 44, 256, table 4.16.

28. Ibid., 237–242, table 4.11.

29. Texas Secretary of State, "History of the Office," www.sos.state.tx.us/about/history.shtml (accessed September 5, 2014).

30. Texas Secretary of State, "Constitutional Duties," www.sos.state.tx.us/about/duties.shtml (accessed September 5, 2014).

31. Texas Department of Transportation, "Texas Transportation Commission FAQs," www.txdot.gov/about_us/commis sion/faqs.htm (accessed September 21, 2012).

32. Texas Department of Transportation, "TxDOT 2015–2019 Strategic Plan," www.txdot.gov/inside txdot/office/state-affairs/strategic-plan.html (accessed August 14, 2014).

33. Texas Department of State Health Services, "Commissioner David L. Lakey, M.D.," www.dshs.state.tx.us/commissioner.aspx (accessed September 5, 2014).

34. Texas Government Code, title 6, subtitle B, chapter 655.

35. Sunset Advisory Commission, "Frequently Asked Questions," www.sunset.texas.gov/about-us/frequently-asked-questions (accessed August 17, 2014).

## CHAPTER 7

1. Morgan Smith, "Chief Justice Delivers State of the Judiciary," *Texas Tribune,* February 23, 2011.

2. Wallace B. Jefferson, "The State of the Judiciary in Texas," February 11, 2009.

3. Wallace B. Jefferson, "Make Merit Matter by Adopting New System of Selecting Judges," *Houston Chronicle,* March 21, 2009.

4. Morgan Smith, "Chief Justice Delivers State of the Judiciary," *Texas Tribune,* February 23, 2011.

5. Ibid.

6. Texas Constitution (1876), art. 5, sec. 1.

7. Office of Court Administration, *Annual Statistical Report for the Texas Judiciary, Fiscal Year 2013* (Austin: Office of Court Administration, 2013).

8. Ibid.

9. Ibid.

10. Texas Constitution (1876), art. 4, sec. 19.

11. *Annual Statistical Report for the Texas Judiciary,* Fiscal Year 2013.

12. *Annual Statistical Report for the Texas Judiciary,* Fiscal Year 2013.

13. Texas Constitution (1876), art. 5, sec. 15.

14. *Annual Statistical Report for the Texas Judiciary,* Fiscal Year 2013.

15. Ibid.

16. Texas Constitution (1876), art. 5, sec. 8.

17. The state's appellate courts have differing opinions on whether the minimal criminal jurisdiction in district-level courts is $200 or $500.

18. Audrey S. Wall, ed., *The Book of the States,* vol. 44 (Lexington, Ky.: Council of State Governments, 2012).

19. Tom Abrahams, "What's the Deal with the Long Ballot?," October 21, 2010, ABC News, http://abc13.com/archive/7736817/ (accessed August 31, 2014).

20. Ibid.

21. Anna Whitney, "Consumer Group: Supreme Court Favors Business," *Texas Tribune,* January 26, 2012.

22. Ibid.

23. Anthony Champagne and Greg Thielemann, "Awareness of Trial Court Judges," *Judicature* 76 (1991): 271–277.

24. Honorable Thomas Phillips, quoted in "The Texas Judiciary: Is Justice for Sale?," League of Women Voters panel discussion, Tyler, Texas, broadcast as part of a PBS *Frontline* special, September 25, 2007.

25. Sommer Ingram, "Perry's Texas Supreme Court Picks Criticized as Too Business Friendly," *Dallas Morning News,* October 31, 2011.

26. Texas Constitution (1876), art. 5, sec. 1A.

27. State Commission on Judicial Conduct, "Fiscal Year 2013 Annual Report," www.scjc.state.tx.us/pdf/rpts/AR-FY13.pdf (accessed July 3, 2014).

28. Eric Dexheimer, "Texas Judges' Misdeeds Often Kept Secret by Oversight Commission," *Austin American Statesman,* April 14, 2012, www.statesman.com/news/statesman-investigates/texas-judges-misdeeds-often-kept-secret-by-oversight-2305404.html (accessed August 31, 2014).

29. Texas Research League, "The Texas Judiciary: A Proposal for Structural-Functional Reform," in *Texas Courts: Report 2* (Texas Research League, 1991), 25.

30. Citizens' Commission on the Texas Judicial System, "Report and Recommendations," 1993, www.courts.state.tx.us/tjc/publications/cc_tjs.pdf (accessed August 31, 2014).

31. Texans for Public Justice, "Billable Ours: Texas Endures Another Attorney-Financed Supreme Court Race," October, 25, 2006.

32. Ibid.

33. Texas Watch Foundation, "Hecht Votes with Mega-Donors to His Personal Legal Fund 89% of the Time: Judge's Actions Raise Serious Questions about His Impartiality," July 17, 2007, www.texaswatch.org/2007/07/hecht-votes-with-mega-donors-to-his-personal-legal-fund-89-of-the-time/ (accessed August 31, 2014).

34. Malia Reddick, Michael J. Nelson, and Rachel Paine Caufield, "Racial and Gender Diversity on State Courts," *The Judges' Journal* 48 (2009): 28–32.

35. Ibid.

## CHAPTER 8

1. Nathan Thornburgh, "Looking Kindly on Vigilante Justice," *Time,* July 3, 2008, www.time.com/time/nation/

article/0,8599,1820028,00.html (accessed September 1, 2014).

2. International Center for Prison Studies, "Highest to Lowest Prison Population Rate," www.prisonstudies.org/highest-to-lowest/prison_population_rate?field_region_taxonomy_tid=All (accessed July 11, 2014).

3. Justice Policy Institute, "Texas Tough: An Analysis of Incarceration and Crime Trends in the Lone Star State," October 2000, www.justicepolicy.org/images/upload/00-10_REP_TXTexasTough1_AC.pdf (accessed September 1, 2014).

4. Bureau of Justice Statistics, "U.S. Prison Population Declined for Third Consecutive Year During 2012," www.bjs.gov/content/pub/press/p12acpr.cfm (accessed July 11, 2014).

5. International Center for Prison Studies, "Highest to Lowest Prison Population Rates."

6. Cal Jillson, *Lone Star Tarnished: A Critical Look at Texas Politics and Public Policy* (New York: Routledge Press, 2012).

7. The Daily Texan Editorial Board, "High Time for Texas to Decriminalize Marijuana," *Daily Texan*, January 30, 2014.

8. Jim Henson and Joshua Blank, "Polling Center: Legal Pot in Texas: Snuff the Thought," *Texas Tribune,* March 20, 2014.

9. "Criminal Justice: Tough on Crime? Check. Smart on Crime? Not So Much," *Austin American Statesman*, December 31, 2009.

10. David Boeri, "Prison Overcrowding, Rising Costs Prompt Surprising Reform," NPR interview, March 30, 2011, www.wbur.org/2011/03/30/tough-on-crime (accessed September 1, 2014).

11. Ibid.

12. Associated Press, "Budget Cuts Might Close Some Prisons: Treatment and Rehab Programs Have Reduced Inmate Numbers," *Houston Chronicle*, May 30, 2010.

13. Pew Center on the States, "Prison Count 2010: State Population Declines for the First Time in 28 Years," April 2010, www.pewstates.org/uploadedFiles/PCS_Assets/2010/Pew_Prison_Count_2010.pdf (accessed September 23, 2012).

14. Renee Lee, "Elderly Inmates Are Putting a Burden on Texas Taxpayers," *Houston Chronicle*, May 16, 2011.

15. Jacquielynne Floyd, "The Crime of Un-air-conditioned Texas Prisons," *Dallas Morning News*, April 24, 2014.

16. Mike Ward, "Officials Dispute That Five of 10 Prisons with Highest Prevalence of Sex Assault Are in State," *Austin American Statesman*, March 28, 2008.

17. Mike Ward, "Privately Run Prisons Come under Fire at Capitol," *Austin American-Statesman,* October 13, 2007.

18. Gregory Hooks, Clayton Mosher, Thomas Rotolo, and Linda Lobao, "The Prison Industry: Carceral Expansion and Employment in U.S. Counties, 1969–1994," *Social Science Quarterly* 85 (March 2004): 1.

19. Ward, "Privately Run Prisons Come under Fire at Capitol."

20. Holly Becka and Jennifer LaFleur, "Texas' Youth Jail Operators Have Troubled Histories," *Dallas Morning News,* July 30, 2007, www.dallasnews.com/sharedcontent/dws/dn/latest news/stories/072907 dnmettyccontracts.37bfd89.html.

21. Erik Kain, "Texas and the Prison-Industrial-Complex," *Forbes*, September 1, 2011.

22. John Burnett, "Private Prison Promises Leave Texas Towns in Trouble," NPR, March 28, 2011, www.npr.org/2011/03/28/134855801/private-prison-promises-leave-texas-towns-in-trouble (accessed September 2, 2014).

23. Michael K. Moore and Allan K. Butcher, "Giving Timbre to Gideon's Trumpet: Evaluating the Administration and Effectiveness of Legal Representation for Texas' Indigent Criminal Defendants," a report to the State Bar of Texas, www.courts.state.tx.us/tidc/pdf/moorebutcherevaleffectiveness reportmay2007.pdf (accessed September 2, 2014).

24. Court Watch, "Thumbs on the Scale: A Retrospective of the Texas Supreme Court, 2000–2010," www.texaswatch.org/wordpress/wp-content/uploads/2012/01/Thumbs-on-the-Scale_CtWatch_Jan2012_Final.pdf (accessed August 31, 2014).

25. John Tedesco, "Damage Claims Hit City One a Day," *San Antonio Express News*, April 1, 2012, www.mysanantonio.com/news/local_news/article/Damage-claims-hit-city-one-a-day-3450565.php (accessed September 20, 2014).

26. Charles M. Silver, "Soapbox: No Better Care, Thanks to Tort Reform," *Texas Weekly*, October 20, 2011.

27. Patrick Michels, "Joe Horn and Five Years with the Texas Castle Doctrine," *Texas Observer*, May 8, 2012.

28. Cheng Cheng and Mark Hoekstra, "Does Strengthening Self Defense Laws Deter Crime or Escalate Violence: Evidence from Expansions to Castle Doctrine", *Journal of Human Resources* 48, no. 3 (2013): 821–854.

29. *Furman v. Georgia*, 408 U.S. 153 (1972).

30. 536 U.S. 304 (2002).

31. Renee Feltz, "Is Texas' Death Penalty Machine Executing the Mentally Disabled?" *Texas Observer*, August 8, 2012.

32. 543 U.S. 551 (2005).

33. David Dobbs, quoted in "The Texas Judiciary: Is Justice for Sale?," League of Women Voters panel discussion, Tyler, Texas, broadcast as part of a PBS *Frontline* special, September 25, 2007.

34. University of Texas/*Texas Tribune,* "Texas Statewide Survey," June 2014, http://s3.amazonaws.com/static.texastribune.org/media/documents/uttt-jun2014-summary-all.pdf (accessed September 2, 2014); Gallup poll on death penalty at http://www.gallup.com/poll/1606/death-penalty.aspx (accessed September 2, 2014).

35. Ross Ramsey, "UT/TT Poll: Texans Stand behind Death Penalty," *Texas Tribune*, May 24, 2012.

36. Chuck Lindale, "Judge Rebuked but Avoids Ouster," *Austin American Statesman*, July 16, 2010, http://www.statesman.com/news/local/judge-rebuked-but-avoids-ouster-807851.html (accessed September 2, 2014).

37. Ford Fessenden, "Deadly Statistics: A Survey of Crime and Punishment," *New York Times,* September 22, 2000.

38. Christy Hoppe, "Executions Cost Texas Millions: Study Finds It's Cheaper to Jail Killers for Life," *Dallas Morning News*, March 8, 1992.

## CHAPTER 9

1. Alexa Ura, "At GOP Convention, Patrick Focuses on Immigration," *Texas Tribune*, June 7, 2014, www.texastribune .org/2014/06/07/gop-convention-patrick-focuses-immigration/ (accessed August 8, 2014).

2. Alexa Ura, "Fact Check: Dan Patrick at the Republican Convention," *Texas Tribune*, July 17, 2014, www .texastribune.org/2014/07/17/truth-teller-dan-patrick-at-republican-convention/ (accessed August 8, 2014).

3. Alexa Ura, "Patrick, Van De Putte Hone Immigration Messages," *Texas Tribune*, June 17, 2014, www.texastribune .org/2014/07/17/lt-gov-candidates-hone-their-immigration-messages/ (accessed August 8, 2014).

4. Alexa Ura, "Fact Check: Dan Patrick at the Republican Convention."

5. Alexa Ura, "At GOP Convention, Patrick Focuses on Immigration."

6. Alexa Ura, "Fact Check: Van De Putte at the Democratic Convention," *Texas Tribune*, July 17, 2014, www.texastribune .org/2014/07/17/truth-teller-leticia-van-de-putte-democratic-conve/ (accessed August 8, 2014).

7. Alex Ura, "Patrick, Van De Putte Hone Immigration Messages."

8. Ross Ramsey, "Analysis: On the Democratic Ticket, Watch the Co-Pilot," *Texas Tribune*, July 11, 2014, www .texastribune.org/2014/07/11/analysis-democratic-ticket-watch-co-pilot/ (accessed August 8, 2014).

9. Ross Ramsey, "Analysis: Will Some Split Ticket Vote? Some Thinks So," *Texas Tribune*, June 10, 2014, www .texastribune.org/2014/06/10/analysis-not-a-thing-without-that-swing/ (accessed August 14, 2014).

10. Matthew Waller, "State Lieutenant Governor Finances," *Corpus Christi Caller*, July 17, 2014, www.caller.com/ news/state_ltgovfinances_13147815 (accessed August 25, 2014).

11. Texas Election Code, chap. 11, sec. 002.

12. Texas Election Code, chap. 16, secs. 002–003.

13. Texas Constitution (1876), art. 7, sec. 3.

14. Ricky F. Dobbs, *Yellow Dogs and Republicans: Allan Shivers and Texas Two-Party Politics* (College Station: Texas A&M University Press, 2005), 80.

15. Michael J. Klarman, "The Supreme Court and Black Disenfranchisement," in *The Voting Rights Act: Securing the Ballot*, ed. Richard M. Valelly (Washington, D.C.: CQ Press, 2006).

16. 383 U.S. 663 (1966).

17. 273 U.S. 534 (1924).

18. 321 U.S. 649 (1944).

19. 345 U.S. 461 (1953).

20. Klarman, "The Supreme Court and Black Disenfranchisement," 154.

21. 557 U.S. 193 (2009).

22. 570 U.S. ___ (2013).

23. Abigail M. Thernstrom, *Whose Votes Count?* (Cambridge, Mass.: Harvard University Press, 1987), 55.

24. Teresa Palomo Acosta, "IN RE RICARDO RODRIGUEZ," Handbook of Texas Online, www.tshaonline .org/handbook/online/articles/ pqitw (accessed August 26, 2012). Published by the Texas State Historical Association.

25. Chandler Davidson, "The Voting Rights Act: A Brief History," in *Controversies in Minority Voting*, eds. Bernard Grofman and Chandler Davidson (Washington, D.C.: The Brookings Institution, 1992).

26. Thernstrom, *Whose Votes Count?*, 52.

27. Ruth P. Morgan, *Governance by Decree: The Impact of the Voting Rights Act in Dallas* (Lawrence: University of Kansas Press, 2004), 50–51.

28. Thernstrom, *Whose Votes Count?*, 56–57.

29. Christopher Smith Gonzalez, "Voter ID Gets Tense Hearing," *Texas Tribune*, March 1, 2011, www.texastribune .org/texaspolitics/voter-id/voter-id-gets-hearing/ (accessed September 24, 2014).

30. Ibid.

31. Julian Aguilar, "Day 24: Stringent Voter ID Law Means Changes at Texas Polls," *Texas Tribune*, August 24, 2011, www .texastribune.org/texas-legislature/82nd-legislative-sesseion/day-24-voter-id-law-means-changes-ballot-box/ (accessed September 24, 2014).

32. Terry Frieden, "Federal Court Strikes Downs Texas Voter ID Law," August 30, 2012, www.cnn.com/2012/08/30/ politics/texas-voter-id-law/ (accessed September 26, 2014).

33. Sari Horwitz, "Texas Voter-ID Law Is Blocked," *Washington Post*, August 30, 2012, www.washingtonpost.com/world/ national-security/texas-voter-id-law-struck-down/2012/08/30/4a07e270-f2ad-11e1-adc6-87dfa8eff430_story.html (accessed September 26, 2014).

34. Frieden, "Federal Court Strikes Down Texas Voter ID Law."

35. 380 U.S. 775 (1965).

36. Texas Secretary of State, "Students," http://votetexas.gov/students/ (accessed September 26, 2014).

37. Texas Constitution (1876), art. 6, sec. 5.

38. 530 U.S. 567 (2000).

39. California Secretary of State, "Top Two Candidates Open Primary Act and Voter Nominated Offices," www.sos.ca.gov/ elections/statewide-elections/2012-primary/new-open-primary-info.pdf (accessed September 8, 2014).

40. John F. Bibby and Thomas M. Holbrook, "Parties and Elections," in *Politics in the American States: A Comparative Analysis*, 8th ed., eds. Virginia Gray and Russell Hanson (Washington, D.C.: CQ Press, 2004), 63.

41. Dobbs, *Yellow Dogs and Republicans*, 70.

42. Ibid., 88.

43. Alexander Heard, *A Two-Party South?* (Chapel Hill: University of North Carolina Press, 1952), 104–105.

44. Audrey S. Wall, ed., *Book of the States*, vol. 44 (Lexington, Ky.: Council of State Governments, 2012), 353, table 6.9.

45. John G. Matsusaka, "2005 Initiatives and Referendums," in *The Book of the States*, vol. 38, ed. Keon Chi (Lexington, Ky.: The Council on State Governments, 2006), 307.

46. In some rare cases, voters do mark local and state races and leave "higher" offices,

such as U.S. senator or U.S. representative, unmarked. However, this pattern is much, much rarer than roll off. As a result, political scientists do not really have a term to describe this phenomenon—"roll on" seems a bit silly.

47. Samuel L. Popkin, "Information Shortcuts and the Reasoning Voter," in *Information, Participation, and Choice,* ed. Bernard Grofman (Ann Arbor: University of Michigan Press, 1993), 19.

48. Ibid., 22–27; Anthony Downs, *An Economic Theory of Democracy* (New York: Harper and Row, 1957), 85.

49. Donald P. Moynihan, "Building Secure Elections: E-Voting, Security, and Systems Theory," *Public Administration Review* 64 (2007): 515–528.

50. Ibid., 518.

51. Paul S. Herrnson et al., "Early Appraisals of Electronic Voting," *Social Science Computer Review* 23 (2005): 274–292.

52. Jeffrey S. Connor, *Amended Texas State Plan Pursuant to the Help America Vote Act of 2002* (Austin: Elections Division, Office of the Secretary of State, 2005), 3.

53. Ibid., 15.

54. Texas Secretary of State, "Election Night Returns," 2010, http://enr.sos.state.tx.us/enr/ (accessed September 8, 2014); Texas Secretary of State, "Turnout and Voter Registration Figures (1970–Current)," 2010, www.sos.state.tx.us/elections/historical/70-92.shtml (accessed September 8, 2014).

55. Karlheinz Reif and Hermann Schmitt, "Nine Second-Order Elections: A Conceptual Framework for the Analysis of European Election Results," *European Journal of Political Research* 8 (1980): 3–44.

56. William H. Riker, *Liberalism against Populism* (Prospect Heights, Ill.: Waveland Press, 1982), 5; Robert A. Dahl, *A Preface to Democratic Theory* (Chicago: University of Chicago Press, 1956), 132.

57. James Endersby, Steven Galatas, and Chapman Rackaway, "Closeness Counts in Canada," *The Journal of Politics* 64, no. 2 (2002): 610–631. Specific cases finding a link in the United States at the state level include Harvey J. Tucker,

"Contextual Models of Participation in U.S. State Legislative Elections," *Western Political Quarterly* 39, no. 1 (1986): 67–78; Gregory A. Caldeira and Samuel C. Patterson, "Contextual Influences on Participation in U.S. State Legislative Election," *Legislative Studies Quarterly* 7, no. 3 (1989): 359–381; and Samuel C. Patterson and Gregory A. Caldeira, "Getting Out the Vote: Participation in Gubernatorial Elections," *American Political Science Review* 77, no. 3 (1983): 675–689.

58. Randolph B. Campbell, *Gone to Texas* (New York: Oxford University Press, 2004), 175.

59. Ibid.

60. James L. Haley, *Passionate Nation: The Epic History of Texas* (New York: Free Press, 2006).

61. Ibid.

62. Matt Stiles, "Interactive: Texas Political Spending: July 1 to Dec. 31, 2010," *Texas Tribune,* February 9, 2011, www.texastribune.org/library/data/texas-political-spending-2010/ (accessed September 9, 2014).

63. Christy Hoppe, "Tweets, Sweets, Other Little Expenses Say Lots about Governor's Race," *Dallas Morning News,* October 17, 2010, www.dallasnews.com/sharedcontent/dws/dn/latestnews/stories/101710dntexpizza.29dc2bd.html (accessed September 8, 2014).

64. *Buckley v. Valeo,* 424 U.S. 1 (1976).

65. Ibid.

66. 558 U.S. 50 (2010).

67. Morgan Smith and Zoë Gioja, "Local Court Runoff Tests Judicial Campaign Fairness Act," *Texas Tribune,* July 26, 2012, www.texastribune.org/texas-courts/texas-judicial-system/local-court-runoff-tests-judicial-campaign-fairnes/ (accessed September 8, 2014).

68. National Institute on Money in State Politics, "Follow the Money: Texas 2010," www.followthemoney.org/database/state_overview.phtml?s=TX&y=2010 (accessed September 28, 2014).

69. National Institute of Money in State Politics, "State at a Glance: Texas 2010 Candidates," www.followthemoney.org/database/StateGlance/state_candidates.phtml?s=TX&y=2010

## CHAPTER 10

1. Alwyn Barr, *Reconstruction to Reform: Texas Politics, 1876–1906* (Dallas: Southern Methodist University Press, 2000), 5.

2. T. R. Fehrenbach, *Lone Star: A History of Texas and the Texans* (Cambridge, Mass.: Da Capo Press, 2000), 618.

3. Ibid., 624.

4. Lewis L. Gould, *Progressives and Prohibitionists* (Austin: University of Texas Press, 1973), 39.

5. Fehrenbach, *Lone Star,* 415.

6. Gould, *Progressives and Prohibitionists,* 39.

7. Randolph B. Campbell, *Gone to Texas* (New York: Oxford University Press, 2004), 350.

8. Earl Black and Merle Black, *The Rise of the Southern Republicans* (Cambridge, Mass.: Belknap Press, 2002), 88.

9. Ibid., 23–24.

10. William H. Riker, *Liberalism against Populism* (Prospect Heights, Ill.: Waveland Press, 1982), 5; Robert A. Dahl, *A Preface to Democratic Theory* (Chicago, Ill.: University of Chicago Press, 1956), 132.

11. James Endersby, Steven Galatas, and Chapman Rackaway, "Closeness Counts in Canada," *The Journal of Politics* 64, no. 2 (2002): 610–631. Specific cases finding a link in the United States at the state level include Harvey J. Tucker, "Contextual Models of Participation in U.S. State Legislative Elections," *Western Political Quarterly* 39, no. 1 (1986): 67–78; Gregory A. Caldeira and Samuel C. Patterson, "Contextual Influences on Participation in U.S. State Legislative Election," *Legislative Studies Quarterly* 7, no. 3 (1989): 359–381; and Samuel C. Patterson and Gregory A. Caldeira, "Getting Out the Vote: Participation in Gubernatorial Elections," *American Political Science Review* 77, no. 3 (1983): 675–689.

12. Edmund Burke, *Works,* vol. I (London: G. Bell and Sons, 1897), 375.

13. Leon Epstein, *Political Parties in Western Democracies* (New York: Praeger, 1967), 9.

14. Angus Campbell, Philip E. Converse, Warren E. Miller, and Donald E. Stokes, *The American Voter* (New York: Wiley), 1960.

15. Quoted in A. James Reichley, *The Life of the Parties* (Boulder, Co.: Rowman & Littlefield Publishers, Inc., 2000), 316.

16. *Eu v. San Francisco County Democratic Central Comm.*, 489 U.S. 214 (1989).

17. Paul Allen Beck, *Political Parties in America*, 8th ed. (New York: Longman, 1997), 67–68.

18. Republican Party of Texas, "Report of Platform Committee," 2014, http://www.texasgop.org/wp-content/uploads/2014/06/2014-Platform-Final.pdf, 12 (accessed July 18, 2014).

19. Marc J. Hetherington and William J. Keefe, *Parties, Politics, and Public Policy in America*, 10th ed. (Washington, D.C.: CQ Press, 2007), 21.

20. John Kenneth White and Daniel M. Shea, *New Party Politics: From Jefferson and Hamilton to the Information Age* (Boston: St. Martin's Press, 2000), 174.

21. V. O. Key, *Southern Politics in State and Nation* (New York: Knopf, 1949), 307.

22. Ibid., 11.

## CHAPTER 11

1. Empower Texans, "About Us," www.empowertexans.com/about/ (accessed September 4, 2014).

2. James Madison, "Federalist Paper No. 10: The Same Subject Continued: The Union as a Safeguard against Domestic Faction and Insurrection," *New York Daily Advertiser*, November 22, 1787, www.ourdocuments.gov/doc.php?doc=10&page=transcript (accessed September 28, 2012).

3. Anthony J. Nownes, *Pressure and Power: Organized Interests in American Politics* (Boston: Houghton Mifflin Company, 2001).

4. Ibid., 8.

5. Randolph Campbell, *Gone to Texas: A History of the Lone Star State* (Oxford, NY: Oxford University Press, 2003).

6. David Truman, *The Governmental Process: Political Interests and Public Opinion*, 2nd ed. (New York: Knopf, 1971).

7. Texans for Public Justice, "Texas PACs: 2010 Election Cycle Spending," August 2011, http://info.tpj.org/reports/pdf/PACs2010.pdf (accessed September 4, 2014).

8. Texans for Public Justice, "Texas PACs: 2012 Election Cycle Spending," October 2013, http://info.tpj.org/reports/pdf/PACs2012.pdf (accessed September 4, 2014).

9. Ibid.

10. Dave Mann, "A Governor's Race Full of Pettiness," *Texas Observer*, August 27, 2010, www.texasobserver.org/contrarian/a-governors-race-full-of-pettiness (accessed September 26, 2012).

11. Kevin McNellis and Robin Parkinson, "Independent Spending's Role in State Elections, 2006–2010," National Institute on Money in State Politics, March 15, 2012, www.followthemoney.org/press/ReportView.phtml?r=481 (accessed September 4, 2014).

12. Pew Research Center for the People & the Press, "Little Public Awareness of Outside Campaign Spending Boom," August 2, 2012, www.people-press.org/2012/08/02/little-public-awareness-of-outside-campaign-spending-boom/ (accessed September 4, 2014).

13. Adam Crowther, "Citizens United Fuels Negative Spending," Public Citizen, November 2, 2012, www.citizen.org/documents/outside-groups-fuel-negative-spending-in-2012-race-report.pdf (accessed July 14, 2014).

14. 548 U.S. 204 (2006).

15. Jim Clancy, Texas Ethics Commission, "In the Matter of Michael Quinn Sullivan before the Texas Ethics Commission," SC-3120487 AND SC-3120488, July 21, 2014, www.ethics.state.tx.us/sworncomp/2012/3120488.pdf (accessed July 24, 2014).

16. Richard West, "Inside the Lobby," *Texas Monthly*, July 1973, www.texasmonthly.com/content/inside-lobby (accessed September 4, 2014).

17. Laylan Copelin, "Wined, Dined and Rubbed the Right Way," *Austin American-Statesman*, January 30, 2007.

18. West, "Inside the Lobby."

19. Edward T. Walker, *Grassroots for Hire: Public Affairs Consultants in American Democracy* (Cambridge, Mass.: Cambridge University Press, 2014), 6.

20. Ibid., 22, 38.

21. Stuart A. MacCorkle and Dick Smith, *Texas Government*, 5th ed. (New York: McGraw-Hill Book Company, 1964), 92.

22. Kevin Bogardus, "Statehouse Revolvers: Study Finds More Than 1,300 Ex-Legislators among 2005 State Lobbying Ranks," Center for Public Integrity, October 12, 2006, www.publicintegrity.org/2006/10/12/5900/statehouse-revolvers (accessed September 5, 2014).

23. Pete Slover and Robert T. Garrett, "'Kinfolk' Lobbyists Prospering," *Dallas Morning News*, May 5, 2005, 1A.

24. Robert A. Dahl, *Who Governs?* (New Haven, Conn.: Yale University Press, 1961).

25. C. Wright Mills, *The Power Elite* (New York: Oxford University Press, 1956).

26. E. E. Schattschneider, *The Semisovereign People* (New York: Holt, Rinehart and Winston, 1960), 34–35.

27. Jonathan Rauch, *Government's End: Why Washington Stopped Working* (New York: Public Affairs, 1999).

## CHAPTER 12

1. Valerie Wigglesworth, "Frisco Family Who Fought HOA over Foreclosure Plans Move to Virginia," *Dallas Morning News*, December 29, 2010, www.dallasnews.com/news/community-news/frisco/headlines/20101229-frisco-family-who-fought-hoa-over-foreclosure-plans-move-to-virginia.ece (accessed September 9, 2014).

2. Ibid.

3. Robert T. Garrett, "State Legislators Told of HOA Fines, Foreclosures," *Dallas Morning News*, April 20, 2010, www

.dallasnews.com/news/politics/texas-legislature/headlines/20100419-State-legislators-told-of-HOA-fines-1617.ece (accessed September 9, 2014).

4. Ron Trevino, "Texas Lawmakers Hear Testimony on Homeowners Associations," *Dallas Morning News,* April 7, 2012, www.khou.com/news/Texas-lawmakers-hear-testimony-on-homeowners-associations-90147157.html (accessed September 9, 2014).

5. Garrett, "State Legislators Told of HOA Fines, Foreclosures."

6. *Clinton v. Cedar Rapids and Missouri River Railroad Co.,* 24 Iowa 455 (1868).

7. *Hunter v. Pittsburgh,* 207 U.S. 161 (1907).

8. Paul Egan, 2012, "Michigan's Toughened Emergency Manager Law Rejected," *Detroit Free Press,* November 7, 2012, www.freep.com/article/20121107/NEWS15/121107008 (accessed September 9, 2014).

9. Texas Constitution (1876), art. 9, sec. 1.

10. Paul Ciotti, "Money and School Performance: Lessons Learned from the Kansas City Desegregation Experiment," *Policy Analysis,* no. 298 (Washington, D.C.: CATO Institute, 1998).

11. Texas State Historical Association, "The Handbook of Texas Online: Loving County," www.tshaonline.org/handbook/online/articles/hcl13 (accessed September 9, 2014).

12. Texas Constitution (1876), art. 9, sec. 1(1).

13. Texas Association of Counties, "Chapter 1: Framework and Function of County Government," www.county.org/texas-county-government/resources/Documents/Chap1.pdf (accessed September 26, 2014).

14. National Association of Counties, "Find a County: Texas," www.naco.org/Counties/Pages/FindACounty.aspx (accessed September 26, 2014).

15. Texas Constitution (1876), art. 9, sec. 14.

16. Texas Local Government Code, chap. 158, sec. 158.001.

17. Paul K. Emmerson, *Texas Counties with Civil Service Systems: Research Report* (Austin: Texas Association of Counties, 2009). Available online at www.county.org/about-texas-counties/county-data/Documents/civil-service2009.pdf (accessed September 9, 2014).

18. Ibid.

19. Texas Local Government Code, chap. 118.

20. "New Recycling Program Biz," *Kennedale News,* January 14, 2010, www.kennedalenews.com (accessed July 9, 2010).

21. Greene County, Missouri, "Personal Property Tax: Frequently Asked Questions," www.greenecountymo.org/spane/personalproperty.htm (accessed July 9, 2014).

22. Texas Local Government Code, chap. 6, sec. 6.001 and chap. 22, secs. 22.031–22.042.

23. Texas Local Government Code, chap. 6, sec. 6.001 and chap. 23.

24. Texas Local Government Code, chap. 6, sec. 6.001; chap. 24; and chap. 25.

25. Ibid., chap. 26.

26. Texas Municipal Association, *Annual Survey of Members* (Denton: Texas Municipal Association, Inc., 2007).

27. Robert Brischetto, "Cumulative Voting at Work in Texas," in *Voting and Democracy Report: 1995* (Takoma Park, Md.: FairVote–Center for Voting and Democracy, 1995).

28. Emily Ramshaw, "State Law Would Usurp City Control of Zoning, Neighborhood Control," *Dallas Morning News,* March 2, 2007.

29. Randy Lee Loftis, "Dallas City Council Passes Restrictive Gas Drilling Ordinance," *Dallas News,* December 11, 2013, http://cityhallblog.dallasnews.com/2013/12/council-now-tackling-gas-drilling-for-the-last-time (accessed July 1, 2014); Randy Lee Loftis, "Dallas Oks Gas Drilling Rules That Are among Nation's Most Restrictive," *Dallas News,* December 11, 2013, www.dallasnews.com/news/metro/20131211-dallas-oks-gas-drilling-rules-that-are-among-natons-most-restrictive (accessed July 1, 2014).

30. Peggy Heinkel-Wolfe, "Fracking Foes Turn to Cities," *Denton Record-Chronicle,* June 21, 2014, www.dentonrc.com/local-news/local-news/headlines/20140621-fracking-foes-turn-to-cities (accessed July 2, 2014).

31. David Spense, "Resolving the State vs. Local Fracking Conflict," *Texas Enterprise,* March 20, 2014, www.texasenterprise.utexas.edu/2014/03/20/policy/resolving-state-vs-local-fracking-conflict (accessed July 1, 2014).

32. Texas Local Government Code, chap. 43, sec. 43.055.

33. Susan McFarland, "Keller Homeowners Say They've Been Shut Out of Association Despite New State Law," July 14, 2012, www.tmcnet.com/usubmit/2012/07/15/6437660.htm (accessed September 10, 2014).

34. Bill Hanna, "New Homeowners Association Laws in Texas Designed to Curb Abuses," December 26, 2011, www.star-telegram.com/2011/12/26/3619134/new-homeowner-association-laws.html (accessed September 28, 2012).

35. McFarland, "Keller Homeowners Say They've Been Shut out of Association Despite New State Law."

36. Texas Constitution (1876), art. 7.

37. Texas Education Code, chap. 11, secs. 11.301 and 11.303.

38. Ibid., chap. 11, secs. 11.051–11.058.

39. Ibid., chap. 11, secs. 11.151.

40. Texas Education Agency, "State Board of Education," www.tea.state.tx.us/index4.aspx?id=25769814582 (accessed September 10, 2014).

41. Texas Constitution, art. 7, sec. 8.

## CHAPTER 13

1. Office of the Governor, "Gov. Perry Announces Toyota Moving North American Headquarters to Plano, Generating 4,000 Jobs," April 28, 2014, http://governor.state.tx.us/news/press-release/19633/ (accessed September 10, 2014).

2. Lauren McGaughy, "State Not Ready to Share Fine Details on Toyota Deal," *Houston Chronicle,* May 29, 2014, http://blog.chron.com/texaspolitics/2014/05/rick-perrys-office-wont-release-details-of-40m-deal-with-toyota/ (accessed September 10, 2014).

3. Office of the Governor, "Texas Enterprise Fund as of August 31, 2014," www.governor.state.tx.us/files/ecodev/TEF_Listing.pdf (accessed November 8, 2014).

4. Sam Wyly and Andrew Wyly, *Texas Got It Right!* (New York: Melcher Media, 2012); Erica Grieder, *Big, Hot, Cheap, and Right: What America Can Learn from the Strange Genius of Texas* (Philadelphia, Pa.: Perseus Books Group, 2013).

5. Gail Collins, *As Texas Goes...: How the Lone Star State Hijacked the American Agenda* (New York, NY: W.W. Norton, 2012), and Cal Jillson, *Lone Star Tarnished: A Critical Look at Texas Politics and Public Policy* (New York, NY: Routledge, 2012).

6. "Texas Goes Sacramento: Republicans Spend Their Energy Gusher, and Then Some," *Wall Street Journal*, June 7, 2013, http://online.wsj.com/news/articles/SB10001424127887324299104578527193464764384 (accessed September 13, 2104).

7. James L. Haley, *Passionate Nation: The Epic History of Texas* (New York: Free Press, 2006), 81.

8. Quoted in Dave McNeely and Jim Henderson, *Bob Bullock: God Bless Texas* (Austin: University of Texas Press, 2008), 174.

9. Scott Drenkard, "State and Local Sales Taxes in 2014," Tax Foundation, March 18, 2014, http://taxfoundation.org/article/state-and-local-sales tax-rates-2014 (accessed August 11, 2014).

10. Lori L. Taylor, "Stop Playing Favorites with the Tax Code," Mosbacher Institute for Trade, Economics, and Public Policy, *The Takeaway* 2, no. 1 (2011), http://bush.tamu.edu/mosbacher/takeaway/TakeAwayVol2Iss1.pdf (accessed September 10, 2014).

11. Scott Drenkard, "The Margin Tax Holds Texas Business Back," *Texas Tribune*, Oct. 23, 2013, http://www.texastribune.org/2013/10/23/guest-column-margin-tax-holds-texas-business-back/ (accessed September 10, 2014).

12. Haley, Passionate Nation, 421.

13. Laurie Fox, "School Districts Opt for Extra Tax," *Dallas Morning News*, September 22, 2006.

14. Legislative Budget Board, "Fiscal Size-Up: 2014–15 Biennium," www.lbb.state.tx.us/Documents/Publications/Fiscal_SizeUp/Fiscal_SizeUp.pdf (accessed May 25, 2014).

15. Quoted in Ignacio Garcia, "Homeowners Say They Might Be Getting Overtaxed," KXAN, May 30, 2014, http://kxan.com/2014/05/30/home-owners-say-they-might-be-getting-overtaxed/ (accessed September 10, 2014).

16. Legislative Budget Board, "Fiscal Size-Up: 2014–15 Biennium," www.lbb.state.tx.us/Documents/Publications/Fiscal_SizeUp/Fiscal_SizeUp.pdf, 32 (accessed May 25, 2014).

17. Haley, Passionate Nation, 231.

18. Texas Constitution (1876), art. 3, sec. 49.

19. Texas Comptroller, "Biennial Revenue Estimate," 2014–2015 Biennium, 83rd Texas Legislature, January 7, 2013, www.texastransparency.org/State_Finance/Budget_Finance/Reports/Biennial_Revenue_Estimate/bre2014/BRE_2014-15.pdf (accessed May 28, 2014).

20. Evan Smith, "One Ticked-Off Grandma," *Texas Monthly*, December 2003, 163.

21. Legislative Budget Board, "Fiscal Size-Up: 2014–15 Biennium," 24, www.lbb.state.tx.us/Documents/Publications/Fiscal_SizeUp/Fiscal_SizeUp_2014-15.pdf (accessed September 11, 2014).

22. Texas Bond Review Board, Local Government Services, www.brb.state.tx.us/lgs/lgspubs2013.aspx (accessed June 10, 2014).

23. Texas Comptroller of Public Accounts, "Your Money and Local Debt," September 2012, www.texastransparency.org/Special_Features/Your_Money/pdf/TexasItsYourMoney-LocalDebt.pdf (accessed June 10, 2014).

24. Rick Perry, "Message," May 26, 2007, www.governor.state.tx.us/divisions/press/bills/letters/letter3-052607 (accessed September 29, 2012).

25. Texas Comptroller of Public Accounts, " Sales Tax Holiday This Weekend - Aug. 8 to 10," August 4, 2014 http://www.window.state.tx.us/news2014/140804-salestax-holiday-reminder.html (accessed November 9, 2014)

26. Joseph Henchman, "Sales Tax Holidays: Politically Expedient but Poor Tax Policy," Tax Foundation, July 30, 2012, http://taxfoundation.org/article/sales-tax-holidays-politically-expedient-poor-tax-policy-3 (accessed September 11, 2014).

27. Sandra Baker, "Helicopter Maker Seeks $13.5 Million Tax Break," *Fort Worth Star Telegram*, November 2, 2011, www.star-telegram.com/2011/11/01/3492198/helicopter-maker-seeks-135-million.html (accessed September 29, 2012).

28. Mitchell Schnurman, "Bell Seeks Tax Breaks but Can Afford to Pay Wall Street," *Fort Worth Star Telegram*, November 5, 2011, www.star-telegram.com/2011/11/05/3501816/bell-seeks-tax-breaks-but-can.html (accessed September 29, 2012).

29. Darrell Preston, "Texas Cities Bear Financial Burden of Rapid Growth," *Fort Worth Star-Telegram*, June 7, 2014, www.star-telegram.com/2014/06/06/5880209/texas-cities-bear-financial-burden.html (accessed September 11, 2014).

30. Darrell Preston and Aaron Kuriloff, "Texas Taxpayers Finance Formula One Auto Races as Schools Dismiss Teachers," Bloomberg.com, May 11, 2011, www.bloomberg.com/news/2011-05-11/texas-taxpayers-finance-formula-one-auto-races-as-schools-dismiss-teachers.html (accessed September 11, 2014).

31. Office of the Governor, "Texas Emerging Technology Fund, FY 2013 Legislative Report, September 1, 2012–August 31, 2013," http://governor.state.tx.us/files/ecodev/etf/TETF_Report_FY2013.pdf (accessed May 29, 2014).

32. Office of the Governor, "Gov. Perry Signs $22 Million Film Incentive Bill," June 7, 2007, http://governor.state.tx.us/news/press-release/2222/ (accessed September 11, 2014).

33. Office of the Governor, "Gov, Perry Signs HB 873 to Provide Incentives for Entertainment Industries," April 23, 2009, http://governor.state.tx.us/news/press-release/12277/ (accessed September 11, 2014).

34. Matt Brian, "Apple Closes Deal to Expand Austin Campus, Moves ahead with $304 Million Texas Investment,"

The Next Web, July 18, 2012, http://
thenextweb.com/apple/2012/07/18/
apple-closes-deal-to-expand-austin-
campus-moves-ahead-with-304-million-
texas-investment/ (accessed September
11, 2014).

35. University of Texas/*Texas Tribune*,
"Texas Statewide Survey, February
11–17," February 2011, http://
s3.amazonaws.com/static.texastribune
.org/media/documents/uttt-
SummaryDoc-day1.pdf (accessed
September 11, 2014).

36. Ross Ramsey, "UT/TT Poll: Water Is
a Priority, but Not a Top Problem,"
*Texas Tribune*, March 7, 2013, www
.texastribune.org/2013/03/07/uttt-
poll-water-priority-not-top-problem/
(accessed June 23, 2014).

## CHAPTER 14

1. Texas Education Agency, Division of
Research and Analysis, Department
of Assessment and Accountability,
"Enrollment in Texas Public Schools,
2012–13," March 2014, www.tea.state
.tx.us/acctres/Enroll_2012-13.pdf
(accessed June 2, 2014).

2. Texas Higher Education Coordinating
Board, "Certified Fall 2013 Texas
Higher Ed Enrollment Data," May 22,
2014, www.txhighereddata.org/index
.cfm?objectid=787E6F83-DA63-ED42-
BBB84792D2E35965 (accessed June 2,
2014).

3. James L. Haley, *Passionate Nation: The
Epic History of Texas* (New York: Free
Press, 2006), 232.

4. Dolph Briscoe, as quoted in Don
Carleton, *Dolph Briscoe: My Life in
Texas Ranching and Politics* (Austin,
Tex.: Center for American History),
100.

5. Texas Education Agency, "Texas
Public School Statistics: Snapshot
2013 Summary Tables, State Totals,"
http://ritter.tea.state.tx.us/perfreport/
snapshot/2013/state
.html (accessed June 3, 2014).

6. Brian Thevenot, "Colbert Report
Satirizes Texas History Textbooks,"

*Texas Tribune*, March 17, 2010, www
.texastribune.org/texas-education/
state-board-of-education/colbert-
report-satirizes-texas-history-textbooks/
(accessed September 11, 2014).

7. 163 U.S. 537 (1896).

8. 347 U.S. 483 (1954).

9. 349 U.S. 294 (1955).

10. Judge Justice's order in the *United States
v. Texas* case is generally referred to as
Civil Order 5821.

11. Amended Complaint, *LULAC v State
of Texas*, Civil Action No. 6:14-CV-
138, www.expressnews
.com/file/825/825-130-Amended-
Complaint-filed-by-LULAC.pdf, 11,
(accessed September 11, 2014).

12. Morgan Smith, "Lawsuit: Texas' English
Language Programs Fall Short," *Texas
Tribune*, June 10, 2014, www
.texastribune.org/2014/06/10/lawsuit-
texas-failing-english-language-students/
(accessed June 19, 2014).

13. Texas Education Agency, Division of
Performance Reporting, Academic
Excellence Indicator System, "2011–12
State Performance Report," http://ritter
.tea.state.tx.us/perfreport/aeis/2012/
state.html (accessed June 3, 2014).

14. 777 S.W. 2d 391 (Tex. 1989).

15. Ross Ramsey, "Sales Tax Plan Would
Redefine School District Wealth," *Texas
Tribune*, April 7, 2014, www
.texastribune.org/2014/04/07/sales-tax-
plan-would-redefine-school-district-
weal/ (accessed June 20, 2014).

16. Jenny Lacoste-Caputo and Gary
Scharrer, "Expect Another School-
Funding Lawsuit," *Houston Chronicle*,
August 1, 2010.

17. Morgan Smith, "Texas School Finance
Trial Goes for Round Two," *Texas
Tribune*, June 19, 2013, www
.texastribune.org/2013/06/19/texas-
school-finance-trial-goes-round-two/
(accessed June 5, 2014).

18. Ross Ramsey, "UT/TT Poll: Partisan
Harmony, Dissonance on Education,"
*Texas Tribune*, February 25, 2014, www
.texastribune.org/2014/02/25/uttt-poll-
partisan-differences-education-also-
some/ (accessed June 24, 2014).

19. Terrence Stutz, "Quirk in Texas Testing
Law Could Cost High Schoolers a Shot
at State Universities," *Dallas Morning
News*, July 10, 2012, www.dallasnews.
com/news/state/headlines/20120710-
quirk-in-texas-testing-law-could-
cost-high-schoolers-a-shot-at-state-
universities.ece (accessed September
11, 2014).

20. Joshua Benton and Holly Hacker,
"Analysis Shows TAKS Cheating
Rampant," *Dallas Morning News*, June 3,
2007.

21. Joshua Benton, "TAKS Analysis Suggests
Many Graduates Cheated," *Dallas
Morning News*, June 11, 2006, 1A.

22. Marie C. Stetser and Robert Stillwell,
"Public High School Four-Year On-
Time Graduation Rates and Event
Dropout Rates: School Years 2010–11
and 2011–12," U.S. Department of
Education, April 28, 2014, http://nces
.ed.gov/pubs2014/2014391.pdf (accessed
June 20, 2014).

23. Robert Stillwell and Jennifer Sable,
"Public School Graduates and
Dropouts from the Common Core
of Data: School Year 2009–10,"
U.S. Department of Education,
January 22, 2013, http://nces.ed.gov/
pubs2013/2013309rev.pdf (accessed
June 20, 2014).

24. Jessica Barnett, "SAT Scores by
State, 2013," Common Wealth
Foundation, October 10, 2013, www
.commonwealthfoundation.org/
policyblog/detail/sat-scores-by-
state-2013 (accessed June 20, 2014).

25. ACT, "2013 ACT National and State
Scores: Average Scores by State," www
.act.org/newsroom/data/2013/states.
html (accessed June 23, 2014).

26. University of Texas/*Texas Tribune*,
"Texas Statewide Survey," February 17,
2014, http://s3.amazonaws.com/static
.texastribune.org/media/documents/
utttpoll-201402-fullsummary.pdf
(accessed June 14, 2014).

27. Lyndsey Layton, "In New Orleans,
Major School District Closes Traditional
Public Schools for Good," *Washington
Post*, May 28, 2014.

28. University of Texas/*Texas Tribune*, "Texas Statewide Survey."

29. National Education Association, "Rankings & Estimates: Rankings of the States 2013 and Estimates of School Statistics 2014," March 2014, table C-11, "Average Salaries of Public School Teachers, 2012–13," www.nea.org/home/rankings-and-estimates-2013-2014.html.

30. Bill Hobby and Saralee Tiede, *How Things Really Work: Lessons from a Life in Politics* (Austin, Tex.: Dolph Briscoe Center for American History, 2010), 97.

31. Jay Mathews, "Caveat Lector: Unexamined Assumptions about Quality in Higher Education," in *Declining by Degrees: Higher Education at Risk*, eds. Richard H. Hersh and John Merrow (New York: MacMillan/Palgrave, 2005), 48.

32. Financial Statements and Independent Auditors' Reports, Permanent University Funds, Years Ended August 31, 2013, www.utimco.org/Funds/Endowment/PUF/PUF2013AuditedFinancials.pdf (accessed June 25, 2014).

33. Hobby and Tiede, *How Things Really Work: Lessons from a Life in Politics*, 124.

34. Charles Miller, "Why Student Regents Shouldn't Vote," *Texas Tribune*, May 13, 2010, www.texastribune.org/texas-education/higher-education/why-student-regents-shouldnt-vote/ (accessed September 11, 2014).

35. Alexa Garcia-Ditta, "Student Regents Have a Voice but No Vote," *Texas Tribune*, May 12, 2010, www.texastribune.org/texas-education/higher-education/student-regents-have-a-voice-but-no-vote/ (accessed September 11, 2014).

36. ACT, "The Condition of College and Career Readiness, 2013," www.act.org/research/policymakers/cccr13/pdf/CCCR13-NationalReadinessRpt.pdf (accessed June 24, 2014).

37. Texas Higher Education Coordinating Board, "Closing the Gaps Spring 2013 Progress Report," June 2013, www.thecb.state.tx.us/reports/PDF/3114.PDF?CFID=12012405&CFTOKEN=15752463 (accessed June 20, 2014).

38. Texas Higher Education Coordinating Board, Division of Planning and Accountability, "Closing the Gaps Progress Report, 2012," June 2012.

39. Reeve Hamilton, "Despite Success, Some Shortcomings in Texas Higher Ed," *Texas Tribune*, July 8, 2014, www.texastribune.org/2014/07/08/deadline-nears-closing-gaps-higher-education/ (accessed July 10, 2014).

40. 78 F.3d 932 (5th Cir. 1996).

41. *Abigail N. Fisher v. University of Texas at Austin, Et Al*, amicus brief, http://chronicle.com/blogs/players/files/2012/08/coaches-amicus.pdf (accessed September 12, 2014).

42. Peter Schmidt, "Supreme Court Is Flooded with Briefs Defending Race-Conscious Admissions," *Chronicle of Higher Education*, August 14, 2012, https://chronicle.com/article/Supreme-Court-Is-Flooded-With/133625/ (accessed September 12, 2014).

43. (5th Cir. 2014) Accessed http://www.ca5.uscourts.gov/opinions/pub/09/09-50822-CV2.pdf

44. Texas Higher Education Coordinating Board, "Overview: Tuition Deregulation," 2010, www.thecb.state.tx.us/Reports/PDF/2266.PDF (accessed September 12, 2014).

45. Hobby and Tiede, *How Things Really Work: Lessons from a Life in Politics*.

46. Office of the Governor, "TETF Annual Report Executive Summary," January 30, 2012, http://governor.state.tx.us/files/ecodev/etf/TETF_Exe_Summary_FY2011.pdf (accessed October 3, 2012).

47. David Muto, "The Brief: Top Texas News for June 19, 2012," *Texas Tribune*, June 19, 2012, www.texastribune.org/texas-newspaper/texas-news/brief-top-texas-news-june-19-2012/ (accessed September 12, 2014).

48. Texas Department of Aging and Disability Services, "Frequently Asked Questions," www.dads.state.tx.us/services/faqs-fact/faq/index.html (accessed June 24, 2014).

49. United States Census Bureau, "Number of People Living in 'Poverty Areas' up, Census Bureau Reports," June 30, 2014, www.census.gov/newsroom/press-releases/2014/cb14-123.html# (accessed September 12, 2014).

50. Texas Health and Human Services Commission, "TANF Statistics," www.hhsc.state.tx.us/research/TANF-Statewide.asp (accessed September 12, 2014).

51. Jeffrey M. Jones, "Texas Widens Gap over Other States in Percentage Uninsured," Gallup Report, March 2, 2012, www.gallup.com/poll/153053/Texas-Widens-Gap-States-Percentage-Uninsured.aspx (accessed September 12, 2014).

52. Texas Health and Human Services Commission, "Medicaid Enrollment by Month," www.hhsc.state.tx.us/research/MedicaidEnrollment/ME-Monthly.asp (access June 24, 2014).

53. "Heal Program Enrolling Fewer Kids," *Dallas Morning News*, March 1, 2006, 4A.

## CHAPTER 15

1. Brantley Hargrove, "State and EPA Battle over Fracking, Flaming Well Water," *Houston Press*, April 25, 2012.

2. Ibid.

3. Jon Hamilton, "Town's Effort to Link Fracking and Illness Falls Short," NPR, May 16, 2012, www.npr.org/2012/05/16/152204584/towns-effort-to-link-fracking-and-illness-falls-short (accessed September 12, 2014).

4. Ibid.

5. Randolph B. Campbell, *Gone to Texas* (New York: Oxford University Press, 2004).

6. Bryan Burrough, *The Rise and Fall of the Greatest Texas Oil Fortunes* (New York: Penguin Press, 2009).

7. Robert Calvert, Arnoldo De León, and Gregg Cantrell, *The History of Texas* (Wheeling, Ill.: Harlan Davidson Press, 2002).

8. Kate Alexander, "Texas Oil and Gas Boom May Ease State Budget Crunch," *Austin American Statesman*, April 7, 2012.

9. Texas Comptroller of Public Accounts, "The Energy Report," May 2008, www.window.state.tx.us/specialrpt/energy/pdf/96-1266EnergyReport.pdf (accessed September 12, 2014).

10. Amy Madden "Texas Oil Boom Means More Money for UT, A&M," *Dallas Morning News*, Nov 22, 2013.

11. Mine K. Yücel and Jackson Thies, "Oil and Gas Rises Again in a Diversified Texas," Federal Reserve Bank of Dallas, *Southwest Economy*, "First Quarter 2011," http://dallasfed.org/research/swe/2011/swe1101g.cfm (accessed September 12, 2014).

12. Texas Comptroller of Public Accounts, "Industry Report," www.window.state.tx.us/specialrpt/tif/gulf/indProfiles.php#oil (accessed September 12, 2014).

13. Brett Shipp, "Scientists: Tests Prove Fracking to Blame for Flaming Parker County Wells," WFAA, June 5, 2014, www.wfaa.com/news/investigates/Scientists-say-state-tests-prove-fracking-to-blame-for-Parker-Co-flaming-wells-262056131.html (accessed September 12, 2014).

14. Forrest Wilder, "Study: In the Midst of Drought Fracking, Industry Does Little to Recycle Water," *Texas Observer*, February 4, 2014, www.texasobserver.org/study-little-progress-made-recycling-water-fracking/ (accessed September 12, 2014).

15. Ricky Jervis, "Fracking Wells Possible Culprit of Texas Earthquakes," *USA Today*, June 1, 2014, www.usatoday.com/story/news/nation/2014/06/01/earthquakes-texas-fracking-wells/9765659/ (accessed September 12, 2014).

16. John Broder and Kate Galbraith, "EPA Is Longtime Favorite Target for Perry," *New York Times*, September 30, 2011.

17. Environmental Protection Agency, "State Energy CO2 Emmissions," http://epa.gov/statelocalclimate/documents/pdf/CO2FFC_2011.pdf (accessed September 12, 2014).

18. Asher Price, "Texas Sues to Stop EPA from Regulating Greenhouse Gases," *Austin American Statesman*, February 16, 2010.

19. Ellen Craft, "State of the Air 2014: 19 Texas Counties Continue to Struggle with Ozone Pollution," Environmental Defense Fund, May 6, 2014, http://blogs.edf.org/texascleanairmatters/2014/05/06/state-of-the-air-2014-19-texas-counties-continue-to-struggle-with-ozone-pollution/ (accessed September 12, 2014).

20. Kate Galbraith, "Drought Caused Big Drop in Texas Portion of Ogallala," *Texas Tribune*, July 3, 2012.

21. "Texas' 2011 Drought Costliest in the State's History," MSNBC, March 22, 2012, www.msnbc.msn.com/id/46821228/ns/weather/t/texas-drought-costliest-state-history/ (accessed October 5, 2012).

22. Theodore Valenti et al., "Influence of Drought and Total Phosphorus on Diel pH in Wadeable Streams: Implications for Econological Risk Assessment of Ionizable Contaminants," *Integrated Environmental Assessment and Management* 7, no. 4 (October 2011): 636–647.

23. American Wind Energy Association, "U.S. Wind Industry First Quarter 2014 Market Report," April 2014, http://awea.files.cms-plus.com/FileDownloads/pdfs/1Q2014%20AWEA%20Public%20Report.pdf (accessed June 11, 2014).

24. Clifford Krauss, "Move Over Oil, There's Money in Texas Wind," *New York Times*, February 23, 2008.

25. American Wind Energy Association, "State Wind Energy Statistics," www.awea.org/Resources/state.aspx?ItemNumber=5183 (accessed June 11, 2014).

26. House Research Organization, "Solar Energy in Texas," July 20, 2010, www.hro.house.state.tx.us/pdf/focus/Solar81-13.pdf (accessed September 12, 2014).

27. Calvert et al., *The History of Texas*.

28. T. R. Fehrenbach, *Lone Star: A History of Texas and the Texans* (Cambridge, Mass.: Da Capo Press, 2000), 319.

29. Ibid., 604.

30. Campbell, *Gone to Texas*, 306

31. Cal Jillson, *Lone Star Tarnished: A Critical Look at Texas Politics and Public Policy* (New York: Routledge Press, 2012); Karl Wallace, "Texas and the Good Roads Movement: 1895 to 1948," master's thesis at the University of Texas at Arlington, 2008.

32. Fehrenbach, *Lone Star: A History of Texas and the Texans*, 319.

33. Wallace, "Texas and the Good Roads Movement: 1895 to 1948."

34. Campbell, *Gone to Texas*, 351.

35. Texas Department of Transportation, "TXDOT History: 1930 to 1917," http://archive.today/vHHB (accessed September 13, 2014).

36. Fehrenbach, *Lone Star: A History of Texas and the Texans*, 649.

37. Calvert et al., *The History of Texas*.

38. Legislative Budget Board, "Texas Highway Funding: Legislative Primer," March 2011, www.lbb.state.tx.us/Transportation/2011%20Texas%20Highway%20Funding%20Primer%200311.pdf (accessed October 5, 2012).

39. David Ellis, Texas A&M Transportation Institute, "Testimony before the Texas House of Representatives Appropriations Sub-Committee on Articles VI, VII and VIII," February 12, 2013, http://tti.tamu.edu/policy/wp-content/uploads/2014/01/David-Ellis-testimony-2-12-13.pdf (accessed September 15, 2014).

40. American Petroleum Institute, "State Motor Fuel Taxes," April 2014, www.api.org/oil-and-natural-gas-overview/industry-economics/~/media/Files/Statistics/state-motor-fuel-taxes-report-summary.pdf (accessed June 1, 2014).

41. Legislative Budget Board, "Texas Highway Funding: Legislative Primer."

42. Patricia Kilday Hart, "Perry's Texas: Transportation Needs Left Unmet," *Houston Chronicle*, August 16, 2011.

43. Ibid.

44. Ibid.

45. Ibid.

46. Legislative Budget Board, "Texas Highway Funding: Legislative Primer."

47. Aman Batheja, "For TXDOT, a $2 Billion 'Perception Problem,'" *Texas Tribune*, June 11, 2012.

48. Ben Wear and Jeremy Schwartz, "Toll Rates Going up on Three Area Roads; Disabled Vets to See Tolls Waived," *Austin American Statesman*, August 30, 2012.

49. Fehrenbach, *Lone Star: A History of Texas and the Texans*, 319.

50. Jillson, *Lone Star Tarnished: A Critical Look at Texas Politics and Public Policy*.

51. Texas Comptroller of Public Accounts, "Undocumented Immigrants in Texas: A Financial Analysis of the Impact to the State Budget and Economy," December 2006, www.window.state.tx.us/ specialrpt/undocumented/ (accessed September 13, 2014).

52. Isabel C. Morales and Al Dia, "Swift Plant Raid Devastated Cactus," *Dallas Morning News*, February 11, 2007.

53. 457 U.S. 202 (1982).

54. Ibid.

55. Katherine Leal Unmuth, "Tyler Case Opened Schools to Illegal Migrants," *Dallas Morning News*, June 11, 2007.

56. "Texas Monday Talks: Dick Armey," *Texas Monthly*, January 2007, 66.

57. Jim Henson and Joshua Blank, "Is Easy Resolution on In-state Tuition a GOP Dream?," *Texas Tribune*, May 8, 2014, www.texastribune.org/2014/05/08/easy-resolution-state-tuition-gop-dream/ (accessed September 13, 2014).

58. Chris Tomlinson, "Poll: Hispanics in Texas More Likely to Favor GOP than the Rest of the Nation," *Austin American Statesman*, February 7, 2014, www.statesman.com/news/news/state-regional-govt-politics/poll-hispanics-in-texas-more-likely-to-favor-gop-t/ndHM2/ (accessed September 13, 2014).

# GLOSSARY

**Administrative federalism:** the process whereby the national government sets policy guidelines then expects state governments to pay for the programs they engender without the aid of federal monies. (Ch. 12)

**Ad-valorem tax:** a tax based on property value, which is subject to periodic appraisals. (Ch. 13)

**Advanced or early voting:** a voting system that allows a voter to cast a ballot before an election without giving a specific reason, thus making voting more convenient for the voter. (Ch. 9)

**Affirm:** appellate court upholds the lower court's decision. (Ch. 7)

**Agenda setting:** the stage in which policymakers prioritize the problems facing the state. (Ch. 13)

**Allocation:** the process by which party rules designate how many of the state's delegates to the national party convention will be pledged to vote for a specific candidate or attend as undecided. (Ch. 10)

**Amendment:** a formal change to a bill made during the committee process or during floor debate in front of the whole chamber. (Ch. 4)

**Annexation:** a process whereby areas adjacent to a city are added to the city, thereby extending the city limits. (Ch. 12)

**Appellate jurisdiction:** the authority to hear an appeal from a lower court that has already rendered a decision; an appellate court reviews the court record from the original trial and does not hear new evidence. (Ch. 7)

**Appointed regulatory commission:** an agency of the state government whose members oversee a specific department of state government, are appointed by the governor, and are confirmed by the Texas Senate. (Ch. 6)

**Appointment power:** the ability to determine who will occupy key positions within the bureaucracy. (Ch. 5)

**Appraisal:** the official estimate of a property's value. (Ch. 13)

**Astroturf lobbying:** a simulation of grassroots support, usually conducted by specialized lobbying firms; involves spending large sums of money to generate the appearance of public support to advance a group's agenda. (Ch. 11)

**At-large election:** an election in which a city or county is treated as a single district and candidates are elected from the entire district as a whole. (Ch. 7)

**Attorney general:** chief legal advisor for the state who represents the state in courts and issues advisory opinions on legal matters to the governor, legislature, and other state agencies. (Ch. 6)

**Auditor:** a county officer appointed by the district judge to oversee county finances. (Ch. 12)

**Beyond a reasonable doubt:** the standard burden of proof necessary to find a defendant guilty in a criminal trial; the defendant is presumed innocent. (Ch. 7)

**Bicameral:** a legislature that consists of two separate chambers or houses. (Ch. 3)

**Bill:** a proposed new law or change to existing law brought before a legislative chamber by a legislative member. (Ch. 3, 4)

**Blanket or wide-open primary:** a primary in which voters do not register party affiliations and receive ballot papers containing the names of all candidates from all political parties running for office; usually voters may choose only one candidate per office rather than one candidate per political party. (Ch. 9)

**Block grant:** national funds given to state and local governments for a broad purpose; comes with fewer restrictions on how the money is to be spent. (Ch. 2)

**Blocking bill:** a bill regularly introduced in the Texas Senate to serve as a placeholder at the top of the Senate calendar; sometimes called a stopper. (Ch. 4)

**Budget power:** the executive's ability to exert influence on the state's budget process. (Ch. 5)

**Bureaucracy:** a method of organizing any large public or private organization that includes hierarchical structure, division of labor, standard operating procedures, and advancement by merit. (Ch. 6)

**Capital punishment:** also known as the death penalty; refers to when the state puts an individual to death for certain crimes (Ch. 8)

**Casework:** the process of solving problems for constituents. (Ch. 9)

**Castle doctrine:** Texas law that allows the use of deadly force to defend your home, or "castle." (Ch. 8)

**Categorical grant:** national money given to states and local governments that must be spent for specific activities. (Ch. 2)

**Ceremonial duty:** an appearance made by the governor as the most visible state officeholder that can function as a source of power; includes appearances at events and performance of ceremonial functions. (Ch. 5)

**Chronic minority:** a group that rarely wins elections or achieves majority status and thus sees few reasons to become actively engaged in politics. (Ch. 10)

**Chubbing:** the act of delaying action on the current bill before the Texas House of Representatives to prevent action on an upcoming bill. (Ch. 4)

**Citizen initiative:** a citizen-initiated petition that forces consideration or votes on certain legislation and amendments rather than having these actions come from the legislature. (Ch. 3)

**Citizen legislature:** a legislature that attempts to keep the role of a state legislator to a part-time function so that many or most citizens can perform it; normally, a citizen legislator is provided minimal compensation, offered few staffing resources, and has short or infrequent legislative sessions. (Ch. 3)

**City charter:** a plan of government that details the structure and function of the city government; similar to a constitution. (Ch. 12)

**Civil case:** a case in which an aggrieved party sues for damages claiming that he or she has been wronged by another individual. (Ch. 7)

**Civil defendant:** the party alleged to have committed the wrong at issue in a civil suit. (Ch. 7)

**Closed primary:** an electoral contest restricted to party loyalists that excludes supporters of other political parties and independent voters. (Ch. 9)

**Closed rider:** a rider that is not made public until after the legislature has voted on the bill; it is made public either when the bill goes to conference committee for reconciliation or when the governor prepares to sign the bill into law. (Ch. 4)

**Cohesion:** unity within a group; in politics, when members of a political party or special caucus vote together on a bill or resolution. (Ch. 4)

**Collective goods:** benefits that, once provided, go to everyone and cannot be effectively denied to others, even those who did not contribute to the effort. (Ch. 11)

**Commissioner of the General Land Office:** administers state-owned lands, controls the Permanent School Fund, and controls leases for the development of mineral and other resources on public lands; the office is sometimes called the land commissioner. (Ch. 6)

**Commissioners court:** the governing body for Texas counties, consisting of four elected commissioners and the judge from the county constitutional court. (Ch. 12)

**Committee:** a formally organized group of legislators that assists the legislature in accomplishing its work, allowing a division of labor and an in-depth review of an issue or a bill before review by the entire chamber. (Ch. 4)

**Compensatory damages:** monetary damages designed to compensate the injured party. (Ch. 7)

**Comptroller of public accounts:** collects fees and taxes, invests state funds, estimates revenue, and oversees payments by the state for goods and services. (Ch. 6)

**Concurrent jurisdiction:** a system in which different levels of courts have overlapping jurisdiction or authority to try the same type of case. (Ch. 7)

**Concurrent powers:** powers such as taxing and spending and the ability to establish courts and charter banks that are shared by the national and state governments. (Ch. 2)

**Concurrent resolution:** a legislative act that expresses an opinion of the legislature; must pass in both houses. (Ch. 4)

**Concurring opinion:** an opinion written by a justice who agrees with the decision but not with the reasoning of the court. (Ch. 7)

**Confederal system:** a type of government in which the lower units of government retain decision-making authority. (Ch. 2)

**Conference committee:** an official legislative work group that meets on a limited basis to reconcile the different versions of a bill that has passed in the Texas House and Senate. (Ch. 4)

**Constable:** an elected county officer who acts as a judicial officer for minor criminal and civil cases; assists the justice of the peace with his or her duties. (Ch. 12)

**Constitution:** a written document that outlines the powers of government and the limitations on those powers. (Ch. 2)

**Contract outsourcing:** a process whereby a government entity contracts with a private company to perform a service that governments traditionally provide, such as a contract to collect trash and garbage. (Ch. 12)

**Conventions (caucuses):** meetings at which party members participate in a range of party business. (Ch. 10)

**Cooperative federalism:** the theory of federalism that suggests both levels of government cooperate across various policy areas rather than maintaining distinct policy arenas.

**County attorney:** the county official who represents the county in legal activities and offers legal advice to the county government. (Ch. 12)

**County chair** (*see* **Precinct chair**)

**County civil service commission:** the agency administering the county's civil service system; develops job definitions, qualification processes, employee classifications, and other aspects of the system. (Ch. 12)

**County clerk:** the elected county official who maintains county records and in some counties oversees elections. (Ch. 12)

**County or senatorial district convention:** a convention in which delegates to the statewide convention are selected; held on the third Saturday after the primary election. (Ch. 10)

**Credit claiming:** the advantage derived from incumbents' ability to point to positive outcomes for which they are responsible. (Ch. 4, 9)

**Criminal case:** a case in which an individual is charged by the state with violating the laws and the state brings the suit. (Ch. 7)

**Criminal defendant:** a person charged with committing a crime. (Ch. 7)

**Crisis manager:** the responsibility to act as a policymaker, coordinator of resources, and point person in the wake of natural and man-made disasters. (Ch. 5)

**Cross-filing:** a system that allows a candidate to run simultaneously as a Democratic and a Republican candidate, essentially competing in both parties' primaries. (Ch. 9)

**Cumulative voting:** a system that allows voters to take the total number of positions to be selected in a district and concentrate their votes among one or a few candidates. (Ch. 7)

**Dark money:** money spent on political activites by a nonprofit organization that does not have to report its sources of funding. (Ch. 11)

**Delegate:** an elected official who acts as an agent of the majority that elected her or him to office and carries out, to the extent possible, the wishes of that majority. (Ch. 3)

**Delegates:** party members elected to attend their party's conventions that are held later at the county level or the Texas senatorial district level. (Ch. 10)

**De novo:** to hear an appeal with a new trial in the absence of an official case record. (Ch. 7)

**Devolution:** returning power to state governments. (Ch. 2)

**Dillon's Rule:** the principle that, regardless of the type of local government, all local governments are creatures of the state government and have only those powers specifically granted to them by the state. (Ch. 12)

**Direct primary:** a primary election in which the winning candidate directly receives the party nomination. (Ch. 9)

**Disclosure:** the reporting of who contributes money to a campaign and how much is contributed by an individual or corporation. (Ch. 9)

**Dissenting opinion:** an opinion written by a justice who disagrees with the decision of the court. (Ch. 7)

**Distributive policy:** moves benefits to meet the needs of citizens but does so without targeting any one group as the source of money. (Ch. 13)

**Disturbance theory:** a theory of group formation that states that as societies become more complex and more diverse, new interests emerge to voice their concerns, prompting established interests to mobilize to protect the status quo. (Ch. 11)

**Dual federalism:** the theory of federalism that suggests state governments and the national government have separate spheres of policy influence and restrict their involvement to policies in their areas.

**Education Reform Act:** a 1984 statute that requires teachers and school administrators to take a test to assure basic competency before being recertified; students are also tested periodically to monitor progress and are required to pass an exam before being allowed to graduate. (Ch. 14)

**Elected board: a** directly elected board, such as the Railroad Commission of Texas, that oversees a specific department of Texas government. (Ch. 6)

**Electioneering:** method used by organized interests to try to shape public policy by influencing who is elected to office, especially by serving as sources of campaign funding. (Ch. 11)

**Electoral competition model:** the view that parties make a pragmatic move to the center of the political spectrum as they attempt to win votes, sacrificing the more purely ideological positions. (Ch. 10)

**Emergency clause:** language that makes a bill effective immediately upon being signed into law rather than subject to the customary ninety-day waiting period. (Ch. 4)

**Emergency legislation:** a designation by the governor that allows proposed legislation to be moved to the beginning of the legislative session and be voted on during the first sixty days of the session. (Ch. 5)

**Eminent domain:** the power of government to take private property for public use, generally for public functions, such as roads. (Ch. 15)

**Empresario:** an entrepreneur who made money colonizing areas of the Mexican territories. (Ch. 1)

**En banc:** an appeal that is heard by the entire court of appeals rather than by a select panel of judges. (Ch. 7)

**Enhanced penalties:** penal code provision that allows repeat offenders to be charged

with a higher-degree offense on subsequent convictions. (Ch. 7)

**Enumerated powers:** the powers listed in Article I, Section 8 of the U.S. Constitution that are expressly granted to the national government. (Ch. 2)

**Equal protection clause:** clause of the Fourteenth Amendment to the U.S. Constitution requiring that state laws and state constitutions treat all citizens the same. (Ch. 9)

**Executive order:** orders issued by the executive to direct existing agencies or create new committees or task forces in order to address a particular policy area. (Ch. 5)

**Excise tax:** a tax paid at the time of purchase, with the cost of the tax included in the price of the product. (Ch. 13)

**Exclusive jurisdiction:** a particular court given the sole right to hear a specific type of case. (Ch. 7)

**Executive committee:** this group, selected at the state party convention, carries on the activities of the party between party conventions; by law, the committee consists of sixty-two members—one man and one woman from each of the state's thirty-one senatorial districts. (Ch. 10)

**Executive order:** orders issued by the executive to direct existing agencies or create new committees or task forces in order to address a particular policy area. (Ch. 5)

**Expressive benefits:** benefits that arise from taking action to express one's views; motivates group membership. (Ch. 11)

**Extradition:** the constitutional requirement that a state deliver someone suspected or convicted of a crime in another state back to the state where the crime allegedly occurred so the accused can face trial or sentencing. (Ch. 2)

**Federalism:** a form of government based on the sharing of powers between the levels of government; in the United States, between the national and state governments. (Ch. 2)

**Filibuster:** an effort to kill a bill by engaging in unlimited debate and refusing to yield the floor to another member, ultimately preventing a vote on the bill. (Ch. 4)

**Fiscal federalism:** use of financial incentives by the national government to encourage policies at the state or local level. (Ch. 2, 12)

**Fiscal policy:** how government seeks to influence the economy through taxing and spending. (Ch. 13)

**Floor debate:** period during which a bill is brought up before the entire chamber for debate. (Ch. 4)

**Floor leader:** a party member who reminds legislators of the party's position on a bill and encourages members to vote with the rest of the party caucus; the floor leader is assisted by one or more deputy floor leaders. (Ch. 4)

**Fracking:** fracturing underground rock formations and using high-pressure injections of chemicals and water to cause natural gas to rise to the surface. (Ch. 15)

**Franchise tax:** the primary tax on businesses in Texas, which is based on the taxable margin of each company. (Ch. 13)

**Free-rider:** problem occurs when citizens who do not contribute to the efforts of a group nevertheless enjoy the results of those efforts. (Ch. 11)

**Full faith and credit clause:** the constitutional requirement that court judgments or legal contracts entered into in one state will be honored by all other states. (Ch. 2)

**General election:** an interparty election in which candidates from two or more political parties and independent candidates compete for actual political office. (Ch. 9)

**General law city:** the default organization for Texas cities, with the exact forms of government, ordinance powers, and other aspects of city government specified in the Texas Local Government Code. (Ch. 12)

**General sales tax:** an across-the-board tax imposed on goods and services sold within a jurisdiction. (Ch. 13)

**Gerrymandering:** the practice of incumbents creating very oddly shaped electoral districts to maximize their political advantage in an upcoming election. (Ch. 3)

**Good Roads Amendment:** state constitutional requirement that 75 percent of road-user fees be spent on building and maintaining roads and the remaining 25 percent be used for education. (Ch. 15)

**Grandfather clause:** the granting of voting rights only to those citizens whose grandfathers had the right to vote; used to bar African Americans from voting in the South after the end of Reconstruction. (Ch. 9)

**Grand jury:** a panel of twelve jurors that reviews evidence, determines whether there is sufficient evidence to bring a trial, and issues an indictment. (Ch. 7)

**Grassroots lobbying:** attempts by organized interests to influence legislators through public opinion; extension of democratic principles in which groups of citizens spontaneously mobilize to build support for a cause. (Ch. 11)

**Grassroots organization:** a group in which power and decision making reside with average citizens; the participation of average citizens is the foundation upon which these groups' legitimacy rests. (Ch. 10)

**Grasstop lobbying:** the attempt to influence legislators through key constituents or friends. (Ch. 11)

**Help America Vote Act (HAVA):** federal statute enacted after the 2000 presidential election to effectively standardize election procedures. (Ch. 9)

**Higher Education Coordinating Board:** a group of nine people appointed by the governor for six-year terms to oversee higher education policy in Texas. (Ch. 14)

**Home rule city:** a city that has been granted greater freedom in the organization and functioning of city government; it can make structural and administrative changes without seeking permission from the state. (Ch. 12)

**Horizontal federalism:** refers to the relationship between the states. (Ch. 2)

**Hyperpluralism:** a view that the system today has evolved beyond simple pluralism and is now one in which many narrow interests are represented, often at the expense of the broader public interest. (Ch. 11)

**Ideological caucus:** a special legislative caucus in the state legislature that promotes an ideological agenda. (Ch. 4)

**Impeachment:** formal procedure to remove an elected official from office for misdeeds; passage of the articles of impeachment by the Texas House merely suggests that there is sufficient evidence for a trial, which is then conducted by the Texas Senate. (Ch. 5)

**Implied powers:** powers beyond those enumerated in the Constitution; implied powers are powers deemed "necessary and proper" to execute the enumerated powers of the national government. (Ch. 2)

**Incarceration rate:** a calculation of how many prisoners a state has per 100,000 people, which controls for population size. (Ch. 8)

**Income tax:** a tax calculated as a percentage of income earned in a year. (Ch. 13)

**Incumbency advantage:** the advantage enjoyed by the incumbent candidate, or current officeholder, in elections; the advantage is based on greater visibility, a proven record of public service, and often better access to resources. (Ch. 7)

**Incumbent:** the current officeholder. (Ch. 9)

**Independent candidate:** a candidate running for office without a political party affiliation. (Ch. 9)

**Independent political expenditures:** spending on behalf of a candidate that is done without coordination with the candidate or his or her campaign. (Ch. 11)

**Indictment:** a document (in the form of a true bill) issued by a grand jury that indicates there is enough evidence to warrant a trial. (Ch. 7)

**Indigent defense:** the requirement that governments provide legal counsel to those charged with serious crimes who cannot afford representation. (Ch. 8)

**Indirect primary:** a primary election in which voters elect delegates to a party convention; delegates are pledged to support a specific candidate seeking the party nomination. (Ch. 9)

**Individualistic political culture:** the idea that individuals are best left largely free of the intervention of community forces such as government and that government should attempt only those things demanded by the people it is created to serve. (Ch. 1)

**Informal power:** an attribute of personal power based on factors such as electoral mandate, political ambition ladder, personal future as governor, and performance ratings rather than on constitutionally enumerated powers. (Ch. 5)

**Initiative:** a mechanism that allows voters to gather signatures on a petition in order to place statutes or constitutional amendments on a ballot. (Ch. 2)

**Instant runoff:** a type of election in which second-place votes are considered in instances where no candidate has received a majority of the vote; a winner is determined by adding together the first- and second-place votes. (Ch. 3)

**Intergovernmental lobby:** the lobbying that occurs between different levels of government, such as between the state and national government or between local governments and the state government. (Ch. 11)

**Interim committee:** a legislative work group that is created during periods when the legislature is not in session to provide oversight of the executive branch and monitor public policy. (Ch. 4)

**Introduce [a bill]:** to officially bring a bill before a legislative chamber for the first time. Introducing a bill is the first step in the formal legislative process. (Ch. 4)

**Issue caucus:** a special legislative caucus in the state legislature that promotes bipartisan and cross-chamber support for policies and bills advocating positions inside a relatively narrow range of policy areas or political issues. (Ch. 4)

**Joint resolution:** a legislative act whose approval by both chambers results in amendment to the Texas Constitution; an amendment must be approved by voters at the next election. (Ch. 4)

**Judicial federalism:** a system in which judicial authority is shared between levels of government. (Ch. 7)

**Jurisdiction:** the court's sphere of authority. (Ch. 7)

**Justice of the peace:** an elected county officer who acts as a judicial officer for minor criminal and civil cases. (Ch. 12)

**Killer amendment:** language added to a bill on an unrelated or controversial topic in order to make the bill unacceptable to the majority of the legislature, which will then be more likely to vote against it. (Ch. 4)

**Labor unions:** organizations that represent the interests of working people seeking better pay and better working conditions. (Ch. 11)

**Legislative Budget Board (LBB):** the group that develops a proposed state budget for legislative consideration. (Ch. 4)

**Legislative Redistricting Board (LRB):** created by a 1948 amendment to the Texas Constitution, this group steps in if the state legislature is unable to pass a redistricting plan or when a state or federal court invalidates a plan submitted by the legislature; the LRB is active only with respect to redistricting of the state legislature. (Ch. 3)

**Legislative role:** the executive's role in influencing the state's legislative agenda. (Ch. 5)

**Lieutenant governor:** the presiding officer of the Texas Senate, elected directly by the voters. Also serves as a member of the Texas executive branch and assumes the duties of the governor when the governor is out of state, dies in office, resigns from office, or is impeached. (Ch. 4, 6)

**Line-item veto:** the ability of the executive to selectively veto only some parts of a bill; in Texas available only on spending bills. (Ch. 4, 5)

**Literacy test:** a test of a prospective voter's ability to read and understand aspects of American government; used to bar African Americans from voting in many parts of the post-Reconstruction South, but not used in Texas. (Ch. 9)

**Lobbying:** direct contact with members of the legislative or executive branch to influence legislation or administrative action. (Ch. 11)

**Long ballot:** a system in which almost all of the positions in a state are elected rather than appointed. (Ch. 2)

**Loser pay law:** Texas law which requires litigants to pay those they sued if they lose their lawsuits in certain cases. (Ch. 8)

**Machine politics:** a system of patronage whereby political organizations, led by a local party boss, disperse city jobs, government contracts, and other benefits to maintain control of city governance; power, once acquired, is typically used for personal gain. (Ch. 12)

**Magistrate functions:** the authority to conduct the preliminary procedures in criminal cases, including issuing search and arrest warrants, conducting preliminary hearings, and setting bail for more serious crimes. (Ch. 7)

**Majority election:** a type of election in which a candidate must receive 50 percent of the vote plus one additional vote to be declared the winner; simply winning the most votes is not sufficient. (Ch. 3)

**Majority opinion:** the official decision and reasoning of the appellate court. (Ch. 7)

**Majority-minority district:** an election district in which the majority of the population comes from a racial or ethnic minority. (Ch. 3)

**Manifest Destiny:** the belief that U.S. expansion across the North American continent was inevitable. (Ch. 2)

**Markup:** process whereby a committee goes line by line through a bill to make changes without formal amendments. (Ch. 4)

**Medicaid:** a federal program providing medical coverage for low-income people and some elderly and disabled people. (Ch. 14)

**Medicare:** a federal health insurance program available to senior citizens who have worked and paid into the Medicare system for ten or more years. (Ch. 14)

**Merit-based civil service system:** a system in which people receive government jobs based upon a set of qualifications and formal training; job promotion and pay raises are based upon job performance. (Ch. 6, 12)

**Minority and women's caucuses:** special legislative caucuses in the state legislature that represent the unique concerns and beliefs of women and ethnic groups across a broad range of policy issues. (Ch. 4)

**Moralistic political culture:** rare in Texas, the view that the exercise of community pressure is sometimes necessary to advance the public good; it also holds that government can be a positive force and citizens have a duty to participate. (Ch. 1)

**Motor Voter Act:** the National Voter Registration Act, which allows citizens to register to vote when applying for or renewing their driver's license. (Ch. 9)

**Multi-member district (MMD):** an election system in which the state is divided into many election districts, but each district elects more than one person to the state legislature. (Ch. 3)

**Municipal bond:** a certificate of indebtedness issued by a city that serves as a pledge by the city to pay back the loan over time with interest; used to raise money for services and infrastructure; may also be issued by other forms of local government, such as counties, school districts, and special districts. (Ch. 12)

**Municipal utility district (MUD):** a special district that provides water, sewer, or similar services to individuals and businesses outside city limits. (Ch. 12)

**Name recognition:** making a voting choice based on familiarity with or previous recognition of a candidate's name. (Ch. 7)

**Negative externality:** an unintended cost imposed on someone who did not participate in the economic transaction. (Ch. 15)

**No Child Left Behind Act (NCLB):** the federal education act based on the Texas standardized testing statutes that requires schools to institute mandatory testing to track student progress and evaluates schools based on that progress. (Ch. 14)

**Nonpartisan or bipartisan independent commission:** a system of drawing electoral district lines that attempts to remove politics from the process of redistricting. (Ch. 3)

**One person, one vote:** shorthand term for the requirement of the U.S. Supreme Court that election districts should be roughly equal in population. (Ch. 3)

**Open primary:** an electoral contest in which voters are not required to declare a party affiliation to participate but must request a specific party's ballot at the primary; voters are subsequently barred from participating in the other party's primary. (Ch. 9)

**Ordinance:** a law enacted by a city government. (Ch. 12)

**Organized interest:** an individual, group of people, or group of businesses that organizes its efforts to influence public policy. (Ch. 11)

**Original jurisdiction:** the authority to hear the initial case; the evidence and the case record are established in this court. (Ch. 7)

**Oversight:** the process whereby the legislature reviews policies and decisions of the executive branch to make sure that the executive branch is following the intentions of the legislature. (Ch. 4)

**Pardon:** an executive grant of release from a sentence or punishment in a criminal case; in Texas, the governor can only grant a pardon upon the recommendation of the state's Board of Pardons and Paroles. (Ch. 5)

**Partisan election:** a type of election in which candidates' names and party affiliations appear on the ballot. (Ch. 12)

**Party affiliation:** a candidate's identifiable membership in a political party, often listed on an election ballot. (Ch. 3)

**Party caucus chair:** a party leader whose main job is to organize party members to vote for legislation on the floor. (Ch. 4)

**Party legislative caucus:** the organization of the members of a specific legislative chamber who belong to a political party; normally shortened to party caucus. (Ch. 4)

**Party-line voting:** process in which voters select candidates by their party affiliation. (Ch. 9)

**Party platform:** the document that officially spells out the issue stands of a party; written and approved at the party conventions. (Ch. 10)

**Party primary:** an electoral contest to win a political party's nomination for the right to appear as its candidate on the ballot in the general election. (Ch. 3)

**Patronage/Patronage system:** when individuals who supported a candidate for public office are rewarded with public jobs and appointments and government contracts. (Ch. 5, 6, 10)

**"Pay-as-you-go" system:** a fiscal discipline, adopted by Texas and many other states, that requires a balanced budget and permits borrowing only under a very few circumstances. (Ch. 13)

**Per curiam opinion:** an opinion issued by the court as a whole. These opinions are not signed by individual justices. (Ch. 7)

**Permanent party organizations:** the party officials selected by the temporary organizations to conduct party business between the primaries, caucuses, and conventions. (Ch. 10)

**Permanent School Fund:** a fund set aside to finance education in Texas; the state's largest source of investment income. (Ch. 6, 13)

**Permanent University Fund (PUF):** an endowment funded by mineral rights and other revenue generated by 2.1 million acres of land set aside by the state; investment returns support schools in the University of Texas and Texas A&M systems. (Ch. 14)

**Petit jury:** a trial jury; jurors attend a trial, listen to evidence, and determine whether a defendant is innocent or guilty. (Ch. 7)

**Plaintiff:** the party claiming to have been wronged that is bringing a civil suit. (Ch. 7)

**Plank:** an individual issue position of the party platform. (Ch. 10)

**Plural executive:** an executive branch in which the functions have been divided among

several, mostly elected, officeholders rather than residing in a single person, the governor. (Ch. 5, 6)

**Pluralist perspective:** a view of politics that argues that democracy is best practiced when citizens participate through groups; a greater number of organized interests means wider participation and a healthier democracy. (Ch. 11)

**Plurality election:** a type of election in which the candidate with the most votes wins the election. (Ch. 3)

**Policy:** the actions and activities of government. (Ch. 13)

**Policy adoption:** the stage in which formal government action takes place. (Ch. 13)

**Policy evaluation:** the stage in which the implementation of a policy is examined to see if policy goals are being met. (Ch. 13)

**Policy formation:** the stage in which possible solutions are developed and debated. (Ch. 13)

**Policy implementation:** the stage in which the policy is carried out in state agencies. (Ch. 13)

**Political action committee (PAC):** the fundraising arm of an interest group that has been organized to meet the requirements of state and federal campaign finance laws. (Ch. 11)

**Political ambition ladder:** the manner in which a political figure has come up through the ranks, working through various levels of state governmental offices and positions on the way to the top position; climbing several levels on the ladder can increase a politician's contacts, allies, and political savvy. (Ch. 5)

**Political culture:** the shared values and beliefs of citizens about the nature of the political world that give the public a common language as a foundation to discuss and debate ideas. (Ch. 1)

**Political party:** any group, however loosely organized, seeking to elect governmental officeholders under a given label. (Ch. 10)

**Politico:** an elected official who is expected to follow the wishes of the electorate on

some issues but on others is permitted more decision-making leeway; a hybrid of the trustee and delegate. (Ch. 3)

**Poll tax:** an annual tax that had to be paid before one was allowed to vote; used in Texas. (Ch. 9)

**Popular mandate:** the claim that a newly elected official's legislative agenda is the will of the people based on a high margin of victory in a general election. (Ch. 5)

**Popular sovereignty:** a government in which the power to govern is derived from the will of the people. (Ch. 2)

**Position taking:** an incumbent's advantage in having an existing record of positions on issues, both from previous elections and in the context of decisions made while in office. (Ch. 9)

**Post-adjournment veto:** a veto that occurs after the legislature has adjourned, leaving the legislature unable to overturn it. (Ch. 5)

**Precinct chair; County chair:** a precinct chair is selected by party members in each voting precinct by majority vote; a county chair is selected by countywide vote. These party officials are responsible for managing the local affairs of their party for the next two years. (Ch. 10)

**Preference primary:** a primary election in which voters indicate their choice to hold office, but the actual selection is left to the political party elites. (Ch. 9)

**Preponderance of evidence:** the burden of proof in a civil case, which is lower than that in a criminal case; the plaintiff must show merely that the defendant is likely to have committed the wrong. (Ch. 7)

**President pro tempore:** a presiding officer elected by the members of the Texas Senate; takes over when the lieutenant governor is unavailable. (Ch. 4)

**Presidential republicanism:** the practice in the South of voting for Republicans in presidential elections but voting for conservative Democrats in other races; this practice continued until animosity over Reconstruction faded and the Republicans

demonstrated their electability in the South. (Ch. 1)

**Primary election:** intraparty election in which candidates compete to determine who will win the party's nomination in the general election. (Ch. 9)

**Principle-agent theory of representation:** theory that citizens, or principles, choose someone to speak or act on their behalf in the government. (Ch 13)

**Private financing:** a system of campaign financing in which citizens, interest groups, labor unions, and corporations donate funds to cover the cost of elections for political parties or candidates. (Ch. 9)

**Private prison:** a private, for-profit prison corporation that staffs and runs prison facilities in a state. (Ch. 8)

**Privatization:** a process whereby a government entity sells off assets or services to a private company that is then responsible for providing a service; for example, a school district sells its buses to a private company and then allows the company to provide transportation to schools. (Ch. 12)

**Privileges and immunities:** the constitutional requirement that states may not fundamentally treat citizens of other states differently than their own citizens. (Ch. 2)

**Professional associations:** organizations that represent the needs of professionals not represented by unions. (Ch. 11)

**Professional legislature:** a legislature that meets annually, often for nine months of the year or more; a professional legislator is provided a professional-level salary and generous allowances to hire and keep support and research staffs. (Ch. 3)

**Progressive tax:** a graduated tax, such as an income tax, which taxes people with higher incomes at higher rates. (Ch. 13)

**Property tax:** a tax on the value of real estate that is paid by the property owner; used by county and local governments to fund such programs as public schools. (Ch. 13)

**Prosecutor:** a lawyer who represents the government and brings a case in criminal trials. (Ch. 7)

**Public financing:** a system of campaign financing in which the government covers the cost of elections for political parties or candidates. (Ch. 9)

**Public interest groups:** organizations that pursue noneconomic policies on behalf of the general public, even if all members of the general public do not agree on these issues or policies. (Ch. 11)

**Public-private partnerships (PPPs):** government infrastructure built by private companies for profit. (Ch. 15)

**Punitive damages:** larger monetary awards designed to punish the defendant and, perhaps, send a message to the larger society. (Ch. 7)

**Quorum:** the minimum number of members in a legislative body who need to be present for the body to conduct business; in the Texas Senate, a quorum is eleven members. In the Texas House of Representatives, a quorum is 100 members. (Ch. 4)

**Recess appointment:** a gubernatorial appointment made while the Texas Senate is not in session; requires Texas Senate approval within ten days of the next legislative session. (Ch. 5)

**Recidivism:** a former inmate's resumption of criminal activity after his or her release from prison. (Ch. 8)

**Redistributive policy:** moves benefits, usually in the form of money, from one group to another in an attempt to equalize society. (Ch. 13)

**Redistricting:** the periodic adjustment of the lines of electoral district boundaries. (Ch. 3)

**Referendum:** a mechanism that allows voters to cast a popular vote on statutes passed by the state legislature; the legislature can place measures on the ballot for voter consideration. (Ch. 2)

**Regressive tax:** a tax that has a greater impact on those with lower incomes. (Ch. 13)

**Regular session:** meetings of a legislature that are required by a constitution or law. In Texas, the Texas Legislature meets every other year for 140 days. (Ch. 3)

**Regulation:** government rulemaking and enforcement intended to protect citizens from being harmed by private firms. (Ch. 15)

**Regulatory policy:** attempts to limit or control the actions of individuals or corporations. (Ch. 13)

**Rehabilitation:** an approach to criminal justice that focuses on therapy or education in order to reform the criminal behavior. (Ch. 8)

**Remand:** appellate court sends the case back to the lower court to be reexamined. (Ch. 7)

**Removal power:** the power of the governor to remove an appointee; in Texas, the governor may remove his or her own appointees with the consent of two-thirds of the Texas Senate. (Ch. 5)

**Representation:** the relationship between an elected official and the electorate. (Ch. 3)

**Reserved powers:** the specification in the Tenth Amendment that all powers not delegated to the national government belong to the states. (Ch. 2)

**Resolution:** a legislative act that expresses the opinion of the legislature on an issue or changes the organizational structure of the legislature. (Ch. 4)

**Responsible party model:** the view that each party should hold firmly to a clear and consistent set of policies with a coherent ideology distinct from that of other parties to present voters with clear choices. (Ch. 10)

**Reverse:** appellate court rejects the lower court's decision. (Ch. 7)

**Revolving door:** the phenomenon of legislators and members of the executive branch moving easily from government office to lucrative positions with lobbying firms. (Ch. 5, 11)

**Rider:** an addition to a bill that deals with an unrelated subject, such as changing some aspect of law or public policy or spending money or creating programs in a specific member's district. (Ch. 4)

**Roll call vote:** a form of voting for which a permanent record of each member's vote is created; used with more important votes. (Ch. 4)

**Roll off:** process in which voters mark off only the "more important" offices on a lengthy ballot—usually national or statewide offices—and leave the county or local office choices blank. (Ch. 9)

**Rule of capture:** Texas law that says property owners own the water below their property. (Ch. 15)

**Runoff election:** a type of election in SMDM that is held when an election fails to yield a clear majority winner in the initial balloting; the runoff is limited to the top two vote-getters from the initial election, ensuring a majority win. (Ch. 3, 9)

**Runoff primary:** a primary that occurs if no nominee receives the required majority of the votes in the primary; the top two finishers face off in a second primary to determine the nominee for the general election. (Ch. 10)

**Second-order elections:** elections for offices below the national executive level in countries with presidential systems like the United States' or the national legislature level in parliamentary countries like Great Britain; generally viewed as less important in scope and impact on a country. (Ch. 9)

**Secretary of state:** this position is responsible for business licensing and regulation and also administrates and supervises elections; also serves as the chief protocol officer of Texas. (Ch. 6)

**Select committee:** a temporary legislative work group created by the lieutenant governor or Speaker of the Texas House of Representatives for a special purpose; called a joint committee when the lieutenant governor and Speaker create a select committee with members from both chambers. (Ch. 4)

**Selective incentives:** benefits exclusively available to members of an organization. (Ch. 11)

**Senatorial courtesy:** the informal requirement that a gubernatorial appointee have approval of her or his own state senator in order to obtain support within the Texas Senate. (Ch. 5)

**Severance tax:** a tax on natural resources charged when the resources are produced or "severed" from the earth. (Ch. 13)

**Sheriff:** the elected county official who oversees county law enforcement. (Ch. 12)

**Simple resolution:** a legislative act that addresses organizational issues; may be limited to a single house. (Ch. 4)

**Sin tax:** a tax on products or activities such as cigarettes or gambling that some legislators would like to discourage. (Ch. 13)

**Single-issue interest groups:** groups usually organized around one side of a single issue, such as pro-choice or anti-abortion groups. (Ch. 11)

**Single-member district (SMD):** an election system in which the state is divided into many election districts, and each district elects just one person to the state legislature. (Ch. 3)

**Solidarity benefits:** the social interactions that individuals enjoy from joining a group and from working together for a common cause. (Ch. 11)

**Speaker of the House:** the presiding officer of the Texas House of Representatives. (Ch. 4)

**Speaker pro tempore:** officer that presides over the House of Representatives when the Speaker is unavailable; akin to the president pro tempore in the Texas Senate. (Ch. 4)

**Special legislative caucus:** an organization of members of the state legislature who share a common interest or have constituencies with a common interest. (Ch. 4)

**Special session:** meetings of a legislature that occur outside the regular legislative session; in Texas, special sessions are called by the governor and last for thirty days. (Ch. 3, 5)

**Standing committee:** a permanent, chamber-specific formal work group that typically exists across sessions and across elections. (Ch. 4)

**State Children's Health Insurance Program (SCHIP):** a federal-state program that offers health insurance and medical care to the children of families that make too much to qualify for Medicaid but not enough to afford private health insurance. (Ch. 14)

**State of the state address:** the constitutional requirement that the governor address the state legislature about the condition of the state; the state of the state address occurs at the beginning of each legislative session and at the end of the governor's term. (Ch. 5)

**State party chair:** individual selected at the state party convention to head the state executive committee; state law mandates that if the chair is a man, a woman must be the vice chair, or vice versa. (Ch. 10)

**Straight-ticket voting:** the practice of selecting all the candidates for office who are running under a party label simply by checking off a single box marked with the party label. (Ch. 7)

**Structuring the vote:** the way in which political parties align support for or opposition to bills. (Ch. 4)

**Subsidy:** incentive designed to encourage the production or purchase of certain goods to stimulate or support some businesses. (Ch. 13)

**Succession:** a set order, usually spelled out in the constitution, denoting which officeholder takes over when the sitting governor resigns, dies, or is impeached. (Ch. 5)

**Suffrage:** the legal right to vote. (Ch. 9)

**Sunset review process:** a formal assessment of the effectiveness of all statutory boards, commissions, and state agencies. (Ch. 6, 15)

**Sunshine laws:** laws designed to make government transparent and accessible. (Ch. 6)

**Super PAC:** An organized group that can raise and spend unlimited amounts of money as long as it does not coordinate with candidate campaigns. (Ch. 11)

**Supplemental Nutritional Assistance Program (SNAP):** program that helps low-income seniors, people with disabilities, single people, and families in need buy food from local retailers. (Ch. 14)

**Supramajority:** a majority that is larger than a simple majority of 50 percent plus 1; supramajorities include requirements of 60 percent, two-thirds, three-fourths, or 80 percent to make a decision. (Ch. 3)

**Supremacy clause:** the section in the U.S. Constitution that guarantees that the national government is the supreme law of the land and that national laws and the national constitution supersede state laws and state constitutions. (Ch. 2)

**Tax assessor:** the elected county officer who collects county taxes and user fees. (Ch. 12)

**Tax expenditure:** any reductions in tax liabilities that result from tax benefits to particular taxpayers rather than taxpayers in general. (Ch. 13)

**Temporary Assistance for Needy Families (TANF):** federal program that provides eligible households with monthly cash payments and Medicaid benefits. (Ch. 14)

**Temporary party organizations:** gatherings of ordinary party members, such as primaries, caucuses, and conventions. (Ch. 10)

**Term limit:** a legal limitation on the number of terms an elected official may serve in office. (Ch. 3)

**Texas Commission on Environmental Quality (TCEQ):** the agency that oversees state environmental policy, including air and water quality. (Ch. 15)

**Tort:** a wrongful act by a person that results in injury to another person or property in civil law. (Ch. 8)

**Trade associations:** organizations of similar businesses that work together to advance shared goals. (Ch. 11)

**Traditionalistic political culture:** the idea, most prevalent in the parts of Texas most like the Old South, that government has a limited role concerned with the preservation of the existing social order. (Ch. 1)

**Treaty of Guadalupe Hidalgo:** signed on February 2, 1848, this agreement between the United States and Mexico ended the Mexican-American War and recognized the Rio Grande as the boundary between Texas, now part of the United States, and Mexico. (Ch. 1)

**Trustee:** an elected official who is entrusted to act in the best interests of the electorate based on his or her knowledge; he or she is understood to be generally better informed than the broader electorate. (Ch. 3)

**Turnover:** when current officeholders step down from office and are replaced by new officeholders; turnover may result from retirement, defeat in an election, or term limits. (Ch. 3)

**Unfunded mandate:** legislation passed by the national government imposing requirements on state and local governments that then bear the costs of meeting those requirements. (Ch. 2)

**Unitary system:** a type of government in which power is vested in a central governmental authority. (Ch. 2)

**Vertical federalism:** the distribution of power between the national and state governments. (Ch. 2)

**Veto power:** the formal power of the executive to reject bills that have been passed by the legislature; in Texas, a veto can be overridden only by a two-thirds vote in both houses. (Ch. 5)

**Voter turnout:** the number of people casting ballots in a given election. (Ch. 9)

**Voting Rights Act of 1965 (VRA):** a federal statute that eliminated literacy tests as a qualification to vote, greatly increasing African Americans' access to the ballot box. (Ch. 9)

**White primary:** the attempt by the Democratic Party in Texas and other southern states to limit the voting in party primaries only to party members; in Texas, this practice was codified in state law. (Ch. 9)

**Writ of habeas corpus:** a court order that requires a prisoner to be brought before the court and informed of the charges against him or her. (Ch. 7)

**Zoning policy:** policy whereby the city restricts what individuals and entities may do with their property, usually by designating certain areas of the city for industrial, commercial, or residential uses. (Ch. 12)

# INDEX

Abbott, Greg
  as attorney general, 38–39, 51,
    189–190, 210, 233, 448, 482, 483
  campaign spending, 304
  educational policies, 453
  election campaigns, 4
  environmental policy, 482, 483
  as governor, 154, 155–156
  highway projects, 495
  marijuana decriminalization, 250
  redistricting plans, 109
  same-sex benefits issue, 400
  voter identification laws, 279
ABC, 305
Abilene, 489
Abortion rights, 47, 76, 86, 121
Absentee voting, 286
ACT scores, 450, 451, 459
Adams, John, 69, 93
Adams, John Quincy, 12, 13
Adams-Onís Treaty (1819), 9
Adams, Samuel, 69
*Adams, Terry v.* (1953), 277
Administrative federalism, 375
Ad valorem tax, 421
Advanced voting, 292, 293 (figure)
Advertising strategies, 304–306,
  328, 330, 355
Affiliations
  political parties, 88–89, 161, 332, 334
  religious affiliations, 97, 97 (table), 348
Affirm, 227
Affordable Care Act (ACA, 2010), 39,
  49, 50, 85, 469, 471
AFL-CIO, 350
African Americans
  citizenship, 53
  comparison studies, 34
  death penalty cases, 264
  female legislators, 98
  judiciary representation,
    234, 235 (figure)
  legislative representation, 96 (table), 97
  population size, 30 (figure), 67
  Reconstruction era, 16, 17

  redistricting impacts, 109
  resident status, 54
  school desegregation, 23, 444–445,
    447, 460–461
  special legislative caucuses, 123
  Supreme Court appointments, 216
  voter turnout, 299, 299 (table), 300
  voting rights, 35, 56, 59, 65–66,
    103, 272, 273–278, 312, 319
Agenda setting, 412, 413 (figure)
Aging prisoners, 251
Agnostics, 31 (figure)
Agriculture, 31, 192–193
Agriculture commissioner,
  188 (table), 192–193
Aikin, A. M., 443
Air-conditioned prisons, 244–245,
  251–252
Air quality, 480, 482–483
Akin, Harry, 330
Alabama
  constitutional amendments, 68
  governor's salary, 165
  legislative representation and size,
    83 (table)
  party competition, 324 (table)
  state constitution comparisons,
    70 (table)
  state expenditures, 431 (figure)
  state treasurer, 191
  taxation, 416
Alamo, 33, 36, 52, 502
Alamo Community College, 463 (table)
Alamo Heights School District, 447
Alaska
  bilingual ballots, 278
  legislative representation and size,
    83 (table)
  local governments, 373 (table)
  party competition, 324 (table)
  primary elections, 285
  redistricting commissions, 104
  special sessions, 84
  state constitution comparisons,
    70 (table)

  state expenditures, 431 (figure)
  taxation, 415, 417
Alaska Natives, 30 (figure)
Albuquerque, New Mexico, 268
Alcoholic beverage tax, 418–419
Alcohol prohibition, 19–20, 21, 317, 318
Alice, 354
Allen, 190
Allen, Ethan, 34
Allen, Oscar K., 179
Allocation, 337–339
Allred, James V., 159 (table)
*Allwright, Smith v.* (1944), 277
Alternative energy resources, 195, 485–486,
  487 (figure), 502
Amarillo, 272
Amarillo College, 463 (table)
Amendments, 63 (table), 67–68, 71,
  72 (figure), 130, 298
America Can Recycle, 383
American Association of Retired Persons
  (AARP), 350
American Cancer Society, 419
American Civil Liberties Union
  (ACLU), 348
American Electric Power, 351 (table)
American Family Association of
  Texas, 348
American immigrants, 8–9, 52–53,
  496–497
American Lung Association, 482
American nations, 25, 26 (map), 27
American Party, 316
American Recovery and Reinvestment Act
  (2009), 203
Americans for a Better Tomorrow,
  Tomorrow, 344
American Wind Energy Association, 485
*amicus curiae* brief, 190
Amnesty International, 260 (figure)
Amusement parks, 3, 387
Andrade, Hope, 196
Andrews County, 486, 488
Angelina College, 405, 463 (table)
Angelina County, 56, 332

Anglo population
    comparison studies, 34
    early settlements, 9–10, 246, 414,
        496–497
    immigration rights, 52–54
    impacts and contributions, 33, 35
    population size, 29, 30 (figure)
Annexation, 13, 15, 55, 386, 398
Ann Richards School for Young Women
    Leaders, 162
*Annual Statistical Report for the Texas
    Judiciary*, 222, 235 (figure)
Antidrug policies, 247, 250
Apaches, 6
Appellate courts, 65, 219, 227–229
    *see also* Supreme Court of Texas; Texas
        Court of Criminal Appeals
Appellate jurisdiction, 219
Apple, 436–437
Appointed regulatory commission, 205
Appointment power, 56, 59, 166, 168–170,
    173, 195, 232–233, 457
Appraisal values, 421–422
Appropriations Committee, 127, 131,
    432, 433 (figure)
Arizona
    female legislators, 91
    governor's residence, 165
    higher education enrollment,
        456 (figure)
    legislative representation and size,
        83 (table)
    party competition, 324 (table)
    redistricting commissions, 104
    redistricting plans, 108
    state constitution comparisons,
        70 (table)
    state expenditures, 431 (figure)
    term limits, 91
Arkansas
    election campaigns, 304
    highway projects, 182
    legislative representation and size,
        83 (table)
    legislative session length, 81
    local governments, 373 (table), 374
    party competition, 324 (table)
    party control, 152
    redistricting commissions, 104
    school districts, 402
    state constitution comparisons,
        70 (table)
    term limits, 90
*Arkansas Democrat-Gazette*, 304
Arlington, 387, 480

Armed services members, 280
Armey, Dick, 387, 500
Asian Americans
    bilingual ballots, 278
    comparison studies, 34
    judiciary representation, 234
    legislative representation, 96 (table), 97
    population size, 30 (figure), 67
    voter turnout, 299 (table)
    voting rights, 103, 311
Astroturf lobbying, 360
AT&T Corp., 351 (table), 363, 442
Atheists, 31 (figure)
*Atkins v. Virginia* (2002), 259
At-large by place election system, 393
At-large election system, 235, 386,
    393, 394–395
Attorney general, 187, 188 (table), 189–190
Auditor, 381
Austin
    immigration policies, 398
    League of United Latin American
        Citizens (LULAC), 354
    legislative compensation, 87
    lobbying activities, 351, 362
    marijuana arrests, 250
    mass transit, 495
    population, 30, 31
    sanctuary cities, 398
    tax breaks, 436
    and the Texas Rangers, 248
    toll roads, 493
Austin Community College, 463 (table)
Austin, Moses, 9
Austin, Stephen F.
    Anglo settlements, 9, 53, 414, 496–497
    debt, 56
    election campaigns, 11, 12
    "Father of Texas," 502
    and Juan Seguín, 33
    as secretary of state, 195–196
    taxation, 414
    Texas independence, 10
    and the Texas Rangers, 248
Australia, 33 (table), 80, 132, 280
Austria, 80
Auto emission standards, 483
Autry, Gene, 248
Aycock, Jimmie Don, 323

Bache, Richard, 13
Back to Basics PAC, 355
Bahia (Goliad), 376
Baker, Louisiana, 402
*Baker v. Carr* (1962), 80, 98, 103

Ballots
    bilingual ballots, 278
    general election ballots, 300–301, 320
    long ballots, 66, 291–292, 311
    mail-in ballots, 286
    paper ballots, 294
    spoiled ballots, 394
    *see also* Primary elections
Baptists, 31, 31 (figure)
Barnes, Ben, 5
Barnett Shale, 474, 479, 480, 488
Barrow, Clyde, 248
Barton, Joe, 414
*Bastrop Independent School District,
    Delgado v.* (1948), 354, 445
Battle of San Jacinto, 11, 52
Battle, William J., 20, 458
Bavaria, Germany, 206–207
Bean, Roy, 223
Bears for a Bearable Tomorrow, 345
Beaumont, 20, 476
Beer tax, 418–419
Bell, Chris, 304
Bell County, 323
Belle Meade, Tennessee, 404
Bell Helicopter, 435
Benzene, 474, 480
Berlanga, Mary Helen, 36
Berry, Nandita, 196
*Best Little Whorehouse in Texas, The*, 253
Bethlehem Baptist Church, 447
Béxar, 11, 52
Bexar County, 259, 278, 376, 383, 446–447
Beyle, Thad, 176, 177
Beyond a reasonable doubt, 241
Bicameral legislatures, 54, 78–80
Biennial budget cycle, 433 (figure)
Big Bend, 4
Big Bend Ranch State Park, 429
Big-business interests, 74
*Big Rich Texas* (television program), 467
*Big Sort, The* (Bishop), 27
Big Tex, 3
Bilingual ballots, 278
Bill Clayton Detention Center, 253
Bill of rights, 54, 56, 62, 63 (table)
Bills
    assignment to committee, 138–139, 142
    bill-to-resolution balance, 146–148,
        147 (figure), 148 (table), 149 (figure)
    committee chairs, 129
    conference committees, 133, 145
    debate, 142–144
    filing and introduction, 137
    geographic representation, 93

governor's veto power, 146
killing a bill, 130, 138
legislative process, 136–139,
    140–141 (figure), 142–148
lieutenant governor, 116
origins, 136–137
parliamentary systems, 132
party caucuses, 120–121
referendum process, 288
Speaker of the House, 117
special legislative caucuses,
    123, 125–126
standing committees, 126–127,
    129–130, 138
voting processes, 142–146
Bipartisan Campaign Reform
    Act (2000), 327
Bipartisan independent commission, 104
Bipartisanship, 112–114, 116–119, 123,
    142, 150–152
Bishop, Bill, 27
Bison, 6
Black Codes, 16
Blackshear, Edward, 19–20
Blanco, Kathleen, 291
Blanket primary, 285
Blinn College, 463 (table)
Block grant, 48
Blocking bill, 139, 142, 150
*Board of Education, Brown v.* (1954),
    23, 445, 447, 460
*Board of Education (II),*
    *Brown v.* (1955), 445
Board of Legal Examiners, 229
Board of Pardons and Paroles,
    173–174, 197, 204, 251, 263
Boards
    gubernatorial appointments, 168–169
    Higher Education Coordinating Board
        (THECB), 440, 457, 459, 464
    independent school districts (ISDs),
        401–402
    origins, 197
    special districts, 405
    staffing resources, 205 (table), 208, 210
    State Board of Education, 36, 85, 107,
        168, 204–205, 302, 403, 443–444
    Texas Board of Pardons and Paroles,
        173–174, 197, 204, 251, 263
    Texas Department of Criminal Justice,
        194, 203–204, 252
    *see also* State agencies
Boehner, John, 499
Bogalusa, Louisiana, 402
Bonds, 398–399, 405, 429, 492

Bonnie and Clyde, 248
B-on-Time program, 186, 464
Border security, 268
Bowdoin, James, 69
Bowie County, 378
Boyd, Jeffrey, 232
Branch, Dan, 310
Branding, cattle, 9
Brazil, 33 (table), 80
Brazos, 376
Brazos River, 489
Brennan, William, 499
Brewster County, 378
Briscoe, Dolph, 158, 160 (table), 164, 230,
    253, 443
British Parliament, 133
Broadcast media, 303–306, 355
Brooks County, 385 (table)
Brothels, 253
Brownsville, 4, 182, 248, 354, 489
*Brown v. Board of Education* (1954),
    23, 445, 447, 460
*Brown v. Board of Education (II)* (1955), 445
*Buckley v. Valeo* (1976), 307
Budget power, 170
Budget, state, 85, 191–192, 427–429,
    432, 438
Buffalo Bayou, 12, 489
Buffalo Gap, 489
Bullock, Bob, 22, 428–429
Bullock's Raiders, 429
Bundesrat, 80
Bureaucracy, 197
Bureaucratic accountability, 185–186,
    210, 211 (figure), 212
Bureau of Land Management (BLM), 39
Burke, Edmund, 323
Burlington, Vermont, 34
Burmese refugees, 497
Burnet County, 323
Burnet, David G., 11–12, 303
Bush, George H. W., 162, 340
Bush, George P., 195
Bush, George W.
    background, 157, 158, 160 (table),
        327, 328
    and Bob Bullock, 22
    education reforms, 449
    as governor, 161, 164, 165, 168, 171, 176
    Iowa Caucuses, 340
    as president, 115, 160, 175

Cabeza de Vaca, Álvar Núñez, 6
Cabinets, 185–186
Cable television, 305–306

Cactus, 498
Caddo people, 6, 27–28
Calendars, 138–139, 139 (table), 142
Calendars Committee, 127, 138–139
California
    auto emission standards, 483
    bilingual ballots, 278
    county government, 378
    death penalty cases, 262–263
    environmental policy, 482
    higher education enrollment,
        456 (figure)
    legislative representation and size,
        80, 81, 83 (table)
    legislative session length, 82
    local governments, 373, 373 (table)
    mass transit funding, 495
    party competition, 324 (table)
    pay and compensation, 87
    primary elections, 285–287
    professional legislatures, 86
    redistricting commissions, 104
    sales tax, 415
    state constitution comparisons,
        70 (table)
    state expenditures, 431 (figure)
    state government employment,
        209 (figure)
    tax breaks, 435
    term limits, 90
    turnover, 91
*California Democratic Party v.
    Jones* (2000), 285
Call, the, 84
Camarillo, Lydia, 104
Campaign financing
    campaign spending, 304, 309–310,
        310 (table)
    contribution disclosures, 308–309
    government regulations, 306–308,
        327, 330, 344, 355–356
    importance, 306
    incumbents, 302
    judicial campaign contributions, 309
    legal loopholes, 344
    legislative campaign committees,
        330–331
    lobbying impact, 302, 310, 359, 361–363
    2014 campaign and election, 269–270
    voluntary spending limits, 309
Campaigns
    costs, 304
    historical perspective, 303
    media strategies, 303–306, 328, 330
    2014 campaign and election, 268–270

Campbell, Thomas M., 19, 159 (table)
Canada, 33 (table), 79, 133, 182–183, 308, 478–479
Candidate qualifications, 88–89
Candidate selection and support, 284, 300–301, 327, 328
    see also Primary elections
Cannibalism, 6
Capital MetroRail, 495
Capital punishment, 258–259, 260 (figure), 261 (figure), 261–264
Carbon dioxide emissions, 482
Carcinogens, 474, 480
Car dealerships, 437
Career College Association, 360
Carlson, Pat, 107
Carona, John, 494
Carpetbaggers, 16–17
Carr, Baker v. (1962), 80, 98, 103
Carrington v. Rash (1965), 280
Carrolton, 30
Carter, Jimmy, 340
Carter, Stefani, 310
Casework, 302
Castle doctrine, 257–258
Categorical grant, 47–48
Catholicism, 8, 10, 31, 31 (figure), 52, 55, 97, 97 (table)
Cats for a Better Tomorrow, Tomorrow, 345
Cattle branding, 9
Caucuses
    candidate selection, 284
    conventions, 331–332, 334
    Democratic Party organization, 118
    functional role, 118, 120–122, 135–136
    Iowa, 340
    Republican Party organization, 118–119
    special legislative caucuses, 122–123, 125 (table), 125–126, 135–136
    structuring the vote, 125–126, 146
    Texas House of Representatives, 118–119
    Texas Senate, 119–120
Cavelier, René-Robert
    see La Salle, René-Robert Cavelier, sieur de
CBS, 305
Centene Corp., 351 (table)
Center for Public Integrity, 363
Center for Responsive Politics, 357
CenterPoint Energy, 351 (table)
Central City, Louisiana, 402
Central Texas, 56–57, 107, 323, 494
Central Texas College, 463 (table)
Ceremonial duties, 174

Chairs, committee, 129
Charter schools, 453–454
Cheating, 450
Chesapeake Energy, 480
Chicken processing plants, 497
Chicken Ranch, 253
Children's Health Insurance Program (CHIP), 469, 471
Childress, George C., 11
China, 33 (table)
Christian affiliations, 97, 97 (table)
Christian Coalition, 355
Christian Social Union (CSU), 206
Christian, Wayne, 107
Christmas Mountains, 195
Chronic minority, 327–328
Chubbing, 143
Cigarette taxes, 419, 420 (table)
Cintra, 493
Cisco College, 463 (table)
Citizen initiative, 90
Citizen legislature, 63, 67, 74, 86, 87–88, 99
Citizens for Lawsuit Reform, 331
Citizens United v. Federal Election Commission (2010), 307, 330, 355–356, 366
City charter, 386
City councils, 390–392
City government
    challenges, 399
    city formation and status, 385–386, 388
    economic development, 398
    election systems, 392–395
    general law cities, 386, 388
    home rule cities, 386, 388, 399
    hydraulic fracking issues, 396–397
    ordinance-making powers, 396–398
    organizational structure, 388, 389–390 (figure), 390–392
    revenue sources, 398–399, 424 (table)
    zoning and planning policy issues, 395–398
Civil appeals, 65
Civil cases, 219, 229, 241
Civil defendant, 241
Civilian-employed population, 32 (table)
Civil rights, 65–66, 108–109, 281, 319, 354, 444–446, 460
Civil Rights Act (1964), 445
Civil service system, 382
Civil War era, 15–16, 38, 57–58
Claiborne, William C. C., 179
Class A misdemeanors, 223, 239, 240 (table)

Class B misdemeanors, 223, 239, 240 (table)
Class C misdemeanors, 221, 222, 239, 240 (table), 250
Clauer, Michael and May, 370–371
Clay, Henry, 13
Clean Air Act (1990), 482, 483
Clean Water Act (1972), 482
Cleburne, 480
Clemency, 174
Clements, William P., 23, 157, 158, 160 (table), 161, 230, 319, 328
Clinton, Bill, 340
Clinton, Hillary, 50, 338
Closed primaries, 284–285, 332
Closed riders, 142
Closing the Gap initiative, 457, 459
Club for Growth, 346, 365
CNN, 306
Coahuila y Tejas, 52, 53
Coahuiltecan tribes, 6
Coal production, 487 (figure)
Coast Coordination Advisory Board, 194
Cockrell, Liz, 23
Coen brothers, 161
Cohesion, 125–126
Coke County, 378
Coke, Richard, 60, 61
Colbert Report, 25, 344
Colbert, Stephen, 25, 344, 443–444
Colbert Super PAC: Americans for a Better Tomorrow, Tomorrow, 344
Colbert Super PAC SSH Institute, 344
Collective goods, 349
College-age voters, 311
College students
    free-rider problem, 349
    higher education costs, 350, 367, 464
    lobbying activities, 360
    state programs and grants, 436
    voting rights, 281
Colleyville, 371
Collier, Mike, 192
Collin County, 28, 190, 388, 493
Collin County Community College District, 463 (table)
Collingsworth County, 58
Collinsworth, James T., 58
Colorado
    legislative representation and size, 83 (table)
    marijuana decriminalization, 250
    party competition, 324 (table)
    redistricting commissions, 104

state constitution comparisons, 70 (table)
state expenditures, 431 (figure)
state government employment, 209 (figure)
women's suffrage, 280
Colquitt, Oscar Branch, 19, 159 (table), 303
Columbia, Texas, 12
Comanche Peak Nuclear Power Plant, 447–448
Combs, Susan, 185, 191, 192, 193, 427, 435
Comedy Central, 268, 344
Commissioner of the General Land Office, 188 (table), 194–195
Commissioners court, 379–380
Commission on Judicial Conduct, 233, 237
Commissions
    Commission on Judicial Conduct, 233, 237
    gubernatorial appointments, 168–169
    Health and Human Services Commission (HHSC), 469
    origins, 197
    Public Utility Commission of Texas (PUC), 205, 207–208
    Railroad Commission of Texas, 18, 21, 168, 201–203, 302, 474, 478, 489–490
    staffing resources, 205 (table), 208, 210
    Sunset Advisory Commission, 210, 212
    Texas Commission on Environmental Quality (TCEQ), 403, 482, 483, 486
    Texas Highway Commission, 492
    Texas Transportation Commission, 197, 198, 201
    see also State agencies
Committee chairs, 129
Committee system
    committee chairs, 129
    functional role, 126, 135
    joint committees, 134
    select committees, 134
    special committees, 132–135
    staffing resources, 131
    standing committees, 126–131, 128 (table), 138
    statutory committees, 131
    subcommittees, 131, 138
Common Core standards, 453
Community College Caucus, 125 (table)
Community college districts, 403, 405, 463 (table), 464
Comparison studies
    auto emission standards, 483
    constitutional comparisons, 64, 69

death penalty cases, 262–263
election systems, 105
employment data, 209 (figure)
ethnic diversity, 34
judicial elections, 239
judicial system, 220
legislative process, 132
lobbying activities, 364
local governments, 373 (table), 391, 404
office of the governor, 179
primary elections, 290–291, 340
redistricting plans, 108
religious freedoms, 64
state constitutions, 64, 69, 70–71 (table)
state expenditures, 431 (figure)
state government, 206–207
state legislatures, 124
taxation, 416
Texas Legislature, 79 (table)
transportation boards, 201
voter turnout, 286, 289 (figure)
Compensation, legislative, 63, 74, 86–88, 99, 122
Compensatory damages, 241
Comptroller of public accounts, 188 (table), 190–192
Compulsory public education, 59, 60, 63 (table), 66
Computer companies, 436–437
Concurrent jurisdiction, 220, 221, 226
Concurrent powers, 44, 45 (figure)
Concurrent resolution, 138
Concurring opinion, 227
Confederal system, 42
Confederate regime, 15–16, 57–58, 376
Confederate sympathizers, 16, 17
Conference committees, 132, 133, 145
Connally, John, 23, 145, 157, 158, 160 (table), 437
Connecticut
    constitutional comparisons, 64
    legislative representation and size, 82 (table)
    local governments, 374
    party competition, 324 (table)
    redistricting commissions, 104
    religious freedoms, 64
    state constitution comparisons, 70 (table)
    state expenditures, 431 (figure)
    taxation, 415, 416
Conservative Christian political groups, 334, 348
Conservative economic policies, 410–411
Constable, 381

Constitution
    appointment approval, 169
    basic concepts, 40
    budget issues, 427
    challenges, 73–74
    city government, 385–386
    Connecticut Constitution, 64
    constitutional amendments, 63 (table), 67–68, 71, 72 (figure), 298
    constitutional conventions, 11, 17, 54, 58, 59
    constitutional revisions, 68–69, 71, 73
    Constitution of 1836, 11, 12, 53, 54–56
    Constitution of 1845, 13, 56–57, 273, 414
    Constitution of 1861, 57–58, 376
    Constitution of 1866, 58–59, 476
    Constitution of 1868, 443
    Constitution of 1869, 59–61, 274
    Constitution of Coahuila y Tejas (1827), 52, 53
    Constitution of the Republic of Texas, 11, 12, 54–56, 273, 376
    criticisms, 67, 68
    distrust of government, 66, 68, 73–75, 156
    education services, 446
    executive branch, 63, 63 (table), 65, 67
    highway construction costs, 491
    historical perspective, 52
    impeachment, 165–166
    individual freedoms, 62
    judicial system, 63 (table), 65, 67, 218–219
    legislative branch, 63, 63 (table), 67, 170–171
    local government power, 374
    Massachusetts Constitution, 69
    Permanent University Fund (PUF), 456–457
    popular sovereignty, 41
    property taxes, 419
    rights of the accused, 254
    special districts, 403
    state constitution comparisons, 70–71 (table)
    statehood constitution, 56–57
    Texas, 273–281
    voter qualifications and registration, 271
    see also U.S. Constitution
Constitutional amendments, 63 (table), 67–68, 71, 72 (figure), 298
Constitutional Convention (1787), 271

Constitutional county courts, 223, 226, 240 (table)
Constitutional governments, 40–41
Constitution of 1876
    Articles, 63 (table)
    basic principles, 61–66
    budget limits, 131
    constitutional amendments, 63 (table), 67–68, 71, 72 (figure), 131, 298
    constitutional comparisons, 64, 69, 71 (table)
    constitutional conventions, 17
    gubernatorial power, 156, 166, 168, 173, 177
    limitations, 18, 37
    pay and compensation, 157, 164
    Permanent University Fund (PUF), 456–457
    poll taxes, 274
    religious freedoms, 64
    school funding, 444
    terms of office, 163
    voter participation, 288
Constitution of Coahuila y Tejas (1827), 52, 53
Consultation (1832), 53
Consultation (1835), 10–11
Continental Airlines, 442
Contract outsourcing, 383
Contributions
    see Campaign financing
Conventions, 331–332, 334, 335, 337–339, 341
    see also Caucuses
Cook County, Illinois, 376, 378
Cooperative federalism, 46, 375
Cornyn, John, 106
Coronado, Francisco Vasquez de, 28
Corporations, 308, 310, 330, 350–351, 351 (table), 355–356, 366, 442
Corpus Christi, 35, 182, 354, 495
Correctional facilities
    associated costs, 249
    health care, 251
    incarceration rates, 247
    prison conditions, 244–245, 250–252
    privatization movement, 252–254
    Texas Department of Criminal Justice, 194, 203–204, 252
Corsicana, 476
Cortéz, Hernando, 6
Cotton farming, 15
Council-manager city government system, 388, 390 (figure), 390–392
Counties, 63 (table)

County attorney, 381
County chair, 333
County civil service commission, 382
County clerk, 381
County constitutional court judge, 380–381
County courts at law, 226, 240 (table)
County district convention, 335
County government
    background and characteristics, 376, 378
    elections, 379, 381
    functional role, 378–379
    organizational structure, 379–382, 380 (figure), 384–385
    population size, 376, 378
    revenue sources, 382–384, 424 (table)
    see also Judicial system
County-level trial courts, 219, 221, 222–223, 226
County populations, 5
Court of Appeals, 220, 228
Court of Criminal Appeals, 65, 219, 227, 228–229, 234, 259, 261, 264
Court system
    see Judicial system
Court Watch, 230
Cowboy image, 17–18, 27
Craddick, Tom, 113, 116, 363
Credit claiming, 137, 302
Criminal appeals, 65
Criminal cases, 219, 227, 238–241
Criminal defendant, 238
Criminal Justice Committee, 135
Criminal justice system
    advantages/disadvantages, 265–266
    civil cases, 241
    criminal cases, 238–241
    criticisms, 241–242
    death penalty cases, 258–259, 260 (figure), 261 (figure), 261–264
    frontier justice, 246
    incarceration rates, 247
    political culture, 246–247, 249–259, 261, 263–265
    rehabilitation approach, 249–250
    rights of the accused, 254–255
Crisis manager, 174
Crockett, Davy, 2
Cromartie, Hunt v. (1999), 103
Cross-filing, 287
Cross-party voting, 290–291
Cruz, Ted, 38, 155, 156, 177, 187, 333, 346, 365
Culberson, Charles A., 159 (table)
Cumulative voting system, 235, 393, 394

Curriculum debates, 444, 451–452
Cyber Crimes Unit, 189
Cypress-Fairbanks Independent School District, 373
Czech immigrants, 497

Dahlonega, Georgia, 201
Dahl, Robert, 366
Daily Show, The, 204, 268
Dallas, 30, 250, 398
Dallas Area Rapid Transit (DART), 495
Dallas County, 93, 101, 219, 231, 259, 383, 484
Dallas County Community College District, 463 (table)
Dallas-Fort Worth Metroplex, 91, 107, 197, 383, 396, 405, 482, 490
Dallas Morning News, 76, 252, 264, 330, 450
Dallas (television program), 467
Daniel, Price, 157, 160, 160 (table)
Dark money, 356
Davidson County, Tennessee, 404
Davis, E. J., 17, 60–61, 62, 63, 166, 177
Davis, Jimmy, 179
Davis, Karina, 143
Davis, Sarah, 78
Davis, Wendy, 76, 77, 86, 93, 121, 304, 360
Dawkins, Johnny, 461
Deadly force law, 257–258
Death penalty cases, 228–229, 258–259, 260 (figure), 261 (figure), 261–264
Debate, 142–144
Debt
    Constitution of 1866, 58
    full faith and credit clause, 45–46
    public debt, 429
    Republic of Texas, 12
    Spanish law, 52
    state constitution guarantees, 56, 62, 378
    state responsibility, 55, 60–61, 66
Deep South, 25, 26 (map)
Deepwater Horizon oil spill, 195
Defense of Marriage Act (1996), 50, 400
Delaware
    county government, 376
    legislative representation and size, 83 (table)
    local governments, 373 (table)
    party competition, 324 (table)
    state constitution comparisons, 70 (table)
    state expenditures, 431 (figure)

Delaying tactics, 143–144
DeLay, Tom, 106
Delegated powers, 44, 45 (figure)
Delegates, 92, 284, 334, 335, 337–339
*Delgado v. Bastrop Independent School District* (1948), 354, 445
Del Mar College, 463 (table)
Democratic Party
  Arizona, 108
  conventions, 334, 337–339, 341
  delegate allocation, 284, 338–339
  electoral competition, 312, 320–321, 322 (table), 323, 324 (table)
  female legislators, 77–78
  Great Depression, 21
  Hispanic population, 30
  historical perspective, 316–320
  internal conflict, 314–315
  Iowa Caucuses, 340
  judicial elections, 230–231
  legislative control, 106–107, 119, 150–152
  legislator qualifications, 88–89
  mid-twentieth century, 23
  national health care policy, 50
  Nebraska, 124
  North Dakota, 105
  office of the governor, 161
  party caucuses, 118, 120–122, 125, 135–136
  party organization, 118
  party platforms, 314–315, 335, 336 (table), 341
  poll taxes, 274
  populism, 19
  post-Reconstruction era, 60–62
  primaries, 275, 284–285, 287, 290–291, 332, 337–339, 341
  Reconstruction era, 17
  redistricting plans, 106–107
  Speaker of the House, 112–114, 117
  standing committees, 129
  2014 campaign and election, 268–270
  voter percentage, 326 (figure)
  white primaries, 277
  *see also* Legislative process
Demographic data
  birth origins, 3
  population growth, 28 (figure), 28–31, 33, 66–67
  population size, 5, 12
  Texas Legislature, 93, 96, 96 (table), 110–111
  Texas versus Vermont, 34

Denied powers, 44, 45 (figure)
De novo, 221, 222
Denton, 396, 398, 481
Denton County, 28, 493
Denton Drilling Awareness Group, 396
Department of Criminal Justice, 194, 203–204, 252
Department of Parks and Wildlife, 130
Department of Public Safety, 248, 500
Department of State Health Services (SHS), 200–201, 257
*Desegregating Texas Schools: Eisenhower, Shivers, and the Crisis at Mansfield High* (Ladino), 447
Desegregation, 23, 374, 444–445, 447, 460–461
Deserts, 4
Detroit, Michigan, 182, 183
Devolution, 46
Dewhurst, David
  attack ads, 365
  campaign spending, 304, 307
  election campaigns, 156, 187
  as lieutenant governor, 129, 143, 164, 186–187
  redistricting plans, 106
  runoff primaries, 333
  special sessions, 172
Dial-controlled computer voting systems, 294
Dietz, John, 448
Diez y Seis de Septiembre, 9
Digital media, 305–306
Dillon, John Forrest, 373
Dillon's Rule, 373
Dimmit County, 385 (table)
Direct democracy elections, 288
Direct primaries, 283, 284
Disclosure, 308–309
Discrimination
  gender, 20
  Hispanic population, 278–279, 445
  reverse discrimination, 460–461
  school desegregation, 23, 444–445, 447, 460–461
  voter identification laws, 279
  voting rights, 103, 273–280, 311
Disenfranchisement, 274–275, 278–279, 311
Dish, 474, 475
Dissenting opinion, 228
Distribution of power, 42, 44, 45 (figure), 46–49, 79
Distributive policy, 413
District clerk, 381

District courts, 219, 220, 226–227, 240 (table)
District of Columbia, 50
Distrust of government, 66, 68, 73–75, 156, 246
Disturbance theory, 348–349
Diverse populations, 29, 34
*Doe, Plyler v.* (1982), 499
Dole, Bob, 340
*Dole, South Dakota v.* (1987), 48
*Dorsey, Fortson v.* (1965), 101
Dos Passos, John, 456
Downs, Anthony, 325
Drinking water quality, 480
*Driscoll Consolidated ISD, Herminca Hernandez et al. v.* (1957), 445
Drought conditions, 484
Drug Enforcement Agency, 247
Drug possession policies, 247, 250
Dual-chamber legislatures, 54, 78–80
Dual federalism, 46, 375
Dukakis, Michael, 340
Duke, David, 290
Duval County, 317, 384, 385 (table)
DVR recordings, 306

Eagle Ford Shale, 474, 479, 488
Eagle Nest, 223
Eagle Rock Energy, 396
Early voting, 292, 293 (figure)
Earthquakes, 480–481
East Texas, 56, 107, 125, 182, 405, 478, 480, 484
Economic and Small Business Development Committee, 131
Economic Development Committee, 131
Economic Stabilization Fund (ESF), 156, 170, 430, 432
*Economist, The*, 414
Economy
  civilian-employed population, 32 (table)
  diversification, 31, 67
  economic development efforts, 398, 410, 437, 466
  gross domestic product, 33 (table)
  growth and size, 31–32
  oil and gas industry, 476–481
  organized interests, 350–351, 351 (table)
  recession impact, 85
Edgewood Independent School District, 446, 448
*Edgewood Independent School District v. Kirby* (1989), 446

Educational attainment
  graduation rates, 451
  legislative representation, 96 (table), 97
Educational policies and services
  accountability, 449–452
  budget cuts, 438
  charter schools, 453–454
  cheating, 450
  civil rights movement, 444–446
  foundation curriculum, 451–452
  funding challenges, 60, 446–449
  graduation rates, 451
  higher education, 454–461, 455 (figure),
    456 (figure), 462–463 (table),
    464–466, 465 (table)
  high-stakes testing, 449–450
  importance, 31, 442
  independent school districts (ISDs),
    401–403, 406
  No Child Left Behind Act (NCLB),
    446, 453
  public education, 59, 60, 63 (table),
    66, 443 (table), 443–452
  reform movements, 442, 449–452
  school enrollment, 442, 443 (table)
  state standards, 440–441
  teacher rewards and incentives, 454
  voucher programs, 348, 452–453
Education Reform Act (1984), 449
Edwards, Edwin, 179, 290
Eisenhower, David, 387
Eisenhower, Dwight D., 177, 287, 319
Elazar, Daniel, 23
Elderly prisoners, 251
Elected boards, 197, 204
Elected officials, 185
  *see also* Plural executive
Election districts, 100–101, 103–105
Electioneering, 353
Election monitors, 277
Elections
  city government, 392–395
  comparison studies, 105
  county government, 379, 381
  direct democracy elections, 288
  early voting, 292, 293 (figure)
  electoral competition, 271, 300–306,
    312, 320–321, 322 (table),
    323, 324 (table), 325
  electronic voting, 293–294
  historical perspective, 312
  judicial elections, 74, 216–217,
    229–231, 234, 309
  legal requirements, 292
  long ballots, 66, 291–292

midterm elections, 89, 298
political action committees (PACs),
  353, 355–357
presidential elections, 299 (table),
  307–308
second-order elections, 298
special elections, 68, 73 (figure),
  297 (figure), 297–298
2014 campaign and election, 268–270
voter qualifications and registration,
  271–273
*see also* Primary elections; Voting rights
Election timing, 89
Election turnout
  college-age voters, 311
  comparison studies, 286, 289 (figure)
  current trends, 295–300, 296 (figure)
  demographic makeup, 299 (table)
  electoral competition, 320
  primary elections, 320, 341
  special elections, 68, 73 (figure),
    297 (figure), 297–298
  voting-age population, 321 (figure)
Electoral competition model, 271,
  300–306, 312, 320–321, 322 (table),
  323, 324 (table), 325
Electoral fusion, 287
Electronic voting, 293–294
Elementary and Secondary Education
  Act (1965), 445
El Norte, 25, 26 (map)
El Paso, 4, 31, 35, 103, 394
El Paso Community College District,
  463 (table)
El Paso County, 93
El Salvador, 500
Emancipation Proclamation (1863), 16
Emergency clause, 146
Emergency legislation, 171
Eminent domain, 184, 479, 485
Emission standards, 483
Emmett, Ed, 183
Employment data, 32 (table)
Empower Texans Foundation, 345
Empower Texans PAC, 345, 355, 359
Empresarios, 9
En banc, 228
Encino, 354
Energy Future Holdings Corp., 351 (table)
Energy production, 195, 487 (figure), 502
English language learners (ELL), 446
English-speaking immigrants, 8–9, 52–53
Enhanced penalties, 239
Entergy Corporation, 207
Enterprise Fund, 156

Enumerated powers, 44
Environmental policy, 481–482, 502
Environmental Protection Agency (EPA),
  480, 482, 483, 486
Epstein, Leon, 325
Equal protection clause, 275, 277
Equal rights, 23, 66, 273–274, 275, 499
Equal Rights Amendment (ERA), 23
Erath County, 193
Erben, Randall H., 361 (table)
eSlates, 294
*Estelle, Ruiz v.* (1972), 250–251
Estelle, William, 251
Ethics Commission, 87, 125, 304, 308,
  356, 359, 361–362
Ethnicity
  *see* Race and ethnicity
European exploration, 6, 8–9, 27–28, 52
Excise tax, 419
Exclusive jurisdiction, 219
Executions, 258–259, 260 (figure),
  261 (figure), 261–264
Executive branch
  Texas Constitution, 63, 63 (table), 65, 67
  *see also* Plural executive
Executive committee, 333, 335, 337
Executive orders, 171–172, 187, 189, 196, 364
Executive role, 166, 168–170
*Ex parte* Rodriguez (1874), 61
Expressive benefits, 348
Extradition, 46

Facebook, 305, 306
Fair Defense Act (2001), 255
Fannin County, 378
Farm and Ranch Lands Conservation
  Council, 194
Farmer Jim
  *see* Ferguson, James E. (Pa)
Farmers' Alliance, 317, 347
Farmers Branch, 498
Farming, 31
Farwest, 26 (map)
Father's Day massacre, 173
Fayette County, 253
Federal Aid Road Act (1916), 490
*Federal Election Commission, Citizens
  United v.* (2010), 307, 355–356, 366
Federal election grants, 307–308
Federal funds
  *see* Grants
Federalism, 41–42, 44–51, 61, 375, 467
Federal policies and control, 38–39,
  47–48
  *see also* States' rights

Federal Telecommunication
    Act (1996), 205
Feldman, David, 400
Felonies, 219, 220, 227, 239, 240 (table)
Female legislators
    *see* Women
Ferguson, James E. (Pa)
    abuse of power, 173
    election campaigns, 303
    as governor, 19–20, 159 (table), 160
    impeachment, 20, 161, 166,
        455–456, 458
    legacy, 21
    political outsiders, 328
    and the Texas Rangers, 248
    and the University of Texas,
        20, 166, 455–456, 458
    white primaries, 319
Ferguson, Miriam (Ma)
    abuse of power, 173
    election campaigns, 458
    as governor, 21, 159 (table), 161, 163, 166
    political appointments, 196
    and the Texas Rangers, 248
*Ferguson, Plessy v.* (1896), 444, 445
Fifteenth Amendment
    (U.S. Constitution), 273
Fifth Amendment (U.S. Constitution), 485
Fifth Circuit Court of Appeals, 262, 263
Filibusters, 76, 121, 143, 150
Filing fees, 300
Film industry, 436
Finance Committee, 131, 432, 433 (figure)
First Amendment (U.S. Constitution), 285,
    307, 355, 365
First Nation, 26 (map)
Fiscal federalism, 47–48, 375, 414
Fiscal policy
    advantages/disadvantages, 436–437
    biennial budget cycle, 433 (figure)
    budget cuts, 438
    definition, 413
    expenditures, 428 (table),
        429, 430 (figure), 431 (figure)
    federal funds, 425, 425 (table),
        426 (figure)
    fiscal federalism, 414
    policymaking process, 412–413,
        413 (figure)
    Rainy Day Fund, 156, 170, 430, 432
    revenue sources, 420 (table),
        422 (figure), 425 (table)
    state budget, 85, 191–192, 427–429,
        432, 438
    subsidies, 435–436

tax expenditures, 434–435
    *see also* Legislative Budget Board (LBB);
        Property taxes; Taxation
Fiscal transfers, 414
Fisher, Abigail, 461
*Fisher v. the University of Texas* (2013), 461
Fitzsimmons, Bob, 223
501(c) nonprofit corporations, 345, 356
Flag etiquette, 56
Floor debate, 142–143
Floor leader, 120
Florida
    female legislators, 91
    governor's salary, 165
    higher education enrollment, 456 (figure)
    legislative representation and size,
        80, 82 (table)
    party competition, 324 (table)
    Spanish legacy, 9
    special sessions, 84
    state constitution comparisons,
        70 (table)
    state expenditures, 431 (figure)
    state government employment,
        209 (figure)
    state treasurer, 191
    term limits, 90, 91
    voting irregularities, 293, 294
Flournoy, Jim, 253
Flower Mound, 396
Ford, Gerald, 340
Foreclosures, 370–371
Formula One racing, 435
Fort Bend County, 28, 277
*Fortson v. Dorsey* (1965), 101
Forts, Spanish, 8
Fort Worth, 394, 435
Fort Worth Firefighters, 355
Founding fathers, 40–42
Fourteenth Amendment (U.S.
    Constitution)
    equal protection clause, 45 (figure),
        80, 100–101, 108–109, 275, 277,
        445, 499
    ratification process, 16, 59
Fox News, 305, 306
Fracking, 396–397, 474–475, 479–481
France, 33 (table), 133
Franchise tax, 418, 420 (table)
Francis, Wayne, 120
Fraudulent voters, 279
Freedmen, 16–17, 18
Freedmen's Bureau, 16
Free enterprise system, 436–437, 481
Free-rider problem, 349

Free speech protections, 307, 355–356, 366
Freestone County, 378
French explorers, 6
Friedman, Kinky, 193, 303–304
Friedman, Thomas, 466
Frisco, 30, 190, 370, 435
Frivolous lawsuits, 256, 257
Frontier justice, 246
*Frontline*, 237
Fruit trees, 21
Fugitive Unit, 189
Fulbright & Jaworski, 236
Full faith and credit clause, 45–46, 50
Fund-raising
    campaign spending, 304, 309–310,
        310 (table)
    contribution disclosures, 308–309
    government regulations, 306–308,
        327, 330, 355–356
    importance, 306
    incumbents, 302
    judicial campaign contributions, 309
    legislative campaign committees,
        330–331
    2014 campaign and election, 269–270
    voluntary spending limits, 309
Fusion, electoral, 287
Future Business Leaders of America, 436

Gallo, Columba Garnicia, 195
Gallup poll, 30, 469
Galveston, 16, 20, 390, 392, 397
Galveston Bay, 405
Galveston College, 463 (table)
Galveston County, 499
Galveston Plan, 397
Gasoline tax, 414, 417–418, 420 (table),
    491, 494–495
Gates, Bill, 453
Gay marriage, 50, 66
Gender
    discrimination, 20
    higher education, 460
    legislative representation, 96 (table), 97
    voter turnout, 299, 299 (table)
General Council, 11
General election ballots, 300–301, 320
General elections, 284, 285, 291
General Investigation and Ethics
    Committee, 127
General Land Office, 106, 165, 194–195
General law cities, 386, 388
General sales tax, 382, 398, 415–416,
    420 (table), 422 (figure), 423
    *see also* Taxation

General services district (GSD), 404
Geographic characteristics, 4–5
Geographic representation, 93
GEO Group, Inc., 252, 253
George Washington's Birthday
　celebration, 27
Georgia
　county government, 376
　higher education enrollment,
　　456 (figure)
　legislative representation and size,
　　82 (table)
　local governments, 374
　party competition, 324 (table)
　runoff elections, 100
　state constitution comparisons,
　　70 (table)
　state expenditures, 431 (figure)
　transportation boards, 201
　voter identification laws, 279
Georgia Department of Transportation
　(GDOT), 201
Georgia Highway 400 (GA 400), 201
Georgia State Transportation Board, 201
Gephardt, Richard, 340
German American population, 15, 16,
　18, 30, 57, 303, 497
Germany, 33 (table), 80, 206–207, 307
Gerrymandering, 104
Ghost votes, 144
Gideon v. Wainwright (1963), 254
Gillespie County, 89
Gilmer-Aikin Act (1949), 443
Gilmer, Claud, 443
Gingles, Thornburg v. (1986), 101
Glen Rose, 447–448
Gonzales, 10, 39, 52
González, Henry B., 35
Gonzalez, Naomi, 93
Gonzalez, Raul A., Jr., 230
Goodlettsville, Tennessee, 404
Good Road Amendment, 491
Gore, Al, 340
Governmental tyranny, 40–41, 42
Government organizational structure,
　43 (figure)
Government public bills, 132
Government rulemaking and
　enforcement, 481
Governorship
　appointment power, 56, 166,
　　168–170, 173, 195, 232–233, 457
　budget power, 170, 432, 433 (figure), 434
　comparison studies, 179
　crisis management, 174

election campaigns, 303–304
executive powers, 56, 59, 63, 65
executive role, 166, 168–170
female governors, 161–163
formal powers, 156–157
governors since 1876, 159–160 (table)
impeachment, 20, 161, 165–166,
　455–456, 458
informal powers, 157, 176–178
institutional powers, 166–176,
　167 (figure), 175 (map),
　178, 180–181
judicial appointments, 232–233, 237
judicial role, 173–174
legislative role, 170–173
Louisiana, 179
military role, 174–176
pay and compensation, 164–165
personal power, 176–178
qualifications and characteristics,
　157–158, 158 (table), 160–161
staffing resources, 165
succession, 164
terms of office, 59, 163–164
veto power, 59, 146, 172–173, 311, 432
Governor's Office of Budget, Planning, and
　Policy (GOBPP), 432
Graded penal code, 238–239,
　240 (table), 257
Graduation rates, 451
Grandfather clause, 274, 275
Grand jury, 238
Grand Prairie, 107, 480
Granger, Gordon, 16
Grange, the, 17, 65, 347
Grants
　block grants, 48
　categorical grants, 47–48
　federal election grants, 307–308
　federal grants, 210, 352, 375, 398, 425,
　　425 (table), 426 (figure), 466, 495
　land grants, 9, 194
　local governments, 435–436, 437
　student grants, 360, 436, 438, 461, 464
Grassroots for Hire (Walker), 360
Grassroots lobbying, 359–360
Grassroots organizations, 331, 341
Grasstop lobbying, 360
Grayson College, 463 (table)
Grayson, Peter, 58
Great Britain, 33 (table), 133, 280
Great Depression, 21, 318–319, 477
Greater Appalachia, 25, 26 (map), 27
Greater Houston area, 91, 107
Greenback Party, 317

Greene County, Missouri, 384
Green, Gene, 103
Greenhouse gases, 482
Green, James, 258
Green Mountain Boys, 34
Green Party, 301, 323
Greenville, 494
Gregg County, 478
Gross domestic product, 33 (table)
Gross state product, 32, 477
Guadalupe Peak, 4
Guatemala, 500
Gubernatorial power and terms,
　56, 59, 63, 65
Guinn v. United States (1919), 275
Gulf Coast, 4
Guzman, Eva, 35

Haas, Rene, 230
Habeas corpus, right to, 62
Hall, Wallace, 456
Hamilton, A. J., 58
Harkin, Tom, 340
Harlingen, 354
Harper v. Virginia Board of Elections
　(1966), 277
Harris County
　county government, 382, 384–385
　death penalty cases, 259
　electronic voting, 294
　judicial elections, 229, 235
　judicial system, 219
　legislative representation, 80
　lobbying activities, 351
　local governments, 373
　population, 5
　population size, 376
　special districts, 405
　toll roads, 383
Harris County Commissioners Court, 405
Harris County Education Department, 373
Harris County Emergency Services District
　9, 373
Harris County Flood Control District, 373
Harris County Hospital District, 373
Hawaii
　county government, 376
　legislative representation and size,
　　83 (table)
　local governments, 373 (table)
　party competition, 324 (table)
　state constitution comparisons,
　　70 (table)
　state expenditures, 431 (figure)
　voter turnout, 299, 299 (table)

Haynesville Shale, 479
Hays County, 28
Hazardous waste storage, 486, 488
Health and human services
    background and characteristics, 467
    federal and state programs, 469–471
    health care services, 469–471
    political challenges, 471
    social welfare programs, 467–469,
        472 (figure)
Health and Human Services Commission
    (HHSC), 469
Health and Human Services
    Committee, 135
Health care legislation, 85–86
Health care services, 31, 469–471
Heat-related prison deaths, 244, 251
Hecht, Nathan, 237
Hegar, Glenn, 192
Help America Vote Act (HAVA), 293–294
Henderson, Jim, 22
Henderson, J. Pinckney, 13
Heritage Lakes Homeowners Association,
    370–371
*Herminca Hernandez et al. v. Driscoll
    Consolidated ISD* (1957), 445
*Herndon, Nixon v.* (1924), 277
Hidalgo y Costilla, Father Miguel, 9
High courts, 219, 227–229
Higher education
    accountability, 464–465, 465 (table)
    admission restrictions, 459–461
    enrollment data, 455 (figure),
        456 (figure)
    funding challenges, 456–457, 459,
        461, 464
    future challenges, 466
    growth and accessibility, 459–461
    institutional system, 454–455
    knowledge resources, 466
    oil boom benefits, 477
    performance measures, 465 (table)
    policymaking process, 457–459
    race-based admissions, 460–461
    state goals, 459
    tuition and fees,
        461, 462–463 (table), 464
Higher Education Committee, 127, 135
Higher Education Coordinating Board
    (THECB), 440, 457, 459, 464
Higher Education Fund (HEF), 457
High-speed rail lines, 197, 490
High-stakes testing, 449–450
Highway construction, 21, 182–184,
    197–198, 490–495

HillCo PAC, 236
Hill County, 61, 317
Hill, John, 253
Hillsboro, 22
Hispanic population
    civil rights movement, 354, 445
    comparison studies, 34
    death penalty cases, 260 (figure), 264
    economic harassment, 278–279
    higher education, 460
    immigration rights, 268–269
    impacts and contributions, 33, 35
    judiciary representation,
        234, 235 (figure)
    legislative representation, 96 (table), 97
    office of the governor, 163
    political challenges, 36
    population size, 29–30, 30 (figure),
        67, 500–501
    Reconstruction era, 17
    redistricting impacts, 108–109
    segregation, 445
    special legislative caucuses,
        108–109, 123
    Supreme Court appointments, 230
    voter turnout, 299 (table), 300
    voting rights, 54, 103, 106–107,
        273, 278–279, 311, 312, 357
Hispanic Republicans for Texas, 195
Historical background
    change effects, 27–33
    Civil War era, 15–16, 38, 57–58
    Confederate regime, 16, 57–58, 376
    Great Depression, 21
    immigrant populations, 33, 35
    Mexican rule, 9–11, 52–54, 55
    Reconstruction era, 16–17, 58–61, 62
    reform movement, 18–21
    Spanish exploration and colonization,
        6, 8–9, 27–28, 52
    statehood, 12, 13, 15, 56–57
    Texas Revolution, 10–12, 55
    transitional years, 23, 25, 27
    *see also* Texas Constitution
Hobby, William P., 145, 159 (table),
    248, 303, 454, 457, 464
Hofheinz, Roy, 387
Hogan, Jim, 193
Hogg, James Stephen, 18, 159 (table),
    161, 189, 201, 202, 317, 489–490
Holder, Eric, 279
*Holder, Northwest Austin Municipal Utility
    District #1 v.* (2009), 277–278
*Holder, Shelby County, AL v.* (2013),
    109, 278, 279

Homeowners associations (HOAs),
    370–372, 399–401
Home ownership, 32, 370–372
Home rule cities, 386, 388, 399
Homestead provisions, 52, 56, 62
Honduras, 500
Hoover, Herbert, 21, 318
*Hopwood v. Texas* (1996), 460
Horizontal federalism, 44–46
Horizontal fracking, 479
Horn, Joe, 258
Horses, 6
Hospital districts, 403
Hotel taxes, 420 (table)
Hot oil wars, 478
House Administration Committee, 127
House Bill (HB) 5, 451–452
House Bill (HB) 8, 459
House Committee on Appropriations,
    127, 131, 432, 433 (figure)
House Environmental Caucus,
    123, 125 (table)
House Progressive Caucus, 123, 125 (table)
House Research Organization, 131
Houston
    air quality, 482
    election systems, 395
    female legislators, 78
    high-speed rail lines, 197, 490
    highway projects, 182, 493
    homeowners associations (HOAs), 371
    lobbying activities, 351
    majority-minority districts, 103
    mass transit, 495
    origins, 12
    population, 5, 30
    same-sex benefits, 400
Houston, Andrew Jackson, 330
*Houston Chronicle*, 410
Houston Community College System,
    405, 463 (table)
Houston County, 388
Houston, Sam
    background, 2
    battle injury, 11–12
    Battle of San Jacinto, 11, 33, 58
    biography, 14
    election campaigns, 303
    as governor, 15–16, 56
    and Native Americans, 12, 14, 427
    political party, 316
    as president, 12, 55, 195
    as senator, 13, 15
    state expenditures, 427
    and the Texas Rangers, 248

Houston Ship Channel, 405
Howard Stern Fans for a Baba Booey Better Tomorrow, Tomorrow, 345
Hubbard, Richard B., 159 (table)
Huckabee, Mike, 340
Hudson High School, 406
*Huffington Post*, 76
Hughes, Bryan, 112
Hulu, 306
Humble Oil, 478
Hunter-gatherer populations, 6
*Hunt v. Cromartie* (1999), 103
Hurricanes, 49, 157, 397
Hutchison, Kay Bailey, 168, 177, 310, 495
Hybrid election systems, 395
Hybrid legislatures, 86–87
Hydraulic fracking, 396–397, 474–475, 479–481
Hyperpluralism, 366

I-2 project, 182
I-30, 494
I-35 corridor, 91, 107, 182, 197
I-369 project, 182
I-69 project, 182–184, 197, 198, 493
I-75, 201
Idaho
    election systems, 105
    legislative representation and size, 83 (table)
    party competition, 324 (table)
    redistricting commissions, 104
    special sessions, 84
    state constitution comparisons, 70 (table)
    state expenditures, 431 (figure)
    term limits, 90, 91
Ideological caucus, 123, 125 (table)
Illegal alcohol distribution, 20
Illegal drugs, 247, 250
Illegal immigrants, 268, 279, 497–501
Illinois
    county government, 376, 378
    higher education enrollment, 456 (figure)
    legislative representation and size, 82 (table)
    legislative terms of office, 89
    local governments, 373, 373 (table)
    party competition, 324 (table)
    state constitution comparisons, 70 (table)
    state expenditures, 431 (figure)

Immigration
    American immigrants, 8–9, 52–53, 496–497
    challenges, 2–3, 501
    city ordinances, 398
    cost-benefit analyses, 498–501
    diverse populations, 29
    educational opportunities, 499–500
    German immigrants, 18, 497
    historical perspective, 496–497
    immigration rights, 53–54, 268–269
    impacts and contributions, 33, 35, 497
    legislative reform, 86, 497–498, 499, 500–501
    Mexican rule, 52–54
    Spanish government, 6, 8–9
    unaccompanied minors, 499, 500
    unauthorized immigrants, 268, 279, 497–501
Immigration and Custom Enforcement (ICE), 498
Impeachment, 20, 63 (table), 161, 165–166, 233, 455–456, 458
Implied powers, 44
Incarceration rates, 247
Income disparities, 32–33, 33 (table)
Income taxes, 47, 63, 415, 422 (figure), 423
Incumbency advantage, 232
Incumbents, 302
Independence movement, 10–12
Independent candidates, 301
Independent political expenditures, 355–356
Independent school districts (ISDs), 401–403, 406
Independent Texas, 7 (map)
India, 33 (table)
Indiana
    highway projects, 182
    legislative representation and size, 82 (table)
    party competition, 324 (table)
    state constitution comparisons, 70 (table)
    state expenditures, 431 (figure)
    voter identification laws, 279
Indianola, 397
Indictments, 238
Indigent defense, 254–255
Indirect primaries, 283, 284
Individual freedoms, 62
Individualistic political culture, 25
Individual responsibility, 255
Informal powers, 157, 176–178
Initiatives, 71, 73, 288

In-N-Out Burger, 435
Instant runoff, 100
Insurance companies, 19
Insurance taxes, 420 (table)
Interest and investment income, 425 (table), 426
Interest groups
    *see* Organized interests
Intergovernmental lobby, 351–352
Interim committees, 134–135
Intermediate appellate courts, 228
International Center for Prison Studies, 247
International Convention of Alcoholics Anonymous, 435
Internet use, 303–304
Interparty elections, 284
Interstate 30, 494
Interstate Highway 69 (I-69) project
    *see* I-69 project
Intimidation tactics, 275, 279
Introduce [a bill], 137
Iowa
    caucuses, 340
    legislative representation and size, 82 (table)
    party competition, 324 (table)
    presidential primaries, 337
    state constitution comparisons, 70 (table)
    state expenditures, 431 (figure)
    voter registration, 272
Iowa Supreme Court, 373
Ireland, John, 159 (table)
Issue caucus, 123, 125 (table)
Italy, 33 (table)
Izzo, Tom, 461

Jackson, Andrew, 2, 13, 14, 316
James, Kenneth, 244
Japan, 33 (table)
Jefferson, Thomas, 204, 444
Jefferson, Wallace, 216–217
Jersey Lilly, 223
Jester, Beauford, 160 (table)
Jewish population, 31 (figure), 97 (table)
Jim Hogg Committee, 138
Jim Hogg County, 385 (table)
Jindal, Bobby, 290–291
Johnson, Ann, 78
Johnson, Lyndon, 21, 23, 157, 283, 317, 319, 330, 387
*Johnson, Miller v.* (1995), 103
Joint committees, 134
Joint resolution, 138

Jones, Anson, 13, 15
*Jones, California Democratic Party v.*
    (2000), 285
Jones, Gene, 145
Jones, Tommy Lee, 248
Jordan, Barbara C., 98
Josephine, 388
Judges and justices, 234–235, 235 (figure),
    238, 239
Judicial Campaign Fairness Act (1995), 237
Judicial elections, 74, 216–217, 229–231,
    234, 309
Judicial federalism, 218–219, 221
Judicial misconduct, 233
Judicial system
    appellate courts, 227–229
    campaign contributions, 309
    campaign donor influences, 236–237
    characteristics, 219, 221
    comparison studies, 220
    county-level trial courts, 219, 221,
        222–223, 226
    criticisms, 236–237
    disadvantages, 241–242
    graded penal code, 238–239,
        240 (table), 257
    gubernatorial appointments,
        232–233, 237
    historical perspective, 216–217
    judges and justices, 234–235,
        235 (figure), 238, 239
    jurisdiction, 218–223, 226–229
    Kansas, 220
    local trial courts, 221–222
    merit-based appointments, 238
    organizational structure, 224–225 (figure)
    partisan elections, 216–217,
        229–231, 234, 238, 239
    racial distribution, 234–235,
        235 (figure)
    removal means, 233
    selection processes, 229–232, 237–238
    state-level trial courts, 219, 226–227
    Texas Constitution, 63 (table),
        65, 67, 218–219
    *see also* County government; Criminal
        justice system
Junell, Rob, 69, 71
Jurisdiction, 218–223, 226–229
Justice, frontier, 246
Justice of the peace, 381
Justice of the peace courts (JP courts),
    219, 222, 240 (table)
Justices, 234–235, 235 (figure)
Justice, William Wayne, 251, 445

Kansas
    judicial system, 220
    legislative representation and size,
        82 (table)
    party competition, 324 (table)
    pay and compensation, 87
    presidential primaries, 337
    state constitution comparisons,
        70 (table)
    state expenditures, 431 (figure)
    taxation, 384
    term limits, 91
Kansas City, Missouri, 374
Kansas Supreme Court, 220
Karankawa tribe, 6
Karnes County, 385 (table)
Katy, 398
Kaufman, David, 13
Kearby, J. C., 317
Keeton-Strayhorn, Carole, 191, 304, 428
Keller, Sharon, 264
Kelley, Russell (Rusty), 361 (table)
Kennedale, 383
Kennedy, John F., 157
Kennedy, Ted, 50
Kentucky
    governor's salary, 165
    highway projects, 182
    legislative representation and size,
        83 (table)
    party competition, 324 (table)
    state constitution comparisons,
        70 (table)
    state expenditures, 431 (figure)
Kerry, John, 340
Key, Francis Scott, 14
Keystone pipeline, 478–479
Key, V. O., 5, 177, 179, 195, 328, 341, 342
Kilgore College, 463 (table)
Killer amendment, 142
Killer Bees, 145
Killing a bill, 130, 138
King, Ken, 93
King, Larry L., 253
*Kirby, Edgewood Independent School
    District v.* (1989), 446
Know Nothing Party, 15–16, 316
Krause, Matt, 107
Krusee, Mike, 144
Ku Klux Klan, 16, 63

Labor unions, 308, 330, 350,
    355–356, 366
Ladino, Robyn Duff, 447
Lafitte, Jean, 179

La Grange, 253
La Grulla, 354
Lakey, David L., 200
Lamar County, 378, 479
Lamar, Mirabeau B., 12, 58, 427, 443
Lamar University, 462 (table)
Lampasas, 317
Lampasas County, 323, 378
Lancaster County Nebraska Republican
    Party, 124
Land commissioner, 188 (table),
    194–195
Land grants, 9, 63 (table)
Landmass, 4–5
Laney, James "Pete", 112, 113, 116
Langtry, George, 223
Langtry, Lillie, 223
Langtry, Texas, 223
Lanham, Samuel, 159 (table)
Laredo, 27, 182, 493
Laredo Community College, 463 (table)
La Salle, René-Robert Cavelier,
    sieur de, 6
Latexo, 388
Lavoro, Jacob, 250
Law of April 6, 1830, 53
League City, 499
League of United Latin American Citizens
    (LULAC), 35, 354, 357, 445, 446
Left Coast, 26 (map)
Legends
    Barbara C. Jordan, 98
    Bob Bullock, 22
    Chicken Ranch, 253
    cowboys, 17–18, 27
    E. J. Davis, 60–61
    Galveston hurricane, 397
    hot oil wars, 478
    immigrant populations, 35
    importance, 3–4
    James Collinsworth, 58
    James E. "Pa" Ferguson, 458
    James Leininger, 348
    Judge Roy Bean, 223
    Killer Bees, 145
    League of United Latin American
        Citizens (LULAC), 354
    Lyndon Baines Johnson, 283
    Mansfield High School, 447
    private property and takings, 485
    Railroad Commission of Texas, 202
    Raul A. Gonzalez Jr., 230
    Republic of Texas, 55–56
    Sam Houston, 14
    Texas Rangers, 248

Texas state capitol building, 81
Tommy Joe Vandergriff, 387
Wilbert Lee (Pappy) O'Daniel, 330
Legislative Air Quality Caucus, 125 (table)
Legislative Appropriation
	Request (LAR), 432
Legislative Audit Committee, 131
Legislative branch, 63, 63 (table), 67
Legislative Budget Board (LBB)
	functional role, 131, 166, 170, 432, 434
	highway construction costs, 491
	origins, 131, 170, 177
	presiding officers, 116, 186
	prison population, 250
	Speaker of the House, 117
Legislative compensation, 63, 74,
	86–88, 99, 122
Legislative Council, 136–137, 177
Legislative organization
	committee system, 126–135,
		128 (table), 138
	Democratic Party organization, 118
	functional role, 114–115
	leadership compensation, 122
	political parties, 117–122
	power and control issues, 150–152
	presiding officers, 115–117, 138,
		150–151, 432
	Republican Party organization,
		118–119
	special legislative caucuses, 122–123,
		125 (table), 125–126, 135–136
Legislative process
	assignment to committee, 138–139, 142
	bill filing and introduction, 136–137,
		140–141 (figure)
	bill-to-resolution balance, 146–148,
		147 (figure), 148 (table), 149 (figure)
	debate, 142–144
	levels of activity, 146–148, 147 (figure),
		148 (table),
		149 (figure)
	power and control issues, 150–152
	resolutions, 137–138, 146–148,
		147 (figure), 148 (table),
		149 (figure)
	voting processes, 142–146
Legislative Redistricting Board (LRB),
	104, 106, 108, 116, 117
Legislative Reference Library, 131
Legislative role, 170–173
Legislative Study Group Caucus,
	123, 125 (table)
Legislative terms, 54, 56
Legislator qualifications, 88–89

Legislature
	alternative energy legislation, 486
	Ann Richards, 162
	antidrug policies, 247, 250
	appointment approval, 169, 232
	bill-to-resolution balance, 146–148,
		147 (figure), 148 (table), 149 (figure)
	budget issues, 85, 191–192, 427,
		432, 433 (figure), 438
	campaign spending, 310
	characteristics, 78–79
	committee system, 126–135,
		128 (table), 138
	comparison studies, 79 (table)
	deadly force law, 257–258
	demographic makeup, 93, 96, 96 (table),
		110–111
	education funding, 446–448, 461, 477
	electoral competition,
		321, 322 (table), 323
	electoral system, 99–101, 103–104,
		106–110
	female legislators, 76–78, 91–92, 96, 98
	functional role, 24 (figure)
	geographic representation, 93
	health care legislation, 85–86
	higher education laws, 460
	highway construction funding, 491–492
	homeowners association (HOA)
		reforms, 401
	immigration issues, 86, 497–498
	impeachment, 20, 165–166, 233
	Killer Bees, 145
	legislative process, 136–139, 142–148
	legislator qualifications, 88–89
	levels of activity, 146–148, 147 (figure),
		148 (table), 149 (figure)
	lobbying impact, 362–365
	lobbying regulation, 361–362, 364
	oil production taxes, 477
	party caucuses, 135–136, 146
	party control, 301–302
	pay and compensation, 63, 74,
		86–88, 99, 122
	political expenditures ban, 356
	power and control issues, 150–152
	presidential primaries, 337
	presiding officers, 115–117, 138,
		150–151, 186–187, 432
	property taxes, 420
	public-private partnerships (PPPs), 493
	rates of incumbency, 91, 92 (table)
	redistricting, 85, 89, 91, 101,
		102 (figure), 103–104, 106–110
	religious affiliations, 97, 97 (table)

representation and size, 80–81,
	82 (table), 93, 96 (table)
session length and frequency,
	81–82, 84–85
special districts, 403, 405
State House districts (2012),
	93, 95 (map)
State Senate districts (2012),
	93, 94 (map)
tax breaks and incentives, 436
tax-free holidays, 434
terms of office, 54, 56, 89
tort reform, 256
turnover, 91, 92 (table)
women's suffrage, 280
zoning and planning policy
	issues, 396
see also Legislative organization;
	Texas House of Representatives;
	Texas Senate
Lehmberg, Rosemary, 173
Leininger, James, 347, 348, 353
Lever-operated voting machines, 294
Levied taxes, 384, 424 (table)
Levin, Lewis C., 13
Lewis, Ron E., 361 (table)
Libertarian Party, 89, 301, 323
Licenses and fees, 425 (table), 426, 491
Lieutenant governor
	bill referrals, 138
	functional role, 115–116, 186–187,
		188 (table)
	leadership influence, 136, 150
	qualifications, 186–187
	special committees, 134, 135
	succession, 164
	2014 campaign and election, 268–270
Lifetime, 305
Light Crust Doughboys, 21, 161, 330
Light rail service, 495
Limestone County, 61
Lincoln, Abraham, 16, 19, 38, 56,
	58, 303
Linebarger Heard Goggan Blair, 351 (table)
Line-item veto, 59, 146, 173, 432
Line of succession, 164
Lipsky, Steve, 474
Liquor smuggling, 20
Literacy tests, 274
Litigation, 357
Little Dribblers' Basketball National
	Tournament, 435
Littlefield, 253
Little Rock, Arkansas, 304
Livingston, Robert, 290

Lobbying/lobbyists
astroturf lobbying, 360
basic concepts, 357, 358 (figure),
359–360
benefits, 359
campaign spending contributions, 310
economic interests, 350–351,
351 (table)
expenditures, 302, 310, 359, 361
government regulations, 361–362, 364
grassroots lobbying, 359–360
grasstop lobbying, 360
intergovernmental lobby, 351–352
lobbyist–legislator relationships,
362–365
policy-influencing role, 355–357,
358 (figure), 359–365
revolving door phenomenon, 170
top lobbyists, 361 (table)
Lobby Registration Act (1957), 361
Local and Consent Calendars Committee,
127, 139
Local government
background and characteristics,
372–376
cities, 385–386, 388, 389–390 (figure),
390–399
comparison studies, 373 (table),
377 (figure), 404
county government, 376, 378–385,
380 (figure), 385 (table)
criticisms, 406–407
homeowners associations (HOAs),
370–372, 399–401
independent school districts (ISDs),
401–403, 406
revenue sources, 382–384,
398–399, 406–407
special districts, 382–383, 403, 405, 406
state–local government relationship,
373–376
township governments, 391
Local political parties, 317, 326–327,
333–335, 341
Local Sales and Use Tax Act (1967), 415
Local sales tax, 415
Local trial courts, 221–222
Locke, John, 204
Lone Ranger, The, 248
Lone Star Card, 469, 472 (figure)
Lone Star College, 405
Lone Star Community College District,
373, 463 (table)
Long ballot, 66, 291–292, 311
Long, Huey, 179

Los Angeles County, California, 378
Loser pay law, 256
Lottery proceeds, 425 (table), 426–427
Louisiana
charter school system, 454
comparison studies, 179, 290–291
highway projects, 182
hybrid legislatures, 86
legislative representation and size,
83 (table)
local governments, 373 (table), 374
office of the governor, 179
party competition, 324 (table)
political machines, 328
primary elections, 285, 287, 290–291
runoff elections, 100
school districts, 402–403
Spanish legacy, 9
state constitution comparisons,
70 (table)
state expenditures, 431 (figure)
taxation, 416, 419
term limits, 91
voting rights, 274
Loving County, 5, 80, 294, 376, 378,
384–385, 385 (table)
Lower courts, 219
Low-income populations
see Social welfare programs
Lubbock Avalanche-Journal, 76
Lufkin, 184, 406
LULAC v. Perry (2006), 106–107, 357
Lumber industry, 21
Lyon, Jeremy, 435

Machine politics, 394
Madden, Jerry, 249
Madison, James, 40, 42, 47, 79, 346, 367
Magistrate functions, 221
Maher, Peter, 223
Mail-in ballots, 286
Maine
governor's salary, 165
legislative representation and size,
82 (table)
legislative session length, 81–82
party competition, 324 (table)
state constitution comparisons, 70 (table)
state expenditures, 431 (figure)
Majority election, 100
Majority-minority districts, 101, 103, 394
Majority opinion, 227
Major league baseball teams, 387
Major-party candidates, 300
Malaysia, 80

Manifest Destiny, 55
Man of the House, 248
Mansfield, 107, 447
Marijuana decriminalization, 247, 250
Marketing strategies, 304–306, 355
Markup, 130
Marriage authority, 49–50
Marriage rates, 29
Marshall, 4, 107, 309
Martial law, 60–61, 63
Martin County, 385 (table)
Martone, Michael David, 244
Maryland
elected officials, 185
female legislators, 92
legislative representation and size,
82 (table)
party competition, 324 (table)
state constitution comparisons,
70 (table)
state expenditures, 431 (figure)
Maryland, McCulloch v. (1819), 44
Massachusetts
constitutional comparisons, 69
governor's residence, 165
higher education enrollment,
456 (figure)
legislative representation and size,
82 (table)
party competition, 324 (table)
same-sex marriage, 50
state constitution comparisons,
70 (table)
state expenditures, 431 (figure)
taxation, 416
term limits, 90
Massive Open Online
Courses (MOOCs), 135
Mass transit, 495
Matamoros, Mexico, 16
Mathews, Jay, 455
Mayor–council city government system,
388, 389 (figure), 390, 392
McAllen, 182, 354, 398
McCain-Feingold Act (2000), 327
McCain, John, 325, 340, 344
McCallum, Jane, 196
McCollum, Larry, 244
McCulloch v. Maryland (1819), 44
McDonald, Bill, 248
McDonald's, 210
McGarah, Carol, 361 (table)
McGarry, Mignon, 361 (table)
McGovern, George, 340
McKinney, 30, 190

McLennan Community College, 463 (table)

McMansions, 396

McNelly, Leander, 248

McWilliams, Andrea, 361 (table)

McWilliams, Dean R., 361 (table)

Media strategies, 303–306, 328, 330, 355

Medicaid, 48, 86, 467, 468, 469, 470–471

Medicare, 86, 467, 471

MegaFest 2013, 435

Meharg, Emma C., 163, 196

Members of the military, 280

Memphis, Tennessee, 182

Merit-based civil service system, 208, 210, 217, 382

Merit-based judicial appointments, 238

Merritt, Tom, 193

Methane, 480

Metropolitan Council, 404

Metropolitan Government, 404

Metropolitan Transportation Authority of Harris County, 351

MetroRail, 495

Mexican American Legislative Caucus (MALC), 108–109, 123, 125, 125 (table)

Mexican-American War (1846-1848), 15

Mexican independence, 9–10

Mexican Texas, 9–11, 52–54, 55, 376, 496–497

Mexican-Texas relations, 196

Mexico, 33 (table), 79–80, 182–183

Michigan
  bill filing, 137
  governor's salary, 165
  higher education enrollment, 456 (figure)
  highway projects, 182, 183
  legislative representation and size, 83 (table)
  legislative session length, 82
  local governments, 373–374
  party competition, 324 (table)
  pay and compensation, 87
  redistricting impacts, 108
  state constitution comparisons, 70 (table)
  state expenditures, 431 (figure)
  state government employment, 209 (figure)
  term limits, 90

Microcosm theory, 93, 96–99, 234

Mid-decade redistricting plans, 106–107, 357

Midland, 31

Midland College, 463 (table)

Midland County, 384, 385 (table)

Midlands, 25, 26 (map), 27

Midterm elections, 89, 298

Midwestern State University, 130, 462 (table)

Migration patterns, 27

Milam County, 317

Military members, 280

Military role, 174–176

Miller, Robert D., 361 (table)

Miller, Sid, 193

Miller v. Johnson (1995), 103

Mills, C. Wright, 366

Mineral rights, 59, 476, 481

Minnesota
  legislative representation and size, 82 (table)
  legislative session length, 81–82
  party competition, 324 (table)
  state constitution comparisons, 70 (table)
  state expenditures, 431 (figure)
  voter registration, 272, 296
  voter turnout, 299, 299 (table)

Minority and women's caucuses, 123, 125 (table)

Minority voting rights, 101, 103, 275, 278–281, 311, 312, 394
  see also African Americans; Voting rights

Minor-party candidates, 301

Misconduct, judicial, 233

Misdemeanors, 239, 240 (table), 250

Missions, 8

Mississippi
  fiscal federalism, 414
  legislative representation and size, 82 (table)
  party competition, 324 (table)
  redistricting commissions, 104
  state constitution comparisons, 70 (table)
  state expenditures, 431 (figure)
  state treasurer, 191
  taxation, 416

Missouri
  female legislators, 91
  hybrid legislatures, 86
  judicial elections, 239
  legislative representation and size, 82 (table)
  party competition, 324 (table)
  school desegregation, 374
  state constitution comparisons, 70 (table)
  state expenditures, 431 (figure)

taxation, 384

term limits, 91

Missouri Compromise, 13

Missouri Plan, 238, 239

Mixed-race population, 30 (figure)

Mondale, Walter, 340

Money
  see Campaign financing; Organized interests

Monroe, Louisiana, 402

Montana
  legislative representation and size, 82 (table)
  legislative session length, 81
  party competition, 324 (table)
  state constitution comparisons, 70 (table)
  state expenditures, 431 (figure)

Montgomery County, 28

Moody, Dan, 159 (table), 189

Moody, Joe, 93

Morales, Dan, 35

Moralistic political culture, 25

Morin, Brad, 309

Mormons, 31 (figure), 97 (table)

Morrill Land-Grant College Act (1862), 477

Mostyn, Steve, 353

Mothers Against Drunk Driving (MADD), 48

Motor fuels taxes, 417–418, 420 (table), 491, 494–495

Motor vehicle taxes, 414, 416, 420 (table), 491

Motor Voter Act (1993), 272, 295, 297

Movie industry, 436

MSNBC, 305

Multi-member district (MMD) election system, 100–101, 104, 105, 109

Municipal bonds, 398–399, 405

Municipal corporations, 63 (table)

Municipal courts, 219, 220, 221–222, 240 (table)

Municipal government
  see City government

Municipal utility districts (MUDs), 391, 403, 405

Murder rates, 264

Muskie, Edmund, 340

Muslims, 97 (table)

Nacogdoches, 13, 182, 371, 497

Nacogdoches County, 101, 376, 476

Nacogdoches County Commissioners Court, 281

Name recognition, 231
Narváez Expedition, 6
Nash, Barbara, 107
Nashville, Tennessee, 404
National Association for the Advancement
    of Colored People (NAACP), 109, 447
National Association of Basketball
    Coaches, 461
National conventions, 284, 337–339, 341
National drinking age, 48
National Guard, 174–175, 499, 500
National health care policy, 39, 49, 50–51,
    85, 469, 471
National income tax, 47
National Institute on Money in State
    Politics, 310
National parliaments, 80
National parties, 341
National Rifle Association (NRA),
    348, 349, 355, 366
National Voter Registration Act (1993),
    272, 295, 297
Nation versus state, 25, 26 (map), 27
Native Americans
    citizenship, 53
    frontier justice, 246
    historical background, 6
    judiciary representation, 234
    legislative representation, 96 (table)
    population size, 12, 30 (figure)
    and Sam Houston, 12, 14, 427
    Spanish exploration and colonization,
        6, 27–28
    Spanish missionaries, 8
    voting rights, 56, 103, 273
Natural disasters, 49, 157, 174,
    175–176, 397
Natural gas production
    economic impacts, 476–481
    fracking, 396–397, 474–475, 479–481
    health concerns, 474–475
    historical perspective, 476
    political impact, 478–479
    severance tax, 418, 420 (table), 477
    see also Oil and gas industry
Natural resources management,
    194–195, 487 (figure), 488, 502
Navarro College, 463 (table)
Navarro County, 317
NBC, 305
NCAA Division I basketball coaches, 461
Nebraska
    legislative representation and size,
        83 (table)
    legislative type, 79, 124

party competition, 324 (table)
    state constitution comparisons,
        70 (table)
    state expenditures, 431 (figure)
Nebraska Democratic Party, 124
Nebraska Legislature, 124
Neff, Pat M., 68, 159 (table)
Negative externalities, 481
Nelson, Jane, 189
Netflix, 306
Nevada
    legislative representation and size,
        83 (table)
    legislative session length, 81
    local governments, 373 (table)
    party competition, 324 (table)
    state constitution comparisons,
        70 (table)
    state expenditures, 431 (figure)
    turnover, 91
New France, 26 (map)
New Hampshire
    legislative representation and size, 80
    party competition, 324 (table)
    representation and size, 82 (table)
    state constitution comparisons,
        70 (table)
    state expenditures, 431 (figure)
    taxation, 415
    term limits, 91
New Jersey
    elected officials, 185
    election systems, 105
    higher education enrollment, 456 (figure)
    legislative representation and size,
        83 (table)
    legislative terms of office, 89
    party competition, 324 (table)
    redistricting commissions, 104
    state constitution comparisons,
        70 (table)
    state expenditures, 431 (figure)
    taxation, 416
New Mexico
    bilingual ballots, 278
    fiscal federalism, 414
    legislative representation and size,
        83 (table)
    local governments, 373 (table)
    party competition, 324 (table)
    state constitution comparisons,
        70 (table)
    state expenditures, 431 (figure)
    state treasurer, 190
    taxation, 419

New Netherland, 26 (map)
New Orleans, Louisiana, 454
News media, 303–306
New South Wales, Australia, 132
New York
    antidrug policies, 247
    governor's salary, 165
    higher education enrollment,
        456 (figure)
    legislative representation and size,
        82 (table)
    legislative session length, 82
    party competition, 324 (table)
    professional legislatures, 86
    school districts, 403
    state constitution comparisons,
        70 (table)
    state expenditures, 431 (figure)
    taxation, 415, 416, 417, 419
New York City, 403
New York Times, 264
New Zealand, 280
Nichols, Robert, 183
Nineteenth Amendment (U.S.
    Constitution), 280
Ninth Circuit Court of Appeals, 262
Nixon, Richard, 23, 48, 98, 157, 247,
    340, 387
Nixon v. Herndon (1924), 277
No Child Left Behind Act (NCLB),
    446, 453
Nolan County, 486
Nominating conventions, 284, 300,
    337–339, 341
Nonpartisan blanket primaries,
    285–287, 290–291
Nonpartisan independent
    commission, 104
Nonpartisan legislatures, 124
Nonpartisan Retention Plan, 239
Norris, Chuck, 248
Norris, George William, 124
North American Free Trade Agreement
    (NAFTA), 182–183, 493
North Carolina
    bill filing, 137
    elected officials, 185
    higher education enrollment,
        456 (figure)
    legislative representation and size,
        82 (table)
    legislative session length, 81, 82
    party competition, 324 (table)
    party control, 152
    pay and compensation, 122

state constitution comparisons, 70 (table)
state expenditures, 431 (figure)
North Central Texas College, 463 (table)
North Dakota
  elected officials, 185
  election systems, 105
  legislative representation and size, 83 (table)
  legislative session length, 81
  party competition, 324 (table)
  pay and compensation, 122
  professional legislatures, 86
  state constitution comparisons, 70 (table)
  state expenditures, 431 (figure)
  voter registration, 272, 296
North Texas, 56–57, 480
North Texas Tollway Authority (NTTA), 494
Northwest Austin Municipal Utility District #1 v. Holder (2009), 277–278
Northwest Ordinance, 391
Nuclear energy, 487 (figure)

Obama, Barack
  campaign financing, 308
  Common Core standards, 453
  health care reform, 50
  immigration policies, 268, 499
  Iowa Caucuses, 340
  presidential primaries, 338
  Stimulus Package, 203
  voter turnout, 299
Obamacare
  see Patient Protection and Affordable Care Act (2010)
O Brother Where Art Thou (film), 161
O'Connor, Sandra Day, 48
O'Daniel, Wilbert Lee (Pappy), 21, 157, 159 (table), 161, 303, 328, 330
Odessa, 31
Odessa College, 463 (table)
Office of Court Administration, 226
Office of the governor
  appointment power, 56, 166, 168–170, 173, 195, 232–233, 457
  budget power, 170, 432, 433 (figure), 434
  comparison studies, 179
  crisis management, 174
  election campaigns, 303–304
  executive powers, 56, 59, 63, 65
  executive role, 166, 168–170
  female governors, 161–163
  formal powers, 156–157
  governors since 1876, 159–160 (table)
  impeachment, 20, 161, 165–166, 455–456, 458
  informal powers, 157, 176–178
  institutional powers, 166–176, 167 (figure), 175 (map), 178, 180–181
  judicial appointments, 232–233, 237
  judicial role, 173–174
  legislative role, 170–173
  Louisiana, 179
  military role, 174–176
  pay and compensation, 164–165
  personal power, 176–178
  qualifications and characteristics, 157–158, 158 (table), 160–161
  staffing resources, 165
  succession, 164
  terms of office, 59, 163–164
  veto power, 59, 146, 172–173, 311, 432
Ogallala Aquifer, 484, 486
Ohio
  female legislators, 91
  higher education enrollment, 456 (figure)
  legislative representation and size, 83 (table)
  legislative session length, 82
  local governments, 373 (table), 374
  party competition, 324 (table)
  redistricting commissions, 104
  state constitution comparisons, 70 (table)
  state expenditures, 431 (figure)
  term limits, 91
  township governments, 391
Oil and gas industry
  campaign spending contributions, 310
  economic impacts, 20–21, 476–481
  energy use and production, 487 (figure)
  health concerns, 474–475
  historical perspective, 476
  hot oil wars, 478
  lobbying activities, 360
  political impact, 478–479, 482
  severance tax, 414, 418, 420 (table), 421, 477
Oil spill management, 194–195
Oklahoma
  bilingual ballots, 278
  death penalty cases, 259
  legislative representation and size, 82 (table)
  local governments, 373, 373 (table)
party competition, 324 (table)
pay and compensation, 122
redistricting commissions, 104
state constitution comparisons, 71 (table)
state expenditures, 431 (figure)
taxation, 419
term limits, 90
Oliveira, René, 112
Oncor Electric Delivery Co., LLC, 351 (table)
121 Tollway, 493–494
130 Tollway, 493
One-Day Republicans, 287
One person, one vote, 80, 101, 103
Open Meetings Act, 210
Open primaries, 285, 290–291
Opinion Committee, 189
Opinion rulings, 189–190
Optical scanners, 294
Ordinances, 386, 388, 390, 392, 396–398
Oregon
  legislative representation and size, 83 (table)
  party competition, 324 (table)
  state constitution comparisons, 71 (table)
  state expenditures, 431 (figure)
  term limits, 90
  voter turnout, 286
Organic Law (1835), 11
Organized crime, 20
Organized interests
  advantages/disadvantages, 366–367
  basic concepts, 346–347
  economic interests, 350–351, 351 (table)
  election spending, 353, 355–357
  formation and motivations, 347–350
  functional role, 352–353
  interest types and characteristics, 350–352
  litigation, 357
  policy-influencing role, 353, 355–357, 358 (figure), 359–365
  political parties, 365
  volunteers, 357
  see also Lobbying/lobbyists
Organized labor, 308, 330, 350, 355–356, 366
Original jurisdiction, 219, 220, 240 (table)
O'Rourke, Robert, 103
Outsourcing, 383, 466
Oversight, 130
Ozone pollution, 482

Paddie, Chris, 107
*Painter, Sweatt v.* (1950), 460
Painter, Theophilus, 460
Panola College, 463 (table)
Panola County, 378
Paper ballots, 294
Pardons, 173–174
Paredes, Raymund A., 457
Parish school boards, 402–403
Paris Junior College, 463 (table)
Parker, Annise, 400
Parker, Bonnie, 248
Parker County, 480
Parks and Wildlife Department, 194
Parliamentary systems, 132, 133
Parliament of New South Wales, 132
Parr, Archer, 317
Parr, George, 317
Partisan blanket primaries, 285
Partisan elections, 216–217, 229–231, 234,
    238, 239, 379
Parton, Dolly, 253
Party affiliation, 88–89, 161, 332, 334
Party caucus chair, 120
Party legislative caucus
    Democratic Party organization,
        118, 135–136
    functional role, 118, 120–122, 135–136
    Republican Party organization,
        118–119, 135
    special legislative caucuses, 122–123,
        125 (table), 125–126, 135–136
    structuring the vote, 125–126, 146
    Texas House of Representatives,
        118–122, 120, 136
    Texas Senate, 119–122, 136
Party-line voting, 230–231, 292
Party organization, 329 (figure),
    331–335, 337–339, 341
Party platforms, 314–316, 335,
    336 (table), 341
Party primary elections
    blanket primaries, 285
    candidate selection, 284, 300, 328
    characteristics, 282–283
    closed primaries, 284–285, 332
    cross-filing, 287
    direct primaries, 283, 284
    indirect primaries, 283, 284
    open primaries, 285, 290–291
    party affiliations, 89
    party organizations,
        329 (figure), 331–335
    presidential primaries, 145, 284,
        337–339

semi-open primaries, 287, 332
    voter turnout, 320, 341
    voting-age population, 321 (figure)
    white primaries, 275, 277, 278, 319
Patient Protection and Affordable Care Act
    (2010), 39, 49, 50, 85, 469, 471
Patrick, Dan, 156, 187, 193, 195,
    268–270, 304
Patronage system, 168, 208, 317,
    381–382, 394
Patrons of Husbandry, 17, 347
Patterson, Jerry, 195
Paxton, Ken, 190
Pay and compensation
    legislators, 63, 74, 86–88, 99, 122
    office of the governor, 164–165
Pay-as-you-go funding system,
    427, 492, 495, 496
Pearsall, 474
Pecos County, 223, 378
Penal code, 238–239, 240 (table), 257
Penn Staters for a Better Tomorrow,
    Tomorrow, 345
Pennsylvania
    governor's salary, 165
    higher education enrollment,
        456 (figure)
    legislative representation and size,
        82 (table)
    legislative session length, 82
    local governments, 373, 373 (table)
    party competition, 324 (table)
    redistricting commissions, 104
    state constitution comparisons,
        71 (table)
    state expenditures, 431 (figure)
People's Party, 19
Per capita income, 32, 467, 472 (figure)
Per curiam opinion, 228
Permanent party organizations, 331
Permanent School Fund, 194,
    204, 426, 444
Permanent University Fund (PUF),
    456–457, 477
Perot, H. Ross, 449
Perry, Bob J., 310
Perry, Doylene, 310
*Perry, LULAC v.* (2006), 106–107, 357
Perry, Rick
    as agriculture commissioner, 193
    background, 160 (table)
    budget issues, 170, 434
    campaign spending, 304, 310,
        310 (table)
    distrust of big government, 38, 50–51

economic development, 410, 437
    environmental policy, 482, 483
    executive orders, 171–172, 189, 196, 364
    as governor, 154–156, 157, 164, 165,
        168, 170–174, 176–178
    highway projects, 177, 183, 493, 494
    Hispanic appointment, 35
    legacy, 154–156
    legislative special session, 86, 106, 109
    legislative strategy, 170–173
    as lieutenant governor, 115
    marijuana decriminalization, 247, 250
    Medicaid, 48
    national health care policy, 50–51, 469
    pay and compensation, 165
    performance rating, 177
    political action committees
        (PACs), 355, 356
    public-private partnerships (PPPs), 493
    redistricting plans, 106–107, 109, 357
    secession movement, 27
    Supreme Court appointments,
        216, 232–233
    tax breaks and incentives, 436
    unaccompanied minors, 499, 500
    university board appointments, 458
    veto power, 311
    vote percentage, 325
    voter identification laws, 279
Personal expenses, 87
Personal property tax, 384
Petit jury, 239–241
Phillips, Thomas, 231
Picard, Theresa, 383
Pickens, T. Boone, 363
Pilgrim, Lonnie (Bo), 361, 497
Pilgrim's Pride, 497
Piney Woods, 4, 125
Pitts, Jim, 365
Pitts, John, 365
Placeholder bills, 139
Plaintiff, 241
Planks, 314–316, 335
Plano, 30, 410
Platforms
    *see* Party platforms; Planks
*Playboy*, 253
*Plessy v. Ferguson* (1896), 444, 445
Plural executive
    advantages/disadvantages, 212–213
    agriculture commissioner, 188 (table),
        192–193
    attorney general, 187, 188 (table),
        189–190
    basic concepts, 168, 185–186

comptroller of public accounts,
188 (table), 190–192
land commissioner,
188 (table), 194–195
lieutenant governor, 186–187,
188 (table)
secretary of state, 188 (table), 195–196
see also Office of the governor
Pluralist perspective, 366
Plurality election, 100
Plyler, Jim, 499
Plyler v. Doe (1982), 499
Pole tax, 419
Policy, 411–413
Policy adoption, 412, 413 (figure)
Policy evaluation, 412, 413 (figure)
Policy formation, 412, 413 (figure)
Policy implementation, 412, 413 (figure)
Policymaking process, 412–413,
413 (figure)
Policy positions
see Planks
Policy Study Group Caucus, 125 (table)
Polish immigrants, 497
Political action committees (PACs),
121, 236, 309, 344–346, 353, 355–357
see also Organized interests
Political ambition ladder, 176–177
Political constitutents, 24 (figure)
Political contributions, 308–309
see also Campaign financing
Political culture
basic concepts, 23, 25
geographic impacts, 5
Political parties
Bavaria, Germany, 206
challenges, 341–342
conventions, 334, 337–339, 341
definitions, 323, 325
delegate allocation, 284, 337–339
electoral competition, 271, 312,
320–321, 322 (table), 323,
324 (table)
functional role, 117–118, 326–328, 341
historical perspective, 316–320
internal conflict, 314–316, 323, 325
Iowa Caucuses, 340
organized interests, 365
party identification, 325–326,
326 (figure)
party organization, 329 (figure),
331–335, 337–339, 341
party platforms, 314–316, 335,
336 (table), 341
poll taxes, 274

voter percentage, 326 (figure)
weak parties, 328, 330–331
see also Democratic Party; Primary
elections; Republican Party
Politico, 93
Polk, James K., 13, 15, 55
Poll taxes, 65–66, 273, 274, 276–277, 278
Pollution, 480, 482–483
Popular mandate, 176
Popular sovereignty, 41, 61
Population growth, 28 (figure),
28–31, 33, 476
Populist Party, 19, 274, 317
Port of Houston Authority, 373, 405
Position taking, 302
Post-adjournment veto, 172, 173
Poster, Steve, 65
Potter, Trevor, 344
Poverty rate, 32, 467, 468 (figure),
472 (figure)
Powers, Bill, 456
Prairie View A&M University, 462 (table)
Prairie View Normal and Industrial
College, 19
Precinct chair, 333
Precinct conventions, 284
Precinct level courts, 222
Pre-clearance provision, 277–278, 279
Preference primaries, 283, 284
Preponderance of evidence, 241
Presbyterians, 31 (figure)
Presidential elections, 299 (table), 307–308
Presidential primaries, 145, 284, 337–339
Presidential republicanism, 23
Presidential terms, 54
President pro tempore, 115, 164
Presiding officers, 115–117, 138,
150–151, 186–187, 432
Presidios, 8
Primary elections
blanket primaries, 285
candidate selection, 284, 300, 328
characteristics, 282–283
closed primaries, 284–285, 332
cross-filing, 287
direct primaries, 283, 284
indirect primaries, 283, 284
open primaries, 285, 290–291
party affiliations, 89
party organizations,
329 (figure), 331–335
presidential primaries,
145, 284, 337–339
semi-open primaries, 287, 332
voter turnout, 320, 341

voting-age population, 321 (figure)
white primaries, 275, 277, 278, 319
Principle-agent theory of representation, 92
Prison system
associated costs, 249
health care, 251
incarceration rates, 247
prison conditions, 244–245, 250–252
privatization movement, 252–254
Texas Department of Criminal Justice,
194, 203–204, 252
Private corporations, 63 (table)
Private financing, 307
Private member bills, 132
Private prisons, 252–254
Private property, 485
Private toll roads, 494
Privatization, 383
Privileges and immunities, 44–45
Procedural standing committees,
127, 138–139
Professional associations, 350
Professional legislature, 63, 73–74, 86
Progressive movement, 19–20, 288,
317–318
Progressive tax, 423
Prohibition, 19–20, 21, 317, 318
Project V.O.T.E. (Voters of Tomorrow
through Education), 196
Pro-life versus pro-choice debate, 47
Property restrictions, 395–396
Property rights, 52, 56
Property taxes
background and characteristics,
419–423
city revenue sources, 398
comparison studies, 422 (figure)
county revenue sources, 382–384,
385 (table)
education funding, 447–448
historical perspective, 414
levied taxes, 384, 424 (table)
school districts, 403, 419–421,
424 (table)
special districts, 405, 406–407
state constitution guarantees, 63
tax breaks, 435
tax burdens, 406–407, 422–423
tax rates, 385 (table)
Proposition 106 (Arizona), 108
Proposition 14 (California), 285–286
Prosecutor, 238
Prostitution, 253
Protestants, 31 (figure), 97, 97 (table)
pro-Union soldiers, 16

Provisional appointments, 169
Public community colleges, 463 (table), 464
Public defenders, 254–255
Public education, 59, 60, 63 (table),
    66, 443 (table), 443–452
Public Education Committee, 135
Public financing, 307
Public Information Act, 210
Public interest groups, 351
Public-private partnerships (PPPs),
    493–495
Public Utility Commission of
    Texas (PUC), 205, 207–208
Puerto Rico, 414
Pulbic lands, 63 (table)
Punch-card ballots, 294
Punitive damages, 241

Qualifications, legislator, 88–89
Quorum, 143–144

Race and ethnicity
    comparison studies, 34
    death penalty cases, 260 (figure), 264
    election campaigns, 303
    election systems, 394, 395
    legislative representation, 96 (table),
        97, 109–110
    minority and women's caucuses,
        123, 125 (table)
    population size, 29–30, 30 (figure)
    school desegregation, 23, 444–445,
        447, 460–461
    voter identification laws, 279
    voter turnout, 299, 299 (table), 300
    voting rights, 101, 103
Racial equality, 16, 19
Radical Republicans, 16–17, 59, 62, 501
Radioactive waste storage, 486, 488
Radio broadcasts, 303–305, 355
Railroad Commission of Texas, 18, 21,
    168, 201–203, 302, 474, 478, 489–490
Railroads, 18–19, 63 (table), 197–198,
    201–203, 317, 489–490
Rainy Day Fund, 156, 170, 430,
    432, 484, 492
Raise Your Hand, Texas, 442
Ramsay, William, 19, 303
Ranching, 31
Ranney Index, 323, 324 (table)
Rape, prison, 252
Rash, Carrington v. (1965), 280
Rates of incumbency, 91, 92 (table)
Ratliff, Bill, 69, 71, 164, 442
Ratliff-Junell constitutional proposal, 69, 71

Rayburn, Sam, 151
Reagan, Ronald, 145, 340, 387
Real estate taxes
    see Property taxes
Recall petition, 288
Recess appointments, 169
Recidivism, 249
Reconciliation, 145
Reconstruction era, 16–17, 58–61, 62, 501
Recycling programs, 383
Redeemers, 17, 60
Redistributive policy, 412–413
Redistricting, 85, 89, 91, 101, 102 (figure),
    103–104, 106–110
Redistricting Committee, 127
Red River, 9
Reeves County, 376
Referendum, 73, 288, 333
Reform movement, 18–21
Regents, 456, 457–459
Regressive tax, 423
Regular sessions, 81–82, 84–85
Regulation, 481
Regulatory policy, 413
Regulatory takings, 485
Rehabilitation, 249–250
Religious affiliations, 97, 97 (table), 348
Religious freedoms, 64
Religious traditions, 31, 31 (figure)
Remand, 227
Removal power, 170
Renewable energy resources,
    195, 487 (figure)
Reno, Shaw v. (1993), 103
Representation
    bicameral legislatures, 79
    comparison studies, 82–83 (table)
    counties as the basis of representation,
        80–81
    demographic data, 96 (table)
    electoral system, 109–110
    geographic representation, 93
    key characteristics, 92–93
    microcosm theory, 93, 96–99
    purpose, 78
    religious affiliations, 97 (table)
    State House districts (2012),
        93, 95 (map)
    State Senate districts (2012),
        93, 94 (map)
Reproductive Health Services,
    Webster v. (1989), 47
Republican Party
    Arizona, 108
    conventions, 334, 337–339, 341

delegate allocation, 284, 338
and E. J. Davis, 60–61, 63
electoral competition, 312, 320–321,
    322 (table), 323, 324 (table)
female legislators, 77–78
Hispanic population, 30, 36
historical perspective, 316–320
immigration reform, 500–501
internal conflict, 314–316, 323, 325
Iowa Caucuses, 340
judicial elections, 230–231
judiciary representation, 234
legislative control, 91, 106–107,
    110, 117, 150–152, 301–302
legislator qualifications, 88–89
mid-twentieth century, 23
national health care policy, 50
Nebraska, 124
North Dakota, 105
office of the governor, 161
party caucuses, 118–122, 125, 135
party platforms, 314–316, 335,
    336 (table), 341
post-Reconstruction era, 60–62
primaries, 284–285, 287, 290–291,
    332, 337–339, 341
Reconstruction era, 16–17, 59, 63
redistricting plans, 36, 106, 106–107
Speaker of the House, 112–114, 117
standing committees, 127, 129
2014 campaign and election,
    268–270
voter identification laws, 279
voter percentage, 326 (figure)
see also Legislative process
Republic of Texas, 11, 12–13, 54–56,
    273, 376, 443, 477, 489
Requirements, legislator, 88–89
Reserved powers, 44, 45 (figure)
Resolutions, 137–138, 146–148,
    147 (figure), 148 (table), 149 (figure)
Responsible party model, 325
Retention election system, 217, 238, 239
Retirement benefits, 87
Retribution, 264
Revenue bonds, 429
Revenue sources
    federal funds, 425, 425 (table),
        426 (figure)
    interest and investment income,
        425 (table), 426
    licenses and fees, 425 (table), 426
    lottery proceeds, 425 (table), 426–427
    tax raids, 429
    see also Taxation

Reverse, 227
Reverse discrimination, 460–461
Revolving door, 363–364
Revolving door phenomenon, 170
Reyes, Silvestre, 103
Reynolds, Burt, 253
*Reynolds v. Sims* (1964), 80, 98
Rhode Island
    constitutional amendments, 68
    governor's residence, 165
    legislative representation and size,
        83 (table)
    local governments, 373 (table), 374
    party competition, 324 (table)
    professional legislatures, 86
    state constitution comparisons,
        71 (table)
    state expenditures, 431 (figure)
    state treasurer, 191
    voter registration, 272
Rice, Ben C., 445
Rice University, 16
Rice, William Marsh, 16
Richard, Michael, 263–264
Richards, Ann, 157, 160 (table), 162, 163
Richmond, 489
Riders, 142–143
Rights of the accused, 254–255
Right to habeas corpus, 62
Rio Grande, 15
Rio Grande Valley, 376
Ritter, Tex, 248
Roads
    funding challenges, 491–492
    historical perspective, 490–491
    public-private partnerships (PPPs),
        493–495
    Texas Department of Transportation
        (TxDOT), 492–493
Road tax, 59
Roberts, Milo, 418
Roberts, Oran M., 159 (table)
Robin Hood plan, 447–448
Robstown, 354
Rockefeller, John D., 187
Rockefeller, Nelson, 247
Rockwall County, 28, 378
Rodríguez, Richard, 278
Rodriguez, Robert, 436
Roemer, Buddy, 290
*Roe v. Wade* (1973), 47
Rogers, Roy, 248
Roll call votes, 144
Roll off, 291–292
Romney, Mitt, 325, 340

Roosevelt, Franklin D., 478
*Roper v. Simmons* (2005), 259
Rosenthal, Alan, 160
Rose, Patrick, 310, 459
Ross, Lawrence Sullivan (Sul), 159 (table)
Ross, Nellie T., 161
Round Rock, 30
Ruiz, David, 250–251
*Ruiz v. Estelle* (1972), 250–251
Rule of capture, 484
Rule of eighty, 165
Rules and Resolutions Committee, 127, 139
Rum Row, 20
Runnels, Hardin R., 15–16
Runoff elections, 100, 287
Runoff primary, 333
Rural Caucus, 123, 125, 125 (table)
Rusk County, 478
Rusk, Thomas Jefferson, 13
Russia, 33 (table)
Rylander, Carole Keeton, 106

Sabine County, 378
Salaries
    legislators, 63, 74, 86–88, 99, 122
    office of the governor, 164–165
Sales tax, 382, 398, 415–416, 420 (table),
        422 (figure), 423
Same-sex marriage, 50, 66, 298, 400
Sam Houston State University, 462 (table)
Sam Rayburn Tollway, 493–494
Samudio, Vanessa, 257
San Antonio
    election systems, 394
    first woman mayor, 23
    high-speed rail lines, 197
    League of United Latin American
        Citizens (LULAC), 354
    mass transit, 495
    Mexican rule, 376
    population, 30
    tax subsidies, 435, 436
Sanchez, Tony, 163
Sanctuary city legislation, 497–498
San Diego, California, 223
San Gabriel, California, 223
San Jacinto Community College,
        405, 463 (table)
Santa Anna, Antonio López de,
        10, 11, 52, 53, 55, 156
Santorum, Rick, 340
SAT scores, 450, 451
Sayers, Joseph D., 159 (table)
Scalawags, 16
Schlueter, Stan, 361 (table)

School desegregation, 23, 444–445,
        447, 460–461
School districts, 401–403, 406, 419–421
    *see also* Educational policies and
        services
School Land Board, 194
School property taxes, 403, 419–421,
        424 (table)
School voucher programs, 348, 452–453
Schwertner, Charles, 93
Scott, Winfield, 15
Secession Convention (1861), 16, 38
Secessionist movements, 16, 38, 56–57
Secession Vote (1861), 57 (map)
Second-order elections, 298
Second Reconstruction Act, 17
Secretary of state, 168, 188 (table), 195–196
Security costs, 165
Segregation, 23, 66, 354, 444–445,
        447, 460–461
Seguín, Juan Nepomuceno, 33
Select committees, 134
Selective incentives, 349–350
Semi-open primaries, 287, 332
Senate Bill 22, 108
Senate Committee on Finance,
        131, 432, 433 (figure)
Senate Research Center, 131
Senatorial courtesy, 169
Senatorial district convention, 335
Seniority, 127
Separate-but-equal policy, 444–445, 460
Servicemembers Civil Relief Act, 371
Seventeenth Amendment (U.S.
        Constitution), 79
Severance tax, 414, 418, 420 (table),
        421, 477
Shale formations, 474, 479, 488
Shami, Farouk, 310
Shankle, Glenn, 486, 488
Sharecroppers, 18
Shared power, 46
Shared values and beliefs, 23
Sharp, John, 466
Sharpstown Scandal, 68
*Shaw v. Reno* (1993), 103
*Shelby County, AL v. Holder* (2013),
        109, 278, 279
Sheppard, Morris, 21, 330
Sheriff, 381
Shivers, Allan, 160 (table), 176–177,
        274–275, 445, 447
Short, Bob, 387
Short-cut voting, 292
Shreveport, Louisiana, 182

*Simmons, Roper v.* (2005), 259
Simple resolution, 137–138
Simpson, David, 112, 493
*Sims, Reynolds v.* (1964), 80, 98
Single-chamber legislatures, 52, 79–80
Single-issue interest groups, 351
Single-member district majority (SMDM)
   election system, 100–101, 287, 393
Single-member district plurality (SMDP)
   election system, 93, 100–101,
   104, 379, 386, 393
Single-member district (SMD) election
   system, 99–101, 109–110, 393–395
Sin taxes, 418–419, 420 (table)
Six Flags Over Texas, 3, 387
*60 Minutes*, 237
Slating, 327
Slavery
   Confederate constitution, 58
   Constitution of the Republic of Texas,
      11, 55, 56
   cotton farming, 15
   East Texas, 56
   federal policies, 38, 42, 46
   German opposition, 16, 57
   Mexican government, 10, 52
   Missouri Compromise, 13
   and Sam Houston, 14, 15
   statehood constitution, 56–57
   termination, 16, 58–59
Smith, Al, 21
Smith County, 263, 383
Smith, Henry, 11, 12
Smith, Preston, 22, 157, 160 (table)
Smith, "Tubby," 461
*Smith v. Allwright* (1944), 277
Smog, 480
Social Democratic Party, 206
Social media, 305
Social welfare programs, 467–469,
   472 (figure)
Solar energy, 486
Solidarity benefits, 347
South Carolina
   legislative representation and size,
      82 (table)
   party competition, 324 (table)
   state constitution comparisons,
      71 (table)
   state expenditures, 431 (figure)
South Dakota
   bilingual ballots, 278
   election systems, 105
   legislative representation and size,
      83 (table)

party competition, 324 (table)
state constitution comparisons,
   71 (table)
state expenditures, 431 (figure)
*South Dakota v. Dole* (1987), 48
South Plains College, 463 (table)
South Texas College, 463 (table)
Southwest Texas Junior College,
   463 (table)
Spain, 33 (table), 496–497
Spanish Caribbean, 26 (map)
Spanish exploration and colonization,
   6, 8–9, 27–28, 52
Speaker of the House, 112–114, 116–117,
   127–129, 134–135, 138, 150
Speaker pro tempore, 117
Special committees, 132–135
Special courts, 219
Special districts, 382–383, 403, 405,
   406, 424 (table)
Special elections, 68, 73 (figure),
   297 (figure), 297–298
Special interest groups, 310, 344–345
   *see also* Organized interests
Special legislative caucuses, 122–123,
   125 (table), 125–126, 135–136
Special sessions, 84, 86, 147–148, 172
Special white primaries, 319
Spending cuts, 438
Spicewood Beach, 484
Spike, 305
Spindletop oil rig, 20, 418, 476
Spoiled ballots, 394
Spoils system
   *see* Patronage system
Sportsmen's Caucus, 123
Square Meals program, 193
Squire, Peverill, 87
STAAR testing system, 85, 449, 450
Staffing resources, 87, 131
Stalling tactics, 143–144
Standardized tests, 441, 442, 448,
   449–450, 452
Standard Oil Company, 187
Standing committees, 126–131,
   128 (table), 138
Staples, Todd, 193
State agencies
   Bavaria, Germany, 206–207
   budget process, 432, 433 (figure), 434
   Department of State Health Services
      (SHS), 200–201
   origins, 197
   policymaking process, 412–413,
      413 (figure)

Public Utility Commission of Texas
   (PUC), 205, 207–208
Railroad Commission of Texas,
   18, 21, 168, 201–203, 302, 474, 478,
   489–490
staffing resources, 205 (table), 208, 210
State Board of Education, 36, 85, 107,
   168, 204–205, 302, 403, 443–444
Texas Department of Criminal Justice,
   194, 203–204
Texas Department of Transportation
   (TxDOT), 182, 184, 197–198,
   199 (figure), 200, 202
State Auditor's Office, 131
State Board of Education, 36, 85, 107,
   168, 204–205, 302, 403, 443–444
State budget, 85, 191–192, 427–429,
   432, 438
State Children's Health Insurance Program
   (SCHIP), 471
State comptrollers, 190–191
State constitution comparisons,
   70–71 (table)
State conventions, 335, 337–339
State executive committee, 335, 337
State government relationships, 373–376
State Guard, 174, 175
State Health Services (SHS), 200–201, 257
State Highway 121, 493–494
State Highway 130, 493
Statehood, 12, 13, 15, 56–57
State House districts (2012), 93, 95 (map)
State legislatures
   background and characteristics,
      78–82, 79 (table)
   comparison studies, 105, 108, 124
   redistricting, 101, 103, 108
   representation and size,
      80, 82–83 (table)
   session length and frequency, 84
   standing committees, 127–128
   typologies, 86–88
   *see also* Legislative organization
State-level trial courts, 219, 220, 226–227
State of Texas Assessments of Academic
   Readiness (STAAR), 85, 449, 450
State of the state address, 170–171
State party chair, 335
State political parties, 326–327, 339, 341
State Preservation Board, 363
State sales tax, 415
State Senate districts (2012), 93, 94 (map)
States' rights, 46, 47–51, 250
State Teachers Association, 349, 350, 352,
   359–360

State treasurers, 190–191
State versus nation, 25, 26 (map), 27
Statutory committees, 131
Statutory courts, 226
Steinbeck, John, 5, 23
Stephen F. Austin State University (SFASU), 281, 462 (table)
Stephenville, 193
Sterling, Ross S., 21, 159 (table), 248, 478
Stevenson, Coke, 159 (table)
Stewart, Jon, 204, 268
Stimulus Package, 203
Stopper, 139, 142
Straight-ticket voting, 230–231, 292
Straus, Joe, 112, 113–114, 116, 121, 129, 135, 190, 310
Strayhorn, Carole Keeton, 191–192, 304, 428
Strong, Charlie, 165
Strong mayor–council city government system, 388, 389 (figure), 392
Structuring the vote, 117, 123, 125–126, 146
Student regents, 458–459
Students for Academic Choice (SAC), 360
Subcommittees, 131, 138
Subsidies, 413, 435–436
Substantive standing committees, 126–127
Succession, 164
Suffrage, 63 (table), 65–66, 273, 280
Suicide, prison, 252
Sullivan, Michael Quinn, 357, 359
Sul Ross State University, 461, 462 (table)
Sunset Advisory Commission, 210, 212, 233
Sunset review process, 210, 211 (figure), 212, 492
Sunshine laws, 210
Super Bowl, 435
Superdelegates, 339
Supermajority, 84, 172
Super PACs, 344–346, 356
Supplemental Nutritional Action Plan (SNAP), 468–469
Supremacy clause, 44, 46
Supreme Court decisions
    abortion rights, 47
    campaign financing, 307, 330, 355–356
    cross-state pollution, 483
    death penalty cases, 259, 263
    education funding, 446
    election laws, 61, 100–101
    free speech protections, 307, 355–356, 366
    health care, 85
    implied powers, 44
    legislative representation, 80, 98, 103
    local government power, 373
    national health care policy, 51
    political party regulation, 331
    poll taxes, 277
    pre-clearance provision, 277–278, 279
    primary elections, 285, 287
    race-based admissions, 460–461
    redistricting plans, 106–107, 109, 357
    right to legal counsel, 254
    school desegregation, 444–445, 447
    separate-but-equal policy, 444, 445, 460
    undocumented immigrants, 499
    use of grants, 48
    voting rights, 103, 109, 275, 280
    white primaries, 277
Supreme Court of Missouri, 239
Supreme Court of Texas, 216, 219, 227, 229–234, 236, 256, 479
Sweatt, Heman Marion, 460, 461
Sweatt v. Painter (1950), 460
Swedish immigrants, 497
Swift meatpacking plants, 498

Taft-Hartley Act (1947), 356
Taking of private property, 485
Tarleton State University, 462 (table)
Tarrant County, 93, 259, 383
Tarrant County College District, 463 (table)
Tauzin, W. J. (Billy), 290
Tax assessor, 381
Taxation
    city government, 398–399
    comparison studies, 422 (figure)
    comptroller of public accounts, 188 (table), 190–192
    Constitution of 1876, 63 (table)
    county government, 382–384, 385 (table)
    criticisms, 423
    education funding, 60, 447–448
    excise tax, 419
    franchise tax, 418, 420 (table)
    gasoline tax, 414, 417–418, 420 (table), 491, 494–495
    general sales tax, 382, 398, 415–416, 420 (table), 422 (figure), 423
    historical perspective, 414
    income taxes, 47, 63, 415, 422 (figure), 423
    levied taxes, 384, 424 (table)
    poll taxes, 65–66, 273, 274, 276–277, 278
    property taxes, 63, 382, 385 (table), 398, 405, 406–407
    revenue sources, 420 (table), 422 (figure), 425 (table)
    road taxes, 59
    severance tax, 414, 418, 420 (table), 421, 477
    sin taxes, 418–419, 420 (table)
    special districts, 405, 406–407
    tax breaks, 434–436
    tax expenditures, 434–435
    tax raids, 429
Tax breaks, 434–436
Tax expenditures, 434–435
Tax Foundation, 416, 434
Tax Freedom Day, 416, 417 (figure)
Tax-free holidays, 434
Taylor County, 378
Taylor, Lori, 415–416
Taylor, Zachary, 15
Teacher rewards and incentives, 454
Tea Party Caucus, 123, 125 (table)
Tea Party movement, 39, 123, 142, 155–156, 268
Teflon Governor, 177
Tejanos
    characteristics, 25
    Civil War era, 16
    impacts and contributions, 33
    Mexican independence, 9
    political involvement, 35, 36
    population size, 12, 15, 35
    Texas independence, 10
    and the Texas Rangers, 248
    voting rights, 278
Telephone service, 205
Television broadcasts, 303–306, 355
Temple College, 463 (table)
Temporary Assistance for Needy Families (TANF), 467, 468
Temporary party organizations, 331
Tenant farmers, 19
Tennessee
    governor's salary, 165
    highway projects, 182
    legislative representation and size, 83 (table)
    legislative session length, 81
    local governments, 374, 404
    party competition, 324 (table)
    state constitution comparisons, 71 (table)
    state expenditures, 431 (figure)
    taxation, 415, 416

Tenth Amendment (U.S. Constitution), 44, 46, 51

Tenther movement, 39, 51

Term limits, 89–92, 163–164

Terms of office
    legislature, 54, 56, 89
    office of the governor, 59, 163–164

Terrell Election Law (1905), 331

*Terry v. Adams* (1953), 277

Tesla Motors, 437

Texans for a Better Tomorrow, Tomorrow, 345

Texans for Fiscal Responsibility, 345, 355

Texans for Gun Safety, 351

Texans for Lawsuit Reform (TLR), 236, 310, 351, 355, 359

Texans for Public Justice, 236, 351, 361

Texans Uniting for Reform and Freedom, 184

Texarkana, 182, 493

Texas
    Anglo settlements, 9–10
    auto emission standards, 483
    bilingual ballots, 278
    change effects, 27–33
    Civil War era, 15–16, 38, 57–58
    Confederate regime, 16, 57–58, 376
    constitutional comparisons, 64, 69
    death penalty cases, 258–259, 260 (figure), 261 (figure), 261–264
    economy, 31–32, 32 (table), 33 (table), 67, 85, 398, 476–481
    election campaigns, 268–270, 303–306
    election systems, 105
    ethnic diversity, 34
    fiscal federalism, 414
    frontier justice, 246
    geography, 4–5
    Great Depression, 21
    gross domestic product, 33 (table)
    historical background, 6
    immigration issues, 2–3
    incarceration rates, 247
    independence movement, 10–12, 52–53, 55
    independent Texas, 7 (map)
    legislative representation, 80–81
    local governments, 373 (table)
    Mexican rule, 9–11, 52–54, 55, 376, 496–497
    military rule, 59
    party competition, 324 (table)
    party identification, 325–326, 326 (figure)
    political ideology, 323, 325, 326 (figure)
    population growth, 28 (figure), 28–31, 33
    presidential primaries, 337
    primary elections, 287, 332
    race and ethnicity, 29, 30 (figure)
    Reconstruction era, 16–17, 58–61, 62
    redistricting plans, 108
    reform movement, 18–21
    religious freedoms, 64
    sales tax, 415–416
    school districts, 401–403, 406
    Spanish legacy, 6, 8–9, 27–28, 52
    state expenditures, 431 (figure)
    state government employment, 209 (figure)
    statehood, 12, 13, 15, 56–57
    transitional years, 23, 25, 27
    voter qualifications and registration, 272–273
    voter turnout, 295, 296 (figure), 297 (figure), 297–300, 299 (table)
    voting rights, 273–281
    *see also* Elections

Texas-21 Transportation Caucus, 125 (table)

Texas A&M International University, 462 (table)

Texas A&M University, 454, 456–457, 462 (table), 466, 477

Texas Abortion and Reproductive Rights Action League, 351

Texas Assessment of Academic Skills (TAAS), 449

Texas Assessment of Knowledge and Skills (TAKS), 449

Texas Association of Builders, 372

Texas Board of Pardons and Paroles, 173–174, 197, 204, 251, 263

Texas Border and Mexican Affairs Division, 196

Texas Bureau of Immigration, 497

Texas Carbon Management Caucus, 123, 125 (table)

Texas Certified Retirement Community Program, 193

Texas Christian Coalition, 348

Texas Commission on Environmental Quality (TCEQ), 403, 482, 483, 486

Texas Comptroller of Public Accounts, 427–429

Texas Conservative Coalition, 123

Texas Constitution
    appointment approval, 169
    budget issues, 427
    challenges, 73–74
    city government, 385–386
    Connecticut Constitution comparison, 64
    constitutional amendments, 63 (table), 67–68, 71, 72 (figure), 298
    constitutional conventions, 11, 17, 54, 58, 59
    constitutional revisions, 68–69, 71, 73
    Constitution of 1836, 11, 12, 53, 54–56
    Constitution of 1845, 13, 56–57, 273, 414
    Constitution of 1861, 57–58, 376
    Constitution of 1866, 58–59, 476
    Constitution of 1868, 443
    Constitution of 1869, 59–61, 274
    Constitution of Coahuila y Tejas (1827), 52, 53
    Constitution of the Republic of Texas, 11, 12, 54–56, 273
    criticisms, 67, 68
    distrust of government, 66, 68, 73–75, 156
    education services, 446
    executive branch, 63, 63 (table), 65, 67
    highway construction costs, 491
    historical perspective, 52
    impeachment, 165–166
    individual freedoms, 62
    judicial system, 63 (table), 65, 67, 218–219
    legislative branch, 63, 63 (table), 67, 170–171
    local government power, 374
    Massachusetts Constitution comparison, 69
    Permanent University Fund (PUF), 456–457
    popular sovereignty, 41
    property taxes, 419
    rights of the accused, 254
    special districts, 403
    statehood constitution, 56–57

Texas Correctional Industries (TCI), 204

Texas Council of Campfire Girls, 429

Texas Court of Criminal Appeals, 65, 219, 227, 228–229, 234, 259, 261, 264

Texas Department of Agriculture, 192–193

Texas Department of Aviation, 492

Texas Department of Criminal Justice, 194, 203–204, 252

Texas Department of Parks and Wildlife, 130

Texas Department of Public Safety, 248, 500

Texas Department of State Health Services, 200–201, 257

Texas Department of Transportation (TxDOT), 182, 184, 197–198, 199 (figure), 200, 202, 492–493

Texas Dream Act (2001), 500, 501

Texas Eagle Forum, 348

Texas Education Agency (TEA), 194, 204, 443, 444

Texas Educational Opportunity Grants, 464

Texas Education Code, 374, 401, 440, 453

Texas Elections Code, 196

Texas Emerging Technology Fund (TETF), 436, 466

Texas Enterprise Fund (TEF), 156, 410, 436

Texas Ethics Commission, 87, 125, 304, 308, 356, 359, 361–362

Texas Examination of Current Administrators and Teachers (TECAT), 449

Texas Farm and Ranch Lands Conservation Council, 194

Texas Grant Program, 464

Texas Health and Human Services Commission (HHSC), 469

Texas Higher Education Coordinating Board (THECB), 440, 457, 459, 464

Texas High Speed Rail Caucus, 123, 125 (table)

Texas Highway Commission, 492

Texas Highway Department, 490–491

Texas, Hopwood v. (1996), 460

Texas Hospitality Association (THA), 350–351

Texas House Farm-to-Table Caucus, 125 (table)

Texas House of Representatives
    budget process, 432, 433 (figure)
    calendars, 138–139, 139 (table)
    campaign spending, 310
    characteristics, 78–79, 79 (table)
    conference committees, 133, 145
    Democratic Party organization, 118, 119
    demographic makeup, 96 (table)
    election districts, 93, 95 (map), 99, 100
    electoral competition, 321, 322 (table), 323
    female legislators, 77–78
    impeachment, 20, 165–166, 233
    interim committees, 134–135
    legislative process, 136–139, 142–148
    legislator qualifications, 88–89
    party caucuses, 118–121, 136
    party control, 106, 301–302

power and control issues, 150–152
    rates of incumbency, 91, 92 (table)
    redistricting plans, 85, 86, 101, 106–109
    representation and size, 81, 82 (table), 103
    Republican Party organization, 118–119
    Speaker of the House, 112–114, 116–117, 127–129, 134–135, 138, 150
    staffing resources, 87
    standing committees, 126–131, 128 (table), 138
    terms of office, 56, 89

Texas Instruments, 442

Texas Legislative Black Caucus (TLBC), 123, 125 (table), 125–126

Texas Legislative Council, 136–137

Texas Legislature
    alternative energy legislation, 486
    antidrug policies, 247, 250
    appointment approval, 169, 232
    bill-to-resolution balance, 146–148, 147 (figure), 148 (table), 149 (figure)
    budget issues, 85, 191–192, 427, 432, 433 (figure), 438
    campaign spending, 310
    characteristics, 78–79
    committee system, 126–135, 128 (table), 138
    comparison studies, 79 (table)
    deadly force law, 257–258
    demographic makeup, 93, 96, 96 (table), 110–111
    education funding, 446–448, 461, 477
    electoral competition, 321, 322 (table), 323
    electoral system, 99–101, 103–104, 106–110
    female legislators, 76–78, 91–92, 96, 98
    functional role, 24 (figure)
    geographic representation, 93
    health care legislation, 85–86
    higher education laws, 460
    highway construction funding, 491–492
    homeowners association (HOA) reforms, 401
    immigration issues, 86, 497–498
    impeachment, 20, 165–166, 233
    Killer Bees, 145
    legislative process, 136–139, 142–148
    legislator qualifications, 88–89
    levels of activity, 146–148, 147 (figure), 148 (table), 149 (figure)
    lobbying impact, 362–365
    lobbying regulation, 361–362, 364

oil production taxes, 477
    party caucuses, 135–136, 146
    party control, 301–302
    pay and compensation, 63, 74, 86–88, 99, 122
    political expenditures ban, 356
    power and control issues, 150–152
    presidential primaries, 337
    presiding officers, 115–117, 138, 150–151, 186–187, 432
    property taxes, 420
    public-private partnerships (PPPs), 493
    rates of incumbency, 91, 92 (table)
    redistricting, 85, 89, 91, 101, 102 (figure), 103–104, 106–110
    religious affiliations, 97, 97 (table)
    representation and size, 80–81, 82 (table), 93, 96 (table)
    session length and frequency, 81–82, 84–85
    special districts, 403, 405
    State House districts (2012), 93, 95 (map)
    State Senate districts (2012), 93, 94 (map)
    tax breaks and incentives, 436
    tax-free holidays, 434
    terms of office, 54, 56, 89
    tort reform, 256
    turnover, 91, 92 (table)
    women's suffrage, 280
    zoning and planning policy issues, 396
    see also Legislative organization; Texas House of Representatives; Texas Senate

Texas Local Government Code, 288, 374, 379, 382, 385, 386

Texas Medical Association, 236, 350, 351 (table)

Texas Monthly, 186–187, 359

Texas Motor Vehicle Commission, 492

Texas Moving Image Industry Incentive Program, 436

Texas Municipal League, 392

Texas National Guard, 174–175, 499, 500

Texas Oil & Gas Association, 351 (table)

Texas Open Meetings Act, 210

Texas Parks and Wildlife Department, 194

Texas penal code, 238–239, 240 (table), 257

Texas Power and Light, 207

Texas Progressive Caucus, 123, 125 (table)

Texas Public and Private Facilities Infrastructure Act (2011), 493

Texas Public Information Act, 210

Texas Railroad Commission, 18, 21, 168, 201–203, 302, 474, 478, 489–490

Texas Rainy Day Fund, 156, 170, 430, 432, 484, 492

Texas Rangers, 145, 162, 223, 248, 429

Texas Rangers (baseball team), 387

*Texas Register*, 196

Texas Research League, 236

Texas Restoration Project, 348

Texas Right to Life Committee, 351

Texas Senate
    appointment approval, 169, 232
    budget process, 432, 433 (figure)
    calendars, 139, 142
    campaign spending, 310
    characteristics, 78–79, 79 (table)
    conference committees, 133, 145
    demographic makeup, 96 (table)
    election districts, 94 (map), 99, 100
    electoral competition, 321, 322 (table)
    female legislators, 77–78
    impeachment, 20, 166, 233
    interim committees, 135
    legislative process, 136–139, 142–148
    legislator qualifications, 88–89
    lieutenant governor, 115–116, 138, 150, 186–187, 188 (table)
    party caucuses, 119–122, 125, 136
    party control, 106, 301–302
    power and control issues, 150–152
    rates of incumbency, 92 (table)
    redistricting plans, 85, 86, 106–107, 109
    representation and size, 81, 103
    staffing resources, 87
    standing committees, 126, 127, 128 (table), 129–131, 138
    terms of office, 56, 89

Texas Southern University, 462 (table)

Texas State Bar Association, 231

Texas State Board of Education, 36, 85, 107, 168, 204–205, 302, 403, 443–444

Texas State Guard, 174, 175

Texas State Rifle Association, 351

Texas State Teachers Association, 349, 350, 352, 359–360

Texas State Technical College institutions, 457

Texas State University, 462 (table)

Texas State University for Negroes, 460

Texas Tech University, 462 (table)

Texas Tourism Caucus, 125 (table)

TEXAS (Towards EXcellence, Access and Success), 436

Texas Traffic Association, 202

Texas Transportation Commission, 197, 198, 201

Texas Trial Lawyers Association, 351 (table)

*Texas Tribune*, 168, 247, 263, 450

Texas Turnpike Authority, 494

Texas Turnpike Corporation, 494

Texas Two-Step, 284, 339

Texas Utilities Code, 374

Texas Veteran's Caucus, 125, 125 (table)

Texas Veterans Commission, 426

Texas Watch, 237, 256

Texas Water Code, 374

Texas Woman's University, 462 (table)

Texas Women's Political Caucus, 123, 125 (table)

Texas Youth Commission (TYC), 252–253

Texline, 4

Theme parks, 3, 387

The Woodlands, 482

Thirteenth Amendment (U.S. Constitution), 16, 59, 273

Thompson, Senfronia, 112

*Thornburg v. Gingles* (1986), 101

Throckmorton County, 385 (table)

Thurgood Marshall School of Law at Texas Southern University, 460

Tidewater, 26 (map)

Tillman, Calvin, 474

Timpson, 480

Tobacco tax, 419, 420 (table)

Togonidze, Alexander, 244

Toll roads, 383, 418, 493–495, 496

Tom Green County, 499

Toomey, Michael, 361 (table)

Top Two Candidates Open Primary Act (2010), 285–286

Tort law/tort reform, 255–257

Touch-screen voting systems, 294

Tower, John, 23, 319

Township governments, 391

Toxic emissions, 482

Toyota, 410

Trade agreements, 182–183

Trade associations, 350–351, 360

Traditionalistic political culture, 25

Traditions
    change effects, 27–33
    religion, 31, 31 (figure)

Trail drives, 17–18, 27

TransCanada, 478–479

Transitional years, 23, 25, 27

Trans-Pecos region, 4

Transportation networks, 182, 184, 197–198, 200

Transportation policy
    challenges, 496
    historical perspective, 488–489
    mass transit, 495
    railroads, 197–198, 489–490
    roads, 490–495

Trans-Texas Corridor, 177, 183, 493

Travis County, 107, 383, 436

Treaty of Guadalupe Hidalgo, 15

Treaty of Velasco, 52, 55

Trial courts
    county-level courts, 219, 221, 222–223, 226
    local courts, 221–222
    state-level trial courts, 219, 220, 226–227

Trial jury, 239–241

Trinity Valley Community College, 463 (table)

Troublemaker Studios, 436

Truman, Harry, 50

Trustee, 92–93

Tuition Equalization Grant program, 464

Tumblr, 305

Turnover, 90–91, 92 (table), 164

Twenty-fourth Amendment (U.S. Constitution), 276

Twenty-sixth Amendment (U.S. Constitution), 280

Twitter, 305

Two-thirds rule, 143–144

TXU Energy, 207

Tyler, 445, 499

Tyler Junior College, 463 (table)

Tyranny, 40–41, 42

Unaccompanied minors, 499, 500

Unauthorized immigrants, 268, 279, 497–501

Unfunded mandate, 48–49

Unicameral legislatures, 52, 79–80, 124

Uninsured populations, 469, 470 (map), 472 (figure)

Unitary system, 42

United Kingdom, 33 (table), 133

United States
    campaign financing, 307–308
    gross domestic product, 33 (table)
    higher education enrollment, 456 (figure)
    incarceration rates, 247
    map of 1837, 51 (map)
    state expenditures, 431 (figure)
    voter turnout, 299, 299 (table)

United States Grand Prix, 435

*United States, Guinn v.* (1919), 275

Universities

   *see* Higher education

University of Houston, 462 (table)

University of North Texas, 462 (table)

University of Texas

   admission restrictions, 460–461

   economic development, 466

   enrollment data, 454

   environmental studies, 480, 481

   legislative oversight, 130

   oil boom benefits, 477

   patronage system, 168

   pay and compensation, 165

   Permanent University Fund (PUF),

     456–457

   political challenges, 20, 166,

     455–456, 458

   and Tommy Joe Vandergriff, 387

   tuition and fees, 461, 462 (table)

*University of Texas, Fisher v. the* (2013), 461

University of Texas Law School,

   216, 251, 460

Unraveling, 349

Upton County, 385 (table)

U.S. 59, 182, 184

U.S. 77, 182

*U.S.A.* (Dos Passos), 456

U.S. Border Patrol, 268

U.S. Bureau of Justice, 252

U.S. Calf Roping Association, 193

U.S. Census Bureau, 28, 66–67, 467

U.S. Citizenship and Immigration

   Services, 498

U.S. Congress

   committee system, 127–128

   comparison studies, 79 (table)

   female legislators, 98

   immigration reform, 86, 499, 500

   intergovernmental lobbying, 352

   legislative representation, 79, 151

   as a model, 78

   Texas statehood, 13

   *see also* Voting Rights Act (1965)

U.S. Constitution

   constitutional amendments, 273

   distribution of powers, 45 (figure)

   election oversight, 271

   functional role, 40–42

   horizontal federalism, 44–46

   judicial system, 218

   legislative representation, 79

   local governments, 374

   Texas Constitution of 1836, 54

Texas statehood, 13

vertical federalism, 42, 44

U.S. Department of Education, 375, 451

U.S. Department of Energy, 479

U.S. Department of Justice, 103, 271,

   277, 445

U.S. Department of Transportation, 182

U.S. Environmental Protection Agency

   (EPA), 480, 482, 483, 486

U.S. House of Representatives

   background and characteristics,

     79, 79 (table)

   election districts, 103, 106

   electoral competition, 321, 322 (table)

   electoral system, 99, 100

   immigration reform, 499

   membership size, 80

   partisan control, 107, 108

   rates of incumbency, 91

   redistricting plans, 86, 106, 108–110

   Texas statehood, 13

U.S. Senate

   background and characteristics,

     79, 79 (table)

   electoral system, 100

   membership size, 80

   rates of incumbency, 91

   Texas statehood, 13

U.S. Supreme Court

   abortion rights, 47

   appeals cases, 229

   campaign financing, 307, 330, 355–356

   cross-state pollution, 483

   death penalty cases, 259, 263

   education funding, 446

   election laws, 61, 100–101, 103

   free speech protections,

     307, 355–356, 366

   health care, 85

   implied powers, 44

   jurisdiction, 218

   legislative representation, 80, 98, 103

   local government power, 373

   national health care policy, 51

   political party regulation, 331

   poll taxes, 277

   pre-clearance provision, 277–278, 279

   primary elections, 285, 287

   race-based admissions, 460–461

   redistricting plans, 106–107, 109, 357

   right to legal counsel, 254

   school desegregation, 444–445, 447

   separate-but-equal policy, 444, 445, 460

   undocumented immigrants, 499

   use of grants, 48

voting rights, 103, 109, 275, 280

white primaries, 277

Utah

   legislative representation and size,

     83 (table)

   party competition, 324 (table)

   pay and compensation, 122

   state constitution comparisons,

     71 (table)

   state expenditures, 431 (figure)

   term limits, 90

Utilities

   *see* Public Utility Commission

     of Texas (PUC)

Utility taxes, 420 (table)

*Valeo, Buckley v.* (1976), 307

Valid elections, 89

Van de Putte, Leticia, 77, 187, 268–270

Vandergriff, Tommy Joe, 387

Veasey, Marc, 144

Vermont

   ethnic diversity, 34

   governor's salary and residence, 165

   legislative representation and size,

     82 (table)

   party competition, 324 (table)

   redistricting commissions, 104

   same-sex marriage, 50

   state constitution comparisons,

     71 (table)

   state expenditures, 431 (figure)

   state treasurer, 190

Vertical federalism, 42, 44, 45 (figure)

Veterans Land Board, 194

Veto power, 59, 146, 172–173,

   311, 432

Victoria College, 463 (table)

Vinson & Elkins, 236

Vinson, Robert, 458

Violence, 275

Virginia

   death penalty cases, 259

   female legislators, 92

   higher education enrollment,

     456 (figure)

   legislative representation and size,

     83 (table)

   legislature naming convention, 79

   local governments, 374

   party competition, 324 (table)

   poll taxes, 277

   state constitution comparisons,

     71 (table)

   state expenditures, 431 (figure)

*Virginia, Atkins v.* (2002), 259
*Virginia Board of Elections, Harper v.*
    (1966), 277
Voice votes, 144
Volatile organic compounds, 480
Voluntary spending limits, 309
Volunteers, 357
Vote-by-mail system, 286
Voter conduct, 281
Voter fraud, 279
Voter identification laws, 279
Voter-led initiatives, 71, 73
Voter qualifications and registration,
    271–273, 295–296, 296 (figure)
Voter turnout
    college-age voters, 311
    comparison studies, 286, 289 (figure)
    current trends, 295–300, 296 (figure)
    demographic makeup, 299 (table)
    electoral competition, 320
    primary elections, 320, 341
    special elections, 68, 73 (figure),
        297 (figure), 297–298
    voting-age population, 321 (figure)
Voting-age population, 295–297,
    296 (figure), 297 (figure), 299 (table),
    300, 321 (figure)
Voting age requirements, 280
Voting machines, 293–294
Voting rights
    African Americans, 35, 56, 59, 65–66,
        103, 272, 273–278, 312, 319
    citizenship, 54
    college students, 281
    historical perspective, 282
    legal barriers, 273–275, 311
    members of the military, 280
    mid-decade redistricting plans,
        106–107, 357
    minority populations, 56, 103,
        273, 278–281, 311, 312, 394
    post-Reconstruction era, 273–275
    Supreme Court decisions, 109
    Texas, 273–281
    voter qualifications and registration,
        271–273
    women, 20, 66, 273, 280
    young adults, 280
Voting Rights Act (1965), 100, 103,
    106–107, 108, 273, 275, 277–278,
    357, 394
Voting Rights Act (1975), 278
Voucher programs, 348, 452–453

Waco City Council, 216
*Wade, Roe v.* (1973), 47
*Wainwright, Gideon v.* (1963), 254
Walker, Edward, 360
*Walker, Texas Ranger*, 248
Wall, Audrey S., 209 (figure)
*Wall Street Journal*, 411
Walmart, 210
War on drugs, 247
Washington (state)
    election systems, 105
    legislative representation and
        size, 83 (table)
    lobbying activities, 364
    marijuana decriminalization, 250
    party competition, 324 (table)
    primary elections, 285, 287
    state constitution comparisons,
        71 (table)
    state expenditures, 431 (figure)
    term limits, 90
Washington, Texas, 11
Waste Control Specialists, 486
Water regulations, 480
Water shortages, 480, 484–485
Waters-Pierce, 187
Ways and Means Committee, 127
Weakened parties, 328, 330–331
Weak mayor–council city government
    system, 388, 389 (figure),
    390, 392
Weatherford, 474
Weatherford College, 463 (table)
Webster, Daniel, 56
*Webster v. Reproductive Health Services*
    (1989), 47
Weights and measures, 192–193
Well-drilling restrictions, 396–397
Weslaco, 230
West, Richard, 359
West Texas, 4, 107, 125, 195, 477,
    479, 486
West Texas A&M University,
    462 (table)
West Virginia
    election systems, 105
    fiscal federalism, 414
    legislative representation and size,
        83 (table)
    party competition, 324 (table)
    state constitution comparisons,
        71 (table)
    state expenditures, 431 (figure)

Wharton County Junior College,
    463 (table)
Whataburger, 435
Whig Party, 316
White, Bill, 304, 310, 310 (table), 355
White, Mark, 160 (table),
    189, 230, 449
White primaries, 275, 277, 278, 319
Whitmire, John, 249, 251
*Who Governs?* (Dahl), 366
Wholesale Beer Distributors of
    Texas, 359
Wichita Falls, 484
Wide-open primary, 285
Wildcatters, 476
Williams, Clayton, 162
Williams, Edith, 77
Williamson County, 28
Wilson, Marvin, 259
Wind energy, 195, 485–486,
    487 (figure)
Windham School District, 203
Wisconsin
    bill filing, 137
    legislative representation and size,
        83 (table)
    legislative session length, 81–82
    party competition, 324 (table)
    state constitution comparisons,
        71 (table)
    state expenditures, 431 (figure)
    voter registration, 272
Women
    abortion rights, 47, 76, 86
    death penalty cases, 264
    legislative involvement, 76–78,
        91–92, 96, 98, 101, 109–110
    minority and women's caucuses,
        123, 125 (table)
    office of the governor, 161–163
    political challenges, 36
    term limit impact, 91–92
    voting rights, 20, 66, 273, 280
Women's Basketball Coaches
    Association, 461
Women's Health Caucus,
    123, 125 (table)
Woodard, Colin, 25, 26 (map)
Woodlands, The, 482
*World Is Flat, The* (Friedman), 466
Wright, Jim, 151
Write-in candidates, 301
Writ of habeas corpus, 228

Written constitutions, 40–41, 69
    see also Constitution
Wylie, 494
Wynne, Angus, Jr., 387
Wyoming
    legislative representation and size,
        83 (table)
    party competition, 324 (table)
    state constitution comparisons,
        71 (table)

    state expenditures,
        431 (figure)
    term limits, 90
    women's suffrage, 280

Yahoo, 306
Yankeedom, 26 (map)
Yarborough, Don, 231
Yarborough, Ralph, 231
Yarbrough, Don, 231

Young adults, 280
YouTube, 305, 306

Zachary, Louisiana, 402
Zavala, Lorenzo de, 11
Zerwas, John, 112
Zindler, Marvin, 253
Zoning policy,
    395–398
Zuñi Indians, 28

**CQ Press**, an imprint of SAGE, is the leading publisher of books, periodicals, and electronic products on American government and international affairs. CQ Press consistently ranks among the top commercial publishers in terms of quality, as evidenced by the numerous awards its products have won over the years. CQ Press owes its existence to Nelson Poynter, former publisher of the *St. Petersburg Times,* and his wife Henrietta, with whom he founded Congressional Quarterly in 1945. Poynter established CQ with the mission of promoting democracy through education and in 1975 founded the Modern Media Institute, renamed The Poynter Institute for Media Studies after his death. The Poynter Institute (www.poynter.org) is a nonprofit organization dedicated to training journalists and media leaders.

In 2008, CQ Press was acquired by SAGE, a leading international publisher of journals, books, and electronic media for academic, educational, and professional markets. Since 1965, SAGE has helped inform and educate a global community of scholars, practitioners, researchers, and students spanning a wide range of subject areas, including business, humanities, social sciences, and science, technology, and medicine. A privately owned corporation, SAGE has offices in Los Angeles, London, New Delhi, and Singapore, in addition to the Washington DC office of CQ Press.

80025 75540